AMERICA

AMERICA

A NARRATIVE HISTORY

VOLUME II

GEORGE BROWN TINDALL

W · W · NORTON & COMPANY · NEW YORK · LONDON

For Bruce and Susan
and For Blair

Time present and time past
Are both perhaps present in time future,
And time future contained in time past.

T. S. Eliot, *Four Quartets*

*The text of this book is composed in Caledonia, with display
type set in Torino Roman. Composition by New England Ty-
pographic Service, Inc. Manufacturing by R. R. Donnelley.
Book design by Antonina Krass.*

First Edition

Library of Congress Cataloging in Publication Data

Tindall, George Brown.
America: a narrative history.

Includes bibliographies and index.
1. United States—History.   I. Title.
E178.1.T55   1984   973   83-22165

W. W. Norton & Company, Inc., 500 Fifth Avenue, New York, N. Y. 10110
W. W. Norton & Company Ltd., 37 Great Russell Street, London WC1B 3NU

2   3   4   5   6   7   8   9   0

CONTENTS

Preface • xi
Acknowledgments • xiii

MAPS

PREFACE

This book is characterized in its subtitle as "A Narrative History." Since professional historians are currently debating the meaning of this term, I'd like to clarify, at least for students and other nonprofessionals, what the term "narrative" suggests about the approach I've taken here.

In *America: A Narrative History* I have tried to fashion the sprawling American past into a story, one brimming with vivid characters and great events. It is a story of promise and achievement, as well as the irony and tragedy of only partially fulfilled ideals. It is a story the events of which are connected in patterns of influence and consequence, not recounted in isolation from one another. By showing connections among past events, I've tried to bring out for readers their significance, their meaning.

With the narrative approach I've taken I've attempted also to put the reader in contact with the personalities and occurrences of the past. Wherever possible, the characters in this story speak with their own voice, the better to convey the flavor of American history.

Does the story I tell have a simple moral? Sir Isaiah Berlin, a distinguished Oxford don, once took as the theme for an essay on Leo Tolstoy's theory of history a fragment from the Greek poet Archilochus which said: "The fox knows many things, but the hedgehog knows one big thing." I prefer to see myself as one who runs with foxes rather than rolls up with hedgehogs. Yet if there were one single idea I should hope to implant with this text, it would be that the lessons of history are not simple lessons, that history is a complex and elusive subject, and that one should be on guard immediately against theories of single causation or pronouncements that begin "History proves. . . ."

The book in hand is designed to serve as an introduction to

American history. However much one might hope to provide a comprehensive account of all the major themes, one cannot pretend in such a limited scope to exhaust the subject. I do hope, however, that this survey will become a gateway through which readers will be drawn to explore more deeply the vast and compelling story of American history.

George B. Tindall
Chapel Hill, North Carolina

ACKNOWLEDGMENTS

A *New Yorker* cartoon of recent vintage has a publisher telling an aspiring author: "Well, it's good, but people just don't write books all by themselves any more." In truth, people don't. The single name on the title page of this book neglects the credit owed to many others. Joseph J. Ellis of Mount Holyoke College, the book's advisory editor, read successive drafts almost from the first, and supplied a judicious mixture of the criticism an author needs and the reassurance he craves. What is more, as deadlines loomed, he sped the author to completion with timely and well-formulated suggestions on the final chapters. Gary R. Freeze, graduate assistant and factotum at the University of North Carolina at Chapel Hill, helped compile the end-of-chapter bibliographies.

The influences which have contributed to this book—teachers, students, books, journals, documents I have encountered over the years, colleagues more than generous in their responses to inquiries—are more than I could acknowledge in a reasonable space, even if I had the gift of total recall. Historians who have read and commented on parts of the typescript in their areas of expertise include Herman J. Belz (University of Maryland), Stephen Botein (Michigan State University), Don E. Fehrenbacher (Stanford University), Michael F. Holt (University of Virginia), Richard B. Latner (Tulane University), Richard L. McCormick (Rutgers University), Drew R. McCoy (University of Texas), Michael R. McVaugh (University of North Carolina), Robert M. Miller (University of North Carolina), Charles W. Royster (Louisiana State University), Ronald E. Shaw (Miami University of Ohio), Michael B. Stoff (University of Texas), Carl Vipperman (University of Georgia), and Peter F. Walker (University of North Carolina).

David B. Parker and Linda W. Sellars, graduate assistants and copyreaders par excellence, saved me from many grotesque constructions, and Parker further checked points of factual accuracy. Jane Lindley, administrative manager of the Department of History in Chapel Hill, routinely passes miracles at expediting administrative details. Over a period of years a number of people who served in the department's secretarial pool have typed parts of various drafts: Jamie Lewis, Pat Maynor, Rosalie I. Radcliffe, and Mary Woodall. Most of the final draft was typed by Mandy Hollowell and Ceci Long, and by Peter Hardy with the help of the Kenan Research Fund when the department was temporarily understaffed.

In the Louis Round Wilson Library at Chapel Hill, Louise McG. Hall, Mary R. Ishaq, Donna P. Cornick, Ridley Kessler, Jr., and their associates have shown the characteristic tenacity of reference librarians in tracking down elusive references.

The Department of History at Chapel Hill and the National Endowment for the Humanities aided a year's stay at the Center for Advanced Study, Stanford, California, by courtesy of Gardner Lindzey and his associates, which helped me immensely in gathering my thoughts for this book as well as other projects. Especially generous to me there were Deanna Dejan at the word processor; Margaret Amara, librarian; and Bruce Harley, on many missions in the book run to the Stanford University library.

At W. W. Norton & Company, James L. Mairs, vice-president, senior editor, and director of production, acted as impresario straordinario from the inception of the project—organizing, supervising, and coordinating, all the while patiently keeping the author's nose to the grindstone and his morale in repair. A year's leave sponsored by the company helped achieve both ends. Steve Forman performed a variety of editorial tasks with unfailing serenity. Fred Bidgood, the copy editor, proved patient and thorough in preparing the manuscript for publication. George P. Brockway, chairman, and Edwin Barber, director of the College Department, both read and marked up the typescript to the author's advantage. Nora Seton and Amy Boesky looked after essential details at crucial times. Antonina Krass designed an elegant book, and Sydney W. Cohen compiled a useful index.

My son Bruce M. Tindall helped with copyreading at this end. To him and his wife, Susan A. McGrath, to my daughter Blair A. M. Tindall, and to my wife Blossom M. Tindall, my love and gratitude, as always.

18

RECONSTRUCTION: NORTH AND SOUTH

THE WAR'S AFTERMATH

In the spring of 1865 the weary war was over, a war whose cost in casualties was greater than all foreign wars down to World War II, and in proportion to population, greater than all other American wars down to the present day. At this frightful cost some old and tenacious issues were finally resolved. As the historian David Potter so graphically put it, "slavery was dead, secession was dead, and six hundred thousand men were dead." American nationalism emerged triumphant, its victory ratified in 1869 when the Supreme Court stamped its approval on the decision of arms. In the case of *Texas v. White*, the Court firmly denied any legality to Rebel state governments while it affirmed the existence of "an indestructible Union, composed of indestructible states." Pursued at first to preserve that Union, the war had turned into a crusade for the total abolition of chattel slavery. Before the end of 1865 all but two border states had voted emancipation. Ratification of the Thirteenth Amendment in December 1865 ended the remnants of slavery in Delaware and Kentucky and overrode any lingering doubts about the legitimacy of Lincoln's Emancipation Proclamation.

DEVELOPMENT IN THE NORTH   The war had been, in the words of Charles and Mary Beard, a Second American Revolution. It was more truly a social revolution than the War of Independence, for it reduced the once-dominant power of planter agrarians in the national councils and elevated that of the "captains of industry."

It is easy to exaggerate the profundity of this change, but government did become subtly more friendly to businessmen and unfriendly to those who would probe into their activities. The Republican Congress had delivered on the major platform promises of 1860, which had cemented the allegiance of northeastern businessmen and western farmers to the party of free labor.

In the absence of southern members, Congress had passed the Morrill Tariff of 1861 which, with later revisions, brought the average level of duties up to about double what it had been on the eve of conflict. The National Banking Act of 1863, reframed in 1864, created a uniform system of banking and banknote currency, and helped to finance the war. Under laws of 1862 and 1864 Congress guaranteed that the first transcontinental railroad would run along a north-central route from Omaha to Sacramento, and donated public lands and public bonds to ensure its financing. In the Homestead Act of 1862, moreover, Congress voted free homesteads of 160 acres to actual settlers who occupied the land for five years, and in the Morrill Land Grant Act of the same year conveyed to each state 30,000 acres of public land per member of Congress from the state, the proceeds from the sale of which went to colleges of "agriculture and mechanic arts."

DEVASTATION IN THE SOUTH   The South, where most of the fighting had occurred, offered a sharp contrast to the victorious North. Along the path of the army led by General Sherman, Carl Schurz reported in 1866, the countryside still "looked for many miles like a broad black streak of ruin and desolation." Columbia, South Carolina, said another observer, was "a wilderness of ruins," Charleston a place of "vacant houses, of widowed women, of rotting wharves, of deserted warehouses, of weed-wild gardens, of miles of grass-grown streets, of acres of pitiful and voiceless barrenness." In the valley of the Tennessee, the British visitor Robert Somers reported: "The trail of war is visible . . . in burnt-up gin houses, ruined bridges, mills, and factories." The border states of Missouri and Kentucky had gone through a guerrilla war which lapsed into postwar anarchy perpetrated by marauding bands of bushwackers turned bank robbers, such as the notorious Younger brothers, Coleman and Jim, and the even more notorious James boys, Frank and Jesse.

Property values had collapsed. Confederate bonds and money became worthless, railroads and rolling stock were damaged or destroyed. Stores of cotton which had escaped destruction were seized as Confederate property or in forfeit of federal taxes. Emancipation at one stroke wiped out perhaps $4 billion in-

Virginia's Capitol, designed by Thomas Jefferson, looms over the ruins of Richmond, Virginia, April 1865. [Library of Congress]

vested in human flesh and left the labor system in disarray. The great age of expansion in the cotton market was over. Not until 1879 would the cotton crop again equal the record crop of 1860; tobacco production did not regain its prewar level until 1880; the sugar crop of Louisiana not until 1893; and the old rice industry of the Tidewater and the hemp industry of the Kentucky Blue Grass never regained their prewar status.

LEGALLY FREE, SOCIALLY BOUND   The newly freed slaves suffered most of all. According to Frederick Douglass, the black abolitionist, the former bondsman "was free from the individual master but a slave of society. He had neither money, property, nor friends. He was free from the old plantation, but he had nothing but the dusty road under his feet. He was free from the old quarter that once gave him shelter, but a slave to the rains of summer and the frosts of winter. He was turned loose, naked, hungry, and destitute to the open sky."

According to a former Confederate general, recently freed blacks had "nothing but freedom." [Library of Congress]

Even dedicated abolitionists in large part shrank from the measures of land reform that might have given the freedmen more self-support and independence. Citizenship and legal rights were one thing, wholesale confiscation and land distribution quite another. Instead of land or material help the freedmen more often got what the historian Leon Litwack called "the moral and economic injunctions and shibboleths that were standard fare in nineteenth-century American society: success came ultimately to the hard-working, the sober, the honest, and the educated, to those individuals who engaged in 'faithful industry,' practiced 'judicious economy,' cultivated habits of thrift and temperance, made their homes 'models of neatness,' and led moral, virtuous, Christian lives."

In 1865 Rep. George Julian of Indiana and Sen. Charles Sumner of Massachusetts proposed to give freedmen forty-acre homesteads carved out of Rebel lands taken under the Confiscation Act of 1862. But their plan for outright grants was replaced by a program of rentals since, under the law, confiscation was effective only for the lifetime of the offender. Discussions of land distribution, however, fueled rumors that freedmen would get "forty acres and a mule," a slogan that swept the South at the end of the war. Its source remains unknown, but the aspirations which gave rise to it are clear enough. As one black man in Mississippi put it: "Gib us our own land and we take care ourselves; but widout land, de ole massas can hire us or starve us, as dey please." More lands were seized as "abandoned lands" under an act of 1864, and for default on the direct taxes which Congress levied in 1861 and 1862, than under the Confiscation Act. The most conspicuous example of confiscation was the estate of Robert E. Lee and the Custis family, which became Arlington National Cemetery, but larger amounts were taken in the South Carolina Sea Islands and elsewhere. Some of these lands were sold to freedmen, some to Yankee speculators.

THE FREEDMEN'S BUREAU   On March 3, 1865, Congress set up within the War Department the Bureau of Refugees, Freedmen, and Abandoned Lands, to provide "such issues of provisions, clothing, and fuel" as might be needed to relieve "destitute and suffering refugees and freedmen and their wives and children." The Freedmen's Bureau would also take over abandoned and confiscated land for rental in forty-acre tracts to "loyal refugees and freedmen," who might buy the land at a fair price within three years. But the amount of such lands was limited. Under Gen. Oliver O. Howard as commissioner, and assistant commis-

Sketch of a primary school set up by the Freedmen's Bureau, Vicksburg, Mississippi, 1866. [The Historic New Orleans Collection]

sioners in each state of the former Confederacy, agents were entrusted with negotiating labor contracts (something new for both freedmen and planters), providing medical care, and setting up schools, often in cooperation with northern agencies like the American Missionary Association and the Freedmen's Aid Society. The bureau had its own courts to deal with labor disputes and land titles, and its agents were further authorized to supervise trials involving Negroes in other courts.

This was as far as Congress would go. Beyond such temporary measures of relief, no program of reconstruction ever incorporated much more than constitutional and legal rights for freedmen. These were important in themselves, of course, but the extent to which even these should go was very uncertain, to be settled more by the course of events than by any clear-cut commitment to equality.

THE BATTLE OVER RECONSTRUCTION

The problem of reconstruction arose first at the very beginning of the Civil War, when the western counties of Virginia refused to go along with secession. In 1861 a loyal state government of Virginia was proclaimed at Wheeling and this government in turn consented to the formation of a new state called West Virginia, duly if irregularly admitted to the Union in 1863. The loyal government of Virginia under Gov. Francis H. Pierpont then carried on from Alexandria, its reach limited to that part of the state which the Union controlled. As Union forces advanced into the South, Lincoln in 1862 named military governors for Tennessee, Arkansas, and Louisiana. By the end of the following year he had formulated a plan for regular governments in those states and any others that might qualify.

LINCOLN'S PLAN AND CONGRESS'S RESPONSE   Acting under his pardon power, President Lincoln issued on December 8, 1863, a Proclamation of Amnesty and Reconstruction under which any Rebel state could form a Union government whenever a number equal to 10 percent of those who had voted in 1860 took an oath of allegiance to the Constitution and Union and received a presidential pardon. Participants also had to swear support for laws and proclamations dealing with emancipation. Excluded from the pardon, however, were certain groups: civil and diplomatic officers of the Confederacy; high officers of the Confederate army and navy; judges, congressmen, and military officers of the United States who had left their posts to aid the rebellion; and those accused of failure to treat captured Negro soldiers and their officers as prisoners of war.

Under this plan loyal governments appeared in Tennessee, Arkansas, and Louisiana, but Congress recognized them neither by representation nor in counting the electoral votes of 1864. In the absence of any specific provisions for reconstruction in the Constitution, there was disagreement as to where authority properly rested. Lincoln claimed the right to direct reconstruction under Article II, Section 2, which set forth the presidential pardon power, and also under Article IV, Section 4, which imposed an obligation on the United States to guarantee each state a republican form of government. Republican congressmen, however, argued that Article IV, Section 4, implied a power of Congress to act. The first congressional plan for reconstruction appeared in the Wade-Davis Bill, sponsored by Sen. Benjamin Wade of Ohio and Rep. Henry Winter Davis of Maryland, which proposed much more stringent requirements than Lincoln had. In contrast to Lincoln's 10 percent plan, the Wade-Davis Bill required that a majority of white male citizens declare their allegiance and that only those who could take an "ironclad" oath (required of federal officials since 1862) attesting to their *past* loyalty could vote or serve in the state constitutional conventions. The conventions, moreover, would have to abolish slavery, exclude from political rights high-ranking civil and military officers of the Confederacy, and repudiate debts incurred "under the sanction of the usurping power."

Passed during the closing day of the session, the bill was subjected to a pocket veto by Lincoln, who refused to sign it but issued an artful statement that he would accept any state which preferred to present itself under the congressional plan. The sponsors responded by issuing to the newspaper the Wade-Davis Manifesto, which accused the president, among other sins, of usurping power and attempting to use readmitted states to ensure his reelection.

Lincoln's last public words on reconstruction came in his last public address, on April 11, 1865. Speaking from the White House balcony, he pronounced the theoretical question of whether the Confederate states were in the Union "bad as the basis of a controversy, and good for nothing at all—a mere pernicious abstraction." These states were simply "out of their proper practical relation with the Union," and the object was to get them "into their proper practical relation." It would be easier to do this by merely ignoring the abstract issue: "Finding themselves safely at home, it would be utterly immaterial whether they had been abroad." At a cabinet meeting on April 14, Lincoln proposed to get state governments in operation before Congress met in December. Secretary Gideon Welles later reported him to have said: "There were men in Congress who, if their motives were good, were nevertheless impracticable, and who possessed feelings of hate and vindictiveness in which he did not sympathize and could not participate." He wanted "no persecution, no bloody work."

THE ASSASSINATION OF LINCOLN   That evening Lincoln went to Ford's Theater and his rendezvous with death. Shot by John Wilkes Booth, a crazed actor who thought he was doing something for the South, the president died the next morning in a room across the street. Accomplices had also targeted Vice-President Johnson and Secretary of State Seward. Seward and four others, including his son, were victims of severe but not fatal stab wounds. Johnson escaped injury, however, because his chosen assassin got cold feet and wound up in the barroom of Johnson's hotel. Had he been murdered, the presidency would have gone to a man whose name is virtually unknown today: Lafayette Sabine Foster, president pro tem of the Senate, a moderate Republican from Connecticut.

Martyred in the hour of victory, Lincoln entered into the national mythology even while the funeral train took its mournful burden north to New York and westward home to Springfield. The nation extracted a full measure of vengeance from the conspirators. Pursued into Virginia, Booth was trapped and shot in a burning barn. Three collaborators were brought to trial by a military commission and hanged, along with Mrs. Mary Surratt, at whose boarding house they had plotted. Against her the court had no credible evidence of complicity. Three others got life sentences, including a Maryland doctor who set the leg Booth had broken when he jumped to the stage. A stagehand at Ford's Theater got six years. All were eventually pardoned by President Johnson, except one who died in prison. The doctor achieved lasting fame by making common a once obscure expression. His name was Mudd. Apart from those cases, however, there was only one other execution in the aftermath of war: Henry Wirz, who commanded the infamous prison at Andersonville, Georgia, where Union prisoners were probably more the victims of war conditions than of deliberate cruelty.

JOHNSON'S PLAN   Lincoln's death suddenly elevated to the White House Andrew Johnson of Tennessee, a man whose state was still in legal limbo and whose party affiliation was unclear. He was a War Democrat who had been put on the Union ticket in 1864 as a gesture of unity. Of humble origins like Lincoln, Johnson had moved as a youth from his birthplace in Raleigh, North Carolina, to Greeneville, Tennessee, where he became proprietor of a moderately prosperous tailor shop. Self-educated with the help of his wife, he had made himself into an effective orator of the rough-and-tumble school, and had become an advocate of the yeomanry against the privileges of the aristocrats. He was one of the few southern men who championed a homestead act. He had served as mayor, congressman, governor, and senator, then as military governor of Tennessee before he became vice-president.

Andrew Johnson. [Library of Congress]

Some of the most advanced Radicals at first thought Johnson, unlike Lincoln, to be one of them—an illusion created by Johnson's gift for strong language. "Treason is a crime and must be punished," he had said. "Treason must be made infamous and traitors must be impoverished." Ben Wade was carried away with admiration. "Johnson, we have faith in you," he said. "By the gods, there will be no trouble now in running this government." But Wade would soon find him as untrustworthy as Lincoln, if for different reasons. Johnson's very loyalty to the Union sprang from a strict adherence to the Constitution. Given to dogmatic abstractions which were alien to Lincoln's temperament, he nevertheless arrived by a different route at similar objectives. The states should be brought back into their proper relation to the Union not by ignoring as a pernicious abstraction the theoretical question of their status, but because the states and the Union were indestructible. And like many other whites, he found it hard to accept the growing Radical movement toward suffrage for blacks. By May he was saying "there is no such thing as reconstruction. Those States have not gone out of the Union. Therefore reconstruction is unnecessary."

Johnson's plan of Reconstruction thus closely resembled Lincoln's. A new Proclamation of Amnesty (May 29, 1865) added to those Lincoln excluded from pardon everybody with taxable property worth more than $20,000. These were the people Johnson believed had led the South into secession. But special applications for pardon might be made by those in the excluded groups, and before the year was out Johnson had issued some 13,000 such pardons. In every case Johnson ruled that pardon, whether by general amnesty or special clemency, restored one's property rights in land. He defined as "confiscated" only lands already sold under court decree. This included lands set aside by General Sherman's expansive Special Field Order No. 15, which had allocated for the exclusive use of freed Negroes a coastal strip thirty miles wide from Charleston south to the St. John's River in Florida.

Johnson's rulings nipped in the bud an experiment in land distribution that had barely begun. More than seventy years later one Thomas Hall, born a slave in Orange County, North Carolina, spoke bluntly of his dashed hopes: "Lincoln got the praise for freeing us, but did he do it? He give us freedom without giving us any chance to live to ourselves and we still had to depend on the southern white man for work, food and clothing, and he held us through our necessity and want in a state of servitude but little better than slavery." Later, a South Carolina Land Commission, established by the Radical state government in 1869, distributed lands to more than 5,000 black families. One black community in the upcountry, Promised Land, still retained its identity more than a century later, an obscure reminder of what might have been.

On the same day that Johnson announced his amnesty, he issued another proclamation which applied to his native state of North Carolina, and within six more weeks came further edicts for the other Rebel states not already organized by Lincoln. In each a native Unionist became provisional governor with authority to call a convention elected by loyal voters. Lincoln's 10 percent requirement was omitted. [Johnson called upon the conventions to invalidate the secession ordinances, abolish slavery, and repudiate all debts incurred to aid the Confederacy.] Each state, moreover, was to ratify the Thirteenth Amendment. Lincoln had privately advised the governor of Louisiana to consider a grant of suffrage to some blacks, "the very intelligent and those who have fought gallantly in our ranks." In his final public address he publicly endorsed a limited black suffrage. Johnson repeated Lincoln's advice. He reminded the provisional governor of Mississippi, for example, that the state conventions might "with perfect safety" extend suffrage to blacks with education or with military service so as to "disarm the adversary"—the adversary being "radicals who are wild upon Negro franchise."

[The state conventions for the most part met Johnson's requirements, although South Carolina and Mississippi did not repudiate their debt and the new Mississippi legislature refused to ratify the Thirteenth Amendment. Presidential agents sent south to observe and report back for the most part echoed General Grant's finding after a two-month tour: "I am satisfied that the mass of thinking men of the south accept the present situation of affairs in good faith." But Carl Schurz of Missouri found "an *utter absence of national feeling* . . . and a desire to preserve slavery . . . as much and as long as possible." The discrepancy between the two reports is perhaps only apparent: southern whites accepted the situation because they thought so little had changed after all. Emboldened by Johnson's indulgence they ignored his counsels of expediency. Suggestions of Negro suffrage were scarcely raised in the conventions, and promptly squelched when they were.

SOUTHERN INTRANSIGENCE   When Congress met in December, for the first time since the end of the war, it had only to accept the accomplished fact that state governments were functioning in the South. But there was the rub. [Southern voters had acted with extreme disregard of northern feelings. Among the new members presenting themselves were Georgia's Alexander H. Stephens, late vice-president of the Confederacy, now claiming a seat in the Senate, four Confederate generals, eight colonels, six cabinet members, and a host of lesser Rebels. That many of them had counseled delay in secession, like Stephens, or actually opposed it until it happened, made little difference given the temper of the times. The Congress forthwith excluded from the roll call and denied seats to all members from the eleven former Confederate states. It was too much to expect, after four bloody years, that Unionists would welcome Rebels like prodigal sons.

Furthermore, the action of southern legislatures in passing repressive Black Codes seemed to confirm Schurz's view that they intended to preserve slavery as nearly as possible. The codes extended to blacks certain rights they had not hitherto enjoyed, but universally set them aside as a separate caste subject to special restraints. Details varied from state to state, but some provisions were common. Existing marriages, including common-law marriages, were recognized, and testimony of Negroes was accepted in cases involving Negroes—in six states in all cases. Blacks could hold property. They could sue and be sued in the courts. On the other hand Negroes could not own farm lands in Mississippi or city lots in South Carolina. In some states they could not carry firearms without a license to do so.

The codes' labor provisions seemed to confirm the worst suspi-

Slavery Is Dead (?) *Thomas Nast's cartoon suggested that, in 1866, slavery was only legally dead.* [Harper's Weekly]

cions. Blacks were required to enter into annual labor contracts, with provision for punishment in case of violation. Dependent children were subject to compulsory apprenticeship and corporal punishment by masters. Vagrants were punished with severe fines and could be sold into private service if unable to pay. To many people it indeed seemed that slavery was on the way back in another guise. The new Mississippi penal code virtually said so: "All penal and criminal laws now in force describing the mode of punishment of crimes and misdemeanors committed by slaves, free negroes, or mulattoes are hereby re-enacted, and decreed to be in full force against all freedmen, free negroes and mulattoes."

[Faced with such evidence of southern intransigence, moderate Republicans drifted more and more toward Radical views] Having excluded southern members, the new Congress set up a Joint Committee on Reconstruction, with nine members from the House and six from the Senate, to gather evidence and submit proposals. Headed by the moderate Sen. William Pitt Fessenden, the committee fell under greater Radical influence as a parade of witnesses testified to the Rebels' impenitence. Initiative on the committee fell to determined Radicals who knew what they wanted: Ben Wade of Ohio, George W. Julian of Indiana, Henry Wilson of Massachusetts, Zachary Chandler of Michigan, James M. Ashley of Ohio—and most conspicuously of all, Thaddeus Stevens of Pennsylvania and Charles Sumner of Massachusetts.

THE RADICALS Their motivations were mixed, and perhaps little purpose is served in attempting to sort them out. Purity of motive is rare in an imperfect world. Most Radicals had been connected with the antislavery cause. While one could be hostile to both slavery and blacks, many whites approached the question of Negro rights with a humanitarian impulse. Few could escape the bitterness bred by the long and bloody war, however, or remain unaware of the partisan advantage that would come to the Republican party from Negro suffrage. But the party of Union and freedom, after all, could best guarantee the fruits of victory, they reasoned, and Negro suffrage could best guarantee Negro rights.

The growing conflict of opinion brought about an inversion in constitutional reasoning. Secessionists—and Johnson—were now arguing that their states had remained in the Union, and some Radicals were contriving arguments that they had left the Union after all. Rep. Thaddeus Stevens spun out a theory that the Confederate states were now conquered provinces, subject to the absolute will of the victors. Sen. Charles Sumner advanced a

Two leading Radicals: Sen. Charles Sumner (left) and Rep. Thaddeus Stevens. [Library of Congress; National Archives]

thesis that the southern states, by their pretended acts of secession, had in effect committed suicide and reverted to the status of unorganized territories subject to the will of Congress. But few ever took such ideas seriously. Republicans converged instead on the "forfeited rights theory" first advanced by Rep. Samuel Shellabarger of Ohio and later embodied in the report of the Joint Committee on Reconstruction. This theory held that the states as entities continued to exist, but by the acts of secession and war had forfeited "all civil and political rights under the constitution." And Congress was the proper authority to determine conditions under which such rights might be restored.

JOHNSON'S BATTLE WITH CONGRESS A long year of political battling remained, however, before this idea triumphed. Radical views had gained a majority in Congress, if one not yet large enough to override presidential vetoes. But the critical year 1866 saw the gradual waning of Johnson's power and influence; much of this was self-induced, for he betrayed as much addiction to "pernicious abstraction" as any Radical. Johnson first challenged Congress in February, when he vetoed a bill to extend the life of the Freedmen's Bureau. The measure, he said, assumed that wartime conditions still existed, whereas the country had returned "to a state of peace and industry." No longer valid as a war measure, the bill violated the Constitution in several ways. It made the federal government responsible for the care of indigents. It was passed by a Congress in which eleven states were denied seats. And it used vague language in defining the "civil rights and immunities" of Negroes. The Congress soon moved to correct that particular defect, but for the time being Johnson's prestige remained sufficiently intact that the Senate upheld his veto.

Three days after the veto, however, Johnson undermined his already weakening prestige with a gross assault on Radical leaders during an impromptu speech on Washington's Birthday. The Joint Committee on Reconstruction, he said, was "an irresponsible central directory" which had repudiated the principle of an indestructible Union and accepted the legality of secession by entertaining conquered-province and state-suicide theories. From that point forward moderate Republicans backed away from a president who had opened himself to counterattack. He was "an alien enemy of a foreign state," Stevens declared. He was "an insolent drunken brute," Sumner asserted—and Johnson was open to the charge because of an incident at his vice-presidential inauguration. Weakened by illness at the time, he had taken a belt of brandy to get him through the ceremony and, under the influence of fever and alcohol, had become incoherent.

In mid-March 1866 Congress passed the Civil Rights Act, which Sen. Lyman Trumbull of Illinois had introduced along with the Freedmen's Bureau Bill. A response to the Black Codes, this bill declared that "all persons born in the United States and not subject to any foreign power, excluding Indians not taxed," were citizens entitled to "full and equal benefit of all laws." The grant of citizenship to native-born blacks, Johnson fulminated, went beyond anything formerly held to be within the scope of federal power. It would, moreover, "foment discord among the races." This time, on April 9, 1866, Congress overrode the presidential veto. On July 16 it enacted a revised Bureau Bill, again overriding a veto. From that point on Johnson steadily lost ground.

THE FOURTEENTH AMENDMENT   To remove all doubt about the constitutionality of the new Civil Rights Act, which was justified as implementing freedom under the Thirteenth Amendment, the Joint Committee recommended a new amendment which passed Congress on June 16, 1866, and was ratified by July 28, 1868. The Fourteenth Amendment, however, went far beyond the Civil Rights Act. It merits close scrutiny because of its broad impact on subsequent laws and litigation. In the first section it did four things: it reaffirmed state and federal citizenship for persons born or naturalized in the United States, it forbade any *state* (the word "state" was important in later litigation) to abridge the "privileges and immunities" of citizens; to deprive any *person* (again an important term) of life, liberty, or property without "due process of law"; or to deny any person "the equal protection of the laws." The last three of these clauses have been the subject of long and involved lawsuits resulting in applications not widely, if at all, foreseen at the time. The "due process clause" has come in the twentieth century to mean that state as well as federal power is subject to the Bill of Rights, and the "due process clause" has been used to protect corporations, as legal "persons," from "unreasonable" regulation by the states. Other provisions of the amendment had less far-reaching effect. Section 4 specified that the debt of the United States "shall not be questioned," but declared "illegal and void" all debts contracted in aid of the rebellion. Section 5 specified the power of Congress to pass laws enforcing the amendment.

Johnson's home state was among the first to ratify. In Tennessee, which had harbored probably more Unionists than any other Confederate state, the government had fallen under Radical control. Gov. W. G. "Parson" Brownlow, in reporting the results to the secretary of the Senate, added: "Give my respects to the dead dog of the White House." His words afford a fair sample of the growing acrimony on both sides of the reconstruction debates. In May and July bloody race riots in Memphis and New Orleans added fuel to the flames. Both incidents amounted to indiscriminate massacres of blacks by local police and white mobs. The carnage, Radicals argued, was the natural fruit of Johnson's policy. "Witness Memphis, witness New Orleans," Sumner cried. "Who can doubt that the President is the author of these tragedies?"

RECONSTRUCTING THE SOUTH

THE TRIUMPH OF CONGRESSIONAL RECONSTRUCTION As 1866 drew to an end, the congressional elections promised to resolve differences in the direction of policy. In August Johnson's friends staged a National Union Convention in Philadelphia. Men from Massachusetts and South Carolina marched down the aisle arm in arm to symbolize national reconciliation. The Radicals countered with a convention of their own and organized a congressional campaign committee to coordinate their propaganda. Johnson responded with a stumping tour of the Midwest, a "swing around the circle," which turned into an undignified contest of vituperation. Subjected to heckling and attacks on his integrity, Johnson responded in kind. "I have been called Judas Iscariot and all that," he said in St. Louis. "If I have played the Judas, who has been my Christ that I have played the Judas with? Was it Thad Stevens? Was it Wendell Phillips? Was it Charles Sumner?" Johnson may have been, as Secretary Seward claimed, the best stump speaker in the country. The trouble was, as Secretary Welles responded, the president ought not to be a stump speaker. It tended to confirm his image as a "ludicrous boor" and "drunken imbecile," which Radical papers projected. When the returns came in, the Republicans had well over a two-thirds majority in each house, by counts of 42 to 11 in the Senate and 143 to 49 in the House, a comfortable margin with which to override any presidential vetoes.

The Congress in fact enacted a new program even before new members took office. Two acts passed in January 1867 extended the suffrage to Negroes in the District of Columbia and the territories. Another law provided that the new Congress would meet on March 4 instead of the following December, depriving Johnson of a breathing spell. On March 2, 1867, two days before the old Congress expired, it passed three basic laws of congressional reconstruction over Johnson's vetoes: the Military Reconstruction Act, the Command of the Army Act (an amendment to an army appropriation), and the Tenure of Office Act.

The first of the three acts prescribed new conditions under which the formation of southern state governments should begin all over again. The other two sought to block obstruction by the president. The Army Act required that all orders from the commander-in-chief go through the headquarters of the general of the army, then Ulysses S. Grant, who could not be reassigned outside Washington without the consent of the Senate. The Radicals had faith in Grant, who was already leaning their way. The Tenure of Office Act required the consent of the Senate for the president to remove any officeholder whose appointment the Senate had to confirm in the first place. The purpose of at least some congressmen was to retain Secretary of War Edwin M. Stanton, the one Radical sympathizer in Johnson's cabinet, but an ambiguity crept into the wording of the act. Cabinet officers, it said, should serve during the term of the president who appointed them—and Lincoln had appointed Stanton, although, to be sure, Johnson was serving out Lincoln's term.

The Military Reconstruction Act, often hailed or denounced as the triumphant victory of "Radical" Reconstruction, actually fell short of a thoroughgoing radicalism. It emerged, the historian Michael Les Benedict wrote, "only after furious tugging and hauling among various Republican factions." As first reported from the Reconstruction committee by Stevens, it would have given military commanders in the South ultimate control over law enforcement and would have left open indefinitely the terms of future restoration. More moderate elements, however, pushed through the "Blaine amendment," which scrapped the prolonged national control under which Radicals hoped to put through the far more revolutionary program of reducing the Rebel states to territories, plus programs of land confiscation and education. With the Blaine amendment in place the Reconstruction program boiled down to little more than a requirement that southern states accept black suffrage and ratify the Fourteenth Amendment. Years later Albion W. Tourgée, after a career as a carpetbagger in North Carolina, wrote: "Republicans gave the ballot to men without homes, money, education, or security, and then told them to use it to protect themselves. . . . It was cheap patriotism, cheap philanthropy, cheap success!"

The act began with a pronouncement that "no legal state governments or adequate protection for life and property now exists in the rebel States. . . . " One state, Tennessee, which had ratified the Fourteenth Amendment, was exempted from the application of the act. The other ten were divided into five military districts, and the commanding officer of each was authorized to keep order and protect the "rights of persons and property." To that end he might use military tribunals in place of civil courts when he judged it necessary. The Johnson governments remained intact for the time being, but new constitutions were to be framed "in conformity with the Constitution of the United States," in conventions elected by male citizens twenty-one and older "of whatever race, color, or previous condition." Each state constitution had to provide the same universal male suffrage. Then, once the constitution was ratified by a majority of voters and accepted by Congress, and once the state legislature had ratified the Fourteenth Amendment, and once the amendment became part of the Constitution, any given state would be entitled to representation in Congress once again. Persons excluded from officeholding by the proposed amendment were also excluded from participation in the process.

Johnson reluctantly appointed military commanders under the act, but the situation remained uncertain for a time. Some people expected the Supreme Court to strike down the act, and for the time being no machinery existed for the new elections.

Congress quickly remedied that on March 23 with the Second Reconstruction Act, which directed the commanders to register for voting all adult males who swore they were qualified. A Third Reconstruction Act, passed on July 19, directed registrars to go beyond the loyalty oath and determine each person's eligibility to take it, and also authorized district commanders to remove and replace officeholders of any existing "so-called state" or division thereof. Before the end of 1867 new elections had been held in all the states but Texas.

Having clipped the president's wings, the Republican Congress moved a year later to safeguard its program from possible interference by the Supreme Court. In two important cases during 1866 the Court had shown a readiness to question certain actions. In *Ex parte Milligan* it struck down the wartime conviction of an Indiana Copperhead tried by court-martial for conspiracy to release and arm Rebel prisoners. The civil courts, the opinion noted, were duly operating in the area, which was far from the front. In *Cummings v. Missouri* the Court ruled void, as *ex post facto*, a Missouri statute which excluded ex-Confederates from certain professions. In *Ex parte Garland* (1867) it made a similar ruling against a test oath which barred ex-Confederates from practice before the Court. On the other hand it had evaded decision on two suits which directly challenged military Reconstruction, *Mississippi v. Johnson* and *Georgia v. Stanton*, on the ground that the suits involved political questions. Nevertheless, another case arising from Mississippi, *Ex parte McCardle*, raised the issue in a different form. McCardle, a Vicksburg editor arrested for criticizing General Ord's administration of the Fourth Military District, sought release under the Habeas Corpus Act of 1867. Congress responded on March 27, 1868, by simply removing the power of the Supreme Court to review cases arising under the law, which Congress clearly had the right to do under its power to define the Court's appellate jurisdiction (Article III, Section 2). The Court accepted this curtailment on the same day it affirmed the notion of an "indestructible Union" in *Texas v. White* (1869). In that case it also asserted the right of Congress under Article IV, Section 4, to reframe state governments.

THE IMPEACHMENT AND TRIAL OF JOHNSON   Congress's move to restrain the Supreme Court preceded by just two days the trial of the president in the Senate on an impeachment brought in by the House. Johnson, though hostile to the congressional program, had gone through the motions required of him. He continued, however, to pardon former Confederates in wholesale lots and replaced several district commanders whose Radical sympathies offended him. He and his cabinet members, moreover, largely ignored the Test Oath Act of 1862 by naming former Confederates to post offices and other federal positions. Nevertheless a lengthy investigation by the House Judiciary Committee, extending through most of the year 1867, failed to convince the House that grounds for impeachment existed.

The occasion for impeachment came when Johnson deliberately violated the Tenure of Office Act in order, he said, to test its constitutionality in the courts. Secretary of War Stanton had become a thorn in the president's side, refusing to resign despite his disagreements with the president's policy. On August 12, 1867, during a recess of Congress, Johnson suspended Stanton and named General Grant in his place. Grant's political stance was ambiguous at the time, but his acceptance implied cooperation with Johnson. When the Senate refused to confirm Johnson's action, however, Grant returned the office to Stanton. The president thereupon named Gen. Lorenzo Thomas as secretary of war after a futile effort to interest Gen. William T. Sherman. Three days later, on February 24, 1868, the House voted impeachment, to be followed by specific charges. In due course a special committee of seven brought in its report.

Of the eleven articles of impeachment, eight focused on the charge that he had unlawfully removed Stanton and had failed to give the Senate the name of a successor. Article 9, the "Emory article," accused the president of issuing orders directly to Gen. William H. Emory in violation of the Army Act. The last two in effect charged him with criticizing Congress by "inflammatory and scandalous harangues" and by claiming that the Congress was not legally valid without southern representatives. But Article 11 accused Johnson of "unlawfully devising and contriving" to violate the Reconstruction Acts, contrary to his obligation to execute the laws. At the least, Johnson had tried to obstruct Congress's will while observing the letter of the law.

The Senate trial opened on March 5 and continued until May 26, with Chief Justice Salmon P. Chase presiding. Seven managers from the House, including Thaddeus Stevens and Benjamin F. Butler, directed the prosecution. The president was spared the humiliation of a personal appearance, and was ably represented by Attorney-General Henry Stanbery, William H. Evarts, Benjamin R. Curtis, and William S. Groesbeck. The defense counsel shrewdly insisted on narrowing the trial to questions that would be indictable offenses under the law, and steered the

*Johnson, impeached by the House, barely survived his trial in the
Senate.* [Harper's Weekly, *April 11, 1868*]

questions away from Johnson's manifest wish to frustrate the will
of Congress. Such questions, they contended, were purely political in nature. In the end enough Republican senators, the
"recusants," joined their pro-Johnson colleagues to prevent
conviction. On May 16 the crucial vote came on Article 9: 35
votes guilty and 19 not guilty, one vote short of the two-thirds
needed to convict. On Articles 2 and 3 the vote was exactly the
same, and the trial adjourned.

In a parliamentary system Johnson probably would have been
removed as leader of the government long before then. But by
deciding the case on the narrowest grounds, the Senate made it
unlikely that any future president could ever be removed except
for the gravest personal offenses, and almost surely not for flout-
ing the will of Congress in his execution of the laws. Impeachment of Johnson was in the end a great political mistake, for the
failure to remove the president was damaging to Radical morale
and support. Nevertheless the Radical cause did gain something.
To blunt the opposition, Johnson agreed not to obstruct the
process of Reconstruction, named as secretary of war Gen. John
M. Schofield, who was committed to enforcing the new laws, and
sent to Congress the new Radical constitutions of Arkansas and
South Carolina. Thereafter his obstruction ceased and Radical
Reconstruction got under way.

REPUBLICAN RULE IN THE SOUTH   In June 1868 Congress agreed
that seven states had met the conditions for readmission, all but

Virginia, Mississippi, and Texas. Congress rescinded Georgia's admission, however, when the state legislature expelled twenty-eight black members on the pretext that the state constitution had failed to specify their eligibility, and seated some former Confederate leaders. The military commander of Georgia then forced the legislature to reseat the Negro members and remove the Confederates, and the state was compelled to ratify the Fifteenth Amendment before being admitted in July 1870. Mississippi, Texas, and Virginia had returned earlier in 1870, under the added requirement that they too ratify the Fifteenth Amendment. This amendment, submitted to the states in 1869, ratified in 1870, forbade the states to deny any person the vote on grounds of race, color, or previous condition of servitude.

Long before the new governments were established, Republican groups began to spring up in the South, chiefly under the aegis of the Union League, founded at Philadelphia in 1862 to promote support for the Union. Emissaries of the league enrolled Negroes and loyal whites, initiated them into the secrets and rituals of the order, and instructed them "in their rights and duties." The league emphasized the display of such symbols as the Bible, the flag, the Constitution, and the Declaration of Independence. The sign of recognition was the recital of the "four Ls": Lincoln, Liberty, Loyal, League. Agents of the Freedmen's Bureau, northern missionaries, teachers, and soldiers aided the cause and spread its influence. When the time came for political action, they were ready. In October 1867, for instance, on the eve of South Carolina's choice of convention delegates, the league reported eighty-eight chapters, which claimed to have enrolled almost every adult black male in the state.

BLACKS IN SOUTHERN POLITICS   It was the new role of Negroes in politics on which attention focused then and afterward. If largely illiterate and inexperienced in the rudiments of politics, they were little different from millions of whites enfranchised in the age of Jackson or immigrants herded to the polls by political bosses in New York and other cities after the war. Some freedmen frankly confessed their disadvantages. Beverly Nash, a black delegate in the South Carolina convention of 1868, told his colleagues: "I believe, my friends and fellow-citizens, we are not prepared for this suffrage. But we can learn. Give a man tools and let him commence to use them, and in time he will learn a trade. So it is with voting."

Brought suddenly into politics in times that tried the most skilled of statesmen, a surprising number of blacks rose to the occasion. Yet it would be absurd to claim, in the phrase of the times, that the "bottom rail" ever got on top. To call what happened "black Reconstruction" is to exaggerate black influence, which was limited mainly to voting, and to overlook the large numbers of white Republicans, especially in the mountain areas of the upper South. Only one of the new conventions, South Carolina's, had a black majority, 76 to 41. Louisiana's was evenly divided between blacks and whites, and in only two other conventions were more than 20 percent of the members black: Florida's, with 40 percent, and Virginia's, with 24 percent. The Texas convention was only 10 percent and North Carolina's 11 percent—but that did not stop a white newspaper from calling it "Ethiopian minstrelsy, Ham radicalism in all its glory," a body consisting of "baboons, monkeys, mules, Tourgee, and other jackasses."

In the new state governments, any Negro participation was a novelty, but no black man ever served as governor and few as judges. There were two Negro senators in Congress, Hiram Revels and Blanche K. Bruce, both from Mississippi, and fourteen black members of the House during Reconstruction. Among these were some of the ablest congressmen of the time. Blacks served in every state legislature, but only in South Carolina did they ever make up a majority in both houses and that only for two years.

CARPETBAGGERS AND SCALAWAGS The top positions in southern state governments went for the most part to white Republicans, whom the opposition whites soon labeled "carpetbaggers" and "scalawags," depending on their place of birth. The men who al-

Hiram R. Revels. Senator from Mississippi, Revels was also a Methodist minister and, later, president of Alcorn College. [Library of Congress]

legedly came south with all their belongings in carpetbags to pick up the political pelf were more often than not men who had arrived as early as 1865 or 1866, drawn south by the hope of economic opportunity and by other attractions that many of them had seen in Union service. Many were teachers or preachers who came on missionary endeavors. Albion W. Tourgée, for instance, a badly wounded Union veteran, moved to North Carolina in 1865, seeking a milder climate for reasons of health. He invested $5,000 in a nursery, and promptly lost it. He would have needed a fine crystal ball indeed to see two years in advance the chance for political office under the Radical program. As it turned out, he served in the state constitutional convention of 1868 and later as a state judge.

The "scalawags," or native white Republicans, were even more reviled and misrepresented. Most had opposed secession, forming a Unionist majority in many mountain counties as far south as Georgia and Alabama, and especially in the Tennessee hills. Not a few in both hills and flatlands attested to the power of what has been labeled "persistent Whiggery." Old Whigs often found Republican economic policies to be in keeping with Henry Clay's American System. Unionists, whether Whig or Democratic before the war, and even some secessionists, agreed with Georgia's Joseph E. Brown, confederate governor and later Democratic senator: "The statesman like the businessman should take a practical view of questions as they arise." For the time a practical view dictated joining the Republicans. Mississippi's James L. Alcorn, wealthy planter and former Whig, was among the prominent whites who joined the Republicans in the hope of moderating Radical policies. Such men were ready to concede Negro suffrage in the hope of influencing Negro voters. Alcorn became the first Republican governor of Mississippi.

THE REPUBLICAN RECORD   The new state constitutions were objectionable to adherents of the old order more because of their origins than because of their contents, excepting their provisions for Negro suffrage and civil rights. Otherwise the documents were in keeping with other state constitutions of the day, their provisions often drawn from the basic laws of northern states. Most remained in effect for some years after the end of Radical control, and later constitutions incorporated many of their features. Conspicuous among Radical innovations were such steps toward greater democracy as requiring universal manhood suffrage, reapportioning legislatures more nearly according to population, and making more state offices elective.

Given the circumstances in which the Radical governments arose and the intense hostility which met them, they made a surprisingly good record of positive achievement. For the first time in most of the South they established state school systems, however inadequate and ill-supported at first. The testimony is almost universal that Negroes eagerly sought education for themselves and their children. Some 600,000 black pupils were in schools by 1877. State governments under the Radicals gave more attention than ever before to poor relief and to public institutions for the disadvantaged and handicapped: orphanages, asylums, institutions for the deaf, dumb, and blind of both races. Public roads, bridges, and buildings were repaired or rebuilt. Blacks achieved new rights and opportunities that would never again be taken away, at least in principle: equality before the law, and the right to own property, carry on business, enter professions, attend schools, and learn to read and write.

In the annals of Reconstruction, partisan historians long denounced the Republican regimes for unparalleled corruption and abuse. That abuses proliferated in those years there is no question. Public money and public credit were often voted to privately owned corporations, especially railroads, under conditions which invited influence-peddling. But governmental subsidies were common before and after Reconstruction, especially for transportation, and the extension of public aid had general support among all elements, including the Radicals and their enemies. Contracts were let at absurd prices and public officials took their cut. Taxes and public debt rose in every state. Yet the figures of taxation and debt hardly constitute an unqualified indictment of Radical governments, since they then faced unusual and inflated costs for the physical reconstruction of public works in the South. Most states, moreover, had to float loans at outrageous discounts, sometimes at 50–75 percent of face value, because of uncertain conditions.

Nor, for that matter, were the breaches of public morality limited to the South or to Republicans. The Democratic Tweed Ring at the time was robbing New York City of more than $75 million, while the Republican "Gas Ring" in Philadelphia was lining its pockets. In national politics it was the time of the Crédit Mobilier, the Whiskey Ring, and other scandals that plagued the Grant administration. Corruption was neither invented by the Radical regimes, nor did it die with them. In Louisiana, the carpetbag governor Henry C. Warmoth found a certain Latin zest in the game: "Why," he said, "down here everybody is demoralized. Corruption is the fashion." In three years Louisiana's printing bill ran to $1.5 million, about half of which went to a newspaper belonging to young Warmoth, who left office with a tidy nest egg and settled down to a long life as a planter. But a later Democratic state treasurer, Maj. E. A. Burke, who decamped for Tegucigalpa in 1890 with the accounts over $1 million short, far outstripped Warmoth's record or anybody else's. About the same time Mississippi's Democratic state treasurer was found to have embezzled over $315,000. During Republican rule in Mississippi, on the other hand, there was no evidence of major corruption.

WHITE TERROR   The case of Mississippi strongly suggests that whites were hostile to Republican regimes less because of their corruption than their inclusion of blacks. Most white southerners remained unreconstructed, so conditioned by slavery that they were unable to conceive of blacks as citizens or even free agents. In some places hostility to the new regimes took on the form of white terror. The prototype of terrorist groups was the Ku Klux Klan, first organized in 1866 by some young men of Pulaski, Tennessee, as a social club with the costumes, secret ritual, and mumbo-jumbo common to fraternal groups. At first a group of Merry Andrews devoted to practical jokes, the founders eventually realized, as two of them wrote in a later account, that they "had evoked a spirit from 'the vasty deep' [which] would not down at their bidding." Pranks turned into intimidation of blacks and white Republicans, and the KKK and imitators like Louisiana's Knights of the White Camellia spread rapidly across the South in answer to the Union League. Klansmen rode about the

Two "carpetbaggers" hanged by the Klan, in the Tuscaloosa Independent Monitor, *1868. [Alabama State Department of Archives and History]*

countryside hiding under masks and robes, spreading horrendous rumors, issuing threats, harassing assertive Negroes, and occasionally running amok in violence and destruction. "Typically the Klan was a reactionary and racist crusade against equal rights which sought to overthrow the most democratic society or government the South had yet known," wrote its historian, Allan W. Trelease. During its brief career it "whipped, shot, hanged, robbed, raped, and otherwise outraged Negroes and Republicans across the South in the name of preserving white civilization."

Militia groups formed by the Radical regimes were hardly able to cope with the underground tactics of the Klan, although their presence may have prevented worse violence. Congress struck back with three Enforcement Acts (1870–1871) to protect Negro voters. The first of these measures levied penalties on persons who interfered with any citizen's right to vote. A second placed the election of congressmen under surveillance by federal election supervisors and marshals. The third (the Ku Klux Klan Act) outlawed the characteristic activities of the Klan— forming conspiracies, wearing disguises, resisting officers, and intimidating officials—and authorized the president to suspend habeas corpus where necessary to suppress "armed combinations." President Grant, in October 1871, singled out nine counties in upcountry South Carolina as an example, suspended habeas corpus, and pursued mass prosecutions which brought an abrupt halt to the Klan outrages. Elsewhere the Justice Department carried out a campaign of prosecution on a smaller scale, while a congressional committee gathered testimony on Klan activity which ran to twelve volumes. The program of federal enforcement broke the back of the Klan, whose outrages declined steadily as conservative southerners resorted to more subtle methods.

CONSERVATIVE RESURGENCE The Klan in fact could not take credit for the overthrow of Republican control in any state. Perhaps its most important effect, Allen Trelease suggested, was to weaken Negro and Republican morale in the South and strengthen in the North a growing weariness with the whole "southern question." Yankees had other fish to fry anyway. Onrushing expansion into the West, Indian wars, economic growth, and political controversy over the tariff and the currency distracted attention from southern outrages. Republican control in the South gradually loosened as "Conservative" parties—Democrats used that name to mollify former Whigs—mobilized the white vote. Scalawags, and many carpetbaggers, drifted away from the Radical ranks

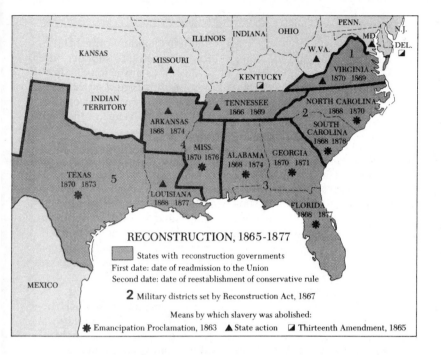

RECONSTRUCTION, 1865-1877

States with reconstruction governments
First date: date of readmission to the Union
Second date: date of reestablishment of conservative rule

2 Military districts set by Reconstruction Act, 1867

Means by which slavery was abolished:
✳ Emancipation Proclamation, 1863   ▲ State action   ☑ Thirteenth Amendment, 1865

under pressure from their white neighbors. Few of them had joined the Republicans out of concern for Negro rights in the first place.

Republican control collapsed in Virginia and Tennessee as early as 1869, in Georgia and North Carolina in 1870, although there was a Republican governor in North Carolina until 1876. Reconstruction lasted longest in the Deep South states with the heaviest Negro population, where whites abandoned Klan masks for barefaced intimidation in paramilitary groups like the Mississippi Rifle Club and the South Carolina Red Shirts. By 1876 Radical regimes survived only in Louisiana, South Carolina, and Florida, and these all collapsed after the elections of that year. Later Daniel H. Chamberlain, the last carpetbag governor of South Carolina, told William Lloyd Garrison that "the uneducated negro was too weak, no matter what his numbers, to cope with the whites."

THE GRANT YEARS

GRANT'S ELECTION   Ulysses S. Grant, who presided over this fiasco, brought to the presidency less political experience than any man who ever occupied the office, except perhaps Zachary Taylor, and arguably less political judgment than any other. But in 1868 the rank-and-file voter could be expected to support "the Lion of Vicksburg" because of his record as a war leader. Both parties wooed him, but his falling-out with President Johnson pushed him toward the Republicans and built trust in him among the Radicals. They were, as Thad Stevens said, ready to "let him into the church." Impeachment proceedings were still in progress when the Republicans gathered in Chicago to name their candidate. Grant was the unanimous choice and House Speaker Schuyler Colfax of Indiana became his running mate. The platform endorsed the Reconstruction policy of Congress, congratulating the country on the "assured success" of the program. One plank cautiously defended Negro suffrage as a necessity in the South, but a matter each northern state should settle for itself. Another urged payment of the national debt "in the utmost good faith to all creditors," which meant in gold. More important than the platform were the great expectations of a soldier-president and his slogan: "Let us have peace."

The Democrats took an opposite position on both Reconstruction and the debt. The Republican Congress, the platform charged, instead of restoring the Union, had "so far as in its power, dissolved it, and subjected ten states, in the time of profound peace, to military despotism and Negro supremacy." As to the public debt, the party endorsed Rep. George H. Pendleton's "Ohio idea" that since most bonds had been bought with depreciated greenbacks, they should be paid off in greenbacks unless they specified payment in gold. With no conspicuously available candidate in sight, the convention turned to Horatio Seymour, war governor of New York and chairman of the convention. His friends had to hustle him out of the hall to prevent his withdrawal. With Francis P. Blair of Missouri in the second place on the ticket, the Democrats made a closer race of it than showed up in the electoral vote. Eight states, including New York and New Jersey, went for Seymour. While Grant swept the electoral college by 214 to 80, his popular majority was only 307,000 out of a total of over 5.7 million votes. More than 500,000 black voters accounted for Grant's margin of victory.

EARLY APPOINTMENTS   Grant had proven himself a great leader in the war, but in the White House he seemed blind to the political forces and influence peddlers around him. He was awe-struck by men of wealth and unaccountably loyal to some who betrayed his trust. The historian Henry Adams, who lived in Washington at the time, noted that to his friends "Grant appeared as intermittent energy, immensely powerful when awake, but passive and plastic in repose. . . . They could never measure his character or be sure when he would act. They could never follow a mental process in his thought. They were not sure that he did think." His conception of the presidency was "Whiggish." The chief executive carried out the laws; in the formulation of policy he passively followed the lead of Congress. This approach endeared him at first to party leaders, but it left him at last ineffective and others disillusioned with his leadership.

At the outset Grant consulted nobody on his cabinet appointments. Some of his choices indulged personal whims; others simply betrayed bad judgment. In some cases appointees learned of their nomination from the newspapers. The first secretary of state, former Rep. Elihu B. Washburne, an old friend from Illinois, served an honorific term of one week before going to his destined post as minister to France. Secretary of the Navy Adolph E. Borie was a casual dinner-table acquaintance and political contributor. A. T. Stewart, a wealthy merchant nominated as secretary of the treasury, was ineligible because of a law which barred anyone in "trade or commerce." As time went by Grant betrayed a fatal gift for losing men of talent and integrity from his cabinet. Secretary of State Hamilton Fish of New York turned out to be a happy exception; he guided foreign policy throughout the Grant presidency.

At first it looked as if Grant's free-wheeling style of choosing a cabinet signaled a sharp departure from the spoils system. But once Grant had taken care of his friends and relatives, he began to take care of party leaders. Cabinet members who balked at the procedure were soon eased out. This strengthened a nascent movement for a merit system in the civil service, modeled on systems recently adopted in Great Britain, Germany, and France. Grant finally approved a measure to set up a commission to look into the matter in 1872, a good gesture in a political year. The group duly brought in recommendations which in turn were duly shelved and forgotten once the election was over.

THE GOVERNMENT DEBT The "sound money" men had more success than the reformers. They claimed that Grant's election had been a mandate to save the country from the Democrats' "Ohio idea." The underlying purpose of the movement to pay off the government debt in greenbacks was to bring about an inflation of the currency. Many debtors and aggressive businessmen rallied to the cause of "easy money," joined by a large number of Radicals who thought a combination of high tariffs and easy money would bring about more rapid economic growth. But creditors stood to gain from payment in gold, and they had the greater influence in Republican circles. They also had the benefit of a strong Calvinistic tendency in the public mind to look upon the cause of hard money as a moral one; depreciated currency was somehow a fraud. In his inaugural address Grant endorsed payment of the debt in gold not as a point of policy but as a point of national honor. On March 18, 1869, the Public Credit Act endorsing that principle became the first act of Congress he signed. Under the Refunding Act of 1870 the Treasury was able to replace 6 percent Civil War bonds with a new issue promising 4–5 percent in gold.

But whatever Grant's convictions respecting a "sound currency," he was not ready to risk a sharp contraction of the greenbacks in circulation. After the war the Treasury had assumed that the $400 million in greenbacks would be retired from circulation. To that end in 1866 Congress gave the Treasury discretionary power to begin the process at a rate of $10 million in the first six months and $4 million a month thereafter. In 1868, however, "soft money" elements in Congress stopped the process, leaving $356 million outstanding. There matters stood when Grant took office.

REFORM AND SCANDAL   Long before Grant's first term was out, a reaction against the Reconstruction measures, and against incompetence and corruption in the administration, had incited mutiny within the Republican ranks. Open revolt broke out first in Missouri where Carl Schurz, a German immigrant and war hero, led a group which elected a governor with Democratic help in 1870 and sent Schurz to the Senate. In 1872 the Liberal Republicans (as they called themselves) held a national convention at Cincinnati which produced a compromise platform condemning the party's southern policy and favoring civil service reform, but remained silent on the protective tariff. The meeting, moreover, was stampeded toward an anomalous presidential candidate: Horace Greeley, editor of the New York *Tribune*, a strong protectionist, and longtime champion of just about every reform of his times. His image as a visionary eccentric was complemented by his record of hostility to Democrats, whose support the Liberals needed. The Democrats nevertheless swallowed the pill and gave their nomination to Greeley as the only hope of beating Grant.

The result was a foregone conclusion. Republican regulars duly endorsed Radical Reconstruction and the protective tariff.

Grant still had seven carpetbag states in his pocket, generous support from business and banking interests, and the stalwart support of the Radicals. Above all he still evoked the imperishable glory of Missionary Ridge and Appomattox. Greeley, despite an exhausting tour of the country—still unusual for a presidential candidate—carried only six southern and border states and none in the North. Greeley's wife had died during the campaign, and worn out with grief and fatigue, he too was gone three weeks after the election.

Within less than a year of his reelection Grant was adrift in a cesspool of scandal. The first hint of scandal had touched Grant in the summer of 1869, when the crafty Jay Gould and the flamboyant Jim Fisk connived with the president's brother-in-law, Abel R. Corbin, to corner the gold market. Gould concocted an argument that the government should refrain from selling gold on the market because a rise in gold prices would raise temporarily depressed farm prices. Grant apparently smelled a rat from the start, but was seen in public with the speculators. Corbin convinced his associates that the president had bought the argument. As the rumor spread on Wall Street, gold rose from $132 to $163 an ounce. When Grant finally persuaded Corbin to pull out of the deal, Gould began quietly selling out. Finally, on "Black Friday," September 24, 1869, Grant ordered the Treasury to sell a large quantity of gold and the bubble burst. Fisk got out by repudiating his agreements and hiring thugs to intimidate his creditors. "Nothing is lost save honor," he said.

During the campaign of 1872 the public first learned about the financial buccaneering of the Crédit Mobilier, a construction company which had milked the Union Pacific Railroad for exorbitant fees to line the pockets of insiders who controlled both firms. Rank-and-file Union Pacific shareholders were left holding the bag. Rep. Oakes Ames had distributed Crédit Mobilier shares at bargain rates where, he said, "it will produce much good to us." The beneficiaries had included Speaker Schuyler Colfax, later vice-president, and Rep. James A. Garfield, later president. This chicanery had transpired before Grant's election in 1868, but it touched a number of prominent Republicans. Of thirteen members of Congress involved, only two were censured by a Congress which, before it adjourned in March 1873, voted itself a pay raise from $5,000 to $7,500—retroactive, it decided, for two years. A public uproar forced repeal, leaving the raises voted the president ($25,000 to $50,000) and Supreme Court justices.

Even more odious disclosures soon followed, and some in-

The People's Handwriting on the Wall. *An 1872 engraving comments on the corruption engulfing Grant. [Library of Congress]*

volved the president's cabinet. Secretary of War W. W. Belknap, it turned out, had accepted bribes from Indian traders at army posts in the West. He was impeached, but resigned in time to elude trial by the Senate. Post-office contracts, it was revealed, went to carriers who offered the highest kickbacks. Secretary of the Treasury W. A. Richardson had awarded a commission of 50 percent for the collection of overdue taxes by John D. Sanborn, a political friend of Massachusetts Rep. Benjamin F. Butler. In St. Louis a "Whiskey Ring" bribed tax collectors to bilk the government of millions in revenue. Grant's private secretary, Orville Babcock, was enmeshed in that scheme, taking large sums of money and other valuables in return for inside information. Before Grant's second term ended, the corruption crossed the Atlantic when Gen. Robert Schenck, minister to London, unloaded worthless stock in "Emma Mines" on gullible Britons. Only a plea of diplomatic immunity and a sudden exit spared him from British justice. There is no evidence that Grant himself was ever involved in, or that he personally profited from, any of the fraud, but his poor choice of associates earned him the public censure that was heaped upon his head.

PANIC AND REDEMPTION Economic distress followed close upon public scandal. Contraction of the money supply and expansion of the railroads into sparsely settled areas had made investors cautious. During 1873 the market for railroad bonds turned sour as some twenty-five roads defaulted on their interest payments before the end of August. The investment banking firm of Jay Cooke and Company, unable to sell the bonds of the Northern Pacific Railroad, financed them with short-term deposits in hope that a European market would develop. But in 1873 the opposite happened when a financial panic in Vienna forced many financiers to unload American stocks and bonds. Caught short, Cooke and Company went bankrupt on September 18, 1873. The ensuing stampede forced the stock market to close for ten days. The Panic of 1873 set off a depression that lasted for six years, the longest and most severe that Americans had yet suffered, marked by widespread bankruptcies, unemployment, and a drastic slowdown in railroad building.

Hard times and scandals hurt Republicans in the midterm elections of 1874. The Democrats won control of the House of Representatives and gained in the Senate. The new Democratic House immediately launched inquiries into the scandals and unearthed further evidence of corruption in high places. The panic meanwhile focused attention once more on greenback currency.

Since greenbacks were valued less than gold, they had become the chief circulating medium. Most people spent greenbacks first and held their gold or used it to settle foreign accounts, which drained much gold out of the country. The postwar retirement of greenbacks had made for tight money. To relieve deflation and stimulate business, therefore, the Treasury reissued $26 million in greenbacks previously withdrawn, raising the total in circulation to about $382 million.

For a time the advocates of easy money were riding high. Early in 1874 they pushed through a bill to issue greenbacks up to the wartime level of $400 million. Here the administration drew the line, however. Grant vetoed the bill in April and in his annual message of December 1874 called for the gradual resumption of specie payments—that is, the redemption of greenbacks in gold. This would make greenbacks "good as gold" and raise their value to a par with the gold dollar. In January, before the Republicans gave up control of the House, Congress obliged by passing the Resumption Act of 1875. The redemption in specie began on January 1, 1879, after the Treasury had built a gold reserve for the purpose and reduced the value of greenbacks in circulation.

THE COMPROMISE OF 1877 Grant, despite everything, was eager to run again in 1876, but the recent scandals discouraged any challenge to the two-term tradition. James G. Blaine of Maine, late Speaker of the House, emerged as the Republican front-runner, but he too bore the taint of scandal. Letters in the possession of James Mulligan of Boston linked Blaine to some dubious railroad dealings. Blaine cajoled Mulligan into turning over a packet of letters, from which he read to Congress selected passages exonerating him. But the performance was a shade too clever. It left doubts which were strengthened by the disclosure of still other "Mulligan letters" that found their way into print.

The Republican convention in Cincinnati therefore eliminated Blaine and several other hopefuls in favor of Ohio's favorite son, Rutherford B. Hayes. Three times elected governor of Ohio, most recently as an advocate of sound money, Hayes had also made a name as a civil service reformer. But his chief virtue was that he offended neither Radicals nor reformers. As Henry Adams put it, he was "a third rate nonentity, whose only recommendation is that he is obnoxious to no one." The vice-presidential nod went to William A. Wheeler of New York.

The Democratic convention in St. Louis was abnormally harmonious from the start. The nomination went on the second ballot to Samuel J. Tilden, millionaire corporation lawyer and reform governor of New York who had directed a campaign to overthrow first the Tweed Ring in New York City and then another ring in Albany which had bilked the state of millions. The convention named Thomas A. Hendricks of Indiana for vice-president.

The campaign generated no burning issues. Both candidates favored the trend toward conservative rule in the South. During one of the most corrupt elections ever, both candidates favored civil service reform. In the absence of strong differences, Democrats waved the Republicans' dirty linen. In response, Republicans waved the bloody shirt, which is to say that they engaged in verbal assaults on former Confederates and the spirit of Rebellion. The phrase "waving the bloody shirt" originated at the impeachment trial of President Johnson when Benjamin F. Butler, speaking for the prosecution, displayed the bloody shirt a Mississippi carpetbagger had been wearing when hauled out of bed and beaten by Ku Kluxers. Reporting such atrocities came to be known to Democrats as "grinding the outrage mills." "Our strong ground," Hayes wrote to Blaine, "is the dread of a solid South, *rebel rule*, etc., etc. . . . It leads people away from 'hard times,' which is our deadliest foe."

On the night of the election early returns pointed to a victory for Tilden, but Republican National Chairman Zachariah Chandler refused to concede. As it fell out, Tilden had 184 electoral votes, just one short of a majority, but Republicans claimed nineteen doubtful votes from Florida, Louisiana, and South Carolina, while Democrats laid a counterclaim to Oregon. But the Republicans had clearly carried Oregon. In the South the outcome was less certain, and given the fraud and intimidation perpetrated on both sides, nobody will ever know what might have happened if, to use a slogan of the day, "a free ballot and a fair count" had prevailed. As good a guess as any may be, as one writer suggested, that the Democrats stole the election first and the Republicans stole it back.

In all three of the disputed southern states rival canvassing boards sent in different returns. In Florida, Republicans conceded the state election, but in Louisiana and South Carolina rival state governments also appeared. The Constitution offered no guidance in this unprecedented situation. Even if Congress was empowered to sort things out, the Democratic House and the Republican Senate proved unable to reach an agreement.

Finally, on January 29, 1877, the two houses decided to set up a special Electoral Commission which would investigate and report back its findings. It had fifteen members, five each from the House, the Senate, and the Supreme Court. Members were so chosen as to have seven from each major party with Justice David Davis of Illinois as the swing man. Davis, though appointed to the Court by Lincoln, was no party regular and was in fact thought to be leaning toward the Democrats. Republicans who voted for the commission, James A. Garfield said, were "fair-minded asses" who thought that "truth is always half way between God and the Devil." The panel appeared to be stacked in favor of Tilden.

But as it turned out, the panel got restacked the other way. Short-sighted Democrats in the Illinois legislature teamed up with minority Greenbackers to name Davis their senator. Davis accepted, no doubt with a sense of relief. From the remaining justices, all Republicans, the panel chose Joseph P. Bradley to fill the vacancy. The decision on each state went by a vote of 8 to 7, along party lines, in favor of Hayes. After much bluster and threat of filibuster by Democrats, the House voted on March 2 to accept the report and declare Hayes elected by an electoral vote of 185 to 184.

Critical to this outcome was the defection of southern Democrats who had made several informal agreements with the Republicans. On February 26, 1877, a bargain was struck at the Wormley House, a Washington hotel, between prominent Ohio Republicans, including Sen. John Sherman and Rep. James A.

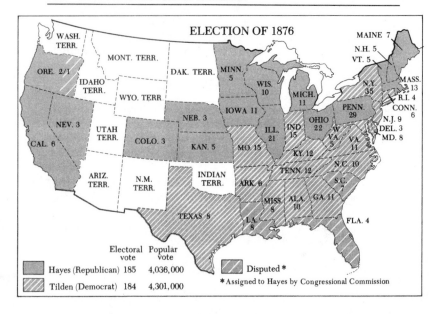

ELECTION OF 1876

	Electoral vote	Popular vote
Hayes (Republican)	185	4,036,000
Tilden (Democrat)	184	4,301,000

Disputed *

*Assigned to Hayes by Congressional Commission

Garfield, and powerful southern Democrats, including Sen. John Brown Gordon of Georgia and Rep. L. Q. C. Lamar of Mississippi. The Republicans promised that, if elected, Hayes would withdraw federal troops from Louisiana and South Carolina, letting the Republican governments there collapse. In return the Democrats promised to withdraw their opposition to Hayes, to accept in good faith the Reconstruction amendments, and to refrain from partisan reprisals against Republicans in the South.

With this agreement in hand, southern Democrats could justify deserting Tilden because this so-called Compromise of 1877 brought a final "redemption" from the "Radicals" and a return to "home rule," which actually meant rule by white Democrats. Other, more informal promises, less noticed by the public, bolstered the Wormley House agreement. Hayes's friends pledged more support for Mississippi levees and other internal improvements, including federal subsidy for a transcontinental railroad along a southern route. Southerners extracted a further promise that Hayes would name a white southerner as postmaster-general, the cabinet position with the most patronage jobs at hand. In return, southerners would let Republicans make James A. Garfield Speaker of the new House.

THE END OF RECONSTRUCTION After Hayes took office, most of these promises were either renounced or forgotten. They had served their purpose of breaking the crisis. In April, Hayes withdrew federal troops from the state houses in Louisiana and South Carolina, and the Republican governments there collapsed—along with much of Hayes's claim to legitimacy. Hayes chose a Tennessean, former Confederate David M. Key, as postmaster-general. But after southern Democrats failed to permit the choice of Garfield as Speaker, Hayes expressed doubt about any further subsidy for railroad building, and none was voted.

As to southern promises regarding the civil rights of blacks, only a few Democratic leaders such as Wade Hampton and Francis T. Nicholls, the new governors of South Carolina and Louisiana, remembered them for long. Over the next three decades those rights crumbled under the pressure of white rule in the South and the force of Supreme Court decisions narrowing the application of the Reconstruction amendments. The Compromise of 1877, viewed in the light of its consequences, might justly bear the label which one historian gave it: "The betrayal of the Negro." But "betrayal" implies that a promise was made in the first place, and Reconstruction never offered more than an uncertain commitment to equality before the law. Yet it left an enduring legacy, the Thirteenth, Fourteenth, and Fifteenth Amendments—not dead but dormant, waiting to be warmed back into life.

FURTHER READING

Over time the various interpretations of Reconstruction have made that period "a dark and bloody ground" for historians. Those interested in following the interplay of interpretation might first turn to works of fiction to understand how the adversaries line up. Albion W. Tourgée's *A Fool's Errand* (1880, 1966)° provides a northern carpetbagger's idealistic view, while Thomas Dixon's *The Clansman* (1905)° applauds the defeated South's heroic casting off of the tyranny of corrupt occupation. This pro-southern viewpoint came to dominate professional scholarship as well after 1900. William A. Dunning's *Reconstruction, Political and Economic, 1865–1877* (1907), sets the tone for numerous monographs sympathetic to white southern suffering under "black rule."

Among the early challengers to the Dunning school are Charles and Mary Beard, whose sweeping *Rise of American Civilization* (1927) assigns largely economic motives to the actors in Reconstruction politics. Howard Beale's *The Critical Year* (1930) sees the Radical Republicans as fanatics who served business interests, and Andrew Johnson as a commonsensical mediator in the controversies of 1866. Among the strongest

°These books are available in paperback editions.

challengers of the pro-southern view is W. E. B. Du Bois's *Black Recon- struction* (1935), which maintains that the Republicans held valid ideals in their defense of freedmen rights.

The civil rights movement of the 1950s and 1960s brought new fresh- ness to the topic. Among the surveys which reflect a new sympathy for the aims of the Radicals and the plight of freedmen are John Hope Franklin's *Reconstruction after the Civil War* (1961) and Kenneth M. Stampp's *The Era of Reconstruction* (1964).° More detailed, but equally valuable, are Rembert W. Patrick's *The Reconstruction of the Nation* (1967), James G. Randall and David Donald's *Civil War and Reconstruc- tion* (1969), and James M. McPherson's *Ordeal by Fire: The Civil War and Reconstruction* (1982).

More specialized works give closer scrutiny to the aims of the princi- pal political figures. William B. Hesseltine's *Lincoln's Plan of Recon- struction* (1960) argues that the president planned postwar policy in the same pragmatic fashion as he directed the Civil War. Peyton McCrary's *Abraham Lincoln and Reconstruction* (1978) deals with the Lincoln poli- cies as they were carried out in Louisiana. Claude G. Bower's *The Tragic Era* (1929) is sympathetic to Johnson, while Eric McKitrick's *Andrew Johnson and Reconstruction* (1960),° John H. and LaWanda C. Cox's *Pol- itics, Principle, and Prejudice* (1963), and William R. Brock's *An Ameri- can Crisis* (1963) sharply criticize the behavior of a president who obstructed Republican policies. Why Johnson was impeached is detailed in Michael L. Benedict's *The Impeachment of Andrew Johnson* (1973)° and H. L. Trefousse's *Impeachment of a President* (1975).

Recent scholars have been far more sympathetic to the aims and mo- tives of the Radical Republicans. Surveys of congressional behavior are Hans F. Trefousse's *The Radical Republicans* (1969)° and Herman Belz's *Reconstructing the Union* (1969). Clearest in dealing with the ideology of these Radicals is Michael L. Benedict's *A Compromise of Principle: Con- gressional Republicans and Reconstruction* (1974). Biographies of Radi- cal leaders include Fawn M. Brodie's *Thaddeus Stevens* (1959)° and David Donald's *Charles Summer and the Rights of Man* (1970).° For an emphasis on the relations of the courts and these congressmen, consult Stanley I. Kutler's *The Judicial Power and Reconstruction Policies* (1968) or Charles Fairman's *Reconstruction and Reunion* (1971).

The intransigence of southern white attitudes is examined in Michael Perman's *Reunion without Compromise* (1973) and Joe G. Taylor's *Loui- siana Reconstructed* (1974). Allen W. Trelease's *White Terror* (1971) covers the various organizations which practiced vigilante tactics, chiefly the Ku Klux Klan. The difficulties former planters had in adjust- ing to the new labor system are documented in James L. Roark's *Masters without Slaves* (1977).°

Numerous works have appeared on the freedmen's experience in the South. Start with Leon Litwack's *Been in the Storm So Long* (1979),° which wonderfully covers the transition from slavey to freedom. Among the best state-level studies are those dealing with South Carolina blacks. Willie Lee Rose's *Rehearsal for Reconstruction* (1964)° examines Union efforts to define the social role of former slaves during wartime emancipation. Joel Williamson's *After Slavery* (1965)° argues that South Carolina freedmen took an active role in pursuing their political and economic rights. A study of Alabama freedmen—Peter Kolchin's *First Freedom* (1974)—should also be consulted. The role of the Freedman's Bureau is explored in George R. Bentley's *A History of the Freedman's Bureau* (1955), William S. McFeely's *Yankee Stepfather: O. O. Howard and the Freedman* (1980),° and Robert C. Morris's *Reading, 'Riting and Reconstruction: The Education of Freedmen in the South, 1861–1870* (1981).

The role of white Republicans in one southern state in the immediate postwar years is traced in William C. Harris's *The Day of the Carpetbagger: Republican Reconstruction in Mississippi* (1979). The land confiscation issue is discussed in Eric Foner's *Politics and Ideology in the Age of the Civil War* (1980),° Beth Bethel's *Promiseland* (1981) on a South Carolina black community, and Janet S. Hermann's *The Pursuit of a Dream* (1981)° on the Davis Bend experiment.

The politics of corruption outside the South is depicted in Allan Nevin's *Hamilton Fish: The Inner History of the Great Administration* (1936) and William S. McFeeley's *Grant: A Biography* (1981).° The influence of Horace Greeley in postwar politics is treated in Eric S. Lunde's *Horace Greeley* (1980). The political maneuvers of the election of 1876 and the resultant crisis and compromise are explained in C. Vann Woodward's *Reunion and Reaction* (1966)° and William Gillette's *Retreat from Reconstruction, 1869–1879* (1979).°

19

NEW FRONTIERS: SOUTH AND WEST

The New South

A FRESH VISION   The major prophet of a New South emerged in an improbable setting—at New York's most elegant restaurant, Delmonico's—where on December 21, 1886, the New England Society of New York held its annual dinner to commemorate the landing of the Pilgrims at Plymouth Rock. The main speaker of the evening was Henry Woodfin Grady, thirty-six-year-old editor of the Atlanta *Constitution*, who had gained notice with his vivid reports of the recent Charleston earthquake. Grady's topic was "The New South," and his eloquent words became certainly the most celebrated statement of the New South Creed, a classic speech that multitudes of schoolboy orators in the South would commit to memory.

In plain yet almost poetic language, Grady set forth the vision that inspired a generation of southerners: "The Old South rested everything on slavery and agriculture, unconscious that these could neither give nor maintain healthy growth. The new South presents a perfect democracy, the oligarchs leading in the popular movement—a social system compact and closely knitted, less splendid on the surface, but stronger at the core—a hundred farms for every plantation, fifty homes for every palace—and a diversified industry that meets the complex need of this complex age."

Many prophets had gone before Grady and still others stood with him as major spokesmen for the New South Creed. In the aftermath of the Civil War these men, and Yankee patrons like William D. "Pig Iron" Kelly of Pennsylvania, preached with evangelical fervor the gospel of industry. The Confederacy, they reasoned, had lost because it relied too much on King Cotton. In the future the South must follow the North's example and industrialize. From that central belief flowed certain corollaries: that a more diversified and efficient agriculture would be a foundation for economic growth, that more widespread education especially vocational training, would promote material success, and that sectional peace and racial harmony would provide a stable environment for economic growth.

By the late 1870s, with Reconstruction over and the panic of 1873 forgotten, a mood of progress permeated the editorials and the speeches of the day. The mood found material expression in a series of industrial fairs whose prototype was Atlanta's International Cotton Exposition of 1881. Organized in response to the call of a Boston capitalist, Edward Atkinson, the exposition would, according to a prospectus, show how the South could become "prosperous in its own right through a liberal development of its own resources." To that end the displays featured machinery for spinning and weaving, and showed the best applications of power. In all some 1,113 exhibits from thirty-three states, the District of Columbia, and six foreign countries were mounted, at an expense of more than $2 million.

ECONOMIC GROWTH   The first and chief fruit of the New South zealots was an expansion of the area's textile production that got under way in the 1880s and eventually overtook the older New

White Oak Cotton Mills, Greensboro, North Carolina. These women are measuring, sewing, and finishing denim. [Brown Brothers]

England industry by the 1920s. In the New South, as in New England and Old England, cotton textiles were the harbingers of the Industrial Revolution. Already in the 1870s new cotton mills had begun to dot the landscape of the Carolina Piedmont, where their promotion generated an almost revivalistic fervor. From 1880 to 1900 the number of cotton mills in the South grew from 161 to 400, the number of mill workers (among whom women and children outnumbered the men) increased fivefold, and the consumption of cotton went up nearly tenfold, from 182,000 bales to 1,479,000. This development was the product mainly of southern capital and southern labor at the outset, though later the decline of the textile industry in New England contributed labor and capital to the South.

Tobacco growth also increased significantly, entering a new era with the development of two varieties of the weed: burley, which appeared in 1864 in southern Ohio, and bright leaf, which was grown on otherwise infertile soils and cured by a charcoal process discovered by a slave in 1839. Knowledge of the bright-leaf type remained chiefly local until, in what seemed a misfortune, Union soldiers swarmed over central North Carolina in 1865.

One victim of their looting was John Ruffin Green, whose bright-leaf tobacco factory was ransacked by soldiers loitering around Durham's Station. Within a few weeks orders began to pour in to Green's factory for the Best Flavored Spanish Smoking Tobacco "that did not bite." With this revival, Green adopted as his trademark a bull's head similar to that on Coleman's mustard, made in Durham, England. It did not take long for Green and his successors to make the image of Bull Durham ubiquitous, so much so that years later Mark Twain, who was not above embellishing a good story, claimed that when he visited Egypt he never got a clear view of the pyramids for the Bull Durham signs.

Even more important in the rise of tobacco and Durham was the Duke family, whose story started at a nearby farm. At the end of the Civil War, the story goes, old Washington Duke had a capital of fifty cents obtained from a Yankee soldier for a souvenir Confederate five-dollar bill. He took a barnful of tobacco, and with the help of his three sons, beat it out with hickory sticks, stuffed it in bags labeled "Pro Bono Publico," hitched up two mules to his wagon, and set out across the state, selling bright leaf as he went. From that start success followed quickly. By 1872 the Dukes had a factory producing 125,000 pounds of leaf annually, and Washington Duke prepared to settle down and enjoy success. His son Buck (James Buchanan Duke), however, had the same drive that animated the Carnegies and Rockefellers of that

From the "Sporting Girls" series of trade cards, W. Duke Sons & Co. These cards were inserted in cigarette packs to promote sales. [W. Duke & Co. Papers, Manuscript Department, Duke University Library]

day. Buck Duke recognized early that the industry was "half smoke and half ballyhoo" and poured large sums into advertising schemes, such as the cigarette coupons for which one could get an album in color entitled "Sporting Girls." Duke also squeezed competitors by underselling them in their own markets, and by cornering the supply of ingredients like glycerin and licorice. Eventually his competitors were ready to take the hint that they join forces, and in 1890 Duke brought most of them into the American Tobacco Company, which controlled nine-tenths of the nation's cigarette production and by 1904 about three-fourths of all tobacco production in the United States. In 1911 the Supreme Court found the company in violation of the Sherman Anti-Trust Act and ordered it broken up, but by then Duke had found new worlds to conquer in hydroelectric power and aluminum.

Systematic use of other natural resources brought into the New South that area along the Appalachian Mountain chain from West Virginia to Alabama. Coal production in the South (including West Virginia) grew from 4.6 million tons in 1875 to 49.3 million tons by 1900. At the southern end of the mountains, Birmingham, Alabama, sprang up during the 1870s in the shadow of Red Mountain, so named for its iron ore, and soon tagged itself the "Pittsburgh of the South." Birmingham's close proximity to coal, iron, and limestone gave it a strong advantage over Chattanooga, which had a meteoric career as an iron center after the war.

With growth came a need for housing, and thus after 1870 lumbering became a ubiquitous industry in the South. Lumber camps and little "peckerwood" mills sprang up all across the mountains and flatlands. By the turn of the century their product, mainly southern pine, had outdistanced textiles in value. Tree cutting seemed to know no bounds. It went on and on, despite the ecological devastation it caused. In time the industry would be saved only by the warm climate, which fostered quick renewal, and the rise of scientific forestry, which had its beginnings on George Vanderbilt's Biltmore Estate near Asheville, North Carolina. Here Dr. Carl Alvin Schenck opened the nation's first school of forestry in 1898.

The South still had far to go to achieve the "diversified industry" that Grady envisioned in the mid-1880s, but a profusion of other products poured from southern plants: phosphate fertilizers from coastal South Carolina and Florida; oysters, vegetables, and fruits from widespread canneries; ships, including battleships, from the Newport News Shipbuilding and Drydock Company; leather products; wagons and buggies; liquors and beverages; paper in small quantities; clay, glass, and stone products.

At the turn of the century two great forces that would impel an even greater industrial revolution were already on the horizon: petroleum in the Southwest and hydroelectric power in the Southeast. The Corsicana field in Texas had been opened in 1895, and in 1901 the Spindletop gusher would bring a great bonanza. Local powerplants dotted the map by the 1890s. Richmond, Virginia, had the nation's first electric streetcar system in 1888, and Columbia, South Carolina, had the first electrically powered cotton mill in 1894. The greatest advance would begin in 1905 when Buck Duke's Southern Power Company set out to develop entire river valleys in the Carolinas.

AGRICULTURE, OLD AND NEW   At the turn of the century, however, most of the South was still undeveloped, at least by northeastern standards. The typical southerner was less apt to be tending a loom or forge than, as the saying went, facing the eastern end of a westbound mule. King Cotton survived the Civil War and expanded over new acreage even as its export markets leveled off. The old tobacco belts of Virginia and Kentucky now reached across North Carolina and touched South Carolina. Louisiana cane sugar, probably the most war-devastated of all crops, flourished again by the 1890s. In 1885 Seaman A. Knapp, an agriculturist from New York by way of Iowa, moved to Louisiana and developed a new rice belt on behalf of an English land company, using machinery imported from the wheatfields. In the process Knapp invented the demonstration methods of agricultural education, which showed farmers the most productive methods on selected plots of land, with the aim of teaching by example.

Knapp later used the demonstration method to fight the boll weevil in Texas. His work led eventually to the national system of county farm and home demonstration agents. In the old rice belt of coastal South Carolina and elsewhere truck farming sprang up with the advent of the railroads and refrigerator cars. Vegetables from the Sea Islands, strawberries from Louisiana, and citrus fruits from Florida combined with other produce to create a cash crop second only to cotton.

In 1880 the poet Sidney Lanier, in one of the perennial essays on "The New South," claimed that "The New South means small farming." The "quiet rise of the small farmer" was "the notable circumstance of the period, in comparison with which noisier events signify nothing." But the growth of small farming remained a statistical illusion. Farms of all sizes were more numerous because new acreage came into cultivation, even in the seaboard states. The census, moreover, counted tenant and sharecropper plots as separate farms.

Sharecropping and tenancy became increasingly prevalent in the aftermath of emancipation, but they seldom produced the self-sufficiency that Lanier envisioned. The sharecropper, who had nothing to offer the landowner but his labor, tilled the land in return for supplies and a share of the crop, generally about half. The tenant farmer, hardly better off, might offer the planter a mule, a plow, and perhaps his own line of credit with the country store, and therefore might claim a larger share, commonly three-fourths of the cash crop and two-thirds of the subsistence crop, which was mainly corn. There were, moreover, infinite variations that ranged from cash rental at best to outright peon-

Black sharecroppers, ca. 1880–1890. [Brown Brothers]

age at worst. From the standpoint of efficiency the system approached the worst conceivable, for the tenant lacked incentive to care for the land and the owner had little chance to supervise the work. In addition the system bred a morbid suspicion on both sides, and the folklore of the rural South was replete with stories of tenants who remained stubbornly shiftless and improvident, and landlords who kept books with crooked pencils.

The crop lien system was equally flawed. At best, it supplied credit where cash was scarce. Country merchants furnished supplies in return for liens (or mortgages) on farmers' crops. To a few tenants and small farmers who seized the chance, the credit offered a way out, but to most it offered only a hopeless cycle of perennial debt. The merchant, who assumed great risks, generally charged markups and interest which ranged, according to one farmer, "from 24 percent to grand larceny." The merchant, like the planter (often the same man), demanded a cash crop that could be readily sold at harvest time. For all the wind and ink expended on preachments of diversification, the routines of tenancy and sharecropping yielded only with difficulty to other arrangements because the marketing, supply, and credit systems were still geared to a staple crop, usually cotton. The stagnation of rural life held millions, white and black, in bondage to privation and ignorance.

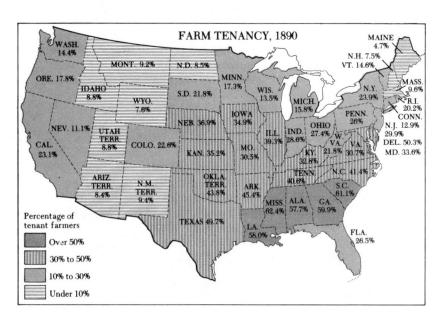

THE BOURBON REDEEMERS   In politics, despite the South's formal democracy, habits of deference still prevailed. "Every community," Union officer John DeForest noted in postwar South Carolina, "had its great man, or its little great man, around whom his fellow citizens gather when they want information, and to whose monologues they listen with a respect akin to humility." DeForest called him the "Central Monkey." After Reconstruction, southern politics was dominated by small coteries of "Central Monkeys" collectively known to history as Bourbons. Like the French Bourbons, the royal family which, Napoleon said, forgot nothing and learned nothing in the ordeal of revolution, the southern Bourbons were said to have forgotten nothing and learned nothing in the ordeal of Civil War. Yet the term, according to one historian, is one of "the most indefinable words ever used to describe Southern persons, places, and things, either solid or liquid."

The word functioned mainly as a hateful epithet, and few could glory in it. But their Republican, Independent, and Populist adversaries fixed the label so firmly in the vocabulary of the times that Bourbon came to signify the leaders of the Democratic party, whether they were real mossbacks or, more commonly, champions of an industrial New South who, if they had forgotten nothing, had at least learned something. They may have worshipped at the shrine of the old order, but they embraced a new order of economic development.

These Bourbons of the New South perfected a political alliance with eastern conservatives and an economic alliance with eastern capitalists. They generally pursued a policy of laissez-faire, except for the tax exemptions and other favors they offered to business. They avoided political initiatives, making the transition from Republican rule to Bourbon rule less abrupt than is often assumed. The Bourbons' favorable disposition toward the railroads was not unlike that of the Radicals. The Louisiana Lottery, a state lottery established during Reconstruction as a private monopoly, paid for "Redemption" from Republican rule in the state and was rewarded by Bourbons with a renewed tenure, written into the state constitution. And despite their reputation for honesty, Bourbon officeholders were occasionally caught with their fingers in the till.

Being basically antigovernment and haunted by the war, the Bourbons made a cardinal virtue of retrenchment. Their parsimony spelled austerity for public services, including the school systems started during Reconstruction. In 1871 the South Atlantic states were spending $10.27 per pupil; by 1880 the figure was down to $6.00 and in 1890 it still stood at $7.63. In 1901 Charles W. Dabney, an educational leader of the time, summarized conditions at the turn of the century: "In the Southern states, in schoolhouses costing an average of $276 each, under teachers receiving an average salary of $25 a month, we are giving children in actual attendance only 5 cents' worth of education a day for eighty-seven days only in the year." Illiteracy rates at the time ran at about 12 percent of the native white population and 50 percent of the black population.

Private philanthropy, however, did help to keep southern schools afloat. In 1867 George Peabody, a London banker born in Massachusetts, established the Peabody Fund for Education, which was to spend some $3.6 million on public schools by 1914, when it was dissolved and most of its capital transferred to the George Peabody College for Teachers, established in 1875 in Nashville. Aid from the Peabody Fund was supplemented by the $1 million in the John F. Slater Fund, established in 1882 by a donor in Connecticut and earmarked for Negro schools. J. L. M. Curry, onetime soldier, preacher, teacher, and politician, became the general agent of both the Peabody and the Slater Funds. A very active man, Curry pursued an extensive program of speaking and building support for education. He set up teachers' associations and started some of the first summer schools for teachers, and in general tried to foster exemplary schools.

The urge to economize created in the penal system one of the darkest blots on the Bourbon record: convict leasing. Necessity gave rise to the practice immediately after the Civil War; economy dictated its continuance. The destruction of prisons and the chaotic poverty of state treasuries combined with the demand for cheap labor on the railroads, in the mines, and in lumber and turpentine camps, to make the leasing of convict labor a way for southern states to avoid expenses and even bring in profits. The burden on the states of detaining criminals grew after the war because freedmen, who as slaves had been subject to the discipline of masters, were now subject to the criminal law. Convict leasing, in the absence of state supervision, allowed inefficiency, neglect, and disregard for human life to proliferate.

The Bourbons scaled down not only expenditures but also the public debt, and by a simple means—they repudiated a vast amount of debt in all the former Confederate states except Florida and Mississippi. The corruption and extravagance of Radical rule were commonly advanced as justification for the process, but repudiation did not stop with Reconstruction debts. Altogether nine states reprediated more than half of what they owed, or nearly $130 million out of an estimated total of $247.6 million. The Bourbons, who respected the sancity of property, were not of one mind about the process, however, and in Virginia their leaders honored the state debt so zealously, and at such cost to public services, that they were temporarily ousted by an Independent rebellion, the Readjuster party.

There are elements of diversity in the Bourbon record, however. Despite their devotion to economy, these parsimonious regimes, so ardently devoted to laissez-faire, did respond to the demand for commisssions to regulate the rates charged by railroads for commercial transport. They established boards of agriculture, boards of public health, agricultural experiment stations, agricultural and mechanical colleges, normal schools and women's colleges, even state colleges for Negroes. Nor will any simplistic interpretation encompass the variety of Bourbon leaders. The Democratic party of the time was a mongrel coalition which threw Old Whigs, Know Nothings, Unionists, secessionists, businessmen, small farmers, hillbillies, planters, and even some Republicans together in alliance against the Reconstruction Radicals. Democrats therefore, even those who willynilly bore the Bourbon label, often heard different drummers.

The effects of Radical and Bourbon rule in the South. This 1880 cartoon shows the South staggering under the oppressive weight of military Reconstruction (left) and flourishing under the "Let 'Em Alone Policy" of Hayes and the Bourbons (right). [The Granger Collection]

And once they got control, the conflicts inherent in any coalition began to assert themselves so that Bourbon regimes never achieved complete unity in philosophy or government.

Independent movements cropped up in all the southern states, endorsing a variety of proposals including debt repudiation, inflation, usury laws, and antimonopoly laws. Locally they fought Bourbon Democrats over fencing laws (poor farmers preferred to let their scrub stock forage for itself), patronage, and issues of corruption. On occasion they joined forces with third parties like the Greenbackers, and sometimes they elected local officials and congressmen. In Tennessee the division became so acute that the Republicans elected a governor in 1880. In Virginia, where the rebels sought reduction of the state debt, a Readjuster party captured the legislature in 1879, elected a governor in 1881, and sent their leader, William E. Mahone, to the United States Senate.

For a brief time there emerged a wholesale collaboration between Republicans and Independents, which Chester A. Arthur promoted after he became president in the fall of 1881. The policy failed to make headway, however, because Republicans had little in common with the Independents except their opposition to the Democrats, and because the Republican machinery in the South had already been devastated by the overthrow of Reconstruction and by President Hayes's policy of reconciliation with the Bourbons immediately afterward. The Republicans maintained a secure foothold only in the Blue Ridge and Smoky Mountains, "the great spine of Republicanism which runs down the back of the South," where stubborn white Unionists passed the faith on to later generations.

Perhaps the ultimate paradox of the Bourbons' rule was that these paragons of white supremacy tolerated a lingering black voice in politics and showed no haste about raising the barriers of racial separation. A number of them harbored at least some element of patrician benevolence toward blacks. The old slaveowner, said a South Carolina editor, "has no desire to browbeat, maltreat, and spit upon the colored man"—clearly in part because the slaveowner saw in freedmen no threat to his status. Blacks sat in the state legislatures of South Carolina until 1900 and of Georgia until 1890; some of these black representatives were Democrats. The South sent black congressmen to Washington in every election down to 1900 except one, though they always represented gerrymandered districts into which most of the state's black voters had been thrown. Under the Bourbons the disfranchisement of black voters remained inconsistent, a local matter brought about mainly by fraud and intimidation, but it occurred enough to ensure white control.

A like flexibility applied to other areas of race relations. The color line was drawn less strictly than it would be in the twentieth century. In some places, to be sure, racial segregation appeared before the end of Reconstruction, especially in schools, churches, hotels and rooming houses, and private social relations. In places of public accommodation such as trains, depots, theaters, and soda fountains, however, discrimination was more capricious. In 1885 a black journalist, T. McCants Stewart, reported from his native state of South Carolina that he rode first-class cars on the railroads and in the streets, was served at saloons and soda fountains, saw Negroes dining with whites at train stations, and saw a black policeman arrest a white man on the streets of Columbia. Fifteen years later such scenes would be rare.

DISFRANCHISING BLACKS   During the 1890s the attitudes that permitted such moderation eroded swiftly. One reason was political. The rise of the Populist party divided the white vote to such an extent that in some places the black vote became the balance of power. Populists made a play for black votes and brought blacks prominently into their councils. "You are kept apart," Georgia's Tom Watson told black and white farmers, "in order that you may be separately fleeced." The Bourbons' reponse to all this was to revive the race issue, which they exploited with seasoned finesse, all the while controlling for their ticket a good part of the black vote in plantation areas. Nevertheless the Bourbons soon argued that the black vote be eliminated completely from southern elections. It was imperative, Gov. Murphy J. Foster told the Louisiana legislature in 1894, that "the mass of ignorance, vice and venality without any proprietary interest in the State" be denied the vote. Some leaders of the farmers hoped that disfranchisement of Negroes would make it possible for whites to divide politically without raising the spectre of "Negro domination."

But since the Fifteenth Amendment made it impossible to disfranchise Negroes as such, the purpose was accomplished indirectly with devices such as poll taxes, head taxes, and literacy tests. Some opposed such devices because they also caught up poor whites in the net. But this white opposition was neutralized by providing loopholes in the literacy tests through which illiterate whites could slip. The Senate buried one last effort to protect black voters in 1890, when Rep. Henry Cabot Lodge sponsored a bill authorizing federal supervisors of elections to pass on the qualifications of excluded voters. Northern sentiment seemed unwilling to support any interference, and the bill failed.

Mississippi led the way to near-total disfranchisement of blacks. The state called a constitutional convention in 1890, while the Lodge Bill was still under consideration, for the express purpose of changing the suffrage provisions of the old Radical constitution of 1868. The Mississippi plan set the pattern that seven more states would follow over the next twenty years. First, a residence requirement—two years in the state, one year in the election district—eliminated those tenants who were in the habit of moving yearly in search of a better chance. Second, voters were disqualified if convicted of certain crimes. Third, all taxes, including a poll tax, had to be paid by February 1 of election year, which left plenty of time to lose the receipt before the fall vote. This proviso fell most heavily on the poor, most of whom were black. Fourth and finally, all voters had to be literate. The alternative, designed as a loophole for whites otherwise disqualified, was an "understanding" clause. The voter, if unable to read the Constitution, could qualify by being able to "understand" it—to the satisfaction of the registrar. Fraud was thus institutionalized rather than eliminated by "legal" disfranchisement.

In other states, variations on the Mississippi plan added a few flourishes. In 1895 South Carolina tacked on the proviso that owning property assessed at $300 would qualify an illiterate voter. In 1898 Louisiana invented the "grandfather clause," which allowed illiterates to qualify if their fathers or grandfathers had been eligible to vote on January 1, 1867, when blacks were still excluded. Negro educator Booker T. Washington sent the convention a sarcastic telegram expressing hope that "no one clothed with state authority will be tempted to perjure and degrade himself by putting one interpretation upon it for the white man and another for the black man. . . ." By 1910 Georgia, North Carolina, Virginia, Alabama, and Oklahoma had all adopted the grandfather clause. The effectiveness of these measures can be seen in a few sample figures. Louisiana in 1896 had 130,000 black voters registered, and in 1900, 5,320. Alabama in 1900 had 121,159 literate Negro males over twenty-one, according to the census; only 3,742 were registered to vote.

More significant than the technical devices for disfranchisement was the futility of attempting to overcome them. The literacy test in fact never had much to do with literacy. It was simply a device that could be used, fraudulently if need be, to exclude blacks. The fraud that had once prevailed at the ballot box was simply moved back one step to the registration process. Years later, when the Republican Calvin Coolidge got 1,000 votes in

South Carolina, Sen. Cole Blease remarked: "I do not know where he got them. I was astonished to know that they were cast and shocked to know that they were counted." Every southern state, moreover, adopted a statewide Democratic primary between 1896 and 1915, which became the only meaningful election outside isolated areas of Republican strength. With minor exceptions, the Democratic primaries excluded black voters altogether.

SEGREGATION SPREADS   "Jim Crow" segregation followed hard on disfranchisement and in some states came first. The symbolic target at first was the railway train. In the 1880s it was still common practice for American trains to have first- and second-class cars, which afforded a degree of racial segregation by the difference in cost. In 1885, nevertheless, George Washington Cable noted that in South Carolina Negroes "ride in first class cars as a right" and "their presence excites no comment." From 1875 to 1883 in fact any racial segregation violated a federal Civil Rights Act, which forbade discrimination in places of public accommodation. But in 1883 the Supreme Court ruled on seven *Civil Rights Cases* involving discrimination against Negroes by corporations or individuals. The Court held, with only one dissent, that the force of federal law could not extend to individual action because the Fourteenth Amendment, which provided that "no State" could deny citizens the equal protection of the laws, stood as a prohibition only against state action.

"Jim Crow," a stock character in the old minstrel shows, became a synonym for racial segregation in the twentieth century. Dan Rice developed the character in the 1830s. [New York Public Library]

This left as an open question the constitutionality of state laws *requiring* separate facilities under the rubric of "separate but equal," a slogan popular with the New South prophets. In 1881 Tennessee had required railroads in the state to maintain separate first-class cars for blacks and whites. In 1888 Mississippi went a step further by requiring passengers, under penalty of law, to occupy the car set aside for their race. When Louisiana followed suit in 1890, the law was challenged in the case of *Plessy v. Ferguson,* which the Supreme Court decided in 1896. The test case originated in New Orleans when Homer Plessy, an octoroon, refused to leave a white car when asked to do so. He was convicted, and the case rose on appeal to the Supreme Court. The Court's majority opinion, written by Justice Henry Billings Brown, a native of Massachusetts, said that segregation laws "have been generally, if not universally recognized as within the competency of state legislatures in the exercise of their police power." The sole dissenter was John Marshall Harlan, a former slaveholder and Whig Unionist from Kentucky, who had written the only dissent in the *Civil Rights Cases.* "In my opinion," Harlan wrote, "the judgment this day rendered will, in time, prove to be quite as pernicious as the decision made by this tribunal in the Dred Scott Case." The Plessy ruling, he predicted, would "stimulate aggressions, more or less brutal, upon the admitted rights of colored citizens. . . . "

Very soon the principle of segregation extended into every area of southern life, including street railways, hotels, restaurants, hospitals, recreations, sports, and employment. If an activity was overlooked by the laws, it was not overlooked in custom and practice. The editor of the Richmond *Times* expressed the prevailing view in his remark on January 12, 1900: "It is necessary that this principle be applied in every relation of Southern life. God Almighty drew the color line and it cannot be obliterated. The negro must stay on his side of the line and the white man must stay on his side, and the sooner both races recognize this fact and accept it, the better it will be for both."

As for the "aggressions, more or less brutal," which Harlan foretold, they were already routine when he pronounced his dissent. From the days of slavery race relations had operated in a context of force and violence. The period of growing discrimination at the turn of the century was one of the worst. In the decade from 1890 to 1899 lynchings in the United States averaged 187.5 per year, 82 percent of which occurred in the South; from 1900 to 1909 they averaged 92.5 per year, 92 percent in the South. Whites constituted 32.2 percent of the victims during the first period, only 11.4 percent in the latter. Edgar Gardner

Murphy, a young Episcopal priest in Montgomery, said that extremists had proceeded "from an undiscriminating attack upon the Negro's ballot to a like attack upon his schools, his labor, his life—from the contention that no Negro shall vote to the contention that no Negro shall learn, that no Negro shall labor, and (by implication) that no Negro shall live."

WASHINGTON AND DU BOIS A few brave souls, black and white, spoke out against the new dispensations, but by and large blacks had to accommodate them as best they could. To be sure, the doctrine of "separate but equal" did open some doors, such as those to black schools, that had once been closed entirely. Some blacks even began to make a virtue of necessity. The chief spokesman for this philosophy was Booker T. Washington, the black prophet of the New South Creed. Born in Virginia of a slave mother and a white father, Washington had fought extreme adversity to get an education at Hampton Institute, one of the postwar missionary schools, and then to build at Tuskegee, Alabama, a leading college for Negroes. Washington argued that American Negroes should first establish an economic base for their advancement. He insisted that Negroes should focus "upon the everyday practical things of life, upon something that is needed to be done, and something which they will be permitted to do in the community in which they reside." In his speech at the Atlanta Cotton States and International Exposition in 1895, which propelled him to fame, Washington advised fellow blacks: "Cast down your bucket where you are—cast it down in making friends . . . of the people of all races by whom we are surrounded. Cast it down in agriculture, mechanics, in commerce, in domestic service, and in the professions." He conspicuously

Booker T. Washington. [New York Public Library]

W. E. B. Du Bois. [The Warder Collection]

omitted politics and let fall an oblique endorsement of segregation: "In all things that are purely social we can be as separate as
the five fingers, yet one as the hand in all things essential to mutual progress."

Some people bitterly criticized Washington in his lifetime and
after for making a bad bargain: the sacrifice of broad education
and of civil rights for the dubious acceptance of white conservatives. W. E. B. Du Bois led blacks in this criticism of Washington.
A native of Massachusetts whose bearing suggested the hauteur
of a Boston Brahmin, Du Bois once said defiantly that he was born
"with a flood of Negro blood, a strain of French, a bit of Dutch,
but thank God! no 'Anglo-Saxon.' " Du Bois first experienced
southern racial practices as an undergraduate at Fisk University
in Nashville, a missionary school which emphasized liberal education. Later he took a Ph.D. in history from Harvard and briefly
attended the University of Berlin. In addition to an active career
in racial protest he left a distinguished record as a scholar and author. On the faculty of Atlanta University he began in 1896 a
series of annual Conferences on Negro Problems which produced some of the earliest sociological research in the South.

Washington, Du Bois argued, preached "a gospel of Work and
Money to such an extent as apparently almost completely to
overshadow the higher aims of life." The education of Negroes,
he argued, should not be merely vocational but should nurture
leaders willing to bid defiance to segregation and discrimination.
Du Bois called Washington's 1895 speech "The Atlanta Compromise" and argued that it had made Washington the leader of
his race by the choice of whites.

MYTH AND THE NEW SOUTH   Du Bois wanted to see a New South for
blacks, one sharply different from the Old. But the connections

between the New and Old South were strong. One connection was ideological. The champions of a New South used the romantic myth of an Old South to bolster their creed while still deploring the backwardness created by slavery and agrarianism. The juxtaposition of old and new was manifested in the offices of the Atlanta *Constitution,* where one could find both Henry Grady, prophet of a New South, and Joel Chandler Harris, creator of Uncle Remus, a character who in turn epitomized the dutiful "darkies" that inhabited the postwar romances of the Old South, along with kindly old massa and his mint julep, the winsome belle, and the gallant suitor.

These New South spokesmen used the Old South myth not because it offered an example for the future, but because it salved the wounds of defeat, bolstered self-esteem, gave a sense of identity, and blunted sectional enmity. By the end of the 1880s the image of the New South itself was moving into the realm of myth, as Paul M. Gaston argued in his book *The New South Creed* (1970). The New South movement's "legacy to the twentieth century was a pattern of belief in which Southerners could see themselves and their section as rich, successful, and just. . . . This picture of a New South had the double effect of ameliorating the bleak realities of the present and winning approbation and respect from the world outside."

The ultimate achievement of the New South prophets and their allies, the Bourbons, was that like all lasting conservative movements they reconciled tradition with innovation. Their relative moderation in racial policy, at least before the 1890s, allowed them to accommodate just enough of the new to disarm adversaries and keep control. By accommodating themselves to the growth of industry, the Bourbons led the South into a new economic era, but without sacrificing what the historian Francis B. Simkins called "the pageantry and rhetoric of the sentimental South." Bourbon rule left a permanent mark on the South, for as C. Vann Woodward has noted, "it was not the Radicals nor the Confederates but the Redeemers who laid the lasting foundations in matters of race, politics, economics and institutions for the modern South."

THE NEW WEST

For vast reaches of western America the great epics of Civil War and Reconstruction were remote events hardly touching the lives of Indians, trappers, miners, and Mormons scattered through the plains and mountains. There the march of Manifest

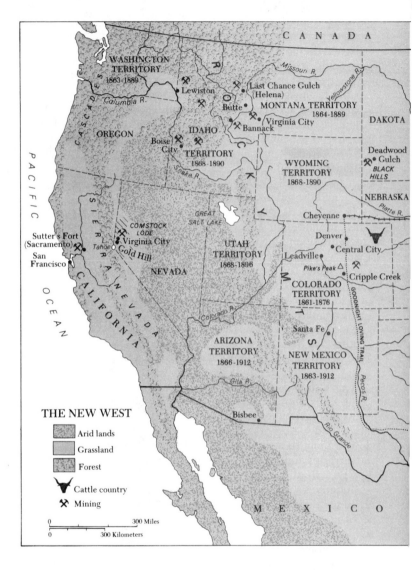

THE NEW WEST

Arid lands

Grassland

Forest

Cattle country

Mining

0   300 Miles

0   300 Kilometers

Destiny continued on its inexorable course. In the second tier of trans-Mississippi states—Iowa, Kansas, Nebraska—and in western Minnesota, the last frontier of farmers was now pressing out onto the Great Plains. From California the miners' frontier scattered enclaves east through the mountains at one new strike after another. From Texas the nomadic cowboys migrated northward into the plains and across the Rockies into the Great Basin. Now there were two frontiers of settlement, east and west, and even a third on the south; in another generation there would be none.

After one final great rush the occupation of the continent would be complete, less than three centuries following the first beachhead at Jamestown.

As settlement moved west, the environment gradually altered. There was no line at which it suddenly changed, but the pathfinders who ventured beyond about 98° West longitude encountered a radically different environment. About two-fifths of the nation's land area was arid, swept by dry winds which had surrendered their moisture successively to the Pacific coastal ranges, the Sierra Nevadas and Cascades, and the Rockies. As Walter Prescott Webb wrote in *The Great Plains*, it was as if "east of the Mississippi civilization stood on three legs—land, water, and timber; west of the Mississippi not one but two of these legs were withdrawn—water and (for want of water) timber—and civilization was left on one leg—land." The scarcity of water and timber rendered useless or impossible the familiar accoutrements of the pioneer: the axe, the log cabin, the rail fence, and the accustomed methods of tilling the soil.

For a long time the region had been called the Great American Desert, a barrier to cross on the way to the Pacific, unfit for human habitation and therefore, to white Americans, the perfect refuge for Indians. But that pattern changed in the last half of the nineteenth century as a result of new finds of gold, silver, and other minerals, completion of transcontinental railroads, destruction of the buffalo, the collapse of Indian resistance, the rise of the range-cattle industry, and the dawning realization that the arid region need not be a sterile desert. With the use of what water was available, techniques of dry farming and irrigation could make the land fruitful after all.

MINING THE WEST   The miners' frontier was in fact not so much a frontier as a scattering of settlements in parts unsuitable for farming, such as steep mountainsides, remote highlands, and barren deserts. The California argonauts of '49 set the typical pattern in which the sudden disorderly rush of prospectors to the new find was quickly followed by the arrival of the campfollowers, a motley crew of sutlers, saloonkeepers, wild women, card sharps, hustlers, and assorted desperadoes, out to mine the miners. Then if the new field panned out, the forces of respectability slowly worked their way in. An era of lawlessness gave place to vigilante rule and, finally, a stable community.

As mining became more dependent on capital, the day of the individual prospector began to wane. The Forty-niners first got at the gold by sifting off dirt and gravel through "placer" mining or "panning," or diverting a stream through a "sluice box" or "long tom." But once the rich diggings tailed off, efficient mining required shafts sunk into the ground or crushing mills built to extract the precious metal locked in quartz. The wild rush then gave way to organized enterprise and the "sourdoughs" either moved on, settled down to work for the bosses, or took up farming in the vicinity.

The drama of the 1849 gold rush was reenacted time and again in the following three decades. Though the California fever had

A sluice box used by gold miners in Auburn Ravine near Virginia City, 1852. [California State Library]

passed by 1851, and no big strikes were made for seven years, new finds in Colorado and Nevada revived hopes for riches. Along Cherry Creek, not far from Pike's Peak in Colorado, a prospecting party found promise of gold in 1858, and stories of success there brought perhaps 100,000 "Fifty-niners" into the country by June 1859, only to find that the rumors had been greatly exaggerated. Wagons that headed west with the legend "Pike's Peak or Bust!" on their sides were soon rumbling back with the sardonic message "Busted, by gosh." Still, a few mines proved out, some new arrivals took up farming to exploit high prices for farm goods in Denver and other mining centers, and the census of 1860 showed 35,000 still in the region. And new discoveries kept occurring: near Central City in 1859, at Leadville in the 1870s, and the last important strikes in the West, again gold and silver, at Cripple Creek in 1891–1894. During these years farming and grazing had given the economy a stable base, and Colorado had become the "Centennial State" in July 1876.

While the early rushers were crowding around Pike's Peak, the Comstock Lode was discovered at Gold Hill, Nevada. H. T. P. Comstock, "Old Pancake," a one-time mountain man, had drifted to the Carson River diggings opened in 1856. Possessed of a glib tongue, he talked his way into a share in a new discovery made by two other prospectors in 1859 and gave it his own name. The lode produced not only gold but a troublesome "blue earth" that turned out to contain silver. Nearby, James Finney, known as "Old Virginia," located a lead to the Ophir vein and gave his nickname to nearby Virginia City. Neither man had the foresight to develop his claim; both sold out for tiny sums what proved to be the two richest fields in the West. Within twenty years the Comstock Lode alone had yielded more than $300 million from shafts that reached hundreds of feet into the mountainside. In 1861 Nevada became a territory and in 1864 the state of Nevada was admitted in time to give its three electoral votes to Lincoln.

The Spaniards had found silver in New Mexico, but mining in Arizona began during the Civil War, when many of Col. James H. Carleton's California volunteers, going to meet a Confederate foray into New Mexico, deserted to the promising mining country near the Colorado River. In both Arizona and Montana the most important mineral proved to be neither gold nor silver, but copper. The richest copper mines included the Anaconda mine in Butte, Montana, and the Phelps-Dodge mine near Bisbee, Arizona.

The last great strike before the Cripple Creek find of the 1890s occurred in 1874–1875 in the Black Hills of South Dakota, which belonged by treaty to the Sioux Indians. Deadwood, the site of the strike, earned brief glory as the refuge of some of the West's most notorious desperadoes: "Calamity Jane," "Wild Bill Hickock," and a host of others. But in Deadwood, as elsewhere, when the gold and silver lodes ran out there was often little to support life in an arid, infertile terrain. The Virginia Citys, the Auroras, the Gold Hills, and others turned into ghost towns until the twentieth century, when shrewd promoters found a new bonanza in mining tourists.

The growing demand for orderly government in the West led to the hasty creation of new territories, and eventually the admission of a host of new states. After Colorado was admitted in 1876, however, there was a long hiatus because of the party divisions in Congress. Democrats were reluctant to create states out of territories that were heavily Republican. After the sweeping Republican victory of 1888, however, Congress admitted the Dakotas, Montana, and Washington in 1889, and Idaho and Wyoming in 1890, completing a tier of states from coast to coast. Utah entered in 1896, after the Mormons abandoned the practice of polygamy, Oklahoma in 1907, and in 1912 Arizona and New Mexico finally rounded out the forty-eight continental states.

THE INDIAN WARS   As the frontier pressed in from east and west, relentless greed and duplicity pursued the Indians into what was supposed to be their last refuge. Mounted on horses which were a legacy of the Spaniards, perhaps 250,000 Indians in the Great

Plains and mountain regions lived mainly off the herds of buffalo which provided food and, from their hides, clothing and shelter. No sooner was the Jacksonian removal policy complete than the onrush of migration in the 1840s began to crowd the Indians' land. Emigrants crossing to Oregon, California, Utah, and Santa Fe came into contact and sometimes into conflict with them. In 1851 the chiefs of the principal plains tribes were gathered at Fort Laramie, where they agreed to accept more or less definite tribal borders and to leave the emigrants unmolested on their trails. It soon became easier to force one tribe to cede its lands without arousing the others, for the Indians could never realize the old dream of Tecumseh, a unified resistance.

From the early 1860s until the late 1870s the frontier was ablaze with Indian wars, and intermittent outbreaks continued through the 1880s. The first serious trouble developed in Minnesota, where a volunteer militia had taken the place of army garrisons fighting in the Civil War. Fighting started in 1862 when a band of Sioux braves, aroused by recent land cessions, killed five whites near New Ulm. Some of the Sioux fled to the west, but others remained and wrought havoc on the frontier, killing or capturing some 1,000 whites until the militia in overwhelming force drove them back and inflicted a devastating revenge. Out of 400 Indians captured, 300 were sentenced to death and eventually 38 were hanged in a mass execution the day after Christmas, 1862.

In Colorado, where chiefs of the Cheyennes and Arapahoes accepted a treaty banishing them westward, protesting braves began sporadic raids on the trails and mining camps. In 1864 the territorial governor persuaded most of the warring Indians to gather at Fort Lyon on Sand Creek, where they were promised protection. Despite this promise, Col. J. M. Chivington's militia fell upon an Indian camp flying the American flag and a white flag of truce, slaughtering 450 peaceful Indians—men, women, and children. Gen. Nelson A. Miles called it the "foulest and most unjustifiable crime in the annals of America." Chivington, a former Methodist minister, later exhibited his personal collection of 100 scalps in Denver. In 1865 the survivors surrendered unconditionally and gave up their Sand Creek reservation for lands farther west.

With other scattered battles erupting, in 1865 a congressional committee began to gather evidence on the grisly Indian wars and massacres. Its 1867 *Report on the Condition of the Indian Tribes* led to an act to establish an Indian Peace Commission charged with ending the Sioux War and removing the causes of

Indian wars in general. Congress decided this was best accomplished at the expense of the Indians, by persuading them to take up life on out-of-the-way reservations. This solution, in short, was to continue the persistent encroachment on Indian hunting grounds.

In October 1867 a conference at Medicine Creek Lodge, Kansas, ended with an agreement that the Kiowa, Comanche, Arapahoes, and Cheyennes would accept lands in western Oklahoma. Smaller tribes from the southern Plains later got reservations in the same area. In the following spring a conference at Fort Laramie resulted in peace with the Sioux, who agreed to settle within the Black Hills reservation in Dakota Territory. But Indian resistance in the southern Plains continued until the Red River War of 1874–1875. In a winter campaign of relentless pursuit, General Sheridan scattered the Indians and finally brought them to terms in the spring of 1875.

By then trouble was brewing once again in the north. In 1874, Gen. George A. Custer led an exploring expedition into the Black Hills, accompanied by gold seekers who began to find what they were after. Miners were soon filtering into the Sioux hunting grounds despite promises that the army would keep them out. The army had done little to protect the Indian lands, but when orders came to move against wandering bands of Sioux hunting on the range according to their treaty rights, the army moved vigorously. After several indecisive encounters, General Custer found the main encampment of Sioux and their Cheyenne allies on the Little Big Horn River. Separated from the main body of his men, Custer and a detachment of 200 were surrounded by a body of warriors numbering about 2,500 and completely annihilated.

But the Battle of the Little Big Horn was only one incident in this war. Instead of following up their victory, the Indians threw away their advantage in celebration and renewed hunting. When the army regained the offensive, the Indians began to melt away into the isolated wilderness. Chief Sitting Bull escaped into Canada, only to return to the Sioux reservation several years later. Crazy Horse was captured and murdered by his guard. The remaining Sioux were forced to give up their hunting grounds and the gold fields around Deadwood in return for payments. When a peace commission imposed this settlement Chief Spotted Tail said: "Tell your people that since the Great Father promised that we should never be removed, we have been moved five times. . . . I think you had better put the Indians on wheels and you can run them about wherever you wish."

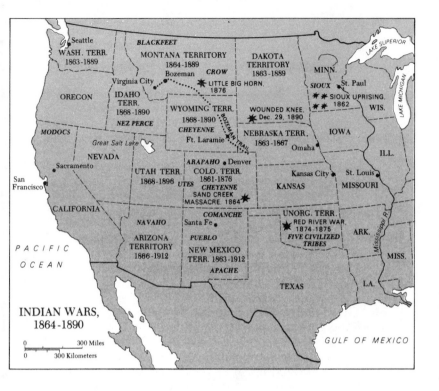

In the Rockies and westward the same story of hopeless resistance was repeated. The Blackfeet and Crows had to leave their homes in Montana. In a war along the California-Oregon boundary the Modocs held out for six months in 1871–1872 before they were overwhelmed. In 1879 the Utes were forced to give up their vast territories in western Colorado after a brief battle. In Idaho the peaceful Nez Perces finally refused to surrender lands along the Salmon River. Chief Joseph tried to avoid war, but when some unruly braves started a fight, he directed a masterful campaign against overwhelming odds, one of the most spectacular feats in the history of Indian warfare. After a retreat of 1,500 miles, through mountains and plains, across the Yellowstone region and through the Bitterroot Mountains of Montana, he was finally caught thirty miles short of the Canadian border, and exiled to Oklahoma.

In his character the heroic Joseph embodied the image of nobility. He maintained strict discipline among his followers, countenanced no scalpings or outrages against civilians, bought supplies which he could have confiscated, and kept his dignity to the end. His eloquent speech of surrender was an epitaph to the warriors's last stand against the march of empire: "I am tired of fighting. Our chiefs are killed. Looking Glass is dead. Toohoolhoolzote is dead. The old men are all dead. . . . I want to have time to look for my children, and see how many of them I can find. . . . Hear me, my chiefs! I am tired. My heart is sick and sad. From where the sun now stands I will fight no more forever."

A generation of Indian wars virtually ended in 1886 with the capture of Geronimo, a chief of the Chiricahua Apaches, who had fought encroachments in the Southwest for fifteen years. But there would be one tragic epilogue. Late in 1888 Wovoka (or "Jack Wilson"), a Paiute in western Nevada, fell ill and in a delirium imagined he had visited the spirit world where he learned of a deliverer coming to rescue the Indians and restore their lands. To hasten the day, he said, they had to take up a ceremonial dance at each new moon. The Ghost Dance craze fed upon old legends of a coming Messiah and spread rapidly. In 1890 the Sioux took it up with such fervor that it alarmed white authorities. An effort to arrest Sitting Bull led to his death and shortly afterward, on December 29, 1890, a bloodbath at Wounded Knee, South Dakota. An accidental rifle discharge led nervous soldiers to fire into a group of Indians who had come to surrender. Nearly 200 Indians and 25 soldiers died in the "Battle of Wounded Knee." The Indian wars had ended with characteristic brutality.

Over the long run the collapse of Indian resistance resulted as much from the killing off of the buffalo herds on which they subsisted as from direct suppression. White hunters felled buffaloes for sport, sometimes firing from train windows for the joy of see-

"Chief Joseph" of the Nez Perce tribe. [The Smithsonian Institution]

Geronimo (seated, left foreground) and his Apache tribesmen in council with the U.S. Army, 1886. [Library of Congress]

ing them die. Systematic slaughter of the buffalo began in the 1870s to satisfy the fashion of buffalo robes and overcoats in the East. By the mid-1880s the herds had reached the verge of extinction.

Most frontiersmen had little tolerance for moralizing on the Indian question. Easterners who were far removed from frontier dangers took a different view. The slaughter of the Indian wars was immensely unpopular. In his annual message of 1877 President Hayes echoed the protest: "Many, if not most, of our Indian wars have had their origin in broken promises and acts of injustice on our part." Statesmen and churchmen spoke out against mistreatment of Indians. In the 1880s Helen Hunt Jackson, a novelist and poet, focused attention on the Indian cause in *A Century of Dishonor* (1881) and *Ramona* (1884), the latter a novel about wrongs inflicted on the California Indians.

INDIAN POLICY Indian policy gradually became more benevolent, but this did little to alleviate the plight of the Indians and actually helped to destroy the remnants of their cultures. The reservation policy inaugurated by the Peace Commission in 1867 did little more than extend a practice that dated from colonial Virginia. Partly humanitarian in motive, this policy also saved money: it cost less to house and feed Indians on reservations than it did to fight them. And one Indian commissioner wrote candidly: "That these reservations will cause any considerable annoyance to the whites we do not believe. They consist, for the most part, of ground unfitted for cultivation, but suited to the peculiar habits of the Indians." Mistakes would be made, of course. Too late it was discovered that the Utes and Osage and some other tribes were left sitting atop rich stores of oil and natural gas.

Well-intentioned reformers sought to "Americanize" the aborigines by dealing with them as individuals rather than as tribes. The fruition of reform efforts came in the Dawes Severalty Act of 1887. Sponsored by Henry M. Dawes of Massachusetts, the act proposed to introduce the Indians to individual land ownership and agriculture. The Dawes Act permitted the president to divide the lands of any tribe and grant 160 acres to each head of family and lesser amounts to others. To protect the Indian in his property, the government held it in trust for twenty-five years, after which the owner won full title and became a citizen. Under the Burke Act of 1906 Indians who took up life apart from their tribes became citizens immediately. Members of the tribes granted land titles became subject to state and federal laws like all other persons. In 1901 citizenship was extended to the Five Civilized Tribes of Oklahoma, and in 1924 to all Indians.

But the more it changed, the more Indian policy remained the same. Despite the best of intentions, the Dawes Act struck a double blow at the Indians. It created an opportunity for more land spoliation, and it disrupted what remained of the traditional cultures. Dawes himself had foreseen the result, but defended his bill as an effort to salvage something for the Indians. Few others had such foresight, except land grabbers and students of Indian "ethnology," the forerunners of the study of anthropology. Lewis H. Morgan, a leading authority, pronounced the Indian "entirely incapable" of dealing with the whites on an individual basis. The result, he predicted, would be "that in a very short time he would divest himself of every foot of land and fall into poverty." And so it happened. Those lands not distributed to Indian families were sold, while others were lost to land sharks because of the Indians' inexperience with private ownership, or simply their powerlessness in the face of fraud. Between 1887 and 1934 they lost an estimated 86 million of their 130 million acres. Most of what remained was unsuited to agriculture.

CATTLE AND COWBOYS   While the West was being taken from the Indians, cattle entered the grasslands where the buffalo had roamed, and the cowboy enjoyed his brief heyday, fading then into the folklore of the Wild West along with the sourdoughs, the desperadoes, and the Plains Indians. From colonial times, especially in the South, cattle raising had been a common enterprise just beyond the fringe of settlement. In many cases the early slaves took care of the livestock. Later, in the West, Negro cowboys were still a common sight, although they were lost from view in the novels and "horse operas" which pictured a lily-white frontier. Much of the romance of the open-range cattle industry derived from its Mexican roots. The Texas longhorns and the cowboys' horses had in large part descended from stock brought over by the Spaniards, and many of the industry's characteristics had been worked out in Mexico first: the cowboy's saddle, his chaps (*chaparajos*) to protect the legs, his spurs, and his lariat.

For many years wild cattle competed with the buffalo in the Spanish borderlands. Natural selection and contact with "Anglo" scrub cattle produced the Texas longhorns: lean and rangy, they were noted more for speed and endurance than for providing a choice steak. They had little value, moreover, because the largest markets for beef were too far away. Occasionally they were driven to market in Austin, Galveston, or New Orleans, and some even to the gold fields of California, Arizona, and Colorado. At the end of the Civil War, perhaps as many as 5 million roamed the grasslands of Texas, still neglected—but not for long. In the upper Mississippi valley, where herds had been depleted by the war, cattle prices ranged from $30 to $50 a head, while the Texas cattle could be had just for the effort of rounding them up.

So the cattle drives began anew after the Civil War, but on a scale far greater than before. In 1866 a large herd set out for Sedalia, Missouri, the western terminus of the Missouri-Pacific Railroad. But that route proved unsuitable because it was subject to raids by postwar bushwhackers, obstructed by woodlands, and opposed by Arkansas and Missouri farmers. New opportunities arose as railroads pushed farther west where cattle could be driven through relatively vacant lands. Joseph G. McCoy, an Illinois livestock dealer, realized the possibilities and showed the way. Officers of the Missouri-Pacific, to whom he turned first, brushed him off as a crank. The result, he later claimed, was that St. Louis took second place to Chicago as a livestock and packing center. The Kansas Pacific finally approved a lenient contract with McCoy, which they later tried to repudiate because they had not foreseen his enormous profits. Another road, the Hannibal and St. Joe, gave McCoy connections to Chicago.

McCoy chose Abilene, Kansas, as the terminus and laid out a trail as far south as Corpus Christi. Abilene was then a sleepy village of about a dozen shacks with so little business that the saloonkeeper raised prairie dogs as curiosities to sell tourists. But the town had water and grass. McCoy threw up stock pens, barns, loading chutes, and a hotel to house the cowboys. In September 1867 the first shipment went to Chicago. Abilene was the first of the great cowtowns, which in their brief day rivaled the mining camps for lawlessness. "On the surface," Walter P. Webb wrote, "Abilene was corruption personified. Life was hectic, raw, lurid, awful. But the dance hall, the saloon, and the red light, the dissonance of immoral revelry punctuated by pistolshots, were but the superficialities. . . . If Abilene excelled all later cowtowns in wickedness, it also excelled them in service, —the service of bartering the beef of the South for the money of the North." As the railroads moved west, so did the cowtowns and the trails. Ellsworth, Wichita, Newton City, Baxter Springs, and Dodge City, all in Kansas, succeeded Abilene, while farther north arose Oglalla, Nebraska, Cheyenne, Wyoming, and Miles City, Montana.

The flush times of the cowtown soon passed, however, and many reverted to sleepy villages with occasional "boot hills" as reminders of the hell-roaring times. The long cattle drives played out too because they were economically unsound. The dangers of the trail, the wear and tear on men and cattle, the charges levied on drives across Indian Territory, and the advance of farms across the trails combined to persuade cattlemen that they could best function near the railroads. As railroads spread out into Texas and the Plains, the cattle business spread with

Lawlessness in the West. [The N. H. Rose Collection]

them over the High Plains as far as Montana and on into Canada.

In the absence of laws governing the range, the cattlemen worked out a code of action largely dictated by circumstances. As a rule the man who staked out a claim, or simply made good his occupation of a stream bank, controlled the grasslands as far back as the next divide since land was useless without access to water. Cowboys would "ride the line" to keep the cattle off the next ranch and conduct spring and fall roundups to separate the mixed herds. In 1873 Joseph Glidden, a farmer of De Kalb, Illinois, invented the first effective barbed-wire, which ranchers used to fence off their claims at relatively low cost. More often than not these were parts of the public domain to which they had no valid title. In 1878 an eastern promoter, John W. "Bet-a-Million" Gates, one of the early agents for Glidden, gave a persuasive demonstration of the barbed-wire in San Antonio. Skeptical cattlemen discovered that their meanest longhorns shied away from the fence which, as Gates put it, was light as air, stronger than whiskey, and cheaper than dirt. Orders poured in, and Gates eventually put together a virtual monopoly in the American Steel and Wire Company. The coming of barbed-wire finally ended the open, free range.

The greatest boom in the range-cattle trade came in the early 1880s, when eastern and European capitalists began to pour money into the "Beef Bonanza." Cattle growing, like mining, entered a season of wild speculation, and then evolved from a romantic adventure into a prosaic business, often a corporate business. A combination of factors conspired to end the open-range industry. Farmers kept crowding in and laying out homesteads on the open range, waging "barbed-wire wars" with cattlemen by either cutting the cattlemen's fences or policing their own. The boundless range was beginning to be overstocked by 1883, and expenses mounted as stock breeders formed associations to keep intruders out of overstocked ranges, to establish and protect land titles, to deal with railroads and buyers, to fight prairie fires, and to cope with rustlers and predatory beasts. The rise of sheep herding by 1880 caused still another conflict with the cattlemen. Warfare between defenders of the bovine and ovine species gradually faded, however, as the sheep for the most part found refuge in the high pastures of the mountains, leaving the grasslands of the Plains to the cattlemen. A final blow to the open-range industry came with two unusually severe winters in 1886 and 1887, followed by ten long years of drought.

For those who survived all the hazards of the range, the response to these problems was to establish legal title and fence in the lands, restrict the herds to a reasonable size, and provide shelter and hay against the rigors of winter. The cowboy settled into a more sedentary existence. Even in the heroic days his life had been a lonely, wearisome affair, the romance of which lay mainly in the pages of books like Owen Wister's *The Virginian* (1902), in which the hero utters the famous line: "When you call me that, *smile!*" Within two short decades, 1866–1886, the glory was ended; it was always more in the eye of the beholder than anywhere else.

FARMERS AND THE LAND Among the legendary figures of the West, the sodbusters projected an unromantic image in contrast to the sourdoughs and cowboys, the Cavalry and the Indians. After 1865, on paper at least, the land laws offered favorable terms to the farmer. Under the old Preemption Act of 1841, if he could locate a claim before the government surveys, he could after six months get 160 acres for $1.25 an acre. Under the Homestead Act of 1862 he could either realize the old dream of free land simply by staking out a claim and living on it for five years, or buy the land at $1.25 an acre after six months. But the land legislation of earlier days was predicated upon an entirely different environment from that of the Plains, and the laws never completely adjusted to the fact that much of the land was suited only for cattle. Cattlemen were forced to garner land by gradual acquisition from homesteaders or land grant railroads.

In the 1870s two new laws at least recognized the shortage of water and timber in the New West. The Timber Culture Act of 1873 permitted any settler to get an additional 160 acres if he maintained 40 acres of woodland for ten years. The act benefited a few farmers of the eastern Plains, but it was subject to such widespread fraud that it was repealed in 1891. The Desert Land Act of 1877 authorized the sale of 640-acre tracts at $1.25 an acre to settlers who irrigated the land within three years. But the act ignored the facts that 640 acres was often not enough to sustain agriculture in arid regions, and that irrigation works were too costly for most settlers. The Timber and Stone Act of 1878 made available 160-acre tracts for $2.50 an acre in areas "unfit for civilization," mostly in California, Nevada, Oregon, and Washington. This amounted to a virtual giveaway of great natural resources in timber and stone which were far more valuable than their purchase price.

The unchangeable fact of aridity, rather than new land laws, shaped institutions in the New West. Where farming was impossible the cattlemen simply established hegemony by control of the water, regardless of the laws. The land laws probably could not have been better designed for fraud and misuse if that had been their purpose. The supposed settler could build a doll-house, twelve by fourteen inches, and swear that a dwelling "twelve by fourteen" stood on the homestead. He might pour out a bucket of water and swear that the land was irrigated. Better yet, he could just perjure himself without bothering with such rigmarole.

Belated legislative efforts to develop irrigable lands finally achieved a major success when the Newlands Reclamation Act (after the aptly named Sen. Francis G. Newlands of Nevada) of 1901 set up the Bureau of Reclamation. The proceeds of public land sales in sixteen states became a fund for irrigation works, and the Reclamation Bureau set about building such major projects as Boulder (later Hoover) Dam on the Nevada-Arizona line, Roosevelt Dam in Arizona, Elephant Butte Dam in Idaho, and Arrowrock Dam in New Mexico.

But the stubborn problem of water remained, rendering much of the west's land useless for field crops. The area in which rainfall averaged ten to twenty inches per year was marginal, but with the techniques of "dry farming" could support such crops as sorghums, kaffir corn, and Turkey wheat. Certain varieties of spring and winter wheat grew at the times of greatest rainfall. The eastern Plains from Minnesota and North Dakota down to Texas emerged as the wheat belt, the new breadbasket of the nation, and behind wheat the corn belt and corn-hog combination edged westward.

The lands of the New West, as on previous frontiers, passed to their ultimate owners more often from private hands than directly from the government. Much of the 274 million acres claimed under the Homestead Act passed quickly to cattlemen or speculators, and thence to settlers. The land-grant railroads got some 200 million acres of the public domain in the twenty years from 1851 to 1871, and sold much of this land to build population and traffic along the lines. The New West of cattlemen and farmers was in fact largely the product of the railroads.

For the first arrivals on the sod-house frontier, life was a grim struggle with adversity and monotony. As the railroads arrived bearing lumber from the wooded regions, farmers could leave their dugouts and homes of "Kansas brick" to build more familiar frame houses. New machinery helped open fresh opportunities for farmers. Back in 1837 John Deere of Illinois had developed the steel-faced plow and moldboard that conquered the clinging humus of the prairie. But its high cost encouraged further exper-

Sod-house farm, Nebraska, 1887. [Nebraska State Historical Society]

iments, and in 1868 James Oliver of Indiana made a successful chilled-iron plow. With further improvements his "sod buster" was ready for mass production by 1878, easing the task of breaking the shallow but tough grass roots of the Plains. Improvements and new inventions in threshing machines, hay mowers, planters, manure spreaders, cream separators, and other devices lightened the burden of labor but added to the capital outlay of the farmer.

In some parts of the West the gigantic "bonanza farms" with machinery for mass production became the marvels of the age, the new corporate plantations complete with mechanized slaves. On one farm in North Dakota, 13,000 acres of wheat made a single field. "You are in a sea of wheat," a bedazzled visitor wrote in 1880. "The railroad train rolls through an ocean of grain. . . . We encounter a squadron of war chariots . . . doing the work of human hands. . . . There are twenty-five of them in this one brigade of the grand army of 115, under the marshalship of this Dakota farmer." Publicized out of proportion to their significance, the bonanza farms disintegrated in the decade of drought after 1885. The land often remained in the same hands, however, operated now on a tenant basis.

The small farmers who diversified their crops fared better, especially those who stayed in the eastern Plains. But even they, to make a go of it, had to make concessions to size. To get a start on a family homestead, the historian Allen G. Bogue estimates, required a minimum capital investment of $1,000. And while the overall value of farm lands and farm products increased in the late nineteenth century, the small farmer did not keep up with the march of progress. His numbers grew, but decreased in proportion to the population at large. Wheat, like cotton in the antebellum period, provided the great export crop which evened America's balance of payments and spurred economic growth. But for a variety of reasons the individual farmer failed to prosper. Something was amiss, he began to reason, and by the decade of the 1890s he was in open revolt against the powers that be.

"THE FRONTIER HAS GONE" American life reached an important juncture in the postbellum years. After the 1890 population count, the superintendent of the census noted that he could no longer locate as before a continuous frontier line beyond which population thinned out to less than two per square mile. This fact inspired the historian Frederick Jackson Turner to develop the influential frontier thesis, first outlined in his paper "The Significance of the Frontier in American History," delivered to the American Historical Association in 1893. "The existence of an area of free land," Turner wrote, "its continuous recession, and the advance of American settlement westward, explain American development." The frontier had shaped the national character in striking ways. It was

> to the frontier [that] the American intellect owes its striking characteristics. That coarseness and strength combined with acuteness and acquisitiveness; that practical, inventive turn of mind, quick to

Oklahoma Territory, 1889. These open-air law and land offices suggest Americans' "masterful grasp of material things" and "restless, nervous energy," which Turner attributed to the frontier experience. [University of Oklahoma Library]

find expedients; that masterful grasp of material things, lacking in the artistic but powerful to effect great ends; that restless, nervous energy; that dominant individualism, working for good and for evil, and withal that buoyancy and exuberance which comes with freedom—these are traits of the frontier, or traits called out elsewhere because of the existence of the frontier.

In 1893 he wrote, "four centuries from the discovery of America, at the end of a hundred years under the Constitution, the frontier has gone and with its going has closed the first period of American history."

FURTHER READING

The concept of the "New South" is explored in Paul W. Gaston's *The New South Creed: A Study in Southern Mythmaking* (1970).° W. J. Cash comments on the boosterism of postwar southerners in *The Mind of the South* (1941).° Biographies of the region's leading proselytizers include Raymond B. Nixon's *Henry W. Grady: Spokesman of the New South* (1969), Joseph F. Wall's *Henry W. Watterson: Reconstructed Rebel* (1956), and John M. Cooper's *Walter Hines Page: The Southerner as American, 1855–1918* (1977).

Scholarship on the textile industry, which formed the heart of New South aspirations, includes Patrick J. Hearden's *Independence and Empire: The New South's Cotton Mill Campaign, 1865–1901* (1982), Dwight G. Billings's *Planters in the Making of a "New South": Class, Politics, and Development in North Carolina, 1865–1900* (1979), and David Carlton's *Mill and Town in South Carolina, 1880–1920* (1982).° For developments in the tobacco industry, consult Robert F. Durden's *The Dukes of Durham, 1865–1929* (1975). For the iron industry, consult Carl V. Harris's *Political Power in Birmingham, 1871–1921* (1977). John F. Stover's *The Railroads of the South* (1955) covers the growth in transportation.

The cultural dimenson of the New South is explored in Daniel J. Singal's *The Conflict Within: From Victorian to Modernist Thought in the South, 1919–1945* (1982).° The religious nature of postwar culture is treated in Charles R. Wilson's *Baptized in Blood: The Religion of the Lost Cause, 1865–1920* (1980), and Thomas L. Connelly's *God and General Longstreet: The Lost Cause and the Southern Mind* (1982). For Bourbon politics after Reconstruction, see Jack P. Maddox's *The Virginia Conservatives, 1867–1879* (1970), and William J. Cooper, Jr.'s *The Conservative Regime: South Carolina, 1877–1900* (1968).°

C. Vann Woodward's *The Strange Career of Jim Crow* (1974)° remains a classic on southern race relations. Some of Woodward's points are challenged in Howard N. Rabinowitz's *Race Relations in the Urban South, 1865–1900* (1978). Other views on race relations are treated in

°These books are available in paperback editions.

August Meier's *Negro Thought in America: Racial Ideologies in the Age of Booker T. Washington, 1880–1915* (1963). The attitudes of the two principal black leaders are defined in Louis R. Harlan's *Booker T. Washington: The Making of a Black Leader, 1865–1901* (1972),° and Elliott M. Rudiwick's *W. E. B. Du Bois: Propagandist of Negro Protest* (1969). J. Morgan Kousser's *The Shaping of Southern Politics: Suffrage Restriction and Establishment of the One-Party South, 1880–1910* (1974), handles disfranchisement.

Race is also a chief component of works on postwar developments in farming. Roger Ransom and Richard Sutch's *One Kind of Freedom: The Economic Consequences of Emancipation* (1977),° Robert W. Higgs's *Competition and Coercion: Blacks in the American Economy, 1865–1914* (1977), Jay R. Mandle's *The Roots of Black Poverty: The Southern Plantation Economy after the Civil War* (1978),° and Jonathan Wiener's *Social Origins of the New South: Alabama, 1860–1865* (1978), all examine the origins of sharecropping.

Both regions surveyed in this chapter receive attention in overall interpretations of post–Civil War development. Robert H. Wiebe's *The Search for Order, 1877–1920* (1968),° and Louis M. Hacker's *The Course of American Economic Development* (1970)° portray the hinterlands as extensions of the more dominant northeastern and midwestern states. C. Vann Woodward also develops the theme of a "colonial economy" in *Origins of the New South, 1877–1913* (1951),° a work which is also the best introduction to the New South. Another overview of the region is John S. Ezell's *The South since 1865* (1975). Overviews of the settlement of the Great Desert include Frederick Merk's *History of the Western Movement* (1978),° and more specifically, Howard R. Lamar's *The Far Southwest, 1846–1912* (1966).

The Turner thesis is best presented by Frederick Jackson Turner himself in *The Frontier in American History* (1920). Ray A. Billington, in his *Frederick Jackson Turner* (1973), analyzes the thesis, and in *Westward Expansion* (1967) applies it. Thomas D. Clark's *Frontier America: The Story of the Westward Movement* (1969) disclaims the centrality of Turner's thesis. A more cultural treatment of the subject of the frontier is Henry Nash Smith's *Virgin Land: The American West as Symbol and Myth* (1950).°

Quite a bit of recent scholarship examines the realities of life among western cowboys. Terry G. Jordan's *Trails to Texas: Southern Roots of Western Cattle Ranching* (1981) finds cowboy origins along the Atlantic seaboard. David Day's *Cowboy Culture: A Saga of Five Centuries* (1981) traces the roots further back. Other studies of various aspects of the cattle trade include J. M. Shagg's *The Cattle Trading Industry* (1973) and Robert R. Dystra's *The Cattle Towns* (1968).°

The sodbusters also have their scholars. Fred A. Shannon's *The Farmer's Last Frontier* (1963),° Gilbert C. Fite's *The Farmer's Frontier, 1865–1900* (1963), and Allen G. Bogue's *From Prairie to Corn Belt* (1963) each details the harsh Great Plains life. The views of important participants are analyzed in Joanna L. Stratton's *Pioneer Women: Voices from the Kansas Frontier* (1981).° Paul W. Gates's *History of Public Land*

Development (1968) concentrates on the effects of the Homestead Law on settlement patterns.

Works which deal with western miners include Rodman W. Paul's *Mining Frontiers of the Far West, 1848–1880* (1963),° and Duane A. Smith's *Rocky Mountain Mining Camps* (1967). Michael P. Molane's *The Battle for Butte: Mining and Politics on the Northern Frontier, 1884–1906* (1981), presents a case study of the copper industry.

The best introduction to the history of the Plains Indians remains Wilcomb E. Washburn's *The Indian in North America* (1975).° The Indian conflict with the encroaching white man is explored in Dee Brown's *Bury My Heart at Wounded Knee* (1970)° and Robert M. Utley's *Last Days of the Sioux Nation* (1963). The white perspective on the issue is presented in Francis Paul Prucha's *American Indian Policy in Crisis: Christian Reformers and the Indians, 1865–1900* (1976), Robert M. Utley's *Frontier Regulars: The United States Army and the Indian* (1973),° and Robert F. Berkhofer, Jr.'s *The White Man's Indian: Images of the American Indian from Columbus to the Present* (1978).° A psychological interpretation of an Indian fighter is in Charles K. Hofling's *Custer and the Little Big Horn: A Psychobiographical Inquiry* (1981).

20

THE RISE OF BIG BUSINESS

The Postbellum Economy

ECONOMIC EFFECTS OF THE CIVIL WAR   America's rise as an industrial giant in the late nineteenth century is a fact of towering visibility. It has led all too easily to the judgement that the demands created by the Civil War powered a "takeoff" in economic growth and that the legislative program of the Republicans at the same time unleashed business, allowing it to guide and continue the process. The Civil War connection seemed to many so obvious as to exclude the need for detailed proof.

But the highly visible success of wartime profiteers in arms and supplies, of speculators in various markets, and of such nabobs as investment banker Jay Cooke, who got rich selling Treasury bonds, have overshadowed the actual setbacks that marked the wartime economy. Estimates of production and income for the nineteenth century prepared by the economic historian Robert E. Gallman have cast much doubt on the conventional story. "Between 1839 and 1899," Gallman wrote, "total commodity output [from farm and factory] increased elevenfold, or at an average decade rate of slightly less than 50 percent. Actual rates varied fairly widely, high rates appearing during the decades ending with 1854 and 1884 and a very low rate during the decade ending with 1869." The decade of the 1860s was the only one in which, on a per-capita basis, output actually decreased, North and South.

Figures for specific goods tend to show the same effect in these years. The output of copper, railroad track, cotton, and woolen textiles all showed the lag. Most surprising of all, pig iron production, which grew 17 percent from 1855 to 1860 (despite a depression in 1857) and 100 percent from 1865 to 1870, grew only 1 percent during the war years. The Civil War, sometimes called the "first modern war," was in large part unmechanized. Rifles, bayonets, sabers, artillery, and ammunition consumed relatively little iron, and army railroads offset only partially the drop in civilian construction. Production declined largely because of unsettled wartime conditions and the loss of southern markets.

Professor Gallman's figures also show that commodity output grew at an annual rate of 4.6 percent from 1840 to 1860, and at a rate of 4.4 percent from 1870 to 1900. Other long-term trends, such as the shift toward manufacturing, seem to have remained relatively constant, except during the 1860s, when the growth of manufactured goods averaged only 2.0 percent per year. In the light of this evidence, economic growth in the 1800s seems now to have been a sustained process, interrupted by the depressions of 1819, 1839, 1857, 1873, and 1893, and by the Civil War.

The postwar expansion, which started from a relatively high base and moved the economy to even higher levels, may have been fueled indirectly by the Civil War. Wartime inflation as usual transferred income to those owning property and making profits, while entrepreneurs forced to save by the war contributed to the immediate postwar period of speculation. It is not clear, though, that postwar Republican policies contributed uniquely to economic expansion. The National Banking Act created a sounder currency, but its effects on the economy were ambiguous. Government aid in building the great transcontinental and regional railroads simply continued the encouragement to railroads long offered by state and federal government. The postwar climate of favoritism to business was but slightly strengthened by the defeat of southern agrarianism. Postwar tariffs also had ambiguous effects, hampering foreign competitors but discouraging American exports. The emotional lift of victory provided an important, if indirect, spur to the economy. After the war Sen. John Sherman of Ohio wrote to his brother, the famous general: "The truth is the close of the war with our resources unimpaired gives an elevation, a scope to the ideas of leading capitalists far higher than anything ever undertaken in this country. They talk of millions as confidently as before of thousands."

BUILDING THE TRANSCONTINENTAL RAILROADS Whatever the explanation, the fact remains that between 1869 and 1899 the population nearly trebled, farm production more than doubled, and the value of manufactures grew sixfold (in constant prices). Basic to this economic transition was the growth of railroads. They were the first big business, the first magnet for the great financial markets, and the first industry to develop a large-scale management bureaucracy. The railroads opened the West, connected raw materials to factories and markets, and in so doing created a national market. At the same time they were themselves gigantic markets for iron, steel, lumber, and other capital goods.

The renewal of railroad building after the Civil War increased the total mileage in roads from 30,600 in 1862 to 53,000 in 1870 and 94,000 by 1880. During the 1880s, the great decade of railroad building, mileage leaped to 167,000 by 1890 and then grew to 199,000 by 1900. Most of this construction filled out the network east of the Mississippi, but the most spectacular exploits were the great transcontinental lines built across the plains and mountains. Running through sparsely settled lands the roads promised little quick return, but they served the national purpose of binding the country together and so received a generous public bounty. Until 1850 constitutional scruples had constrained federal aid, although many states had subsidized railroads within their borders, but in 1850 Stephen Douglas secured from Congress a grant of public lands to subsidize two north-south roads connecting Chicago and Mobile: the Illinois Central and the Mobile and Ohio. Over the next twenty years federal land grants, mainly to transcontinentals, amounted to a net figure of some 129 million acres. In addition to land the railroads received financial aid from federal, state, and local governments. Altogether, according to one railroad authority, the roads got about $707 million in cash and $335 million in land.

Before the Civil War, sectional differences over routes held up the start of a transcontinental line. Secession finally permitted passage of the Pacific Railway Bill, which Lincoln signed into law on July 1, 1862. The act authorized a line along a north-central route, to be built by the Union Pacific railroad westward from Omaha and the Central Pacific railroad eastward from Sacramento. As amended in 1864, the act donated to these two corporations twenty sections of land per mile of track, in alternating blocs of railroad and government property, and loans of $16,000, $32,000, and $48,000 per mile, depending on the difficulty of the terrain. Security for the loans after 1864 was a second mortgage on the property, which permitted the roads to float their own bonds secured by a first mortgage.

Both roads began construction during the war, but most of the work was done after 1865 as the companies raced to build most of the line and get most of the subsidy. Under Gen. Grenville

Dodge, who became chief engineer in 1866, the Union Pacific pushed across the plains at a rapid pace, piercing the Rockies through Cheyenne Pass. The work crews, with large numbers of ex-soldiers and Irish immigrants as laborers, had to cope with bad roads, water shortages, alternately hot and cold weather, and Indian marauders. The moveable encampments with their retinue of sutlers, gamblers, and prostitutes, were aptly dubbed "Hell-on-wheels." Construction was hasty and much of it so flimsy that it had to be redone later, but the Union Pacific pushed on to its rendezvous with the Central Pacific.

The Central Pacific was the brainchild of the engineer Theodore P. Judah, but it was organized and, after Judah's untimely death, dominated by the Sacramento shopkeepers who made an indelible imprint on their state as the California "Big Four": Charles Crocker, Mark Hopkins, Collis P. Huntington, and Leland Stanford, who was elected governor in 1862. The Central Pacific used mainly Chinese crews and early encountered the Sierra massif, but cut through by way of Dutch Flat and Donner Pass to more level country in Nevada. The Union Pacific had built 1,086 miles to the Central Pacific's 689 when the race ended on the salt plains of Utah near Ogden, at Promontory Point. There, on May 10, 1869, Leland Stanford drove a gold spike which symbolized the road's completion as the telegraph lines signaled the taps of the hammer to a celebrating nation.

It was twelve years before the next transcontinental was completed, when the Atchison, Topeka and Santa Fe made contact

Union Pacific Railroad announces the "Great Event," the opening of the nation's first transcontinental line. For "Gold, Silver, and Other Miners, Now is the time to seek your Fortunes" in the West. [Union Pacific Railroad Museum Collection]

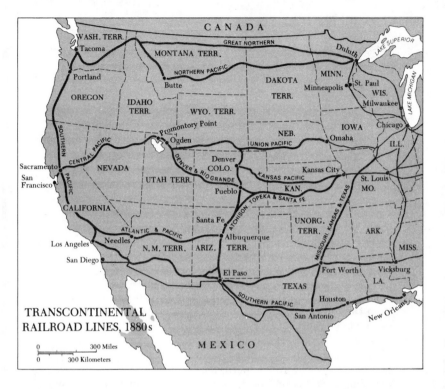

TRANSCONTINENTAL
RAILROAD LINES, 1880s

0 ____ 300 Miles
0 ____ 300 Kilometers

with the Big Four's Southern Pacific at the Needles in southern California. The Santa Fe built on to San Diego by 1884. Meanwhile the Southern Pacific, which had absorbed the Central Pacific, built on by way of Yuma to El Paso in 1882, where it made connections to St. Louis and New Orleans. To the north the Northern Pacific had connected Lake Superior with Portland by 1883, and ten years later the Great Northern, which James J. Hill had slowly and carefully extended westward from Minneapolis, thrust its way through Marias Pass and on to Tacoma—and Hill did it without a land grant. Thus before the turn of the century five trunk lines existed, supplemented by connections which afforded other transcontinental routes. In 1909 another trunk line was completed: the Chicago, Milwaukee, St. Paul, and Pacific.

FINANCING THE RAILROADS The financial practices attending the construction was enough to give railroading a bad name. The financial doings of railroad men in fact gave rise to the label of "robber barons," an epithet soon extended to the "captains of industry" as well. The building of both the Union Pacific and Central Pacific was accompanied by shameless profiteering through construction companies, controlled by insiders, which drained off the resources of the railroad companies. The Crédit Mobilier Company, according to a congressional investigation, bought congressmen like sacks of potatoes and charged the Union Pacific $94 million for construction that cost at most $44 million. In one year, 1868, a holder of Crédit Mobilier stock took dividends that amounted to 230 percent in Union Pacific bonds and 515 percent in Union Pacific stock, on top of 60 percent in cash. The Credit and Finance Corporation, controlled by the California Big Four, did almost as well, taking the Central Pacific for $79 million, of which an estimated $36 million was profit. When the same men began building the Southern Pacific northward and southward, then eastward to El Paso, the Western Development Company looted the new road just as effectively. The vast economic and political power wielded by the four men in California was lambasted by Frank Norris in a novel entitled *The Octopus*, but the book could not alter the facts. Each of the Big Four at his death left an estate of $40 million or more.

In the long run, nevertheless, the federal government recovered much if not all of its investment in transcontinentals and accomplished the purpose of linking the country together. The Union Pacific, for example, repaid in full its second mortgage loan in 1897. The roads increased incalculably the value of the alternate sections of land that remained in government hands, and until 1946 the government shipped freight and military personnel over land-grant roads at half fare.

The transcontinentals were trunk lines from the start, but in the East trunk lines were formed by continued expansion and combination. Eastern lines, like those in the West, were subject to financial buccaneering, which centered first on the Erie Railroad, the favorite prey of manipulators. Prince of the railroad buccaneers was Jay Gould, a secretive trickster who developed on a grand scale the fine art of buying up run-down railroads, making cosmetic improvements, paying dividends out of capital, and selling out at a profit, meanwhile using corporate treasuries for personal speculation and judicious bribes. Ousted by a reform group after having looted the Erie, Gould moved on to bigger things in western roads and a variety of other corporations, including Western Union. Nearly every enterprise he touched was either compromised or ruined, while Gould was building a fortune that amounted to $100 million upon his death at age fifty-six.

Few railroad fortunes were built in those free-wheeling times by methods of pristine purity, but compared to such as Gould, most railroaders were giants of probity. They at least took some interest in the welfare of their companies, if not always in that of the public. Cornelius Vanderbilt, called "Commodore" by virtue of his early exploits in steamboating, stands out among the railroad barons. Already rich before the Civil War, he decided to give up the hazards of wartime shipping and move his capital into land transport. Under his direction the first of the major eastern consolidations took form. Back in 1853 the New York Central Railroad had brought eleven roads into a line that paralleled the Erie Canal from Albany to Buffalo. For connections into New York City, however, it depended on two other lines, especially when river steamboats quit running in winter. In 1862 Vanderbilt began to secure control of these, first the New York and Harlem, then the Hudson River line. He may have been after the Central from the start, but in any case it soon fell into his hands. In 1867, as a result of disagreements over money owed the Hudson River line by the Central, Vanderbilt refused to transfer any traffic to and from his Hudson lines to the Central. Driven to the wall by Vanderbilt, the Central's stockholders conceded him a controlling interest. When protest arose at his embargo on traffic, he asked innocently: "Can't I do what I want with my own?"

In December 1867 he became president of the Central and soon combined it with the other lines. Next he tried to corner the stock of his chief competitor, the Erie, but Daniel Drew, Jim Fisk, and Jay Gould beat him there by the simple expedient of printing new stock faster than he could buy it. In 1873, however, he bought the Lake Shore and Michigan Southern road, which gave his lines connections into Chicago. After the Commodore's death in 1877, his son William Henry extended the Vanderbilt lines to include more than 13,000 miles in the Northeast. By similar acts of acquisition and combination about two-thirds of the nation's railroad mileage fell under the control of only seven major groups.

ADVANCES IN MANUFACTURING The story of manufacturing after the Civil War shows much the same pattern of expansion and merger in both old and new industries. The Patent Office, which had recorded only 276 inventions during its first decade of existence, the 1790s, registered 234,956 in the decade of the 1890s. And whether or not necessity was the mother of invention, invention was the mother of new industries—and new departures in old ones. New processes in steelmaking and refining, for instance, were the foundation of the Carnegie and Rockefeller enterprises. The refrigerator car made it possible for the beef, mutton, and pork of the New West to reach a national market, giving rise to the great packinghouse enterprises of Gustavus V. Swift in Chicago and Philip D. Armour in Minneapolis. The use of corrugated rollers to crack the hard spicy wheat of the Plains provided impetus to the flour milling that centered in Minneapolis under the control of the Pillsburys, Washburns, and Crosbys. Technological improvements in papermaking, which occurred first in Europe, made it possible to satisfy the appetite of continuous-action roller presses with cheap paper made from woodpulps. Glassmaking became a mechanized industry. In 1884 tobacco manufacturing moved into a new stage when the Duke interests employed a machine to roll cigarettes.

The list of industrial innovations can be extended indefinitely: barbed-wire, farm implements, George Westinghouse's air brake for trains (1868), steam turbines, gas distribution and electrical devices, Christopher Schole's typewriter (1867), J. W. McGaffey's vacuum cleaner (1869), and countless others. Before the end of the century the internal combustion engine and the motion picture, each the work of many hands, were laying foundations for new industries of the twentieth century.

These advances in technology altered the lives of ordinary people far more than the activities of the political or intellectual realms. In no field was this more true than in the applications of electricity to communications and power. Few if any inventions of the times could rival the importance of the telephone, which Alexander Graham Bell patented in 1876 and demonstrated at the Philadelphia Centennial Exposition the same year. In 1877 he staged a conversation between Boston and New York. To promote the new device the inventor and his supporters formed the Bell Telephone Association, out of which grew in 1879 the National Bell Telephone Company. Almost from the beginning the Bell interests had to defend their patent against competitors. The most dangerous threat came from Western Union which, after turning down a chance to buy Bell's "toy," employed Thomas Edison to develop an improved version. Edison's telephone became the prototype of the modern instrument, with its separate transmitter and receiver. But Bell had a prior claim on the basic principle and Western Union, rather than risk a legal defeat, sold its rights and properties for a tidy sum, clearing the way for the creation of a monopoly. In 1885 the Bell interests, led by Theodore N. Vail, organized the American Telephone and Telegraph Company. By 1899 it was a holding company, capitalized at $120 million, in control of forty-nine licensed subsidiaries and itself an operating company for long-distance lines.

EDISON'S INVENTIONS   In the rise of electrical industries the name of Thomas Alva Edison stands above that of other inventors. He started his career at an early age as a railway news butcher, selling papers and candies on trains, soon learned telegraphy, and began making improvements in that and other areas. In 1876, at quarters in Menlo Park, New Jersey, Edison went full-time into the "invention business"; eleven years later he moved into enlarged quarters in West Orange, New Jersey. He invented the phonograph in 1877, the first successful incandescent light bulb in 1879, and altogether through his invention factories created or perfected hundreds of new devices and processes including the storage battery, dictaphone, mimeograph, dynamo, electric transmission, and the motion picture. In 1882, with the backing of J. P. Morgan, the Edison Electric Illuminating Company began to supply current to eighty-five customers from its Pearl Street Station in New York City, beginning the great electric utility industry. A number of companies making light bulbs merged into the Edison General Electric Company in 1888. Financially secure, Edison retired from business to devote full-time once again to invention.

The use of direct current limited Edison's lighting system to a radius of about two miles. To get more distance required an alternating current, which could be transmitted at high voltage and then stepped down by transformers. George Westinghouse, inventor of the air brake, developed the first alternating-current system in 1886 and manufactured the equipment through the Westinghouse Electric Company. Edison resisted the new method on the ground that it was too dangerous, but just as Edison's instrument supplanted Bell's first telephone, the Westing-

Thomas Edison in his laboratory. [Photoworld]

house system won the "Battle of the Currents," and the Edison companies had to switch over. After the invention of the alternating-current motor in 1888 by Nikola Tesla, a Croatian immigrant, Westinghouse acquired and improved the motor and worked a revolution by enabling factories to disperse widely. They no longer had to cluster around waterfalls and coal supplies.

Edison and Westinghouse were rare examples of inventors with the luck and foresight to get rich from the industries they created. The great captains of industry were more often pure entrepreneurs, men skilled mainly in organizing and promoting industry. Three stand out both for their achievements and for their special contributions: John D. Rockefeller, for his innovations in organization; Andrew Carnegie, for his own achievements in organization and for contributions to the philosophical rationale for entrepreneurial activity; and J. Pierpont Morgan, for his development of investment banking.

ENTREPRENEURS

ROCKEFELLER AND THE OIL TRUST Born in New York state, Rockefeller moved as a youth to Cleveland, where railroad and ship connections provided a strategic location for servicing the oil fields of western Pennsylvania, which were later found to extend into Ohio and West Virginia. Oil had long been known to exist in the region. One branch of the Allegheny River was called Oil Creek, from which farmers skimmed off the stuff to grease their wagon wheels. Medicine men bottled it and claimed it had miraculous curative powers. One of these men, "Doc" Samuel M. Kier, distilled what he called "carbon oil" for use in a lamp burner, but the resulting odor made it impractical. The problem remained unsolved until the late 1850s when Yale's Dr. Benjamin Silliman, Jr., at the behest of a local promoter, showed that the oil could be refined into a good illuminant (kerosene) which served also for heating and cooking. The promoter, George Henry Bissell, set a friend to drilling on his lease near Titusville, Pennsylvania, where in 1859 the first well was struck, producing oil at a rate of twenty-five barrels a day. This proved the start of a great industry, based at first mainly on the sale of kerosene.

In economic importance the Pennsylvania oil rush far outweighed the California gold rush of just ten years before. If it duplicated many of the earlier scenes of disorder, it ended by

Drums of oil leaving Rouseville, Pennsylvania, by train. Rouseville was one of the centers of the Pennsylvania oil rush. [Drake Well Museum]

yielding more wealth. Well before the end of the Civil War derricks checkered the area and refineries sprang up in Pittsburgh and Cleveland. Of the two cities, Cleveland had the edge in transportation, and John D. Rockefeller made the most of it. He started as a bookkeeper, but before age twenty-one was already a partner in a wholesale house. While other young men were going off to war, Rockefeller moved into the oil business. In 1860, sent out by business friends to look over the Pennsylvania fields, he advised against the risks of sinking wells, but saw that refining, a strategic bottleneck, promised great profits at little risk. In 1862 he backed a refinery started by his friend, Samuel Andrews. He then quit merchandising to form a partnership with Andrews, and in 1867 added H. M. Flagler to create the firm of Rockefeller, Flagler, and Andrews. In 1870 Rockefeller incorporated his various interests as the Standard Oil Company of Ohio, capitalized at $1 million.

Rockefeller was already the largest refiner, but as he put it, "the butcher, the baker, and the candlestick maker began to refine oil." As a result, "the price went down and down until the trade was ruined." Rockefeller resolved to bring order out of chaos, which is to say he decided to weed out the competition. Soon a useful device presented itself. In 1872 Rockefeller acquired the South Improvement Company, which he made the marketing agent for a large percentage of his oil shipments. By controlling this traffic, he gained clout with the railroads, which gave him large rebates on the standard rates in order to keep his business. In some cases they even gave him information on competitors' shipments. Rockefeller then approached his Cleveland competitors and offered to buy them out at his own price. Most of them saw the wisdom of this course. As Rockefeller put it, "the conditions were so chaotic [i.e., competitive] that most of the refiners were very desirous to get out of the business." By 1879 Standard Oil had come to control 90–95 percent of the oil refining in the country.

Much of Rockefeller's success was based on his determination to "pay nobody a profit." Instead of depending on the products or services of other firms, Standard undertook to make its own barrels, cans, staves, and whatever else it needed. In economic terms this was vertical integration. The company kept large amounts of cash reserves to make it independent of banks in case of a crisis. In line with this policy, Rockefeller set out also to control his transportation needs. By 1879 most of the pipelines in the Appalachian field had come under United Pipe Lines Company, a Standard subsidiary. With Standard owning most of the pipelines leading to railroads, plus the tank cars and the oil-storage facilities, it was able to dissuade the railroads from servicing eastern competitors. Those competitors who insisted on holding out then faced a giant marketing organization capable of driving them to the wall with price wars.

Eventually, in order to consolidate scattered business interests under a more efficient control, Rockefeller and his friends resorted to the legal device of the trust. Long established in law to enable one or more people to manage property belonging to others, such as children or the mentally incompetent, the trust now was used for a new purpose—centralized control of business. Since Standard Oil of Ohio was not permitted to hold property out of state, it began in 1872 to place properties or companies acquired elsewhere in trust, usually with Henry M. Flagler, company secretary. This became impractical, however, since the death of the trustee would endanger the trust. To get around this problem, in 1882 all of the thirty-seven stockholders in various Standard Oil enterprises conveyed their stock to nine trustees, getting "trust certificates" in return. The nine trustees were thus empowered to give central direction to all the Standard companies.

The original plan, never fully carried out, was to organize a Standard Oil Company in each state in which the trust did business. But the trust device, widely copied in the 1880s, proved legally vulnerable to prosecution under state laws prohibiting monopoly or restraint of trade. In 1892 the Supreme Court of Ohio ordered the Standard Oil Trust dissolved. For a while the company maintained a unified control by the simple device of interlocking directorates, through which the board of directors of one company was made identical or nearly so to the boards of the others. Gradually, however, Rockefeller took to the idea of the holding company: a firm which controlled other companies by holding all or at least a majority of their stock. The Pennsylvania Railroad had adopted the device as early as 1870; American Bell Telephone did the same in 1880. New Jersey favored the device under a law enacted in 1888 and clarified in the 1890s. In 1899 Rockefeller brought his empire under the direction of the Standard Oil Company of New Jersey, a holding company. Though less vulnerable to prosecution under state law, some holding companies proved vulnerable to the Sherman Anti-Trust Act of 1890. (This story will be told later.) Meanwhile the term "trust" had become so fixed in the public lexicon that it was used to describe large combinations under holding companies as well.

CARNEGIE'S GOSPEL OF WEALTH   Andrew Carnegie, like Rockefeller, experienced the untypical rise from poverty to riches that came to be known in those days as "the typical American success story." Born in Dunfermline, Scotland, son of a hand weaver who fell upon hard times, he migrated in 1848 with his family to Allegheny, Pennsylvania. Then thirteen, he started out as a bobbin boy in a textile mill at wages of $1.20 per week. At fourteen he was getting $2.50 per week as a telegraph messenger and im-

Andrew Carnegie, apostle of "The Gospel of Wealth." [Carnegie Library, Pittsburgh]

proved himself in his spare time by learning to read messages by ear. Soon he was promoted to telegrapher and in 1853 became personal secretary and telegrapher to Thomas Scott, then district superintendent of the Pennsylvania Railroad and later its president. When Scott moved up, Carnegie moved into his job and was soon on his way. During the Civil War, when Scott became assistant secretary of war in charge of transportation, Carnegie went with him, developed a military telegraph system, and personally helped evacuate the wounded from Bull Run.

Carnegie kept on moving—from telegraphy to railroading to bridge building and then to iron and steel making. He used personal connections and borrowed money to enter these fields, usually moving into the next one before dropping the last. Tom Scott got Carnegie started in investments with a hot tip on American Express stock. Carnegie mortgaged his mother's home to buy it. A chance venture in the Pennsylvania oilfields, which Rockefeller shunned, netted Carnegie a gusher. Because of his help in promoting sleeping cars, he got an eighth share in the venture, after which he bought into the Iron City Forge Company and organized the Keystone Bridge Company. He then persuaded officials of the Pennsylvania Railroad to finance his plan to make bridges for the road.

In 1865 Carnegie quit the railroad to devote full time to his own interests. These were mainly in iron and bridge building, but the versatile entrepreneur also made money in oil and sold railroad bonds in Europe. In 1872 he netted $150,000 on one trip, and on that trip met Sir Henry Bessemer, inventor of a new process of steelmaking. The next year Carnegie resolved to concentrate on steel, or as he put it, to put all his eggs in one basket and then watch that basket. He began first the J. Edgar Thompson Steel Works, which he shrewdly named after the head of the Pennsylvania Railroad. In addition to the Bessemer process, Carnegie soon began using the open-hearth process, developed first in Germany. As competitors arose, Carnegie picked them off one by one. In 1882 when the Pittsburgh Bessemer Steel Company ran into labor troubles and slackening demand, Carnegie bought out their almost-new Homestead works approximately at cost. When the Duquesne Bessemer Steel Company ran afoul of a smear campaign describing their rails as unsafe, Carnegie bought them out at less than cost—and in bonds which were paid off in five years out of profits from the Duquesne plant. By 1900 Carnegie Steel was paying dividends of $40 million.

Carnegie was never a technical expert on steel. He was a promoter, salesman, and organizer with a gift for finding and using men of expert ability. He always insisted on up-to-date machinery and equipment, and shrewdly used times of recession to expand more cheaply.

In much of this Carnegie was a typical businessman of the time, if abler and luckier than most. But he stands out from the lot especially as a thinker who fashioned and publicized a philosophy for big business, a conservative rationale that became deeply implanted in the conventional wisdom of Americans. Carnegie argued that however harsh their methods at times, the captains of industry were on the whole public benefactors. At thirty-three he confided to his diary an ambition to retire early and devote his time to self-improvement, to being a "distributor" of wealth (he disliked the word "philanthropy"), and perhaps to public service. He did finally achieve that goal, but not until age sixty-five. Meanwhile, however, he found time to write articles for current magazines and to produce a modest shelf of books.

His best remembered piece was an essay, "Wealth," published by the *North American Review* in 1889, and retitled "The Gospel of Wealth" when reprinted in the *Pall Mall Gazette* of London. In this basic statement of his philosophy Carnegie drew upon the ideas of Charles Darwin and especially Darwin's English interpreter Herbert Spencer, who had invented the phrase "survival of the fittest." In the evolution of society, Carnegie argued, the contrast between the millionaire and the laborer measures the distance society has come. "Not evil, but good, has come to the race from the accumulation of wealth by those who have the ability and energy that produces it." The process had been costly in many ways, but the law of competition was "best for the race, because it insures the survival of the fittest in every department."

Carnegie then moved on to a sermon on the proper uses of wealth. Carnegie professed no religious faith, but surely had absorbed from his Presbyterian origins the Christian doctrine of stewardship. A rich man could leave his fortune to his children, Carnegie said, but experience suggested that this was not always wise or even kind. He might leave it at his death for public uses, but in his absence it would likely be misused. The best way to dispense a fortune was to administer it during one's lifetime for the public good. One should first set an example of humble living—in Carnegie's case this included Skibo Castle in Scotland—and provide for his dependents, then consider the rest a trust fund for the public good. One should avoid alms-giving, but rather provide means for people to help themselves by supporting universities, libraries, hospitals, parks, halls for meetings and concerts, swimming baths, and church buildings—in that order. To his credit, Carnegie meant it, devoting his wealth to many such benefactions and to the cause of world peace. Rockefeller too gave many gifts, mainly to education and medicine, but apparently at least in part because he was persuaded it would make for good public relations.

Carnegie's gospel of wealth found widespread acceptance in the late nineteenth century's worship of success, an attitude of respect for the self-made man that owed perhaps more to the *Autobiography* of Benjamin Franklin and the sayings of Franklin's Poor Richard than to Charles Darwin and his interpreters. The popularity of such attitudes was shown by the market for inspirational literature touting the ancient verities of thrift, integrity, and hard work. Among the sages of that school none was better known than Horatio Alger, whose very name became a byword for success. A Unitarian minister in New York, he wrote novels for boys, mostly about poor boys who made good, with titles like *Ragged Dick* (1867), *Luck and Pluck* (1869), and *Tattered Tom* (1871). More often than not, however, Horatio Alger heroes made it, like Carnegie, by winning the favor of some well-placed man. William Makepeace Thayer's biographies of self-made men such as Franklin, Lincoln, and Grant became the nonfiction counterparts to Alger's novels. On the Chautauqua circuit the star was Russell Conwell, a Baptist minister who delivered his lecture, "Acres of Diamonds," more than 6,000 times. The message was that opportunity, in effect acres of diamonds, was at everybody's doorstep. "I say, get rich, get rich." It was a social and Christian duty.

J. P. MORGAN, THE FINANCIER   J. Pierpont Morgan, who was born to wealth and increased it enormously, was about as far from being a Horatio Alger hero as one could get. Born in Connecticut, he was the son of Junius Spencer Morgan, partner in the banking house of George Peabody and Company of London, which later became J. S. Morgan and Company. Young Pierpont attended preparatory school in Switzerland and the University of Gottingen in Germany, where he proved so adept at mathematics that a chance was held out to him to become a professor. It was a skill not without its uses for a young financier. After a brief apprenticeship, he was sent in 1857 to work in a New York firm which represented his father's London firm, and in 1860 set himself up as its New York agent under the name of J. Pierpont Morgan and Company. This firm, under various names, chan-

J. Pierpont Morgan. [The Pierpont Morgan Library]

neled much European capital into the country and grew into a financial power in its own right.

Morgan was an investment banker, which meant that he was engaged in a marketing operation. He would buy corporate shares and bonds wholesale and then sell them at a profit, much as other merchants would market, say, hardware, but on a larger scale. The growth of large corporations put Morgan's and other investment firms in a more and more strategic position in the economy. The financial world began to take notice in 1869 when Morgan actually beat the wily Jay Gould and Jim Fisk in a fight to control a New York railroad. Other major signs of his growing stature came in 1872 when Morgan was able quietly to sell a large bloc of New York Central stock in England before the news could adversely affect the American markets, and in 1873 when he secured the division of a Treasury loan with Jay Cooke and Company, which had held a virtual monopoly on the sale of government bonds since the Civil War.

Railroads were the key to the times and they became a special concern of Morgan's; he picked up and reorganized one line after another. After the Panic of 1893 Morgan took over the Erie, Philadelphia and Reading, the Northern Pacific, and organized the Southern Railway; he already had a hand in the Vanderbilt and Pennsylvania lines. Since the investment business depended on the general good health of client companies, investment bankers became involved in the operation of their clients' firms, demanding places on boards of directors and helping to shape their fiscal dealings. By these means bankers could influence company policies, which, technicians often argued, resulted in heavy emphasis on fiscal matters to the detriment of technical innovation. Eventually people were speaking of the "money trust," the greatest trust of all, with its hand in all kinds of other enterprises.

To Morgan, however, the stability brought by his operations was plain common sense. The railroad people and other businessmen, if unrestrained, acted like anarchists. Morgan, the historian Joseph F. Wall wrote,"felt that the American economy should ideally be like a company organizational chart, with each part in its proper place, and the lines of authority clearly designated. He did not really believe in the free-enterprise system, and like the most ardent socialists, he hated the waste, duplication, and clutter of unrestrained competition." In this view, the difference between the Morgans and Rockefellers on one side and the socialists on the other was chiefly over who would control the system, "the state or an oligopoly." While most Americans loudly professed belief in the "American system" of free enterprise, Wall wrote, "a few men like Morgan, with an efficiency and power that the socialists could never achieve in America, went about in their quiet way, building combines and trusts and interlocking directorates that would forever eliminate that wasteful competitive system."

Morgan's crowning triumph was consolidation of the steel industry, to which he was introduced by his interests in railroading. In 1898 a rapid series of mergers in the iron and steel industry was brought on mainly by two groups: one centered on the American Steel and Wire Company, formed by William H. Moore and John W. "Bet-a-Million" Gates, both longtime speculative plungers; the other group comprised the Morgan interests, chiefly the National Tube Company and the Federal Steel Company, headed by Judge Elbert Gary, who urged Morgan to buy out Carnegie and the other interests.

In 1901 Carnegie sold out to Morgan at his own price, which came to nearly $500 million, of which his personal share was nearly $300 million. In rapid succession Morgan added the Moore-Gates interests and the Rockefeller holdings in both the Mesabi ore range and a Great Lakes ore fleet. Altogether the new United States Steel Corporation, a holding company for these varied interests, was capitalized at $1.4 billion, a total that was heavily watered (well above the company's actual assets) but was soon made solid by large profits. The new giant was a marvel of the new century, the first billion-dollar corporation, the climactic event in that age of consolidation. By 1904, the financial writer John Moody recorded in *The Truth about the Trusts*, there were some 318 industrial trusts capitalized at over $7 billion,

A lavish dinner celebrated the merger of the Carnegie and Morgan interests into U.S. Steel in 1901. These executives are seated at a table shaped like a huge rail. [Carnegie Library, Pittsburgh]

with nearly 5,300 distinct plants. Of these trusts, 236, holding five-sixths of the capital, had incorporated since January 1, 1898, most under New Jersey law.

ADVANCES FOR LABOR

THE DISTRIBUTION OF WEALTH   Accompanying the spread of such industrial combinations was a rising standard of living for most people. If the rich were still getting richer, a lot of other people were at least better off, and the pre–Civil War trend toward even higher concentrations of wealth slacked off. This, of course, is far from saying that disparities in the distribution of wealth had disappeared. One set of estimates by Robert E. Gallman has it that in both 1860 and 1900 the richest 2 percent of American families owned more than a third of the nation's physical wealth, while the top 10 percent owned almost three-fourths and all the nation's physical assets were in the hands of half its families. Studies of social mobility in towns across the country show, moreover, that while the rise from rags to riches was rare, "upward mobility both from blue-collar to white-collar callings and from low-ranked to high-ranked manual jobs was quite common."

The continuing demand for unskilled or semi-skilled workers meanwhile was filled by new groups entering the workforce at the bottom: immigrants above all, but also growing numbers of women and children. Because of a long-term decline in prices and the cost of living, real wages and earnings in manufacturing went up about 50 percent between 1860 and 1890, and another 37 percent from 1890 to 1914. By latter-day standards, however, working conditions then were dreary indeed. At the turn of the century the average hourly wage in manufacturing was 21.6¢, and average annual earnings were $490. The average work week was fifty-nine hours, which amounted nearly to six ten-hour days, but that was only an average. Most steelworkers put in a twelve-hour day, and as late as the 1920s a great many worked a seven-day or eighty-four-hour week. Oil and pipeline crews were still doing such stints into the 1930s.

A NEW SOCIAL WORLD Rising wages in no way discount the high social costs of industrialization. In the crowded tenements that grew up in major cities the death rates ran substantially higher than in the countryside. Factories often maintained poor health and safety conditions. In 1913, for instance, there were some 25,000 factory fatalities and some 700,000 injuries that required at least four weeks' disability—more than half the number of American casualties in World War I. A fundamental social fact in this new bureaucratic world was the dependence of ever-larger numbers of people on the machinery and factories of owners whom they seldom if ever saw. In the simpler world of small shops, workers and employers could enter into close personal relationships; the larger corporation, on the other hand, was likely governed by a bureaucracy in which ownership was separate from management.

The coming of the railroads was basic to this development. The roads, the business historian Alfred Chandler wrote, "caused entrepreneurs to integrate and subdivide their business activities and to hire salaried managers to monitor and coordinate the flow of goods through their enlarged enterprises." What Chandler called the "visible hand" of management increasingly replaced the "invisible hand" which in Adam Smith's theory guided the marketplace through multitudes of individual decisions. As an old formulation had it, the corporation "has no soul to be damned and no body to be kicked." Much of the social history of the modern world in fact turns on the transition from a world of personal relationships to one of impersonal and contractual relationships.

DISORGANIZED PROTEST In these circumstances, it was far more difficult for thousands and millions of workers to organize for mutual benefit than for a few captains of industry to organize for profit. Public opinion was likely to respect property rights more than any right that inhered in labor. Many businessmen held to the viewpoint that a "labor supply" was simply another commodity to be procured at the lowest possible price.

Among workers still rooted in an agrarian world the idea of durable unions was slow to take hold. Immigrant workers came from many cultures and spoke many tongues. Many if not most saw their jobs as transient, the first rung on the ladder to success. They hoped to move on to a homestead, or having made their fortunes, to return to the old farms of their European homelands. With or without unions, though, workers often staged impromptu strikes in response to grievances such as wage cuts. But impromptu action often led to violence, and three violent incidents of the 1870s colored much of the public's view of labor unions thereafter.

The decade's early years saw a reign of terror in the eastern Pennsylvania coal fields, attributed to an Irish group called the Molly Maguires. Taking their name from an Irish patriot who had directed violent resistance against the British, the group aimed to right perceived wrongs against Irish workers by such methods as intimidation, beatings, and killings. Their actions excited high emotions which were reflected in later chronicles depicting them as either heroic defenders of the workingman in a genuine class war, or early practitioners of labor racketeering. The terrorism reached its peak in 1874–1875. In the meantime Franklin P. Gowen, president of a railroad which owned a number of the mines, had hired Pinkerton detectives to stop the movement. James McParlan, the most effective of the agents who infiltrated the Mollies, produced enough evidence to indict the leaders of the movement. At trials in 1876 twenty-four of the Molly Maguires were convicted. Ten of them were hanged. The trials also resulted in a wage reduction in the mines and the final destruction of the Miners' National Association, a weak union the Mollies had infiltrated. Later investigations have shown that agents of the mine operators themselves stirred up some of the trouble. Nobody came out of the affair smelling like a rose, except perhaps a few Catholic priests who, at some risk to themselves, urged their Irish brethren to abjure violence and secret societies.

THE RAILROAD STRIKE OF 1877 Far more significant, because more widespread, was the Great Railroad Strike of 1877, the first major interstate strike. For many people it raised the spectre of a social revolution led by workers, like the short-lived Paris Commune of 1871. Wage cuts caused the walkout. After the Panic of 1873 the major rail lines in the East had cut wages, and then in 1877 effected another 10 percent cut. This cut went into effect on July 16, and the next day most of the railroad workers at Martinsburg, West Virginia, walked out and blocked the tracks. Without organized direction, however, their movement degenerated into a mob which burned and plundered railroad property.

Walkouts and demonstrations of sympathy spread spontaneously from Cumberland, Maryland, to Chicago and San Francisco. The greatest outbreak began at Pittsburgh on July 19, when the Pennsylvania Railroad put on "double-headers" (long trains pulled by two locomotives) in order to reduce crews. Public sympathy for the strikers was so great at first that local militiamen, called out to suppress them, instead fraternized with them. But militiamen from Philadelphia were called, and after dispersing one crowd at the cost of twenty-six lives, found themselves besieged in the railroad's roundhouse, where the commander disbanded them and advised them to escape as best they could. Looting and rioting went on for another day until the frenzy wore itself out. Public opinion, sympathetic at first, tended to blame the strikers for the violence. Eventually the workers, lacking organized bargaining power, had no choice but to drift back to work. Everywhere the strikes failed.

In California, however, they indirectly gave rise to a political movement. At San Francisco's "Sand Lot" a meeting to express

The railroad strike of 1877. Railroad workers in Pittsburgh reacted violently to wage cuts. [Carnegie Library, Pittsburgh]

sympathy for the strikers ended with attacks on some passing Chinese. Within a few days sporadic anti-Chinese riots led to a mob attack on Chinatown. Depression had hit the West Coast especially hard, and the Chinese were a handy scapegoat for the frustrations of the time. Soon an Irish immigrant, Dennis Kearney, organized the "Workingmen's Party of California" mainly on the platform of Chinese exclusion. A gifted agitator, himself only recently naturalized, he harangued the "sand lotters" about the "foreign peril" and assaulted the rich for exploiting the poor —sometimes at gatherings beside their mansions on Nob Hill. In 1878 his new party won a good number of seats in a state constitutional convention, but managed to incorporate in the state's basic law little more than ineffective attempts to regulate the railroads. The workingmen's movement peaked in 1879 when it elected many members of the new legislature and the mayor of San Francisco. Kearney lacked the gift for building a durable movement, but as his party went to pieces his anti-Chinese theme became a national issue, and in 1882 Congress voted to prohibit Chinese immigration for ten years.

TOWARD PERMANENT UNIONS Meanwhile efforts to build a permanent union movement had begun to bear fruit. Earlier efforts, in the 1830s and 1840s, had largely been dominated by reformers with schemes that ranged from free homesteads to utopian socialism. But the 1850s had seen the beginning of "job-conscious" unions in certain skilled trades: first the National Typographical Union (1852), then the Stone Cutters (1853), Hat Finishers (1854), Iron Molders (1859), and Machinists and Blacksmiths (1859). By 1860 there were about twenty such unions, and during the Civil War, because of the demand for labor, such unions grew in strength and numbers.

Until after the war, however, there was no overall federation of these groups. In August 1866 some seventy-seven delegates organized the National Labor Union at a convention in Baltimore and chose as their leader William H. Sylvis, a Philadelphian who headed the Iron Molders. Essentially the NLU comprised congresses of delegates from labor and reform groups more interested in political and social reform than in bargaining with employers. The groups espoused such ideas as the eight-hour day, workers' cooperatives, greenbackism, and equal rights for women and blacks. In 1869 Sylvis died suddenly, still only forty-one, after which trade union support fell away quickly. Only a remnant of reformers was left in 1872 when the union reorganized as the National Labor Reform party, but its candidate for president, Justice David Davis of Illinois, withdrew and the movement collapsed. The National Labor Union cannot be put down as a total failure, however. It was influential in persuading Congress to enact an eight-hour day for federal employees and to repeal the Contract Labor Law, which had been passed during the Civil War to encourage the importation of labor. The union, moreover, undertook to encourage the organization of black workers, but with little success.

THE KNIGHTS OF LABOR   Before the National Labor Union collapsed, another group had emerged which soon claimed national standing, the Noble and Holy Order of the Knights of Labor. The name betokened a tendency to copy the forms of fraternal orders and to evoke the aura of medieval guilds. The founder of the Knights of Labor, Uriah S. Stephens, a Philadephia tailor, was a habitual "joiner" involved with several secret orders, including the Masons. His early training for the Baptist ministry also affected his outlook. Secrecy, he felt, along with a semi-religious ritual, would protect members against retaliation and at the same time create a sense of solidarity.

In 1869, with Stephens as leader, nine Philadelphia tailors founded the order. At first it grew slowly, but in 1873 formed the first district assembly in the Philadelphia area. During the years of depression, as other unions collapsed, it spread more rapidly and in 1878 its first General Assembly established a national organization. Its preamble and platform endorsed the reforms advanced by previous workingmen's groups, including producers' and consumers' cooperatives, homesteads, bureaus of labor statistics, mechanics' lien laws (to ensure payment of salaries), elimination of convict-labor competition, the eight-hour day, and greenbacks. One plank in the platform, far ahead of the times, called for equal pay for equal work by both sexes.

Throughout its existence the Knights emphasized reform measures and preferred boycotts to strikes as a way to put pressure on employers. The constitution of the order allowed as members all who had ever worked for wages except lawyers, doctors, bankers, and those who sold liquor. Theoretically it was one big union of all workers regardless of race, color, creed, or sex, skilled and unskilled. Each local assembly was to be formed on such a basis, but in practice some local and district assemblies were organized on a craft basis, such as the telegraphers and cigarmakers. Above these stood the General Assembly, a General Executive Board, and at the head of the organization a Grand Master Workman.

Stephens was the first elected to this office, but he stepped down in 1879 to protest a relaxation of secrecy. Secret labor groups had become suspect after the Molly Maguires, and had been the objects of the Catholic church's disapproval for some time. When the General Assembly allowed local and district groups to emerge into the open, Stephens gave way to Terence V. Powderly, the thirty-year-old mayor of Scranton, Pennsylvania. Born of Irish immigrant parents, Powderly had become a switchtender at sixteen but soon moved into the machine shop. In many ways he was unsuited to the new job. At once mayor, head of the Knights, county health officer, and part-owner and manager of a grocery store, he had too many irons in the fire. He was physically frail, sensitive to criticism, and indecisive at critical moments. He was temperamentally opposed to strikes, and when they did occur, did not always back up the local groups involved. Yet the Knights owed their greatest growth to strikes that occurred under his leadership.

In the mid-1880s the union had a meteoric rise. In 1884 a successful strike against wage cuts in the Union Pacific shops at Denver led many railroad workers to form new assemblies. Then, in 1885, the Knights scored a startling victory over Jay Gould. Late the previous year and early in 1885 Gould had cut wages on the Missouri, Kansas, and Texas and Wabash roads. A spontaneous strike on these lines in February 1885 spread to Gould's Missouri-Pacific, and as organizers from the Knights of Labor moved in, Gould restored the wage cuts. In June another strike on the Wabash against the firing of union members brought another victory. These successes allowed the Knights to grow rapidly from about 100,000 members to more than 700,000 in 1886, a memorable year in the history of organized labor for several reasons.

One was that the Knights peaked and then went into rapid decline. Jay Gould, taken by surprise in 1885, set a trap for the Knights in 1886. He spoke favorably of unions, expressed his wish that all railroad workers were organized, but in February 1886 he provoked another strike by firing a foreman in the Texas-Pacific shops at Marshall, Texas. When the Knights struck, Gould refused arbitration and hired Pinkerton agents to harass strikers and keep the trains running. On May 4 the Knights had to call off the strike. The organization was further damaged by an incident in Chicago that very night, with which the Knights had little to do but which provoked widespread revulsion against labor groups in general.

THE HAYMARKET AFFAIR   The Haymarket Affair grew indirectly out of agitation for the eight-hour day. The lead on this issue had been taken by a little-known organization with an unwieldy name, forerunner to the American Federation of Labor, the Federation of Organized Trades and Labor Unions of the United States and Canada. In 1884 this group had set May 1, 1886, as the deadline for the eight-hour day in all trades. Powderly declined to join the federation in a call for strikes on that day, but some assemblies of the Knights did. Chicago became the center of the movement, and on May 3 the International Harvester plant became the site of an unfortunate clash between strikers and policemen in which one striker was killed.

Leaders of a minuscule anarchist movement in Chicago scheduled an open meeting the following night at Haymarket Square to protest the killing. After listening under a light drizzle to lengthy speeches promoting socialism and anarchism, the crowd was beginning to break up when a group of policemen arrived and called upon the meeting to disperse. At that point somebody threw a bomb at the police, killing one and wounding others. The police responded by firing into the crowd. In a trial marked by prejudice and hysteria, seven anarchist leaders were sentenced to death despite the lack of any evidence linking them to the bomb-thrower, whose identity was never established. Of these, two were reprieved and some years later pardoned, one committed suicide in prison, but four were actually hanged. All but one of the group were German-speaking, but that one, Albert Parsons, held a membership card in the Knights of Labor.

Despite his best efforts, Powderly could never dissociate in the public mind the Knights from the anarchists. He clung to leadership until 1893, but after that the union evaporated and by the turn of the century it was but a memory. A number of problems accounted for the Knights' decline other than widespread fantasies of radicalism: a leadership devoted more to reform than to the nuts and bolts of organization, the failure of the Knights' cooperative enterprises, and a preoccupation with politics which led the Knights to sponsor labor candidates in hundreds of local elections. They won a surprising number of races in 1886, but their political efforts proved in the end to be a flash in the pan. The Knights may be credited with some lasting achievements among them the creation of the federal Bureau of Labor Statistics in 1884 as well as several state bureaus; the Foran Act of 1885 which, though weakly enforced, penalized employers who imported contract labor (an arrangement similar to the indentured servitude of colonial times in which workers were committed to a term of labor in exchange for transportation to America); and a national law enacted in 1880 for the arbitration of labor disputes.

The Knights by example also spread the idea of unionism and initiated a new type of union organization: the industrial union, an industry-wide union of the skilled and unskilled, begun in special assemblies of railway and telegraph workers. Industrial unions would have the power to match that of the organized concentrations of capital, but not for some time.

The craft unions were successful earlier. They organized workers who shared special skills, such as typographers or cigarmakers. In 1881 the Federation of Organized Trades and Labor Unions came into being as a group similar to the old National Labor Union; it was primarily an association of national craft unions but with representation of state and local assemblies as well. The craft unions were at first inclined to cooperate with the Knights, but the two groups were organized on different principles. Leaders of the crafts feared that joining with the unskilled would mean a loss of their separate craft identities and a loss of the bargaining power held by skilled workers.

GOMPERS AND THE AFL As it turned out, however, the main threat to the Federation came from another direction when the Knights themselves organized a few special assemblies along craft lines. An effort by the Knights' District Assembly 49 to organize a separate union in the New York cigar trade led the Cigarmakers International Union to call for stronger unity among the existing craft unions. In May 1886 delegates from twenty craft unions met in Philadelphia and called on the Knights to cease organizing in trades for which a national union already existed. When the Knights failed to heed the suggestion, a second conference met at Columbus, Ohio, and organized the American Federation of Labor (AFL). In structure it differed from the Knights in that it was a federation of national organizations, each of which retained a large degree of autonomy. The structure, it was sometimes said, was typically American because it followed the federal model of the Constitution; actually it followed very closely the model of the British Trades Union Congress.

Samuel Gompers served as president of the AFL from its start until his death in 1924 with only one year's interruption. Born in London of Dutch-Jewish ancestry, Gompers came to the United States as a teenager, joined the Cigarmakers Union in 1864, and became president of his New York local in 1877. This background was significant. The Cigarmakers were the intellectuals of the labor movement; to relieve the tedium of their task, they hired young men to read aloud as they worked, and debated such weighty topics as socialism and Darwinism. But Gompers and

Samuel Gompers, head of the American Federation of Labor. [AFL-CIO]

other leaders of the union focused on concrete economic gains, avoiding involvement with utopian ideas or politics. "At no time in my life," Gompers once said, "have I ever worked out a definitely articulated economic theory." Adolph Strasser head of the Cigarmakers, put it more strongly: "We have no ultimate ends," he told a Senate hearing. "We are going on from day to day. We are fighting only for immediate objects—objects that can be realized in a few years."

Such job-consciousness became the policy of the AFL under Gompers, whose lifetime concern was the effectiveness of the federation. He hired organizers to spread unionism, and worked as a diplomat to prevent overlapping unions and to settle jurisdictional disputes. The federation represented workers in matters of national legislation and acted as a sounding board for their cause. On occasion it exercised its power to request from members dues for the support of strikes. Gompers, it turned out, was temperamentally more fitted than Powderly for the rough-and-tumble world of unionism. He had a thick hide, liked to talk and drink with the boys in the back room, and did not shy off from using the strike to achieve labor's objectives. His preference, though, was to achieve these objectives by trade agreements including provisos for union recognition in the form of closed shops (which could hire only union members) or union-preference shops (which could hire others only if no union members were available).

One great objective which Gompers achieved at least in principle was making the eight-hour day standard. In 1889 the AFL voted to revive its May Day demonstrations for the eight-hour day abandoned after the Haymarket Affair. But within a few years the demonstrations underwent a curious change. In July

1889 the founding congress of the Socialist International in Paris voted to sponsor demonstrations for the eight-hour day worldwide. Later, these evolved into demonstrations for general worker demands, labor solidarity, and socialism. Still later, Communists took up the May Day celebrations and, in the supreme irony, paraded their armor through Moscow to observe a holiday which, its origins forgotten, began with an American demand for the eight-hour day.

The AFL at first grew slowly, but by 1890 it had already surpassed the Knights of Labor in membership. By the turn of the century it claimed 500,000 members in affiliated unions; in 1914, on the eve of World War I, it had 2 million and in 1920 reached a peak of 4 million. But even then it embraced less than 15 percent of the nonagricultural workers, and all unions, including the unaffiliated railroad brotherhoods, accounted for little more than 18 percent of these workers. Organized labor's strongholds were in transportation and the building trades. Most of the larger manufacturing industries, including steel, textiles, tobacco, and packing houses remained almost untouched. Gompers never frowned on industrial unions, and several became important affiliates of the AFL: the United Mine Workers, the International Ladies' Garment Workers, and the Amalgamated Clothing Workers. But the AFL had its greatest success in organizing skilled workers.

THE HOMESTEAD STRIKE Two violent incidents in the 1890s nipped the emerging industrial union movement, and set it back for forty years to come—the Homestead Steel Strike of 1892 and the Pullman Strike of 1894. The Amalgamated Association of Iron and Steel Workers, founded in 1876, had by 1891 a membership of more than 24,000 and was probably the largest craft union at that time. But it excluded the unskilled and had failed to organized the larger steel plants. The Homestead Works at Pittsburgh was an important exception. There the union had enjoyed friendly relations with the Carnegie company until H. C. Frick became its president in 1889. A showdown was delayed, however, until 1892 when the union contract came up for renewal. Andrew Carnegie, who had expressed sympathy for unions in the past, had gone to Scotland and left matters in the hands of Frick. Carnegie, however, knew what was afoot: a cost-cutting reduction in the number of workers through the use of labor-saving devices, and a deliberate attempt to smash the union.

As negotiations dragged on, the company announced it would treat with workers as individuals unless an agreement was reached by June 29. A strike, or more properly a lockout of unionists, began on that date. Even before the negotiations ended, Frick had hired as plant guards 300 Pinkerton detectives whose specialty was union-busting. But on the morning of July 6, when the Pinkertons came up the Monongahela River on barges, unionists were waiting behind breastworks on shore. Who fired the first shot remains unknown, but a battle broke out in which six workers and three Pinkertons died. In the end the Pinkertons surrendered and were marched away, subjected to taunts from crowds in the street. Six days later the state militia appeared at the plant. The strike dragged on until November, but by then the union was dead at Homestead. It did not help the labor cause that anarchist Alexander Berkman tried to help out by killing Frick. Armed with both knife and gun he still botched the job, although he wounded the company president severely.

THE PULLMAN STRIKE The Pullman Strike of 1894 involved a dispute at the "model" town of Pullman, Illinois, which housed workers of the Pullman Palace Car Company. The idyllic appearance of the town was deceptive. Employees were required to live there, pay rents and utility costs higher than in nearby towns, and buy goods from company stores. During the Depression of 1893 George Pullman laid off 3,000 of 5,800 employees, and cut wages 25–40 percent, but not his rents and other charges. When Pullman fired three members of a grievance committee, a strike began on May 11, 1894. Pullman workers had been joining the American Railway Union, founded the previous year by Eugene V. Debs. Once secretary-treasurer of the Brotherhood of Locomotive Firemen, Debs had decided that such brotherhoods were too exclusive and set out to organize an industrial union to include all railway workers. Late in June union workers ceased to handle Pullman cars and by the end of July had tied up most of the roads in the Midwest.

The roads brought strikebreakers from Canada and elsewhere, instructing them to connect mail cars to Pullman cars so that interference with Pullman cars meant also interference with the mails. Attorney-General Richard Olney swore in 3,400 special deputies to keep the trains running, and when clashes occurred between these and some of the strikers, lawless elements exploited the situation to repeat some of the scenes of the 1877 strike. Finally, on July 3 President Grover Cleveland answered an appeal from the railroads that he send federal troops into the Chicago area, where the strike was centered. Illinois Gov. John Peter Altgeld insisted that the state could keep order, but Cleveland claimed authority and a duty to ensure delivery of the mails. "If it takes every dollar in the Treasury and every soldier in the United States to deliver a postal card in Chicago," he vowed, "that postal card should be delivered."

Meanwhile Olney had got an injunction from the federal district court forbidding any interference with the mails or any combination to restrain interstate commerce; the principle was that a strike or boycott violated the Sherman Anti-Trust Act. On July 13 the union called off the strike and on the same day Debs was cited for violating the injunction and sentenced to six months in jail. The Supreme Court upheld the decree in the case of *In re Debs* (1895) on broad grounds of national sovereignty: "The strong arm of the national government may be put forth to brush away all obstructions to the freedom of interstate commerce or the transportation of the mails." Debs served his term, during which time he read deeply in socialist literature, and emerged to devote the rest of his life to that cause.

SOCIALISM AND THE UNIONS   The major American unions, for the most part, never allied themselves with the socialists as many European labor movements did. But socialist ideas had been abroad in the country at least since the time Robert Owen visited America in the 1820s. Marxism, a strain of socialism, was imported mainly by German immigrants. Karl Marx's International Workingmen's Association, the First International, founded in 1864, inspired a few affiliates in the United States. In 1872, at Marx's urging, the headquarters was moved from London to New York as a precaution against the growing influence of anarchists in the movement. In 1876 the First International expired, but the next year followers of Marx in America organized the Socialist Labor party, a group so heavily made up of immigrants that German was its official language in the first years. The movement gained little notice before the rise of Daniel DeLeon in the 1890s. As editor of its paper, *The People*, he became the dominant figure in the party. A native of the Dutch West Indies, DeLeon had studied law and lectured for some years at Columbia University. DeLeon proposed to organize industrial unions with a socialist purpose, and to build a political party which would abolish the state once it gained power, after which the unions of the Socialist Trade and Labor Alliance would become the units of control. His ideas seem to have influenced Lenin, leader of the Bolshevik Revolution of 1917, but DeLeon preached revolution at the ballot box, not by violence.

Debs was more successful at building a socialist movement in

America. To many, DeLeon seemed doctrinaire and inflexible. Debs, however, built his new party by following a method now traditional in the United States: he formed a coalition, one which embraced viewpoints ranging from moderate reform to doctrinaire Marxism. In 1897 Debs organized the Social Democratic party from the remnants of the American Railway Union, and got over 4,000 votes as its candidate for president in 1900. In 1901 his followers joined a number of secessionists from DeLeon's party, led by Morris Hillquit of New York, to set up the Socialists Party of America. In 1904 Debs polled over 400,000 votes as the party's candidate for president and more than doubled that to almost 900,000 votes in 1912, or 6 percent of the popular vote. In 1910 the Socialists of Milwaukee elected Emil Seidel mayor and sent Victor Berger to Congress.

By 1912 the party seemed well on the way to becoming a permanent fixture in American politics. Thirty-three cities had Socialist mayors, including Berkeley, California; Butte, Montana; Flint and Jackson, Michigan; as well as Milwaukee. The party sponsored five English daily newspapers, eight foreign-language dailies, and a number of weeklies and monthlies. Its support was not confined to urban workers and intellectuals. In the Southwest the party built a sizable grass-roots following among farmers and tenants. Oklahoma, for instance, had in 1910 more paid-up party members than any other state except New York, and in 1912 gave 16.5 percent of its popular vote to Debs, a greater proportion than any other state. But the party reached its peak in 1912. During World War I it was wracked by disagreements over America's participation, and was split thereafter by desertions to the new Communist party. A brief revival during the Great Depression served only to interrupt, not halt, its decline.

THE WOBBLIES During the years of Socialist party growth there emerged a parallel effort to revive industrial unionism, led by the Industrial Workers of the World (IWW). The chief base for this group was the Western Federation of Miners, organized at Butte, Montana, in 1893. Over the next decade the Western Federation was the storm-center of violent confrontation with unyielding bosses who mobilized private armies against it at Leadville and Cripple Creek in Colorado, in the Coeur d'Alenes of Idaho, and elsewhere. In June 1905 the founding convention of the IWW drew a variety of people who opposed the AFL's philosophy. Debs participated, although many of his comrades preferred to work within the AFL. DeLeon was of course happy at

*"One Big Union." The Arlington, Virginia, branch of the
Industrial Workers of the World. [Archives of Labor and
Urban Affairs, Wayne State University]*

this chance to strike back at craft unionism. A radical manifesto
issued from the meetings, arguing that the IWW "must be
founded on the class struggle, and its general administration
must be conducted in harmony with the recognition of the irre-
pressible conflict between the capitalist class and the working
class."

But the IWW waged class war better than it articulated class
ideology. Like the Knights of Labor, it was designed to be "One
Big Union," including all workers, skilled or unskilled. Its roots
were in the mining and lumber camps of the West, where unsta-
ble conditions of employment created a large number of nomadic workers, to whom neither the AFL's pragmatic approach nor
the socialists' political appeal held much attraction. The revolutionary goal of the Wobblies, as they came to be called, was an
idea labeled syndicalism by its French supporters: the ultimate
destruction of the state and its replacement by one big Union.
"We have been *naught*—We shall be *All!*" went their version of
the *Internationale*. "The industrial Union Shall be the Human
Race." But just how it would govern remained vague.

Like other radical groups it was split by sectarian disputes. Because of policy disagreements all the major founders withdrew,
first the Western Federation of Miners, then Debs, then De-
Leon. William D. "Big Bill" Haywood of the Western Federation remained, however, and as its leader held the group
together. But the Wobblies were reaching out to the fringe elements of least power and influence, chiefly the migratory

workers of the West and the ethnic groups of the East. Always ambivalent about diluting their revolutionary principles, they scorned the usual labor agreements, even when they participated in them. Consequently they engaged in spectacular battles with capital but scored few victories, the largest of which was a textile strike at Lawrence, Massachusetts, in 1912, which ended with wage raises, overtime pay, and other benefits. But the next year a strike of silk workers at Paterson, New Jersey, ended in disaster, and the IWW entered a rapid decline.

The IWW was effectively destroyed during World War I, when most of its leaders were jailed for conspiracy because of their militant opposition to the war. Big Bill Haywood fled to the Soviet Union, where he died and was honored by burial in the Kremlin wall. But the IWW, decried as a conduit for alien ideas, was actually an American original, born of the rough-and-tumble world of western miners and migrants. The Wobblies left behind a rich folklore of nomadic working stiffs and bindlebums, martyrs like the Swedish songster and labor organizer Joe Hill, framed (so the faithful assumed) for murder and executed in Utah, and the folk music of *The Little Red Song Book*, rediscovered by singers of a later generation.

FURTHER READING

All surveys of the Gilded Age deal extensively with developments in business and labor. Consult the relevant chapters in Robert H. Wiebe's *The Search for Order, 1877–1920* (1966),° John A. Garraty's *The New Commonwealth, 1877–1890* (1968),° and Samuel P. Hays's *The Response to Industrialism, 1885–1914* (1957).° Other works deal more strictly with the development of commerce. They include Howard M. Jones's *The Age of Energy: Varieties of American Experience, 1865–1915* (1970),° Thomas C. Cochrane and William Miller's *The Age of Enterprise* (1942),° Edward C. Kirkland's *Industry Comes of Age* (1961), and Glenn Porter's *The Rise of Big Business, 1860–1910* (1973).° Of particular interest are Sidney Fine's *Laissez-Faire and the General-Welfare State: A Study of Conflict in American Thought, 1865–1901* (1956), which gauges public opinion about the effects of business, and Alfred D. Chandler's *The Visible Hand: The Managerial Revolution in American Business* (1977),° which details the strategies of the early corporate managers. Also useful is Douglass C. North's quantitative *Growth and Welfare in the American Past* (1966).°

Scholarship on the growth of transportation includes George R. Taylor and Irene D. Neu's *The American Railroad Network, 1861–1890*

°These books are available in paperback editions.

(1956), Robert W. Fogel's *Railroads and American Economic Growth* (1964), and John F. Stover's *The Life and Decline of the American Railroad* (1970). Matthew Josephson's *The Robber Barons* (1934)° denounces the methods used by men like Jay Gould, while Thomas C. Cochrane's *The Railroad Leaders* (1953) is more sympathetic to the entrepreneurs as a group. Gabriel Kolko's *Railroads and Regulation, 1877–1916* (1965),° argues that the entrepreneurs themselves sought regulation.

For an overview of the entrepreneurial leaders, consult Jonathan Hughes's *The Vital Few* (1966). Allen Nevins's *Study in Power: John D. Rockefeller, Industrialist and Philanthropist* (1953), and David F. Hawke's *John D.: The Founding Father of the Rockefellers* (1980) scrutinize that vital individual. Harold F. Williamson and Arnold R. Daum et al., in *The American Petroleum Industry* (2 vols.; 1959–1963), also treat Rockefeller's rise to power. In the iron and steel sector, Peter Temin's *Iron and Steel in Nineteenth Century America: An Economic Inquiry* (1964) surveys development, while Harold Livesay's *Andrew Carnegie and the Rise of Big Business* (1975)° treats the titan of the steel mills. The best available biographies of J. P. Morgan are Andrew Sinclair's *Corsair: The Life of J. Pierpont Morgan* (1981) and George Wheeler's *Pierpont Morgan and Friends: The Anatomy of a Myth* (1973).

Nathan Rosenberg's *Technology and American Economic Growth* (1972) and Elting E. Morison's *From Know-How to Nowhere: The Development of American Technology* (1974) document the growth of invention during the period. More specific are Matthew Josephson's *Edison* (1959), which emphasizes the innovations which came from Edison's laboratory, and R. V. Bruce's *Alexander Graham Bell and the Conquest of Solitude* (1973), which stresses the social impact of technology.

The best introduction to the justification for business growth is Richard Hofstadter's *Social Darwinism in American Thought* (1959). Irwin G. Wyler's *The Self-Made Man in America* (1964) treats the Horatio Alger myth. Robert G. McCloskey's *American Conservatism in the Age of Enterprise* (1951)° and James Weinstein's *The Corporate Ideal in the Liberal State* (1960)° critically analyze laissez-faire capitalism.

Much of the recent scholarship on labor in the Gilded Age stresses the traditional values and the culture of work which the workforce brought to the factory. Herbert G. Gutman's *Work, Culture, and Society in Industrializing America* (1976)° best introduces these themes. Also helpful are Daniel T. Rodgers's *The Work Ethic in Industrial America, 1850–1920* (1974), and Daniel Nelson's *Managers and Workers: Origins of the New Factory System in the United States, 1880–1920* (1975).° Two brief surveys which have chapters on the Gilded Age are Joseph G. Rayback's *A History of American Labor* (1959)° and Henry Pelling's *American Labor* (1959). More specific to the Gilded Age is Melvyn Dubofsky's *Industrialism and the American Worker, 1865–1920* (1975).° David Montgomery, in *Beyond Equality: Labor and the Radical Republicans, 1862–1872* (1975),° and *Workers' Control in America: Studies in the History of Work, Technology, and Labor Struggles* (1979), analyzes the evolution of the work environment.

As for labor groups, Gerald N. Grob's *Workers and Utopia* (1961)° examines the difference in outlook between the Knights of Labor and the American Federation of Labor. For the Knights, see Terence V. Powderly's autobiography, *Thirty Years of Life and Labor, 1859–1889* (1890), and Melton McLaurin's *The Knights of Labor in the South* (1978). Two recent works on the leader of the AFL are Harold C. Livesay's *Samuel Gompers and Organized Labor in America* (1978)° and Stuart Kaufman's *Samuel Gompers and the Origins of the American Federation of Labor* (1978). To trace the rise of socialism among organized workers, see Nick Salivatore's *Eugene V. Debs: Citizen and Socialist* (1983) and Patrick Renshaw's *The Wobblies: The Story of Syndicalism in the United States* (1967).

In addition to the relevant essays in the Gutman volume, Gilded Age strikes and strikers are handled in Daniel Walkowitz's *Worker City, Company Town: Iron and Cotton Worker Protest in Troy and Cahoes, New York, 1855–1884* (1978).

21

THE EMERGENCE OF
MODERN AMERICA

AMERICA'S MOVE TO TOWN

EXPLOSIVE URBAN GROWTH   The frontier was a safety valve, Frederick Jackson Turner said in his influential thesis on America. Its cheap lands afforded a release for the population pressures mounting in the cities. If there was such a thing as a safety valve in his own time, however, he had it just backward. The flow of population toward the city was greater than toward the west, and "country came to town" epitomized the American people better than the occasional city "dude" who turned up in cow country. Much of the westward movement in fact was itself an urban movement, spawning new towns near the mining digs or at the railheads, forming in the arid regions what a later historian would call an "oasis civilization." More often than not, western towns anticipated settlement. They supplied headquarters for the land boomers and services for the hinterlands. On the Pacific coast a greater portion of the population was urbanized than anywhere else; its major concentrations were around San Francisco Bay at first, and then in Los Angeles, which became a boom town after the arrival of the Southern Pacific and Santa Fe Railroads in the 1880s. Remarkably, its salubrious climate and clean air were among Los Angeles's chief selling points. Seattle grew quickly, first as the terminus of three transcontinental railroad lines, and by the end of the century as the staging area for the Yukon gold rush. Minneapolis, St. Paul, Omaha, Kansas City, and Denver were no longer the mere villages they had been in 1860. The

South, too, produced new towns: Durham and Birmingham, which were centers of tobacco and iron manufactures, and Houston, which handled cotton and cattle, and soon, oil.

Trade and transportation had been the city builders of the past. Eight of the nine cities that by 1860 had passed 100,000 in population were ports, and the ninth (Brooklyn) was a suburb to the largest port. By the late nineteenth century no city could hope to thrive without at least one railroad, and most could boast a cluster of railroads. But it was the explosion in industry that powered the growth of new cities during this period. Industry brought huge concentrations of labor, and both required the proliferation of services that became synonymous with city life.

The emergence of the major cities was completed during the years from 1860 to 1910. After that, new cities sprang up only in unusual circumstances: Miami was the product of tourism brought by the coastal railroad, while Tulsa was the product of an oil boom. In those fifty years, population in incorporated towns of 2,500 or more grew from 6.2 million to 44.6 million, or from 19.8 to 45.7 percent of the nation's total population. After 1920 more than half the nation's population would be urban.

While the Far West had the greatest proportion of urban population, the Northeast had far greater numbers of people in the teeming cities north of the Ohio River and east of the Mississippi. There the situation that Jefferson had so dreaded was coming to pass: the people "piled high up on one another in the cities," and worse, these people increasingly were landless, tool-less, and homeless—an urban proletariat with nothing but their labor to sell. By 1900 more than 90 percent of the residents in Manhattan lived in rented homes or tenements. In Boston, Fall River, Jersey City, Memphis, four-fifths of the inhabitants were renters.

The cities expanded both vertically and horizontally to absorb their huge populations. In either case progress in the means of conveyance played an important role: the elevator, the streetcar, and before the end of the century the first automobiles. The first safety elevator, which would not fall if the rope or cable broke, was developed in 1852 by Elisha Graves Otis. In 1889 the Otis Elevator Company installed the first electric elevator, which made possible the erection of taller buildings. Before the 1860s few structures had gone higher than three or four stories.

Another support for the vertical city came from the engineers who developed cast-iron and steel-frame construction. Much of the impulse to new design centered in Chicago, which had to rebuild after the great fire of 1871. There William LeBaron Jenney built a metal skeleton for the ten-story Home Life Insurance

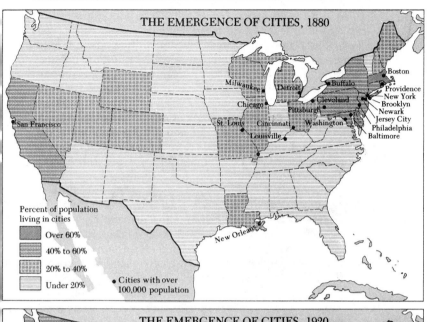

THE EMERGENCE OF CITIES, 1880

Milwaukee
Detroit
Buffalo
Boston
Chicago
Cleveland
Providence
New York
Pittsburgh
Brooklyn
Newark
San Francisco
St. Louis
Cincinnati
Washington
Jersey City
Louisville
Philadelphia
Baltimore

New Orleans

Percent of population
living in cities

Over 60%
40% to 60%
20% to 40%
Under 20%

● Cities with over
100,000 population

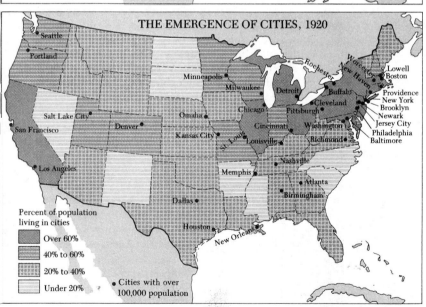

THE EMERGENCE OF CITIES, 1920

Seattle
Portland
Minneapolis
Rochester
Worcester
New Haven
Lowell
Boston
Milwaukee
Detroit
Buffalo
Providence
Salt Lake City
Chicago
Cleveland
New York
Pittsburgh
Brooklyn
San Francisco
Denver
Omaha
Cincinnati
Washington
Newark
Kansas City
St. Louis
Louisville
Jersey City
Los Angeles
Richmond
Philadelphia
Baltimore
Nashville
Memphis
Atlanta
Dallas
Birmingham
Houston
New Orleans

Percent of population
living in cities

Over 60%
40% to 60%
20% to 40%
Under 20%

● Cities with over
100,000 population

building, finished in 1885. Other architects added a sense of style to the new techniques. Louis Sullivan, whose motto was "Form Follows Function," pioneered a plain functional style in reaction against elaborate Victorian decoration. Other popular architectural styles included the Romanesque, with elaborate stone and masonry, the Italian Renaissance style, and the neoclassical.

Before the 1890s the chief sources of urban transport were either animals or steam. Horse- and mule-drawn streetcars had appeared in antebellum cities, but they were slow and cumbersome, and cleaning up after the animals added to the cost. Animal power, like the automobile later, contributed to severe pollution, but in its own way. In 1873 San Francisco became the first city to use cable cars which clamped onto a moving underground cable driven by a central power source. In the twentieth century it would become the last to use cable cars, after a few other cities tried and gave them up. Some cities used steam-powered trains on elevated tracks, but by the 1890s electric trolleys were replacing these. The electrical traction system in Richmond, Virginia, completed by Frank J. Sprague in 1888, is generally regarded as the first successful trolley system in a city of any size. Such systems spread rapidly, and in some places mass-transit companies began to dig underground passages for their cars. Around the turn of the century subway systems began to function in Boston, New York, and Philadelphia. Advances in bridge building through the use of steel and the perfection of the steel-cable

Carson, Pirie, Scott & Co. Louis Sullivan designed this Chicago store, built in the 1890s. [Chicago Architectural Photo Company]

The Elevated Rail Road, looking north on Eighth Avenue in New York City, 1883. Here, mass transit preceded urban growth. [Library of Congress]

suspension bridge also enlarged the reach of commuters. The marvels of the age were James B. Eads's cantilevered steel bridge over the Mississippi at St. Louis (1874) and John A. and Washington Roebling's cable-supported Brooklyn Bridge (1883), which linked Brooklyn to Manhattan.

The spread of mass transit made it possible now for large numbers of people to become commuters, and a growing middle class (working people often could not afford even the nickel fare) retreated to quieter tree-lined "streetcar suburbs" whence they could travel into the central city for business or entertainment. The pattern of urban growth often became a sprawl, however, since it took place usually without plan, in the interest of a fast buck, and without thought to the need for parks and public services. But some cities and developers had the wit to look ahead. New York in the early 1850s had set up a park commission which hired Frederick Law Olmstead as superintendent to plan Central Park. Olmsted later planned parks and even new subdivisions in San Francisco, Brooklyn, Chicago, and other cities.

CITY PLANNING   Chicago's World Fair, the Columbian Exposition of 1893–1894, gave impetus to a "city beautiful" movement. The fair was of such size that a whole new city had to be built on Chicago's South Side lakefront and supplied with a complex of services. Olmsted helped with the choice of a site, and the planning brought together leading architects and engineers. One planning session was called "the greatest meeting of artists since the fifteenth century."

The success of what visitors took to calling the "White City" stirred a new interest in city planning. Among the early fruits of the enthusiasm was a project to commemorate Washington, D.C.'s centennial in 1900 by completing L'Enfant's plan for a mall from the Capitol to the Potomac and the landscaping of Rock Creek Park. New civic centers sprang up in San Francisco, Cleveland, and Chicago, and new riverfront and lakefront plans in Harrisburg and Chicago. Hartford created the first city-planning commission in 1907, and in 1916 the American City Planning Institute, a professional organization of planners, met for the first time.

CITY PROBLEMS AND POLITICS   Although housing conditions in the mill villages of the New South could be bad indeed, one observer who saw laborers going to work through the pine woods at Lyman, South Carolina, noted the contrast to "the stuffy, crowded subways and the crowded elevated" of the metropolis. But workers in the big cities often had no choice other than crowded tenements, most of which were poorly designed. The new dumbbell tenements that began to appear in New York in the late 1870s derived their name from their shape: a narrow airshaft on either side at the middle made possible, even for a building crowded into a standard 25- by 100-foot lot, at least a small window in every room, giving some measure of light and ventilation. By the time the state adopted a stricter tenement law in 1901 the dumbbells had spread across the city. In 1900 Manhattan numbered 42,700 tenements which housed almost 1.6 million people, an average of 33.58 residents per building. Before the day of high-rise apartments this represented an extremely high density. Other cities were less densely populated, but the spread of slums with urban growth created immense problems of health and morale. The sheer size of these cities helped create a new politics. Since individuals could hardly provide for themselves such necessary services as transit, paving, water, sewers, street lighting and cleaning, and fire and police protection, they came increasingly to rely on city government for these things. Before city agencies took over these functions, operating with some degree of efficiency, they were handled by local political bosses who traded in patronage favors, and graft. Big-city machines were not altogether sinister in their effects: they provided food and money for the poor, fixed problems at city hall, and generally helped immigrants in their adjustment to a new life. Martin Lomasney, a ward boss in Boston, said: "There's got to be in every ward somebody that any bloke can come to—no matter what he's done—

*Overcrowding in New York. Jacob Riis took this photograph of a
tenement on Bayard Street in 1889. [Museum of the City of New York]*

and get help. Help, you understand, none of your law and justice,
but help."

In return the political professionals felt entitled to some reward for having done the grubby work of the local organization.
George Washington Plunkitt, for instance, a power in Tammany
Hall (New York City's Democratic organization) at the turn of
the century, saw nothing wrong with a little honest graft. "Well,
I'm tipped off, say, that they're going to lay out a new park at a
certain place. . . . I go to that place and buy up all the land I can in
the neighborhood. . . . Ain't it perfectly honest to charge a good
price and make a profit on my investment and foresight?" Dis-
honest graft would consist of "robbin' the city treasury or levyin'
blackmail on disorderly houses or workin' in with the gamblers
and lawbreakers." For his own epitaph Plunkitt proposed: "He
Seen His Opportunitities, and He Took 'Em."

MOVING FROM COUNTRY TO CITY   But whatever the problems of the
cities, the wonder of their glittering new arc and electric lights,
their streetcars, telephones, amusements, newspapers and magazines, and a thousand other things exerted a magnetic lure on the
youth of the farms. Hamlin Garland told in his autobiography, *A
Son of the Middle Border,* of his mixed sense of dread and wonder
at first visiting Chicago with his brother. The city first appeared
from the train window enveloped in clouds of smoke, "the soaring banners of the great and gloomy inland metropolis, whose
dens of vice and houses of greed had been so often reported to
me." Later the two young men wandered the streets: "Everything interested us. The business section so sordid to others was
grandly terrifying to us. . . . Nothing was commonplace, nothing
was ugly to us."

Luck and Pluck. *The young hero of Horatio Alger's story leaves his home in the country for the city where, with some luck and pluck, he will make good. [New York Public Library]*

The new cities threw into stark contrast the frustration of unending toil, the isolation and loneliness of country life. In times of rural depression thousands left for the cities in search of the opportunity that Horatio Alger and other writers of success literature dangled before their eyes. The exodus from the countryside was especially evident in the East, where the census documented the shift in population from country to city, and stories began to appear of entire regions where buildings were abandoned and going to ruin, where the wilderness was reclaiming farms that had been wrested from it during the previous 250 years.

The New Immigration

AMERICA'S PULL   Newcomers to the cities arrived not only from the surrounding hinterland but from Europe as well. European immigrants also were often moving from country to city, and increasingly from the great agricultural areas of eastern and southern Europe directly to the foremost cities of America. They gathered in these cities in order to live with others of like language, customs, and religion, and also because they lacked the means to go west and take up farms. Though cities of the South and West (excepting the Far West) drew their populations mainly from the native-born of their regions, American cities as a whole drew more residents from abroad. During the peak decade of immigration, 1900–1910, 41 percent of the urban newcomers arrived from abroad, while 29.8 percent were native Americans, 21.6 percent were the products of natural increase, and 7.6 percent lived in areas annexed to the cities.

Ethnic neighborhoods, "Little Italys," "Hunkertowns," "Chinatowns," sometimes populated by those from a single province or town, preserved familiar ways and shielded newcomers from the shocks of a strange culture. Such communities grew to be so large they soon overshadowed their Old World counterparts. In 1890 four out of five New Yorkers were foreign-born, a higher proportion than any other city in the world. It had twice as many Irish as Dublin, as many Germans as Hamburg, and half as many Italians as Naples. "A map of the city, colored to designate nationalities," Jacob Riis (a native of Denmark) wrote in *How the Other Half Lives* (1890), "would show more stripes than . . . a zebra, and more colors than any rainbow." In 1893 Chicago claimed the largest Bohemian (Czech) community in the world, and by 1910 the size of its Polish population ranked behind only Warsaw and Lodz.

This nation of immigrants continued to draw new inhabitants for much the same reasons as always, and from much the same strata of society. Immigrants came in flight from famine or the grinding lack of opportunity in their native lands. They fled racial, religious, and political persecution, or the imposition of compulsory military service. Yet one historian has claimed that "the desire to get cheap labor, to take in passenger fares, and to sell land have probably brought more immigrants than the hard conditions of Europe, Asia, and Africa have sent."

More immigrants probably were pulled by America's promise than were pushed by conditions at home. American industries, seeking cheap labor, kept agents abroad and at American ports to solicit members of depressed groups. Railroads, eager to sell land and build up the traffic on their lines, put out tempting propaganda in a medley of languages. Many of the western and southern states set up official bureaus and agents to attract immigrants. Under the Contract Labor Law of 1864 the federal government itself encouraged immigration by providing a lien on the immigrant's wages in order to pay for his or her passage. The law was repealed in 1868, but not until 1885 did the government forbid companies to import contract labor, which had put immigrant workers under the control of their employers. Domestic service and some skilled occupations were exempted from the ban, and evasion was easy.

From 1820 (when by requirement of Congress official statistics on immigration began to be kept) to 1900 about 20 million immigrants entered American ports, more than half of them coming after the Civil War. The tide of immigration rose from just under 3 million in the 1870s to more than 5 million in the 1880s, then fell to a little over 3.5 million in the depression dec-

Immigrants about to arrive at New York's Ellis Island in 1906. [Library of Congress]

ade of the 1890s, and rose to its high-water mark of 8.8 million in the first decade of the new century. The numbers declined to 5.7 million in the 1910s and 4.1 million in the 1920s, after which official restrictions cut the flow of immigration down to a negligible level.

A NEW WAVE   During the 1880s the continuing search for cheap labor combined with renewed persecutions in eastern Europe to bring a noticeable change in the source of immigration, one fraught with meaning for American social history. Before 1880 immigrants were mainly of Teutonic and Celtic origin, hailing from northern and western Europe. But by the 1870s there were signs of a change. The proportion of Latin, Slavic, and Jewish peoples from southern and eastern Europe rose sharply. After 1890 these groups made up a majority of the newcomers, and by the first decade of the new century they formed 70 percent of the immigrants to this country. Among these new immigrants were Italians, Hungarians, Czechs, Slovaks, Poles, Serbs, Croats, Slovenes, Russians, Rumanians, and Greeks—all people of markedly different cultural and language stocks from those of western Europe, and most followers of different religions, including Judaism and Catholicism.

THE NATIVIST RESPONSE   Many Americans of native stock saw the new immigration as a threat, not as an enrichment of American culture. The "clannishness" of these new ethnic communities posed a problem of assimilation far more complex than that which had once alarmed Benjamin Franklin, whose colonial Pennsylvania had only to assimilate Germans and Ulster Scots to a still-formative culture. The new immigrants found in America attitudes like those of Prof. Ellwood P. Cubberley of Stanford University, who called them "Illiterate, docile, lacking in self-reliance and initiative, and not possessing the Anglo-Teutonic conceptions of law, order, and government. . . ." The undercurrent of nativism so often present in American culture now surfaced mainly in anti-Catholic, and secondarily anti-Semitic, sentiments. The Catholic church in America, long dominated by the English-speaking Irish, now became a polyglot group all the more subject to misunderstanding and persecution. Similarly, Russian and Polish Jews came from a far different tradition than the Sephardic and German Jews who preceded them. Their unruly beards, long black coats, and their distinctive language, Yiddish, made them seem almost as strange to old Jewish stock as to other Americans.

More than religious prejudice underlay hostility toward the latest newcomers. Cultural differences confirmed in the minds of nativists the assumption that the Nordic peoples of the old immigration were superior to the Slavic and Latin peoples of the new immigration. Many of the new immigrants were illiterate, and more appeared so because they could not speak English. Some

An immigrant family, Ellis Island, New York, ca. 1910. The unfamiliar ways of immigrants from southern and eastern Europe reawakened nativist sentiment in America. [Library of Congress]

resorted to crime in order to survive in the new land, encouraging suspicions that criminals were being quietly helped out of Europe just as they had once been transported from England to the colonies. Italians from Sicily knew the tradition of Mafia, which bred a spirit of defiance to law and its enforcers. In the early 1890s vendettas among Italian gangs in New Orleans led to the murder of the police chief and the lynching of eleven Italian suspects, an incident which convinced many that the new immigrants were criminals.

The success of the Irish in city politics was emulated by the newer groups, who also thereby offended the sensibilities of well-born natives. Political and social radicals turned up among these immigrant groups in sufficient numbers to encourage nativists to blame labor disputes on alien elements. Such charges harbored a fine irony, however, because mainline labor organizations generally favored restricting immigration to keep down the competition for jobs. Employers sometimes used immigrants as strikebreakers; those who came from peasant origins, and were unfamiliar with strikes, were apt as not to think they were merely taking jobs that others had abandoned. Employers also learned quickly that a babel of tongues could confound unity of action among workers.

A resurgence of nativism in the 1880s was marked by the growth of groups devoted to saving the country from imaginary papal conspiracies. The most successful of these nativist groups, the American Protective Association, operated mainly in Protestant strongholds of the upper Mississippi Valley. Its organizer, Henry F. Bowers of Clinton, Iowa, seemed addicted to paranoid fantasies of Catholic conspiracies, and was especially concerned to keep the public schools free from Jesuit control. The movement grew slowly until 1893, when keen leaders took advantage of a severe depression to draw large numbers of the frustrated to its ranks. The APA soon vanished, swallowed up in the Populist and free-silver agitations, but while it lasted it promoted restricted immigration, more stringent naturalization requirements, refusal to employ aliens or Catholics, and the teaching of the "American" language in the schools.

IMMIGRATION RESTRICTION   The movement to restrict immigration had little success beyond the exclusion of certain individuals deemed undesirable. In 1875, for instance, a new law refused entry to prostitutes and to convicts whose sentences had been remitted in other countries on condition they leave. In 1882 a more general law added lunatics, idiots, and persons likely to become public charges, and over the years other specific undesirables joined the list. In 1891 Rep. Henry Cabot Lodge of Massachusetts took up the cause of excluding illiterates—a measure that would have affected most of the new immigration. Bills embodying the restriction were vetoed by three presidents on the ground that they penalized people for lack of opportunity: Cleveland in 1897, Taft in 1913, and Wilson in 1915 and 1917. The last time, however, Congress overrode the veto.

The one group specifically excluded as a nationality were the Chinese, who were victims of everything the European immigrants suffered, plus color prejudice as well. By 1880 there were some 75,000 Chinese in California, about one-ninth of the population. Their nemesis there was himself an immigrant (from Ireland), Dennis Kearney, leader of the Workingmen's party. Many white workers resented the Chinese for accepting lower wages, but their greatest sin, the New York *Nation* opined, was perpetuating "those disgusting habits of thrift, industry, and self-denial."

Exclusion of the Chinese was prevented by the Burlingame Treaty, which in 1868 gave China most-favored-nation status (the same as the best conceded to any other country) with respect to travel and immigration. But by 1880 the urgent need for railway labor had ebbed, and a new treaty with China permitted the United States to "regulate, limit, and suspend" Chinese immigration. In 1882 President Arthur vetoed a twenty-year suspension of immigration from China as actually a prohibition, but accepted a ten-year suspension. This was periodically extended until it was made permanent in 1904.

Chinese immigrants are unfairly excluded from the United States in this 1882 cartoon by Thomas Nast. [The Warder Collection]

April 1, 1882

E Pluribus Unum (Except the Chinese).

PUBLIC EDUCATION

THE SPREAD OF SCHOOLS The spread of public education helped quicken the emergence of a new America. "The spirit of American institutions is to be looked for in the public schools to a greater degree than anywhere else," wrote William T. Harris, the superintendent of St. Louis schools, philosopher, and proponent of graded schools and professional administration. By the time Harris wrote this in his annual report for 1871, America's commitment to public education was well nigh universal, though performance often fell short of the ideal.

The growing importance of public education is evident in statistics compiled by the national commissioner of education, whose office was created in 1867. In 1870 there were 6.8 million pupils in public schools; by 1920 the number had risen to 21.6 million. The percentage of school-age children in attendance went from 57 to 78 during these years, expenditures from $63 million to over $1 billion, and expenditures per pupil from $9 to $48. City schools quickly became schools of several rooms and separate grades with a teacher for each. In rural areas one-room schools lingered on into the twentieth century, when good roads made it possible to bus children to "consolidated schools." Despite these signs of progress, educational leaders all too often had to struggle against a pattern of political appointments, corruption, and incompetence in the public schools.

The spread of secondary schools accounted for a good bit of the increased enrollment in public schools. In antebellum America private academies prepared those who intended to enter college. At the beginning of the Civil War there were only about 100 public high schools in the whole country, but in the next decades their number grew rapidly to about 800 in 1880 and 6,000 at the turn of the century. Their curricula at first copied the academies' emphasis on higher mathematics and classical languages, but the public schools gradually accommodated their programs to those not going on to college, devising vocational training in such arts as bookkeeping, typing, drafting, and the actual use of tools.

VOCATIONAL TRAINING Vocational training was most intensely promoted after the Civil War by missionary schools for blacks such as Hampton Institute in Virginia, which trained Booker T. Washington, founder of Tuskegee Institute in Alabama. Another major prophet of the movement was Prof. Calvin M. Woodward

The beginnings of Tuskegee Institute. These three buildings first housed the school, an early leader in providing vocational training for blacks. [Library of Congress]

of St. Louis, who in setting up a school of engineering found his students woefully inept at the use of simple tools. He called on the public schools to teach manual skills as well as more abstract knowledge. Prodded by the National Society for the Promotion of Industrial Education, high schools installed workshops for training in carpentry, printing, drafting, bricklaying, and machine work, and for home management, or "home economics," as well. Under the Smith-Hughes Act of 1917 the national government provided dollar-matching grants for such programs.

Congress had supported vocational training at the college level for many years. The Morrill Act of 1862 granted each state warrants for 30,000 acres per representative and senator, the income from which was to be applied to teaching agriculture and the mechanic arts in what came to be known as the "land-grant colleges." In 1890 a Second Morrill Act began the practice of making federal grants to these colleges. Their outreach, first attempted in Farmers' Institutes, greatly expanded with the rise of the demonstration technique perfected by Seaman A. Knapp, "schoolmaster to American agriculture." In 1903, about a decade after the Mexican boll weevil crossed the Rio Grande, Knapp set up near Terrell, Texas, a demonstration of the best techniques then known to fight the pest. From this beginning, with the support of the Rockefellers' General Education Board, the demonstration technique spread rapidly as a means of getting knowledge into the field. The Smith-Lever Act of 1914 subsidized a permanent Extension Service of county demonstration agents who worked closely with land-grant colleges and state agricultural experiment stations.

HIGHER EDUCATION   American colleges at this time, whether church schools or state "universities," sought to instill discipline, morality, and a curriculum heavy on mathematics and the classics (and in church schools, theology), along with ethics and rhetoric. History, modern languages and literature, and some science were tolerated, although laboratory work would likely be limited to a professor's demonstration to his class. The ill-assorted collection of books that passed for libraries drove faculties to take refuge in textbooks, which often represented the limits of their own knowledge. The college teacher was all too apt to be a young man seeking temporary refuge or a broken-down preacher seeking safe harbor. In 1871 a writer in *The Galaxy* called the typical professor "nondescript, a jack of all trades, equally ready to teach surveying and Latin eloquence, and thankful if his quarter's salary is not docked to whitewash the college fence." A case in point, the versatile J. L. M. Curry of Richmond College, sometime congressman, soldier, preacher, and lawyer, taught English, philosophy, and international and constitutional law. An even more heroic scholar at Columbia University taught mental and moral philosophy, English literature, history, political economy, and logic. One cannot help thinking that the subject matter must have run thin somewhere.

Nevertheless the increasing demand for higher learning drove the college student population up from 52,000 in 1870 to 157,000 in 1890 and to 600,000 in 1920. During the same years the number of institutions rose from 563 to 998 and then to 1,041, and the number of faculty from 5,553 to 15,809 to 48,615. To accommodate the diverse needs of these growing numbers, colleges moved away from rigidly prescribed courses toward an elective system. In 1866 Washington College in Virginia, under its president, Robert E. Lee, adopted electives, and after 1869 Harvard College did so under its young president Charles W. Eliot. The new approach allowed students to favor their strong points and colleges to expand their scope to include all knowledge instead of a few set disciplines. But as Henry Cabot Lodge complained, it also allowed students to "escape without learning anything at all by a judicious selection of unrelated subjects taken up only because they were easy or because the burden imposed by those who taught them was light."

Women's access to higher education improved markedly in

the period. Before the Civil War some colleges had already gone coeducational, and state universities in the West were commonly open to women from the start. But colleges in the South and East fell in line very slowly. Of the women's colleges, Vassar (1865) was the first to teach by the same standards as the best of the men's colleges, though it had to maintain a Preparatory Department for twenty-three years to upgrade poorly prepared entrants. In 1875 two more excellent women's schools appeared in Massachusetts: Wellesley and Smith, the latter being the first to set the same admission requirements as men's colleges. The older women's colleges moved fast to upgrade their standards in the same way.

The dominant new trend in American higher education after the Civil War was the rise of the graduate school. The versatile professors of the old school had a knowledge more broad than deep. With some notable exceptions they engaged in little research, nor were they expected to advance the frontiers of knowledge. But gradually more and more Americans experienced a different system at the German universities, where training was more systematic and focused. After the Civil War the German system became the basis for the modern American university. Yale awarded its first Ph.D. in 1861, and Harvard its first in 1872.

The Johns Hopkins University, opened in Baltimore in 1876, set a new precedent by making graduate work its chief concern. The graduate students gathered in seminar rooms or laboratories, where under the guidance of an experienced scholar they learned a craft, much as journeymen had in the medieval guilds. The crowning achievement, signifying admission to full membership in the craft, was a masterpiece—in this case the Ph.D. dissertation, which it was expected would make an original contribution to knowledge. Clark University at Worcester, Massachusetts, founded in 1887 under the guidance of the prominent psychologist G. Stanley Hall, followed the model of Johns Hopkins. In the early 1890s two more major universities were founded to spread the gospel of Germanic education. The first, established by railroad magnate Leland Stanford (and named after his son, Leland Stanford, Jr.), opened at Palo Alto, California, in 1891, and the following year the University of Chicago, endowed by oil baron John D. Rockefeller, began operation. Meanwhile other established institutions, including Harvard, Columbia, Cornell, Michigan, and Wisconsin, also set up graduate schools, and by 1900 American universities annually conferred upward of 300 doctorates. The Ph.D. was fast becoming the ticket of admission to the guild of professors.

THE RISE OF PROFESSIONALISM   The Ph.D. revolution, moreover, was but one aspect of a growing emphasis on professionalism, with its imposition of standards, licensing of practitioners, and accreditation of professional schools. The number of professional schools grew rapidly in fields such as theology, law, medicine, dentistry, pharmacy, and veterinary medicine. While these fields accounted for 60 schools in 1850, there were 146 in 1875 and 283 in 1900. Growth in numbers brought pressures for higher standards. At Harvard in 1870 one could qualify for a medical degree by attending two lecture courses for four months, proving three years of medical experience, and passing a simple examination. Harvard President Eliot then insisted on requiring three years of class attendance, together with laboratory and clinical work. In 1870 the Harvard Law School developed a rough equivalent to the laboratory by introducing the "case method," which required students to dig out the rules for themselves.

Along with advanced schooling went a movement for licensing practitioners in certain fields. The first state licensing law for dentistry, for instance, came in 1868, for pharmacy in 1874, for veterinary medicine in 1886, for accounting in 1896, and for architecture in 1897. By 1894 twenty-one states held standard examinations for doctors, and fourteen others recognized only graduates from accredited medical schools. Licensing benefited the public by certifying competence in a given field, but it also benefited members of the profession by limiting competition.

A Red Sox home game, 1897. Professional baseball became a major attraction in the late nineteenth century. [Library of Congress]

Learned and professional associations now began to proliferate. Earlier societies, such as the American Association for the Advancement of Science (1848), which had seemed specialized enough, made way for still more specialized groups such as the American Chemical Society (1876), the American Ornithologists' Union (1883), and the National Statistical Association (1888). Modern-language scholars organized in 1883, American historians in 1884, economists in 1885, political scientists in 1889, folklorists in 1888, and all sponsored meetings and journals to keep members in touch with developments in the field. A host of commonplace and simple jobs entered the ranks of the "professions," including barbering, playing baseball, and planning vacations.

THEORIES OF SOCIAL CHANGE

Every field of thought in the postbellum years felt the impact of Charles Darwin's *On the Origin of Species* (1859), which argued that existing species, including humanity itself, had evolved through a long process of "natural selection" from less complex forms of life. Those species adapted to survival by reason of quickness, shrewdness, or other advantages reproduced their kind, while others fell by the wayside. The idea of species evolution shocked those of conventional religious views by contradicting a literal interpretation of the creation stories in Genesis. Heated arguments arose among scientists and clergymen, and the two leading scientists at Harvard took opposing positions, with Asa Gray defending Darwin's theory against Louis Agassiz's denial of its validity. Some of the faithful rejected Darwin's doctrine, while others found their faith severely shaken not only by evolutionary theory but also by the urging of professionals to apply the critical standards of scholarship to the Bible itself, and by the study of comparative religion, which found parallels to biblical stories and doctrines in other faiths. Most of the faithful, however, came to reconcile science and religion. Men like Joseph Le Conte, a scientist at the University of California, and James McCosh, a theologian and president of Princeton, came to view evolution as the Divine Will, as one of the secondary causes through which God worked.

SOCIAL DARWINISM   Though Darwin's theory applied only to biological phenomena, other thinkers drew broader inferences from it. The temptation to apply evolutionary theory to the social world proved irresistible. Darwin's fellow Englishman Herbert

Spencer became the first major prophet of Social Darwinism, and an important influence on American thought. Spencer, whose first works anticipated Darwin, brought forth in eight weighty tomes his *System of Synthetic Philosophy* (1862–1893), an effort to embrace all fields of knowledge within an overall system of Darwinian evolution. He argued that human society and institutions, like organisms, passed through the process of natural selection, which resulted, in Spencer's phrase, in the "survival of the fittest." For Spencer, social evolution implied progress, ending "only in the establisment of the greatest perfection and the most complete happiness."

If, as Spencer believed, society naturally evolved for the better, then the right of the individual to do as he pleased was inviolable, and organized interference with the process of social evolution was a serious mistake. This view amounted to a more ponderous version of Carnegie's "Gospel of Wealth"; it used biological laws to justify the workings of the free market. Social Darwinism implied a governmental policy of hands-off; it decried the regulation of business, the graduated income tax, sanitation and housing regulations, and even protection against medical quacks. All these would only impede progress by contributing to the survival of the unfit. The only acceptable charity was voluntary, and even that was of dubious value. Spencer warned that "fostering the good-for-nothing at the expense of the good, is an extreme cruelty."

Accumulated wealth was the best evidence of fitness. Successful businessmen and corporations were the engines of progress. If small business were crowded out by trusts and monopolies, that too was part of the process. Thus John D. Rockefeller told his Baptist Sunday school class: "The growth of a large business is merely a survival of the fittest. . . . The American Beauty rose can be produced in the splendor and fragrance which bring cheer to its beholder only by sacrificing the early buds which grow up around it. This is not an evil tendency in business. It is merely the working-out of a law of nature and a law of God."

The ideas of Darwin and Spencer were quickly popularized in America. John Fiske, a historian and lecturer, was one of the chief spokesmen for Social Darwinism, writing copiously and speaking to audiences all over the country. In 1872 Edward Livingston Youmans founded *Popular Science Monthly*, which soon became the chief medium for popularizing Darwinism. That same year Darwin's chief academic disciple, William Graham Sumner, took up the new chair of political and social science at Yale. Trained for the ministry and formerly an Episcopal rector, he was given to preaching the gospel of natural selection under titles such as *What Social Classes Owe to Each Other* (1883) and "The Absurd Effort to Make the World Over" (1894).

Sumner's most lasting contribution, made in his book *Folkways* (1907), was to argue that social conditions were set by the working of tradition, or the customs of a community, and not by reason or natural laws. The implication here too was that it would be a mistake for government to interfere with established customs in the name of ideals of equality or natural rights. Democracy, according to Sumner, was a condition based not on reason but on customs arising from the availability of much free land in America. As available land diminished, customs would slowly change, showing democracy to be merely a temporary condition.

REFORM DARWINISM The influence of Darwin and Spencer over the American mind did not go without challenge. Social Darwinism itself was partly a defense against critics of industrial society. Reform found its major philosopher in an obscure Washington civil servant, Lester Frank Ward, who had fought his way up from poverty and never lost his empathy for the underdog. Ward's book *Dynamic Sociology* (1883) singled out one product of evolution that previous pundits had neglected, the human brain. Man, unlike the animals, had a mind that was "telic," that could shape his ends and purposes. Far from being the helpless pawn of evolution, Ward argued, humanity could improve its situation by reflecting upon it and then acting. People thus had reached a stage at which they could control the process of evolution. The competition extolled by Sumner was in fact highly wasteful, and so was the natural competitive process: plant or cattle breeding, for instance, could actually improve on the results of natural selection.

Ward's Reform Darwinism challenged Sumner's conservative Social Darwinism, holding that cooperation, not competition, would better promote progress. Sumner's "irrational distrust of government" might have been justified in an earlier day of autocracy, but no longer under a representative system. Government could become the agency of progress by striving to reach two main goals: to ameliorate poverty, which impeded the development of the mind, and to promote the education of the masses. "Intelligence, far more than necessity," Ward wrote, "is the mother of invention," and "the influence of knowledge as a social factor, like that of wealth, is proportional to the extent of its distribution." Intellect, rightly informed by science, could plan successfully. In the benevolent "sociocracy" of the future, legislatures would function mainly to sanction decisions worked out in the sociological laboratory.

REALISM IN FACT AND FICTION

HISTORY AND THE SOCIAL SCIENCES   The pervasive effect of Darwinism in late nineteenth-century America was comparable to the effect of romanticism in the first part of the century. Like the earlier reaction against the Enlightenment's praise of reason, the trend in social thought now was, as one scholar put it, the "revolt against formalism," that is, a turn against abstract logic and toward concrete reality. The revolt had two salient features: its emphasis on history, on looking to the past for explanations, and its interest in investigating reality broadly through a variety of the social sciences. A succinct expression of the first feature as applied to the law lay in the book by Oliver Wendell Holmes, Jr., *The Common Law* (1881). "The life of the law has not been logic; it has been experience," Holmes explained. And experience was history. "The law embodies the story of a nation's development through many centuries," Holmes wrote, "and it cannot be dealt with as if it contained only the axioms and corollaries of a book of mathematics."

In the milieu of Darwinism the study of history flourished. The historian, like the biologist, studied the process of development, but in the origins and the evolution of society. Under the influence of German scholarship, and the new emphasis on science, history aspired to become "scientific." This meant examining documents and manuscripts critically, using external and internal evidence to determine validity and relevancy. The ideal of the scientific historian was to reproduce history with perfect objectivity, as Leopold von Ranke suggested, as it actually was—a noble if unreachable goal. At the new Johns Hopkins University, Herbert Baxter Adams instilled into a whole generation of historians the "germ theory" of history, which held that the truth about things was to be found in their origins. For most American institutions the germ theory led to the forests of ancient Germany. Frederick Jackson Turner, a student of Adams's, carried to his work on the American frontier his teacher's approach to history as an evolutionary process of adaptation.

Henry Adams spent half a long lifetime in vain quest for the "laws" of history, and ended with the chilling thought that human history was a cycle marked by the accelerating capture and dissipation of energy, so that standards of living rose sharply, but with disruptive effects. "Power leaped from every atom," he wrote. "Man could no longer hold it off. . . . The railways alone approached the carnage of war; automobiles and fire-arms ravaged society, until an earthquake became almost a nervous relaxation." There was much to be said for the new rigor in historical study, less to be said for a growing notion in academe that literary style was irrelevant to the science of history. But Henry Adams presided over a happy marriage of science with art in his nine-volume *History of the United States during the Administrations of Jefferson and Madison* (1889–1891).

Lester Frank Ward's achievements in *Dynamic Sociology* (1883) qualified him as the father of American sociology, but he, like many others, thought of the book as a broad synthesis of the social studies. It fell to Albion W. Small, head of the department at the University of Chicago, to define the field specifically. In his *General Sociology* (1905) Small confined it to the scientific analysis of social phenomena with emphasis on groups in human society. As founder and editor of the *American Journal of Sociology* (1895–present) Small wielded a strong influence in turning sociology from abstract speculation to the study of actual human relations. Theory, once all there was to sociology, gave way to a multitude of special interests: population, the family, ethnic groups, social class, public opinion, and social movements, to name but a few.

Economists made the same transition from abstract theory to the study of actual conditions. This transition was reflected in the statement of principles of the American Economics Association, founded in 1885 by a group of young scholars including Richard T. Ely, Simon Patten, and John Bates Clark. These economists looked "not so much to speculation as to historical and statistical study of actual conditions of economic life for the satisfactory accomplishment of [economic] study" and upheld the state "as an agency whose positive assistance is one of the indispensable conditions of human progress." Simon Patten, an economist at the University of Pennsylvania, argued that the economic problem would soon no longer be scarcity, since modern technology would make possible a surplus of goods, but distribution: how best to distribute goods and services. Wesley C. Mitchell of Columbia and the New School for Social Research carried further the "revolt against formalism" in economics by pioneering the statistical study of business cycles and economic trends.

PRAGMATISM Around the turn of the century the evolutionary idea found expression in a philosophical principle set forth in mature form by William James in his book *Pragmatism: A New Name for Some Old Ways of Thinking.* James, a professor of philosophy and psychology at Harvard, like Lester Frank Ward was concerned with the role of ideas in the process of evolution. Truth, to James, arose from the testing of new ideas, the value of which lay in their practical consequences. Similarly, scientists could test the validity of their ideas in the laboratory, and judge their import by their applications. James applied the principles of pragmatism even to religion in *Varieties of Religious Experience* (1902), where he noted that prayer in some cases seemed to raise the energy and potential of an individual, making prayer a true and valid experience for those people. Pragmatism reflected a quality often looked upon as genuinely American: the inventive, experimental spirit.

John Dewey, who would become the chief philosopher of pragmatism after James, preferred the term "instrumentalism," by which he meant that ideas were instruments, especially of social reform. Dewey, unlike James, threw himself into movements for the rights of labor and women, the promotion of peace, and the reform of education. Dewey believed that education was the process through which society would gradually progress toward the end of economic democracy. Dewey became the founder of an experimental laboratory school at the University of Chicago in 1895 and the prophet of what was later labeled "progressive education." He emphasized the teaching of history, geography, and science in order to enlarge the child's personal experience. Dewey also pointed out that social conditions had so changed that schools had to find ways to inculcate values once derived from participation in family and community activities. Another important goal of the schools was to keep habits plastic and flexible to prepare children for a changing world. They needed not just knowledge but a critical intelligence to cope with a complex, modern world.

THE LOCAL COLORISTS   American literature responded in different ways to the changes in American life and thought. The local color movement, which emerged after the Civil War, reflected a reunited nation engrossed with the diversity of its peoples and cultures. This movement also expressed the nostalgia of a people moving from a rural to an urban culture and longing for those places where the old verities survived. In California Bret Harte, the editor of the *Overland Monthly*, burst upon the national consciousness in the late 1860s with colorful stories of the gold country such as "The Outcasts of Poker Flat," "The Luck of Roaring Camp," and his best known poem, "Plain Language from Truthful James," about the "Heathen Chinee." Hamlin Garland, in *Main Traveled Roads* (1891), pictured the hardscrabble existence of farmers and their wives in his native country, the upper Midwest from Wisconsin to the Dakotas. Sarah Orne Jewett depicted the down-easters of her native Maine, most enduringly in the stories and sketches collected in *The Country of the Pointed Firs* (1896), while Mary E. Wilkins Freeman wrote stories of village life in Vermont and Massachusetts gathered in *A Humble Romance* (1887) and other works.

Once the passions of war and Reconstruction were spent, the South became for many northern readers an inexhaustible gallery of quaint types. George Washington Cable exploited the local color of the quaint Louisiana Creoles and Cajuns in *Old Creole Days* (1879), *The Grandissimes* (1880), *Madame Delphine* (1881), and other books. Joel Chandler Harris, a newsman and columnist, wove authentic Afro-American folk tales into the unforgettable stories of Uncle Remus, gathered first in *Uncle Remus: His Songs and His Sayings* (1880). Few Americans, whether they have read the stories or not, can long remain ignorant of the wonderful tar-baby or the brier patch.

TWAIN, HOWELLS, AND JAMES   The best of the local colorists could find universal truths in local life, but Samuel Langhorne Clemens (Mark Twain) transcended them all. A native of Missouri, Clemens was forced to work from the time he was twelve, becoming first a printer and then a Mississippi riverboat pilot. When the Civil War shut down the river traffic, he briefly joined a Confederate militia company, then accompanied his brother Orion to Nevada, where he wrote for the *Territorial Enterprise.* He moved on to California in 1864, where he first gained widespread notice with his tall tale of the gold country, "The Jumping Frog of Cala-

Samuel Langhorne Clemens, or Mark Twain. [Mark Twain Memorial, Hartford, Conn.]

veras County" (1865). In 1867 the San Francisco *Alta Californian* staked him to a tour of the Mediterranean, and his humorous reports on the trip, revised and collected into *Innocents Abroad* (1869), established him as a funny man much in demand on the lecture circuit. With the success of *Roughing It* (1871), an account of his western years, he moved to Hartford and was able to set up as a full-time author and lecturer.

Clemens was the first great American writer born and raised west of the Appalachians. His early writings accentuated his western background, but for his greatest books he drew heavily upon his boyhood in a border slave state and the tall-tale tradition of southwestern humor. In *The Adventures of Tom Sawyer* (1876) he evoked in fiction the prewar Hannibal, Missouri, where his own boyhood was cut so short. Its story of childhood adventures is firmly etched on the American memory. *Life on the Mississippi* (1883), based on articles written eight years before, drew upon what Clemens remembered as his happiest days as a young riverboat pilot before the war.

Twain's masterpiece, *The Adventures of Huckleberry Finn* (1884), created unforgettable characters in Huck Finn, his shiftless father, Nigger Jim, the Widow Douglas, the "King," and the "Duke." The product of an erratic upbringing, Huck Finn embodied the instinct of every red-blooded American boy to "light out for the territory" whenever polite society set out to civilize him. Huck's effort to help his friend Jim escape bondage expressed well the moral dilemmas imposed on everyone by slavery. Many years later another great American writer, Ernest Hemingway, would claim that "All modern literature comes from one book by Mark Twain, called *Huckleberry Finn*."

Twain wrote other memorable books, but nothing to equal those three. Like many humorists he had a broad streak of pessimism. He preferred to laugh rather than gaze into the abyss, but eventually the laughter stopped. Speculative investments bankrupted him during the Panic of 1893 and sent him back to the lecture circuits. Then his oldest daughter died of meningitis and his wife went into a long decline. His later writings, many not published before his death, expressed despair about what Clemens took to calling "that damned human race," but he himself remained a revered national treasure. As his friend William Dean Howells observed, he was unique among his contemporaries: "Emerson, Longfellow, Lowell, Holmes—I knew them all and all the rest of our sages, poets, seers, critics, humorists; they were like one another and like other literary men; but Clemens was sole, incomparable, the Lincoln of our literature."

Howells himself was unique, for no other American writer ever so dominated the scene as literary arbiter. Born in Ohio, he went to Boston in 1867 and soon became editor of the influential *Atlantic Monthly*. He left that post in 1881 to devote himself to novel writing, but later served better than two decades as a columnist and critic for *Harper's Monthly*. Howells proclaimed the doctrine of realism, a sort of literary version of scientific history's effort to reproduce the past as it actually happened. He wrote that realism "was nothing more or less than the truthful treatment of . . . the motives, the impulses, the principles that shape the life of actual men and women." The realist commonly wrote of the middle class in a simple and direct language, taking a pragmatic, objective point of view.

Howells wrote novels, plays, travel books, criticism, essays, biography, and autobiography. Amid the varied output of a long and productive life, *The Rise of Silas Lapham* (1885) stands out as his most famous novel. In it Howells presented a sympathetic portrayal of a *nouveau riche* manufacturer from the West, and one of the earliest fictional treatments of an American businessman. Soon after its publication, however, at the height of his career, Howells felt that "the bottom had dropped out" of his life. Converted to socialism by reading Tolstoy, horrified by the "civic murder" of the Haymarket anarchists, he entered a new phase. In *A Hazard of New Fortunes* (1890) he offered less sympathetic views of businessmen, included scenes of squalor and misery in the Bowery, and introduced a German-American socialist who lost his life in a police beating during a violent streetcar strike.

The third major literary figure of the times, Henry James, moved in a world far different from those of Clemens or Howells. Brother of the pragmatist philosopher William James, Henry spent most of his adult life as a voluntary expatriate in London, where he produced elegant novels that for the first time explored the international society of Americans in Europe. In novels such as *Daisy Miller* (1878), *Portrait of a Lady* (1881), *The Ambassadors* (1903), and *The Golden Bowl* (1904), James explored the tensions that developed between direct, innocent, and idealistic Americans (most often young women) and sophisticated, devious Europeans. James typically wrote of the upper classes, and his stories turned less on plot than on moral dilemmas. His intense exploration of the inner selves of his characters brought him the titles of "father of the psychological novel" and "biographer of fine consciences." What was more, he could produce spine-tingling ghost stories such as "The Turn of the Screw"

(1898) and "The Jolly Corner" (1907). In his later work he pioneered the technique of removing the author from the reader's awareness, becoming "invisible," as T. S. Eliot said, a technique commonplace among later authors.

LITERARY NATURALISM   During the 1890s the naturalists emerged as a new literary school, the heralds of twentieth-century modernism. Naturalism reacted against realism as realism had reacted against romanticism. The naturalists imported scientific determinism into literature, viewing man as part of the animal world, prey to natural forces and internal drives without control or full knowledge of them. From Darwin, their greatest inspiration, they drew biological determinism, from Newton a mechanistic determinism, and from Karl Marx a type of historical determinism. Frank Norris, who drew inspiration from the French novelist Emile Zola, pictured in *McTeague* (1899) the degeneration of a San Francisco dentist and his wife into madness, driven by greed, violence, and lust. Norris's *The Octopus* (1901), first of an unfinished trilogy on the lives of wheat farmers, presented the attempt of railroad owners to squeeze out the ranchers from the wheatfields of California. Stephen Crane in *Maggie: A Girl of the Streets* (1893) and *The Red Badge of Courage* (1895) pictured people caught up in situations beyond their control. *Maggie* depicted a girl driven to prostitution and death amid scenes so sordid that Crane had to finance publication himself. *The Red Badge of Courage*, his masterpiece, told the story of a young man going through his baptism of fire in the Civil War, and evoked nobility and courage amid the ungovernable carnage of war. Crane himself had had no experience of battle, which made his achievement the more remarkable.

Two of the naturalists achieved a degree of popular success: Jack London and Theodore Dreiser. Jack London of California was both a professed socialist and a believer in the philosopher Friedrich Nietzsche's doctrine of the superman. In adventure stories like *Call of the Wild* (1903) and *The Sea Wolf* (1904) London celebrated the triumph of brute force and the will to survive. He reinforced his point about animal force in the *Call of the Wild* by making his protagonist not a superman but a superdog who reverted to the wild in Alaska and ran with a wolf pack.

Theodore Dreiser shocked the genteel public probably more than the others with protagonists who sinned without remorse and without punishment. *Sister Carrie* (1900), a companion piece to *Maggie*, departed from it in having Carrie Meeber survive illicit loves and go on to success on the stage. In *The Finan-*

cier (1912) and *The Titan* (1914) Dreiser pictured in Frank Cowperwood (modeled on the Chicago speculator Charles T. Yerkes) a sexual athlete and a man of elemental force who rose to a dominant position in business and society. *An American Tragedy* (1925), generally regarded as Dreiser's masterpiece, pictured a less successful young man driven by the desire for sex and money to murder his pregnant mistress in order to marry wealth. He eventually was convicted and executed.

SOCIAL CRITICISM   Behind their dogma of determinism the naturalists harbored intense outrage at human misery. Other writers addressed themselves more directly to protest and reform. Henry George, a California printer and journalist, was suddenly struck on a visit to New York by the contrast the city offered between wealth and poverty. "Once, in daylight, and in a city street, there came to me a thought, a vision, a call. . . . And there and then I made a vow." The vow was to seek out the cause of poverty in the midst of progress. Back in California, the spectacle of land boomers grabbing choice sites brought George a new insight. The basic problem, he reasoned, was the unearned increment in wealth that came to those who owned the land. The fruit of his thought, *Progress and Poverty* (1879), a thick and difficult book, started slowly but by 1905 had sold about 2 million copies in several languages.

George held that everyone had as much right to the use of the land as to the air she breathed. Nobody had a right to the value that accrued from the land, since that was created by the community, not by its owner. Labor and capital, on the other hand, did have a just claim on the wealth they produced. One justifiable solution to the problem of unearned wealth was to socialize all property in land, but that would have been too disruptive. Better simply to tax the unearned increment in the value of the land, or the rent. George's "single-tax" idea was intended to free capital and labor from paying tribute for the land, and to put to use lands previously held out of production by speculators. George's idea was widely propagated and actually affected tax policy here and there, but his influence on the thinking of the day came less from his "single-tax" panacea than from the paradox he posed in his title, *Progress and Poverty*.

The journalist and freelance writer Henry Demarest Lloyd addressed himself to what many found a more vital issue than Henry George's, not the monopoly in land but industrial monopoly. His best known book, *Wealth Against Commonwealth* (1894), drew on more than a decade of studying the Standard Oil

Company. Lloyd, like Lester Frank Ward, saw the key to progress in cooperation rather than competition. Economic activities in their cooperative aspects demonstrated a civilizing process; Lloyd argued that "the spectacle of the million or more employees of the railroads . . . dispatching trains, maintaining tracks, collecting fares and freights . . . is possible only where civilization has reached a high average of morals and culture. . . ." But those in charge of the machinery of industry were concerned only with wealth, not with promoting civilization. "Of gods, friends, learning, of the uncomprehended civilization they overrun, they ask but one question: How much? What is a good time to sell? What is a good time to buy?" To avoid destruction, civilization required changes. The cooperative principle should be applied "to all toils in which private sovereignty has become through monopoly a despotism over the public." Where monopoly had developed, it should be transferred to public operation in the public interest. In 1903, just before his death, Lloyd joined the Socialist party.

Thorstein Veblen brought to his social criticism a background of formal training in economics and a purpose of making economics more an evolutionary or historical science. By all accounts he taught miserably, even inaudibly, and seldom held a job for long, but he wrote brilliantly. In his best known work, *The Theory of the Leisure Class* (1899), he examined the pecuniary values of the middle classes and introduced phrases that have since become almost clichés: "conspicuous consumption" and "conspicuous leisure." With the advent of industrial society, Veblen argued, property became the conventional basis of reputation. For the upper classes, moreover, it became necessary to consume time nonproductively as evidence of the ability to afford a life of leisure. In this and later works such as *The Theory of Business Enterprise* (1904) and *The Engineers and the Price System* (1921), Veblen held that the division between industrial experts and business managers was widening to a dangerous point. The businessman's interest in profits combined with his ignorance of productive efficiency to produce wasteful organization and a failure to realize the full potential of modern technology.

Edward Bellamy's *Looking Backward, 2000–1887* (1888) typified another genre of reform literature, the utopian novel. In Bellamy's futuristic story, a Bostonian who falls asleep in 1887 awakens in the year 2000 to find that the millennium has genuinely arrived. More than a hundred years in the future Julian West discovers a society transformed. The revolution which led to political equality has led on, by the democratic method, to a

"Nationalist" society of economic equality under socialism. Everybody gets an equal share of the national product and labor is shared by the simple method of reducing the hours for distasteful jobs until someone is willing to do the work. All this is accomplished by public control under national planning. The book enjoyed a temporary vogue, became a bestseller, and led to the founding of Nationalist Clubs, numbering 163 by 1891. The popularity of Bellamy's book gave rise to a spate of utopian novels, and some antiutopian ones depicting model societies gone wrong.

THE SOCIAL GOSPEL

RISE OF THE INSTITUTIONAL CHURCH   The churches responded slowly to the mounting social criticism, for American Protestantism had become one of the main props of the established order. The Rev. Henry Ward Beecher, pastor of the fashionable Plymouth Congregational Church in Brooklyn, preached success, Social Darwinism, and the unworthiness of the poor. Rudyard Kipling in 1899 reported a visit to a church in Chicago where the minister pictured "a heaven along the lines of the Palmer House (but with all the gilding real gold, and all the plate-glass diamond). . . . One sentence . . . caught my delighted ear. It was apropos of some question of the Judgment, and ran: 'NO! I tell you God doesn't do business that way!'"

As the middle classes moved out to the streetcar suburbs, their churches followed. In the years 1868–1888, for instance, seventeen Protestant churches abandoned the areas below Fourteenth Street in Manhattan. In the center of Chicago 60,000 residents had no church, Protestant or Catholic. Where churches became prosperous they fell easily under the spell of respectability and Social Darwinism. Working-class people sometimes felt out of place in opulent edifices with stained-glass windows: "opera-singing churches," revivalist Dwight L. Moody called them.

Many churches responded to the growing secularism of the time by undertaking earthly functions in addition to saving souls. The institutional church devoted most of its resources to community service and care for the unfortunate. The Young Men's Christian Association had entered the United States from England in 1850s and grew rapidly after 1870; the Salvation Army, founded in London in 1876, entered the United States four years later.

Churches in urban districts began to develop institutional features that were more social than strictly religious in function. Before the Civil War William A. Muhlenberg, an Episcopal minister in New York, organized St. Luke's Hospital and St. Johnland, a rural settlement in the Hudson Valley, as a refuge for slum dwellers. In the postbellum years this kind of work spread as church buildings acquired gymnasiums, libraries, lecture rooms, and other facilities for social programs. By 1894 there were enough such churches to form the Open and Institutional Church League. St. George's Episcopal Church exemplified the success of the institutional church: when it first offered institutional features in 1882 it had 75 members; by 1897 it had over 4,000 members. Russell Conwell's Baptist Temple in Philadelphia included, among other features, a night school for working people which grew into Temple University.

RELIGIOUS REFORMERS   The involvement of Conwell, a leading spokesman for the gospel of success, signified that the institutional movement might be consistent with a conservative outlook. But other church leaders built upon the institutional movement by preaching what came to be called the social gospel. One of the earliest, Washington Gladden of Columbus, Ohio, managed to preach the social gospel from the pulpit of a middle-class Congregational church. The new gospel in fact expressed the social conscience of the middle class. Gladden accepted the new ideas of evolution and textual criticism of the Bible, which he said relieved him of defending the literal truth of the story of Jonah and the whale. In *Working People and Their Employers* (1878), *Applied Christianity* (1886), and numerous other books, Gladden set forth the idea that true Christianity lies not in rituals, dogmas, or even in the mystical experience of God, but in the principle that "Thou shalt love thy neighbor as thyself." Christian law should govern the operation of industry, with worker and employer united in serving each other's interest. He argued for labor's right to organize, and complained that the class distinctions of society had invaded and split congregations as well.

The acknowledged intellectual leader of the social gospel movement, however, was the Baptist Walter Rauschenbusch, professor at the Colgate-Rochester Theological Seminary—appropriately located in the unofficial capital of the old Burnt-Over District. In *Christianity and the Social Crisis* (1907) and other works he developed a theological basis for the movement in the Kingdom of God. This kingdom existed in the churches themselves, but it embraced far more than these: "It is the Christian transfiguration of the social order. The church is one social institution alongside of the family, the industrial organization of society, and the State. The Kingdom of God is in all these, and realizes itself through them all. . . ." The church was indispensable to religion, but "the greatest future awaits religion in the public life of humanity."

THE CATHOLIC CHURCH   In the postbellum years Catholics remained inhibited from support of the new social movements by the *Syllabus of Errors* (1864), issued by Pope Pius IX, which declared erroneous such current ideas as progress, liberalism, rationalism, and socialism. James Cardinal Gibbons of Baltimore was instrumental, however, in moderating the effects of the *Syllabus*. In 1886 he forestalled an official condemnation of the Knights of Labor, which had abandoned secrecy and was headed by a Catholic, Terence Powderly. Gibbons also prevented the listing of *Progress and Poverty* on the *Index of Forbidden Books*. The church's outlook altered drastically in 1891 when Pope Leo XIII issued his encyclical, *Rerum novarum* ("Of modern things"). This new expression of Catholic social doctrine upheld private property as a natural right but condemned capitalism where it had imposed poverty and degredation on workers. It upheld the right of Catholics to join labor unions and socialist movements insofar as these were not antireligious. But American Catholics for the most part remained isolated from reform movements until the twentieth century, though they themselves were among the victims of the slums.

EARLY EFFORTS AT URBAN REFORM

THE SETTLEMENT HOUSE MOVEMENT   While preachers of the social gospel dispensed inspiration, dedicated reformers attacked the problems of the slums from residential and community centers called settlement houses. The movement sprang from the example of Toynbee Hall, founded in London's Whitechapel industrial district, where an English vicar, Samuel A. Barrett, invited students to join him in "settling" in a deprived section. Stanton Coit, an early American visitor, established the Neighborhood Guild on New York's Lower East Side in 1886. By 1900 perhaps a hundred settlement houses existed, some of the best known being Jane Addams's and Ellen Starr's Hull House in Chicago (1889), Jane E. Robbins's and Jean Fine's College Settlement in New York (1889), Robert A. Woods's South End House in Boston (1891), and Lillian Wald's Henry Street Settlement in New York.

Jane Addams. [New York Public Library]

The settlement houses were populated mainly by idealistic middle-class young people, a majority of them college-trained women who found the world unready to employ them except in nurturing roles. Settlement workers sought to broaden the horizons and improve the lives of slum dwellers in diverse ways. At Jane Addams's Hull House, for instance, workers sought to draw the neighborhood children into clubs and kindergartens, and a day nursery served the infant children of working mothers. The program gradually expanded as Hull House sponsored health clinics, lectures, music and art studios, an employment bureau, men's clubs, training in skills such as bookbinding, a gymnasium, and a savings bank. The Hull House Players helped initiate the Little Theater movement. Jane Addams and other settlement house leaders realized, however, that the spreading slums made their work as effective as bailing out the ocean with a teaspoon. They therefore spoke out and organized political support for housing laws, public playgrounds, juvenile courts, mothers' pensions, workmen's compensation laws, and legislation against child labor. Lillian Wald promoted the establishment of the federal Children's Bureau in 1912 and Jane Addams, for her work in the peace movement, received late in her life the Nobel Peace Prize for 1931.

The settlement house movement was not all of one piece, however. Critics accused settlements of subtle and not-so-subtle forms of social control, and of attempts to assimilate the poor to middle-class standards. The cultural gap between middle-class social workers and slum dwellers could often lead to misunderstanding, and in the effort to "Americanize" immigrants, the settlement houses and agencies of education sometimes lacked sensitivity to the values of other cultures. But on balance their contributions were more positive than negative. By the end of the century both the Catholic church and Jewish agencies were taking up the settlement house movement.

THE WOMEN'S SUFFRAGE MOVEMENT   Settlement house workers, insofar as they were paid, of course made up but a fraction of all gainfully employed women. With the growth of population the number of employed women steadily increased, as did their percentage of the labor force and of the total female population. The greatest leaps forward came in the decades of the 1880s and the 1900s, both of which were also peak decades of immigration, a correlation which can be explained by the immigrant's need for income. The number of employed women went from over 2.6 million in 1880 to 4 million in 1890, then from 5.1 million in 1900 to 7.8 million in 1910. "Between 1880 and 1900 the employment of women in most parts of the economy became an established fact," wrote one historian. "This was surely the most significant event in the modern history of women." Through all those years domestic work remained the largest category of employment for women; teaching and nursing also remained among the leading fields. The main change was that clerical work (bookkeeping, stenographic work, and the like) and sales jobs became increasingly available to women.

These changes in occupational status had little connection with the women's rights movement, which increasingly focused on the issue of suffrage. Immediately after the Civil War, Susan B. Anthony, a seasoned veteran of the movement though still in her forties, demanded that the Fourteenth Amendment include a guarantee of the vote for women as well as black males. She made little impression on the defenders of masculine prerogative, however, who kept intact the notion that women belonged in the domestic sphere. "Their mission is at home, by their blandishments and their love to assuage the passions of men as they come in from the battle of life . . ." said New Jersey's Senator Frelinghuysen. "It will be a sorry day for this country when those vestal fires of love and piety are put out."

In 1869 the unity of the women's movement was broken in a manner reminiscent of the antislavery rift three decades before. The question once again was whether or not the movement should concentrate on one overriding issue. Anthony and Elizabeth Cady Stanton founded the National Woman Suffrage Association to promote a woman suffrage amendment to the constitution, but they looked upon suffrage as but one among many feminist causes to be promoted as well. Later that same year Lucy Stone, Julia Ward Howe, and other leaders formed the American Woman Suffrage Association, which focused single-mindedly on the suffrage as the first and basic reform.

It would be another half century before the battle could be won, and the long struggle for referenda and state legislation on the issue focused the women's cause ever more on the primary objective of the vote. In 1890, after three years of negotiation, the rival groups united as the National American Woman Suffrage Association, with Elizabeth Cady Stanton as president for two years, to be followed by Susan B. Anthony until 1900. The work thereafter was carried on by a new generation, led by Anna Howard Shaw and Carrie Chapman Catt. Over the years the movement slogged its way to some local and some partial victories, as a few states granted woman suffrage in school board or municipal elections, or bond referenda. In 1869 the Territory of Wyoming granted full suffrage to women, and after 1890 retained woman suffrage as a state. Three other western states soon followed suit: Colorado in 1893, Utah and Idaho in 1896. But woman suffrage lost in a California referendum in 1896 by a dishearteningly narrow margin of 27,000 votes.

The movement remained in the doldrums thereafter until the cause won a Washington state referendum by a two-to-one margin in 1910, and then carried California by a close majority of 3,500 in 1911. The following year three more western states—Arizona, Kansas, and Oregon—joined in to make a total of nine western states with full suffrage. In 1913 Illinois granted women presidential and municipal suffrage. Not until New York acted in 1917 did a state east of the Mississippi adopt universal suffrage. In 1878 California's Sen. A. A. Sargent introduced the "Anthony Amendment," which remained before Congress until 1896 and then vanished until 1913. It was word for word the woman suffrage amendment eventually ratified, but that triumph required another schism in the movement brought on by a new generation of militants who had been fired up by the direct action of the British suffragists (see Chapter 26).

Despite the focus on the vote, women did not confine their public work to that issue. In 1866 a Young Women's Christian Association, a parallel to the YMCA, appeared in Boston and spread elsewhere. The New England Women's Club, started in 1868 by Julia Ward Howe and others, was an early example of the women's clubs which then proliferated to the extent that a General Federation of Women's Clubs tied them together in 1890. Many women's clubs confined themselves to "literary" and social activities, but others became deeply involved in charities and reform. The New York Consumers League, formed in 1890, and the National Consumers League, formed nine years later, sought to make the buying public, chiefly women, aware of labor conditions. One of its devices was the "White List" of firms which met its minimum standards. The National Women's Trade Union League, founded in 1903, performed a similar function of bringing educated and middle-class women together with working women for the benefit of women unionists. These and the many other women's groups of the time may have aroused the fear in opponents to woman suffrage that voting women would tilt toward reform. This was the fear of the brewing and liquor interests, large business interests generally, and political machine bosses. Others, mainly in the South, expressed opposition to woman suffrage on the ground that black women would be enfranchised, or because of states'-rights views.

A JUDICIAL HARBOR FOR LAISSEZ-FAIRE   Even without the support of voting women in most places, the states groped toward rudimentary measures to regulate big business and labor conditions in the public interest. By the end of the century nearly every state had provided for the regulation of railroads, if not always effectively, and had moved to supervise banks and insurance companies. North Carolina in 1899 created the first corporation commission, with jurisdiction over railroads, banks, and public utilities. Between 1887 and 1897, by one count, the states and territories passed 1,639 laws relating to conditions of work, which limited the hours of labor, provided special protection for women, limited or forbade child labor, required regular wage payments in cash, called for factory inspections, and outlawed blacklisting or the importation of "Pinkerton men." Nearly all states had boards or commissioners of labor, and some had boards of conciliation and arbitration. As one writer noted at the turn of the century, the labor laws of the time were designed "to secure the liberty of one class by curbing the license of another." Still, the effect of the effort was limited by poor enforcement and a sizable body of contrary opinion which found a special lodgment in the courts, where conservative judges in this era were busily reading laissez-faire into the Constitution.

Their chief devices were either higher-law doctrines or, more often, a revised interpretation of the Fourteenth Amendment's clauses which forbade the states to "deprive any person of life, liberty or property without due process of law" or to deny any person "the equal protection of the laws." Two significant steps of legal reasoning turned the due-process clause into a bulwark of property. First, the judges reasoned that the word "person" in the clause included corporations, which in other connections were legally artificial persons with the right to own property, buy and sell, sue and be sued like natural persons—even though, in a common expression, they had neither tail to kick nor soul to be damned. Second, the courts moved away from the old view that "due process" referred only to procedural rights and toward a doctrine of "substantive due process" which allowed court review of the substance of an action. Under this line of reasoning it was possible for legislatures by perfectly proper procedures to pass laws so extreme (in the view of the judges) as to deprive persons of property to an unreasonable degree, and thereby violate due process.

The Supreme Court first accepted the personality of the corporation in a tax case, *Santa Clara County v. Southern Pacific Railroad Company* (1886). That same year the Court in *Stone v. Farmers Loan and Trust Company* (1886) recognized the authority of Mississippi to regulate railroad rates, but declared that there might be cases in which the Court could review the rates: "Under pretense of regulating fares and freights, the State cannot require a railroad corporation to carry persons or property without reward." In *Chicago, Milwaukee and St. Paul Railway Company v. Minnesota* (1890) the justices declared unconstitutional a state law which forbade judicial review of rates set by a railroad commission. "The question of the reasonableness of a rate of charge . . . is eminently a question for judicial investigation," the Court ruled, "requiring due process of law for its determination." This was a direct reversal of the ruling in *Munn v. Illinois* (1877) that regulation was a legislative prerogative. It remained only for the Court to overturn rates set directly by a state legislature. That it did in *Smyth v. Ames* (1898), in which it struck down a Nebraska law for setting rates so low as to be, in the Court's view, unreasonable.

From the due-process clause the Court also derived a new doctrine of "liberty of contract," defined as being within the liberties protected by the due-process clause. This fine-spun theory first surfaced in *Allgeyer v. Louisiana* (1897), in which the Court struck down a Louisiana law forbidding a citizen to buy an insurance policy from a company that had not qualified to do business in the state. Liberty, the Court ruled, involved "not only the right of the citizen to be free from the mere physical restraint of his person, . . . but the term is deemed to embrace the right of the citizen to be free in the enjoyment of all his faculties," and free "to enter into all contracts" proper to carrying out such purposes. When it came to labor laws, this translated into an employee's "liberty" to contract for work under the most oppressive conditions without interference from the state. The courts continued to apply such an interpretation well into the twentieth century.

Judges in some of the lower courts found no need to spin their theories so fine. In 1886 the Pennsylvania Supreme Court, in striking down an act to protect workers against payment in commodities instead of in cash, declared it "an insulting attempt to put the laborer under a legislative tutelage, which is not only degrading to his manhood, but subversive of his rights as a citizen of the United States." The high court of West Virginia in 1889 condemned a similar law as an attempt to "foist upon the people a paternal government of the most objectionable character, because it assumes that the employer is a knave, and the laborer an imbecile." At least equally boggling in its blindness to reality was the opinion expressed by New York's Judge Robert Earl in the case of *In re Jacobs* (1885), in which he ruled against a law forbidding cigarmaking in tenements. "It cannot be perceived," Earl said, "how the cigarmaker is to be improved in his health or his morals by forcing him from his home and its hallowed associations and beneficent influences, to ply his trade elsewhere."

As the turn of the century neared, opinion in the country stood poised between such conservative rigidities and a growing sense that new occasions teach new duties. "By the last two decades of the century," wrote one observer, "many thoughtful men had begun to march under various banners declaring that somewhere and somehow the promise of the American dream had been lost—they often said 'betrayed'—and that drastic changes needed to be made to recapture it."

The last two decades of the nineteenth century had already seen a slow erosion of laissez-faire values, which had found their most secure home in the courts. From the social philosophy of the reformers, Social Gospelers, and Populists there emerged a concept of the general-welfare state which, in the words of the historian Sidney Fine, sought "to promote the general welfare not by rendering itself inconspicuous but by taking such positive action as is deemed necessary to improve the condition under which its citizens live and work." The reformers supplied no agreed-upon blueprint for a general-welfare utopia, but "simply assumed that government could promote the public interest by appropriate positive action . . . whenever the circumstances indicated that such action would further the common weal." The conflict between this notion and laissez-faire values went on into the new century, but by the mid–twentieth century, after the Progressive Movement, the New Deal, and the Fair Deal, the conflict would be "resolved in theory, in practice, and in public esteem in favor of the general-welfare state."

FURTHER READING

No one work synthesizes fully all aspects of Gilded Age life covered in this chapter. John A. Garraty's *The New Commonwealth, 1877–1890* (1968),° deals well with trends during the 1880s, while Robert H. Wiebe's *The Search for Order, 1877–1920* (1967),° thoroughly depicts the changes which began to transform American thought near the turn of the twentieth century. Other interpretations can be found in Howard Mumford Jones's *The Age of Energy: Varieties of American Experience* (1970) and Alan Trachtenberg's *The Incorporation of America: Culture and Society in the Gilded Age* (1982).°

Recent surveys of urbanization include Howard Chudacoff's *The Evolution of American Urban Society* (1975), Zane Miller's *The Urbanization of America* (1973), and A. Theodore Brown's *A History of Urban America* (1967). Stephen Thernstrom's *The Other Bostonians: Poverty and Progress in the American Metropolis, 1880–1970* (1973),° and Howard Chudacoff's *Mobile Americans: Residential and Social Mobility in Omaha, 1880–1920* (1972), present case studies on how some Americans fared with city life. Urban politics is treated in John M. Allswang's *Bosses, Machines, and Urban Voters* (1977), Zane Miller's *Boss Cox's Cincinnati* (1968),° and Jay Mandelbaum's *Boss Tweed's New York* (1965).° Sam Bass Warner examines how space and distance changed urban configurations in *Streetcar Suburbs: The Process of Growth in Boston, 1870–1900* (1971).° How cities dealt with growth and clutter is handled by Thomas L. Philpott in *The Slum and the Ghetto* (1978). Barbara Rosencrantz provides a kindred treatment of urban blight in *Public Health and the State* (1972). James F. Richardson's *The New York Police* (1970) examines the changing nature of crime and law enforcement.

Immigration has an extensive scholarship. Other general surveys include Leonard Dinnerstein and David Reimers's *Ethnic Americans: A History of Immigration and Assimilation* (1975)° and Maldwyn A. Jones's *American Immigration* (1960). Oscar Handlin's *The Uprooted* (1951)° and Philip Taylor's *The Distant Magnet: European Immigration to the U.S.A.* (1970)° are helpful in interpreting the European background which sent the immigrants over. John Higham's *Strangers in the Land: Patterns of American Nativism* (1955)° examines how old-stock residents reacted to the influx of new citizens.

More specific studies of different ethnic groups include Rowland

°These books are available in paperback editions.

Berthoff's *British Immigrants in Industrial America* (1953), John B. Duff's *The Irish in the United States* (1971), Josef Barton's *Peasants and Strangers: Italians, Rumanians, and Slovaks in an American City* (1975), Humbert Nelli's *The Italians of Chicago, 1880–1920* (1970), Irving Howe's *The World of Our Fathers: The Journey of the East European Jews to America and the Life They Made and Found* (1976),° and Stanford M. Lyman's *Chinese Americans* (1974).

Much of the recent work on education stresses how schools were designed to assimilate these new arrivals. This work includes Marvin Lazerson's *Origins of the Urban Schools* (1971), Selwyn K. Troen's *The Public and the Schools* (1975), and David Tyack's *The One Best System: A History of American Urban Education* (1974). For trends in higher education, consult Lawrence Veysey's *The Emergence of the American University* (1965) and Hugh Hawkins's *Pioneer: A History of the Johns Hopkins University* (1960) and *Between Harvard and America: The Educational Leadership of Charles W. Elliott* (1972). Burton J. Bledstein's *The Culture of Professionalism: The Middle Class and the Development of Higher Education in America* (1976)° is particularly insightful.

Sidney Fine's *Laissez-Faire and the General Welfare State* (1956)° and Morton and Lucia White's *The Intellectuals vs. the City* (1962)° survey the insights provided by the Gilded Age's leading thinkers. Richard Hofstadter's *Social Darwinism in American Thought* (1945), Robert Bannister's *Social Darwinism: Science and Myth in Anglo-American Thought* (1979), and Bruce Curtis's *William Graham Sumner* (1981) examine the impact of the theory of evolution. To trace the contours of pragmatism, consult Bruce Kuklick's *The Rise of American Philosophy* (1977).° Other intellectual trends are traced in Nathan G. Hale, Jr.'s *Freud and America: The Beginnings of Psychoanalysis in America, 1876–1917* (1971), George Dykhuizen's *The Life and Mind of John Dewey* (1973), Samuel Chugerman's *Lester F. Ward: The American Aristotle* (1936), and David Hershoff's *American Disciples of Marx: From the Age of Jackson to the Progressive Era* (1967).

Literature is treated in Jay Martin's *Harvest of Change: American Literature, 1865–1914* (1967), and Maxwell Geismer's *Rebels and Ancestors: The American Novel, 1890–1915* (1953). Larzer Ziff's *The American 1890s: The Lost Generation* (1966)° covers writers during that crucial decade. Specific studies include Justin Kaplin's *Mr. Clemens and Mark Twain* (1966),° Kenneth S. Lynn's *William Dean Howells: An American Life* (1970), and Louis D. Rubin, Jr.'s *George Washington Cable: The Life and Times of a Southern Heretic* (1969).

John L. Thomas's *Alternative America: Henry George, Edward Bellamy, Henry Demarest Lloyd, and the Adversary Tradition* (1983) and Nick Salvatore's *Eugene V. Debs: Citizen and Socialist* (1983) provide the best introductions to the social critics of the Gilded Age. Also helpful is James Weinstein's *The Decline of Socialism in America* (1967). For the Social Gospel, consult Paul A. Carter's *The Spiritual Crisis of the Gilded Age* (1971)° and Michael D. Clark's *Wordly Theologians: The Persistence of Religion in Nineteenth Century America* (1981).

William O'Neill's *Everyone Was Brave: The Rise and Fall of Feminism in America* (1969) and Eleanor Flexnor's *Century of Struggle: The Women's Rights Movement in the United States* (1959) present good introductions to the condition of women in the Gilded Age. More culturally oriented are Sheila M. Rothman's *Woman's Proper Place: A History of Changing Ideals and Practices, 1870 to the Present* (1980), and Lois Banner's *American Beauty* (1983). To gauge the impact of the increasing numbers of working women, see Carl N. Degler's *At Odds: Women and the Family in America from the Revolution to the Present* (1980),° Barbara Wertheimer's *We Were There: The Story of Working Women in America* (1977), and Susan E. Kennedy's *If All We Did Was to Weep at Home: A History of White Working-Class Women in America* (1979).

Innovations in architecture are handled in Henry Russell Hitchcock's *The Architecture of Henry H. Richardson and His Times* (1966) and Paul R. Baker's *Richard Morris Hunt* (1980). Peggy Samuels and Harold Samuels examine elements of Gilded Age art in *Frederick Remington: A Biography* (1982). An important profession is analyzed in Paul Stone's *The Social Transformation of American Medicine* (1982). George Juergens's *Joseph Pulitzer and the New York World* (1966) looks at journalistic developments. For the growth of urban leisure and sports, see Gunther Barth's *City People: The Rise of Modern City Culture in Nineteenth Century America* (1980)° and John A. Lucas and Ronald Smith's *Saga of American Sport* (1978). E. Reid Badger's *The Great American Fair: The World's Columbian Exposition and American Culture* (1979) explores the cultural implications of the Chicago World's Fair.

22

GILDED AGE POLITICS
AND AGRARIAN REVOLT

PARADOXICAL POLITICS

In 1873 Mark Twain and Charles Dudley Warner created an enduring tag for their times when they collaborated on a novel entitled *The Gilded Age*. The most unforgettable character in the book was an engaging mountebank, Col. Beriah Sellers, who always had afoot some slippery scheme to trade on political favors. Sellers had enough counterparts in the real politics of the day to enliven that story too, and their humbuggery reinforced the novelists' judgment that it was above all an age of jobbery, profiteering, and false glitter.

Perspectives on the times would eventually change, but generations of historians reinforced the two novelists' judgment. "No period so thoroughly ordinary had been known in American politics since Christopher Columbus first disturbed the balance of American society," Henry Adams wrote of the years 1870–1896. The real movers and shakers of American life were not the men who sat in the White House but the captains of industry who flung railroads across the continent and decorated its cities with their plumed smokestacks and gaudy mansions. Those presidents from Hayes to Harrison, novelist Thomas Wolfe wrote, became for later generations "the lost Americans: their gravely vacant and bewhiskered faces mixed, melted, swam together in the depths of a past intangible, immeasurable, and unknowable as the buried city of Persepolis."

Lord James Bryce, the most acute foreign observer of America in the late nineteenth century, suggested in *The American Commonwealth* (1888) that the American system, unlike the parliamentary system, tended to bring mediocre men to the top. "Since the heroes of the Revolution died with Jefferson and Adams and Madison," he wrote, "no person except General Grant has reached the [presidential] chair whose name would have been remembered had he not been President, and no President except Abraham Lincoln has displayed rare or striking qualities in the chair."

On the national issues of the day the major parties pursued for the most part a policy of evasion. Only on the tariff were there clear-cut traditions of division between protectionist Republicans and low-tariff Democrats, but there were individual exceptions even on that. On questions of the currency, regulation of big business, farm problems, civil service reform, internal improvement, and immigration, one would be hard put to distinguish between the parties. Europeans, accustomed to more ideological parties, were repeatedly perplexed at the situation until, in Lord Bryce's words, the truth began to dawn that "neither party has any principles, any distinctive tenets. Both have traditions. Both claim to have tendencies. Both have certainly war cries, organizations, interests enlisted in their support. But those interests are in the main the interests of getting or keeping the patronage of government. Tenets and policies, points of political doctrine and points of political practice, have all but vanished. They have not been thrown away but have been stripped away by Time and the progress of events, fulfilling some policies, blotting out others. All has been lost, except office or the hope of it."

What distinguished the American system was that the parties themselves comprised vast coalitions. In a country so large and diverse, James Madison had long ago argued in *The Federalist* Number 10, no one group, no one region, no one idea, no one interest could hope to constitute a majority. Such a situation protected liberty, he asserted. Any party with an expectation of governing had to include a variety of groups, interests, and ideas. The process was not unknown to European parliaments. There, splinter parties might form governing coalitions after elections. American parties simply moved the process forward one step, forming their coalitions at the party coventions in the course of choosing presidential candidates and writing platforms. The American system for electing presidents bent politics toward a two-party system.

Two things, above all, accounted for the muddled politics of this period. Americans had before them the fearsome lesson of what had happened in 1860, when parties had taken clear-cut stands on a deeply felt moral issue, with bloody consequences. But the more compelling cause of political inertia was the even division between the parties. From 1869 to 1913, from Grant to Taft, Republicans occupied the White House except during the two nonconsecutive terms of Grover Cleveland, but Republican domination was more apparent than real. In the years between 1872 and 1896 no president won office with a majority of the popular vote. In 1888 Benjamin Harrison failed to muster even a plurality over Cleveland, but carried the election anyway because his popular vote was concentrated in the states with the larger electoral votes. And while Republicans usually controlled the Senate, Democrats usually controlled the House. Only during the years 1881–1883 and 1889–1891 did a Republican president have a Republican Congress; and only between 1893 and 1895 did a Democratic president have a Democratic Congress— the only time this occurred between the Civil War and 1913, and that during a period of severe depression and turmoil.

No chief executive between Lincoln and Theodore Roosevelt could be described as a "strong" president. With the exception of Grant's their administrations were reasonably effective and honest, but none seriously challenged the prevailing view that the formulation of policy belonged to Congress. The function of the chief executive, to these presidents, was to administer the government, just as the prewar Whigs had always insisted. At the same time the almost equal strength of the parties in Congress worked against any vigorous new departures there, since most bills required bipartisan support to pass both houses. Congress thus was caught up in political maneuvers and could not come to grips with national issues.

Under such static conditions, politicians thought twice before rocking the boat. The parties became machines for seeking office and dispensing patronage. In the choice of candidates, more than ever, "availability" outweighed ability. The ideal presidential candidate had an affable personality, willingness to cooperate with the bosses, an ability to win votes from various factions, residence in a pivotal state, and a good war record. He had no views that might alienate powerful voting blocs, and few or no political enemies. Vice-presidential candidates were chosen to balance the ticket, to placate a disappointed faction, or to improve the party's chances in a key state. This process placed a premium on candidates who were relatively obscure or at least removed from national party battles capable of arousing opposition.

The Bosses of the Senate. *Joseph Keppler's 1889 cartoon bitingly portrays the alliance between big business and politics in this period. [Library of Congress]*

An alliance of business and politics, which was characteristic of the period, lent credence to the cynical maxim that the central institution of every government was the hog trough. This alliance was not necessarily corrupt, since many a politician favored business out of conviction. Nor was the public as sensitive to conflicts of interest as it would be later. So James G. Blaine of Maine, and hosts of his supporters, saw nothing wrong in his accepting stock commissions from an Arkansas railroad after helping it win a land grant from Congress. It was, they thought, a reward after the event, not a bribe in advance. John Brown Gordon of Georgia freely accepted a retainer fee of $10,000 from the Southern Pacific Railroad, a sum larger than his salary as senator, without losing his standing with his constituents. Railroad passes, free entertainment, and a host of other favors were freely given to and accepted by politicians, editors, and other leaders in positions to influence public opinion.

POLITICS AND THE VOTERS   But if many observers considered this a time of political futility in which the parties refused to face up to such "real issues" as the growth of an unregulated economy and the social injustices which resulted, it is nonetheless clear that the voters of the time thought more was at stake. Voter turnout was commonly about 70–80 per cent, even in the South, where the disfranchisement of blacks was not yet complete. (By contrast, the turnout for the 1980 presidential election was only

52.6 percent.) How was it then that leaders who failed to face up to the real issues presided over the most highly organized and politically active electorate in American history?

The answer is partly that the politicians and the voters deeply believed that they *were* dealing with crucial issues, such as the tariff, monopolies, the currency, civil service reform, and immigration. They turned out in heavy numbers for political rallies and parades. Probably more than any other generation of Americans they had the patience to follow the intricacies of lengthy debates and heavy tomes on such matters. If the major parties then failed to resolve these issues, no later generation has resolved them either, and they remain live issues, still relevant to American life a century later.

A NEW VIEW OF POLITICAL HISTORY   But what motivated party loyalties and voter turnout more than anything else in these years were intense cultural conflicts among ethnic and religious groups. Recent practitioners of what has been called the "new political history" have come to this view by analyzing American politics into local, ethnic, cultural, and religious divisions. These historians approach politics less as a simple contest among economic interests, as the "progressive" historians of the earlier twentieth century saw it, than as a complex interplay of motivations, a struggle in which voters follow not simply their pocketbooks but prejudice, heritage, and convictions as well. According to Robert Kelley, one of the new political historians: "It has become clear to us . . . that the energies shaping public life are emotional as well as rational, cultural as well as economic."

Far from being like two empty bottles that differed only in their labels, as Woodrow Wilson said of the parties before the turn of the century, each party contained a different mixture of ingredients picked up in the course of its history. The Republican party, legitimate heir to the Whig tradition, attracted political insiders and active reformers. Party members were mainly Protestants of British descent or established American stock. In their own eyes, and in the eyes of many immigrants, they were prototypical Americans. Their native seat was New England, and their other strongholds were New York and the upper Middle West, both of which they had seeded with Yankee stock. Legitimate heirs to the abolitionist tradition, Republicans drew to their ranks a host of reformers and moralists, spiritual descendants of the perfectionists who populated the revivals and the reform movements of the antebellum years. The party's heritage of anti-

Catholic nativism, dating from the 1850s when the Republican party had become a haven for former Know-Nothings, would also make a comeback in the 1880s.

The Democrats, by contrast, tended to be outsiders. Since the days when Jefferson and Madison had linked up with New York's Tammany Hall, the Democrats had been a heterogeneous, often unruly coalition of unlikely allies. What they had in common was that in one way or another they differed from the Republicans. The Democratic party embraced southern whites, immigrants and Catholics of any origin, Jews, freethinkers, skeptics, and all those repelled by the "party of morality." The Democrats were the "party of personal liberty," a commitment which sometimes proved volatile. Democratic conventions tended to be more disorderly than Republican gatherings, and often the more interesting for it. There were exceptions to these broad generalizations, of course, including black Americans who though outsiders for sure, clung to the party of Lincoln, and some Protestant immigrants drawn to the Republicans by the party's image of uprightness.

The new immigration of the postbellum years, coming largely from Catholic and Jewish strongholds in eastern and southern Europe, reinforced the Democratic ranks. One result was the rebirth of nativism. In 1887 a nativist group called the American Protective Association sprang up in Clinton, Iowa, and over the next few years spread like a prairie fire through the Middle West, which became its chief stronghold. In that region especially, Republicans pressed nativist causes, calling for tighter naturalization laws, restrictions on immigration and the employment of foreigners, and greater emphasis on the teaching of the "American" language in the schools. Nativists saw as a threat those parochial schools, usually but not always Catholic, which sought to preserve Old Country cultures. German Lutherans, for instance, often maintained their own schools, and while as Protestants they gravitated to the Republicans, as Germans they were driven toward the Democrats by Republican campaigns for cultural conformity.

Prohibitionism revived along with nativism in the 1880s. Among the immigrants who crowded into the growing cities were numbers of hard-drinking Irish, beer-drinking Germans, and wine-bibbing Italians. Democratic constituents in general were more bibulous than Yankees, who increasingly saw saloons as the central social evil around which all others revolved, including vice, crime, political corruption, and neglect of families. Republicans across New England and the Middle West took up the cause of prohibition and local option, and were joined after 1869 by a Prohibition party, after 1874 by the Women's Christian Temperance Union, and after 1893 by the Anti-Saloon League. But before the turn of the century these groups attracted few Democrats to their camp.

CORRUPTION AND REFORM

CIVIL SERVICE REFORM   In the aftermath of Reconstruction, Rutherford B. Hayes admirably embodied the "party of morality." Hayes brought to the White House in 1877 a new style of uprightness that contrasted with the graft and corruption of the Grant administration. The son of an Ohio farmer, Hayes attended Kenyon College and Harvard Law School, and was admitted to the Ohio bar in 1845. He entered politics as a Whig but became one of the early Republicans, was wounded four times in the Civil War, and was promoted to major-general of volunteers. As a member of the House of Representatives for one term, from 1865 to 1867, he supported the congressional reconstruction program. Elected governor of Ohio in 1867, he served two terms and was then elected to a third nonconsecutive term in 1875, a bad year for Republicans, which marked him as presidential timber. Honest and respectable, competent and dignified, he lived in modest style. His wife startled Washington society and won the sobriquet of "Lemonade Lucy" by her refusal to serve strong drink on social occasions.

Yet Hayes's tenure was besmirched by the manner of his elec-

Rutherford B. Hayes. [Library of Congress]

tion. Snide references to him as "Old 8 to 7," the "*de facto* President," and "His Fraudulence," dogged his steps and denied him any chance at a second term, which he renounced from the beginning. Hayes's own party was split between Stalwarts and Half-Breeds, led respectively by Sen. Roscoe Conkling of New York and James G. Blaine of Maine. The difference between these Republican factions was murkier than that between the parties. The Stalwarts generally supported Grant, a Radical southern policy, and the spoils system. The Half-Breeds took a contrary view on the first two and were even vaguely touched by the sentiment for civil service reform. But for the most part the factions were loose alliances aimed at personal advancement.

Hayes himself played by the rules of the game enough to pay his political debts. All members of the Louisiana electoral returns board, which had helped elect Hayes, got jobs. But Hayes nevertheless aligned himself with the growing public discontent over the corruption and jobbery that had prevailed under Grant. American leaders were just learning about the merit system long established in the bureaucracies of France and Germany, and the new British Civil Service Act of 1870 under which jobs were filled by competitive examination. Prominent leaders such as James A. Garfield in the House and Carl Schurz in the Senate joined in the cause of civil service reform, and important journals like *Harper's Weekly* under George William Curtis and the New York *Nation* under Edwin L. Godkin endorsed the idea. A New York Civil Service Reform League appeared in 1877, and out of that grew the National Civil Service Reform League of 1881.

Before Hayes took office the most significant result of the agitation had been Grant's gesture of naming a commission to recommend measures for a merit system in the civil service. Its report was conveniently forgotten. Both Hayes and Tilden raised the issue again during the corrupt campaign of 1876, and Hayes repeated his support for reform in his inaugural address. While he failed to get legislation on the subject, he did take administrative measures for a change.

Hayes included in his cabinet such supporters of reform as Carl Schurz (Interior), John Sherman (Treasury), and William M. Evarts (State). In letters to his cabinet members and in an Executive Order of June 22, 1877, Hayes laid down his own rules for merit appointments: those already in office would be dismissed only for the good of the government and not for political reasons; party members would have no more influence in appointments than other equally respectable citizens; no assessments for political contributions would be permitted; and no office holder could manage election campaigns or political organizations, although all could vote and express opinions.

Schurz and Sherman, especially, tried to carry out the new policy. The customs houses, which fell within the Treasury Department, were notorious centers of corrupt politics, filled with political appointees with little or nothing to do but draw salaries and run political machines. Merchants sometimes found that they might gain favor by cooperating with corrupt customs officials, and might be punished for making trouble. John Sherman ordered an inquiry and laid before Hayes evidence that both Collector Chester A. Arthur and Naval Officer Alonzo Cornell were guilty of "laxity" and of using the New York Customs House for political management on behalf of Sen. Roscoe Conkling's organization. When hints went out that resignations would be welcomed, Conkling responded with an attack on reformers in a speech to the state Republican convention: "Their vocation . . . is to lament the sins of other people. Their stock in trade is rancid, canting self-righteousness. . . . When Dr. Johnson defined patriotism as the last refuge of a scoundrel, he was unconscious of the then undeveloped capabilities and uses of the word 'Reform!' " Political parties, Conkling reminded the delegates, "are not built up by deportment, or by ladies' magazines, or by gush!"

On October 15, after removing Arthur and Cornell, Hayes named replacements only to have the nominees rejected when Conkling appealed to the "courtesy of the Senate," an old custom whereby senators might control appointments in their own states. During a recess in the summer of 1878, however, Hayes appointed new replacements. When Congress reassembled, the administration put pressure on senators and, with Democratic support, carried the nominations. Even this, however, did not end the New York Customs House episode; it would flare up again under the next president.

For all his efforts to clean house, Hayes's vision of government's role remained limited. On the economic issues of the day he held to a conservative line which would guide his successors for the rest of the century. His solution to labor troubles, demonstrated in the great railway strike of 1877, was to send in troops and break the strike. His answer to demands for an expansion of the currency was to veto the Bland-Allison Act which, passed over his veto, required only a limited expansion of silver currency through the government's purchase for coinage of $2–$4 million worth of silver per month.

GARFIELD AND ARTHUR   With Hayes unavailable for a second term, the Republicans were forced to look elsewhere in 1880. The Stalwarts, led by Conkling, brought Grant forward for a third time, still a strong contender despite the tarnish of his administration's scandals. For two days the Republican convention in Chicago was deadlocked, with Grant leading but strongly challenged by Blaine and John Sherman. On the thirty-fifth ballot Wisconsin suddenly switched sixteen votes to former House Speaker (now Senator-elect) James A. Garfield, Sherman's campaign manager. Garfield rose to protest but was ruled out of order, and on the thirty-sixth ballot the convention stampeded to the dark-horse candidate, carrying him to the nomination. The Stalwarts stubbornly stood by Grant and went down, 399 to 306, but as a sop to the losing faction the convention named Chester A. Arthur of Custom House fame for vice-president.

The Democrats named Winfield Scott Hancock, a Union commander at Gettysburg, to counterbalance the Republicans' Brigadier-General Garfield and thus ward off "bloody-shirt" attacks on their party as the vehicle of Rebellion. Old Rebels, nevertheless, advised their constituents to "vote as you shot"—that is, against Republicans. In an election characterized by widespread bribery, which may have carried Indiana for Garfield, and publication of a forged letter in which Garfield allegedly championed the importation of cheap Chinese labor, the substantive highlight may have been Hancock's observation that the tariff question was a local one. Republicans ridiculed his lack of understanding, but the remark was actually a profound judgment, for tariffs were commonly produced by deals among localities, each seeking protection for its own products. The election turned out to be the closest of the century. Garfield eked out a plurality of only 39,000 votes with 48.5 per cent of the vote, but with a comfortable margin of 214 to 155 in the electoral college.

A native of Ohio, Garfield had shown the foresight to be born in a log cabin and to have a brief career on a canal towpath. Both became political assets in his rise from canal boy to president, as Horatio Alger put it in the title of a campaign biography. A graduate of Williams College, Garfield became president of Hiram College, was admitted to the bar, and won election to the Ohio Senate as a Republican in 1859. During the Civil War he distinguished himself at Shiloh and Chickamauga, served on General Rosecrans's staff, and was mustered out as a major-general when he went to Congress in 1863. Noted for his oratory and parliamentary skills, he became one of the outstanding leaders in the House and eventually its Speaker. His early appointments as president reflected the fact that he had been the candidate of a faction-ridden party. Garfield made Blaine his secretary of state, a reward for service as campaign manager in the election. The appointment of Wayne MacVeagh as attorney-general was another blow directed at the Stalwarts, since MacVeagh opposed Senator Cameron's machine in Pennsylvania—even though he was Cameron's son-in-law. But the naming of Stalwart Thomas James as postmaster-general was an important concession to the other faction.

On July 2 Garfield started on a vacation in New England to get away from the siege of office seekers. As the president passed through the Baltimore and Potomac station a deranged office seeker named Charles Guiteau shot him in the back. "I am a Stalwart," Guiteau explained to the arresting officers. "Arthur is now President of the United States," an announcement that would prove crippling to the Stalwarts. Garfield lingered for two long, hot months, his suffering eased by a contrived air conditioner—a blower rigged up by navy engineers to pass air over a vault of ice into the president's sickroom. Finally, on September 19, Garfield died of complications resulting from the shooting, having been president for a little over six months and able to transact business for less than four.

One of the chief henchmen of Stalwart leader Roscoe Conkling was now president. "Chet Arthur, President of the United States?" one of his friends exclaimed. "Good God!" Little in Arthur's past, save his record as an abolitionist lawyer who had helped secure the freedom of a fugitive slave, raised hopes that he would rise above custom-house politics. A native of Vermont, he had attended Union College, become a lawyer, and made a political career in appointive offices, most notably as New York quartermaster-general during the Civil War and collector of customs from 1871 to 1878. But Arthur demonstrated rare and striking qualities as president. He began by distancing himself from Conkling and the Stalwarts and establising a genuine independence, almost a necessity after Guiteau's announcement.

As president he vigorously prosecuted the Star Route Frauds, a kickback scheme which involved the secretary of the Republican National Committee and an assistant postmaster-general, both old political cronies of Arthur's. The president further surprised Washington in 1882 with the veto of an $18-million river and harbors bill, a "pork barrel" measure that included something for most congressional districts. He also vetoed the Chinese Exclusion Act (1882) which in his view violated the Burlingame Treaty of 1868. Congress proceeded to override both vetoes.

Most startling of all was Arthur's emergence as something of a civil service and tariff reformer. Stalwarts had every reason to expect him to oppose the merit system, but instead he allied himself with the reformers. While the assassin Guiteau had unwittingly added a certain urgency to the public support of reform, the defeat of a reform bill in 1882 sponsored by "Gentleman George" Pendleton, Democratic senator from Ohio, aroused public opinion further. The Pendleton Civil Service Act passed in January 1883, setting up a three-member Civil Service Commission independent from the regular cabinet departments, the first such federal agency established on a permanent basis. About 14 percent of all government jobs came under the category of "classified services," in which new appointments had to be made on the basis of competitive examinations. What was more, the president could enlarge the classified services at his discretion. This had important consequences over the years because after each of the next four presidential elections the "outs" emerged as victors. Each new president thus had a motive to enlarge this category because it would shield his own appointees from political removal.

The high protective tariff, a heritage of the Civil War, had by the early 1880s raised revenues to the point that the government actually enjoyed an embarrassment of riches, a surplus which drew money into the Treasury and out of circulation. Some argued that lower tariff rates would reduce prices and the cost of living, and at the same time leave more money in circulation. In 1882 Arthur named a special commission to study the problem. The appointment of John L. Hayes, secretary of the protectionist National Association of Wool Manufacturers, struck many low-tariff advocates as setting the fox to guard the henhouse. The Tariff Commission, however, brought in a recommendation for a 20–25 percent rate reduction, which gained Arthur's support, but Congress's effort to enact the proposal was marred by logrolling to further local interests, resulting in the "Mongrel Tariff" of 1883, so called because of its diverse percentage. The tariff provided for a slight rate reduction, perhaps by 5 percent, but it actually hiked the duty on some articles still imported in volume.

SCURRILOUS CAMPAIGN   When the next election came around, Arthur's record might have commended him to the voters, but it did not set well with the other leaders of his party. He had been weakened, moreover, by a political setback in his home state of New York, where his treasury secretary William J. Folger lost the 1882 governor's race to Grover Cleveland, despite Arthur's support. An even more compelling reason for Arthur's withdrawal was the fact, unknown to the public, that he had contracted Bright's disease, a fatal kidney inflamation from which he would die in 1886.

So the Republicans turned instead to the glamorous Sen. James G. Blaine of Maine, longtime leader of the Half-Breeds, and chose the Stalwart John A. Logan of Illinois as his running mate. A man with the personal magnetism a later generation would call "charisma," Blaine was the consummate politician. He never forgot a name or a face, he inspired the enthusiasm of the party faithful with his oratory, and at the same time he knew how to wheel and deal in the backrooms. He managed eloquence even when spouting the platitudes of party loyalty, waving the bloody shirt, and twisting the British lion's tail—the last of which held special appeal for the Irish, a group not normally drawn to Republican candidates.

Back in 1876 Blaine had been nominated for the presidency by Robert Ingersoll, who in an eloquent flight of oratory of his own, had announced:

> The people called for the nomination of the man who has torn from the throat of treason the tongue of slander—for the man who has snatched the mask of Democracy from the hideous face of rebellion. . . . Like an armed warrior, like a plumed knight James G. Blaine marched down the halls of American Congress and threw his shining lance full and fair against the brazen forehead of the defamers of his country and maligners of his honor.

To his followers in 1884 Blaine was still the plumed knight, but in Democratic newspapers he became the plumed knave. The "defamers of his honor" were those who found in the "Mulligan letters" evidence that Blaine was up for sale to the railroads.

During the campaign more letters surfaced with disclosures embarrassing to Blaine. For the reform element of the Republican party, this was too much, and one after another prominent leaders and supporters of the party bolted the ticket: George W. Curtis of *Harper's*, E. L. Godkin of the New York *Nation*, Carl Schurz, Charles Francis Adams, Jr., Thomas Wentworth Higginson, James Russell Lowell, Henry Ward Beecher, President Eliot of Harvard, and the New York *Times*. Party regulars scorned them as "goo-goo"—the "good-government" crowd who ignored partisan realities—and editor Charles A. Dana of the New York *Sun* jokingly called them Mugwumps, after an Algonquian word meaning a great chieftain. To regulars, in what soon became a stale joke, Mugwumps were unreliable Republicans who had their "mugs" on one side of the fence and their "wumps" on the other.

The rise of the Mugwumps, however, influenced the Democrats to nominate Stephen Grover Cleveland as a reform candidate. Cleveland experienced a rapid rise from obscurity to the White House. One of many children in the family of a small-town Presbyterian minister, he had been forced by his father's death to go to work at an early age. He got a job as clerk in a law office, read law, passed the bar examination, became an assistant state attorney-general in New York in 1863 and sheriff of Erie County in 1870. He first attracted national attention as mayor of Buffalo, elected in 1881, for battling graft and corruption. In 1882 the Democrats elected him governor, where he continued to build a reform record by fighting New York's Tammany Hall organization. Cleveland saw the corruption of government by the rich and powerful as a constant danger. As mayor and as governor he repeatedly vetoed what he considered special-privilege bills serving sordid and selfish interests.

A stocky 250-pound man with a droopy mustache, Cleveland seemed the stolid opposite of Blaine. He possessed little charisma, but impressed the public with something that was more important that year, a stubborn integrity. One supporter called him an "Ugly-honest man," and another said that "We love him for the enemies he has made." Cleveland the reformer was a godsend to Democrats who at last sighted the Promised Land, the White House. George Washington Curtis said the main issue of the campaign was not political but moral.

Then the Buffalo *Evening Telegraph* revealed some of bachelor Cleveland's earlier escapades with an attractive Buffalo widow, Maria Halperin. Mrs. Halperin had named Cleveland as the father of a child born to her in 1874, though there was no proof of paternity. Cleveland, it seemed, was only one of several likely fathers, but he took responsibility and provided for the child.

Another Voice for Cleveland. *This 1884 cartoon attacks "Grover the Good" for allegedly fathering an illegitimate child.*

The Bloody Banquet. *Republican candidate James G. Blaine is caricatured at a "royal feast" with "the money kings," while a starving family begs for morsels. [New York* World, *1884]*

When supporters asked Cleveland what to say, he answered "Tell the truth." Later he said: "The Republicans can have a monopoly of all the dirt in this campaign." Of course they did not, and the respective escapades of Blaine and Cleveland provided some of the most colorful battle cries in American political history. "Blaine, Blaine, James G. Blaine, the continental liar from the state of Maine," Democrats chanted. Republicans countered with "Ma, ma, where's my pa? Gone to the White House, ha, ha, ha!" Many voters, sorting out the scandals, seem to have made the same distinction between the public and private spheres as a voter in Chicago: "We should elect Mr. Cleveland to the public office which he is so admirably qualified to fill, and remand Mr. Blaine to the private life which he is so eminently fitted to adorn."

Near the end of the campaign Blaine and his supporters committed two fateful blunders. At New York's fashionable Delmonico's restaurant Blaine went to a private dinner with a clutch of millionaire bigwigs, including John Astor and Jay Gould, to discuss campaign finances. Cartoons and accounts of "Belshazzar's Feast" festooned the opposition press for days to come. And when a delegation of Protestant ministers visited Republican headquarters in New York, the Rev. Samuel D. Burchard referred to the Democrats as the party of "rum, Romanism, and rebellion." The judgment had a certain validity, but the tone was insolent. Blaine, who was present, let pass and perhaps failed to catch the implied insult to Catholics—a fatal oversight, since he had always cultivated Irish-American support with his anti-

British talk and public reminders that his mother was Catholic. Democrats spread word that he had let the insult pass, even that he had made it himself.

The incident may have tipped the election. The electoral vote in Cleveland's favor stood at 219 to 182, but the popular vote ran far closer; Cleveland's plurality was fewer than 30,000 votes.

CLEVELAND AND THE SPECIAL INTERESTS   For all Cleveland's hostility to the spoils system and politics as usual, he represented no sharp break with the conservative policies of his pedecessors, except in opposing governmental favors to business. "A public office is a public trust" was one of his favorite mottoes. He held to a strictly limited view of government's role in both economic and social matters, a rigid philosophy illustrated by his 1887 veto of the Texas Seed Bill, an effort to appropriate $10,000 to meet the urgent need of drought victims for seed grain. Back to Congress it went with a lecture on the need to limit the powers and functions of government—"though the people support the government the government should not support the people," Cleveland said.

For a man who took such high ground philosophically, he had a mixed record on the civil service. Cleveland had good intentions, but he also had a hungry party which had not elected a president since Buchanan in 1856. Before his inauguration Cleveland arranged to have the National Civil Service Reform League send him a letter warning that the spoils system would be a sensitive issue in the new administration. In response he repeated his support for the Pendleton Act and his intention to follow its spirit even where it did not apply; he would not remove able men on partisan grounds, he said. But he inserted one significant exception: those who had used federal jobs to forward the interests of the opposition party. In many cases, especially in the post offices, he thus had ample excuse to remove men who had practically made their offices into Republican headquarters.

Party pressures gradually forced Cleveland's hand. To a friend he remarked: "The damned everlasting clatter for office continues . . . and makes me feel like resigning and hell is to pay generally." When he left office about two-thirds of the federal officeholders were Democrats, including all internal revenue collectors and nearly all the heads of customs houses. But at the same time Cleveland had extended the classified civil service to cover about 27,000 employees, whereas about 14,000 had been covered when he came in. The result was that he satisfied neither Mugwumps nor spoilsmen, indeed he managed to antagonize both.

On other matters Cleveland's stubborn courage and concern for the public treasury led him into costly conflicts with predatory interests, conflicts which eventually cost him the White House. One such dispute arose over misue of the public domain in the West. Secretary of the Interior L. Q. C. Lamar and W. A. J. Sparks, commissioner of the General Land Office, uncovered one case after another of fraud and mismanagement: bogus surveys by govenment surveyors, public lands used fraudulently by lumbermen, mine operators, and cattlemen with the collusion of government officials, and at least 30 million acres of railroad land grants subject to forfeiture because the required lines were not built.

The administration brought suits against railroads to recover such lands, and against the Montana Improvement Company, subsidiary of the Northern Pacific Railroad, for cutting trees on public forestlands. It nullified exploitive leases of Indian lands, such as that of one cattle company which had leased 6 million acres from the Cherokees for $100,000 and subleased the land for about five times as much. Cattle barons were ordered to remove fences enclosing waterholes and grasslands on the open range. In all, during Cleveland's first term about 81 million acres of public lands were restored to the federal government.

Cleveland incurred the wrath of Union veterans by his firm stand against pension raids on the Treasury. Congress had passed the first general Civil War pension law in 1862 to provide for veterans disabled in service and for the widows, orphans, and dependents of veterans. By 1882 Cpl. James Tanner, commander of the Grand Army of the Republic, an organization of Union veterans and a powerful pressure group, was trying to get pensions paid for any disability, no matter how it was incurred. Meanwhile many veterans enjoyed such benefits by having private pension bills put through an obliging Congress. In Washington a large tribe of lawyers built careers on filing claims and pushing special laws for veterans.

Insofar as time permitted Cleveland examined such bills critically and vetoed those which seemed to him dubious. Although he signed more than any of his predecessors, running pension costs up from $56 million to $80 million, he also vetoed more. A climax came in January 1887 when Congress passed the Dependent Pension Bill, which provided funds for all ninety-day veterans dependent upon manual labor and unable to work for any reason, whether or not the reason was service conected. Cleveland sent it back with a ringing veto, declaring that the pension list would become a refuge for frauds rather than a "roll of honor." On June 5, 1887, Cleveland compounded his sins in the eyes of the old soldiers when he signed an order for the return of captured Confederate battleflags to the South. Although the order had originated in the War Department, Cleveland was the target of a stormy protest. "May God palsy the hand that wrote that order," said Commander Lucius Fairchild of the GAR. "May God palsy the brain that conceived it, and may God palsy the tongue that dictated it." Faced with such a tempest, Cleveland made the convenient discovery that he lacked authority to issue the order and revoked it after eight days. The flags finally went back with congressional approval in 1905, when Theodore Roosevelt was president.

About the middle of his term Cleveland set out after new special interests, leading in the adoption of an important new policy, railroad regulation. Since the late 1860s state after state had adopted regulatory laws, and from the early 1870s Congress had debated federal legislation to regulate the railroads. In 1886 a Supreme Court decision finally spurred action. In the case of *Wabash Railroad v. Illinois* the Court denied the state's power to regulate rates on interstate traffic. Cleveland urged in his annual message in December that since this "important field of control and regulation [has] thus been left entirely unoccupied," Congress should act.

In February Cleveland signed into law an act creating the Interstate Commerce Commission, the first such independent regulatory commission. The law empowered its five members to investigate carriers and prosecute violators. All rates had to be "reasonable and just." Railroads were forbidden to grant rebates, discriminate against persons, places, and commodities, or enter into pools (agreements to fix rates). The commission's actual powers, however, proved to be weak when first tested in the courts. If creating the ICC seemed to conflict with Cleveland's fear of big government, it accorded with his Jacksonian fear of great combinations of capital. The Interstate Commerce Act, to his mind, was a legitimate exercise of sovereign power.

Cleveland's most dramatic challenge to special interests came in his efforts to force action on tariff reform. He had entered office as the leader of the traditional low-tariff party, but his party was far from unified on the issue, and Cleveland himself confessed at first to little understanding of the tariff issue. Like most politicians of the time, he hesitated to plunge into that tangled thicket. But with greater exposure to the question and further study he decided that the rates were too high and included many inequities. Near the end of 1887 Cleveland decided on the deliberate step of dramatizing the issue by devoting his entire annual

Grover Cleveland made the issue of tariff reform central to the politics of the late 1880s. [Library of Congress]

message to the subject. He did so in full knowledge that he was focusing attention on a political minefield on the eve of an election year, against the warnings of his advisers. "What is the use of being elected if you don't stand for something?" he asked.

Cleveland's message was a classic summary and exposition of the current arguments against protection. He noted that tariff revenues had bolstered the surplus, making the Treasury "a hoarding place for money needlessly withdrawn from trade and the people's use." It pushed up prices for everybody, and while it was supposed to protect American labor against the competition of cheap foreign labor, the most recent census showed that of 17.4 million Americans gainfully employed only 2.6 million were in "such manufacturing industries as are claimed to be benefitted by a high tariff." It was evident, moreover, that while business combinations could push prices up to the artificial level set by the prices of dutied foreign goods, prices often fell below that level when domestic producers were in competition, "proof that someone is willing to accept lower prices for such commodity and that such prices are renumerative." Congress, Cleveland argued, should study the more than 4,000 articles subject to duties with an eye to cutting the cost of necessities and of the raw materials used in manufacturing. "Our progress toward a wise conclusion will not be improved by dwelling upon the theories of protection and free trade. . . . It is a condition which confronts us, not a theory." The final sentence became an epigram so infectious that for the next few years public speakers worked it nearly to death.

That did not stop Blaine and other Republicans from denouncing the message as pure "free trade," a doctrine all the more suspect because it was also British policy. The House Ways and Means Committee soon reported a bill calling for modest reductions from an average level of about 47 percent of the value of imported goods to about 40 percent. House Democrats rallied to its support, some of them under assurances that it could not become law. Passed by the House, the bill stalled in the Republican Senate and finally died a lingering death in committee. If Cleveland's talk accomplished his purpose of drawing party lines more firmly, it also confirmed the fears of his advisers. The election of 1888 for the first time in years highlighted a difference between the major parties on an issue of substance.

Cleveland was inevitably the nominee of his party. The platform endorsed "the views expressed by the President in his last message to Congress." The Republicans passed up old warhorses like Blaine and Sherman and turned to the obscure Benjamin Harrison, who had all the attributes of availability. Grandson of a former president, a flourishing lawyer in Indiana, the diminutive Harrison resided in a pivotal state, and had a good war record and little in his political record to offend any voter. He had lost a race for governor and served one term in the Senate (1881–1887). For vice-president the party named Levi P. Morton of New York. The Republican platform picked up the gauntlet thrown down by Cleveland, accepted the protective tariff as the chief issue, and promised generous pensions to veterans.

The campaign thus became the first waged mainly on the tariff issue. Sen. Matthew Quay, Harrison's campaign chairman and Republican boss of Pennsylvania, took the advice of a friend to "put the manufacturers of Pennsylvania under the fire and fry all the fat out of them." As insurance against tariff reduction, manufacturers obligingly larded the campaign fund, which was used to denounce Cleveland's un-American "free trade," his pension vetoes, and his Confederate battleflag order. In Indiana party workers were told: "Divide the floaters into blocks of five and put a trusted man in charge . . . with the necessary funds, and make him responsible that none get away, and that all vote our ticket." Democratic poll-watchers claimed that floaters got $15 to $20 each for their votes.

Personal attacks too were leveled against Cleveland. The old charges of immorality had played out. After Cleveland entered the White House he had married young Frances Folsom, who later presented him with a daughter whose name would be immortalized one day by the "Baby Ruth" candy bar. During the campaign, though, the rumor went abroad that a drunken Cleveland had taken to wife-beating. On the eve of the election Cleveland suffered a more devastating blow from the phony "Murchison letter." A California Republican named George A.

Osgoodsby had written British Minister Sir Lionel Sackville-West over the false name "Charles F. Murchison." Posing as an English immigrant he asked advice on how to vote. Sackville-West, engaged at the time in sensitive negotiations over Canadian fisheries, hinted that he should vote for Cleveland. Published on October 24, the letter aroused a storm of protest against foreign intervention and further linked Cleveland to British free-traders. Democratic explanations never caught up with the original sense of outrage.

The outcome was very close. Cleveland was vindicated in the popular vote by 5,538,000 to 5,447,000, but that was poor comfort. The distribution was such that Harrison, with the key states of Indiana and New York on his side, carried the electoral college by 233 to 168. For once the country had not only a minority president, but one who lacked even a plurality in the popular vote.

REPUBLICAN REFORM UNDER HARRISON   Harrison became a competent and earnest figurehead, overshadowed by his secretary of state, James G. Blaine. He proved something of a cold fish in personal relations. "Harrison can make a speech to ten thousand men and every man of them will go away his friend," said one observer. "Let him meet the same ten thousand in private and every one will go away his enemy." When Sen. Matthew Quay came to call with the election returns, Harrison exclaimed fervently: "Providence has given us the victory." The cynical Quay later remarked that Harrison "ought to know that Providence hadn't a damn thing to do with it" and opined that the president "would never know how close a number of men were compelled to approach a penitentiary to make him president."

Harrison had aroused the hopes of civil service reformers. "In appointments of every grade and department," he said, "fitness and not party service should be the essential and discriminating test, and fidelity and efficiency the only sure tenure of office." Nevertheless he appointed John Wanamaker, the Philadelphia merchant prince, as his postmaster-general, allegedly as a reward for a generous contribution. J. S. Clarkson, the first assistant postmaster-general, announced less than a year later: "I have changed 31,000 out of 55,000 fourth-class postmasters and I expect to change 10,000 more before I finally quit." Harrison made a few feckless efforts to resist partisan pressures, but the party leaders had their way. His most significant gesture at reform was to name young Theodore Roosevelt to the Civil Service Commission.

BILLION- DOLLARISM ᵀ HOLE

A cartoon attacking Benjamin Harrison's spending policies. He is shown pouring Cleveland's huge surplus down a hole. [W. Bencough, Democratic National Committee]

Harrison owed a heavy debt to the old-soldier vote, which he discharged by naming Cpl. James Tanner of the GAR to the office of pension commissioner. "God help the surplus," Tanner reportedly exclaimed, and proceeded to approve pensions with such abandon that Secretary of the Interior J. W. Noble removed him six months and and several million dollars later. In 1890 Congress passed, and Harrison signed, the Disability Pension Act, substantially the same measure that Cleveland had vetoed. Any ninety-day veteran unable to make a living by manual labor was granted $6 to $12 a month according to the degree of his disability. The pension rolls shot up from 490,000 in 1889 to 966,000 in 1893, and the program's costs from $89 million to $175 million. Eventually, in 1904 a presidential order placed all veterans over age sixty-two on the pension rolls, and by 1936 Civil War pensions had totaled near $8 billion, not counting the pensions paid by southern states to old Confederates, their widows and dependents.

During the first two years of Harrison's term the Republicans controlled the presidency and both houses of Congress for the only time in the twenty years between 1875 and 1895. They were positioned to have pretty much their own way, and they made the year 1890 memorable for some of the most significant legislation enacted in the entire period. In addition to the Dependent Pension Act, Congress and the president approved the Sherman Anti-Trust Act, the Sherman Silver Purchase Act, the McKinley Tariff, and the admission of the last of the "omnibus states," Idaho and Wyoming, which followed the admission of the Dakotas, Montana, and Washington in 1889.

Both parties had pledged themselves to do something about the growing power of trusts and monopolies. The Sherman Anti-Trust Act, named for Sen. John Sherman, chairman of the Senate Judiciary Committee that drafted it, sought to incorporate into federal law a long-standing principle of the common law against "restraint of trade." It forbade contracts, combinations, or conspiracies in restraint of trade or in the effort to establish monopolies in interstate or foreign commerce. A broad consensus put the law through, but its passage turned out to be largely symbolic. The common law prevailed only in state courts, and the largest corporations had grown well beyond the boundaries of a single state, and beyond the ability of state courts to control them. During the next decade successive administrations expended little effort on the act's enforcement. From 1890 to 1901 only eighteen suits were instituted, and four of those were against labor unions.

Congress meanwhile debated currency legislation against the backdrop of growing distress in the farm regions of the West and South. Hard-pressed farmers were now agitating to inflate the currency by an increased coinage of silver. Increased coinage would raise prices, making it easier for farmers to raise the money with which to pay their debts. The silverite forces were also strengthened, especially in the Senate, by members from the new omnibus states, which had silver-mining interests. The pro-silver Senate easily passed the new measure, and in the House the western silverites struck a bargain with eastern protectionists strengthening support for both an increased silver coinage and a higher tariff. The new Sherman Silver Purchase Act, passed on July 14, replaced the Bland-Allison Act of 1878; it required the Treasury to purchase 4.5 million ounces of silver each month and to issue in payment Treasury notes redeemable in either gold or silver. The act failed to satisfy the demands of the silverites, however. Although it approximately doubled the amount of silver purchased, that was still too little to have an inflationary impact on the economy. Eastern business and financial groups, on the other hand, saw a threat to the gold reserve in the growth of paper currency which holders could redeem in gold at the Treasury. The stage was set for the currency issue to eclipse all others in a panic that swept the country three years later.

Republicans took their victory over Cleveland as a mandate not just to maintain the protective tariff but to raise it. But the mandate was less than clear, in view of Cleveland's plurality, and passage of the new tariff remained doubtful until its backers struck their bargain with western silverites. Piloted through by

William McKinley, House Ways and Means chairman, and Sen. Nelson W. Aldrich, the McKinley Tariff of 1890 raised duties on manufactured goods to an average of about 49.5 percent, the highest to that time. And it included three interesting new departures. First, the protectionists reached out for farmers' votes with high duties on agricultural products. Second, they sought to lessen the tariff's impact on consumers by putting sugar, a universal necessity, on the free list—thus reducing its cost—and then compensating Louisiana and Kansas sugar growers with a bounty of two cents a pound out of the federal treasury. And third, the measure included a reciprocity section which empowered the president to hike duties on sugar, molasses, tea, coffee, and hides to pressure countries exporting those items into reducing unreasonably high duties on American goods.

The absence of a public concensus for higher tariffs became clearly visible in the 1890 elections. By the time the November congressional election returns were in it seemed apparent, at least to Democrats, that the voters had repudiated the McKinley tariff, which had become law in October, with a landslide of Democratic votes. In the new House Democrats outnumbered Republicans by 235 to 88; in the Senate the Republican majority was reduced to 8. One of the election casualties was McKinley himself, the victim of a few tricks the Democrats used to reinforce the widespread revulsion against the increased duties. In McKinley's Ohio district itinerent peddlers offered household utensils at exorbitant prices, explaining that the McKinley Tariff had caused the price increases. But there was more to the election than the tariff. Voters reacted also against the baldly partisan measures of the Harrison administration and its extravagant expenditures on pensions and other programs. Democrats raised a ruckus about the Republicans' "billion-dollar Congress," to which Speaker Thomas B. Reed responded with the question: "Isn't this a billion dollar country?" But with expenditures rising and revenues dropping, largely because the tariff was not high enough to discourage imports, the nation's surplus was shrinking at a rapid pace.

The large Democratic vote in 1890 may have also been a reaction to Republican efforts to legislate against alcohol and parochial schools. In the years from 1880 to 1890 sixteen out of twenty-one states outside the South held referenda on constitutional prohibition, and a number of state legislatures provided for votes on the issue of local option. In the referenda only six states voted dry (for prohibition), however, and one of these, Rhode Island, reversed its dry vote of 1886 three years later. With the politics of righteousness, then, Republicans were playing a losing game, arousing wets (antiprohibitionists) on the Democratic side. In 1889 Wisconsin Republicans compounded their party's problems by pushing through a law which struck at parochial schools. The law held that a school could be accredited only if it taught the basic subjects in the English language. That was the last straw: it turned hordes of threatened and outraged immigrants into Democratic activists. In 1889 and 1890 the Democrats swept state after state.

The election returns reflected something even more than a re-action against the Republican tariff, spoils politics, extravagance, and moralizing. The returns revealed a deep-seated unrest in the farming communities of the South and West that was beginning to find voice in the new People's party. In the Fifty-second Congress there would be eight Populist representatives and two Populist senators.

THE PROBLEMS OF FARMERS

ECONOMIC CONDITIONS For some time farmers had been subject to worsening economic and social conditions. The source of their problem was a long-term decline in commodity prices from 1870 to 1898, the product of domestic overproduction and growing international competition for world markets. The vast new lands brought under cultivation in America poured an ever-increasing supply of farm products into the market, driving down prices. This effect was reinforced as innovations in transportation and communications brought American farmers ever more into competition with farmers around the world, further increasing the supply of farm commodities. Considerations of abstract economic forces, however, puzzled many farmers. They would never quite understand how want could be caused by plenty. They shared the puzzlement that Kansas's Populist Gov. Lorenzo Dow Lewelling professed at a friend's argument in the 1890s that "there were hungry people . . . because there was too much bread" and "so many . . . poorly clad . . . because there was too much cloth." How could one speak of overproduction when so many remained in need? Instead there must be a screw loose somewhere in the system.

The railroads and the middlemen who handled the farmers' products became the prime villains. Farmers felt victimized by the high railroad rates which prevailed in farm regions that had no alternative forms of transportation. Individual farmers could not get the rebates the Rockefellers could extract from railroads, and could not exert the political influence wielded by the railroad lobbies. In other ways farmers found themselves with little bargaining power either as buyers or sellers. When they went to sell wheat or cotton, the buyer set the price; when they went to buy a plow point, the seller set the price.

High tariffs operated to the farmers' disadvantage because they protected manufacturers against foreign competition, allowing them to raise the prices of factory goods on which farmers depended. Farmers, however, had to sell their wheat, cotton, and other staples in the world market, where competition lowered prices. Tariffs inflicted a double blow on farmers because insofar as they hampered imports, they indirectly hampered exports by making it harder for foreign buyers to get the necessary American currency or exchange to purchase American goods.

Debt has been a perennial problem of agriculture. After the Civil War farmers became ever more enmeshed in debt, western farmers in mortgages to cover the costs of land and machinery, southern farmers in crop liens. As prices dropped, the burden of debt grew because farmers had to cultivate more wheat or cotton to raise the same amount of money; and by growing more they furthered the vicious cycle of surpluses and price declines.

AN INADEQUATE CURRENCY   Currency deflation was yet another cause of declining prices. Ultimately, farm discontent became focused on the currency issue, magnifying this grievance out of proportion to all others. The basic problem with the nation's currency in the late nineteenth century was that it lacked the flexibility to grow along with America's expanding economy. From 1865 to 1890 the amount of currency in circulation decreased from about $30.20 to $27.06 per capita. Three types of currency existed in those days: greenbacks, national banknotes, and hard money (gold and silver coins or certificates). The amount of greenback money in circulation had been set at $346 million in 1878, and had remained fixed at that amount, despite agitation for more paper money by debtors (largely farmers) and expansion-minded businessmen. National banknotes, based on government bonds, actually contracted in volume as the government paid off its bonds, which it was able to do rapidly with revenues from tariffs and land sales.

Metallic currency dated from the Mint Act of 1792, which authorized free and unlimited coinage of silver and gold at a ratio of 15:1 in weight.° The phrase "free and unlimited coinage" sim-

°The ratio meant that the amount of precious metal in a silver dollar weighed fifteen times as much as that in a gold dollar. This reflected the relative values of silver and gold at the time.

ply meant that owners of precious metals could have any quantity of their gold or silver coined free, except for a nominal fee to cover costs. A fixed ratio of values, however, could not reflect fluctuations in the market value of the metals. When gold rose to a market value higher than that reflected in the official ratio, owners ceased to present it for coinage. The country was actually on a silver standard until 1837, when Congress changed the ratio to 16:1, which soon reversed the situation. Silver became more valuable in the market than in coinage, and the country drifted to a gold standard. This state of affairs prevailed until 1873, when Congress passed a general revision of the coinage laws and, without fanfare, dropped the then-unused provision for the coinage of silver. The action came, however, just when silver production began to increase, reducing its market value through the growth in supply. Under the old laws this would have induced owners of silver to present it at the mint for coinage. Soon advocates of currency inflation began to denounce the "crime of '73," which they had scarcely noticed at the time. Gradually a suspicion, and in some cases a belief, grew that creditor interests had conspired in 1873 to ensure a scarcity of money. But the silverites had little more legislative success than the advocates of greenback inflation. The Bland-Allison Act of 1878 and the Sherman Silver Purchase Act of 1890 provided for some silver coinage, but too little in each case to offset the overall contraction of the currency.

Aside from economic and political forces, physical problems of geography and climate conspired to torment farmers with problems of drought, flood, blizzards, soil depletion, and insects. The farmers' response to these problems was crippled by the American ideal of the individual family farm, which in fostering their social and intellectual isolation made it more difficult for them to act collectively.

AGRARIAN REVOLT

THE GRANGER MOVEMENT When the Department of Agriculture sent Oliver H. Kelley on a tour of the postbellum South in 1866, it was the farmers' isolation which most impressed him. Resolving to do something about it, Kelley and some government clerks in 1867 founded the Patrons of Husbandry, better known as the Grange. In the next few years the Grange mushroomed, reaching a membership as high as 1.5 million by 1874. The Grange started as a social and educational response to the farmers' isolation, but as it grew it began to promote farmer-owned cooperatives for buying and selling and soon became indirectly involved in politics through independent third parties, especially in the Midwest, during the early 1870s.

The Grangers' political goal was chiefly to regulate the rates charged by railroads and warehouses. In five states they brought about the passage of "Granger Laws" which at first proved relatively ineffective, but laid a foundation for stronger legislation later. Owners subject to their regulation challenged these laws in cases which soon rose to the Supreme Court, where the plaintiffs in the "Granger Cases" claimed to have been deprived of property without due process of law. In a key case involving warehouse regulation, *Munn v. Illinois* (1877), the high court ruled that the state under its "police powers" had the right to regulate property in the interest of the public good where that property was clothed with a public interest. If regulatory power were abused, the ruling said, "the people must resort to the polls, not the courts." Later, however, the courts would severely restrict state regulatory powers.

The Granger movement gradually declined (but never disappeared) as members' energies were drawn off into cooperatives, many of which failed, and into political action. Out of the independent political movements of the time there grew in 1875 a party calling itself the Independent National party, more commonly known as the Greenback party because of its emphasis on that issue. In 1876 it nominated philanthropist Peter Cooper of New York for president, but polled only 82,000 votes for its slate. In the 1878 midterm elections it enjoyed greater success, polling over 1 million votes and electing fifteen congressmen. But in 1880 the party's fortunes declined, and it disintegrated after 1884.

FARMERS' ALLIANCES   The more direct antecedents of the People's party were the Farmers' Alliances which grew with startling speed as the Greenback agitation petered out. By 1890 there were two major groups: the northwestern Alliance, organized in 1880 by Milton George, editor of the *Western Rural* in Chicago, was never effective and by the late 1880s was mostly a paper organization; the southern Alliance, which had various official names in its brief heyday, proved the more militant, the more effective, the more radical, and ultimately the more national of the two. The southern group, which started as a frontier farmers' club in Lampasas County, Texas, in 1877, grew into the Grand State Alliance in 1879. In 1886 Dr. Charles W. Macune became its leader and dazzled members with a glittering vision of large-

After Reconstruction ended, many black families (called "Exodusters") left the South to farm in Kansas. They laid the groundwork for later organizations like the Colored Farmers Alliance. Kansas State Historical Society]

scale cooperatives, which drew new converts rapidly to the organization. By absorbing existing farm groups and organizing new locals, the Alliance swept the cotton belt and established strong positions in Kansas and the Dakotas. By 1890 it had members from New York to California numbering about 1.5 million. A parallel Colored Farmers Alliance claimed over 1 million members.

The Alliance had an elaborate social and educational program, and about 1,000 affiliated newspapers. But unlike the Grange, the Alliance proposed from the beginning an elaborate economic program. In 1890 Alliance agencies and exchanges in some eighteen states claimed a business of $10 million, but they soon went the way of the Granger cooperatives, victims of discrimination by wholesalers, manufacturers, railroads, and bankers, but above all victims of inexperienced management and overextended credit. Increasingly farmers decided that they could not lift themselves by their own bootstraps, that they needed political power to secure railroad regulation, currency inflation, fertilizer inspections, state departments of agriculture, antitrust laws, farm credit, and the other measures they sought.

In 1890 Alliance members plunged headlong into politics. In the West, where hard times had descended after the collapse of land values in 1887, farmers were ready for third-party action. In the South, however, white Alliancemen hesitated to bolt the Democratic party, seeking instead to influence or control it. Both approaches gained startling success. Independent parties under various names upset the political balance in western states, electing a governor under the banner of the People's party in Kansas, and taking control of one house of the legislature there and both houses in Nebraska. In South Dakota and Minnesota

"Sockless Jerry" Simpson, on the stump at Harper, Kansas, 1892. [Kansas State Historical Society]

they gained a balance of power in the legislatures, while Kansas and Nebraska sent Populists to the Senate. The Populists produced colorful leaders, especially in Kansas, where the popular imagination was captured by: Mary Elizabeth Lease, who advised farmers "to raise less corn and more hell"; Rep. "Sockless Jerry" Simpson, who got his nickname as a riposte to his own charge that his Republican opponent, "Prince Hal," wore silk stockings; and William Alfred "Whiskers" Peffer, a Topeka editor and senator.

In the South the Alliance won equal if not greater success by forcing the Democrats to nominate candidates pledged to their program. The southern states elected four pro-Alliance governors, seven pro-Alliance legislatures, forty-four pro-Alliance congressmen, and several senators. Few of these officials, however, supported the subtreasury plan, which southern Alliancemen saw as the cure for their ills. Under this plan, formulated by C. W. Macune, farmers could store their crops in government warehouses and secure government loans for up to 80 percent of their crops' value at 1 percent interest. Besides credit, the plan allowed the farmer the leeway to hold his crop for a good price, since he would not have to sell it immediately at harvest time to pay off debts, and it promoted inflation because loans to farmers would be made in new legal-tender notes. The plan went before Congress in 1890 but was never adopted.

THE POPULIST PARTY   In May 1891 a conference in Cincinnati brought together delegates from farm, labor, and reform organizations to discuss strategy. The meeting endorsed a national third party and formed a national executive committee of the People's party. Few southerners were at Cincinnati, but many endorsed the third-party idea after their failure to move the Democratic party toward the subtreasury plan. In February 1892 a larger meeting at St. Louis called for a national convention of the People's party at Omaha on July 4 to adopt a platform and choose candidates. The stirring platform, written by Ignatius Donnelly of Minnesota, typified the apocalyptic, almost paranoid, style that increasingly characterized both the farmers' movement and its opponents:

> We meet in the midst of a nation brought to the verge of moral, political, and material ruin. Corruption dominates the ballot-box, the Legislatures, the Congress, and touches even the ermine of the bench. The newspapers are largely subsidized or muzzled, public opinion silenced, business prostrated, homes covered with mortgages, labor impoverished, and the land concentrating in the hands of the capitalists. . . . A vast conspiracy against mankind has been organized. . . . If not met and overthrown at once it forebodes terrible social convulsions . . . or the establishment of an absolute despotism.

The platform itself focused on issues of finance, transportation, and land. Its financial program demanded the new legal-tender currency proposed in the subtreasury plan, or a variation on it, free and unlimited coinage of silver at the 16:1 ratio, an increase in the amount of money in circulation to $50 per capita, an income tax, and postal savings banks to protect depositors who otherwise risked disastrous losses in small-town banks vulnerable to farm depression. As to transportation, the time had come "when the railroad corporations will either own the people or the people must own the railroads." Let government therefore nationalize the railroads, and the telephone and telegraph systems as well. For land, "the heritage of the people," the Populist remedy was for the government to reclaim from railroads and other corporations lands "in excess of their actual needs," and to forbid land ownership by aliens. Finally, the platform endorsed the eight-hour day and restriction of immigration, and denounced the use of Pinkerton agents as strikebreakers. The party took these positions to win support from the urban workers, whom Populists looked upon as fellow "producers."

The party's platform turned out to be more exciting than its candidate. The front-runner for the nomination, the southern Alliance's president Leonidas L. Polk of North Carolina, suddenly fell ill and died just before the convention. The party then turned to James B. Weaver of Iowa. The choice was unfortunate, for Weaver, an able and prudent man, carried the stigma of his defeat on the Greenback ticket twelve years before. To balance Weaver, a Union general, the party named James G. Field of Virginia, a former Confederate general, for vice-president.

The third party was the startling new feature of the 1892 campaign, but for the major parties it was a repetition of 1888, with Grover Cleveland the Democratic candidate and Benjamin Harrison the Republican, and with the tariff the chief issue between them. The outcome, however, was different. Both major candidates polled over 5 million votes, but Cleveland carried a plurality of the popular votes and the electoral college. Weaver polled over 1 million votes, and carried Colorado, Kansas, Nevada, and Idaho, for a total of twenty-two electoral votes. Alabama was the banner Populist state of the South, with 36.6 percent of its vote for Weaver, even as reported by a Democratic returns board.

THE DEPRESSION OF 1893 Cleveland's second administration came to grief early. Before it ended, Cleveland had antagonized every major segment of the public: the farmers and silverties opposed his efforts to maintain the gold standard, business groups disliked his attempt to lower the tariff, and a large segment of labor was alienated when he put down the Pullman Strike. Worst of all, his second term coincided with one of the worst depressions in history, set off just before he took office by the failure of the Philadelphia and Reading Railroad and a panic on Wall Street. By 1894 many people had reached bottom. That year some 750,000 workers went out on strike, including the Pullman workers; millions found themselves unemployed; railroad construction workers, laid off in the West, began tramping east and, to the dismay of alarmists who sniffed revolution in the air, talked of marching on Washington. Few of the groups made it to the capital. One that did was the Army of the Commonweal of Christ, led by Jacob S. Coxey, an Ohio Populist, who demanded mass employment on public works. When "Coxey's Army" of about 400 finally straggled into Washington, Coxey was arrested for walking on the grass.

In this climate of anxiety the midterm elections took place. The outcome disappointed the Populists, who had expected to profit from the discontent. In North Carolina a Populist fusion with Republicans actually captured the legislature from the Democrats, after which the fusionists named to the Senate one Populist and one Republican. But it was the only southern legislature lost by the Democrats, and that only for four years. Nationally, the elections amounted to a severe setback for

Democrats, and the Republicans were the chief beneficiaries. The Populists emerged with six senators and seven representatives. They had polled 1.5 million votes for their congressional candidates and still expected the simmering discontent to carry them to power in 1896.

SILVERITES VS. GOLDBUGS   The course of events, however, would dash that hope. In the mid-1890s events conspired to focus all agitations on the currency issue. One of the causes of the depression had been the failure of the British banking house of Baring Brothers, which led many British investors to unload American investments in return for gold. Soon after Cleveland's inauguration the gold reserve fell below $100 million. To plug this drain on the Treasury the president sought repeal of the Sherman Silver Purchase Act in order to stop the issuance of silver notes redeemable in gold. Cleveland won the act's repeal in 1893, but at the cost of irreparable division in his own party. To further build the gold reserve, the administration floated four bond issues in the years 1894 to 1896. The first two brought little response, but in 1895 the administration made a deal with J. P. Morgan and other financiers, who promised to get from abroad half the gold needed to buy the bonds, and to use their influence to stop demands on the Treasury. The deal worked, but it created the unfavorable image of Cleveland and the financial oligarchy working hand in glove.

Meanwhile the American Bimetallic League, heavily financed by silver miners, raised the agitation for silver coinage to a crescendo. Their greatest propaganda windfall came from the appearance in mid-1894 of William H. Harvey's book *Coin's Financial School,* which soon became a bestseller, the *Uncle Tom's Cabin* of the silver movement. In the book the youthful "Professor Coin" delivered lectures in which he resolutely confounded the "goldbugs" with his logic. The growing importance of the currency issue presented a dilemma for Populists: Should the party promote the whole spectrum of reform it advocated, or should it try to ride the silver issue into power? The latter was the practical choice, so the Populist leaders decided, over the protest of more radical members, to hold their 1896 convention last, confident that the major parties would at best straddle the silver issue and that they would then reap a harvest of bolting silverites.

THE ELECTION OF 1896   Contrary to these expectations the major parties took opposite positions on the currency issues. The Republicans, as expected, chose William McKinley on a gold-

*William Jennings Bryan at the
Democratic convention in 1896.
[Culver Pictures]*

standard platform. McKinley, a former congressman and governor of Ohio, benefited from the political steamroller organized
by his campaign manager, Marcus A. Hanna. On the Democratic
side, early organizing paid off for the prosilver forces, who captured the convention for their platform. William Jennings Bryan
arranged to give the closing speech for the silver plank. A two-
term congressman from Nebraska who had been swept out in the
Democratic losses of 1894, Bryan had distinguished himself
mainly with an exhausting three-hour speech he gave against repeal of the Sherman Silver Purchase Act. In the months before
the convention he had traveled the South and West, speaking for
free silver. His rehearsed phrases swept the convention into a
frenzy:

> I come to speak to you in defense of a cause as holy as the cause of
> liberty—the cause of humanity. . . . We have petitioned, and our
> petitions have been scorned. We have entreated, and our entreat-
> ies have been disregarded. We have begged, and they have mocked
> when our calamity came. We beg no longer, we entreat no more;
> we petition no more. We defy them!

By the time he reached his peroration there was little doubt
that he would get the nomination: "You shall not press down
upon the brow of labor this crown of thorns. You shall not crucify
mankind upon a cross of gold!"

When the Populists met in St. Louis two weeks later they faced
an impossible choice. They could name their own candidate and
divide the silver vote or endorse Bryan and probably lose their
identity. In the end they named Bryan, but chose their own vice-
presidential candidate, former Rep. Thomas E. Watson of Georgia, and invited the Democrats to drop their vice-presidential

nominee, Arthur Sewall—an action which Bryan refused to countenance. Given the workings of the electoral college, the two different candidates for vice-president might have caused a split in the silverite vote had the parties insisted on separate slates. Some diehard Populists did, but in twenty-eight of the forty-four states Democrats and Populists put out fusion slates which carried candidates for elector from both parties.

The thirty-six-year-old Bryan, the "boy orator of the Platte," traveled the country and exploited his spellbinding eloquence, while McKinley conducted a "front-porch campaign," receiving selected delegations at his home in Canton, Ohio, and giving only prepared responses. At the battle's end the Democratic-Populist-Silverite candidates were overwhelmed by the well-organized and well-financed Republican campaign directed by Mark Hanna. McKinley carried the popular vote by 7.1 million to 6.5 million and the electoral college by 271 to 176. Bryan carried most of the West and the South below the border states, but the problem neither the Populists nor Bryan ever overcame was that of breaking into metropolitan centers east of the Mississippi and north of the Ohio and Potomac. In the critical midwestern battleground, from Minnesota and Iowa eastward to Ohio, Bryan carried not a single state. Despite efforts on his behalf by reformers and unionists in the Midwest and East, unorganized workers found it easier to identify with McKinley's "full dinner pail" than

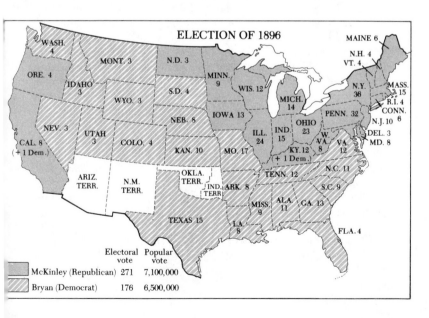

with Bryan's free silver. Some workers may have been intimi-
dated by businessmen's threats to close shop if the "Demopop"
heresies triumphed. Many ethnic voters, normally drawn to the
Democrats, were no doubt repelled by Bryan's flamboyant evangelical style. Farmers in the Northeast, moreover, were hurting
less than farmers in the wheat and cottonbelts.

A NEW ERA   It had been a climactic political struggle, falling almost precisely in the middle of what the historian Walter Nugent
called the Grand Conjuncture between rural and metropolitan
America, 1870–1920. And metropolitan America had won.
Henry Adams, who lived through the 1890s, wrote in *The Education of Henry Adams:*

> For a hundred years . . . the American people had hesitated, vacil-
> lated, swayed forward and back, between two forces, one simply
> industrial [productive], the other capitalistic, centralizing and me-
> chanical. . . . the majority at last declared itself, once and for all, in-
> favor of the capitalistic system with all its necessary machinery. All
> one's friends, all one's best citizens, reformers, churches, colleges,
> educated classes, had joined the banks to force submission to capi-
> talism. . . .

The first important act of the McKinley administration was to
call a special session of Congress to raise the tariff again. The
Dingley Tariff of 1897 became the highest to that time. By 1897
prosperity was returning, helped along by inflation of the currency, which bore out the arguments of greenbackers and silverites. But the inflation came, in one of history's many ironies, from
neither greenbackers nor silver, but from a new flood of gold into
the market and into the mints. During the 1880s and 1890s new
discoveries of gold in the South African Rand, the Canadian
Yukon, and in Alaska, aided by the development of a new cya-
nide process for extracting gold from its ore, led to spectacular
new gold rushes. The Yukon alone, from 1897 to 1904, was estimated to have added some $100 million worth of gold to the
world's store. In1900 Congress passed a Gold Standard Act,
which marked the temporary passing of the silver issue.

The old issues of tariffs and currency were now swallowed up
by the Spanish-American War, which ushered in a new era. "The
Spanish War finished us," said old Populist Tom Watson. "The
blare of the bugle drowned the voice of the Reformer." And yet
to compound the irony, most of the Populists' Omaha platform,
which seemed so radical at the time, would be in effect within
two decades.

FURTHER READING

Overviews of the Gilded Age deal in detail with politics. Vincent P. DeSantis's *The Shaping of Modern America, 1877–1916* (1973),° gives a clear narrative of political tangles, while Robert H. Wiebe's *The Search for Order, 1880–1920* (1967),° is more interpretive. Matthew Josephson's *The Politicos, 1865–1896* (1938),° argues the traditional view that those in power lacked principle. More comprehensive and sweeping in its coverage of change is Morton Keller's *Affairs of State: Public Life in Nineteenth Century America* (1977),° an indispensable guide to the forces which positively affected politics.

Some scholars treat the subject by focusing on party process. Leonard D. White's *The Republican Era, 1869–1901* (1958), concentrates on activities at the federal level. H. Wayne Morgan's *From Hays to McKinley: National Party Politics, 1877–1896* (1966), takes an organizational approach. Also party-specific are Robert D. Marcus's *GOP: Political Structure in the Gilded Age, 1880–1896* (1971), and Horace S. Merrill's *Bourbon Democracy in the Midwest, 1865–1896* (1967).° David J. Rothman concentrates on one legislative group in *Politics and Power: The United States Senate, 1869–1901* (1966).

Much recent scholarship concentrates on the ethnocultural thesis which stresses that community values as represented by religious affiliation separated the voters. Paul Kleppner's *The Cross of Culture: A Social Analysis of Midwestern Politics, 1850–1900* (1970), and *The Third Electoral System, 1852–1892* (1979), are salient works for this approach. Others include Samuel T. McSeveney's *The Politics of Depression: Political Behavior in the Northeast, 1893–1896* (1972), and Richard J. Jensen's *The Winning of the Midwest: Social and Political Conflicts, 1888–1896* (1971).

For reviews of the administrations of Gilded Age presidents, see William S. McFeeley's *Grant: A Biography* (1981),° Justis D. Doenecke's *The Presidencies of James A. Garfield and Chester A. Arthur* (1981), Allan Peskin's *Garfield: A Biography* (1978), Thomas C. Reeves's *Gentleman Boss: The Life of Chester Alan Arthur* (1975), and Lewis L. Gould's *The Presidency of William McKinley* (1980).

Biographies on other notables include David D. Anderson's *William Jennings Bryan* (1981), a short introduction, and David Jordan's *Roscoe Conkling of New York* (1971).

Issues and interest groups also receive special attention. Mary R. Dearing's *Veterans in Politics* (1952) details the influence of the veterans' lobby. John G. Sproat's *The Best Men: Liberal Reformers in the Gilded Age* (1968),° Gerald W. McFarland's *Mugwumps, Morals, and Politics, 1884–1920* (1975), and Ari Hoogenboom's *Outlawing the Spoils: A History of the Civil Service Reform Movement, 1865–1883* (1961), all examine the issue of government service. Tom E. Terrill's *The Tariff, Pol-*

°These books are available in paperback editions.

itics, and American Foreign Policy, 1874–1901 (1973), lends clarity to that complex issue. The finances of the Gilded Age are covered in Irwin Unger's *The Greenback Era: A Social and Political History of American Finance, 1865–1879* (1964),° Walter T. K. Nugent's *Money and American Society, 1865–1880* (1968), and Allen Weinstein's *Prelude to Populism: Origins of the Silver Issue, 1867–1878* (1970).

The study of issues and interest groups comes together in books on populism. The most comprehensive and controversial work on the subject is Lawrence Goodwyn's *Democratic Promise: The Populist Moment in America* (1976), also available in condensed form as *The Populist Moment* (1978).° Goodwyn's emphasis on the cooperative nature of agrarian protest contradicts the interpretations of John Hicks in *The Populist Revolt* (1931),° which portrays agrarians as forerunners of liberal reform, and Richard Hofstadter's *The Age of Reform* (1954),° which depicts them as reactionary. Norman Pollack's *The Populist Response to Industrial America* (1966) is more Marxist in tone.

State-level studies add to the diversity of interpretation. Among the better works are Sheldon Hackney's *From Populism to Progressivism in Alabama* (1969), William W. Rogers's *One-Galloused Revolution: Agrarianism in Alabama, 1865–1896* (1970), Walter T. K. Nugent's *The Tolerant Populists: Kansas, Populism, and Nativism* (1963), and O. Gene Clanton's *Kansas Populism: Ideas and Men* (1969).

Robert McMath's *Populist Vanguard: A History of the Southern Farmers Alliance* (1975),° J. Morgan Kousser's *The Shaping of Southern Politics: Suffrage Restriction and the Establishment of the One-Party South, 1880–1910* (1974),° and Bruce Palmer's *Man over Money: The Southern Populist Critique of American Capitalism* (1980) each deals with selected aspects of the agrarian cause.

Biographies of leading agrarians include C. Vann Woodward's *Tom Watson, Agrarian Rebel* (1938),° Stuart Noblin's *Leonidas Lafayette Polk: Agrarian Crusader* (1949), Peter Argersinger's *Populism and Politics: William Alfred Peffer and the People's Party* (1974), and Louis W. Koenig's *Bryan: A Political Biography of William Jennings Bryan* (1971).° For the role of leading populists in the election of 1896, consult Paul W. Glad's *McKinley, Bryan, and the People* (1964) and Robert F. Durden's *The Climax of Populism: The Election of 1896* (1965).°

23 ❧

THE COURSE OF EMPIRE

Toward the New Imperialism

DIPLOMACY AFTER THE CIVIL WAR Foreign affairs remained low on the horizon of public awareness, throughout most of the late nineteenth century. The overriding concerns of the time were the development of industry, settlement of the West, and domestic politics. Compared to these, foreign relations simply were not important to the vast majority of Americans. The major issues of foreign affairs stemming from the Civil War were settled within a few years of its end, after which few conflicts or major issues arose to trouble the American people. A mood of isolation settled upon the United States, favored since the War of 1812 with what the historian C. Vann Woodward called "free security:" wide oceans as buffers on either side, the British navy situated between America and the powers of Europe, and militarily weak neighbors in the Western Hemisphere.

At the end of the Civil War Lincoln's Secretary of State William H. Seward continued to serve under President Johnson and persisted in his policy of protest and watchful waiting on the French occupation of Mexico, which had begun while the United States was distracted by its domestic conflicts. His patience paid off when the growing power in Europe of Bismarck's Prussia impelled Napoleon III to end his Mexican adventure in 1867, four years after it began, in order to bolster French defenses at home. Napoleon's puppet in Mexico, Emperor Maximilian, continued a hopeless fight, but without French troops to prop him up was soon overwhelmed and executed by Mexican forces under Benito Juarez, who became president of a restored republic in June 1867. In the same year Seward negotiated the puchase of Alaska from the Russians for $7.2 million, thus removing the most recent colonial power from the New World. "Seward's folly" of buying the Alaskan "icebox" proved in time to be the biggest bargain for the United States, economically and strategically, since the Louisiana Purchase. Seward's effort to buy the Virgin Islands from Denmark for $7.5 million met with rebuff from the Radicals in Congress, but his proclamation of annexation of the Midway Islands (1867) was carried without effective challenge.

Seward's successor under Grant, Hamilton Fish, proceeded to settle the outstanding issues in controversy with Great Britain through the 1871 Treaty of Washington. Under the treaty an arbitration panel of five nations settled the "Alabama claims" brought by the government for destruction wrought by Confederate raiders built in Britain. The panel awarded some $15 million to the United States but partially balanced that off with $5.5 million to the British for damages suffered during the Civil War. The disputed ownership of the San Juan Islands was settled when the German kaiser ruled that they lay on the American side of the main channel between Vancouver Island and the state of Washington. Finally, mutual agreement was reached on fishing rights for Americans off Canada and for Canadians south to the Thirty-ninth Parallel. With these decisions, foreign affairs receded for a time.

EXPANSION IN THE PACIFIC   Yet the spirit of Manifest Destiny remained alive, if muted. Expansionism surfaced in Grant's attempt to annex Santo Domingo in 1870, which was defeated in the Senate. Seward had articulated a vision of empire which "must continue to move on westward until the tides of the renewed and the decaying civilizations of the world meet on the shores of the Pacific Ocean." Seward, whom the historian Walter LaFeber called "the prince of players" in this drama, was followed at the State Department by a line of secretaries who never completely lost sight of this expansionist vision, including Fish, James G. Blaine, and Richard Olney.

The Pacific Ocean remained the major field of overseas activity. America's interest in the area was nearly as old as the Republic. The China trade, begun in 1784, had been a steady if minor part of the nation's foreign trade ever since, and had brought with it a variety of other contacts in the Pacific. Whalers, first active in the colonial period, pursued their prey into the Pacific. The missionary impulse had taken Americans into India and Burma as early as 1812, into Hawaii by the 1820s, and into China by the 1830s.

The urge to annex islands in the Pacific was first expressed by Commodore Perry in 1853–1854. Perry had his eye on the Bonin Islands, off the coast of Japan. He was overruled, but in the flush years of expansionism during the 1850s the United States laid claim to various small islands and coral atolls of the mid-Pacific, sometimes in conflict with the claims of other nations. Among these islands, two inhabited groups occupied especially strategic positions about twenty degrees from either side of the equator: Samoa on the south and Hawaii (the Sandwich Islands) on the north. Both had major harbors, Pago Pago and Pearl Harbor respectively, with which Americans had made contact as early as the 1820s. In the years after the Civil War American interest in these islands gradually deepened.

SAMOA   In 1872 U.S.Navy Commander R. W. Meade negotiated a treaty with a Samoan chieftain giving the United States a naval station at Pago Pago. The Senate took no action on the treaty. Col. A. B. Steinberger, a special agent of Grant, then organized a government on his own initiative and installed himself as prime minister of Samoa, but was soon overthrown and deported on a British vessel. Finally, in 1878, a permanent American presence was established. The Samoans signed a treaty with the United States which granted a naval base at Pago Pago, extraterritoriality for Americans (meaning that in Samoa they remained subject only to American law), exchanged trade concessions, and called for the United States to extend its good offices in case of a dispute with another nation. The Senate ratified this accord and in the following year the German and British governments worked out similar arrangements on other islands of the Samoan group.

There things rested until civil war broke out in 1887 when the Germans backed a pretender against the native Samoan king and finally installed him under a German protectorate. The sequel to this incident was a conference in Berlin, called at the suggestion of German Chancellor Bismarck, which established a tripartite protectorate, with Germany, Great Britain, and the United States in an uneasy partnership.

HAWAII   In Hawaii the Americans had more nearly a clear field. The islands, a united kingdom since 1795, had a sizable settlement of American missionaries and planters and were strategically more important to the United States. Occupation by another major power might have posed a threat to American commercial interests and even to American defense. As early as 1842 Secretary of State Daniel Webster said that the United

States would be "dissatisfied" to see any other power take posession.

In 1875 the kingdom entered a reciprocal trade agreement under which Hawaiian sugar entered the United States duty free. Hawaii also promised that none of its territory would be leased or granted to a third power. In 1884 the agreement was renewed but it was not ratified by the Senate until 1887, when it was amended to grant the United States exclusive right to a fortified naval base at Pearl Harbor, near Honolulu. These agreements resulted in a boom in sugar growing, and American settlers in Hawaii came to have a dominant position economically. The fortunes of white planters were based on cheap immigrant labor, mainly Chinese, Japanese, and Portuguese. By the 1890s the native population had been reduced to a minority by smallpox and other foreign diseases, and Orientals quickly became the most numerous group in Hawaii. In 1887 the Americans forced King Kalakaua to grant a constitutional government which they dominated.

Things changed sharply when the king's sister, Queen Liliuokalani, ascended the throne in 1891 and began efforts to restore absolute power. Shortly before that the McKinley Tariff had destroyed Hawaii's favored position in the sugar trade by putting the sugar of all countries on the free list and granting growers in the United States a two-cent bounty. The resultant discontent led the white population to stage a revolt early in 1893. A committee of public safety under Sanford B. Dole, justice of the Hawaiian Supreme Court, seized power. The American minister, John L. Stevens, brought in marines from the cruiser *Boston* to

Queen Liliuokalani. [Public Archives of Hawaii]

support the coup. Within a month a committee of the new government turned up in Washington and in February signed a treaty of annexation with Secretary of State John W. Foster.

The treaty, however, came just weeks before President Harrison left office, and Democratic senators blocked ratification. On March 9 President Cleveland withdrew the treaty and sent former Rep. James H. Blount of Georgia as a special commissioner to investigate. Blount withdrew the American marines and reported that Stevens had acted improperly. Most Hawaiians opposed annexation, Blount said. He thought that the revolution had been engineered mainly by sugar planters hoping to get the domestic sugar bounty by annexation. Cleveland therefore proposed to restore the queen in return for amnesty to the revolutionists. The provisional government refused and on July 4, 1894, proclaimed the Republic of Hawaii, which had in its constitution a standing provision for American annexation, presumably after Cleveland yielded to a president whose sensibilities were less easily offended.

STEPS TO WORLD POWER

The antebellum spirit of expansionism thus had neither died out with the 1850s nor gone completely dormant. It would return full blown in the 1890s with the addition of some new flourishes. European powers from about 1870 on set an example with a new surge of imperialism in Africa and Asia, where they acquired colonies, protectorates, and economic privileges. All of Africa except Liberia and Ethiopia fell under outside dominion. Above all, the new imperialism was economic, a quest for markets and raw materials, and to more than one American the European example seemed relevant to the American experience. The closing of the frontier, brought forcefully to public attention by the census of 1890 and by Frederick Jackson Turner's classic essay on the significance of the frontier in 1893, might well signal the end of a constantly growing market and a need to seek markets overseas, many people reasoned. Turner himself had written: "He would be a rash prophet who would assert that the expansive character of American life has now entirely ceased. Movement has been its dominant fact, and, unless this training has no effect upon a people, the American energy will continually demand a wider field for its exercise."

Most Americans shared a concern with world markets as developments in transportation and communication quickened the pace of commerce and diplomacy. From the first, exports of farm products had been the basis of American economic growth. Now the conviction grew that American manufactures had matured to the point that they could outsell foreign goods in the world market. The new conviction challenged an old Republican principle that industry must be protected against foreign competition in the domestic market. But should the expansion of markets lead to territorial expansion as well? Or to intervention in the internal affairs of other countries? On this point Americans disagreed, but a growing minority in public life were ready to entertain the idea of overseas possessions; they were led by Sen. Albert J. Beveridge of Indiana and Henry Cabot Lodge of Massachusetts, Theodore Roosevelt, and not least of all, Capt. Alfred Thayer Mahan.

NAVAL POWER   Captain Mahan, son of Dennis T. Mahan, West Point's one-time strategist of land war, became himself a leading advocate of sea power. A graduate of Annapolis, he served for years as president of the Naval War College at Newport, Rhode Island. A series of his lectures on naval history grew into a volume published in 1890, *The Influence of Sea Power upon History, 1660–1783*, in which he argued that national greatness and prosperity flowed from sea power, which had a fundamentally economic importance. To Mahan, economic development called for a big navy, a strong merchant marine, foreign commerce, colonies, and naval bases. The age of steam made coaling stations a new matter of strategic concern. Mahan expounded on America's destiny to control the Caribbean, build an isthmian canal, and spread Western civilization in the Pacific. His ideas were widely circulated in popular journals.

Even before Mahan's writings became influential a gradual expansion of the navy had gotten under way, after a season of post–Civil War neglect led the *Army and Navy Journal* in 1874 to call the American fleet a "heterogeneous collection of naval trash." In 1880 the nation had fewer than a hundred sea-going vessels, many of them rusting or rotting at the docks. By the time Cleveland entered office four new steel vessels had been authorized, and Cleveland's navy secretary, William C. Whitney, got funds in 1886 for twenty more, including the battleships *Maine* and *Texas*. By 1896 eleven battleships had been built or authorized. The depression of the 1890s was little felt at the Newport News Shipbuilding and Drydock Company and other shipyards. In 1897 Theodore Roosevelt, as assistant secretary of the navy under John D. Long in the McKinley administration, worked overtime to get the new navy in condition for a war he expected —and even wanted.

The battleship Maine, *funded in 1886, shown here entering Havana Harbor in 1898. [National Archives]*

RACIAL THOUGHT   Meanwhile certain intellectual currents of the day workd to bolster the new Manifest Destiny. The Darwinian idea of natural selection afforded a handy argument for imperialism. If natural selection worked in the biological realm, would it not apply also in human society? Among nations, as among individuals, the fittest survive and prevail. "There is apparently much truth in the belief that the wonderful progress of the United States, as well as the character of the people, are the results of natural selection," Darwin himself wrote in *The Descent of Man* (1871), "the more energetic, restless and courageous men from all parts of Europe having emigrated during the last ten or twelve generations to that great country and having there succeeded best." Darwin himself, however, cannot fairly be tagged a champion of imperialism or of racial "purity."

John Fiske, the historian and popular lecturer on Darwinism, nevertheless developed racial corollaries from Darwin's idea. In *American Political Ideas* (1885) he stressed the superior character of "Anglo-Saxon" institutions and peoples. The English "race," he argued, was destined to dominate the globe: in the institutions, traditions, language, even in the blood of the world's peoples. John W. Burgess, a historian and political scientist at Columbia University, argued similarly that the Teutonic peoples had a superior political talent and a duty to spread the blessings of their superior institutions.

Josiah Strong, a Congregational minister, added the sanction of religion. In his book *Our Country: Its Possible Future and Its Present Crisis* (1885), Strong argued that "Anglo-Saxons" embodied two great ideas: civil liberty and "a pure spiritual Christianity." The Anglo-Saxon was "divinely commissioned to be, in a pecular sense, his brother's keeper." Expansion to establish foreign missions found favor in both Protestant and Catholic churches, the chief opposition coming from minority groups like the Quakers and Unitarians.

LATIN AMERICA   By the 1890s events drew the United States more and more into the orbit of world affairs. One significant step came with the First International American Conference in Washington, which met from late 1889 through early 1890. The idea of closer commercial and cultural ties with Latin America had been for years associated with the name of James G. Blaine. Like Henry Clay, whose "American System" he admired, Blaine hoped to expand trade with Latin America and bring the American republics closer together. Named secretary of state by Garfield, late in 1881 he sent out invitations to a general peace conference of American republics to meet in November 1882. The succession of Arthur brought Blaine's resignation and the plan fell through.

Blaine's vindication awaited yet another administration. In 1888 Congress authorized President Cleveland to call a conference of American states, but when the First International American Conference met on October 2, 1889, Blaine was again secretary of state, this time under Harrison. Seventeen Latin American states sent delegates. Blaine's ultimate hope was to establish a customs union and to initiate free trade among American nations. The Latin delegates, however, were afraid of damaging their ties with Europe for the benefit of manufacturers in the United States. They resolved therefore in favor of reciprocity agreements, and over the next few years Blaine secured tariff concessions from ten Latin countries by executive agreements under the provisions of the McKinley Tariff. Though it failed to set up machinery for the arbitration of disputes, the conference did establish a permanent agency as a clearinghouse for information: the Bureau of American Republics, later the Pan-American Union, which in 1948 became the Organization of American States.

CANADA AND SOUTH AMERICA   But not all was sweetness and light in the Western Hemisphere. In the 1880s and 1890s incidents in the Bering Sea, in Chile, and in Venezuela stirred the bumptious spirit of national pride that never lay far below the surface. At issue in the Bering Sea was the practice of pelagic (oceanic) sealing by foreign nationals, mostly Canadians, in offshore waters where the difficulty of distinguishing males and females resulted in the loss of many pups when their mothers were killed. This was an issue because a caprice of fashion had put sealskin coats and muffs much in demand. In 1886 American revenue cutters began seizing Canadian ships engaged in the practice, and in 1889 Congress declared the Bering a closed sea under United States dominion. In an exchange of notes in 1890, however, British Foreign Minister Lord Salisbury refused to accept the legitimacy of Congress's claim. There was a flurry of bluster in the American press, but never much chance that the two countries would come to blows over what a Spokane Falls newspaper called "a few greasy, ill-smelling sealskins." Eventually, under an arbitration treaty of 1892, it was decided that while the Bering was an open sea, by mutual agreement pelagic sealing was forbidden within sixty miles of the Pribilof Islands. Later, in 1911, by treaty with Britain, Russia, and Japan, pelagic sealing was prohibited throughout the North Pacific and Bering Sea.

Trouble in Chile flared intensely, but passed quickly. When civil war broke out in that country in 1891, American authorities briefly detained a rebel ship carrying arms from San Diego, then found that there had been no violation of neutrality laws. This left a lingering resentment among the rebels, who soon took over Chile's government. In October 1891, when the cruiser *Baltimore* called at Valparaiso, a mob attacked sailors returning from the True Blue Saloon. Two sailors were killed and seventeen hurt in the fracas, and some were thrown into jail. For a season tempers ran hot as the countries exchanged imprecations. By January 1892 Secretary Blaine was theatening to break off relations, and President Harrison waxed bellicose in a special message to Congress. Happily, tempers cooled in Valparaiso and Chile offered an apology and an indemnity of $75,000.

Far more serious was the Venezuelan boundary dispute with British Guiana, which had simmered since colonial days but took on new urgency when gold was found in the disputed area. When Venezuela suspended diplomatic relations with Britain in 1887, the American State Department suggested arbitration, but the matter was still unsettled in 1892 when Cleveland was reelected to the White House. In 1895 Congress passed a resolution for arbitration, largely at the instigation of William L. Scruggs, who had been Harrison's minister to Venezuela. Cleveland was almost forced to "twist the lion's tail" or see his political opponents do it. He may even have found the occasion a welcome diversion from his domestic problems. His secretary of state, Richard L. Olney, got up a note dated July 20 in which he invoked the Monroe Doctrine against British interference in the affairs of the New World. Cleveland claimed to have softened the "verbiage" a bit, but still dubbed it a "20 inch gun" note.

> Today [Olney wrote] the United States is practically sovereign on this continent, and its fiat is law upon the subjects to which it confines its interposition. Why? ... It is because, in addition to all other grounds, its infinite resources combined with its isolated position render it master of the situation and practically invulnerable as against any or all other powers.

The note was calculated to provoke a quick reply, but Lord Salisbury let it lie for a maddening four months. The British government was preoccupied elsewhere and assumed the note was largely for domestic American consumption anyway. When Salisbury did respond on November 26, he rejected the demand for arbitration and noted that the Monroe Doctrine was not recognized international law, and in any case was irrelevant to a boundary dispute. Clevelend pronounced himself "mad clear through" at such a rebuff to the "friendly" suggestion of the United States. Congress, at Cleveland's request, unanimously voted for a boundary commission to run the line in spite of the British. Enthusiasm swept the country. Theodore Roosevelt vented his opinion that "this country needs a war." But cooler heads soon prevailed. The British faced more urgent problems in South Africa and a growing German navy, and through the good offices of the United States finally came around to an arbitration treaty with Venezuela, signed in 1897. By the time an international commission handed in its findings in 1899, the focus of public attention was elsewhere. The settlement turned out to be about what the British had offered in the first place.

THE SPANISH-AMERICAN WAR

"CUBA LIBRE" Until the 1890s a certain ambivalence about overseas possessions had checked America's drive to expand. Suddenly in 1898 and 1899 the inhibitions collapsed and American power thrust its way to the far reaches of the Pacific. The occasion for this explosion of imperialism lay neither in the Pacific nor in the quest for bases and trade, but to the south in Cuba. The chief motive was a sense of outrage at another country's imperialism.

After the age of filibustering in the 1850s diplomatic interest in Cuba had waned; it revived only briefly during a ten-year insurrection, from 1868 to 1878. After the insurrection was brought under control in 1878, American investments in Cuba, mainly in sugar and mining, rose to about $50 million. The United States in fact traded more with Cuba than Spain did. On February 24, 1895, insurrection broke out again. Simmering discontent with Spanish rule had been aggravated by the Wilson-Gorman Tariff of 1894, which took sugar off the free list in the midst of a depression already damaging to the market for Cuban sugar. Public feeling in the United States was with the rebels, and many Americans extended help to the Cuban Revolutionary party which organized the revolt from headquarters in New York. Its leader, José Marti, returned to the island soon after the outbreak and was killed in a skirmish with Spanish troops. Leadership then fell to Maximo Gomez, a native Santo Domingan, who had led the earlier Ten Years' War.

The insurrectionists' strategy was to wage guerrilla warfare and to damage the economic life of the island, which in turn would excite the concern of American investors. The strategy dictated hit-and-run attacks on trains, railways, and plantations. The movement found one source of income by selling "protection" against attack. Such tactics forced people either into the insurgent forces or into garrisoned towns, which in turn might be cut off from food supplies. Revolutionary propaganda of course presented the effort in a different light, and Americans were more than ready to look upon the insurrection in the light of their own War of Independence. American attentions were distracted by the Venezuelan crisis and the election of 1896, but Spanish authorities insisted that only aid from the United States kept the revolt alive.

The strategies needed to counter guerrilla warfare nearly always cast their practitioners in a bad light. In 1896 Spanish Gen. Valeriano Weyler adopted a policy of gathering Cubans behind Spanish lines, often in detention *(reconcentrado)* centers so that no one could join the insurrections by night and appear peaceful by day. In some of the centers a combination of tropical climate, poor food, and unsanitary conditions soon brought a heavy toll of disease and death. The American press promptly christened the Spanish commander "Butcher" Weyler.

Events in Cuba supplied exciting copy for the popular press. Chance had it that William Randolph Hearst's New York *Journal* and Joseph Pulitzer's New York *World* were at the time locked in a monumental struggle for circulation. "It was a battle of gigantic proportions," the journalist Walter Millis wrote, "in which the sufferings of Cuba merely chanced to furnish some of the most convenient ammunition." Another device of the circulation war was the new-fangled comic strip and one of the most popular was "The Yellow Kid," the cartoonist for which Hearst lured from Pulitzer with a high salary. Hence, by association, the unbuttoned sensationalism at which the papers vied came to be called "yellow journalism." Hearst emerged as the undisputed champion. Frederick Remington, the artist best known for his cowboy pictures, supplied Hearst's *Journal* an imaginary picture which left the impression that three Cuban women on a detained American ship had been forced to disrobe in the presence of male Spanish officers. Pulitzer was able to demonstrate the falsity of the report, but truth was a poor substitute for titillation. A Hearst reporter, by means of bribery and intrigue, spirited one Evangeline Cisneros out of a Spanish prison and away from Cuba, whereupon a member of Congress suggested hiring a thousand such reporters to liberate the whole island. The *Journal* excelled also at invective against "Weyler the brute, the devastator of haciendas, the destroyer of men."

At the outset the Cleveland administration tried to protect American rights but avoided involvement beyond an offer of mediation. Mounting public sympathy for the cause, however, manifested itself in Congress. By concurrent resolution on April 6, 1896, the two houses endorsed recognition of the Cuban belligerents and urged the president to seek a peace on the basis of Cuban independence. Cleveland, however, denied any designs against Spanish rule and offered to cooperate with Spain in bringing peace on the basis of home rule. The Spanish politely refused. Meanwhile America's revenue service and naval forces did their best to break up filibustering and gun-running expeditions launched from the Atlantic and Gulf coasts.

PRESSURE FOR WAR   The posture of neutrality changed sharply when McKinley entered office. He had been elected on a platform that endorsed independence for Cuba, as well as American control of Hawaii and of an isthmian canal. In October a new Spanish commander, Ramon Blanco, set out to liberalize the reconcentration system and in November Spain's queen regent offered Cuba autonomy in return for peace. What the Cubans might once have welcomed, however, they now rejected, insurrectionists and Spanish loyalists alike. Spain was impaled on the horns of a dilemma, unable to end the war and unready to give up Cuba.

Early in 1898 events moved rapidly to arouse opinion against Spain. On January 12 a riotous demonstration of loyalists in Havana denounced Weyler's recall and the offer of autonomy. Consul-General Fitzhugh Lee seized the occasion to request a warship nearby, perhaps at Key West, to help assure the security of American citizens and property. The battleship *Maine* showed up on January 25, but in Havana harbor, ostensibly on a courtesy call. On February 9 Hearst's New York *Journal* released the text of a letter from Spanish Minister Depuy de Lôme to a friend in Havana, stolen from the post office by a Cuban spy. In the letter de Lôme called President McKinley "weak and a bidder for the admiration of the crowd, besides being a would-be politician who tries to leave a door open behind himself while keeping on good terms with the jingoes of his party." This was hardly more extreme than what McKinley's assistant secretary of the navy Theodore Roosevelt had said about him: "no more backbone than a chocolate eclair." But that comment had remained private. De Lôme resigned to prevent further embarrassment to his government.

Six days later, on February 15, the *Maine* exploded in Havana harbor and sank with a loss of 260 men. A naval court of inquiry reported in March that an external mine had set off an explosion in the ship's magazine. Lacking evidence, the court made no effort to fix the blame, but the yellow press had no need of evidence. The outcry against Spain reached a crescendo in the words "Remember the Maine!" Never mind that one cannot imagine any advantage Spain could derive from such an act. What actually happened, whether accidentally or on purpose, remains a mystery.

Hearst's Journal *reports the sinking of the* Maine. *The uproar created by the incident and its coverage in the "yellow press" edged McKinley toward war. [New York Historical Society]*

McKinley, under the mounting pressure of public excitement, tried to maintain a steady course but requested and quickly got from Congress on March 9 a $50-million appropriation for defense. One month later the Spanish government ordered General Blanco to suspend hostilities unilaterally. On April 10 the Spanish minister gave the State Department a message that amounted to a surrender: the United States should indicate the nature and duration of the armistice; Cuba would have an autonomous government; and the two countries would submit the question of the *Maine* to arbitration. On the same day United States Minister Stewart L. Woodford cabled from Madrid an expression of hope that McKinley would get full authority from Congress to secure peace by negotiations. "I hope nothing will now be done to humiliate Spain, as I am satisfied that the present government is going, and is loyally ready to go, as fast and as far as it can." McKinley, he predicted, could win settlement by August 1 on any terms: autonomy, independence, or cession of Cuba to the United States.

The following day found McKinley sending Congress what amounted to a war message. He asked for power to use armed forces in Cuba to abate a nuisance off the United States' shores and to protect American property and trade. The Cuban situation, McKinley said, was a constant menace to the peace. Back to the president came a joint resolution of Congress, which went beyond endorsing the use of the armed forces: it declared Cuba independent an demanded withdrawal of Spanish forces. The Teller Amendment, added on the Senate floor, disclaimed any American designs on Cuban territory. McKinley signed the resolution and a copy went off to the Spanish government, with notice that McKinley would execute it unless Spain gave a complete and satisfactory response by noon, April 23. Meanwhile, on April 22 the president announced a blockade of Cuba's northern coast and the port of Santiago. Under international law this was an act of war. Rather than give in to an ultimatum, the Spanish government declared war on April 24. Congress then, determined to be first, declared war on April 25, retroactive to April 21.

Why such a rush into war after Woodford had predicted that Spain would cave in before the summer was out? Chiefly because too much momentum and popular pressure had already built up for a confidential message to change the course of events. Also, leaders of the business community, which tolerates uncertainty poorly, were demanding a quick resolution of the problem. Many lacked faith in the willingness or ability of the Spanish government to carry out a moderate policy in the face of a hostile public opinion. Still, it is fair to ask why McKinley did not take a stand for peace, knowing what he did. He might have defied Congress and public opinion, but in the end the political risk was too high. The Democrats were likely to adopt the popular cause of Cuba. The ultimate blame for war, if blame must be levied, belongs to the American people for letting themselves be whipped up into such a hostile frenzy.

DEWEY TAKES MANILA The war itself was short, lasting four months, and for America, victorious. John Hay called it "a splendid little war." The war's end was also the end of Spain's once-great New World empire, which had begun with Columbus. It marked as well the emergence of the United States as a world power. If American participation saved many lives by ending the insurrection in Cuba, it also led to American involvement in another insurrection, in the Philippines, and created a host of problems that persisted into the twentieth century.

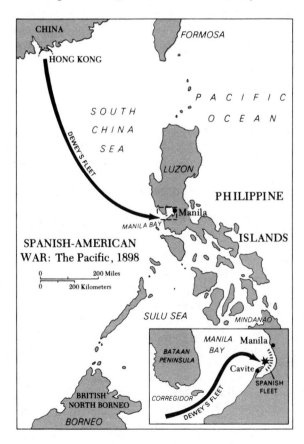

SPANISH-AMERICAN WAR: The Pacific, 1898

The war was barely under way before the navy produced a quick, spectacular victory in an unexpected quarter—Manila Bay. While public attention was fixed on Cuba, young Theodore Roosevelt was thinking of the Philippines. As assistant secretary of the navy, he had Commodore George Dewey appointed commander of the small Asiatic squadron, and had seen to it that ample supplies went out to the squadron at Hong Kong along with orders to engage Spain in the Philippines in case of war. President McKinley had approved those orders.

Arriving late on April 30 with four cruisers and two gunboats, Dewey proceeded on May 1 to destroy or capture all the Spanish warships in Manila Bay. The Spanish force lost 381 men killed, while Dewey's squadron suffered casualties of 8 wounded. Dewey, without a force of occupation, was now in awkward posession of Manila Bay. Promised reinforcements, he stayed while foreign warships, including a German force equal if not superior to Dewey's, hung about the scene like watchful vultures. Land reinforcements finally arrived, and with the help of Filipino insurrectionists under Emilio Aguinaldo, Dewey's forces entered Manila on August 13.

THE CUBAN CAMPAIGN While these events transpired halfway around the world, the war reached a quick climax closer to home, which was surprising because American preparation for this war was spotty. The navy was fit, but the army could muster only an ill-assorted guard of 28,000 regulars and about 100,000 militiamen. Altogether during the war about 200,000 more militiamen were recruited, chiefly as state volunteers. The armed forces suffered badly from both inexperience and maladministration, with the result that more died from disease than from enemy action. The United States' salvation was that Spanish forces were even worse off, their morale infinitely so.

Events pushed the United States into a Cuban campaign sooner than at first planned. On April 29 Spanish Adm. Pascual Cervera left the Cape Verde Islands with four cruisers and three destroyers, turning up finally in Santiago de Cuba where the U.S. Navy put the Spanish fleet under blockade. Adm. William T. Sampson soon arrived to assume command, and found a situation in need of land forces. The navy could not venture too close to shore, land troops might force Cervera to flee bombardment from land batteries and risk battle at sea.

So it fell out that land and sea battles around Santiago early in July broke Spanish resistance and ended the war within another month. A force of some 17,000 troops hastily assembled at

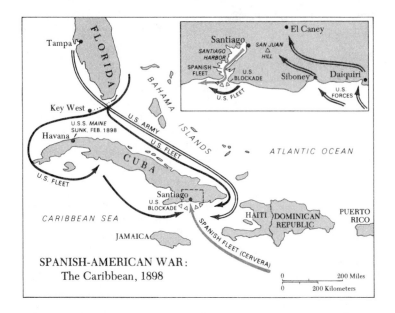

SPANISH-AMERICAN WAR:
The Caribbean, 1898

Tampa under the command of General Shafter. One significant element of that force was Col. Leonard Wood's First Volunteer Cavalry, better known as the "Rough Riders" and best remembered because Lt.-Col. Theodore Roosevelt was second in command. Eager to get "in on the fun," Roosevelt had quit the Navy Department to join a colorful volunteer regiment of eastern dudes and southwestern deadshots. At Tampa Roosevelt found three regiments assigned to a ship that could hold but one, whereupon he double-timed the Rough Riders on board. "There was a great deal of expostulation," he wrote later, "but we had possession." There they sat for six days in a stream of sewage. Their landing at Daiquiri was an equally mad scramble. The horses went somewhere else leaving the horseless Rough Riders "Wood's Weary Walkers." The disorganized army might have been defeated by a determined attack at that point.

The major land action of the campaign occurred on July 1. About 7,000 Americans took the fortified village of El Caney from about 600 of the enemy garrison. While a much larger force attacked San Juan Hill, a smaller unit, including the dismounted Rough Riders, together with black soldiers from the Ninth and Tenth Cavalry seized the enemy position atop nearby Kettle Hill. The two battles put American forces atop heights from which to the west and south they could bring Santiago and the Spanish fleet under seige. On July 3 Admiral Cervera made a gallant run for it, but his decrepit ships were little more than sitting ducks for the newer American fleet, which included five battleships and two cruisers. The casualties were as one-sided as at Manila: 474 Spanish were killed and wounded and 1,750 were taken prisoner, while only one American was killed and one wounded. The timely battle afforded Fourth of July orators the rarest opportunity they had had since the twin Union victories of Vicksburg and Gettysburg thirty-five years before. Santiago surrendered with a garrison of 24,000 on July 17. On July 25 a force under Gen. Nelson A. Miles moved into Puerto Rico against minor resistance. What was to have been the first action of the war became, in the words of Finley Peter Dunne's Mr. Dooley, fictional Irish bartender and commentator on the passing scene, General Miles's "gran' picnic and moonlight excursion."

The day after Miles landed the Spanish government sued for peace through the French ambassador in Washington. After discussions lasting two weeks, an armistice was signed on August 12, less than four months after the war's start and the day before Americans entered Manila. The peace protocol specified that Spain should give up Cuba, and that the United States should annex Puerto Rico and one island in the Ladrones (later called the Marianas), and should occupy the city, bay, and harbor of Manila pending disposition of the Philippines. Among more than 274,000 Americans who served during the war and the ensuing demobilization, 5,462 died, but only 379 in battle. The total wounded numbered 1,704.

THE DEBATE OVER ANNEXATION   On October 1, a delegation headed by Secretary of State William R. Day opened negotiations that led to the Treaty of Paris, signed on December 10. Most of the major points had been settled in the peace protocol, but Guam was now designated as the island in the Ladrones to be annexed. Two fundamental questions remained: the Cuban debt and the Philippines. The United States simply refused to assume the Cuban government's debt of $400 million, incurred in the first place largely to subdue the insurrection. The Philippines posed a harder question, indeed one of the biggest decisions to face United States foreign policy to that time, and one that was sprung upon the country without preparation. At first, Mr. Dooley remarked, the American people "did not know whether the Philippines were islands or canned goods." McKinley, who claimed that at first he himself could not locate them within two thousand miles, gave ambiguous signals to the peace commission. The commission itself was divided.

There had been no demand for annexation before the war, but

Dewey's victory quickly kindled expansionist fever. Businessmen began thinking of the commercial possibilities not so much in the islands as in the nearby continent of Asia, such as oil for the lamps of China and textiles for its teeming millions. Missionary societies saw the chance to save the "little brown brother." The Philippines promised to provide a useful base for all such activities. It was neither the first nor the last time that Americans would get caught up in fantasies of saving Asia or getting rich there. McKinley pondered the alternatives and later explained his reasoning to a group of Methodists:

> And one night late it came to me this way—I don't know how it was, but it came: (1) that we could not give them back to Spain— that would be cowardly and dishonorable; (2) that we could not turn them over to France or Germany—our commercial rivals in the Orient—that would be bad business and discreditable; (3) that we could not leave them to themselves—they were unfit for self-government—and they would soon have anarchy and misrule over there worse than Spain's was; and (4) that there was nothing left for us to do but to take them all, and to educate the Filipinos, and uplift and civilize and Christianize them, and by God's grace do the very best we could by them, as our fellowmen for whom Christ also died. And then I went to bed, and went to sleep and slept soundly.

In one brief statement he had summarized the motivating ideas of imperialism: (1) national honor, (2) commerce, (3) racial superiority, and (4) altruism. So despite the fact that these candidates for conversion were already largely Catholic, the word went forth to take the Philippines. Spanish negotiations raised the delicate point that American forces had no claim by right of conquest, and had even taken Manila after the armistice. American negotiators finally offered the Spanish compensation of $20 million.

The treaty then added to American territory Puerto Rico, Guam, and the Philippines. Meanwhile Americans had taken other giant steps in the Pacific. Hawaiian annexation, promised in McKinley's platform, failed to get a two-thirds majority in the Senate, but the war demonstrated the islands' strategic importance all the more. The administration therefore moved to annex Hawaii, like Texas, by joint resolution. The resolution passed on July 7, 1898, in the midst of the war. Within a year of the peace treaty, in 1899, after another outbreak of fighting over the royal succession in Samoa, Germany and the United States agreed to partition the Samoan Islands. The United States annexed Tutuila and the other easternmost islands; Germany took the rest, including the largest island, Upolu. Britain ceded its claims in Samoa in return for German concessions in the Pacific (the Tongas and the Solomons) and in Africa. Meanwhile the United States laid claim to Wake Island (1898), which would be a vital link in a future trans-Pacific cable line.

The Treaty of Paris had yet to be ratified in the Senate, where most Democrats and Populists, and some Republicans, opposed it. Anti-imperialists argued that acquisition of the Philippines would undermine American democracy. They appealed to traditional isolationism, American principles of self-government, the inconsistency of liberating Cuba and annexing the Philippines, the involvement in foreign entanglements that would undermine the logic of the Monroe Doctrine, and the danger that the Philippines would become an Achilles heel, expensive if not impossible to defend. The prospect of incorporating so many alien peoples into American life was not the least of some people's worries. "Bananas and self-government cannot grow on the same piece of land," Senator Pettigrew said.

The opposition may have been strong enough to kill the treaty had not William Jennings Bryan influenced the vote for approval. Ending the war, he argued, would open the way for the future independence of Cuba and the Philippines. Finally, ratification came on February 6, 1899, by a vote of 57 to 27. On February 14 the deciding vote of Vice-President Garret A. Hobart defeated a resolution for Philippine independence. That same month in *McClure's* magazine Rudyard Kipling's poem, "The White Man's Burden," called the American people to a new duty:

> Take up the White Man's burden—
>   Send forth the best ye breed—
> Go, bind your sons to exile
>   To serve your captive's need;
> To wait in heavy harness
>   On fluttered folk and wild—
> Your new-caught sullen peoples,
>   Half devil and half child.

By this time Americans had already clashed with Filipino insurrectionists near Manila. The Filipino leader, Emilio Aguinaldo, was in exile until Commodore Dewey brought him back to Luzon to make trouble for the Spanish. Since Aguinaldo's forces were more or less in control of the islands outside of Manila, what followed was largely an American war of conquest which lasted more than two years. Organized Filipino resistance was broken by the end of 1899, but even after the capture of Aguinaldo in

Philippine insurrectionists, led by Emilio Aguinaldo. [Library of Congress]

March 1901 sporadic guerrilla action lasted until mid-1902. It was a sordid little war, marked by massacre and torture on both sides.

Against the backdrop of this agony the great debate over imperialism continued. The treaty debates inspired a number of anti-imperialist groups which united in October 1899 as the American Anti-Imperialist League. The league attracted members representing many shades of opinion; the main thing they had in common was that most belonged to an older generation. George S. Boutwell, the old Stalwart from Massachusetts, was president, but the group included as well Democrat "Pitchfork Ben" Tillman of South Carolina. Andrew Carnegie footed the bills, but on imperialism at least Samuel Gompers was in agreement with him. The group included such prominent figures as Sens. George F. Hoar and George F. Edmunds, Carl Schurz, Charles Francis Adams, Jr., House Speaker Thomas B. Reed, and John Sherman. Presidents Charles Eliot of Harvard and David Staff Jordan of Stanford supported the group, along with social reformer Jane Addams and editor E. L. Godkin of the *Nation.* The drive for power, said the philosopher William James, had caused the nation to "puke up its ancient soul." Mark Twain addressed a letter "To the Person Sitting in Darkness" (McKinley) suggesting that, given current policies, the flag should have "the white stripes painted black and the stars painted by the skull and cross bones."

ROOSEVELT'S RISE   In the fall elections of 1898 Republicans benefited from the euphoria of victory and increased their majority in

Congress. That hardly amounted to a mandate for imperialism, however, since the election preceded most of the debates on the issue. In 1900 the Democrats turned once again to Bryan, who sought to make imperialism the "paramount issue" of the campaign. The Democratic platform condemned the Philippine involvement as "an unnecessary war" which had "placed the United States, previously known and applauded throughout the world as the champion of freedom, in the false and un-American position of crushing with military force the efforts of our former allies to achieve liberty and self-government."

The Republicans welcomed the issue. They renominated McKinley, and to fill the vacancy left by the death of Vice-President Hobart they turned to Theodore Roosevelt, who after his role in both the Philippine and Cuban action was virtually "Mr. Imperialism." Somehow, whether by luck or design, Roosevelt always had correspondents nearby to report on his actions. And lest the public forget, he had hastened into print with his own account of the Rough Rider—a book the wry Mr. Dooley said should have been entitled "Alone in Cuba." After his triumphant return as a war hero Roosevelt had been elected governor of New York in the fall of 1898. Now he profited from support in the West as well as the East, and perhaps as well from the eagerness of New York's Boss Platt to kick the independent Roosevelt upstairs into the harmless post of vice-president.

"Don't haul down the flag!" was a Republican slogan. The question, Bryan retorted, was "Who will haul down the President?" The trouble with Bryan's idea of a solemn referendum on imperialism was the near impossibility of making any presiden-

This 1900 cartoon shows the Republican vice-presidential candidate, Theodore Roosevelt, overshadowing his running mate, President McKinley. [Horace Taylor, January 1, 1900]

tial contest so simple. Bryan himself complicated things by insisting once again on free silver, and the tariff became an issue again too. The Republican's biggest advantage was probably the return to prosperity, which they were fully ready to take credit for. So those who opposed imperialism but also opposed free silver or tariff reduction faced a bewildering choice. One voter was said to have reasoned finally: "It is a choice between evils, and I am going to shut my eyes, hold my nose, vote, go home and disinfect myself."

The outcome was a victory for McKinley greater than his last, by 7.2 million to 6.4 million in the popular vote and by 292 to 155 in the electoral vote. If there had been no clear-cut referendum on annexations, the question was settled nonetheless, although it would take yet another year and a half to subdue the Filipino rebels. The job would be finished, however, under the direction of another president.

On September 6, 1901, while McKinley attended a reception at the Pan-American Exposition in Buffalo, a fanatical anarchist named Leon Czolgosz approached him with a gun concealed in a bandaged hand and fired at point-blank range. McKinley died six days later and Theodore Roosevelt was suddenly elevated to the White House. "Now look," Mark Hanna erupted, "that damned cowboy is President of the United States!" Six weeks short of his forty-third birthday, Roosevelt was the youngest man ever to reach the office, but he brought to it more experience in public affairs than most and perhaps more vitality than any.

Descended from a line of well-to-do New Yorkers and from the Bullochs of Georgia, son of a wealthy merchant, he grew up in surroundings of comfort and culture, visited Europe as a child, spoke German fluently, and finished Harvard in 1880. A sickly, asthmatic, astigmatic child, he built himself up by force of will into a physical and intellectual athlete, a lifelong preacher and practitioner of the "strenuous life," ready, willing, and able to express opinions on any and all subjects.

After Harvard, Roosevelt read law briefly and within two years of graduation won election to the New York legislature and published *The Naval War of 1812*, the first of a number of historical, biographical, and other writings to flow from his pen. After the untimely death of his first wife he moved west to take up the cattle business on the Dakota frontier. His western career was brief, but he never quite got over being a cowboy. Back in New York he ran for mayor, and later served as civil service commissioner, New York City police commissioner, assistant secretary of the navy, colonel of the "Rough Riders," and governor of New York.

TR *on the stump.*
[Library of Congress]

Teddy Roosevelt was an American original, the embodiment of many a Boy Scout's fantasies. His glittering spectacles and glistening teeth, along with his bouncing ebullience, were a godsend to the cartoonists, who added another trademark when he pronounced the adage: "Speak softly, and carry a big stick." Along with his boundless energy went an unshakable conviction of righteousness and a tendency to cast every issue in moral terms. But appearances were deceiving. The boundless energy left a false impression of impulsiveness and the talk of morality cloaked a cautious pragmatism. Roosevelt could get carried away on occasion, but as he said of his foreign policy steps, this was likely to happen only when "I am assured that I shall be able eventually to carry out my will by force."

ORGANIZING THE NEW ACQUISITIONS   Soon it would be Roosevelt, one of the chief proponents of the American Empire, who would round out its organization. In the Philippines McKinley had already moved toward setting up a civil government. The commission of five he sent to study the situation in the Philippines suggested delay because of unsettled conditions. In 1900 another commission went out under Federal Circuit Judge William Howard Taft with instructions to set up a civil government. Unlike some of the Americans on the scene, Taft seemed genuinely to like the Filipinos and gradually established a rapport with his "little brown brothers." He encouraged them to participate, and eventually to sit on the commission itself.

On July 4, 1901, military government ended and under an act of Congress Taft became the civil governor with appointed provincial governors under his authority. The five-man Philippine Commission continued to function, with three Filipino members added. The Philippine Government Act, passed by Congress on July 1, 1902, made the Philippine Islands an "unorganized territory" and made the inhabitants citizens of the Philippines. When the first elective assembly met in 1907 the commission became the upper house of the legislature—much as the governor's council had been in colonial America. In 1916 the Jones Act made both houses elective and affirmed America's intention to grant the Philippines independence at an indefinite date. Finally, the Tydings-McDuffie Act of 1934 offered independence after a tutelary period of ten more years. A constitution was drafted and ratified, and on September 17 Manuel Quezon was elected the first president of the Philippines. Independence, delayed by World War II, finally took effect on July 4, 1946.

Puerto Rico had been acquired from Spain ostensibly in lieu of a Spanish indemnity, but also as an American outpost on the approaches to the Caribbean and any future isthmian canal. On April 12, 1900, the Foraker Act established a civil government on the island. This act would resemble the one passed two years later for the Philippines. The president appointed a governor and eleven members of an executive council, and an elected house of Delegates made up the lower house of the legislature. Residents of the island were citizens of Puerto Rico but not of the United States until 1917 when the Jones Act granted United States citizenship and made both houses of the legislature elective. In 1947 the governor also became elective, and in 1952 Puerto Rico became a commonwealth with its own constitution and elected officials, a unique status. Like a state, Puerto Rico is free to change its constitution insofar as it does not conflict with the United States Constitution.

The Foraker Act of 1900 also levied a temporary duty on imports from Puerto Rico. The tariff was challenged in the federal courts on the grounds that the island had become part of the United States. In *Downes v. Bidwell* the Supreme Court upheld the tariff. In this and other "Insular Cases" federal judges faced a question which went to the fundamental nature of the American Union, and to the civil and political rights of the people in America's new possessions. In public discussions of the day the issue was summed up in the question: Does the constitution follow the flag? The Court ruled in effect that it did not unless Congress extended it. A concurring opinion by Justice Edward D. White advanced the doctrine of "incorporation." Always before, territories treated as an integral part of the United States had been "incorporated" either by treaty or by act of Congress. Puerto Rico had not, the Court ruled. White suggested "that there may be a distinction between certain natural rights enforced in the Constitution . . . and what may be termed artificial or remedial rights."

Justice John Marshall Harlan confessed that "this idea of 'incorporation' has some occult meaning which my mind does not apprehend." In rapid order, nevertheless, it became an operative doctrine in other cases. The effect was that none of the overseas possessions was declared by the courts "incorporated," not even Hawaii under the Organic Act of 1900, which established a territory in the manner of those on the mainland. Only Alaska was ruled incorporated, although it did not have a territorial government until 1912. In short, outside continental North America Congress could deal with territorial possessions pretty much as it saw fit, except with respect to such fundamental rights as free speech and religion, due process of law, and equal protection of the law.

American authorities soon learned that "Cuba libre" posed problems at least as irksome as those in the new possessions. Cuba's insurgent government was weak and its economy in a state of collapse. Bad relations between American soldiers and Cubans set in almost immediately. General Shafter would not even let the rebels have a hand in the formal surrender of Santiago, and when McKinley set up a military government for the island late in 1898, it was at odds with rebel leaders almost immediately.

Many Europeans expected annexation, and Gen. Leonard Wood, who became Cuba's military governor in December 1899, thought this the best solution. But the United States finally did fulfill the promise of independence for Cuba after the military regime had restored order, gotten schools under way, and improved sanitary conditions. The problem of disease in Cuba provided a focus for the work of Dr. Walter Reed, who made an outstanding contribution to the health of people in warm climates around the world. Named head of the Army Yellow Fever Commission in 1900, he directed experiments with volunteers which proved the theory of Cuban physician Dr. Carlos Finlay that yellow fever was carried by stegomyia mosquitoes. This led the way to effective control of the disease.

In 1900, at President McKinley's order, General Wood called an election for a Cuban constitutional convention. The convention met in November 1900 and drafted a basic law modeled on that of the United States. The Platt Amendment to the Army Appropriation Bill passed by Congress in March 1901, however, sharply restricted the independence of the new government. The amendment required Cuba never to impair its independence by treaty with a third power, to maintain its debt within the government's power to repay out of ordinary revenues, and to acknowledge the right of the United States to intervene for the preservation of Cuban independence and the maintenance of "a government adequate for the protection of life, property, and individual liberty." Finally, Cuba was called upon to sell or lease to the United States lands to be used for coaling or naval stations—a proviso which eventuated in an American naval base at Guantanamo Bay. Under pressure, on June 12, 1901, the Cuban delegates added the Platt Amendment as an appendix to their own constitution. The new Cuban government, established May 20, 1902, then incorporated its provisions in a treaty with the United States signed a year later. As early as August 1906 an insurrection arose against the new government, and President Theodore Roosevelt responded by sending Secretary of War William Howard Taft to "sit on the lid"—weighing in at more than 300 pounds, he was not a bad choice for the job. Backed up by American armed forces Taft assumed full governmental authority, as he had in the Philippines, and the American army stayed until 1909 when a new president was peacefully elected. Further interventions would follow for more than two decades: in 1912 under President Taft, in 1917 under Woodrow Wilson, and in 1933 when President Franklin D. Roosevelt dispatched warships to Cuba. In 1934, however, as part of his "Good Neighbor Policy," Roosevelt negotiated a new treaty which abrogated the Platt Amendment.

IMPERIAL RIVALRIES IN THE FAR EAST

CHINA AND THE "OPEN DOOR"   During the 1890s not only the United States but also Japan emerged as a world power. Commodore Perry's voyage of 1853–1854 had opened Japan to Western ways and the country began modernization in earnest after the 1860s, when the Meiji Restoration overthrew the old shogunate. Flexing its new muscles, Japan engaged the moribund Chinese Empire in the Sino-Japanese War (1894–1895) and as a result picked up the Pescadores Islands and the island of Taiwan (renamed Formosa). China's weakness, demonstrated in the war, brought the great powers into a scramble for leaseholds and "spheres of influence" on that remaining frontier of imperialist expansion. Russia secured the privilege of building a railroad across Manchuria and established itself in Port Arthur and the

U.S. INTERESTS IN THE PACIFIC
Dates indicate year of acquisition
or occupation by U.S.

Liaotung Peninsula. The Germans moved into Shantung, the French into Kwangchow Bay, the British into Wei-hai-wei.

The bright prospect of American trade with China dimmed with the possibility that the great powers would throw up tariff barriers in their own spheres of influence. The British, ensconced at Hong Kong since 1840, had more to lose though, for they already had far and away the largest foreign trade with China. Just before the Spanish-American War, in March 1898, British Minister Sir Julian Pauncefote suggested joint action with the United States to preserve the integrity of China, and renewed the proposal early in 1899. Both times it was rejected by the Senate because it risked an entangling alliance.

In its origins and content, what soon came to be known as the Open Door Policy was reminiscent of the Monroe Doctrine. In both cases the United States proclaimed unilaterally a hands-off policy which the British had earlier proposed as a joint statement. The policy outlined in Secretary of State John Hay's Open Door Note, dispatched on September 6, 1899, to London, Berlin, and St. Petersburg, and a little later to Tokyo, Rome, and Paris, proposed to keep China open to trade with all countries on an equal basis. More specifically it called upon foreign powers, within their spheres of influence: (1) not to interfere with any treaty port (a port open to all by treaty) or any vested interest, (2) to permit Chinese authorities to collect tariffs on an equal basis, and (3) to show no favors to their own nationals in the matter of harbor dues or railroad charges. Hay's request that each of the powers accept these principles was, the diplomat George Kennan later wrote, like asking everyone who believes in truth to stand: the liars would be the first on their feet. As it turned out, none except Britain accepted Hay's principles, but none rejected them either. The rest gave equivocal answers, usually conditioned on the action of the others. On March 20 Hay blandly announced that all powers had accepted the policy. None stood to deny it.

Soon after that a new crisis arose. In June 1900 a group of Chinese nationalists known to the Western world as Boxers ("Fists of Righteous Harmony") rose in rebellion against foreign encroachments on China laying siege to foreign embassies in Peking. An international expedition of British, German, Russian, Japanese, and American forces was quickly mounted to relieve the embassy compound. Hay, fearful that the intervention might become an excuse to dismember China, seized the chance to further refine the Open Door Policy. The United States, he said in a circular letter of July 3, 1900, sought a solution which would "preserve Chinese territorial and administrative integrity" as well as "equal and impartial trade with all parts of the Chinese Empire."

On August 14 the expedition reached Peking and broke the

This Puck *cartoon shows "Civilization" accusing the Chinese government of complicity in the Boxer Rebellion.* [Library of Congress]

Boxer Rebellion. The occupying powers then agreed to settle for an indemnity from China of approximately $333 million. Of this total the United States got $25 million, of which nearly $11 million was refunded once all claims were paid. Most of this the Chinese government put into a fund to support Chinese students in American colleges.

The Open Door Policy, if rooted in the self-interest of American businessmen eager to exploit the markets of China, also tapped the deep-seated sympathies of those who opposed imperialism, especially as it endorsed China's territorial integrity. But it had little more legal standing than a pious affirmation. When the Japanese, concerned about Russian pressure in Manchuria, asked Hay how he intended to enforce the policy, Hay replied that the United States was "not prepared . . . to enforce these views on the east by any demonstration which could present a character of hostility to any other power." So it would remain for forty years, until American insistence upon the integrity of China would bring war with Japan in 1941.

THE RUSSO-JAPANESE WAR   For the time being, however, Hay's policy was hailed as a brilliant success. It worked after a fashion, but less because of its moral authority than because the powers meddling in China tended to balance each other off. The balance was upset, however, when rivalries between Russia and Japan flared into a fight over the prostrate forms of China and Korea. Russian encroachments had brought about a fifteen-year defensive treaty with China in 1896, in which China conceded to Russia the right to build the Chinese Eastern Railway across Manchuria, providing a shorter route to Vladivostok. In 1898 Russia secured a leasehold at Port Arthur on the Liaotung Peninsula with the right to build a rail line southward from Harbin, Manchuria. Russian ambitions soon extended to Korea, in which Japan too was interested, prompting Japan to make a defensive alliance in 1902 with Great Britain, which feared Russian threats to her interests in Asia and the Mediterranean.

On February 8, 1904, war broke out when the Japanese launched a surprise attack on Port Arthur, devastated the Russian fleet, occupied Korea, and drove the Russians back into Manchuria. But neither side could score a knockout blow, and neither relished a long stalemate. When the Japanese signaled President Roosevelt that they would welcome help in a settlement, the president agreed to sponsor a peace conference in Portsmouth, New Hampshire. In the Treaty of Portsmouth, signed on September 5, 1905, the concessions all went to the

Japanese. Russia acknowledged Japan's "predominant political military, and economic interests in Korea" (Japan would annex the kingdom in 1910), and ceded to Japan the leasehold at Port Arthur, railroad rights, and the southern half of Sakhalin Island. Both powers agreed to evacuate Manchuria.

AMERICA'S RELATIONS WITH JAPAN   American sentiment at first favored the Japanese as a counterweight to Russian aggression, but Japan's show of strength in the war raised doubts about the security of the Philippines. During the Portsmouth talks Roosevelt sent William Howard Taft to meet with the Japanese foreign minister in Tokyo and the two men arrived at the Taft-Katsura Agreement of July 29, 1905, in which the United States accepted Japanese control of Korea and Japan disavowed any designs on the Philippines. The understanding was reinforced by the Root-Takahira Agreement on November 30, 1908, negotiated by Secretary of State Elihu Root and the Japanese ambassador, in which both sides endorsed the status quo, promised to respect the other's possessions, and reinforced the Open Door Policy by supporting "the independence and integrity of China" and "the principle of equal opportunity for commerce and industry in China."

Behind the diplomatic facade of goodwill, however, lay mutual distrust. At Portsmouth the Japanese had hoped to get financial indemnities from Russia; they blamed their failure on the United States, and especially President Roosevelt, who had indeed opposed indemnities. For many Americans the Russian threat in East Asia now gave way to the "yellow peril" of Japan.° Racial animosities on the West Coast helped sour relations with Japan. In October 1906 the San Francisco school board ordered students of Chinese, Japanese, and Korean descent to attend a separate public school. The Japanese government sharply protested this show of prejudice, and President Roosevelt managed to talk the school board into changing its mind after making sure that Japanese authorities would not issue passports to "laborers" except former residents of the United States, the parents, wives, or children of residents, or those who already possessed interest in an American farming enterprise. This "Gentlemen's Agreement" of 1907, the precise terms of which have never been revealed, halted the influx of Japanese immigrants and brought some respite in racial agitations in California.

°The term "yellow peril" was apparently coined by Kaiser Wilhelm II of Germany.

TR's FOREIGN POLICY

BUILDING THE PANAMA CANAL   After the Spanish-American War
the United States became more deeply involved in the Caribbean area. One issue overshadowed every other in the region:
the Panama Canal. The narrow isthmus of Panama had excited
dreams of an interoceanic canal ever since Balboa's crossing in
1513. Admiral Mahan regarded a canal as important to American
commerce and naval power, a point dramatized in 1898 by the
long voyage of the battleship *Oregon* around South America's
Cape Horn to join the fleet off Cuba.

Transit across the isthmus had first become a strong concern of
the United States in the 1840s when it became an important
route to the California gold fields. Two treaties dating from that
period loomed years later as obstacles to construction of a canal.
The Bidlack Treaty (1848) with Colombia (then New Granada)
guaranteed both Colombia's sovereignty over Panama and the
neutrality of the isthmus, so that "free transit . . . not be embarrassed in any future time." In the Clayton-Bulwer Treaty (1850)

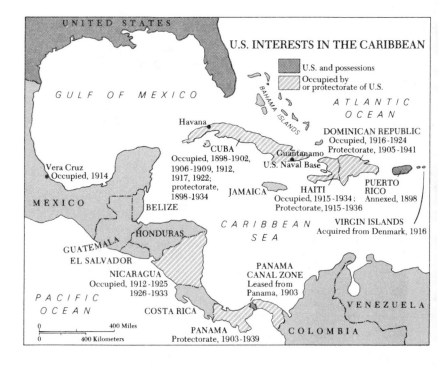

the British agreed to acquire no more Central America territory, and the United States joined them in agreeing to build or fortify a canal only by mutual consent.

After the Spanish-American War, Secretary Hay commenced talks with the British ambassador to estsablish such consent. The outcome was the Hay-Pauncefote Treaty of February 1900, but the Senate rejected it on the grounds that it forbade fortification of the canal and required that the canal be neutral even in time of war. By then a bill was already pending in Congress for a Nicaraguan canal and the British apparently decided to accept the inevitable. In November 1901 the Senate ratified a second Hay-Pauncefote Treaty which simply omitted reference to the former limitations.

Other obstacles remained, however. From 1881 to 1887 a French company (Compagnie Universelle du Canal Interocéanique) under Ferdinand de Lesseps, who had engineered the Suez Canal in 1877, had spent nearly $300 million and some 20,000 lives to dig less than a third of the canal through Panama. The company now wanted $109 million for its holdings. Consequently an Isthmian Canal Commission, appointed by McKinley, reported in 1901 that a Nicaraguan route would be cheaper. When the House of Representatives quickly passed an act for construction there, the Panama Company lowered its price to $40 million and the Canal Commission made Panama its first choice.

Meanwhile Secretary Hay had opened negotiations with Ambassador Thomas Herrán of Colombia. In return for a Canal Zone six miles wide, the United States agreed to pay $10 million in cash and a rental fee of $250,000 a year. The United States Senate ratified the Hay-Herrán Treaty in 1903, but the Colombian Senate held out for $25 million in cash. At this action of those "foolish and homicidal corruptionists at Bogotá," Theodore Roosevelt, by then president, flew into a rage punctuated by references to "dagoes" and "contemptible little creatures." Meanwhile in Panama, an isolated province long at odds with the remote Colombian authorities in Bogotá, feeling was heightened by Colombia's rejection of the treaty. One Manuel Amador, an employee of the French canal company, then hatched a plot in close collusion with the company's representatives Philippe Bunau-Varilla and William Nelson Cromwell. Bunau-Varilla paid visits to Roosevelt and Hay and, apparently with inside information, informed the conspirators that the U.S.S. *Nashville* would call at Colón in Panama on November 2.

With an army of some 500, reinforced by Colón's fire department, Amador staged a revolt the next day. Colombian troops,

A *New York* Times *cartoon suggests that Bunau-Varilla*
and TR were behind Panama's revolt against Colombia.
Their aim: to secure American rights to build a Panama-
nian canal. [Drake in the New York Times]

who could scarcely penetrate the overland jungle, found American ships athwart the sea lanes. On November 13 the Roosevelt
administration received its first ambassador from Panama, whose
name happened to be Philippe Bunau-Varilla, and on November
18 signed a treaty which extended the Canal Zone from six to ten
miles in width. For $10 million down and $250,000 a year the
United States got "in perpetuity the use, occupation and control" of the zone. Just who got the $40 million paid to the French
canal company remains unknown. Attorney-General Philander
C. Knox, asked to supply a legal opinion upholding Roosevelt's
actions, responded wryly: "No, Mr. President, if I were you I
would not have any taint of legality about it."

In 1904 Congress created a new Isthmian Canal Commission
to direct construction. Despite sanitary problems, the biggest
obstacle at first, Roosevelt instructed the commission to make
the "dirt fly." Speaking to an audience at the University of California in 1911, he said: "If I had followed traditional, conservative methods I would have submitted a dignified State paper of
probably 200 pages to Congress and the debates on it would
have been going on yet; but I took the Canal Zone and let Congress debate; and while the debate goes on the Canal does also."

And so did a rankling resentment in Colombia. By needlessly
offending Latin American sensibilities, Roosevelt had committed
one of the greatest blunders in American foreign policy. Colombia eventually got its $25 million from the Harding administra-
tion, but only once America's interest in Colombia oil had
lubricated the wheels of diplomacy. There was no apology, but
the payment was made to remove "all misunderstandings grow-

ing out of the political events in Panama, November, 1903."
Meanwhile the canal had opened on August 15, 1914, less than
two weeks after the outbreak of World War I in Europe.

THE ROOSEVELT COROLLARY   Even without the canal, the United
States would have been concerned with the stability of the Caribbean area, and particularly with the activities of any hostile
power. A prime excuse for intervention in those days was to
force the collection of debts owed to foreign nationals. In 1904 a
crisis over the debts of the Dominican Republic gave Roosevelt
an opportunity to formulate American policy. In his annual address to Congress in 1904 he set forth what came to be known as
the Roosevelt Corollary to the Monroe Doctrine: the principle,
in short, was that since the Monroe Doctrine enjoined intervention in the region by Europeans, the United States was justified
in intervening first to forestall the actions of outsiders.

In the president's words the Roosevelt Corollary held that:
"Chronic wrongdoing . . . may in America, as elsewhere, ultimately require intervention by some civilized nation, and in the
Western Hemisphere the adherence of the United States to the
Monroe Doctrine may force the United States, however reluctantly, in flagrant cases of such wrongdoing or impotence, to the
exercise of an international police power." As put into practice
by mutual agreement with the Dominican Republic in 1905, the
Roosevelt Corollary called for the United States to install and
protect a collector of customs who would apply 55 percent of his
revenues to debt payments.

The World's Constable. *TR, shown here as the world's
policeman, wields the "big stick" symbolizing his
approach to diplomacy. [Library of Congress]*

DOLLAR DIPLOMACY The principle, applied peaceably in 1905, became the basis for more forcible interventions later. During President Taft's term (1909–1913) refinements of the policy earned from its opponents the less exalted—if fairly descriptive—title of "dollar diplomacy." The policy so tagged had its origin in China in 1909, when President Taft personally cabled the Chinese government on behalf of American financiers interested in an international consortium to finance railroad lines in the Yangtze Valley. Philander C. Knox, by then secretary of state, wrote that the government regarded such cooperation "as best calculated to maintain the Open Door and the integrity of China." In 1911 the Americans were let in on the deal with British, French, and German capitalists, and in 1912 entered an even larger scheme to make a gigantic loan to the new Chinese Republic. Both schemes were repudiated, however, when Woodrow Wilson became president in 1913, and the American investors, lacking support from the government, withdrew.

In Latin America "dollar diplomacy" worked differently and with somewhat more success. The idea was to encourage American bankers to help prop up the finances of shaky governments in the Caribbean region. In 1910 Knox got several lenders to invest in the national bank of Haiti. In 1911 he signed treaties with Nicaragua and Honduras providing them with private loans to bolster their treasuries and ensuring payment by installing American collectors of customs. The Senate refused to go along with the treaties, but the administration continued its private appeals for American bankers to assume debts in the region.

In 1912, however, when the Nicaraguan president asked for help in putting down disorders, American marines entered the country. An American collector of customs was then installed and the government placed on a monthly allowance doled out by a commission of two Americans and one Nicaraguan. American forces stayed until 1925, then returned in 1926 to stay until 1933. Similar forcible interventions occurred in Haiti in 1915 and the Dominican Republic in 1916.

THE UNITED STATES AND EUROPE During the years of expansionism the United States was looking mainly westward and southward. Toward Europe's affairs the fixed policy was, as Admiral Mahan affirmed it should be, abstention. Differences between the United States and European powers usually had to do with possessions in the Western Hemisphere, and one such matter came to a head during Roosevelt's presidency: the Alaskan boundary dispute. Years before the American purchase in 1867 an Anglo-

Russian Treaty of 1825 had given the boundary of the Alaska panhandle a geographically impossible definition. Nobody cared much until 1896, when gold was discovered in the Canadian Klondike to which the panhandle offered the readiest access. The Canadians then pressed an extreme claim whereby they would control the heads of the major inlets.

In 1899 Secretary Hay proposed a commission of six, three chosen by each side, to draw the line. A renewal of the offer in 1902 led to a treaty early the next year. The "impartial jurists" named for the panel by Roosevelt included Secretary of War Elihu Root, Roosevelt's close friend Henry Cabot Lodge, and George Turner, a former senator from Washington, a state with an intense interest in the boundary. Roosevelt also got word indirectly to the British leaders that if the commission decided wrongly, he planned to run the line by force, if need be. As it turned out only the two Canadian members of the board held out for their extreme claim. The one British member voted with the Americans for a line that would give the United States control of the major inlets. It was the third major understanding between the two powers in a dozen years (the fur seal and Venezuelan settlements were the others) and it opened the way to a growing rapprochement in Anglo-American relations.

To Roosevelt, however, total abstention from European affairs was an improper stance for a newly arrived world power. While he was moving toward mediation of the Russo-Japanese War in 1905, another dangerous crisis began heating up in Morocco. There, on March 31, 1905, German Kaiser Wilhelm II stepped ashore at Tangier and gave a saber-rattling speech defending the independence of the sultan. This was a deliberate response to growing French influence there, and particularly to the Franco-British Entente of 1904, under which Britain recognized French dominance in Morocco in return for French recognition of British dominance in Egypt. The kaiser's speech aroused a diplomatic storm of dangerous proportions. Roosevelt felt that the United States had something at stake in preventing the outbreak of a major war. At the kaiser's behest he talked the French and British into attending an international conference at Algeciras, Spain, with American delegates present. Roosevelt then maneuvered the Germans into accepting his lead.

The Act of Algeciras, signed on April 7, 1906, affirmed the independence of Morocco and guaranteed an open door for trade there, but provided for the training and control of Moroccan police by France and Spain. The United States Senate ratified the agreement, but only with the provison that it was not to be construed as a departure from America's traditional policy of noninvolvement in European affairs. It was, of course, and one that may well have prevented a general war, or at least postponed it until 1914. Roosevelt received the Nobel Peace Prize in 1906 for his work at Portsmouth and Algeciras. For all his bellicosity on other occasions, he had earned it.

Before Roosevelt left the White House he celebrated America's rise to world power with one great flourish. In December 1907 he sent the United States Navy, by then second only to the British, on a grand tour around the world, their commander announcing he was ready for "a feast, a frolic, or a fight." He got mostly the first two, and none of the last. At every port of call the "Great White Fleet" set off rousing celebrations, down the Atlantic coast of South America, up the west coast, out to Hawaii, and down under to New Zealand and Australia. It was the first such show of American naval might in the Pacific, and many feared the reaction of the Japanese, for whose benefit Roosevelt had in fact staged the show. They need not have worried, for in Japan the flotilla got the greatest welcome of all. Thousands of schoolchildren turned out waving tiny American flags and singing "The Star Spangled Banner" in English. The triumphal procession continued home by way of the Mediterranean, and steamed back into American waters in February 1909, just in time to close out Roosevelt's presidency on a note of success.

But it was a success that would have mixed consequences. As one close student of Roosevelt's role in America's rise to world power wrote: "One comes away from the study with admiration for Roosevelt's ability, his energy, and his devotion to his country's interests as he saw them but with a sense of tragedy that his abilities were turned toward imperialism and an urge for power, which were to have consequences so serious for the future." Roosevelt had influenced the United States "in a direction that . . . was to bring her face to face with grave dangers" before the mid–twentieth century.

FURTHER READING

Two recent surveys trace Gilded Age diplomacy and lend a balanced treatment to current interpretations: consult Charles S. Campbell's *The Transformation of American Foreign Relations, 1865–1900* (1976),° and Robert L. Beisner's shorter *From the Old Diplomacy to the*

°These books are available in paperback editions.

New, 1865–1900 (1975).° Ernest R. May's *Imperial Democracy: The Emergence of America as a Great Power* (1961)° is more traditional. Relevant chapters in Lloyd C. Gardner, Walter LaFeber, and Thomas McCormick's *The Creation of the American Empire* (1973)° give condensed treatment to revisionist interpretations. William Appleman Williams's *The Tragedy of American Diplomacy* (1972)° advances most clearly the economic interpretation. Marilyn B. Young (ed.), *American Expansion: The Critical Issues* (1973), reviews the scholarly debate over imperialistic motives.

Particularly useful as background for the events of the 1890s are Walter LaFeber's *The New Empire: An Interpretation of American Expansion, 1860–1898* (1963), and Milton Plesur's *America's Outward Thrust: Approaches to Foreign Affairs, 1865–1890* (1971).° Also useful is David Pletcher's *The Awkward Years: America's Foreign Relations under Garfield and Arthur* (1962). To elaborate on the influence of A. T. Mahan, consult Peter Karster's *The Naval Aristocracy* (1972). Richard Hofstadter's *Social Darwinism in American Thought* (1949) details the intellectual justifications for expansion.

An early dispute over American policy in the Pacific is covered in Thomas J. Osborne's *"Empire Can Wait": American Opposition to Hawaiian Annexation, 1893–1898* (1981), and William A. Russ, Jr.'s *The Hawaiian Republic, 1894–98, and Its Struggle to Win Annexation* (1961).

David Healy's *United States Expansion: The Imperialist Urge in the 1890s* (1970) provides a survey of that decade, while David F. Transk's lengthy *The War with Spain* (1981) is the comprehensive volume on that conflict. Other accounts include H. Wayne Morgan's concise *America's Road to Empire: The War with Spain and Overseas Expansion* (1965)° and Frank Friedel's *The Splendid Little War* (1958). More detailed and revisionist is Philip S. Foner's *The Spanish-Cuban American War and the Birth of American Imperialism* (2 vols.; 1972). A special angle is taken in Charles H. Brown's *The Correspondents' War: Journalists in the Spanish-American War* (1967). For the role played by political leadership, see Lewis L. Gould's *The Presidency of William McKinley* (1980). Richard Challener's *Admirals, Generals, and American Foreign Policy, 1889–1914* (1973), stresses the influence of the military in the war, while Graham A. Cosmos's *An Army for Empire: The United States Army in the Spanish-American War* (1971) concentrates on infantry operations in Cuba.

The effects of victory in the Pacific are gauged by James Thomson, Jr., Peter Stanley, and John C. Perry in *Sentimental Imperialists: The American Experience in East Asia* (1981).° More specific are Stuart C. Miller's *"Benevolent Assimulation": American Conquest of the Philippines, 1899–1903* (1982), and Peter Stanley's *A Nation in the Making: The Philippines and the United States* (1974). Also useful is Glenn May's *Social Engineering in the Philippines* (1980). For the debate over annexation, see Robert L. Beisner's *Twelve against Empire: The Anti-Imperialists, 1898–1900* (1968), and E. Berkeley Tompkins's *Anti-Imperialism in the United States: The Great Debate, 1890–1920* (1970).

A good introducton to American interest in China is Robert McClellan's *The Heathen Chinese: A Study of American Attitudes toward China* (1971). More expansive is Marilyn B. Young's *The Rhetoric for Empire: America's China Policy, 1893–1901* (1968). Two interpretations of the Open Door are Thomas McCormick's *China Market: America's Quest for Informal Empire, 1893–1901* (1967),° and Paul A. Varg's *The Making of a Myth: The United States and China, 1899–1922* (1968). For the immediate consequences of the Open Door, see Warren Cohen's *America's Response to China* (1971) and Jerry Israel's *Progressivism and the Open Door: America and China, 1905–1921* (1971). Kenton J. Clymer's *John Hay: The Gentleman as Diplomat* (1975) examines the role of this key secretary of state in forming policy.

Works which deal with the role of Theodore Roosevelt in foreign policy both before and during his time as president include Howard K. Beale's *Theodore Roosevelt and the Rise of America to World Power* (1956), Raymond A. Esthus's *Theodore Roosevelt and the International Rivalries* (1970), and Edmund Morris's *The Rise of Theodore Roosevelt* (1979).° Roosevelt's influence also shows through in Robert A. Hart's *The Great White Fleet: Its Voyage around the World* (1965) and Robert C. Hildebrand's *Power and the People: Executive Management of Public Opinion in Foreign Affairs, 1897–1921* (1981).

David McCollough's *Path between the Seas: The Creation of the Panama Canal, 1870–1914* (1977),° presents the fullest account of how the United States secured the canal. Walter LaFeber's *The Panama Canal: The Crisis in Historical Perspective* (1970)° gives a revisionist interpretation of American policy on the canal. Dwight C. Miner's *Fight for the Panama Canal* (1966) covers the political intrigues involved. Policy subsequent to Roosevelt is the subject of Walter V. Scholes and Marive V. Scholes's *The Foreign Policies of the Taft Administration* (1970) and Dana G. Muroe's *Intervention and Dollar Diplomacy in the Caribbean, 1900–1921* (1964).

24

PROGRESSIVISM: ROOSEVELT, TAFT, AND WILSON

Elements of Reform

Theodore Roosevelt was an ambitious man whose eagerness to leave his mark moved easily from the world arena to his own country. But Roosevelt was more calculating in domestic politics than in foreign affairs and more inclined to follow the dictates of experience. He recognized that 1901 was no time for a "big stick" domestic policy.

The prudence Roosevelt displayed in making domestic policy, if uncharacteristic of the man, was a necessity of the time. Roosevelt's emergence as a national leader coincided roughly with the onset of progressivism, a reform movement so broad-gauged it almost defied definition.

The Progressives saw themselves as engaged in a democratic reform movement against the abuses of Gilded Age bosses and robber barons. Their goals were greater democracy, good government, the regulation of business, social justice, and public service. But the Kansas editor William Allen White hinted at a paradox in the movement when he called progressivism just populism that had "shaved its whiskers, washed its shirt, put on a derby, and moved up into the middle class." As White suggested, urban business and professional leaders brought to progressivism a certain respectability that populism had lacked. They also brought a more businesslike, efficient approach to reform. While progressivism still had about it the glorious glow of agrarian democracy and its antitrust traditions, newer themes of efficiency soon gained ascendancy. Even farm groups abandoned the mass movement for more bureaucratic forms of organization. In so doing, they and other Progressives may have been trying to find identity, no longer derived from the local community, in business and professional groups.

Another paradox in the movement was that it contained an element of conservatism. In some cases the regulation of business turned out actually to be regulation *by* businessmen, who preferred stability to the chaos and uncertainty of unrestrained competition. It should be clear, then, that when we speak of a Progressive movement, we refer to the common spirit of an age rather than to an organized group or party. Much like the reform spirit of the 1830s and 1840s, once called Jacksonian Democracy, progressivism was diverse in both origins and tendencies. Few people adhered to all progressive causes. Most, like Theodore Roosevelt, were selective.

ANTECEDENTS TO PROGRESSIVISM   Populism was indisputably one of the harbingers of progressivism. The program the Populists set forth in their platform of 1892 outlined many reforms that would be accomplished in the progressive era. Many old populists, in addition, believed that their movement achieved vindication in the progressive era. William Allen White wrote that populism "was the beginning of a movement that in another decade was to change the politics of the nation: indeed it was a symptom of a world wide drift to liberalism, which reached its peak in Christendom twenty-five years later."

After the collapse of the farmers' movement the focus of the reform spirit shifted to cities, where middle-class reformers had for years attacked the problems of political bossism and urban development. The Mugwumps, those gentlemen reformers who had fought the spoils system and promoted a civil service based on merit, supplied the Progressive movement with an important element of its thinking, the good-government ideal. Over the years their ranks had been supplemented and the good-government outlook broadened by leaders who confronted such new urban problems as crime, vice, and the efficient provision of gas, electricity, water, sewers, mass transit, and garbage collection.

Finally, a minor but significant force in fostering the spirit of progressivism was the growing familiarity of socialist doctrines and their critiques of living and working conditions. The Socialist party of the time can be considered the left wing of progressivism. Still, most Progressives found socialist remedies unacceptable, and the Progressive reform impulse grew in part from a desire to counter the growing influence of socialist doctrines. More important in spurring Progressive reform, however, were those social critics who over the years had attacked the social evils of American life. Chief among these were thinkers such as Lester F. Ward, Henry George, Henry Demarest Lloyd, Jacob Riis, and Thorstein Veblen.

THE MUCKRAKERS In the early twentieth century the exposure of social evils became a profitable enterprise. The writers who thrived on exposing scandal got their name when Theodore Roosevelt compared them to a character in John Bunyan's *Pilgrim's Progress:* "A man that could look no way but downwards with a muckrake in his hands." The "muckrakers" (and TR was no mean muckraker himself) "are often indispensable to ... society," Roosevelt said, "but only if they know when to stop raking the muck."

Henry Demarest Lloyd is sometimes cited as the first of the muckrakers for his critical examination of the Standard Oil Company and other monopolies, *Wealth against Commonwealth* (1894). Lloyd exposed the growth of corporate giants responsible to none but themselves, able to corrupt if not control governments. Another early muckraker was Jacob August Riis, a Danish immigrant who as an influential New York journalist exposed slum conditions in *How the Other Half Lives* (1890) and *The Battle with the Slum* (1902). The chief outlets for these social critics were the cheap popular magazines which began to flourish in the 1890s, such as *The Arena* and *McClure's Magazine,* founded in 1893 by Samuel S. McClure, an Irish immigrant who had begun the first newspaper syndicate in the country.

The golden age of muckraking is sometimes dated from October 1902 when *McClure's* began to run articles by the reporter Lincoln Steffens on municipal corruption, later collected into a book: *The Shame of the Cities* (1904). *McClure's* also ran Ida M. Tarbell's *History of the Standard Oil Company* (1904). McClure had set her to research on the project more than three years before. The result was a more detailed treatment than the earlier book by Lloyd, but all the more damaging in its detail. Other outstanding books which began as magazine articles included Thomas Lawson's *Frenzied Finance* (1904), on stock-market manipulation; Charles Edward Russell's *The Greatest Trust in the World* (1905), on the meat industry; David Graham Phillip's *The Treason of the Senate* (1906), on the influence of special interests; Burton J. Hendrick's *The Story of Life Insurance* (1907); and Ray Stannard Baker's *Following the Color Line* (1908). The inexhaustible market for scandal even absorbed such tomes as Gustavus Myers's *History of the Great American Fortunes* (3 vols., 1910).

Without the muckrakers, progressivism surely would never have achieved the popular support it had. In feeding the public's appetite for facts about their new urban industrial society, the muckrakers demonstrated one of the salient features of the Progressive movement, and one of its central failures. The Progressives were stronger on diagnosis than on remedy, thereby reflecting a naïve faith in the power of democracy. Let the people know, expose corruption, and bring government close to the people, went the rationale, and the correction of evils would follow automatically. The cure for the ills of democracy was more democracy.

THE FEATURES OF PROGRESSIVISM

DEMOCRACY   The most important reform with which the Progressives tried to democratize government was the direct primary or the nomination of candidates by the vote of party members. Under the existing convention system, the reasoning went, only a small proportion of the voters attended the local caucuses or precinct meetings which sent delegates to county, and in turn to state and national, conventions. While the system allowed seasoned leaders to sift the candidates, it also lent itself to domination by political professionals who were organized to turn out early and stay late. Direct primaries at the local level had been held sporadically since the 1870s, but after South Carolina adopted the first statewide primary in 1896 the movement spread within two decades to nearly every state.

The primary was but one expression of a broad movement for direct democracy. In 1898 South Dakota became the first state to adopt the initiative and referendum, procedures which allowed voters to enact laws directly. If a designated number of voters petitioned to have a measure put on the ballot (the initiative), the electorate could then vote it up or down (the referendum). Oregon, largely through the influence of William S. U'Ren, a blacksmith turned editor and lawyer, adopted a whole spectrum of reform measures including a voter registration law (1899); the initiative and referendum (1902); the direct primary (1904); a sweeping corrupt-practices act (1908); and the recall (1910), whereby public officials could be removed by petition and vote. Within a decade nearly twenty states had adopted the initiative and referendum and nearly a dozen the recall.

Most states came to use the party primary even in the choice of United States senators. Nevada was first, in 1899, to let voters express a choice which state legislators of their party were expected to follow in choosing senators. The popular election of senators required a constitutional amendment, and the House of Representatives four times adopted such an amendment (in 1894, 1898, 1900, and 1902) only to see it defeated in the Senate, which came under increasing attack as a "millionaire's club." By 1912 thirty states had provided preferential primaries. The Senate in that year finally accepted the inevitable and agreed to the Seventeenth Amendment, authorizing popular election of senators. The amendment was ratified in 1913.

EFFICIENCY A second major theme of progressivism was the "gospel of efficiency," which found a home in both private and public bureaucracies. In the business world during those years Frederick W. Taylor, the original "efficiency expert," was developing the techniques he summed up in his book *The Principles of Scientific Management* (1911): efficient management of time and costs, the proper routing and scheduling of work, standardization of tools and equipment, and the like. In government, efficiency demanded the reorganization of agencies to prevent overlapping, to establish clear lines of authority, and to fix responsibility. One long-held theory had it that the greater the number of offices chosen by popular vote the greater the degree of democracy, but Progressives considered this inefficient. They believed that voters could make wiser choices if they had a shorter ballot and chose fewer officials in whom power and responsibility were clearly lodged. Many states and localities worked at rationalizing their finances by equalizing tax assessments, and during the first decades of the twentieth century by adopting budget systems. The federal government finally got around to a budget system with passage of the Budget and Accounting Act in 1921.

Two new ideas for making municipal government more efficient gained headway in the first decade of the new century. The commission system, first adopted by Galveston, Texas, in 1901, when local government there collapsed in the aftermath of a hurricane and tidal wave, placed ultimate authority in a board composed of elected administrative heads of city departments—commissioners of sanitation, police, utilities, and so on. The more durable idea, however, was the city-manager plan, under which a professional administrator ran the government in accordance with policies set by the elected council and mayor. Staunton, Virginia, first adopted the plan in 1908. By 1914 the

National Association of City Managers heralded the arrival of a new profession.

When America was a preindustrial society, Andrew Jackson's notion that any reasonably intelligent citizen could perform the duties of any public office may have been true. In the more complex age of the early twentieth century it was apparent that many functions of government and business had come to require expert specialists. This principle was promoted by progressive Gov. Robert M. La Follette of Wisconsin (1901–1906), who established a Legislative Reference Bureau to provide research, advice, and help in the drafting of legislation. The "Wisconsin Idea" of efficient government was widely publicized and copied. La Follette also worked for such reforms as the primary, stronger railroad regulation, the conservation of natural resources, and workmen's compensation. Counterparts to La Follette appeared as progressive governors in other states. In 1905 Joseph W. Folk was elected governor of Missouri after prosecuting and convicting a ring of boodlers (corruptionists) in St. Louis. As counsel to a legislative committee in New York, Charles Evans Hughes became a national figure by uncovering spectacular insurance frauds and won the governorship in 1906. In Georgia and Alabama that year Hoke Smith and Braxton Bragg Comer won governorships by promising to regulate the railroads. Hiram Johnson of California, after getting in 1908 a conviction of Abe Ruef, the grafting boss of San Francisco, won the governorship in 1910 on the promise of reining in the Southern Pacific Railroad.

REGULATION   Of all the problems facing American society, one engaged a greater diversity of reformers, and elicited more—and more controversial—solutions than any other: the regulation of giant corporations, which became a third major theme of progressivism. Concern over the concentration of economic power had brought bipartisan support to the passage of the Sherman Anti-Trust Act in 1890, but in its effects the act had turned out to be more symbolic than effective.

The problem of economic power and its abuse offered a dilemma for Progressives. Four broad solutions were available, but of these, two were extremes which had limited support: letting business work out its own destiny under a policy of laissez-faire, or adopting a socialist program of public ownership. At the municipal level, however, the socialist alternative was rather widely adopted in public utilities and transportation—so-called gas and water socialism—but otherwise was not seriously considered as a general policy. The other choices were either to adopt a policy of trust-busting in the belief that restoring old-fashioned competition would best prevent economic abuses, or to accept big business in the belief that it brought economies of scale, but to regulate it to prevent abuses.

Efforts to restore the competition of small firms proved unworkable, partly because breaking up large combinations was complex and difficult. The trend over the years was toward regulation of big business. To some extent regulation and "stabilization" won acceptance among businessmen who, whatever respect they paid to competition in the abstract, preferred not to face it in person. In the long run, although it was not at first apparent, regulation posed the problem raised in the old maxim: Who will guard the guards? Regulatory agencies often came under the influence or control of those they were supposed to regulate. Railroad men, for instance, generally had more intimate knowledge of the intricate details involved in their business, giving them the advantage over the outsiders who might be appointed to the Interstate Commerce Commission.

SOCIAL JUSTICE   A fourth important feature of the progressive spirit was the impulse toward social justice, which motivated diverse actions from private charities to campaigns against child labor and liquor. The settlement house movement of the late nineteenth century had spawned a corps of social workers and genteel reformers devoted to the uplift of slum dwellers. But with time it became apparent that social evils extended beyond the reach of private charities and demanded the power of the state. Progressives found that old codes of private ethics and accountability scarcely applied to a complex industrial order. In his book *Sin and Society* (1907) the sociologist E. A. Ross observed: "Unlike the old time villain, the latter-day malefactor does not wear a slouch hat and a comforter, breathe forth curses and an odor of gin, go about his nefarious work with clenched teeth and an evil scowl. . . . The modern high-powered dealer of woe wears immaculate linen, carries a silk hat and a lighted cigar, sins with calm countenance and a serene soul, leagues or months from the evil he causes. Upon his gentlemanly presence the eventual blood and tears do not obtrude themselves."

Labor legislation was perhaps the most significant reform to emerge from the drive for social justice. The National Child Labor Committee, organized in 1904, led a movement for laws banning the still widespread employment of young children. Through propaganda, the organization of state and local committees, and a telling documentation of the evils of child labor by

Girl at work in a North Carolina textile mill, 1908. Photograph by Lewis Hine. [Library of Congress]

the photographer Lewis W. Hine, the committee within ten years brought about legislation in most states banning the labor of underage children (the minimum age varied from twelve to sixteen) and limiting the hours of older children. Many states also outlawed night work and labor in dangerous occupations for both women and children. But numerous exemptions and inadequate enforcement often virtually nullified the laws.

The Supreme Court pursued a curiously erratic course in ruling on state labor laws. In *Holden v. Hardy* (1898) it upheld a Utah law limiting the working day in mining and smelting to eight hours as a proper exercise of the state police power to protect the health and safety of workers. The Court even referred to the unequal bargaining power of workers and employers as a justification for state action. In *Lochner v. New York* (1905), however, the Court voided a ten-hour day because it violated workers' "liberty of contract" to accept any terms they chose. Justice Oliver Wendell Holmes, Jr., dissented sharply. "The 14th Amendment does not enact Mr. Herbert Spencer's *Social Statics*," he said, meaning it did not enact Spencer's laissez-faire dogmas. Then in *Muller v. Oregon* (1908) the high court upheld a ten-hour law for women largely on the basis of sociological data which Louis D. Brandeis presented regarding the effects of long hours on the health and morals of women. In *Bunting v. Oregon* (1917) the Court accepted a ten-hour day for both men and women, but held out for twenty more years against state minimum-wage laws.

Legislation to protect workers against accidents gained impetus from disasters like the 1911 fire at the Triangle Shirtwaist Company in New York in which 146 people, mostly women, died for want of adequate exits. They either were trapped on the three upper floors of a ten-story building or plunged to the street below. Stricter building codes and factory inspection acts followed. One of the most important advances along these lines was the series of workmen's compensation laws enacted after Maryland led the way in 1902. Accident insurance systems replaced the old common-law principle that an injured worker was entitled to compensation only if he could prove employer negligence, a costly and capricious procedure from which the worker was likely to win nothing, or as often happened, excessive awards from overly sympathetic juries.

For many the cause of prohibition absorbed the yearnings for reform. Opposition to strong drink was an ideal cause in which to merge the older private ethics and the new social ethics. Given the moral disrepute of saloons, prohibitionists could equate the "liquor traffic" with progressive suspicion of bossism and "special interests." When reform pressures mounted, prohibition offered an easy outlet, bypassing the complexities of corporate regulation.

The battle against booze dated far back into the nineteenth century. The Women's Christian Temperance Union had promoted the cause since 1874 and a Prohibition party had entered the field in 1876. But the most successful political action followed the formation in 1893 of the Anti-Saloon League, an organization which pioneered the tactics of the single-issue pressure group. By singleness of purpose it forced the prohibition issue into the forefront of state and local elections. At its "Jubilee Convention" in 1913 the Anti-Saloon League endorsed a prohibition amendment to the Constitution, adopted by Congress that year. By the time it was ratified six years later, state and local action already had dried up areas occupied by nearly three-fourths of the nation's population.

ACTIVE GOVERNMENT   A fifth feature of progressivism, and perhaps the most significant of all in its long-term impact, was its emphasis on the public-service functions of government. Governments were now called upon to extend a broad range of direct services: schools, good roads (a movement propelled first by cyclists and then by automobilists), conservation, public health and welfare, care of the handicapped, farm loans, and farm demonstration agents, among other things.

The good-roads movement, the automobile-age equivalent of the nineteenth-century railroad movement, went forward first by means of conventions, associations, and heroic caravans in dusters and goggles, and finally triumphed through broad-gauged planning of integrated networks with the Federal Highways Acts of 1916 and 1921 and the development of state systems. A bewildering profusion of local associations followed the founding of the magazine *Good Roads* (1892), the National Good Roads Association (1900), and the American Automobile Association (1902). In the first flush of excitement over the liberation brought by the automobile, few foresaw the dependence it would later entail or the devastating effect it would eventually have on rail transit. Good roads were in fact often promoted at first as feeders to the existing rail network.

ROOSEVELT'S PROGRESSIVISM

Theodore Roosevelt's version of Progressive reform was a cautious one. As a reformer he best displayed his political skills. He cultivated party leaders in Congress, and steered away from such political meat-grinders as the tariff and banking issues. And when he did approach the explosive issue of the trusts, he always took care to reassure the business community. For him, politics was the art of the possible. Unlike the more advanced progressives and the doctrinaire "lunatic fringe," as he called them, he would take half a loaf rather than none at all. Roosevelt acted in large part out of the conviction that reform was needed to keep things on an even keel. Control should rest in the hands of sensible Republicans, and not with irresponsible Democrats or, worse, the growing socialist movement.

EXECUTIVE ACTION At the outset of his presidency in 1901 Roosevelt took up McKinley's policies and promised to sustain them. He touched base with McKinley's friend and manager Mark Hanna, and worked with Republican leaders in Congress, against whom the minority of new Progressives was as yet powerless. Republican Speaker Joe Cannon, who now wielded the dictatorial powers once held by "Czar" Reed, was able to announce on one occasion to a helpless House, "We will now perpetrate the following outrage."

Roosevelt, it turned out, would accomplish more by vigorous executive action than by passing legislation, and in the exercise of executive power he was not inhibited by points of legal detail.

The president, he argued, might do anything not expressly forbidden by the Constitution. The Constitution, he said later, "must be interpreted, not as a straight jacket, not as laying the hand of death upon our development, but as an instrument designed for the life and healthy growth of the Nation." He was even credited with asking: "What's the Constitution between friends?" but that query seems to have been apocryphal.

Caution suffused Roosevelt's first annual message, delivered in December 1901, but he felt impelled to take up the trust problem in the belief that it might be more risky to ignore it. The message carefully balanced arguments on both sides of the question. "The mechanism of modern business is so delicate," he warned, "that extreme care must be taken not to interfere with it in a spirit of rashness or ignorance." A widespread belief nevertheless held the great corporations "in certain of their features and tendencies hurtful to the general welfare." The president endorsed the "sincere conviction that combination and concentration should be, not prohibited, but supervised and within reasonable limits controlled. . . ." The first essential was "knowledge of the facts—publicity . . . the only sure remedy we can now invoke." Later would follow regulatory legislation, perhaps based on the experience of the Interstate Commerce Commission (ICC).

Finley Peter Dunne's Mr. Dooley summarized the essence of Roosevelt's message this way: "Th' trusts, says he, are heejoous monsthers built up be the enlightened intherprise iv th' men that have done so much to advance progress in our beloved country, he says. On wan hand I wud stamp thim undher fut; on th' other hand not so fast." The result, in fact, was not so fast. But in August 1902 Roosevelt carried the trust issue to the people on a tour of New England and the Midwest. He endorsed a "square deal" for all, calling for enforcement of existing antitrust laws and stricter controls on big business.

From the outset, however, Roosevelt believed that wholesale trust-busting was too much like trying to unscramble eggs. Effective regulation, he believed, was better than a futile effort to restore small business, which might be achieved only at a cost to the efficiencies of scale gained in larger operations. Roosevelt nevertheless soon acquired a reputation as a "trustbuster."

Because Congress boggled at regulatory legislation, Roosevelt sought to force the issue by a more vigorous prosecution of the Sherman Anti-Trust Act. He chose his target carefully. In the case against the Sugar Trust (*United States v. E. C. Knight and Company,* 1895) the Supreme Court had declared manufacturing a strictly intrastate activity. Railroads, however, were beyond question engaged in interstate commerce and thus subject to federal authority. In February 1902 Roosevelt ordered Attorney-General Philander C. Knox to move against the Northern Securities Company, a firm vulnerable to both the law and public opinion. That company, formed the previous year, had taken shape during a gigantic battle in the New York Stock Exchange between E. H. Harriman of the Union Pacific and James J. Hill and J. P. Morgan of the Great Northern and Northern Pacific. The stock battle raised the threat of a panic, and led to a settlement in which the chief contenders made peace. They formed Northern Securities as a holding company to control the Great Northern and Northern Pacific.

At about the time Roosevelt ordered suit against Northern Securities in 1902, he balanced his action with a speech at the South Carolina and West Indian Exposition in Charleston denouncing demagogues who raved "against the wealth which is simply the form of embodied thrift, foresight, and intelligence." But when J. P. Morgan invited Roosevelt to "send your man to my man and they can fix it up," the president refused. Hill complained: "It seems hard that we should be compelled to fight for our lives against the political adventurers who have never done anything but pose and draw a salary. . . ." Knox pressed the case and in 1904 the Supreme Court ordered the combination dissolved. "What has been the result?" Hill asked. "To the owners . . . merely the inconvenience of holding two certificates of stock of different colors instead of one. To the public, no difference at all except that it has missed the advantages which the simpler and more businesslike plan would have secured."

THE COAL STRIKE   Support for Roosevelt's use of the "big stick" against corporations was strengthened by the stubbornness of mine owners in the anthracite coal strike of 1902. On May 12 the United Mine Workers (UMW), led by John Mitchell, walked out demanding a 20 percent wage increase, a reduction in hours from ten to nine, and union recognition. The mine operators, having granted a 10 percent raise two years before, dug in their heels against further concessions, and shut down in preparation for a long struggle to starve out the miners. Their spokesman, George F. Baer, president of the Reading Railroad, helped the union cause more than his own with an arrogant pronouncement: "The rights and interests of the laboring man will be protected and cared for," he said, "not by the labor agitators, but by the Christian men to whom God in his infinite wisdom has given control of the property interests of the country."

The prospect of a coal shortage seemed real. Roosevelt called a conference at the White House on October 3 and the operators came but refused even to speak to the UMW leaders. The enraged president confessed a temptation to throw Baer bodily through a window of the White House. When the conference ended in an impasse, Roosevelt threatened to take over the mines and run them with the army. It would have been an act of dubious legality, but the owners feared that TR might actually do it and that public opinion would support him.

The coal strike ended in October with an agreement to submit the issues to an arbitration commission named by the president. After a last-minute flurry over the operators' refusal to accept a union man on the panel, the president blithely reclassified the head of the railway conductors' union, E. E. Clark, as an "eminent sociologist." The agreement enhanced the prestige of both Roosevelt and union leader Mitchell, although it produced only a partial victory for the miners. By the arbitrators' decision of March 21, 1903, the miners won only a 10 percent wage increase and a nine-hour day, but no union recognition.

TOWARD A SECOND TERM   Roosevelt continued to use his executive powers to enforce the Sherman Act, but he avoided conflict in Congress by drawing back from further antitrust legislation. Altogether his administration brought about twenty-five antitrust suits, the most notable victory coming in *Swift and Company v. United States* (1905), a decision against the "beef trust" through which most of the packers had avoided competitive bidding in

No Lack of Big Game. *A 1905 cartoon shows TR going after the trusts.* [Library of Congress]

NO LACK OF BIG GAME
The President Seems to Have Scared Up Quite a Bunch of Octopi.

the purchase of livestock. In this decision the Supreme Court put forth the "stream of commerce" doctrine which overturned its previous holding that manufacturing was strictly intrastate. Since both livestock and the meat products of the packers moved in the stream of interstate commerce, the Court reasoned, they were subject to federal regulation. This interpretation of the interstate commerce power would be broadened in later years until few enterprises would remain beyond the reach of federal regulation.

In 1903 Congress came around to legislation that somewhat strengthened both antitrust enforcement and governmental regulation. Within one week in February of that year, Congress approved three important measures: the Expedition Act, whereby circuit courts had to give priority to antitrust suits upon request of the attorney-general; an act creating the Department of Commerce and Labor, including the Bureau of Corporations; and the Elkins Act, which made it illegal to take as well as to give rebates.

The new Bureau of Corporations had no direct regulatory powers, but it did have a mandate to study and report on the activities of interstate corporations. Headed by James R. Garfield, son of the former president, the bureau followed a policy of concord rather than conflict. Its findings could lead to antitrust suits, but its purpose was rather to help corporations correct malpractices and avoid the need for lawsuits. Many companies, among them United States Steel and International Harvester, worked closely with Garfield, but others held back. When Standard Oil refused to turn over records, the government brought an antitrust suit which resulted in its dissolution in 1911. The American Tobacco Company was dissolved at the same time. This approach fell short of the direct regulation which Roosevelt preferred, but without a congressional will to pass such laws, little more was possible. Trusts which cooperated were left alone; others had to run the gauntlet of antitrust suits.

Roosevelt's policies built a coalition of progressive- and conservative-minded voters which assured his election in his own right in 1904. He had skillfully used patronage, and his progressive policies, achieved mainly by executive action, had not challenged congressional conservatives. Nor did Roosevelt try to take on the Old Guard at the Chicago convention in June. He accepted a harmless platform which dwelt on past achievements, and the convention chose him by acclamation. The Democrats, having lost with Bryan twice, turned to Alton B. Parker who, as chief justice of New York, had upheld labor's right to the closed shop and the state's right to limit hours of work. Despite his liberal record party leaders presented him as a safe conservative, and his acceptance of the gold standard as "firmly and irrevocably established" bolstered such a view. The effort to present a candidate more conservative than Roosevelt proved a futile gesture for the party which had twice nominated Bryan. Despite Roosevelt's trust-busting proclivities, most businessmen, according to the New York *Sun*, preferred the "impulsive candidate of the party of conservatism to the conservative candidate of the party which the business interests regard as permanently and dangerously impulsive." Even J. P. Morgan and E. H. Harriman contributed handsomely to Roosevelt's campaign chest. Parker made little headway with his charge that businessmen expected favors in return.

An invincible popularity plus the sheer force of personality swept Roosevelt to an impressive victory by a popular margin of 7.6 million to 5.1 million. Parker carried only the Solid South of the former Confederacy and two border states: Kentucky and Maryland. It was a great personal triumph for Roosevelt. Amid the excitement of election night he announced that he would not run again, a statement he later had reason to regret.

LEGISLATIVE LEADERSHIP   Elected in his own right, Roosevelt approached his second term with heightened confidence and a stronger commitment to progressive reform. In December 1905 he devoted most of his annual message to the regulation and control of business. He took aim at the railroads first, and it was with reference to railroads that his demands most nearly approached success. The Elkins Act of 1903, finally outlawing rebates, had been a minor step. Railroad men themselves welcomed it as an escape from shippers clamoring for special favors. But the new Hepburn proposal was something else again, for it would both extend the authority of the ICC and give it effective control over rates for the first time.

Roosevelt had to mobilize all the pressure and influence at his disposal to push through the bill introduced by Rep. Peter Hepburn of Iowa. Nelson Aldrich, leader of the Senate conservatives, sought to embarrass the president by making the Democrat "Pitchfork Ben" Tillman floor manager for the bill, but Roosevelt and the South Carolinian put aside partisan differences to get it passed. Enacted on June 29, 1906, the Hepburn Act for the first time gave the ICC power to set maximum rates. The commission no longer had to go to court to enforce its decisions. While the carriers could challenge the rates in court, the burden of proof now rested on them rather than on the ICC. As part of the compromise required to pass the law, however, new rates under challenge would be suspended pending decision of the courts. In other ways too the Hepburn Act enlarged the mandate of the ICC. Its reach now extended beyond railroads to pipelines, express companies, sleeping-car companies, bridges, and ferries, and it could prescribe a uniform system of bookkeeping to provide uniform statistics. In addition, the act forbade carriers to grant free passes except to their own employees, or to carry commodities they had produced themselves, such as coal or timber, except for their own use.

For more dedicated progressives like Senator La Follette, the Hepburn Act was but half a loaf. They would have preferred that ICC rates continue in effect while appeals were pending, and to have the ICC estimate the overall value of the roads as a basis for rate-fixing. Before many years, though, they would get both of these.

Railroads took priority, but a growing movement for the regulation of meat-packers, food processors, and makers of drugs and patent medicines reached fruition, as it happened, on the very day after passage of the Hepburn Act. Discontent with abuses in these fields had grown rapidly as a result of the muckrakers' reports. Dr. W. H. Wiley, chief chemist of the Agriculture Department, and Dr. E. F. Ladd, food commissioner of North Dakota, supplied telling evidence of harmful preservatives and adulterants in the preparation of "embalmed meat" and other food products. Edward Bok and Mark Sullivan in the *Ladies Home Journal,* and Samuel Hopkins Adams in *Colliers,* provided evidence of false claims and dangerous ingredients in patent medicines, what Adams called "The Great American Fraud." One of the more notorious nostrums, Lydia Pinkham's Vegetable Compound, was advertised to work wonders in the relief of "female complaints"; it was no wonder, for the compound was 18 percent alcohol.

But perhaps the most telling blow against such abuses was struck by Upton Sinclair's novel *The Jungle* (1906). Sinclair meant the book to be a tract for socialism, but its main impact came from its portrayal of filthy conditions in Chicago's meat-packing industry: "It was too dark in these storage places to see well, but a man could run his hand over these piles of meat and sweep off handfuls of the dried dung of rats. These rats were nuisances, and the packers would put poisoned bread out for them, they would die, and then rats, bread, and meat would go into the hoppers together." Roosevelt, an omnivorous reader, read *The Jungle*—and reacted quickly. He sent two agents to Chicago and their report confirmed all that Sinclair had said: "We saw meat

A Modern First Class Pork Packing & Canning Establishment. *Upton Sinclair's exposé of the filthy conditions in meat-packing plants belied the pristine surroundings pictured here.* [Chicago Historical Society]

shovelled from filthy wooden floors, piled on tables rarely washed, pushed from room to room in rotten box carts, in all of which processes it was in the way of gathering dirt, splinters, floor filth, and the expectoration of tuberculous and other diseased workers."

The Meat Inspection Act of June 30, 1906, required federal inspection of meats destined for interstate commerce and empowered officials in the Agriculture Department to impose standards of sanitation. The Pure Food and Drug Act, enacted the same day, placed restrictions on the makers of prepared foods and patent medicines, and forbade the manufacture, sale, or transportation of adulterated, misbranded, or harmful foods, drugs, and liquors.

Thus during one week of February 1903, and during two days of June 1906, Theodore Roosevelt's campaign for regulatory legislation reached its chief goals: in 1903 the Expedition Act, the Elkins Act, and the establishment of the Department of Commerce and Labor with its Bureau of Corporations; in 1906 the Hepburn Act, the Meat Inspection Act, and the Pure Food and Drug Act. If in later years these would seem modest achievements for all of Roosevelt's bluster, they had moved the federal government a great distance from the laissez-faire policies which had prevailed before the turn of the century.

CONSERVATION One of the most enduring legacies of the Roosevelt years was the push he gave to the conservation movement.

Concern for protecting the environment grew with the rising awareness that the frontier was being exhausted by the end of the nineteenth century. A large section of Roosevelt's first annual message was devoted to the subject. As early as 1872 Yellowstone National Park had been set aside as a public reserve (the National Park Service would be created in 1916 after other parks had been added). In 1881 Congress had created a Division of Forestry in the Department of Agriculture, and Roosevelt's appointment of Gifford Pinchot, one of the country's first scientific foresters, as chief brought vigorous administration of forests on public lands. After 1891 the Forest Reserve Act had permitted the president to exclude certain timberlands from settlement. When Roosevelt took office approximately 46 million acres had been set aside; by the end of his presidency some 172 million acres had been withdrawn, including acreage important mainly for coal, phosphates, and waterpower.

Forestry Chief Pinchot worked vigorously, with TR's full support, to develop programs and public interest in conservation. In 1903 a Public Lands Commission called for a review of the nation's resources by the Geological Survey. In 1907 an Inland Waterways Commission proposed regional development with an eye to reviving steamboats on the rivers. Congressional resistance to this and other proposals led Pinchot and Roosevelt to publicize the cause through a White House Conference on Conservation in 1908, and later that year by setting up a National Conservation Commission which proposed a thorough survey of resources in minerals, water, forests, and soil. Within eighteen months some forty-one state conservation commissions sprang up, and a number of private groups took up the cause. The movement remained divided, however, between those who wanted to conserve resources for continuous human use and those who wanted to set aside wilderness areas. Pinchot, for instance, won the enmity of naturalist John Muir in 1906 when he endorsed a water reservoir in the wild Hetch Hetchy Valley of Yosemite National Park to supply the needs of San Francisco.

From Roosevelt to Taft

Unlike most presidents, Roosevelt was strong enough to handpick a successor to carry out "the policies." He decided that the heir to the White House should be Secretary of War William Howard Taft, and the Republican convention ratified the choice on its first ballot in 1908. The Democrats, whose conservative strategy had backfired in 1904, decided to give William Jennings

Bryan one more chance at the highest office. Still vigorous at forty-eight, Bryan retained a faithful following. But once again it was not enough. The Republican platform declared its support of Roosevelt's policies, including conservation and further strengthening of the ICC. On the tariff and the use of labor injunctions the platform made vague references to revision but without any specifics. The Democratic platform hardly differed on regulation, but endorsed a lower tariff and an AFL-supported plank opposing court injunctions against labor actions. Bryan himself went beyond support of regulation by calling for federal incorporation of interstate business and even government ownership of railroads, "not as an immediate issue, but as an ultimate solution." In the end the voters opted for Roosevelt's chosen successor, leaving Bryan only the southern states plus Nebraska, Colorado, and Nevada. Taft swept the electoral college by 321 to 162.

Once out of office, still only fifty, Roosevelt left on a big-game hunt in Africa, followed by a triumphant procession through Europe. The new president he left behind was an entirely different kind of political animal, in fact hardly a political animal at all. Offspring of a family long prominent in Cincinnati—his father Alphonso had been Grant's attorney-general—Taft had progressed through appointive offices, from judge in Ohio to solicitor in the Justice Department, federal judge, commissioner and governor-general in the Philippines, and secretary of war. The presidency was the only elective office he ever held. Later he would be chief justice (1921–1930), a job more suited to his temperament. Weighing in at some 300 pounds, Taft was more

William Howard Taft, on the golf course. [Culver Picture Service]

attuned to the sedentary reflections of the bench than to the active give and take of the political arena. "I don't like politics," he wrote once. "I don't like the limelight." The political animal in the family was his wife, who had wanted the White House more than he. One of the major tragedies of Taft's presidency was that Helen Taft fell seriously ill soon after they entered the White House, and for most of his term remained unable to serve as his political adviser.

TARIFF REFORM   Contrary to Republican tradition, Taft preferred a lower tariff. This he made the first important issue of his presidency. Once a student of William Graham Sumner at Yale, Taft had absorbed the laissez-faire views of his mentor and had since differed with orthodox Republican protectionism. Early in the campaign, and contrary to TR's advice, he had clarified the vague tariff plank in the platform by affirming that it meant revision downward. In keeping with the platform pledge for a special session, Taft called Congress to meet on March 15, 1909, eleven days after his inauguration. But if, in pressing an issue that TR had skirted, Taft seemed the bolder of the two, he proved the less adroit.

A bill sponsored by Sereno E. Payne of New York passed the House with surprising ease. It lowered rates less than Taft would have preferred but made some important reductions and enlarged the free list. But the chairman of the Senate Finance Committee, Nelson W. Aldrich, guided through a bill drastically revised by more than 800 changes. Many of these were "jokers" which concealed increases by changing specific duties to *ad valorem* duties (in proportion to value) or the other way around. Finley Peter Dunne's Mr. Dooley ridiculed the free list which, he said, included such important things as divvy-divvy, spunk, silkworm eggs, stilts, skeletons, and leeches. "The new tariff bill," he said, "puts these familyar commodyties within the reach iv all." What finally came out of a conference committee was a measure close to the Senate version, although Taft did get some reductions on important items: hides, iron ore, coal, oil, cottons, boots, and shoes.

In response to the higher rates in Aldrich's bills, a group of midwestern Republicans took the Senate floor to fight what they considered a corrupt throwback to the days when the Republican party had served big business unquestioningly. In all, ten progressive Republicans joined the Democrats in an unsuccessful effort to defeat the bill. Taft at first agreed with them; then, fearful of a party split, backed the majority and agreed to an imperfect bill. He lacked TR's love of a grand battle as well as his gift for working both sides of the street. Temperamentally conservative, inhibited by scruples about interfering too much with the legislative process, he drifted into the orbit of the Republican Old Guard and quickly alienated the progressive wing of his party, whom he tagged "assistant Democrats." Aware of rising discontent in the corn and wheat belts, Taft embarked in late summer on a speaking tour of the West only to make things worse when he pointedly ignored insurgent senators and pronounced the Payne-Aldrich Act the best tariff bill the Republican party had ever passed.

BALLINGER AND PINCHOT In 1910 Taft's policies drove the wedge deeper between the Republican factions. The Ballinger-Pinchot controversy made Taft appear to be a less reliable custodian of TR's conservation policies than he actually was. Taft's secretary of the interior, Richard A. Ballinger of Seattle, was well aware that many westerners opposed conservation programs on the grounds that they held back full development of the region. The strongest conservation leaders were often easterners like TR and Gifford Pinchot of Pennsylvania. Ballinger threw open to use more than a million acres of waterpower sites which Roosevelt had withdrawn in the guise of ranger stations. Ballinger's reasoning was that the withdrawal had "gone far beyond legal limitations," and Taft agreed. At about the same time Ballinger turned over certain coal lands in Alaska to a group of Seattle men, some of whom he had represented as a lawyer. Apparently without Ballinger's knowledge, this group had already agreed to sell part of the lands to a Morgan-Guggenheim syndicate.

This was too much for Louis R. Glavis, an investigator with the General Land Office, who went to Chief of Forestry Pinchot with evidence of the collusion. Pinchot in turn called it to the attention of Taft, who then fired Glavis for his pains. When Pinchot went public with the controversy, he in turn was fired for insubordination early in 1910. A joint congressional investigation of Ballinger exonerated him from all charges of fraud or corruption, but progressive suspicions created such pressures that he resigned in 1911.

Taft acted on the strictly legal view which his training had taught him to value, but circumstances tarnished his image in the public mind. "In the end," one historian has written, "the Ballinger-Pinchot affair had more impact on politics than it did on conservation." Taft had been elected to carry out the Roosevelt policies, his opponents said, and he was carrying them out—"on a stretcher." Pinchot was soon off to Africa carrying the word to Roosevelt.

Meanwhile, in the House of Representatives rebellion had broken out among the more progressive Republicans. When the regular session opened in March 1910 the insurgents joined Democrats in voting to investigate Ballinger. Flushed with that victory, they resolved to clip the wings of Speaker Joseph G. Cannon (R-Ill.), a conservative who held almost a stranglehold on procedures by his power to appoint all committees and their chairmen, and especially by his control of the Rules Committee, of which he was a member. A Democratic-insurgent coalition overrode a ruling from the Speaker and proceeded to adopt new rules offered by George W. Norris (R-Neb.) which enlarged the Rules Committee from five to fifteen members, made them elective by the House, and excluded the Speaker as a member. About forty Republicans joined the Democratic minority in the move. In the next Congress the rules would be further changed to make all committees elective.

In all these matters, events had conspired to cast Taft in a conservative role at a time when progressive sentiment was riding high in the countryside. The result was a severe rebuke to the president in the congressional elections of 1910, first by the widespread defeat of pro-Taft candidates in the Republican primaries, then by the election of a Democratic majority in the House and of enough Democrats in the Senate that insurgent Republicans could wield the balance of power.

TAFT AND ROOSEVELT In June 1910 Roosevelt had returned from his travels abroad. He had been reading new accounts and letters about the Taft "betrayal," but unlike some of his supporters, he refused to break with his successor. With rather severe politeness, however, Roosevelt refused an invitation to visit the White House. But, he wrote Taft: "I shall keep my mind open as I keep my mouth shut." Neither was easy for Roosevelt, who was beset by followers urging him to action. Soon he was rallying support for gubernatorial candidate Henry L. Stimson in New York, and then he was off on a speaking tour of the West in advance of the congressional elections. At Osawatomie, Kansas, on August 31, 1910, he gave a catchy name to his principles, the "New Nationalism," and issued a stirring call for stronger regulatory power and new measures of direct democracy. Most offensive to conservatives, perhaps, was his support for the recall of judicial decisions by popular vote.

Relations between Roosevelt and Taft remained tense, but it

was another year before they came to an open break. It happened in the fall of 1911 when the Taft administration announced an antitrust suit against United States Steel, citing specifically as cause the company's acquisition of Tennessee Coal and Iron Company in 1907, a move to which TR had given tacit approval in the belief it would avert a panic. In mid-November Roosevelt published a sharp attack on Taft's "archaic" attempt to restore competition. The only sensible response to the problem, he argued, was to accept business combinations in modern circumstances but to enlarge the government's power to regulate them. His entry into the next presidential campaign was now only a matter of time.

Not all progressive Republicans wanted TR back in the White House. A sizable number proposed to back Senator La Follette in 1912, but some of La Follette's supporters were ready to switch if TR entered the race. An opening came on February 2, 1912, when La Follette betrayed signs of nervous exhaustion in a rambling speech at a publishers' dinner in Philadelphia. As his following began to drop away, a group of seven Republican governors met in Chicago on February 10 and called on Roosevelt to become a candidate. On February 24 Roosevelt threw his hat in the ring. "I hope that so far as possible the people may be given the chance, through direct primaries," Roosevelt wrote the governors, "to express their preference. . . ."

The rebuke implicit in Roosevelt's decision to run against Taft, his chosen successor, was in many ways undeserved. During Taft's first year in office one political tempest after another left his image irreparably damaged. The three years of solid achievement that followed came too late to restore its luster or to reunite his divided party. Taft had at least attempted tariff reform, which TR had never dared. He replaced Ballinger with Walter Fisher of Chicago and Pinchot with Henry S. Graves, former head of the Yale Forestry School, both men of impeccable credentials in conservation matters. He won from Congress the power to protect public lands for any reason, and was the first president to withdraw oil lands from use. Under the Appalachian Forest Reserve Act (1911) he enlarged the national forests by purchase of lands in the East. In the end his administration withdrew more public lands in four years than TR's had in nearly eight, and brought more antitrust suits, by a score of eighty to twenty-five.

In 1910, with Taft's support, Congress passed the Mann-Elkins Act, which empowered the ICC for the first time to initiate rate changes, extended regulation to telephone and telegraph companies, and set up a Commerce Court to expedite appeals from the ICC rulings. Taft's reform record was further extended by passage of a postal-savings law (1910) and a parcel-post law (1913), the establishment of the Bureau of Mines and the Federal Children's Bureau (1912), and the provision of statehood for Arizona and New Mexico and territorial government for Alaska (1912). The Sixteenth Amendment (1913), authorizing a federal income tax, was ratified with Taft's support before he left office, and the Seventeenth Amendment (1913), providing for the popular election of senators, was ratified soon after he left office.

Despite this record, Roosevelt now hastened Taft's demise. In all but two of the thirteen states which held presidential primaries, Roosevelt won, even in Taft's Ohio. But the groundswell of popular support was no match for Taft's decisive position as president and party leader. In state conventions the party regulars held the line, so that Roosevelt entered the Republican national convention about 100 votes short of victory. The regulars' control of the convention machinery, operating under established rules, ensured their triumph and the Taft forces proceeded to nominate their man by the same "steamroller" tactics that had nominated Roosevelt in 1904. Outraged at such "naked theft," the Roosevelt delegates assembled in a rump convention. "If you wish me to make the fight I will make it," Roosevelt told the delegates, who then issued a call for a Progressive party convention, which assembled in Chicago on August 5. TR appeared, feeling "fit as a bull moose." He was "stripped to the buff and ready for the fight," he said. "We stand at Armageddon and we battle for the Lord." But the convention was filled with advanced

A skeptical view of TR, the Bull Moose candidate in 1912. [Library of Congress]

thinkers, social workers like Jane Addams of Hull House and the New Jersey business progressive George L. Record, and few professional politicians turned up. Progressive Republicans decided to preserve their party credentials and fight another day. For the time being, with the disruption of the Republican party, the progressive torch was about to be passed on to the Democrats.

WILSON'S PROGRESSIVISM

WILSON'S RISE   The emergence of Thomas Woodrow Wilson as the Democratic nominee climaxed a political rise even more rapid than that of Cleveland. In 1910, before his nomination and election as governor of New Jersey, Wilson had been president of Princeton University, but had never run for public office. Born in Staunton, Virginia, in 1856, Wilson had grown up the son of a Presbyterian minister in Georgia and the Carolinas during the Civil War and Reconstruction. He attended Davidson College for one year, finished his undergraduate career at Princeton in 1879, and after law school at the University of Virginia he tried a brief and profitless law practice in Atlanta. From there he went to the new Johns Hopkins University in Baltimore, where he found his calling in the study of history and political science under Herbert Baxter Adams.

Wilson's dissertation, *Congressional Government,* published in 1885, outlined the operation of the committee system, until then little understood except among politicians, and the view, later elaborated in *Constitutional Government in the United States* (1908), that the president, like the British prime minister, should be the leader of party government, as active in directing legislation as in the administration and enforcement of laws. In calling for a strong presidency he expressed views closer to those of Roosevelt than those of Taft, but over the years more typical of Democratic than of Republican presidents.

After Johns Hopkins, Wilson taught at Bryn Mawr, moved to Princeton in 1890, and twelve years later became its president. In that position he showed the first evidence of reform views and a tenacity buttressed by his Presbyterian sense of righteousness. At Princeton he started a preceptorial system to supplement lectures, but met defeat when he tried to democratize student life by banning the exclusive dining clubs and putting the graduate school at the center of the campus as a leaven for undergraduate programs. When these plans were blocked by the opposition of alumni and the dean of the graduate school, Wilson faced a choice of giving up or leaving.

Woodrow Wilson. [National Archives]

At this juncture James Smith, the Democratic boss of New Jersey, offered Wilson his support for the 1910 gubernatorial nomination, and Wilson accepted. Smith sought a respectable candidate to ward off progressive challengers. He discovered, too late, that the supposedly innocent schoolmaster actually had a will of iron. Elected as a reform candidate, Wilson proceeded to push progressive measures through the legislature. Wilson, for instance, insisted that the legislature honor the senatorial nomination won by James E. Martine in the Democratic primary—despite Smith's desire for the job. The legislature heeded Wilson. Under pressure from the governor the lawmakers also enacted a workmen's compensation law, a corrupt-practices law, measures to regulate public utilities, and ballot reforms. Such strong leadership in a state known as the "home of the trusts" for its lenient corporation laws brought Wilson to national attention.

THE ELECTION OF 1912   In the spring of 1911 a group of southerners resident in New York opened a Wilson presidential campaign headquarters, and Wilson set forth on strenuous tours into all regions of the country, denouncing special privilege and political bossism. But by convention time, despite a fast start, the Wilson campaign seemed headed for defeat by Speaker Bennett Champ Clark of Missouri, who garnered supporters among Bryanites, the Hearst newspapers, and party hacks. Clark had enough for a majority in the early ballots, but the Wilson forces combined with supporters of Oscar Underwood of Alabama to prevent a two-thirds majority. On the fourteenth ballot Bryan came over to Wilson. When Roger Sullivan, Democratic boss of Illinois, deserted Clark on the forty-second ballot and the Underwood delegates went over to Wilson on the forty-sixth, he swept to the nomination.

It quickly became clear that in a three-man race Taft was out of the running. "There are so many people in the country who don't like me," he lamented. The campaign settled down to a running debate over the competing ideologies of the two front-runners: Roosevelt's "New Natonalism" and Wilson's "New Freedom." The inchoate ideas that Roosevelt fashioned into his New Nationalism had first been presented systematically in *The Promise of American Life* (1909), a treatise by Herbert Croly, a then-obscure New York journalist. Its central point was often summarized in a useful catch-phrase: Hamiltonian means to achieve Jeffersonian ends, meaning that Hamilton's program of governmental intervention, once indentified with the business interests, should be used to achieve democratic and egalitarian Jeffersonian goals. The times required progressives to give up Jeffersonian prejudices against big government and use a strong central government to achieve democratic ends in the interest of the people.

The old nationalism had been used "by the sinister . . . special interests," TR said. The New Nationalism would enable government to achieve social justice, and more specifically to effect such reforms as graduated income and inheritance taxes, workmen's compensation, regulation of the labor of women and children, and a stronger Bureau of Corporations. These and more went into the platform of the Progressive party, which called for a federal trade commission with sweeping authority over business and a tariff commission to set rates on a "scientific basis." The Progressive platform, the historian Arthur Link has written, "provided the basis for the future development of the progressive movement in the United States after 1912, just as the Populist platform of 1892 had earlier provided a foundation for the first phase of American progressivism."

Before the end of his administration, Wilson would be swept into the current of the new nationalism too. But for now he spoke for the decentralizing antitrust traditions of his party. Before the start of the campaign Wilson conferred with Louis D. Brandeis, a progressive lawyer from Boston who focused Wilson's thought much as Croly had focused Roosevelt's. The central idea of the New Freedom was that government should "so restrict the wrong use of competition that the right use of competition will

Wilson's view of Roosevelt's New Nationalism.
Wilson argued that TR's program of monopoly
regulation played into the hands of the big trusts.
[Library of Congress]

destroy monopoly." This was the dream of restoring an economy of small-scale competitive units, and Roosevelt dismissed it as illusory.

The Republican schism opened the way for Woodrow Wilson to win by 435 electoral votes to 88 for Roosevelt and 8 for Taft. But in popular votes Wilson had only 42 percent of the total. It was the victory of a minority over a divided opposition. The election of 1912 assumes significance in several ways. First, it was a high-water mark for progressivism. The election was the first to feature presidential primaries. The two leading candidates debated the basic issues of progressivism in a campaign unique for its focus on vital alternatives and for its high philosophical tone. Taft too, despite his temperament and associations, showed his own progressive instincts. And the Socialist party, the left wing of progressivism, polled over 900,000 votes for Eugene V. Debs, about 6 percent of the total vote, its highest proportion ever.

Second, the election brought the Democrats back into effective national power for the first time since the Civil War. For two years during the second Cleveland administration, 1893–1895, they had held the White House and majorities in both houses of Congress, but they quickly fell out of power during the most severe depression in American history to that time.

Third, the election of Wilson brought southerners back into the orbit of national and international affairs in a significant way for the first time since the Civil War. In Washington, one reporter said, "you feel it in the air . . . you listen to evidence of it in the mellow accent with which the South makes our English a musical tongue." Wilson himself once said that "the only place in the world where nothing has to be explained to me is the South." Five of his ten cabinet members were born in the South, three still resided there, and William Jennings Bryan, the secretary of state, was an idol of the southern masses. At the president's right hand, and one of the most influential members of the Wilson circle, at least until 1919, was Col. Edward M. House of Texas. On Capitol Hill southerners, by virture of their seniority, held the lion's share of committee chairmanships. As a result much of the progressive legislation of the Wilson era would bear the names of the southerners who guided it through Congress.

Fourth and finally, the election of 1912 had begun to alter the character of the Republican party. Even though most party pro-

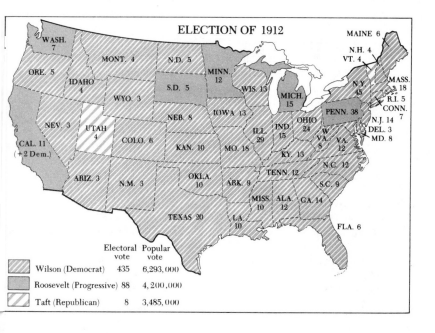

ELECTION OF 1912

	Electoral vote	Popular vote
Wilson (Democrat)	435	6,293,000
Roosevelt (Progressive)	88	4,200,000
Taft (Republican)	8	3,485,000

fessionals remained, the defection of the Bull Moose Progressives had weakened the party's progressive wing. The leader of the Republican party which would return to power in the 1920s would be more conservative in tone and temperament.

WILSONIAN REFORM   Inauguration day of 1913 was "one of the most perfect March days Washington had ever known," a happy omen it seemed as the former Confederate, Chief Justice Edward Douglass White of Louisiana, gave the oath. Wilson's address voiced in eloquent tones the ideals of social justice that animated many progressives. "We have been proud of our industrial achievements," he said, "but we have not hitherto stopped thoughtfully enough to count the human cost . . . the fearful physical and spiritual cost to the men and women and children upon whom the dead weight and burden of it all has fallen pitilessly the years through." He promised specifically a lower tariff and a new banking system. "This is not a day of triumph; it is a day of dedication. Here muster, not the forces of party, but the forces of humanity."

Wilson offered his party its first chance since the Civil War to make a record of achievement. Democrats were bound to him by their need to disprove the slur voiced by Republican Rep. Nicholas Longworth that they were "the organized incapacity of the country." They were bound even more by Wilson's determination to be their leader. If Roosevelt had been a strong president by force of personality, Wilson became a strong president by force of conviction. The president, he wrote in *Constitutional Government,* "is . . . the political leader of the nation, or has it in his choice to be. The nation as a whole has chosen him, and is conscious that it has no other political spokesman. His is the only national voice in affairs."

Wilson courted popular support, but he also courted members of Congress through personal contacts, invitations to the White House, and visits to the Capitol. He used the patronage power to reward friends and punish enemies. He might have acted through a progressive coalition, but chose instead to rely on party loyalty. "I'd rather trust a machine Senator when he is committed to your program," he told Navy Secretary Josephus Daniels, "than a talking Liberal who can never quite go along with others because of his admiration of his own patented plan of reform." Wilson therefore made use of the party caucus, in which disagreements among Democrats were settled, and often directed caucus strategy.

Wilson's leadership got its first big test on the issue of tariff reform. Wilson summoned Congress into special session on April 7, 1913, and the day after it convened he went before it in person —the first president to do so since John Adams. (Roosevelt was said to have asked, "Why didn't I think of that?") "The object of the tariff duties henceforth laid must be effective competition," Wilson said, "the whetting of American wits by contest with the wits of the rest of the world." Congress now acted vigorously on tariff reductions. In the House, where Oscar Underwood's Ways and Means Committee had been working since January, the outcome was never in doubt. Only four Democrats bolted the party line as the bill passed the House easily.

The crunch came in the Senate, the traditional graveyard of tariff reform. Swarms of lobbyists got so thick in Washington, Wilson said, that "a brick couldn't be thrown without hitting one of them." But Wilson turned the tables with a public statement that focused the spotlight on the "industrious and insidious" tariff lobby. "It is of serious interest to the country," he said, "that the people at large should have no lobby and be voiceless in these matters, while great bodies of astute men seek to create an artificial opinion and to overcome the interests of the public for their private profit." In the end the two "sugar senators" from Louisiana were the only Democrats to vote against the bill, which received the president's signature on October 3.

The Underwood-Simmons Tariff of 1913, based throughout on *ad valorem* duties, reduced import duties on 958 items, raised them on only 86, and left 307 the same, with the effect of lowering the overall average duty from about 37 to about 29 percent. A free list of some 300 items, about 100 of them new to the list, included important consumer goods and raw materials: sugar, wool, iron ore, steel rails, agricultural implements, cement, coal, wood and woodpulp, and many farm products.

The act lowered tariffs but raised internal revenues with the first income tax levied under the newly ratified Sixteenth Amendment: 1 percent on incomes over $3,000 ($4,000 for married couples) and a surtax graduated from 1 percent on incomes of about $20,000 to 6 percent on incomes above $500,000. The highest total tax thus would be 7 percent. Opponents objected that the tax was class legislation and a sectional raid on eastern wealth, but Cordell Hull (D-Tenn.), who guided it through the House, disclaimed any purpose of sharing the wealth and justified the tax on the principle that eastern profits derived from all parts of the country.

Before the new tariff had cleared the Senate, the administration proposed the first major banking and currency reform since the Civil War. The need for a change had been acknowledged since the brief panic of 1907, which threatened to bring on widespread bank failures. The panic had occasioned the appointment of a National Monetary Commission headed by Sen. Nelson W. Aldrich, which in 1912 recommended creation of a National Reserve Association with fifteen branches. The plan aimed to strengthen the banking system by pooling bank reserves and maintaining a flexible currency.

But to progressive Democrats it seemed a plan to revive the second Bank of the United States, which Jackson had destroyed, and to extend the Wall Street "Money Trust's" control of business and finance, which a House committee under A. P. Pujo (D-La.) began to expose in the fall of 1912. Dominant figures in framing the Democrats' counterproposal were Rep. Carter Glass, a pugnacious redhead from Virginia, and the economist H. Parker Willis. Glass's chief contribution was a provision, which appealed to traditional Democratic fears of centralization, for regional reserve banks to be owned by member banks. Wilson, however, insisted on a central board of governors, comprising only a minority of bankers, as the capstone of the system.

A group of radical agrarians, with support from William Jennings Bryan, insisted that the entire system, including the banks and the governing board, should be under governmental control. They won a compromise arrangement excluding bankers' representatives from the central board, making Federal Reserve Notes obligations of the federal government, and providing short-term, ninety-day farm loans as well as business loans. The Glass-Owen Federal Reserve Act, signed into law two days before Christmas 1913, created a new banking system along regional lines, with twelve Federal Reserve Banks, each owned by member banks in its district. All national banks became members; state banks and trust companies could join if they wished. Each member bank had to subscribe 6 percent of its capital to the Federal Reserve Bank and deposit a portion of its reserve there, the amount depending on the size of the community.

These "bankers' banks" dealt chiefly with their members and not at all with individuals. Along with other banking functions, the chief service to member banks was to rediscount their loans, that is, to take them over in exchange for Federal Reserve Notes, which member banks might then use to make further loans. The Federal Reserve Notes in turn were based 40 percent on government gold and 60 percent on commercial and agricultural paper (the promissory notes signed by borrowers). This arrangement made it possible to expand both the money supply and bank

Reading the Death Warrant. *Wilson's plan for banking and currency reform spells the death of the "Money Trust" according to this New York World cartoon. [C. R. Macauley]*

credit in times of high business activity, or as the level of borrowing increased. A Federal Reserve Board with seven members (eight after 1922) named three of the nine members on each Reserve Bank's board (member banks chose the remaining six) and exercised general supervision, including review of the rediscount rates. These rates might be raised to fight inflation by tightening credit or lowered to stimulate business by making credit more easily available.

This new system corrected three great defects in the previous arrangements. Now reserves could be pooled, affording greater security; both the currency and bank credit became more elastic; and the concentration of reserves in New York was lessened. The system represented a new departure in active governmental intervention and control in one of the most sensitive segments of the economy.

The next major issue confronting Wilson, after tariffs and banking, concerned the antitrust laws. In his campaign Wilson had made trust-busting the central focus of the New Freedom, and information gathered by the Pujo Committee showed that the concentration of economic power had continued to grow despite the Sherman Act and the Bureau of Corporations. Wilson's solution to the problem was revision of the Sherman Act to define more explicitly what counted as "restraint of trade."

During the summer of 1914, while Congress took up several bills, Wilson suddenly reversed himself and, influenced by attorneys Brandeis and George Rublee, decided to make a strong Federal Trade Commission the cornerstone of his antitrust program.

Created by an act of September 1914, the five-member commission replaced Roosevelt's Bureau of Corporations and assumed new powers to define "unfair trade practices" and to issue "cease and desist" orders when it found evidence of unfair competition.

Having embraced the Brandeis principle of "controlled competition," Wilson seemed to lose interest in the antitrust bill drafted by Henry D. Clayton (D-Ala.) of the House Judiciary Committee, which followed the president's original idea of defining specific acts in restraint of trade. The Clayton Antitrust Act, passed in October 1914, outlawed such practices as price discrimination (charging different customers different prices for the same goods), "tying" agreements which limited the right of dealers to handle the products of competing manufacturers, interlocking directorates connecting corporations with a capital of more than $1 million (or banks with more than $5 million), and corporations' acquisition of stock in competing corporations. In every case, however, conservative forces in the Senate qualified these provisions by tacking on the weakening phrase "where the effect may be to substantially lessen competition" or words of similar effect. In accordance with the president's recommendation, however, corporate officials were made individually responsible for any violations. Victims of price discrimination and tying agreements could sue for compensation three times the amount of damages suffered.

Agrarian radicals, in alliance with organized labor, won a stipulation which supposedly exempted farm labor organizations from the antitrust laws, but actually only declared them not to be, per se, unlawful combinations in restraint of trade. Injunctions in labor disputes, moreover, were not to be handed down by federal courts unless "necessary to prevent irreparable injury to property." Hailed by Samuel Gompers as labor's "Magna Carta," these provisions were little more than pious affirmations, as later court decisions would demonstrate. Wilson himself remarked that the act did little more than affirm the right of unions to exist by forbidding their dissolution for being in restraint of trade.

Administration of the antitrust laws generally proved disappointing to the more vehement progressives under Wilson. In the wake of a business setback late in 1913 Wilson set out to reassure business that his purposes were friendly. As Secretary of Commerce William C. Redfield put it later, Wilson hoped to "create in the Federal Trade Commission a counsellor and friend to the business world." Its first chairman, Joseph E. Davies of

Wisconsin, lacked forcefulness, and under Edward N. Hurley, a Chicago industrialist who succeeded Davies in June 1916, the FTC practically abandoned its function of watchdog. Under Attorney-General McReynolds the Justice Department offered help and advice to businessmen interested in arranging matters so as to avoid antitrust prosecutions. The appointment of conservative men to the Interstate Commerce Commission and the Federal Reserve won plaudits from the business world and profoundly disappointed progressives.

The fact was that Wilson had never been a strong progressive of the social-justice persuasion. He had carried out promises to lower the tariff, reorganize the banking system, and strengthen the antitrust laws. Swept along by the course of events, and the pressures of more far-reaching progressives, he was pushed farther than he intended to go on some points. The New Freedom was now complete, he wrote Treasury Secretary McAdoo late in 1914; the future would be "a time of healing because a time of just dealing." Although Wilson endorsed state action for women's suffrage, he declined to endorse a suffrage amendment because his party platform had not. He had cultivated the support of black voters, but let members of his cabinet extend Jim Crow practices in the federal government and froze out all but a few black appointees. He withheld support from federal child labor legislation because he regarded it a state matter. He opposed a bill for federal support of rural credits on the ground that it was "unwise and unjustifiable to extend the credit of the government to a single class of the community." Not until the second anniversary of his inauguration (March 4, 1915) did Wilson sign an important piece of social-justice legislation, the La Follette Seamen's Act. The product of stubborn agitation by Andrew Furuseth, eloquent president of the Seamen's Union, the act strengthened safety requirements, reduced the power of captains, set minimum food standards, and required regular wage payments. Seaman who jumped ship before their contracts expired, moreover, were relieved of the charge of desertion.

PROGRESSIVE RESURGENCE   It was the need to weld a winning coalition in 1916 that pushed Wilson back on the road of reform. Progressive Democrats were restless, and after war broke out in Europe in August 1914, further divisions arose over defense and foreign policy. At the same time the Republicans were repairing their own rift, as the Progressive party showed little staying power in the midterm elections and Roosevelt showed little will to preserve it. It was plain to most observers that Wilson could shape a majority only by courting progressives of all parties. In January 1916 Wilson scored points with them when he nominated Louis D. Brandeis to the Supreme Court. Conservatives waged a vigorous battle against Brandeis, but Senate progressives rallied to win confirmation of the social-justice champion, the first Jewish member of the Supreme Court.

Meanwhile Wilson began to embrace a broad program of farm and labor reforms. On farm credit, after having first opposed it he reversed himself abruptly, supporting early in 1916 a proposal to set up land banks to sponsor long-term farm loans. With this boost the Federal Farm Loan Act became law on July 17. Under the control of a Federal Farm Loan Board, twelve Federal Land Banks, each with a minimum capital of $750,000, paralleled the Federal Reserve Banks and offered farmers loans of five to forty years' duration at low interest rates.

Thus the dream of cheap rural credits, sponsored by a generation of Alliancemen and Populists, came to fruition. Democrats never embraced the Populist subtreasury plan, but made a small step in that direction with the Warehouse Act of 1916. This measure authorized federal licensing of private warehouses; federal backing made their receipts for stored produce more acceptable as collateral for short-term bank loans. Other concessions to farm demands came more readily in the Smith-Lever Act of 1914 and the Smith-Hughes Act of 1917, both of which passed with little controversy. The first, sponsored by Sen. Hoke Smith (D-Ga.) and Rep. A. F. Lever (D-S.C.), provided federal grants-in-aid for farm demonstration agents under the supervision of land-grant colleges. The measure made permanent a program that had started in Texas in 1903 and that had already spread to many localities with help from the Agriculture Department and the General Education Board. In 1923 the county farm agents were organized into an Extension Service supervised by state land-grant colleges. The second measure, sponsored by Smith and Rep. Dudley M. Hughes (D-Ga.), extended agricultural and mechanical education to high schools through grants-in-aid.

Farmers with automobiles had more than a passing interest as well in the Federal Highways Act of 1916, which provided dollar-matching contributions to states with highway departments that met certain federal standards. The measure authorized distribution of $75 million over five years, and marked a sharp departure from Jacksonian opposition to internal improvements at federal expense, just as the Federal Reserve System departed from Jacksonian banking principles. Although the argument that highways were one of the nation's defense needs weakened constitutional scruples against the act, it still restricted support to "post roads." A renewal act in 1921 would mark the beginning of a systematic network of numbered United States highways.

The progressive resurgence of 1916 broke the logjam on labor reforms as well. With newfound support from the administration, the Kern-McGillicuddy Bill, a workmen's compensation measure for federal employees, passed in August. Advocates of child-labor legislation persuaded Wilson that social-justice progressives would regard his stand on the issue as an important test of his humanitarian concerns, and Wilson overcame doubts of its constitutionality to support and sign the Keating-Owen Child Labor Act, which excluded from interstate commerce goods manufactured by children under fourteen. Both the Keating-Owen Act and a later act of 1919 to achieve the same purpose with a prohibitory tax were ruled unconstitutional by the Supreme Court on the grounds that regulation of interstate commerce could not extend to the conditions of labor. Effective action against the social evil of child labor had to await the New Deal, although it seems likely that discussion of the issue contributed to the sharp reduction in the number of underage workers during the next few years. Another important accomplishment was the eight-hour day for railroad workers, a measure that the Supreme Court upheld. The Adamson Act of 1916 was brought about by a threatened strike of railroad brotherhoods demanding the eight-hour day and other concessions. Wilson, who objected to some of the union demands, nevertheless went before Congress to request action on the hours limitation. The resulting Adamson Act required an eight-hour day, beginning January 1, 1917, with time and a half for overtime, and appointed a commission to study the problem of railroad labor.

In Wilson's first term progressivism reached its zenith. A creative time, the age of progressivism set at the beginning of the twentieth century a framework within which American politics and society would still function, by and large, near the end of the century. Progressivism had conquered the old dictum that the government is best which governs least, whatever political rhetoric might be heard to the contrary, and left the more extreme doctrines of limited government as dead as Herbert Spencer. Progressivism, an amalgam of agrarian, business, governmental, and social reform, amounted in the end to a movement for positive government. From two decades of ferment (three, if the Populist years be counted) the great fundamental contribution of progressive politics was the firm establishment and general acceptance of the public-service concept of the state.

THE LIMITS OF PROGRESSIVISM

The Progressive period was an optimistic age in which reformers of various hues were persuaded, in Walter Lippmann's
terms, that drift would give way to mastery over social ills and
that no problem lay beyond solution. But like all great historic
movements, progressivism had elements of paradox and irony.
Despite its talk of democracy, it was the age of disfranchisement
for southern blacks—an action seen by many whites as progressive. The initiative and referendum, supposed democratic reforms, proved subject to manipulation by well-financed publicity campaigns. And much of the public policy of the time
came to be formulated by experts and members of appointed
boards, not by broad segments of the population. There is a fine
irony indeed in the fact that the drive to increase the political
role of ordinary people moved parallel with efforts to strengthen
executive leadership and exalt expertise. This age of efficiency
and bureaucracy, in business as well as government, brought into
being a society in which more and more of the decisions affecting
people's lives were made by faceless policy-makers.

Progressivism was largely a middle-class movement in which
the poor and unorganized had little influence. The supreme
irony was that a movement so dedicated to the rhetoric of democracy should experience so steady a decline in voter participation. In 1912, the year of the Bull Moose campaign, voting
dropped off by between 6 and 7 percent. The new politics of
issues and charismatic leaders proved to be less effective in turning out voters than party organizations and bosses had been. And
by 1916 the optimism of an age that looked to infinite progress
was already confronted by a vast slaughter. Europe had already
stumbled into war, and America would soon be drawn in. The
twentieth century, which dawned with such bright hopes, held
in store episodes of horror unparalleled in history.

FURTHER READING

A good introduction to the issues which faced the Progressives can
be found in William L. O'Neill's *The Progressive Years: America Comes
of Age* (1975).° Otis L. Graham, Jr.'s *The Great Campaigns: Reform and
War in America, 1900–1928* (1971), reviews the scholarly interpretations and carries the Progressive impulse in its altered forms up to the

°These books are available in paperback editions.

depression. George E. Mowry's *The Era of Theodore Roosevelt* (1958)°
and Arthur S. Link's *Woodrow Wilson and the Progressive Era* (1954)°
block out the periods of reform according to which party held power.
Lewis L. Gould's *Reform and Regulation: American Politics, 1900–1916*
(1978), is a more recent review of scholarship on the entire period.

Progressivism has been interpreted in many ways. Lewis L. Gould
(ed.), *The Progressive Era* (1973),° and David M. Kennedy (ed.), *Progressivism: The Critical Issues* (1971),° each provides a variety of short essays
on the subject. Robert H. Wiebe's *The Search for Order, 1877–1920*
(1966),° presents the organizational model for reform. Richard Hofstadter's *The Age of Reform: From Bryan to FDR* (1955)° examines the
consensus at the basis of reform. Christopher Lasch counters that view in
The New Radicalism in America, 1889–1963 (1965),° and John P. Diggins
supports the Lasch view in *The American Left in the Twentieth Century*
(1973).° Gabriel Kolko sees reform as another means of social control in
The Triumph of Conservatism (1963).° John D. Buenker's *Urban Liberalism and Progressive Reform* (1973)° stresses the role played by immigrant voters in supporting reformers. Other interpretative works include Samuel P. Hays's *The Response to Industrialism, 1885–1914*
(1957),° James Weinstein's *The Corporate Ideal in the Liberal State,
1900–1918* (1968),° Arthur Ekrich's *Progressivism in Practice* (1974),
and Jean Quandt's *From the Small Town to the Great Community: The Social Thought of Progressive Intellectuals* (1970).

Scholars disagree not only about the goals of the Progressives but
about just who the Progressives were. George E. Mowry's *The California
Progressives* (1951)° and Richard Hofstadter's *The Age of Reform*
(1955)° argue that the reform impulse originated out of old-stock voter
anxieties over the new immigration. David P. Thelen, among others,
argues in *The New Citizenship: Origins of Progressivism in Wisconsin,
1885–1900* (1972), that reform groups were diverse coalitions interested in efficiency. Sheldon Hackney's *Populism to Progressivism in Alabama* (1969) sees the two reform groups as coming from different classes
in society. Jack T. Kirby's *Darkness at the Dawning: Race and Reform in
the Progressive South* (1972) documents how blacks were excluded from
certain areas of "progress." Robert H. Wiebe's *Businessmen and Reform*
(1962) locates the reform impulse in the hands of an emerging economic
interest group.

Biographers of the three progressive presidents elaborate on the
complexity of reform. Edmund E. Morris's *The Rise of Theodore Roose-
velt* (1979),° a favorable account, can be balanced with G. Wallace
Chessman's *Theodore Roosevelt and the Politics of Power* (1968) and
William H. Harbaugh's *Power and Responsibility: The Life and Times of
Theodore Roosevelt* (1961).° Also helpful is John M. Blum's *The Republi-
can Roosevelt* (1954).° Taft receives sympathetic treatment in Paolo E.
Colletta's *The Presidency of William Howard Taft* (1973) and more criti-
cal assessment in Donald E. Anderson's *William Howard Taft* (1973).
For Wilson, begin with the multivolume biography (1947–1965) by Ar-
thur S. Link, particularly *The New Freedom* (1956). Other treatments of
Wilson's domestic policies are John M. Blum's *Woodrow Wilson and the*

Politics of Morality (1956)° and John A. Garraty's *Woodrow Wilson* (1956).°

Different scholarly approaches detail the impact of reform at the urban level. A survey of a state's efforts to cope with urban problems is Richard N. Abrams's *Conservatism in a Progressive Era: Massachusetts Politics, 1900–1912* (1964). Roy Lubove's *The Progressives and the Slums* (1962), Jack Hall's *Juvenile Reform in the Progressive Era* (1971), and Allen Davis's *Spearheads for Reform: The Social Settlements and the Progressive Movement, 1890–1919* (1967),° all examine the problem of urban decay. Steven A. Reiss's *Touching Base: Professional Baseball and American Culture in the Progressive Era* (1980) and Dominick Cavallo's *Muscles and Morals: Organized Playgrounds and Urban Reform, 1880–1920* (1981), link athletics to new forms of organization and socialization. Health issues are covered in David M. Kennedy's *Birth Control in America: The Career of Margaret Sanger* (1970),° David J. Rothman's *Conscience and Convenience: The Asylum and Its Alternatives in Progressive America* (1980),° and John Ettling's *The Germ of Laziness: Rockefeller Philanthropy and Public Health in the New South* (1981).

Other aspects of the progressive impulse receive focus in James H. Timberlake's *Prohibition and the Progressive Movement, 1900–1920* (1963),° Samuel Haber's *Efficiency and Uplift: Scientific Management in the Progressive Era* (1964), David M. Chalmers's *The Social and Political Ideas of the Muckrakers* (1964),° and Harold S. Wilson's *McClure's Magazine and the Muckrakers* (1970). Samuel P. Hayes's *Conservation and the Gospel of Efficiency: The Progressive Conservation Movement, 1890–1920* (1959),° James L. Penick's *Progressive Politics and Conservation: The Ballinger-Pinchot Affair* (1968), and Harold T. Pinkett's *Gifford Pinchot: Private and Public Forester* (1970) cover that controversy.

Labor studies include Stephen Meyer III's *The Five Dollar Day: Labor Management and Social Control in the Ford Motor Company, 1908–1921* (1981), Peter R. Shergold's *Working Class Life: The "American Standard" in Comparative Perspective, 1899–1913* (1982), and Tamara K. Hareven's *Family Time and Industrial Time: The Relationship between the Family and Work in a New England Industrial Community* (1982).°

Biographies of public figures during the Progressive Era include Richard Lovitt's *George W. Norris: The Making of a Progressive* (1963), Louis R. Harlan's *Booker T. Washington: The Wizard of Tuskegee, 1901–1915* (1982),° Michael E. Parrish's *Felix Frankfurter and His Times: The Reform Years* (1982), George H. Nash's *The Life of Herbert Hoover: The Engineer, 1874–1914* (1983), David P. Thelen's *Robert M. La Follette and the Insurgent Spirit* (1976),° John Braeman's *Alfred J. Beveridge* (1971), and R. F. Wessner's *Charles Evans Hughes: Politics and Reform in New York, 1905–1910* (1967).

25

WILSON AND THE
GREAT WAR

WILSON AND FOREIGN AFFAIRS

When Woodrow Wilson was sworn in as the president of
the United States in March 1913 the former historian brought to
the office little background in the study of diplomacy and none at
all in its practice. Wilson tacitly admitted this when he remarked
just before taking office, "It would be an irony of fate if my administration had to deal chiefly with foreign affairs." But events
in Europe were to make the irony all too real. From the summer
of 1914, when the guns of August heralded a World War, foreign
relations increasingly overshadowed all else, including Wilson's
domestic program, the New Freedom.

AN IDEALIST'S DIPLOMACY   Although lacking in international experience, Wilson did not lack ideas or convictions in this area. The
product of a Calvinist past, Wilson brought to diplomacy a version of progressivism more than a little touched with Calvinist
righteousness. Both Wilson and his secretary of state, William
Jennings Bryan, believed that America had been called to advance democracy and moral progress in the world. If they did not
always follow principle at the expense of national self-interest,
they did in many respects try to develop a diplomatic policy
based on idealism.

The teetotaling Bryan, undismayed by ridicule of his "grape
juice diplomacy," during 1913–1914 negotiated some thirty
"cooling-off" treaties under which participating nations pledged
themselves not to go to war over any disagreement for a period of

twelve months pending arbitration by an international panel. Arbitration treaties were in fact not an invention of Bryan's, although the "cooling-off" feature gave them a new twist. In any case the treaties were of little consequence, soon forgotten in the revolutionary sweep of world events that would make the twentieth century the bloodiest in recorded history.

One of the first applications of Wilsonian idealism to foreign policy came when the president renounced dollar diplomacy. The government, he said, was not supporting any "special groups or interests." As good as his word, on March 18, 1913, he withdrew governmental support of the Six-Power Consortium then preparing to float a large loan to China. Such a monopolistic grant, he said, would compromise China's integrity and possibly involve the United States in a future intervention. Without governmental backing, American bankers withdrew.

INTERVENTION IN MEXICO   Closer to home Wilson found it harder to take such high ground. Nor did the logic of his "missionary diplomacy" always imply nonintervention. Mexico, which had been in the throes of revolution for nearly three years, presented a thorny problem. For most of the thirty-five years from 1876 to 1911 President Porfirio Diaz had dominated Mexico. As military dictator he had suppressed opposition and showered favors on his followers and on foreign investors, who piled up holdings in Mexican mines, petroleum, railroads, and agriculture. But eventually the dictator's hold slipped, and in 1910 popular resentment boiled over in revolt. In May 1911 revolutionary armies occupied Mexico City and Diaz fled.

The leader of the rebellion, Francisco I. Madero, proved unable to manage the tough customers drawn by the scramble for power. In February 1913 Gen. Victoriano Huerta assumed power and Madero was murdered soon afterward. Confronted with this turn to rule by a military dictator, Wilson enunciated a new doctrine of nonrecognition: "We hold, as I am sure all thoughtful leaders of republican government everywhere hold, that just government rests upon the consent of the governed," he said. Recognition, formerly extended routinely to governments which exercised *de facto* power, now might depend on judgments of their legality: an immoral government presumably would not pass muster.

Huerta's hold on power was still unsure, and for a while Wilson resisted the impulse to intervene. In October 1913 he sought to quiet fears of intervention with a statement that the United States "will never again seek one additional foot of territory by conquest." Nevertheless he obliquely expressed sympathy with the revolutionary movement and began to put diplomatic pressure on Huerta. "I am going to teach the South American republics to elect good men," he told a visiting British diplomat. Early in 1914 he removed an embargo on arms to Mexico in order to help the resurgent revolutionaries under Venustiano Carranza of the Constitutionalist party, and stationed warships off Vera Cruz to halt arms shipments to Huerta.

On April 9, 1914, several American sailors, gathering supplies in Tampico, strayed into a restricted area and were arrested. The local commander, a Huertista, quickly released them and sent an apology to Adm. Henry T. Mayo, the American naval commander. There the incident might have ended, but Mayo demanded a salute to the American flag. Wilson backed him up and got from Congress authority to use force to bring Huerta to terms. Before the Tampico incident could be resolved, Wilson authorized a naval force to enter Vera Cruz and stop the imminent landing of an arms shipment. American marines and sailors went ashore on April 21, 1914, and occupied the town at a cost of 19 killed and 47 wounded. The Mexicans lost at least 200 killed and 300 wounded.

In Mexico the occupation aroused the opposition of all factions, and Huerta tried to rally support against foreign invasion. At this juncture Wilson accepted an offer of mediation by the ABC powers (Argentina, Brazil, and Chile), which in June proposed withdrawal of United States forces, the removal of Huerta, and installation of a provisional government sympathetic to reform. Huerta refused, but the moral effect of the proposal, his isolation abroad, and the growing strength of his foes forced him to leave office in July. In August the Carranzistas entered Mexico City, and in November the Americans left Vera Cruz. Finally, in October 1915 the United States and several Latin American governments recognized Carranza as president of Mexico.

Still, the troubles south of the border continued. The disorders had spawned independent bands of freebooters, Pancho Villa's among the wildest. All through 1915 fighting between the forces of Villa and Carranza swayed back and forth. In January 1916 Villa seized a train at Santa Ysabel and murdered eighteen American mining engineers in a deliberate attempt to provoke American intervention, discredit Carranza, and build himself up as an opponent of the "Gringos." That failing, he crossed the border on raids into Texas and New Mexico. On March 9 he entered Columbus, New Mexico, burned the town, and killed seventeen Americans.

Wilson then had to abandon his policy of "watchful waiting." With the reluctant consent of Carranza, he sent Gen. John J.

Pancho Villa (center) and his generals. [National Archives]

Pershing across the border with a force of some 15,000 men and mobilized 150,000 National Guardsmen along the frontier. For nearly a year Pershing went on a wild-goose chase after Villa through northern Mexico and, missing his catch, was ordered home in January 1917. Carranza then pressed his own war against the bandits and put through a new liberal constitution in 1917. Mexico was by then well on the way to a more orderly government.

PROBLEMS IN THE CARIBBEAN   In the Caribbean Wilson found it as hard to act on his ideals as in Mexico. Despite Wilson's stand against dollar diplomacy, American marines who had entered Nicaragua in 1912 stayed there to prevent renewed civil war. In July 1915 American marines landed in Haiti after two successive revolutions and subsequent disorders. Later that year a new Haitian government imposed by the American military signed a treaty which placed the United States in control of customs collections. The American forces stayed until 1934. Disorders in the Dominican Republic brought American marines to the country in 1916; they remained until 1924.

The Great War and America

Such problems in Latin America and the Caribbean loomed larger than the gathering storm in Europe. When the thunderbolt of war struck Europe in the summer of 1914 it came to most Americans, one North Carolinian wrote, "as lightning out of a clear sky." Whatever the troubles in Mexico, whatever disorders and interventions agitated other countries, it seemed unreal that civilized Europe could descend into such an orgy of destruction. Since the fall of Napoleon in 1815, Europe had known local wars but only as interruptions of a general peace that contributed to a century of unprecedented material progress. But the assassination in Sarajevo of Austrian Archduke Franz Ferdinand by a Serbian nationalist, Austria-Hungary's determination to punish Serbia, and Russia's mobilization in sympathy with her Slavic brothers in Serbia suddenly triggered a European system of alliances: the Triple Alliance or Central Powers (Germany, Austria-Hungary, and Italy) and the Triple Entente (France, Great Britain, and Russia). When Russia refused to stop its mobilization, Germany declared war on Russia on August 1, 1914, and on Russia's ally France two days later. Germany then invaded Belgium to get at France, which brought Great Britain into the war on August 4. Japan, eager to seize German holdings in the Pacific, declared war on August 23 and Turkey entered on the side of the Central Powers a week later. Italy stayed out, however, and struck a bargain under which she joined the Allies in 1915.

AMERICA'S INITIAL REACTIONS   The initial reaction of shock in the United States was followed by gratitude that an ocean stood between America and the battlefields. "Our isolated position and freedom from entangling alliances," said the *Literary Digest,* "inspire our press with cheering assurance that we are in no peril of being drawn into the European quarrel." Beginning on August 4 President Wilson issued routine declarations of neutrality. On August 19 he urged the American people to be "impartial in thought as well as action."

That was more easily said than done, not least for Wilson himself. Americans might want to stay out, but most of them cared which side won. In the 1910 population of 92 million, more than 32 million were "hyphenated Americans," first- or second-generation immigrants who retained ties to their old countries. Among the more than 13 million from the countries at war, by far the largest group were 8 million German-Americans. And 4 million Irish-Americans harbored a deep-rooted enmity to Britain, further heightened by British suppression of the Irish Easter Rebellion of 1916. These groups instinctively leaned toward the Central Powers.

But old-line Americans, largely of British origin, were sympathetic to the Allies. If, as has been said, Britain and the United States were divided by a common language, they were united by ties of culture and tradition. Since the British had yielded on the Venezuelan and Alaskan boundary disputes, a grand rapprochement in sympathy and good relations had occurred. Americans identified also with France, which had contributed to American culture and ideas, and to independence itself. Britain and France, if not their ally Russia, seemed the custodians of liberal democracy, while Germany more and more seemed the embodiment of autocracy and militarism. If not a direct threat to the United States, Germany would pose at least a potential threat if it destroyed the balance of power in Europe. High officers of the United States government were pro-British in thought from the outset. Robert Lansing, first counselor of the State Department, Walter Hines Page, ambassador to London, and Col. Edward House, Wilson's close adviser, saw in German militarism a potential danger to America.

Just what effects the propaganda of the warring powers had is unclear. The Germans and the British were particularly active, but German propaganda, which played on American dislike of Russian autocracy and Russian anti-Semitism, fell mainly upon barren ground. Only German- and Irish-Americans responded to a "hate England" theme. From the outset the British had one su-

Most Americans leaned toward the Allies, but all were shocked at the outbreak of the Great War. In this cartoon, the Samson-like War pulls down the temple of Civilization. [Harding in the Brooklyn Eagle]

preme advantage in this area. Once they had cut the direct cable from Germany early in the war, nearly all news from the battle fronts had to clear through London. Wellington House, the British propaganda agency, used the services of Viscount James Bryce, a close student of the American scene, among others, and reports of German atrocities endorsed by Bryce were convincing to Americans. Some of these stories later proved to be highly embellished, but there were real atrocities enough in the German occupation of Belgium to affront American feelings. Most Americans already knew pretty well which way they were leaning.

A STRAINED NEUTRALITY   At first the war brought a slump in American exports and the threat of a depression, but by the spring of 1915 the Allies' demand for supplies generated a wartime boom. The Allies at first financed their purchases by disposing of American securities, but ultimately they needed loans. Early in the war Secretary Bryan informed J. P. Morgan that loans to any warring nation were "inconsistent with the true spirit of neutrality." Money, he warned, "is the worst of all contrabands because it commands everything else." Still, by October 1914 Wilson quietly began approving short-term credits to sustain trade with the Allies. When in September 1915 it became apparent that the Allies could no longer carry on without long-term credit, the administration raised all restrictions and Morgan soon extended a loan of $500 million to England and France. American investors would advance over $2 billion to the Allies before the United States entered the war, and only $27 million to Germany.

The administration nevertheless clung to the fond hope of

neutrality through two and a half years of warfare in Europe and tried to uphold the traditions of "freedom of the seas" which had guided American policy since the Napoleonic Wars. As the German drive through Belgium and toward Paris finally ground down into the stalemate of trench warfare, trade on the high seas assumed a new importance. In a war of attrition survival depended on access to supplies, and in such a war British naval power counted for a great deal. With the German fleet outclassed and bottled up almost from the outset, the war in many ways assumed the pattern that had once led America into war with Britain in 1812. Indeed, as British Orders in Council (familiar from a century before) restricted trade with central Europe, they once again raised some of the old issues. Wilson remarked that only two Princeton men had been president, and that both he and Madison faced similar problems of "freedom of the seas."

On August 6, 1914, Secretary Bryan called upon the belligerents to accept the Declaration of London, drafted and signed in 1909 by leading powers but never ratified by the British. That document, the culmination of nineteenth-century liberal thought on the rules of warfare, reduced the list of contraband items and specified that a blockade was legal only when effective just outside enemy ports. The Central Powers promptly accepted. The British almost as promptly refused, lest they lose some of their advantage in sea power. Beginning with an Order in Council of August 20, 1914, Britain gradually extended the list of contraband goods to include all sorts of things formerly excluded, such as food, cotton, wood, and certain ores. Wilson protested, but Ambassador Page, personally pro-British, assured Foreign Minister Sir Edward Grey that the two could find ways of getting around the problem. The British consequently gave little serious heed to further protests.

In November 1914 the British declared the whole North Sea a war zone, sowed it with mines, and ordered neutral ships to enter only by the straits of Dover, where they could be easily searched. In March 1915 they further announced that they would detain and carry into port ships carrying goods of presumed enemy destination, ownership, or origin. Previous rules had required search on the high seas and this, combined with Britain's new policy, caused extended delays, sometimes running into months. The same order also directed British ships to stop vessels carrying German goods via neutral ports. When the State Department protested, Earl Grey reminded the Americans that this was the same doctrine of continuous voyage on which the United States had acted in the 1860s to keep British goods out of the Confederacy.

NEUTRAL RIGHTS AND SUBMARINES   British actions, including black-listing of companies that traded with the enemy and censorship of the mails, raised some old issues of neutral rights, but the German reaction introduced an entirely new question. With the German fleet bottled up, only German submarines could venture out to harass the enemy. On February 4, 1915, in response to the "illegal" British blockade, the German government proclaimed a war zone around the British Isles. Enemy merchant ships in those waters were liable to sinking, the Germans declared, "although it may not always be possible to save crews and passengers." Since the British sometimes flew neutral flags as a ruse, neutral ships in the zone would also be in danger. U-boat (*Unterseeboot*) warfare violated the established procedure of stopping enemy vessels on the high seas and providing for the safety of passengers and crews, since the chief advantage was in surprise.

The United States pronounced the German policy "an inde-fensible violation of neutral rights" and warned that Germany would be held to "strict accountability" for any destruction of American lives and property. If the meaning of the phrase was unclear, the stern tone of the note was unmistakable. The admin-istration asked the British to give up flying neutral flags and its blockade of foodstuffs in return for German renunciation of sub-marine warfare, but nothing came of the effort. On March 28, 1915, one American drowned when the Germans sank the Brit-ish steamer *Falaba* in the Irish Sea. On May 1 the American tanker *Gulflight* went down with a loss of two lives. The adminis-

Cunard announces the sailing of the Lusitania. The German Embassy warns travelers that British ships sailing in the war zone are "liable to destruction."
[New York Public Library]

tration was divided on the proper course of action. Bryan wanted to say that American citizens entered the war zone at their own risk; his counselor, Robert Lansing, and Colonel House wanted to imply a possible break in diplomatic relations with Germany. Then, as Wilson pondered the alternatives, the sinking of the British Cunard liner *Lusitania* provoked a crisis.

On May 7, 1915, the captain of the German U-20 sighted a four-stack liner moving slowly through the Irish Sea and fired a torpedo. It hit the mark, and the ship exploded and sank within eighteen minutes. Only as it tipped into the waves was he able to make out the name *Lusitania* on the stern. Before the ship left New York bound for Liverpool the German Embassy had published warnings in the American press against travel to the war zone, but among the 1,198 persons lost were 128 Americans.

The American public was outraged. It was an act of piracy, Theodore Roosevelt declared. In an effort to quiet the uproar Wilson, speaking to newly naturalized citizens in Philadelphia, said: "There is such a thing as a man being too proud to fight. There is such a thing as a nation being so right that it does not need to convince others by force that it is right." Wilson's previous demand for "strict accountability," however, forced him to make a strong response. On May 13 Bryan reluctantly signed a note demanding that the Germans abandon unrestricted submarine warfare, disavow the sinking, and pay reparations. The Germans responded that the ship had been armed (which it was not) and carried a cargo of small arms and ammunition (which it did). A second note on June 9 repeated American demands in stronger terms. The United States, Wilson asserted, was "contending for nothing less high and sacred than the rights of humanity." Bryan, unwilling to risk war on the issue, resigned in protest and joined the peace movement as a private citizen. His successor, Robert Lansing, signed the note. A third note on July 21 warned that repetition of such sinkings would be regarded as "deliberately unfriendly."

Before the lengthy exchange ended in February 1916, other events took the spotlight and aroused further hostility to the Central Powers. In New York a German agent, Dr. Heinrich Albert, absent-mindedly left his briefcase on a subway where an alert American agent picked it up. On August 15, 1915, the New York *World* began to publish letters revealing Albert's subversive activities, which included subsidizing pro-German speakers and efforts to buy up munitions plants. More damaging were papers which fell into British hands, revealing that Austrian Ambassador Dr. Constantin Dumba was attempting to foment strikes in war industries, and finally, that German attachés Franz von Papen and Karl Boy-ed were fomenting sabotage.

In response to the uproar over the *Lusitania*, the German government had secretly ordered U-boat captains to avoid sinking large passenger vessels. When, despite the order, two American lives were lost in the sinking of the British liner *Arabic*, bound for New York, German Ambassador Count von Bernstorff demanded and got from Berlin an offer of indemnity and a public assurance which he delivered on September 1, 1915: "Liners will not be sunk by our submarines without warning and without safety of the lives of non-combatants, provided that the liners do not try to escape or offer resistance." With this "Arabic pledge" Wilson's resolute stand seemed to have resulted in a victory for his policy.

During the fall of 1915 Wilson's trusted advisor Edward M. House proposed to renew a mediation effort he had explored on a visit to London, Paris, and Berlin the previous spring—before the *Lusitania* sinking. In January and February 1916 House visited those capitals again, but found neither side ready to begin serious negotiations. The French and British would soon be engaged in destructive battles, the French at Verdun and the British at the Somme, and both were determined to fight until they could bargain from strength.

Peace advocates in Congress now rose up to challenge the administration's policy on neutral rights. In February 1916 Rep. Jeff McLemore (D-Tex.) and Sen. Thomas P. Gore (D-Okla.) introduced similar resolutions warning Americans against traveling on armed belligerent vessels. Such surrender to the German threat, Wilson asserted, would be a "deliberate abdication of our hitherto proud position as spokesmen, even amidst the turmoil of war, for the law and the right." Once accept a single abatement of right and "the whole fine fabric of international law might crumble under our hands piece by piece." The administration worked desperately to bring Democratic congressmen in line, and with the help of some Republicans managed to defeat both resolutions by a solid margin. On March 24, 1916, a U-boat torpedoed the French steamer *Sussex* with injury to two Americans. This time Wilson threatened to break off relations with Germany, but got a renewed pledge that U-boats would not torpedo merchant and passenger ships.

THE DEBATE OVER PREPAREDNESS   The *Lusitania* incident, and more generally the quarrels over neutral commerce, contributed to a growing demand for a stronger army and navy. Even before the end of 1914 spokesmen for preparedness included Elihu Root,

Lansing, Roosevelt, Sen. Henry Cabot Lodge, and editors George Harvey of the *North American Review* and Lyman Abbott of the *Outlook*. On December 1, 1914, the champions of preparedness organized the National Security League to promote their cause. After the *Lusitania* sinking the outcry from such people grew into a clamor. Although Wilson did not announce his intentions until November 4, 1915, war preparation plans were public knowledge the previous July, when Wilson asked the War and Navy Departments to draft proposals. In his annual message in December Wilson alerted Congress to forthcoming requests.

The response was far from unanimous. Progressives and pacifists, and a broad-based antiwar sentiment running through the rural South and West, awakened the traditional American suspicion of military establishments, especially standing armies, which dated back to the colonial period. The new Democratic leader in the house, Claude Kitchin of North Carolina, opposed "the big Navy and big Army program of the jingoes and war traffickers." In the East, leaders of the peace movement organized a League to Limit Armament. Jane Addams and suffragist Carrie Chapman Catt organized a Women's Peace party. Bryan, La Follette, and other leaders lent their voices to the peace movement.

Secretary of War Lindley M. Garrison's plan to enlarge the regular army and create a national reserve force of 400,000 ran into stubborn opposition in the House Military Affairs Committee. Wilson was forced to accept a compromise between advocates of an expanded force under federal control and advocates of a traditional citizen army. The measure finally passed after Secretary Garrison gave up his office to Newton D. Baker, the mayor of Cleveland, a step which reassured progressives. The National Defense Act of June 3, 1916, expanded the regular army from 90,000 to 175,000 and permitted gradual enlargement to 223,000. It also authorized a National Guard of 440,000, made provision for their training, and gave federal funds for summer training camps for civilians. In August the Army Appropriation Act provided for a Council of National Defense to include six cabinet members, and a civilian National Defense Advisory Commission.

The bill for an increased navy had less trouble because of the general feeling expressed by Secretary Josephus Daniels that there was "no danger of militarism from a relatively strong navy such as would come from a big standing army." The Naval Construction Act of August 15 authorized between $500 million and $600 million for a three-year program of enlargement, and another act on September 7 created the United States Shipping Board, empowered to spend up to $50 million for the building or purchase of merchant vessels suitable for use as naval auxiliaries. Forced to relent on preparedness, progressive opponents of the action like Claude Kitchin and Sen. George Norris determined that the financial burden should rest on the wealthy people they held responsible for the effort. The income tax became their weapon. Supported by a groundswell of popular support, they wrote into the Revenue Act of 1916 changes which doubled the basic income tax from 1 to 2 percent, lifted the surtax to a maximum of 13 percent (a total of 15 percent) on incomes over $2 million, added an estate tax graduated up to a maximum of 10 percent, levied a 12½ percent tax on gross receipts of munitions makers, and added a new tax on corporation capital, surplus, and undistributed profits. The new taxes on wealth amounted to the most clear-cut victory of radical progressives in the entire Wilson period, a victory further consolidated and advanced after war came. It was the capstone to the edifice of progressive legislation which Wilson supported in preparation for the election of 1916.

THE ELECTION OF 1916   Republicans started that year hoping to regain their normal majority, and Roosevelt started out hoping to be their leader again. But he had committed the deadly sin of bolting his party and, what was more, expressed a bellicosity on war issues that would scare off voters. Needing somebody who would draw Bull Moose Progressives back into the fold, the regulars turned to Justice Charles Evans Hughes, who had made a progressive record in New York where he was governor from 1907 to 1910. On the Supreme Court since then, he had neither taken a stand in 1912 nor spoken out on foreign policy. To round out the ticket the party named Roosevelt's vice-president, Charles W. Fairbanks (Ind.), once again. The remnants of the Progressive party gathered in Chicago at the same time as the Republicans. Roosevelt had held out the vain hope of getting both nominations, but he now declined to lead a moribund party. Two weeks later the Progressive National Committee disbanded the party and endorsed Hughes; a minority, including their vice-presidential nominee, John M. Parker (La.), came out for Wilson.

The Democrats, as expected, chose Wilson and Marshall once again, and in their platform endorsed a program of social legislation, neutrality, and reasonable preparedness. The party further commended women's suffrage to the states, denounced groups that placed the interests of other countries above those of the United States, and pledged support for a postwar League of Nations to enforce peace with collective security measures against aggressors. The Democrats found their most popular issue, how-

ever, when former New York Gov. Martin H. Glynn in the key-
note speech got an unexpected response to his recital of historic
cases in which the United States had refused under provocation
to go to war. As he mentioned successive examples, the crowd
chanted "What did we do? What did we do?" and Glynn responded: "We didn't go to war! We didn't go to war!" The peace
theme, refined into the slogan "He kept us out of war," became
the rallying cry of the campaign, one that had the merit of taking
credit without making any promises for the future.

Rooseveltians found themselves drawn in large numbers to
Wilson who, according to Walter Lippmann, "is temporarily at
least creating, out of the reactionary, parochial fragments of the
Democracy, the only party which at this moment is national in
scope, liberal in purpose, and effective in action." The impression of Democratic purpose and effectiveness was heightened by
Republican feuding and ineptitude. On foreign policy Hughes
worked both sides of the street. While trying to keep the votes of
German-Americans and other "hyphenates," Hughes refused to
disavow Roosevelt, who was going about the country denouncing the kaiser. On social reform issues Wilson was far ahead of
Hughes, and Hughes found himself often the captive of old-line
Republican bosses more eager to punish Bull Moose Progressives
by excluding them than to win the election for Hughes.

In the end Wilson's twin rallying cries of peace and
progressivism, a unique combination of issues forged in the
legislative and diplomatic crucibles of 1916, brought victory.

Peace with Honor. *Wilson's neutral policies proved
popular in the 1916 campaign. [United Press Interna-
tional]*

Early returns showed a Republican sweep in the East and Mid-west, signaling a victory for Hughes, but the outcome remained in doubt until word came that Wilson had carried California by 3,772 votes, where one incident may have decided the outcome. While visiting California Hughes unintentionally snubbed the popular Gov. Hiram Johnson who, without Hughes's knowledge, was in the same hotel. The final vote showed a Democratic sweep of the Far West and South, enough for victory in the electoral college by 277 to 254, and in the popular vote by 9 million to 8.5 million. "It is the combination which made Jefferson and Jackson," the historian William E. Dodd exulted. "It is the South and the West united; the farmers, small businessmen and perhaps a large sprinkle of Union labor against the larger industrial, transportation and commercial interests." Dodd might have added that Wilson also carried many social-justice Progressives who had previously supported the Bull Moose campaign.

LAST EFFORTS FOR PEACE Late in the 1916 contest Wilson expressed a belief that this was the last world war the United States could keep out of, although as a historian he should have known that America had been drawn into every general European war since colonization began. Relations with Britain in 1916 had become almost as troubled as relations with Germany. The British dragged their heels on Colonel House's mediation offer; they put down the Irish Easter Rebellion so severely that they offended American opinion in general; they stepped up their economic warfare, and blacklisted firms suspected of dealing with the Central Powers. Immediately after the election Wilson began to plan another peace move, but before he was ready the German government announced on December 12 its readiness to begin discussion of peace terms.

Six days later Wilson sent identical notes to the belligerent powers, asking each to state its war aims. The Germans responded promptly that they would state theirs only to a conference of the belligerents at a neutral site. In January 1917 the Allies made it plain that they intended to exact reparations, break up the Austro-Hungarian and Ottoman Empires, and destroy German power. Wilson then decided to make one more appeal, in the hope that public opinion would force the hands of the warring governments. Speaking before the Senate on January 22, 1917, he asserted the right of the United States to a share in laying the foundations for a lasting peace, which would have to be a "peace without victory" for only a "peace among equals" could endure. The peace must be based on the principles of government by the consent of the governed, freedom of the seas, and disarmament, and must be enforced by an international league for peace established to make another such catastrophe impossible. "I would fain believe," the president ended, "that I am speaking for the silent mass of mankind everywhere who have as yet had no place or opportunity to speak their real hearts out concerning the death and ruin they see to have come already upon the persons and homes they hold most dear."

Although Wilson did not know it, he was already too late. Exactly two weeks before he spoke, German leaders had decided to wage unrestricted submarine warfare. They took the calculated risk of provoking American anger in the hope of scoring a quick knockout. On January 31 the new policy was announced, effective the next day. All vessels in the war zone, belligerent or neutral, would be sunk without warning, with the exception that one American passenger ship could approach Falmouth weekly, provided it were painted with red and white stripes and carried a checkered flag, but no contraband. "Freedom of the seas," said the Brooklyn *Eagle,* "will now be enjoyed by icebergs and fish."

On February 3, 1917, Wilson told a joint session of Congress that the United States had broken diplomatic relations with the German government. He added that he still did not believe the Germans would do what they said they felt at liberty to do—only overt acts would persuade him that they actually intended to sink neutral ships. In case of such acts, he would take measures to protect American seamen and citizens. On February 26 Wilson went before another joint session to ask for authority to arm American merchant ships and "to employ any other instrumentalities or methods that may be necessary and adequate to protect our ships and our people." There was little quarrel with arming merchantmen, but bitter opposition to Wilson's vague reference to "any other instrumentalities or methods." A group of eleven or twelve die-hard noninterventionists including Senators La Follette and Norris filibustered the measure until the regular session expired on March 4. Thus, in Wilson's words: "A little group of willful men, representing no opinion but their own, have rendered the great Government of the United States helpless and contemptible." On March 12 the State Department announced that a forgotten law of 1792 allowed the arming of merchant ships regardless of congressional inaction.

In the midst of the debate, on March 1, news of the Zimmerman Note broke in the American press. Word had reached Wilson four days earlier from Ambassador Page in London that the British had intercepted and decoded an important message from

German Foreign Secretary Alfred Zimmerman to his ambassador in Mexico. The note instructed the envoy to offer an alliance and financial aid to Mexico in case of war between the United States and Germany. In return for diversionary action against the United States, Mexico would recover "the lost territory in Texas, New Mexico, and Arizona." Carranza, moreover, should invite Japan to swap sides and join the coalition. All this was contingent on war with the United States, but an electrified public read in it an aggressive intent. Then, later in March a revolution overthrew Russia's czarist government and established the provisional government of a Russian Republic. The fall of the czarist autocracy allowed Americans the illusion that all the major Allied powers were now fighting for constitutional democracy. Not until November 1917 was this illusion shattered when the Bolsheviks seized power in Russia.

AMERICA'S ENTRY

The overt acts Wilson awaited came in March when German submarines sank five American merchant vessels. On March 20 Wilson's cabinet unanimously endorsed a declaration of war and the following day the president called a special session of Congress. When it met on April 2, Wilson asked Congress to recognize the war that Imperial Germany was already waging against the United States, then turned to a discussion of the issues. The German government had revealed itself as a natural foe of liberty, and therefore "The world must be made safe for democracy. Its peace must be planted upon the tested foundations of political liberty." The war resolution passed the Senate by a vote of 82 to 6 on April 4. The House concurred, 373 to 50, and Wilson signed the measure on April 6. It was Good Friday.

How had it come to this, less than three years after Wilson's proclamation of neutrality? Prominent among the various explanations of America's entrance into the war are the effects of British propaganda, and America's deep involvement in trade with the Allies, which some observers then and later credited to the intrigues of war profiteers and munitions makers. Some Americans thought German domination of Europe would be a threat to American security, especially if it meant the destruction or capture of the British navy. But whatever the influence of such factors, they likely would not have been decisive without the issue of submarine warfare. This issue need not have become decisive, since such neutrals as Norway, Sweden, and Denmark took relatively heavier losses and yet stayed out of the war. But once Wilson had taken a stand for the traditional rights of neutrals and noncombatants, he was to some extent at the mercy of decisions by the German high command and was led step by step into a war over what to a later generation would seem a rather quaint, if noble, set of principles.

AMERICA'S EARLY ROLE   Having entered the war, the scope of America's role remained unclear. Few on either side of the Atlantic expected more from the United States than a token military effort. Despite Congress's preparedness measures the army remained small and rudimentary. The navy also was largely undeveloped. A few days before the declaration of war, however, Rear Adm. William S. Sims was given command of American ships in European waters, and he then systematically built up the United States Navy. He brought the first contingent of six American destroyers to Queenstown, Ireland, on May 4, and more came later. The Americans, in addition, made two important contributions to Allied naval strategy. Previously, merchant ships had survived through speed and evasive action. Sims persuaded the Allies to adopt a convoy system of escorting merchant ships in groups, and the result was a decrease in Allied shipping losses from 881,000 tons in April 1917 to 289,000 in November of the same year. Later the United States Navy conceived and laid a gigantic minefield across the North Sea which practically eliminated the U-boats' access to the North Atlantic.

Within a month of the declaration of war, British and French missions arrived in the United States. First they requested money with which to buy supplies, a request Congress had already anticipated in the Liberty Loan Act of April 24, which added $5 billion to the national debt in "Liberty Bonds." Of this amount, $3 billion could be loaned to the Allied powers. The United States was also willing to furnish naval support, credits, supplies, and munitions, but to raise and train a large army, equip it, and send it across a submarine-infested ocean seemed out of the question. Marshal Joffre, who came with the French mission, nevertheless insisted that the United States send a token force to bolster morale, and on June 26, 1917, the first contingent of Americans, about 14,500 men commanded by Gen. John J. Pershing, began to disembark at St. Nazaire. Pershing and his troops were able to fight their way to Paris by July 4. On the scene, Pershing soon decided that the war-weary Allies would be unable to mount an offensive by themselves. He advised the War Department that plans should be made to send a million American troops by the following spring. It was done.

Fresh recruits sign up for the Marines, 1917.
[Library of Congress]

When the United States entered the war the combined strength of the regular army and National Guard was only 378,619; at the end it would be 4.8 million. The need for such large numbers of troops converted Wilson to the idea of conscription. Under the Selective Service Act of May 18, 1917, all men aged twenty-one to thirty (later, from eighteen to forty-five) had to register for service. Registrants went into five classes, the first being able-bodied unmarried men without dependents. From this group alone came all the 2.8 million ultimately drafted. All told, about 2 million Americans crossed the Atlantic and about 1.4 million saw some action. Training of the soldiers went on in some thirty-two camps located mostly in the South for reasons of climate. The example of the Spanish-American War was well learned: the camps were for the most part sanitary and equipped with modern plumbing, hospitals, and recreation centers.

MOBILIZING A NATION   The war required of all belligerent nations complete economic mobilization on the home front. "In the sense in which we have been wont to think of armies," Wilson said, "there are no armies in this struggle; there are entire nations armed." Germany especially had perfected this kind of mobilization under a system that came to be known as War Socialism. A group of War Companies fixed prices, allocated materials, set priorities, and dictated what should be produced throughout the economy. In the United States, war brought more regulation of industry than most progressives had dreamed of.

The Army Appropriation Act of August 1916 had created a Council of National Defense, which in turn led to the creation of more new wartime agencies. The United States Shipping Board, started in 1916, operated the Emergency Fleet Corporation, which by the fall of 1918 had more than forty steel and ninety wooden ships coming off the ways monthly. The Lever Food and Fuel Control Act of August 1917 created a Food Administration, headed by Herbert Hoover, a future president, and a Fuel Administration, under Harry A. Garfield, son of a former president. Both had begun as committees under the Council of National Defense. Hoover, a mining engineer and former head of the Commission for Relief in Belgium, had the responsibility of raising production while reducing civilian use of foodstuffs. "Food will win the war" was the slogan. Hoover had coercive authority, but preferred to use voluntary methods and directed a propaganda campaign which "Hooverized" the country with "Wheatless Mondays," "Meatless Tuesdays," "Porkless Thursdays," the planting of victory gardens, and the use of leftovers.

Garfield's Fuel Administration introduced the country to Daylight Saving Time and "heatless Mondays." His greatest crisis came in January 1918 when a severe winter caused a coal shortage that held up the departure of munitions ships and shut down all factories east of the Mississippi for five days. The Railroad Administration, created in December 1917 and headed by Treasury Secretary William G. McAdoo, operated the nation's roads as a single unitary system, giving priority to military traffic. The War Trade Board, run by Vance McCormick, a publisher in Harrisburg, Pennsylvania, sought to reduce nonessential imports and exports in order to free shipping for the war effort, and tried to keep American goods from finding their way into Germany. The Trading with the Enemy Act of October 1917 also granted the president the right to seize and administer enemy property in the United States.

In July 1917 the Council for National Defense established the War Industries Board (WIB), which would become the most important of all the mobilization agencies. For nearly a year, however, this body floundered in confusion. The solution came on March 4, 1918, when Wilson summoned Bernard Baruch, a brilliant Wall Street speculator, to head the board, giving him a virtual dictatorship over the economy. Under Baruch the purchasing bureaus of the United States and Allied governments submitted their needs to the board, which set priorities and planned production. The board could allocate raw materials, tell manufacturers what to produce, order construction of new plants, and with the approval of the president, fix prices. For the sake of greater efficiency the WIB standardized product styles and designs.

The National War Labor Board (WLB), set up in April 1918 under former President Taft and the labor lawyer Frank P. Walsh, encouraged conciliation and mediated labor disputes that could not be settled otherwise. Where settlement proved impossible the government resorted to coercion. When the Smith and Wesson Arms Company of Springfield, Massachusetts, rejected a WLB decision, the War Department took over the plant. Munitions workers who struck in defiance of the board were threatened with loss of their draft exemptions. AFL President Samuel Gompers built goodwill with a policy of limiting labor disputes. A separate War Labor Policies Board, under a young lawyer, Felix Frankfurter, standardized policies regarding wages, hours, and working conditions in the war industries.

With the high wartime demand for labor and the movement of many men from the labor force into the armed services, labor was in a position to score solid advances in employment and wages, despite the rise in prices. A newly created United States Employment Service placed some 4 million workers in war-related jobs. Labor unions benefited from expanded employment, the increased demand for labor, government policies favorable to collective bargaining, and the goodwill built by Gompers. From 1913 to 1918 the AFL increased its membership by 37 percent.

The war mobilized more than economic life: the progressive gospel of efficiency suggested mobilizing public opinion as well. On April 14, 1917, eight days after the declaration of war, an ex-

A poster calling for cooperation between American "wage-payers" and "wage-earners" to defeat the "common foe—Autocracy."
[Wisconsin Historical Society]

ecutive order established the Committee on Public Information, composed of the secretaries of state, war, and the navy. Its executive head, George Creel, a Denver newsman, sold Wilson on the idea that the best approach to influencing public opinion was "expression, not repression"—propaganda instead of censorship. Creel's purpose was to organize a propaganda machine that would carry word of the Allies' war aims to the people, and above all to the enemy, where it might encourage the forces of moderation.

To sell the war Creel gathered a remarkable group of journalists, photographers, artists, entertainers, and others useful to his purpose. Charles Dana Gibson, James Montgomery Flagg, and other artists contributed posters. Historians under the direction of Guy Stanton Ford turned out little "Red, White, and Blue Books" with such titles as *How the War Came to America, German War Practices*, and *Conquest and Kultur.* A film division produced such pictures as *The Beast of Berlin*, starring, as the spike-helmeted embodiment of Prussian villainy, Erich von Stroheim. Hardly any public group escaped a harangue by one of the 75,000 Four-Minute Men, organized to give short speeches on Liberty Bonds, the need to conserve food and fuel, and other timely topics. Creel took special pains to get propaganda into Germany, where it was more likely to accentuate the size of the American war effort, Wilson's idealism, and offers of an easy peace if the German people would rebel against their government.

CIVIL LIBERTIES   The ultimate irony in Creel's "expression, not repression," however, was that the one led to the other. By arousing public opinion to such a pitch of excitement, the war effort channeled the crusading zeal of progressivism into grotesque campaigns of "Americanism" and witch-hunting. Wilson had foreseen such consequences. "Once lead this people into war," he told Frank Cobb, the editor of the New York *World*, "and they'll forget there even was such a thing as tolerance." Popular prejudice equated anything German with disloyalty. Schools dropped courses in the German language, violinist Fritz Kreisler was prevented from giving concerts, and patriots translated sauerkraut into "liberty cabbage," German measles into "liberty measles," and dachshunds into "liberty pups." In New Orleans Berlin Street became General Pershing Street.

While mobs hunted spies and chased rumors, the federal government stalked bigger game, with results often as absurd. Under the Espionage and Sedition Acts, criticism of government leaders and war policies was in effect outlawed. The Espionage Act of June 15, 1917, set penalties of up to $10,000 and twenty years in prison for those who gave aid to the enemy, who incited or tried to incite insubordination, disloyalty, or refusal of duty in the armed services, or who circulated false reports and statements with intent to interfere with the war effort. The postmaster-general could bar from the mails anything which violated the act or which advocated treason, insurrection, or forcible resistance to any United States law. The Sedition Act of May 16, 1918, extended the penalties to those who did or said anything to obstruct the sale of Liberty Bonds or advocate cutbacks in production, and—just in case something had been overlooked—for saying, writing, or printing anything "disloyal, profane, scurrilous, or abusive" about the American form of government, the Constitution, or the armed forces.

The penalties applied under these acts by the Democratic successors of Jefferson exceeded in both absurdity and severity anything done under the infamous Alien and Sedition Acts of John Adams. Under those acts of 1798, 25 prosecutions had resulted in 10 convictions; under Wilson's Espionage and Sedition Acts more than 1,500 prosecutions resulted in more than 1,000 convictions. According to one professor of law: "It became criminal to advocate heavier taxation instead of bond issues, to state that conscription was unconstitutional though the Supreme Court had not yet held it valid, to say that the sinking of merchant vessels was legal, to urge that a referendum should have preceded our declaration of war, to say that war was contrary to the teachings of Christ." One patriotic film producer drew a ten-year sentence for making a film on the American Revolution, *The Spirit of Seventy-six*, because it risked stirring sentiment against the British!

The impact of the acts fell with most severity upon Socialists and other radicals. Victor Berger, Socialist congressman from Milwaukee, got a twenty-year sentence for editorials in the Milwaukee *Leader* which called the war a capitalist conspiracy. Eugene V. Debs, who had polled over 900,000 votes for president in 1912, got twenty years for statements that had a "tendency" to bring about resistance to the draft. In 1920, still in jail, he polled nearly 1 million votes for president. In Chicago over 100 leaders of the Industrial Workers of the World went on trial before Judge Kenesaw Mountain Landis for opposing the war effort. All were found guilty. The IWW never fully recovered from the blow.

In two important decisions just after the war the Supreme

Court upheld the Espionage and Sedition Acts. *Schenck v. United States* (1919) upheld the conviction of a man for circulating anti-draft leaflets among members of the armed forces. In this case Justice Holmes said: "Free speech would not protect a man in falsely shouting fire in a theater, and causing a panic." The act applied where there was "a clear and present danger" that speech in wartime might create evils Congress had a right to prevent. In *Abrams v. United States* (1919) the Court upheld conviction of a man who circulated pamphlets opposing intervention in Russia. Here Holmes and Brandeis dissented. The "surreptitious publishing of a silly leaflet by an unknown man," they argued, posed no real danger to government policy.

"THE DECISIVE POWER"

American troops took little more than a token role in the fighting until the end of 1917. American units were parceled out in quiet sectors mainly to show the flag and bolster the morale of British and French soldiers. All through 1917 the Allies remained on the defensive and late in the year their situation turned desperate. In October the Italian lines collapsed at Caporetto and the Austrians swarmed into the plain of Friuli. With the help of Allied forces from France the Italians finally held along the Piave. In November the Bolshevik Revolution overthrew the infant Russian Republic, and the new Soviet government dropped out of the war.

ALLIED VICTORIES   With the Central Powers now free to concentrate their forces on the Western Front, the American war effort became a "race for France" to restore the balance of strength. By May 1918 Pershing had his 1 million men, and by November 2 million were "over there." The Allied lines held, and with the arrival of fresh troops the Allies' growing numerical majority finally turned the tide. "America," wrote German Commander-in-Chief von Ludendorff, "thus became the decisive power in the war." Meanwhile, on March 21 the Germans had begun their great offensive to end the war before the Americans arrived in force. On the Somme they broke through at the juncture of British and French sectors and penetrated about thirty-five miles, nearly to the rail and supply center at Amiens. Farther north, the Germans struck on April 9 in Flanders, where the Allies still held a corner of Belgium, broke through at Lille, and pushed the British back along a front from Ypres to Armentières. At this critical

THE WESTERN FRONT, 1918

—— The Western Front, March 1918
······ German offensive, spring 1918
⇒ Allied counteroffensive
▬▬ The Western Front, November 1918

point, on April 14 the Allies made French Gen. Ferdinand Foch the supreme commander of all Allied forces.

On May 27 the Germans began their next drive along the Aisne River, took Soissons, and pushed on to the Marne along a forty-mile front. To that time only token American forces had joined the defensive effort, but now the fresh American troops for the first time made a difference. In a counterattack American forces took Cantigny on May 28 and held it. A week later, on June 2–3, a marine brigade of the Second Division with the help of French colonials blocked the Germans at Château-Thierry and threw them back across the Marne. On June 5 the Second Division took the offensive at Bellau Wood and in three weeks cleared out the Germans and pushed them back. Though these actions had limited military significance, their effect on morale was immense. Each was a solid American success, and together they reinforced Pershing's demand for a separate American army.

Before that could come to pass, the turning point in the campaign came on July 15 in the Second Battle of the Marne. On both sides of Rheims, the eastern end of a great bulge toward Paris, the Germans commenced their push against the French lines. Their heaviest attack came at Château-Thierry where the American and French forces held off the threat to the French capital. Elsewhere the Germans made slight gains, but little progress. Within three days they had shot their bolt, and the Allies went on the offensive to wipe out German troops on the Marne, a job completed by August 6.

Soon the British along the Somme River and the French along the Oise-Aisne began to roll the German front back toward and into Belgium. American forces helped on both fronts. Then on August 10 the First U.S. Army was organized with the consent of General Foch and assigned the task of liquidating the Germans at St. Mihiel, southeast of Verdun. There, on September 12, an army of more than 500,000 staged the first strictly American offensive of the war. Within twenty-four hours the Germans had been cut off. Pershing wanted to push on from there to the fortress city of Metz, a German supply center, but Foch wanted to use the First Army to the west of Verdun, between the Marne and the Argonne Forest. The Meuse-Argonne offensive, begun September 26, employed every available American division in a drive toward Sedan and its railroad to Metz. The largest American action of the war, it involved some 1.2 million American troops and cost 117,000 American casualties. Through October and early November the battle raged. By the first week of November the Americans were at the outskirts of Sedan and had cut the railroad from Metz. All along the front from Sedan to Flanders the Germans were in retreat.

THE FOURTEEN POINTS   The approaching end of the war brought to the point of decision the question of war aims. Neither the Allies nor the Central Powers, despite Wilson's prodding, had stated frankly and openly what they hoped to gain. Wilson insisted throughout that the Americans had no selfish ends. "We desire no conquest, no dominion," he said in his war message. "We seek no indemnities for ourselves, no material compensation for the sacrifices we shall freely make. We are but one of the champions of the rights of mankind." Unfortunately for his purpose, after the Bolsheviks seized power in November 1917 they captured and published copies of secret treaties in which the Allies had promised territorial gains in order to win Italy, Rumania, and Greece to their side. When an Interallied Conference in Paris late in 1917 failed to agree on a statement of aims, Colonel House advised Wilson to formulate his own.

During 1917 House had been drawing together an informal panel of American experts called "The Inquiry" to formulate plans for peace. With advice from these experts, Wilson drew up a statement which would become the famous Fourteen Points. These he delivered to a joint session of Congress on January 8, 1918, "as the only possible program" for peace. The first five points in general terms called for open diplomacy, freedom of the seas, removal of trade barriers, reduction of armaments, and an impartial adjustment of colonial claims based on the interests of the populations involved. Most of the remainder called on the Central Powers to evacuate occupied lands and endorsed self-determination for various nationalities. Point 13 endorsed an independent Poland with access to the sea. Point 14, the capstone in Wilson's thinking, championed a general association of nations to secure guarantees of independence and territorial integrity to all countries, great and small.

The Fourteen Points set forth a firm commitment in which Wilson persisted, but they also served the purposes of psychological warfare. One of their aims was to keep Russia in the war by a more liberal statement of purposes—a vain hope, as it turned out. Another was to reassure the Allied peoples that they were involved in a noble cause. A third was to drive a wedge between the governments of the Central Powers and their people by the offer of a reasonable peace. Wilson's promise of "autonomous development" for the subject nationalists of Austria-Hungary (Point 10) might have weakened the unity of the polyglot Habsburg Empire, though it was no part of his purpose to break up the empire. But the chaos into which central Europe descended in 1918, and the national aspirations of the empire's peoples, took matters out of his hands.

On September 29, 1918, German Commander-in-Chief Erich von Ludendorff advised his government to seek the best peace terms possible. On October 3, a new chancellor, Prince Max of Baden, made the first German overtures for peace on the basis of the Fourteen Points. A month of diplomatic fencing followed between Colonel House and Allied representatives. Finally, a threat by House to pursue separate negotiations led the Allies to accept the Fourteen Points as a basis of peace, but with two significant reservations: they reserved the right to discuss freedom of the seas further, and they demanded reparations for war damages.

Meanwhile the German home front was being torn apart by a

naval mutiny at Kiel, a revolution in Bavaria, and disturbances elsewhere. Germany's allies had dropped out of the war: Bulgaria on September 29, Turkey on October 30, and Austria-Hungary on November 3. On November 8 a German delegation crossed the lines to meet with General Foch at Compiègne; the next day the kaiser abdicated and a German Republic was proclaimed. On November 11, at 5:00 A.M., an armistice was signed. Six hours later, at the eleventh hour of the eleventh day of the eleventh month, the guns fell silent. Under the Armistice the Germans had to evacuate occupied territories, pull back behind the Rhine, and surrender their submarines, railroad equipment, and other materials. The naval blockade would continue until a final peace settlement was reached, and the Germans were assured that the Fourteen Points would be the basis for the peace conference.

THE FIGHT FOR THE PEACE

WILSON'S ROLE   Wilson now made a fateful decision to attend in person the peace conference which convened in Paris on January 18, 1919. It shattered precedent for a president to leave the country for so long a time, but it dramatized all the more Wilson's desire to ensure his goal of a lasting peace. From one viewpoint it was a shrewd move, for his prestige and determination made a difference in Paris. But he lost touch with developments at home. His progressive coalition was already unraveling under the pressures of wartime discontent. Western farmers complained about the government's control of wheat prices while southern cotton rode the wartime inflation. Eastern businessmen chafed at revenue policies designed, according to the New York *Sun*, "to pay for the war out of taxes raised north of the Mason and Dixon Line." Labor, despite manifest gains, was unhappy with inflation and the problems of reconversion to a peacetime economy.

In the midterm elections of 1918, Wilson made matters worse with a partisan appeal for a Democratic Congress to ensure support of his foreign policies. Republicans, who for the most part had supported war measures, took affront. In elections held on November 5, a week before the Armistice, the Democrats lost control of both houses of Congress. Wilson thus lost face at home just as he prepared to go abroad. With an opposition majority in the new Congress, he further weakened his standing by failure to involve a single prominent Republican in the negotiations. The

United States Peace Commission, in addition to Wilson, consisted of Colonel House, Secretary Lansing, Gen. Tasker Bliss, and Henry White, a career diplomat and a nominal Republican.

When Wilson reached Europe in December, riotous demonstrations of affection greeted him on his tour of England, France, and Italy. The cheering millions had found a symbol of hope and a spokesman for humanity. Their heartfelt support no doubt strengthened his hand at the conference. But in Paris Wilson had to deal with some tough-minded statesmen. The conference comprised a body of delegates from all countries that had declared war or broken diplomatic relations with Germany. It was dominated at first by the Council of Ten (two each from Japan, Britain, France, Italy, and the United States), but ended with major decisions controlled by the Big Four: the prime ministers of Britain, France, and Italy, and the president of the United States. Japan restricted its interests to Asia and the Pacific. French Premier Georges Clemenceau, as John Maynard Keynes put it, had but one illusion—France—and insisted on stern measures to weaken Germany and ensure French security. Lloyd George of England was a gifted politician fresh from electoral victory on the slogan "Hang the Kaiser." Vittorio Orlando of Italy was there to pick up the spoils promised in the secret Treaty of London (1915) and, if possible, also the Adriatic port of Fiume.

"Vive Wilson." Paris welcomes the American president as a hero. [National Archives]

THE LEAGUE OF NATIONS   Wilson carried the point that his cherished League of Nations must come first, in the conference and in the treaty provisions. Whatever compromises he might have to make, whatever mistakes might result, Wilson believed that a permanent agency of peace would assure international stability. Wilson presided over the commission set up to work out a charter for the League.

The security-conscious French advanced a plan for an international general staff and a League army to enforce the peace. Wilson knew that Senate ratification would be foredoomed by such a provision, and with the help of Lloyd George he squelched the plan. Article X of the covenant, which Wilson called "the heart of the League," pledged members to consult on military and economic sanctions against aggressors. The use of arms would be a last (and an improvised) resort. The League, it was assumed, would exercise enormous moral influence, but when push came to shove it would have little force at its disposal. The League structure allowed each member an equal voice in the Assembly; the Big Five (Britain, France, Italy, Japan, and the United States) and four other nations would make up the Council; the administrative staff in Geneva would make up the Secretariat; and finally, a Permanent Court of International Justice (set up in 1921 and usually called the World Court) could "hear and determine any dispute of an international character." All treaties had to be registered with the Secretariat to be valid.

On February 14 Wilson reported the finished draft to the plenary session of the conference and departed the next day for a month-long visit home to see after routine business and talk up the League. Already he faced rumblings of opposition, and shortly before his return to Paris, Sen. Henry Cabot Lodge brought forward a statement that the League covenant was unacceptable "in the form now proposed." The Round Robin, as Lodge's statement of March 4 was called, bore the signatures of thirty-nine Republican senators or senators-elect, more than enough to block ratification. That evening Wilson confidently retorted: "When the treaty comes back, gentlemen on this side will find the covenant not only in it, but so many threads of the treaty tied to the covenant that you cannot dissect the covenant from the treaty without destroying the whole vital structure."

TERRITORY AND REPARATIONS   Yet, back in Paris, Wilson found it politic to seek amendments to meet the objections at home. These provided that any member nation could withdraw from the League on two years' notice, that none could be required to take a mandate to administer former enemy possessions now under League supervision, that domestic affairs remained outside League jurisdiction, and that regional understandings like the Monroe Doctrine would remain undisturbed. All these went pretty much without saying, but the French exploited Wilson's discomfort to press for harsh measures: territorial concessions and reparations from Germany to keep her weak for years to come. Wilson clashed sharply with Clemenceau, and after the president threatened to leave the conference they settled on French recovery of Alsace-Lorraine (lost in 1870), a demilitarized Rhineland (up to fifty kilometers beyond the river), French occupation of this zone for fifteen years, and League administration of the Saar Basin. France could use Saar coal mines for fifteen years, after which a plebiscite would determine the region's status.

In other territorial matters Wilson had to compromise his principle of national self-determination. There was in fact no way to make boundaries correspond to ethnic divisions. The folk wanderings of centuries had left mixed populations scattered through central Europe. In some areas, moreover, national self-determination yielded to other interests: the Polish Corridor, for instance, gave Poland its much-needed outlet to the sea through German territory, and the South Tyrol, home for some 200,000 German-speaking Austrians, gave Italy a more defensible frontier at the Brenner Pass. One part of the Austro-Hungarian Empire became Czechoslovakia, which included the German-speaking Sudetenland, an area favored with good defenses. Another part of the empire united with Serbia to create the kingdom of Yugoslavia. Still other substantial parts passed to Poland (Galicia), Rumania (Transylvania), and Italy (Trentino and Trieste). Fiume on the Adriatic, claimed also by Yugoslavia, had not been promised to Italy, but it had been occupied by freebooters led by the poet Gabrial d'Annunzio, a romantic Italian nationalist. The conference finally left the matter for future settlement. In 1921 Italy and Yugoslavia divided the adjacent lands and made Fiume a free city, but in 1924 Yugoslavia accepted Italian annexation.

Where political decisions did not override considerations of nationality the Big Four could more easily follow recommendations from the committees of experts who made exhaustive studies of history, geography, and populations. Because of Colonel House's body of experts, The Inquiry, the American delegation was probably better informed than other delegations. In a few cases issues in doubt were decided by plebiscites of the people

EUROPE AFTER VERSAILLES
.... 1914 boundaries
New nations
Plebiscite areas
Occupied area

themselves. All in all, despite some aberrations, the new boundaries more nearly followed the ethnic divisions of Europe than the prewar lines.

The discussion of reparations began after the French felt they had already given up a great deal in territorial matters. Britain and France both sought reparations, and the French wanted enough to cripple Germany. Discussions of the issue were among the longest and most bitter at the conference. Despite a pre-Armistice agreement that Germany would be liable only for civilian damages, Clemenceau and Lloyd George proposed reparations for the entire cost of the war. On this point Wilson made perhaps his most fateful concessions. He accepted in the treaty a clause by which Germany confessed responsibility for the war and thus for its entire costs. The "war guilt" clause was an offense to all Germans and a source of persistent bitterness. A down payment of $5 million was to be extracted from Germany immediately; in 1921 a Reparations Commission estimated that Germany owed $33 billion in all.

On May 7 the victorious powers presented the treaty to the German delegates, who returned three weeks later with 443 pages of criticism protesting that the terms violated the Armistice agreement to abide by the Fourteen Points. A few small changes were made, but when the Germans still refused to sign Marshal Foch prepared to move across the Rhine. On June 28 they gave in and signed the treaty in the Hall of Mirrors at Versailles, where France had capitulated to Bismarck and Kaiser Wilhelm I in 1871. Treaties with the lesser powers followed the arrangements already made. Each, like the Versailles Treaty, bore the name of the palace near Paris were it was signed: St. Germain (with Austria), Trianon (with Hungary), Neuilly (with Bulgaria), and Sèvres (with Turkey).

WILSON'S LOSS AT HOME Wilson returned home with the Versailles Treaty on July 8. Two days later he called on the Senate to accept "this great duty." The force of Wilson's idealism struck deep, and he returned amid a great clamor of popular support. A third of the state legislatures had endorsed the League, as had thirty-three of forty-eight governors. Sen. Henry Cabot Lodge, chairman of the Senate Foreign Relations Committee, later said: "What I may call the vocal classes of the community . . . were friendly to the League as it stood and were advocating it."

But Lodge, a partisan Republican who nourished an intense dislike for Wilson, was now sharpening his knives. He, like other senators, knew all too well the fickle nature of popular acclaim. He knew also the undercurrents already stirring up opposition to the treaty: the resentment of German, Italian, and Irish "hyphenates," the disappointment of liberals at Wilson's compromises, the postwar letdown, the distractions of demobilization and resulting domestic problems, and the revival of isolationism. In the Senate a group of "irreconcilables," fourteen Republicans

Sen. Henry Cabot Lodge, leader of the opposition to the League. [Library of Congress]

and two Democrats, were unwilling to allow America entrance to the League on any terms. They were mainly western or midwestern progressives who stood on principle. The irreconcilables would be useful to Lodge's purpose, but he belonged to a larger group of "reservationists" who were ready to go partway with Wilson, but insisted on limiting American participation in the League and its actions. Wilson of course said that he had already amended the covenant to these ends, pointing out that with a veto in the League Council the United States could not be obligated to do anything against its will.

Lodge resorted to delays. First he arranged a reading of the entire treaty to a nearly empty committee room—the 264 pages consumed two weeks—then held lengthy hearings in which every critic could get in his licks. Lodge, who set more store by the old balance of power than by the new idea of collective security, brought forward a set of amendments, or reservations. Wilson responded by agreeing to interpretive reservations, but to nothing that would reopen the negotiations. He especially opposed weakening Article X, which provided for collective action against aggression.

By September, with momentum for the treaty slackening, Wilson decided to go to the people and, as he put it, "purify the wells of public opinion." Bold appeals to public opinion had helped get the New Freedom through Congress—why not the treaty? Against the advice of doctors and friends he set forth on a swing through the Midwest to the West Coast, pounding out speeches on his typewriter between stops. In all he traveled 8,000 miles in twenty-two days, gave thirty-two major addresses and eight minor ones, refuted his opponents, and voiced warnings. "Everywhere we go, the train when it stops is surrounded with little children . . ." he said in Tacoma, Washington. "These glad youngsters with flags in their hands—I pray God that they may never have to carry that flag upon the battlefield!"

For a while he seemed to be regaining the initiative, but then his body rebelled. His six years as president, during which he wrestled with major issues of war and peace, had depleted his resources. After a speech at Pueblo, Colorado, on September 25, the signs of exhaustion were so clear that his doctor canceled the tour and hurried the president's train back to Washington. On October 2 Wilson suffered a severe stroke and paralysis on his left side, leaving him helpless for weeks. He never recovered completely. For more than seven months he did not meet the cabinet, and was kept isolated from all but the most essential business by a protective wife. The illness intensified his traits of stubbornness and hostility. He might have done better to stay in the White House and secure the best compromise possible, but now he refused to yield anything. Wilson ended up committing what the historian Thomas A. Bailey called the supreme infanticide, the destruction of his own brainchild.

Between November 7 and 19 the Senate adopted fourteen reservations presented by Lodge, most having to do with the League. Wilson especially opposed the reservation to Article X which, he said, "does not provide for ratification but, rather, for the nullification of the treaty." As a result the Wilsonians found themselves thrown into an unlikely combination with irreconcilables who opposed the treaty under any circumstances. The Senate vote was 39 for and 55 against. On the question of taking the treaty without reservations, irreconcilables and reservationists combined to defeat ratification again, with 38 for and 53 against. The American public, however, would not permit the treaty to be laid aside because senators professing support could not reach agreement on a few reservations. In the face of public reaction the Senate voted to reconsider. But Wilson remained adamant: "Either we should enter the league fearlessly, accepting with responsibility and not fearing the role of leadership which we now enjoy, contributing our efforts toward establishing a just and permanent peace, or we should retire as gracefully as possible from the great concert of powers by which the world was saved." On March 19, 1920, twenty-one Democrats deserted Wilson and joined the reservationists, but the treaty once again fell short of a two-thirds majority by a vote of 49 yeas and 35 nays. The real winners were the smallest of the three groups in the Senate, neither the Wilsonians nor the reservationists but the irreconcilables.

Three Senators Refuse the Lady a Seat. *Americans reacted against the Senate's defeat of the Versailles peace treaty.* [Library of Congress]

Wilson still nourished the hope that he could make the next presidential election a "solemn referendum" on the League of Nations. He deluded himself, as Bryan had in 1900, for presidential elections are touched by many issues. When Congress declared the war at an end by joint resolution on May 20, 1920, Wilson vetoed the action; it was not until after he left office, on July 2, 1921, that a joint resolution ended the state of war with Germany and Austria-Hungary. Peace treaties with Germany, Austria, and Hungary were ratified October 18, 1921, but by then Warren Gamaliel Harding was president of the United States.

LURCHING FROM WAR TO PEACE

The Versailles Treaty, for all the time it took in the Senate, was but one issue competing for public attention in the turbulent year after the war. But on the domestic scene Wilson's leadership was missing. He had been preoccupied by the war and the League, and once broken by his illness became strangely grim and peevish. His administration floundered through its last two years.

Demobilization proceeded without plan, indeed without much sense that a plan was needed once the war was over. The War Industries Board closed shop on January 1, 1919, and vanished so quickly that Bernard Baruch paid out of his pocket travel expenses home for some of his aides. The sudden cancellation of war contracts left workers and businessmen to cope with reconversion on their own. By April 1919 the armed forces were discharging about 4,000 men daily, and within a year the process was nearly complete.

THE ECONOMIC TRANSITION Events once again bore out the adage that there seems to be a special providence for fools, drunkards, and the United States of America. An unforeseen postwar boom eased the country over the difficult economic transition from war to peace. The boom fed on markets renewed by pent-up demand and wartime savings, and on overseas trade left open because German and British shippers had been weakened by wartime damage. Both farmers and businessmen benefited. The $2-billion cotton crop, which resulted from a happy mix of high prices and high production in 1919, was the most valuable ever. Reports from the southern countryside marveled at the unaccustomed wealth to be found among tenants and sharecroppers, but this was soon ended by a drop in farm prices in 1920 and a general business slump in 1921.

Government quickly extracted itself from "war socialism" in communications and transport. Telegraph, telephone, cable, and radio facilities were back in private hands by August 1919. On Christmas Eve 1919 Wilson announced that the railroads would go back to their owners on March 1, and Congress responded quickly. The Esch-Cummins Transportation Act of February 28, 1920, undertook to retain some of the advantages of unified operation. Unlike previous railroad laws, it gave up the pretense of enforcing competition and instead encouraged consolidation. The ICC, now enlarged from nine to eleven members, was authorized to work out plans to eliminate wasteful competition. It acquired in addition powers over the issuance of securities, the construction or abandonment of track, and the fixing of minimum as well as maximum rates. The commission was to evaluate all railroad property and thereby fix a fair rate of return to stockholders and fair rates for freight and passengers. Transferring the nation's great merchant fleet from public management to private management was less successful. Demand for the merchant fleet did not revive after the war. As a result, many of the ships were left to rot or rust.

The problems of postwar readjustment were worsened by general labor unrest. Prices rose along with employment after the war, and discontented workers, released from wartime constraints, were more willing to strike for their demands. In 1919, more than 4 million workers went out in thousands of disputes. Some workers in the East won their strike demands early in the year, but after a general strike in Seattle public opinion began to turn hostile. Seattle Mayor Ole Hansen denounced the general walkout of 60,000 workers as evidence of Bolshevik influence. The strike lasted only five days, but public alarm at the affair damaged the cause of unions across the country.

An AFL campaign to organize steelworkers suffered from charges of radicalism against its leader, William Z. Foster, a former Bryanite who joined the Socialists in 1900 and later emerged as a Communist. Attention to Foster's radicalism obscured the squalid conditions which had marked the steel industry since the Homestead strike of 1892. The twelve-hour day, often combined with a seven-day week, was common for steelworkers. On September 22, 1919, after U.S. Steel refused to talk, about 340,000 men walked out, mainly in the Chicago-Gary and western Pennsylvania areas. But the union succumbed to a back-to-work movement and gave up the strike four months later. When information about conditions became widely known, public opinion turned in favor of the steelworkers, but too late: the strike was over.

The most celebrated postwar labor dispute was the Boston Police Strike. If less significant than the steel strike in the numbers involved, it inadvertently launched a presidential career. When a local society of police, the Boston Social Club, applied to the AFL for a union charter, the Boston police commissioner dismissed eight members. A citizens' committee named by the mayor to investigate suggested arbitration and reinstatement of the fired officers, but the commissioner responded by firing nineteen more. On September 9, 1919, most of Boston's police force went out on strike. Gov. Calvin Coolidge mobilized the National Guard to keep order, and after four days the strikers were ready to return, but the commissioner refused to take them. When Samuel Gompers appealed that they be reinstated, Coolidge responded in words that suddenly turned him into a national figure: "There is no right to strike against the public safety by anybody, anywhere, any time."

RACIAL FRICTION   The summer of 1919 also brought a season of race riots, both North and South. Within a few weeks of the Armistice rumors began to circulate about black soldiers who had been "French-women ruined" or who had fallen under Bolshevik influence. What black leader James Weldon Johnson called "The Red Summer" ("Red" here signified blood) began in July, when whites invaded the black section of Longview, Texas, in search of a teacher who had allegedly accused a white woman of a liaison with a black man. They burned a number of shops and homes and ran several blacks out of town. A week later in Washington reports of black attacks on white women aroused white mobs and for four days gangs of white and black rioters waged race war in the streets until soldiers and driving rains ended the fighting. These were but preliminaries to the Chicago riot of late July in which 38 people were killed and 537 injured. The climactic disorders of the summer occurred in the rural area around Elaine, Arkansas, where black tenant farmers tried to organize a union. According to official reports 5 whites and 25 blacks died, but whites told one reporter in the area that more than 100 blacks died. Altogether twenty-five race riots took place in 1919, and more were threatened.

THE RED SCARE   Public reaction to the wave of strikes and riots was influenced by the impact of the Bolshevik Revolution. A mi-

Red Scare. A 1920 cartoon reflects popular alarm at the "Red menace" in America. [New York Public Library]

WHOSE COUNTRY IS THIS, ANYHOW?

nority of radicals thought America's domestic turbulence, like that in Russia, was the first scene in a drama of revolution. A much larger public was persuaded that they might be right. After all, a tiny faction in Russia had exploited confusion to impose its will. In 1919 the Socialist party, already depleted by wartime persecution, suffered the further defection of radicals inspired by the Russian example. Left-wing members formed the Communist and the short-lived Communist Labor parties. Wartime hysteria against all things German was readily transformed into a postwar Red Scare.

Fears of revolution might have remained latent except for the actions of a lunatic fringe. In April 1919 the post office intercepted in all nearly forty bombs addressed to various prominent citizens. One slipped through and blew off the hands of Georgia Sen. Thomas R. Hardwick's maid. In June another destroyed the front of Attorney-General A. Mitchell Palmer's home in Washington. Assistant Navy Secretary Franklin D. Roosevelt and his wife, who had just entered their house across the street, had a narrow escape. The random violence of these criminals formed no part of Bolshevik tactics, but many Americans saw Red on all sides and condoned attacks on all kinds of minorities in retaliation.

Soon the government itself was promoting witch-hunts. Attorney-General Palmer, a Pennsylvania Quaker and once a progressive congressman with prolabor leanings, harbored an entrenched distrust of aliens and a strong desire for the presidency. In June 1919 the Justice Department decided to deport radical aliens, and Palmer set up as the head of the new General Intelligence Division the young J. Edgar Hoover, who began to collect an index file on radicals. Raids began on November 7, 1919, when agents swooped down on the Union of Russian Workers in twelve cities. On December 22 the transport ship *Buford*, dubbed the "Soviet Ark," left New York for Russia with 249 people, including assorted anarchists, criminals, and public charges. All were deported without the benefit of a court hearing. On January 2, 1920, a series of raids by police in dozens of cities swept up some 6,000 suspects, often taken from their homes without search warrants, of whom about half were kept in custody. That same month the New York legislature expelled five duly elected Socialist members.

Basking in popular approval, Palmer continued to warn of the Red menace, but like other fads and alarms, the mood passed. Widespread disruptions predicted for May 1 never took place. Acting Secretary of Labor Louis F. Post began to scrutinize arrest warrants that required his approval. By the summer of 1920 the Red Scare had begun to evaporate. Communist revolutions in Europe died out, leaving Bolshevism isolated in Russia; bombings tapered off; the strike wave and race riots receded. Congress refused to pass peacetime sedition bills, although thirty-two states enacted criminal laws which made it illegal to join groups that called for the overthrow of the government by force. The attorney-general and his mimics began to seem more threatening to civil liberties than a handful of radicals. By September 1920, when a bomb explosion at the corner of Broad and Wall Streets in New York killed thirty-three people, Americans were ready to take it for what it was, the work of a crazed mind and not the start of a revolution. The Red Scare nevertheless left a lasting mark on American life. Part of its legacy was the continuing crusade for "100 percent Americanism" and restrictions on immigration. It left a stigma on labor unions and contributed to the anti-union open-shop campaign—the "American Plan," its sponsors called it. But for many Americans the chief residue of the Great War and its disordered aftermath was the profound disillusionment which pervaded American thought in the postwar decades.

FURTHER READING

Different interpretations of why the United States entered the First World War appear in George F. Kennan's *American Diplomacy, 1900–1950* (1951), and William Appleman Williams's *The Tragedy of American Diplomacy* (1959). Also valuable are Foster R. Dulles's *America's Rise to World Power, 1898–1954* (1955), John A. S. Grenville and

George B. Young's *Politics, Strategy, and American Diplomacy, 1873–1917* (1966), and Lloyd C. Gardner, Walter LaFeber, and Thomas McCormick's *The Creation of the American Empire* (1973). Otis L. Graham, Jr.'s *The Great Campaigns: Reform and War in America, 1900–1928* (1971), shows the link between progressive reform and the impulse for war. Good for background about American relations with the British is Bradford Perkins's *The Great Rapprochement: England and the United States, 1895–1914* (1968).

A number of scholars concentrate on the neutrality issue. Arthur S. Link, Woodrow Wilson's biographer, is sympathetic to the ideals of the president in *Wilson the Diplomatist* (1957) and *Woodrow Wilson: War, Revolution, and Peace* (1979). Other, more critical, efforts are Ernest R. May's *The World War and American Isolation, 1914–1917* (1959), John M. Cooper, Jr.'s *The Vanity of Power: American Isolation and the First World War, 1914–1917* (1969), Carl P. Parrini's *Heir to Empire: United States Economic Diplomacy, 1916–1923* (1969), and Ross Gregory's *The Origins of American Intervention in the First World War* (1971). John W. Coogan's *The End of Neutrality: The United States, Britain, and Maritime Rights, 1899–1915* (1981), argues that the issue of maritime rights was resolved before the war.

Other scholars have attempted to understand Wilsonian diplomacy by examining the president's actions in the Caribbean. For the Mexican intervention, consult P. Edward Haley's *Revolution and Intervention: The Diplomacy of Taft and Wilson with Mexico, 1910–1917* (1970), and Robert E. Quirk's *An Affair of Honor: Woodrow Wilson and the Occupation of Vera Cruz* (1962).° Frederick Katz's *The Secret War in Mexico: Europe, the United States, and the Mexican Revolution* (1981) gives an international perspective to the conflict. To gain a comparative perspective, see Hans R. Schmidt's *The United States Occupation of Haiti, 1915–1934* (1971).

Daniel M. Smith's *The Great Departure: The United States in World War I, 1914–1920* (1965), briefly surveys the war's impact both at home and abroad, while Frederick L. Paxton's *American Democracy and the World War* (3 vols.; 1936–1948) provides a lengthier treatment. Russell F. Weigley's *The American Way of War: A History of United States Military Strategy and Policy* (1973) has good interpretative chapters on the Expeditionary Force. Edward M. Coffman's *The War to End Wars: The American Military Experience in World War I* (1968) is a detailed presentation of America's military involvement.

David M. Kennedy's *Over Here: The First World War and American Society* (1980)° is an important recent survey of the impact of the war on the home front. Other studies of mobilization include Charles Gilbert's *American Financing of World War I* (1970), Robert Cuff's *The War Industries Board: Business-Government Relations during World War I* (1973), and Maurine Wiener Greenwald's *Women, War, and Work: The Impact of World War I on Women Workers in the United States* (1980).

William Preston, Jr., fits opposition to the war into a general pattern

°These books are available in paperback editions.

of dissent in *Aliens and Dissenters: Federal Suppression of Radicals, 1903–1933* (1953). More specific for the war period are Frederick C. Luebke's *Bonds of Loyalty: German-Americans and World War I* (1974) and Paul L. Murphy's *The Meaning of Freedom of Speech: First Amendment Freedoms from Wilson to FDR* (1972).

The tensions of the immediate postwar years are chronicled in Robert K. Murray's *Red Scare: A Study of National Hysteria, 1919–1920* (1955), and William Tuttle, Jr.'s *Race Riot: Chicago and the Red Summer of 1919* (1970). Other perspectives on these tensions can be found in Stanley Coben's *A. Mitchell Palmer: Politician* (1963) and A. E. Barbeau and Florette Henri's *The Unknown Soldiers: Black American Troops in World War I* (1974). Labor tensions are examined in Robert L. Friedheim's *The Seattle General Strike* (1964), David E. Brody's *Labor in Crisis: The Steel Strike of 1919* (1965), and Francis Russell's *A City in Terror: 1919, the Boston Police Strike* (1975).

How American diplomacy fared in the making of peace received considerable attention. In addition to the Link books on Wilson, the role of the president is treated in Arno J. Mayer's *Politics and Diplomacy in Peacemaking: Containment and Counterrevolution at Versailles, 1918–1919* (1967), and N. Gordon Levin, Jr.'s *Woodrow Wilson and World Politics: America's Response to War and Revolution* (1968).° The treaty controversy is handled in Thomas A. Bailey's *Woodrow Wilson and the Lost Peace* (1944) and *Woodrow Wilson and the Great Betrayal* (1945). Another perspective can be found in John A. Garraty's *Henry Cabot Lodge* (1953) and Ralph A. Stone's *The Irreconcilables: The Fight against the League of Nations* (1970). Peter G. Filene in *Americans and the Soviet Experiment* (1967) and Betty M. Unterberger in *America's Siberian Expedition* (1956) investigate American response to the Bolshevik takeover.

26

THE MODERN TEMPER

On August 5, 1914, the day after Britain entered the Great War, the American novelist Henry James wrote to a friend: "The plunge of civilization into this abyss of blood and darkness . . . so gives away the whole long age during which we have supposed the world to be . . . gradually bettering, that to have to take it all now for what the treacherous years were all the while really making for and *meaning* is too tragic for any words." The war, as James foresaw, dealt a shattering blow to what another author called "the prevailing Meliorist myth," that civilization was progressing, moving forward, a myth which had dominated the public consciousness for a century and which had been so powerful a stimulant to progressivism. The fighting imprinted on modern memory scenes of carnage worse than those once supposedly consigned to a barbaric past. The postwar disillusionment hastened a growing challenge in modern thought to all the old values. Ernest Hemingway wrote in his war novel *A Farewell to Arms* (1929) that "abstract words such as glory, honor, courage or hallow were obscene beside the concrete names of villages, the number of roads, the names of rivers, the numbers of regiments and dates." Young men had simply gone off to die for a European civilization that was, in the words of the poet Ezra Pound, "an old bitch gone in the teeth, . . . a botched civilization."

To many others, watching the postwar wave of strikes, bombings, red scares, and race riots, it seemed that America had entered a frightening new terrain of diversity and change in which there lurked a thousand threats to the older orthodoxies. And those threats centered in the polyglot cities teeming with immigrants and foreign ideas. The defensive mood of the 1920s fed on a growing tendency to connect American nationalism with nativism, Anglo-Saxon racism, and militant Protestantism.

NATIVISM   The foreign connections of so many radicals strengthened the sense that sedition was chiefly foreign-made. That it went hand in hand with crime seemed confirmed by the most celebrated case of the times, which involved two Italian-born anarchists, Nicola Sacco and Bartolomeo Vanzetti. Arrested on May 5, 1920, for a payroll robbery and murder in South Braintree, Massachusetts, they were brought for trial before Judge Webster Thayer, who privately referred to the defendants as "those anarchist bastards." In the courtroom, wrote Felix Frankfurter of the Harvard Law School, Thayer allowed the prosecutor to exploit the Communist hysteria and "thus to divert and pervert the jury's mind." The question of the two men's guilt remains in doubt, though not the bias of the court, and the belief persists that they were sentenced for their beliefs and their ethnic origins rather than for any crime they had committed. The case became a great radical and liberal cause célèbre of the 1920s, but despite pleas for mercy and public demonstrations around the world on behalf of the two men, they went to the electric chair on August 23, 1927, their last appeals denied.

The surging postwar nativism brought an end to three centuries of immigration that dated from the first European settlements. The push to restrict immigration was reinforced by a pseudo-scientific racism which found expression in two widely read books: Madison Grant's *The Passing of the Great Race* (1916)—the great race being the Nordics of northern Europe, threatened by the Slavic and Latin people of eastern and southern Europe—and Lothrop Stoddard's *The Rising Tide of Color* (1920). The flow of immigrants, slowed by the war, rose again at its end. From June 1920 to June 1921 more than 800,000 per-

Sacco (middle) and Vanzetti (right) in court. [Brown Brothers]

sons entered the country, 65 percent of them from southern and eastern Europe; and more were on the way. An alarmed Congress passed the Emergency Immigration Act of 1921, which restricted new arrivals each year to 3 percent of the foreign-born of any nationality as shown in the 1910 census. A new quota law in 1924 reduced the number to 2 percent based on the 1890 census, which included fewer of the "new" immigrants. This law set a permanent limitation, which became effective in 1929, of slighty over 150,000 per year based on the "national origins" of the American people as of 1920. Since national origins could not be determined with precision, officials were called upon to use available statistics on migration, natural increase, and "such other data as may be found reliable." However inexact the quotas, the purpose clearly was to tilt the balance in favor of the old immigration from northern and western Europe, which was assigned about 85 percent of the total. The law completely excluded people from East Asia—a gratuitous insult to the Japanese, who were already kept out by their "Gentlemen's Agreement" with Theodore Roosevelt.

On the other hand the law left the gate open to new arrivals from Western Hemisphere countries, so that an ironic consequence was a great increase in the United States' Hispanic Catholic population. The legal arrivals from Mexico peaked at 89,000 in 1924. Lower figures after that date merely reflect policies of the Mexican government to clamp down on the outflow of labor and stronger American enforcement of old regulations like the 1882 exclusion of those immigrants likely to become public charges. Uncounted illegal immigrants continued to come, however, in response to southwestern agriculture's demand for "stoop" labor. People of Latin American descent (chiefly Mexicans, Puerto Ricans, and Cubans) became the fastest growing ethnic minority in the country.

THE KLAN During the postwar years the nativist tradition adopted a new form, a revived Ku Klux Klan modeled on the group founded during Reconstruction, but in a striking departure from its predecessor, devoted to "100 percent Americanism" and restricted in membership to native-born white Protestants. America was no melting pot, its founder William J. Simmons warned: "It is a garbage can! . . . When the hordes of aliens walk to the ballot box and their votes outnumber yours, then that alien horde has got you by the throat." A habitual joiner and promoter of fraternal orders, Simmons had gathered a hooded group atop Stone Mountain near Atlanta on Thanksgiving night, 1915. There, "bathed in the sacred glow of the fiery cross, the invisible empire was called from its slumber of half a century to take up a new task." It was a "living memorial" to the earlier Klan, but also something of a fraternal order with an elaborate ceremonial and secret passwords, all of which the founder took care to copyright in his name—thereby making the "secrets" available through copies in the Library of Congress.

The KKK had little success before 1920, when Simmons made a fateful alliance with Edward Young Clarke and Mrs. Elizabeth Tyler, two promoters who had honed their skills in the Red Cross and other wartime drives. Granted exclusive rights to publicize and propagate the Klan, the two got $8 out of each $10 Klecktoken (initiation fee), from which they paid all promotional expenses. By shrewd exploitation of ballyhoo, they transformed bigotry into big business. In the "idea of selling people their own prejudices," a sardonic editor remarked in Charleston, South Carolina, Simmons had displayed a genius "almost equal to the old bunco game of selling a hick the Capitol." The Klan always had about it a taint of racketeering—and its promoters also developed a profitable business in bedsheets on the side.

In 1921 a sensational exposé by the New York *World* and a congressional investigation only publicized the Klan further. In living testimony to the cynical adage that there is no such thing as bad publicity, the Klan thrived on the exposure. In going nativist, the Klan had gone national and was no longer restricted to the South. Its appeal reached areas as widely scattered as Oregon and Maine. It flourished mainly among the uprooted and insecure newcomers to the cities and towns. The robes, the flaming crosses, the eerie processionals, the kneeling recruits, the occult liturgies—all tapped a deep American urge toward mystery and brought drama into the dreary routine of a thousand communities.

A Klan rally on a baseball field in Beckley, West Virginia, 1923. [Library of Congress]

At the same time it was paradoxically a reflex against the strange and exotic, against shifting moral standards, the declining influence of churches, the broadmindedness of cities and colleges. It represented a degradation of the hopes aroused by progressivism and the war. In the Southwest it became more than anything else a moral crusade. "It is going to drive the bootleggers forever out of this land," declared a Texan. "It is going to bring clean moving pictures . . . clean literature . . . break up roadside parking . . . enforce the laws . . . protect homes." All these things it set out to achieve by nightriding and floggings. Enemies of the Klan, said a Kentucky Klansman, were uncertain who its members were, or how many. "It is the invisible something that gets their goat."

Simmons, always something of a dreamer, betrayed a fatal inability to control the tough customers attracted to the Klan by the scramble for power and booty. In 1922 a palace revolution toppled Simmons who, threatened with violence, sold his copyright on the Klan and abdicated to a new Imperial Wizard, Hiram Wesley Evans, a dentist from Dallas. The hooded order became a political power in thousands of communities. Officeholders either cultivated the Klan or were struck dumb on the subject. But the Klan never achieved much politically beyond securing the dismissal of a Catholic here and there or afflicting officials with blindness to floggings. Diligent research has uncovered only one Klan-inspired law, an Oregon act requiring Catholic children to attend public schools—and it was found unconstitutional. The order had neither a political program nor a dynamic leadership. Unlike kindred movements in postwar Europe, it conjured up no Mussolini, no Hitler.

Estimates of its peak membership, probably inflated, range from 3 million to 8 million, but the Klan's influence decayed as quickly as its numbers grew. For one thing, the Klan suffered from a decline in nativist excitement after passage of the 1924 immigration law. For another, it suffered recurrent factional quarrels and schisms. And its moral pretensions were tarnished by the violence it perpetrated, by charges of dubious relations between the promoters Clark and Tyler, and above all by a sordid scandal involving the Indiana Klan leader. Grand Dragon David C. Stevenson organized a political machine which for a while dominated the state through control of the Republican party, but the whole thing collapsed in 1925 after he forced a State House secretary aboard a train and fatally assaulted her. Convicted of second-degree murder, Stevenson got a life sentence. When the governor (elected as his stooge) refused to pardon him, Stevenson drew from a "little black box" the evidence that sent a congressman and several other officials to jail. The governor barely escaped a bribery charge. The "best people" of many towns had joined what they thought was an agency of reform, but drifted away as the Klan became a cloak for outrage; in that respect, at least, the organization repeated the history of its ancestor.

FUNDAMENTALISM   While the Klan saw a threat mainly in the alien menace, many adherents of the old-time religion saw threats from modernism in the churches: new ideas that the Bible should be studied in the light of modern scholarship (the "higher criticism") or that it could be reconciled with evolution. With the dawning knowledge that such notions had infected schools and even pulpits, orthodoxy took on a new militancy in fundamentalism. The movement had acquired a name and definition from a series of pamphlets, *The Fundamentals* (1910), published in Los Angeles. Armed with the "Five Points" fundamental to the faith —an inerrant Bible, the Virgin Birth, the Vicarious Atonement, the Resurrection, and the Second Coming of Christ—the fundamentalists were distinguished less by their belief in a faith which many others shared than by their posture of hostility toward any other belief.

Among the movement's leaders only William Jennings Bryan had the following and the eloquence to make the movement a popular crusade. In 1921 he sparked a drive for laws to prohibit the teaching of evolution. Bryan denounced Darwin with the same zeal he had once directed against the goldbugs. Many old-time admirers thought he had gone over to the forces of reaction, but to Bryan's mind the old reformer still spoke through the new fundamentalist. "Evolution," he said, "by denying the need or possibility of spiritual regeneration, discourages all reforms, for reform is always based upon the regeneration of the individual." Antievolution bills began to turn up in the hoppers of legislatures in the Midwest and South, but the only victories came to the South—and there were few of those. Some officials took direct action without legislation. Gov. Miriam "Ma" Ferguson of Texas ordered elimination from state schools of textbooks upholding Darwinism. "I am a Christian mother . . .," she declared, "and I am not going to let that kind of rot go into Texas schoolbooks."

The climax came in Tennessee, where in 1925 an obscure legislator, John Washington Butler, introduced a bill to outlaw the teaching of evolution in public schools and colleges. The bill passed by overwhelming majorities and the governor, unwilling to endanger a pending school program, signed with the observa-

Ballyhoo surrounding "the monkey trial" in Dayton, Tennessee. William Jennings Bryan and the Rev. T. T. Martin were leaders of the fundamentalist crusade. [Library of Congress]

tion that it would probably never be applied. He reckoned without the civic boosters of Dayton, Tennessee, who inveigled a young high school teacher, John T. Scopes, into accepting an offer of the American Civil Liberties Union to defend a test case —chiefly to put their town on the map. They succeeded beyond their wildest hopes: the publicity was worldwide, and enduring. Before the opening day of the "monkey trial" on July 13, 1925, the streets of Dayton swarmed with sundry oddments of humanity drawn to the carnival: publicity hounds, curiosity-seekers, professional evangelists and professional atheists, a blind mountaineer who proclaimed himself the world's greatest authority on the Bible, hot-dog and soda-pop hucksters, and a miscellany of reporters.

The two stars of the show—Bryan, who had offered his services to the prosecution, and Clarence Darrow, renowned trial lawyer of Chicago and self-confessed agnostic—united at least in their determination to make the trial an exercise in public education. When Judge John T. Raulston ruled out scientific testimony, however, the defense called Bryan as an expert witness on biblical interpretation. In his colloquy with Darrow, he repeatedly entrapped himself in literal-minded interpretations and indeed his ignorance of biblical history and scholarship. He stated a belief that a "great fish" actually swallowed Jonah, that Joshua literally made the sun stand still, that the world was created in 4004 B.C.—all, according to Darrow, "fool ideas that no intelligent Christian on earth believes."

But the only issue before the court, the judge ruled, was whether or not Scopes had taught evolution, and no one denied that he had. He was found guilty, but the Tennessee Supreme Court, while upholding the act, overruled the $100 fine on a legal technicality. The chief prosecutor accepted the higher court's advice against "prolonging the life of this bizarre case" and dropped the issue. With more prescience than he knew, Bryan had described the trial as a "duel to the death." A few days after it closed he died suddenly of a heart condition aggravated by heat and fatigue.

After Dayton the rest was anticlimactic. No other leader could assume Bryan's mantle, but in Mississippi the Bible Crusaders, led by the Rev. T. T. Martin, author of *Hell and the High Schools*, descended on the state legislature and got another antievolution law in 1926. One final fundamentalist victory came in Arkansas by the use of two progressive reforms, the initiative and the referendum, in 1928. With that, the fundamentalists had spent their fury. Their very victories were self-defeating, for they served to publicize what they opposed as heresy. The states that went through the fiercest controversies became prime markets for books on evolution, and the movement roused a liberal defense of academic freedom. Fundamentalists, usually defeated, suffered the complacent scorn of those people the sociologist Howard Odum called the "learned ignoranti," whose contempt for the beliefs of plain folk mirrored the intolerance of fundamentalists and whose own belief in science mirrored the fundamentalists' belief in the "Five Points."

PROHIBITION   Prohibition offered another example of reforming zeal channeled into a drive for moral righteousness and conformity. Around the turn of the century the leading temperance organizations, the Women's Christian Temperance Union and the Anti-Saloon League, had converted from efforts to change individuals to a campaign for legal prohibition. Building upon the general moral disrepute of saloons, they were able to equate the "liquor traffic" with the trusts and "special interests." For the churches, prohibition could easily become, as one historian put it, "a surrogate for the Social Gospel." At the same time, contrary to certain oldtime folk beliefs that alcohol was beneficial, medical and scientific opinion now showed that it did more harm than good. By the 1910s the Anti-Saloon League had become one of the most effective pressure groups in American history, mobilizing Protestant churches behind its single-minded battle to elect "dry" candidates.

"Close the Saloons." A Prohibition poster of the 1920s. [American Heritage Society]

At its "Jubilee Convention" in November 1913 the league endorsed a national prohibition amendment to the Constitution. That December some 4,000 White Ribboners marched on the Capitol to present resolutions for a constitutional amendment. The 1916 elections finally produced two-thirds majorities for prohibition in both houses of Congress. Soon the wartime spirit of sacrifice, the need to use grain for food, and wartime hostility to German-American brewers transformed the cause virtually into a test of patriotism. On December 18, 1917, Congress passed and sent to the states the Eighteenth Amendment which, one year after ratification on January 16, 1919, banned the manufacture, sale, or transport of intoxicating liquors.

By then, however, about three-fourths of the American people already lived in states and counties that were legally dry. The wartime Lever Food and Fuel Control Act, moreover, had banned the use of grain for distilling and brewing. In 1919 the Volstead Act extended the ban and defined as "intoxicating" all beverages containing more than 0.5 percent alcohol, which became illegal once the Eighteenth Amendment went into effect on January 16 ,1920. On that date the corpse of John Barleycorn arrived in Norfolk, Virginia, on a special train. While his Satanic Majesty trailed along in deep mourning and anguish, twenty pallbearers carried an enormous coffin to a tabernacle where evangelist Billy Sunday preached the funeral oration to more than 10,000 people.

But John Barleycorn, like the labor hero Joe Hill, never died. The Eighteenth Amendment had been effective less than eight months when authorities found a still with a daily capacity of 130

gallons near Austin, Texas, on a farm belonging to Morris Shep-
pard, the "Father of National Prohibition." Congress never supplied adequate enforcement, if such were indeed possible given
the public thirst, the spotty support of local officials, and the
profits to be made in bootlegging. With 1,520 agents in the Prohibition Bureau in 1920 and 2,836 ten years later, the government could hardly plug up all the leaks in the coastline and the
borders. Rumrunning into Florida provided the Bahamas enough
revenue to get out of debt. In Detroit, just across the river from
Ontario, the liquor industry was second in size only to automobiles. From Vancouver Island in the Northwest ships left with
booze consigned to Mexico and returned empty within twenty-
four hours—most likely not having gotten much beyond Seattle!

Imported liquors tended to be the real thing, but a lucrative
trade developed in denatured grain alcohol, which could be re-
distilled or "cooked" to make it potable and treated with flavor-
ing and artificial coloring to impress desperate palates as
facsimiles of bourbon, rye, or gin. But as "forbidden fruit," even
fake liquor was all the more enticing and arrests for public drunk-
enness went up sharply. Speakeasies, hip flasks, and cocktail parties were among the social innovations of the prohibition era,
along with increased drinking by women.

It would be too much to say that prohibition gave rise to organized crime, for organized vice, gambling, and extortion had
long been practiced, and often tied in with the saloons. But prohibition supplied criminals an enormous new source of income,
while the automobile and the submachine gun provided greater
mobility and firepower. Gangland leaders showed remarkable
gifts for exploiting loopholes in the law, when they did not simply buy up policemen and politicians. George Remus, a crime
boss who operated in the Midwest, bought a chain of drugstores
so he could order medicinal liquors and then hijack his own
trucks as they transported the goods.

But the most celebrated gangster and racketeer (a word
coined in the 1920s) was "Scarface" Al Capone, who moved
from New York to Chicago in 1920 and within a few years became the city's leading bootlegger, and gambling and vice lord.
By 1927 he had an income of $60 million a year and a private
army of gunmen. He asked once: "What's Al Capone done, then?
He's supplied a legitimate demand. Some call it bootlegging.
Some call it racketeering. I call it business. They say I violate the
prohibition law. Who doesn't?" The widespread toleration of
such "business" by its customers began to wear thin, however, in
the face of the St. Valentine's Day Massacre in 1929, in which
seven members of Chicago's Dion O'Banion gang were gunned

"Scarface" Al Capone.
[Brown Brothers]

down by members of a rival gang dressed as policemen. No indictments were ever made. Law-enforcement officials were unable to pin anything on Capone until a Treasury agent infiltrated his gang and got evidence to nail him in 1929 for income-tax evasion.

It came as no great surprise in 1931 when a commission under former Attorney-General George W. Wickersham reported evidence that enforcement of prohibition had broken down. Of the commission's eleven members only five approved continued efforts to enforce prohibition without change, four favored modifications, and two personally favored repeal. Still, the commission as a whole voted for further trial, and President Hoover chose to stand by what he called the "experiment, noble in motive and far-reaching in purpose."

The Roaring Twenties

In many ways the defensive temper of the 1920s and the repressive movements to which it gave rise seem the dominant trends of the times, but they arose in part as reactions to a social and intellectual revolution that seemed about to sweep America away from its old moorings. In various labels given to the times, it was an era of excess, the jazz age, the era of wonderful nonsense, the roaring twenties, the ballyhoo years, the aspirin age. During those years a new America confronted an old America, and cultural conflict reached new levels of tension.

The smart set of the sophisticated metropolis developed an active disdain for the old-fashioned rural–small-town values of the

hinterlands. In Sinclair Lewis's novel *Main Street* (1920), for instance, one encountered the stifling, mean, and cramped life out
there on the prairie, a theme continued in his *Babbitt* (1922). In
Look Homeward, Angel (1929), Thomas Wolfe scandalized his
native Asheville, North Carolina, with his unrelenting drive to
escape the encircling hills for the "billion-footed city." The banality of small-town life became a pervasive theme in the literature of the time and the popular outlook of city folk. Writing for
the *Smart Set* and *American Mercury*, H. L. Mencken was the
most merciless in his attacks on the American "booboisie." The
daily panorama of America, he wrote, has become "so inordi-
nately gross and preposterous . . . that only a man who was born
with a petrified diaphragm can fail to laugh himself to sleep
every night, and to awake every morning with all the eager, un-
flagging expectation of a Sunday-school superintendent touring
the Paris peep-shows." The hinterlands responded with coun-
terimages of alien cities infested with vice, crime, corruption,
and foreigners. The tension erupted into the national political
arena on several occasions, and rather than let the growing cities
register their increase in Congress, traditionalists managed (for
the only time in American history) to block any reapportionment
of the House of Representatives after the census of 1920.

THE NEW MORALITY   Much of the shock to oldtimers came from
the revolution in manners and morals, evidenced first among
young people, and especially in the college campuses, where
H. L. Mencken had become a hero. Folkways seemed to be
changing faster than William Graham Sumner would ever have
believed possible. In *This Side of Paradise* (1920), a novel of student life at Princeton, F. Scott Fitzgerald wrote of "the great
current American phenomenon, the 'petting party.' " None of
the Victorian mothers, he said, "had any idea how casually their
daughters were accustomed to be kissed." One of the old
muckrakers, Samuel Hopkins Adams, published a novel under
the pen name of Warner Fabian, *Flaming Youth* (1923), which
gave an enduring tag to the phenomenon. From such novels and
from current magazine pieces the heartland learned about the
"accent on youth," wild parties, bathtub gin, promiscuity, the
new uses to which automobiles were put on secluded lovers'
lanes, speakeasies, roadhouses, and "shimmy dancers" imitating
Gilda Gray, who titillated the boys by shaking her chemise.

If flaming youth generated perhaps more smoke than fire,
taboos were nonetheless loosening and remained loosened in the
1930s. Some young women abandoned corsets because, as one

said: "The men won't dance with you if you wear corsets." By the mid-1920s women's fashion called for a cloche hat that fit tightly over bobbed hair, thin dresses with short sleeves, tightly strapped bust, waistlines where hips used to be, and hemlines that rose to alarming heights. On the feet, at least in John Held's cartoons in the old *Life*, fashionable women wore unfastened galoshes, and hence were called "flappers." Ironically, the more boyish the look, the more the flapper painted her face. Cosmetics joined other growth industries of the decade.

Whatever people did, however few flappers went "all the way," sex came to be discussed with a frankness once unheard of. One father, Frederick Lewis Allen reported, said his daughter "would talk about anything; in fact, she hardly ever talked about anything else." Much of the talk derived from a spreading awareness of Dr. Sigmund Freud, the Viennese father of psychoanalysis. When Freud visited Clark University in 1909, he was surprised to find himself so well known "even in prudish America." The following year appeared the first English translation of his *Three Contributions to a Theory of Sex*. By the 1920s and 1930s his ideas had begun to percolate into the popular awareness, and the talk spread in society and literature about libido, inhibitions, Oedipus complexes, transference, sublimation, and repression.

An obsession with sex permeated much of the literature and popular media of the day. James Branch Cabell, who became famous when his novel *Jurgen* (1919) was banned in Boston, exploited his "phallic candour" in a string of novels, while Eugene O'Neill used Freudian themes onstage in *Desire under the Elms* (1924), *Mourning Becomes Electra* (1931), and other plays. Sex became the stock-in-trade of a prosperous tabloid press, and a new form of literature, the confession magazine, featured lurid

Sweet Sexteen. *One of cartoonist John Held's "flappers" reading up on her Freud.* [Life *magazine*]

stories about women who had gone wrong. Pulp magazines like *Spicy Stories, Paris Nights,* or *Flapper Experiences* aroused interest and sales. In motion pictures "America's Sweetheart," the maidenly Mary Pickford, yielded stardom to the "vamp," Theda Bara, and the "It" girl, Clara Bow, followed in the 1930s by Jean Harlow, the movies' first "platinum blonde." A rising protest over such movie fare as *Up in Mable's Room, Sinners in Silk,* and *Her Purchase Price* impelled the movie industry to follow the example of organized baseball, which had made Judge Kenesaw Mountain Landis its commissioner or "czar" after Chicago White Sox players were charged with selling out their team in the 1919 World Series. In 1922 Postmaster-General Will H. Hays became the "Judge Landis of the Movies."

By 1930 the thrill of rebellion was waning; the revolution against Victorian codes had run its course. Its extreme expressions in time aroused doubts that the indulgence of lust equaled liberation. Frederick Lewis Allen wrote of a fictional "Mrs.Y, who had so stoutly believed in her right to sleep where she pleased and had been sure that she didn't care with whom Mr. Y slept, had found she couldn't take it after all and had marched off to Reno"—a discovery more than one generation had to make for itself. Women's styles never went back to the layered look of an earlier day, but they did once again acknowledge and exploit the difference between the sexes. Still, some new folkways had come to stay. In "Middletown" (Muncie, Indiana), where Robert and Helen Lynd had researched a classic community study in the mid-1920s, a young man told them on their return in 1935 that young people had "been getting more and more knowing and bold. The fellows regard necking as a taken-for-granted part of a date." In the late 1930s a survey disclosed that among college women almost one-half (47 percent) had yielded their virginity before marriage, but of these three-quarters had had sexual relations only with their future spouses. Most of them no doubt would have been shocked to discover that colonial Puritans accepted that much, if reluctantly.

The most pervasive change brought by the new moral code was in its views of marriage. The old Victorian code had made the husband head and master of the family, responsible for its support, while limiting the wife's "sphere" to the care of the home and the children, and the nurturing and gentling of the male animal. Children learned respect for parental authority. By the 1930s a code exalting romantic love and companionship as the basis for marriage had gained ascendancy. The sociologist Ernest R. Groves, in *The American Family* (1934), announced that the "breaking of the former taboo on sex has made possible for younger men and women a healthier attitude toward marital relationship" and a greater chance for mutual happiness. More important than breaking taboos may have been the social and economic evolution of a century which had taken away functions the family once had and delivered them to the factory, the school, and other institutions. Much alarm was expressed in the 1920s at the rising divorce rate. The rate declined briefly with the onset of the Great Depression in 1929, but picked up again during the later 1930s and 1940s. The divorce rate reflected perhaps less an increase in unsatisfactory marriages than a greater willingness and ability to abandon an intolerable situation.

THE WOMEN'S MOVEMENT Equal suffrage for women arrived in 1920. It had been an unconscionably long time in coming. A span of seventy-two years separated the Seneca Falls Declaration of 1848, which marked the start of the political movement for women's rights, from ratification of the Nineteenth Amendment, which secured women the vote. The suffrage movement, which had been in the doldrums since 1896, sprang back to life in the second decade of the new century. In 1912 Alice Paul, a Quaker and social worker, returned from an apprenticeship with the militant suffragists of England, and became chairman of the National American Woman Suffrage Association's Congressional Committee. The day before Wilson's inauguration in 1913, when Washington was full of visitors, she organized a march to promote the suffrage amendment. When unruly crowds nearly broke up the parade, the resultant publicity revitalized the suffrage campaign. Paul's militant tactics and single-minded focus on the federal amendment, however, increasingly drove a wedge between her and the larger national group. The Congressional Union, formed by her committee in 1913, became a separate organization in 1915 and changed its name to the Woman's party in 1916. This group copied the British suffragists in holding the party in power responsible for failure to act, a reasonable stance under a parliamentary system but one which led them to oppose every Democrat, which the mainline suffragists found self-defeating in America. Alice Paul nevertheless knew how to get publicity for the cause. By 1917 she and her followers were engaged in picketing the White House and deliberately provoking arrests, after which they went on hunger strikes in prison. The authorities obligingly cooperated in making martyrs by the hundreds.

Women suffragists picketing the White House in 1917. Their sign points up the irony of Wilson's aim to make the world safe for democracy. [Library of Congress]

Meanwhile, Carrie Chapman Catt became head of the National Suffrage Association once again in 1915 and revived it through her gift for organization. She brought with her a legacy of about $1 million from Mrs. Frank Leslie, publisher of *Leslie's Weekly,* dedicated "to the furtherance of the cause of woman suffrage." The money became available in 1917 and contributed to organizing the final campaigns for voting rights. For several years President Wilson evaded the issue of an amendment, but he voted for suffrage in a New Jersey referendum and supported a plank in the 1916 Democratic platform endorsing state action for woman suffrage, addressed the National Suffrage Organization that year, and thereafter worked closely with its leaders.

Finally, in 1918, after the House had passed the "Anthony Amendment," Wilson went before the Senate on September 30 to plead for its passage there. The Senate fell short of the two-thirds majority by two votes, but the attention centered on the issue helped defeat two antisuffrage senators. On June 4, 1919, the Senate finally adopted the amendment by a bare two-thirds majority. Ratification of the Nineteenth Amendment took another agonizing fourteen months. The Tennessee legislature had the distinction of completing the ratification, on August 21, 1920. It was one of the climactic achievements of the progressive era.

Even before ratification the suffrage organization began transforming itself into the League of Women Voters, founded in 1919, and women thereafter entered politics in growing numbers. But, it was often noted, this did not usher in a political millennium or any sudden release of women from all the trammels of custom and law. What was more, the suffrage victory left the broader feminist movement prey to a letdown that lasted for a generation. A few years after the triumph Carrie Chapman Catt wrote that suffragists were disappointed "because they miss the exaltation, the thrill of expectancy, the vision which stimulated them in the suffrage campaign. They find none of these appeals to their aspiration in the party of their choice."

One group, however, wanted to advance equality yet further. Alice Paul and the Woman's party set a new feminist goal, first introduced in Congress in 1923: an Equal Rights Amendment which would eliminate any remaining legal distinctions between the sexes—including the special legislation for the protection of working women put on the books in the previous fifty or so years. Feminists who had been caught up in the social-justice movement considered this a sacrifice of gains painfully accomplished. If would be another fifty years before Alice Paul would see Congress adopt her amendment in 1972; she did not live, however, to see it fall short of ratification.

The sharp increase in the number of women in the workforce during World War I proved ephemeral, but in the longer view a steady increase in the numbers of employed women occurred in the 1920s and, surprisingly, continued through the depression decade of the 1930s. Still, this phenomenon represented more evolution than revolution. The greatest breakthroughs had come in the nineteenth century, and by 1900 women had at least a token foothold in most of the gainful occupations. By 1910 they made up almost a quarter of all nonagricultural workers, and in 1920 were found in all but 35 of the 572 job categories listed by the census. The continued entry of women into the workforce brought their numbers up from 8.2 million in the 1920 census to 10.4 million in 1930, and 13 million in 1940. Still these women remained concentrated in traditional occupations: domestics, office workers, teachers, clerks, salespeople, dressmakers, milliners, and seamstresses. In manufacturing they were found mainly in related work, such as textiles or garment making. On the eve of World War II women's work was little more diversified than it had been at the turn of the century, but by 1940 it was on the eve of a great transformation.

THE "NEW NEGRO" The discriminations that have befallen blacks and women have many parallels, and the loosening of restraints for both have often gone together. The most significant development in black life during these years was the Great Migration, which one historian pronounced "the greatest watershed in American Negro history" after emancipation. The movement of blacks northward got under way in 1915–1916 when war industries were depleting the ranks of common labor at a time when the war prevented replacement by foreign immigrants; legal restrictions on immigration continued the movement in the 1920s. Altogether, between 1910 and 1920 the Southeast lost some 323,000 blacks, or 4.9 percent of the native black population, and by 1930 had lost another 615,000, or 8.2 percent of the native black population in 1920. With the migration a slow but steady growth in black political influence set in, for not only were blacks freer to speak and act in a northern setting; they gained political leverage by concentrating in large cities located in states with many electoral votes.

Along with political activity came a bristling spirit of protest among blacks, a spirit which received cultural expression in a literary and artistic movement tagged the "Harlem Renaissance." Claude McKay, a Jamaican immigrant, was the first significant writer of the movement which was a rediscovery of black folk culture and an emancipation from the genteel tradition. Poems collected in McKay's *Harlem Shadows* (1922) expressed defiance in such titles as "If We Must Die" and "To the White Fiends." Other emergent writers included the versatile and prolific Langston Hughes, poet, novelist, and columnist; Zora Neal Hurston, folklorist and novelist; Countée Cullen, poet and novelist; and James Weldon Johnson, who pictured the Negro mecca in *Black Manhattan*. Perhaps the greatest single creation of the

Major figures of the Harlem Renaissance. From left, Langston Hughes, Charles Johnson, and the historian E. Franklin Frazier. [Schomberg Collection, New York Public Library]

time was Jean Toomer's novel *Cane,* which pictured the lives of simple blacks in Georgia's black belt and the sophisticated inhabitants of Washington's brown belt. White writers like Eugene O'Neill, DuBose Heyward, Julia Peterkin, and Sherwood Anderson also took up the theme of what Alain Locke in 1925 called "The New Negro," but more often than not they merely abandoned the old stereotype of the "darkie" for a new stereotype of the exotic primitive, a caricature the more fully alive for its want of inhibitions.

In its extreme expression the spirit of the New Negro found outlet in what came to be called "Negro nationalism," which exalted blackness, black cultural expression, and black exclusiveness. The leading spokesman for such views was Marcus Garvey, who in 1916 brought to New York the United Negro Improvement Association (UNIA), which he had started in his native Jamaica two years before. His organization grew rapidly under the strains of the postwar years. Racial bias, he said, was so ingrained in whites that it was futile to appeal to their sense of justice. The only hope for blacks was to flee America and build a Negro republic in Africa. Garvey began to organize ancillary groups such as the Universal African Legion, the Universal Black Cross Nurses, and the Black Star Steamship Line. Much of their appeal paralleled that of fraternal groups which enjoyed parading in uniform. Garvey quickly enlisted half a million members and claimed as many as 6 million by 1923. At that point he was charged with fraudulent use of the mails in raising funds for his steamship line. Found guilty, he went to the Atlanta penitentiary in 1925, where he remained until President Coolidge pardoned and deported him to Jamaica in 1927. Garvey, one biographer concluded, had suffered from a lack of business experience rather than from an intent to defraud. He died in obscurity in London in 1940, but the memory of his movement kept alive an undercurrent of Negro nationalism which would reemerge later under the slogan of "black power."

The year in which the Great Migration began, 1915, marked another milestone with the passing of Booker T. Washington. His position of race leadership was taken up not by a single spokesman but more and more by an organization, the National Association for the Advancement of Colored People (NAACP). It had started with writer William English Walling's call in *The Independent* for a revival of the abolitionist spirit in response to a 1908 race riot in Springfield, Illinois, Lincoln's hometown. Plans laid at a meeting in May 1909 led to a formal organization in 1910. Two participants supplied a direct link to the abolitionists: Oswald Garrison Villard, who was the grandson of William Lloyd Garrison, wrote the call for the 1909 meeting, and Moorefield Storey, in his youth the secretary to the abolitionist Charles Sumner, became the organization's first president. Black participants came mainly from a group associated with W. E. B. Du Bois since 1905 called the Niagara Movement, which had met each year at a place associated with antislavery (Niagara Falls, Oberlin, Boston, Harper's Ferry) and issued a defiant statement against discrimination. Du Bois became the NAACP's director of publicity and research, and editor of its journal, *The Crisis.*

Although most progressives were not in harmony with the NAACP, the new group took seriously the progressive idea that the solution to social problems began with informing the people, and it planned an active press bureau to accomplish this. Its main strategy, however, came over the years to be legal action aimed at warming the Fourteenth and Fifteenth Amendments back to life. One early victory came with *Guinn v. United States* (1915), in which, after the NAACP submitted a friend of the court brief, the Supreme Court struck down Oklahoma's grandfather clause, used in the state to deprive blacks of the vote. In *Buchanan v. Worley* (1917) the Court invalidated a residential segregation ordinance in Louisville, and in *Moore v. Dempsey* (1923) ruled that trials of blacks after the Elaine, Arkansas, riots in 1919 violated due process because they took place in an atmosphere of mob hysteria.

Meanwhile, in 1919 the NAACP launched a campaign against lynching with a statistical survey of the practice and a conference. Rep. L. C. Dyer of St. Louis introduced an antilynching bill to make mob murder a federal offense. The bill passed the House in 1922, but lost to a filibuster by southern senators. The bill stayed before the House until 1925, and NAACP Field Secretary James Weldon Johnson believed the continued agitation of the issue did more than the bill's passage would have to reduce lynchings, which fell off to a third of what they had been the previous decade.

The emergent black political renaissance found expression in two events: Oscar DePriest's election from a Chicago district in 1928 as the first black congressman since 1901, the first ever from the North; and the fight against the confirmation of Judge John J. Parker for the Supreme Court in 1930. When President Hoover submitted Parker's name the NAACP found that as the 1920 Republican candidate for governor of North Carolina Parker had pronounced Negro suffrage "a source of evil and danger." The NAACP conducted its campaign, Du Bois said, "with a snap, determination, and intelligence never surpassed in colored America." Parker lost by the close vote of 41 to 39 to a convergence of unlikely allies: the AFL, unhappy at a Parker labor decision, insurgents who found him too conservative, and southern Democrats opposed to a southern Republican. His defeat nevertheless represented the first instance of significant black impact on Congress since Reconstruction.

In 1930 the NAACP began laying plans for a legal assault on segregation in American life. The administration of Franklin D. Roosevelt saw the political influence of blacks grow further after 1933. Like Wilson, Roosevelt did not give a high priority to Negro affairs, but he tolerated people in his administration who did. By 1936 there was a "Black Cabinet" of some thirty to forty advisors in government departments and agencies, and black voters were fast transferring their political loyalty from Republicans to Democrats.

During the 1930s the NAACP's legal campaign gathered momentum. A major setback occurred in *Grovey v. Townsend* (1935), which upheld the Texas Democrats' white primary as the practice of a voluntary association and thus not state action. But the *Grovey* decision held up for only nine years and marked the end of major decisions that for half a century had narrowed application of the Reconstruction Amendments. A trend in the other direction had already set in. Two important precedents arose from the celebrated Scottsboro case of 1931, in which nine black youths were convicted of raping two white women while riding a freight train in Alabama. The first verdict failed, the high court ruled in *Powell v. Alabama* (1932), for want of due process because the judge's appointing "all of the members of the bar" to defend the accused was "little more than an expensive gesture imposing no substantial or definite obligation upon anyone." Another verdict fell to a judgment in *Norris v. Alabama* (1935) that the systematic exclusion of Negroes from Alabama juries had denied the defendants equal protection of the law—a principle that had significant and widespread impact on state courts.

THE CULTURE OF MODERNISM

SCIENCE AND SOCIAL THOUGHT As the twentieth century advanced, the easy faith in progress and reform expressed by social gospelers and other liberals fell victim to a series of frustrations and disasters: the Great War, failure of the League of Nations, the failure of prohibition, the Great Depression, the rise of Communist and fascist dictators, continuing world crises. New currents in science and social thought also brought shocks to the easy faith in a rational or melioristic universe. Darwin's biology portrayed man as more akin to apes than to angels. Darwin's contemporary Karl Marx influenced even people who rejected his Communist doctrine but saw relevance in his emphasis on the material, economic basis of society. In capitalist society, Marx argued, freedom was an illusion: people were actually driven by impersonal economic forces. In Freud's psychology people were also driven, but by needs arising from the depths of the unconscious. If Darwin, Marx, and Freud suggested that rational man was not the master of his fate, startling new findings in physics further shook the verities underlying American life and thought in the progressive period.

Modern times began, one writer has asserted, on May 29, 1919, when photographs taken during a solar eclipse confirmed Albert Einstein's theory of relativity by showing that the sun's gravitational pull actually bent rays of light from distant stars. The new findings in physics altered the image of the cosmos in ways that seemed almost a calculated assault on common sense. The conventional wisdom since Sir Isaac Newton held the universe to be governed by laws which the scientific method could ultimately uncover. The world was a machine, a scientific writer of the early twentieth century said. "In its motions there is no uncertainty, no mystery." A world of such certain order bolstered hopes of infinite progress in human knowledge, and good Victorians of the nineteenth century could readily accommodate even Darwinism to their optimistic outlook.

This world of order and certainty came apart when Albert Einstein, a young German physicist working in the Swiss patent office, puzzled over recent experiments and reasoned that space, time, and mass were not absolutes but relative to the location and motion of the observer. In 1905 he published a paper, "On the Electrodynamics of Moving Bodies," which became known as the special theory of relativity. Ten years later he elaborated his general theory of relativity, which covered gravitational fields and challenged the Newtonian cosmos. Newton's mechanics, according to Einstein, worked well enough at relatively slow speeds, but the more nearly one approached the velocity of light (about 186,000 miles per second) the more all measuring devices would change accordingly, so that yardsticks would become shorter, clocks and heartbeats would slow down. An observer on another planet moving at a different speed would see a quite different universe from the one we see. Even more incredibly, a

Albert Einstein. [United Press International]

person traveling on a spaceship at immense velocity, and unaware that for him time had slowed relative to earth time, might return to find that centuries had passed in his absence.

Certainty dissolved the farther one reached out into the universe. The same thing happened the farther one reached down into the minute world of the atom. The discovery of radioactivity in the 1890s showed that atoms were not irreducible units of matter but that some of them emitted particles of energy. What this meant, Einstein noted, was that mass and energy were not separate phenomena but interchangeable. In 1907 Einstein quantified this relationship in the famous and deceptively simple formula $E = mc^2$, energy equals mass times the speed of light squared. Meanwhile the researches of Max Planck in Berlin had led Planck to find that electromagnetic emissions of energy, whether as electricity or light, came in little bundles which he called quanta. The development of quantum theory suggested that atoms were far more complex than once believed and, as German physicist Werner Heisenberg stated in his principle of uncertainty in 1927, ultimately indescribable. One could never know both the position and the velocity of an electron, Heisenberg concluded, because the very process of observation would inevitably have an impact on the behavior of the particle, altering its position and velocity.

Heisenberg's thesis meant that beyond a certain point things could not possibly be measured, so that human knowledge had limits. "The physicist thus finds himself in a world from which the bottom has dropped clean out," a Harvard mathematician wrote in 1929. He had to "give up his most cherished convictions and faith. The world is not a world of reason, understandable by the intellect of man, but as we penetrate ever deeper, the very law of cause and effect, which we had thought to be a formula to which we could force God Himself to subscribe, ceases to have any meaning." Hard for the public to grasp, such findings proved too much even for Einstein, who spent much of the rest of his life in quest of an explanation through a unified field theory which would combine electromagnetism and gravitation in one system and unify the relativity and quantum theories. "I shall never believe that God plays dice with the world," Einstein said.

Though few people understood it, Einstein's theory especially captured the imagination of a public whose common experience told them that observers differently placed got a different view of things. Just as Enlightenment thinkers drew on Newton's laws of gravitation two centuries before to formulate their views on the laws governing society, the ideas of relativity and uncertainty in the twentieth century carried over into denials of absolute values in any sphere of society, and thus undermined the concepts of personal responsibility and absolute standards. Anthropologists aided the process by transforming the word "culture," which had before meant refinement, into a term for the whole system of ideas, folkways, and institutions within which any group lived. Even the most primitive groups had cultures and, all things being relative, one culture had no place imposing its value judgments on another. Two students of Columbia University anthropologist Franz Boas, Ruth Benedict and Margaret Mead, were especially effective in spreading this viewpoint. Benedict's *Patterns of Culture* (1934), a steady seller, introduced millions to the different values of unusual cultures from the North American Indians to the Melanesians, and Mead's *Coming of Age in Samoa* (1928) celebrated the healthfulness of the uninhibited sex she observed there. The uncertainty principle got an ironic twist in Mead's case, however, when over fifty years later another anthropologist insisted that she was the victim of a gigantic put-on by Samoans who told her what they thought she wanted to hear.

MODERNIST LITERATURE   The cluster of scientific ideas associated with Darwin and Einstein inspired a revolution in the minds of intellectuals and creative artists which they expressed in a new modernism. Some observers now count this new intellectual current as ranking with the Enlightenment, romanticism, or Victorianism in its sweep and significance. The historian Daniel J. Singal has identified certain major features of the modernist movement. First, it undertook "to plumb the nether regions of the psyche," to explore the irrational as an essential part of human nature. Second, it viewed the universe as turbulent and

Louis Armstrong's Hot Five. Jazz emerged during this period as an especially American expression of the modernist spirit. Black artists bent musical conventions to give fuller reign to improvisation. [United Press International]

unpredictable, and presented uncertainty as a desirable condition. Third, it displaced the Victorian ideals of "bliss" and "peace" with a positive view of conflict. Finally, the modernist displayed "a critical temperament uninhibited by considerations of formal manners," for rules of gentility had to yield to the urge to make contact with "reality," no matter how distasteful. In the various arts related technical features appeared: abstract painting which represented an inner mood rather than an image of an object, atonal music, free verse in poetry, stream-of-consciousness narrative, and interior monologues in stories and novels. Writers dramatized our separation from the past. They showed an intense concern with new forms in language in an effort to avoid outmoded forms and structures and to violate expectations and shock their audiences.

The search for the new centered in America's first major artistic bohemias: Chicago, where cheap housing built for visitors to the Columbian Exposition offered a haven on the South Side; and New York, where the area in lower Manhattan soon known as Greenwich Village offered a lure for aspiring artists, and radicals —and their camp followers. In the words of the radical writer John Reed, the Village featured "inglorious Miltons by the score, and Rodins, one to every floor." As early as 1909 the photographer Alfred Stieglitz hung Matisse paintings in his Photo-Secession gallery on Fifth Avenue. At Mabel Dodge's Fifth Avenue salon intellectuals rubbed shoulders with IWW leader Big Bill Haywood and discussed the new ideas. In 1913 the Armory Show in New York, which went then to Chicago, Philadelphia, and Boston, shocked traditionalists with its display of the latest in experimental and nonrepresentational art: post-impressionists, Fauvists, expressionists, primitives, and cubists. ablo Picasso's work made its American debut there. Mabel Dodge thought the show the most important event in America since 1776. It aroused a portion of shocked indignation and not a little good-natured ridicule, but it was a huge success. Audiences flocked to the show and buyers afterward snapped up the pieces for sale.

Suddenly everything was new: the "New Freedom," the "New Nationalism," the new poetry, the new art, the new ethics, the new marriage. In 1913 James Harvey Robinson of Columbia announced in *The New History* a purpose of making history a pragmatic science oriented toward explaining the present, and in the same year his colleague Charles A. Beard sent out shock waves with *An Economic Interpretation of the Constitution.* Late in 1912 Max Eastman had taken over the socialistic *Masses* and turned it into a lively magazine; in 1914 Herbert Croly established the less radical *New Republic.* Literary magazines mushroomed: the *Seven Arts, Dial*, the *Little Review*, the *Bohemian*, the *Criterion*, and many others.

"The fiddles are tuning as it were all over America," the Irish painter John Butler Yeats wrote. In Chicago, Harriet Monroe provided a sounding board in *Poetry: A Magazine of Verse.* A poet of some local renown, author of the official ode for the Columbian Exposition, and already past fifty when she started *Poetry* in 1912, she found her vocation as patron to a renaissance. Within a few years she had brought to light a dozen and more major figures: Carl Sandburg, celebrator of Chicago, "Stormy, husky, brawling, City of the Big Shoulders"; Vachel Lindsay, vagabond poet who sought to restore the "primitive singing voice" in poems like "General Booth Enters Heaven" and "The Congo"; the lyricists Sara Teasdale, Elinor Wylie, and Edna St. Vincent Millay; Robinson Jeffers, poet of tragic despair; the imagists Amy Lowell, Conrad Aiken, and William Carlos Williams. To her eternal regret Harriet Monroe "missed" Edgar Lee Masters, a lawyer resident in Chicago and author of *Spoon River Anthology* (1915), his poetic epitaphs for middle western types. She also missed Sherwood Anderson, whose stories of midwestern characters in *Winesburg, Ohio* (1919), offered a prose parallel to *Spoon River.*

The chief American prophets of modernism were in neither Chicago nor New York, but emigrés in Europe: Ezra Pound and T. S. Eliot in London, and Gertrude Stein in Paris, all deeply concerned with creating new and often difficult styles of expression. Pound, as foreign editor for *Poetry*, became the conduit through which many American poets achieved publication in America and Britain. At the same time he became the leader of the imagist movement, a revolt against the ornamental verbosity of Victorian poetry in favor of the concrete image, exclusion of "superfluous words," and the rhythm of the "musical phrase" rather than the "sequence of a metronome." In the course of a long life, Pound was to embrace a number of causes, continue his expatriation in Paris and Italy, encourage new writers, seek new poetic techniques, and compose as his lifetime project an endless series of difficult and obscure *Cantos*.

Pound's supreme protégé was T. S. Eliot, who in 1915 contributed to *Poetry* his first major poem, "The Love Song of J. Alfred Prufrock," the musings of an ineffectual man who "after tea and cakes and ices" could never find "the strength to force the moment to its crisis." Eliot's "The Waste Land" (1922) made few concessions to readers in its arcane allusions, its juxtaposition of unexpected metaphors, its deep sense of postwar disillusionment and melancholy, and its suggestion of a burnt-out civilization; but it became for a generation almost the touchstone of the modern temper along with the Irishman James Joyce's stream-of-consciousness novel *Ulysses*, published the same year. As poet and critic in *The Criterion*, which he founded in 1922, Eliot became the arbiter of modernist taste in Anglo-American literature.

Gertrude Stein, in voluntary exile since 1903, was with her brother Leo an early champion of modern art and a collector of early Cézannes, Matisses, and Picassos. Long regarded as no more than the literary eccentric who wrote "Rose is a rose is a rose is a rose" and "Pigeons on the grass alas," she came later to be recognized as one of the chief originators and propagators of modernist style, beginning with *Three Lives* (1906). Included in this work is the classic "Melanctha," perhaps the first story by a white author to treat a black character as something other than a stereotype. Having studied psychology under William James, Stein sought to develop in writing the equivalent of nonrepresentational painting; her work captured interior moods in such books as *The Making of Americans* (1911, published 1925) and *Tender Buttons* (1914).

But she was long known chiefly through her influence on such 1920s expatriates as Sherwood Anderson and Ernest Hemingway, whom she told: "All of you young people who served in the war, you are the lost generation." The earliest chronicler of that generation, F. Scott Fitzgerald, blazed up brilliantly and then quickly flickered out, like all the tinseled, blithesome, sad young people of his novels. Successful and famous at age twenty-four with *This Side of Paradise* (1920), along with his wife Zelda he lived in and wrote up the "greatest, gaudiest spree in history," and then both had their crack-up in the Great Depression. What gave depth to the best of his work was what a character in *The Great Gatsby* (1925), his finest novel, called "a sense of the fundamental decencies" amid all the surface gaiety—and almost always a sense of impending doom.

Hemingway's first novel, *The Sun Also Rises* (1926), pictures an even more desperate search for life by the expatriate crowd, chasing about frantically from the bistros of Paris to the bullrings of Spain. Young Jake Barnes, emasculated by a war wound, cannot marry his love, Lady Brett Ashley. "Oh, Jake," she says in the poignant ending, "we could have had such a damned good time together." "Yes," he replied. "Isn't it pretty to think so?" Hemingway's second novel, *A Farewell to Arms* (1929), is another tale of lost love. Based on Hemingway's experience in the ambulance corps in northern Italy, where he had caught shrapnel in both legs during the retreat from Caporetto, it pursues the love affair of a driver and a nurse who abandon the war for Switzerland, where the young woman dies in childbirth.

Already in these novels are found the lively, even frenetic action, and the cult of athletic masculinity (epitomized by the bullfighter), which became the stuff of the public image which Hemingway cultivated for himself and the hallmark of such novels as *Death in the Afternoon* (1932), *To Have and Have Not* (1937), *For Whom the Bell Tolls* (1940), and *The Old Man and the Sea* (1952). Hundreds of writers tried to imitate Hemingway's terse style, but few had his gift, which lay less in what he had to say than in the way he said it. The critic Alfred Kazin passed judgment in one short sentence: "He brought a major art to a minor vision of life."

THE RETURN OF SOCIAL SIGNIFICANCE   In view of the studied alienation of writers caught in the materialistic world of the 1920s, one might have expected the onset of the Great Depression in 1929 to deepen the despair. Instead it brought a renewed sense of commitment and affirmation, as if people could no longer afford the art-for-art's-sake affectations of the 1920s. The surprisingly popular musical show *Pins and Needles* (1936), put on by members of the International Ladies' Garment Workers Union, caught the new feeling of dedication in one of its numbers: "Sing Me a Song with Social Significance."

In the early 1930s the commitment sometimes took the form of allegiance to revolution. For a time leftist politics and rhetoric made significant inroads in literary circles. By the summer of 1932 even the "golden boy" of the lost generation, F. Scott Fitzgerald, was saying that "to bring on the revolution, it may be necessary to work within the Communist party." In September 1932 fifty-three artists and intellectuals signed an open letter endorsing William Z. Foster, the Communist party candidate for president, and many writers flocked into the party's John Reed Clubs, named for the American journalist who had observed and written about the Bolshevik revolution.

Until 1935, following the line laid down by the Soviet dictator Joseph Stalin, the Communist party refused to collaborate with other groups. In 1935 the party line switched to endorse a broad "popular front" with democratic and socialistic groups opposed to fascism. In 1935 the John Reed clubs gave way to the more broadly based League of American Writers, which held an annual American Writers' Congress for several years. It paralleled other popular-front groups like the American Youth Congress, the American Negro Congress, and the American League for Peace and Democracy. It drew into its activities, among others, Hemingway, Erskine Caldwell, Waldo Frank, Archibald MacLeish, Richard Wright, John Dos Passos, Theodore Dreiser, John Steinbeck, and Langston Hughes. But few remained for long. Writers being a notoriously independent lot, they rebelled at demands to hew to a shifting line. Over the years a series of shocks persuaded most of them that Joseph Stalin practiced tyranny and terror more efficient and more bloody than anything under the czars. The climactic events were the staged treason trials of Stalin's former comrades in 1936 and Stalin's Non-Aggression Pact with Hitler in 1939 which opened the way for World War II in Europe.

In the heyday of the "Red Decade" there was much talk of a proletarian literature, but the only product of lasting significance to come out of the leftist cultural movement was the *Partisan Review,* founded in 1934 as the organ of New York's John Reed Club and, after a brief hiatus in 1936–1937, revived as an anti-Stalinist literary journal. Among the writers who sang songs with social significance at least three novelists deserve special notice: John Dos Passos, John Steinbeck, and Richard Wright.

After Harvard and a stint as an ambulance driver in France and Italy during the Great War, Dos Passos first got wide notice with *Three Soldiers* (1921), an exposé of the sordid and brutal nature of war. *Manhattan Transfer* (1925) presented a similar picture of modern urban society and began to use the kaleidoscopic techniques of his great trilogy *U.S.A.* (1930–1936), which undertook no less than a panorama of American society from 1900 to 1936. In its three parts—*The Forty-second Parallel, 1919,* and *The Big Money*—the sprawling story line served mainly as a device to place its eleven major characters at crucial junctures of the national experience. Three structural devices lent a special flavor to the book. One, the "Newsreel," presented a collage of newspaper stories and headlines, popular songs, and quotations from public figures to evoke a feeling of the times. The second, the "Camera Eye," gave brief impressionistic sketches of responses to the issues and scenes of the times. Third was the series of biographies of public figures such as Isadora Duncan, Robert La Follette, Thomas A. Edison, and many others. The trilogy ends by contrasting a hungry, dirty hitchhiker by a roadside to a wealthy, well-fed executive passing overhead on a transcontinental plane. The scene underscored the radical vision of the trilogy that America had become divided into "two nations." A lengthy flirtation with Communist causes in the 1920s and early 1930s ended in disillusionment at the Communists' use of violence against Socialist opponents who preferred democratic methods. After the mid-1930s his viewpoint moved away from Marxism and ever more toward affirmations of patriotism, but his creative powers never again equaled those which produced *U.S.A.*

The single piece of fiction that best captured the ordeal of the depression, John Steinbeck's *The Grapes of Wrath* (1939), was also the most memorable "proletarian" novel of the times because it escaped political formula to treat workers as people. Steinbeck had taken the trouble to travel with displaced "Okies" driven from the Oklahoma Dust Bowl by bankers and farm combines to pursue the illusion of jobs in the fields of California's Central Valley. The story focused on the Joad family as they made their painful journey from Oklahoma west along U.S. 66, enticed by job ads aimed really at producing a labor surplus and depressed wages. Met chiefly with contempt and rejection, caught up in labor agitations, Ma Joad strove to keep hope alive and at the end, even as the family was breaking up under the pressure, she grasped at a broader loyalty: "Use'ta be the fambly was fust. It ain't so now. It's anybody. Worse off we get, the more we got to do." The novel was more than a period piece about the depression. As one critic observed: "It is an allegory that is applicable wherever prejudice and a sense of self-importance inhibit co-operation."

Steinbeck produced a bountiful harvest of writing, most suc-

Migrant Mother, *photograph by Dorothea Lange, 1936. This care-worn but proud migrant mother appears the real-life counterpart to Steinbeck's Ma Joad. [Library of Congress, FSA Collection]*

cessfully when he dealt with his native California, as in "The Red Pony" (1933, 1938), the story of a boy's maturing through experience of the tragic nature of life, or *Tortilla Flat* (1935) and *Cannery Row* (1935), which celebrated the vagabond lives of the mixed-blood *paisanos* and dockside bums of Monterey. Fame arrived for Steinbeck with *In Dubious Battle* (1936), about a strike of fruit pickers exploited both by the bosses for profit and by their Communist leader for the sake of power, and with *Of Mice and Men* (1937), about the tragedy of two ranchhands. He continued writing into the 1960s, but *The Grapes of Wrath* remained his masterpiece.

Among black novelists the supreme genius was Richard Wright. Born on a plantation near Natchez, Mississippi, the son of a matriarch whose husband deserted the family, Wright grew up in the course of moving from town to town, ended his formal schooling with the ninth grade (as valedictorian of his class), worked in Memphis, and greedily devoured books he borrowed on a white friend's library card, all the while saving up to go north. In Chicago, where he arrived on the eve of the depression, the Federal Writers' Project gave him a chance to perfect his talent, and his period as a Communist from 1934 to 1944 gave him an intellectual framework, Marxism, which did not, however, overpower his fierce independence. His first book, *Uncle Tom's Children* (1938), a collection of four novellas, and his autobiographical *Black Boy* (1945) revealed in their very rebellion against racial injustice his ties to the South, for, he wrote, "there had been slowly instilled into my personality and consciousness, black though I was, the culture of the South."

Native Son (1940), Wright's masterpiece, was set in the Chicago he had come to know before moving on to New York. It was the story of Bigger Thomas, a product of the black ghetto, a man hemmed in and finally impelled to murder by forces beyond his control. "They wouldn't let me live and I killed," he said unrepentently at the end. Somehow Wright managed to sublimate into literary power his bitterness and rage at what he called "The Ethics of Living Jim Crow," an art he never quite mastered. In the black experience, he wrote, America had "a past tragic enough to appease the spiritual hunger of even a James; and . . . in the oppression of the Negro a shadow athwart our national life dense and heavy enough to satisfy even the gloomy broodings of a Hawthorne."

THE SOUTHERN RENAISSANCE   In different ways southern whites had shared that tragic past. Out of the memory and the consciousness of change the writers among them nurtured a renaissance that burgeoned into one of the most notable literary growths since the flowering of New England a century before. There was little reason to expect it in 1920 when H. L. Mencken published in his *Prejudices: Second Series* his essay "The Sahara of the Bozart," which described the southern cultural landscape as a barren wasteland: "One thinks of the interstellar spaces, of the colossal reaches of the now mythical ether. . . . It would be impossible in all history to match so complete a drying-up of civilization." Among the writers Mencken missed was Ellen Glasgow, of Richmond, Virginia, who in the Victorian twilight at the turn of the century had begun a lonely revolt against the "twin conventions of prudery and platitude" in her "Novels of the Commonwealth," a realistic social history of Virginia from the Civil War. *Barren Ground* (1925), about a heroic female figure of endurance, brought her recognition that was long overdue.

What Mencken's essay had also missed was that the South had reached a historical watershed, that it stood between two worlds: the dying world of tradition and the modern, commercial world struggling to be born. The resultant conflict of values, felt more intensely in the South than in the North, aroused the Ku Klux Klan and fundamentalist furies, but had quite another effect on the South's young writers. Allen Tate, a talented young poet, novelist, and critic, saw in the South the "curious burst of intelligence that you get at a crossing of the ways, not unlike, on an infinitesimal scale, the outburst of poetic genius at the end of the sixteenth century when commercial England began to crush feudal England."

That Mencken had touched a sensitive nerve was apparent from the frequent references to him in the literary groups and little magazines that sprang to life in his Sahara. The Poetry Society of South Carolina noted in its first *Year Book* (1921) that the desert had already sprouted oases where the fig trees were not entirely barren. In New Orleans *The Double Dealer* (1921–1926) became the focus of a literary bohemia which for a time included Sherwood Anderson and William Faulkner. In Nashville *The Fugitive: A Journal of Poetry* (1922–1925) announced the arrival of the most influential group in American letters since the New England transcendentalists.

The Fugitive poets began as a group of student intellectuals at Vanderbilt University who first gathered for discussions in 1915, then regrouped after the war with young Prof. John Crowe Ransom as their dean and mentor. Four of the group eventually stood out in their commitment to literature as a profession: Ransom, Donald Davidson, Allen Tate, and Robert Penn Warren. The Fugitives admired T. S. Eliot and were committed to the new doctrines of modernism in literature. They cultivated a style distinguished by attention to form and language, by complexity and allusion that yielded only to the closest study. They began in revolt against the twin images of southern sentimentalists and commercial boosters. "*The Fugitive,*" Ransom wrote, "flees from nothing faster than from the high-caste Brahmins of the Old South."

It dawned on them that they had protested too much, however, when reporters drawn to the Scopes trial vied with Mencken in mocking the Bible Belt and the benighted South. In reaction the Fugitives began to seek a usable past in the southern agrarian tradition. They brought others into the project, and their manifesto, *I'll Take My Stand* (1930), by twelve southerners, appeared fortuitously just when industrial capitalism seemed on the verge of collapse. In reaction against images of the New South and the Benighted South, the Vanderbilt agrarians championed, in Donald Davidson's words, a "traditional society . . . that is stable, religious, more rural than urban, and politically conservative," a society in which human needs were supplied by "Family, bloodkinship, clanship, folkways, custom, community. . . ." In the end their agrarianism proved less important as a social-economic force than as a context for creative literature. Yet their image of the agrarian South, as Louis Rubin later wrote, provided "a rich, complex metaphor through which they presented a critique of the modern world." Their critique of the frenzy of modernism "has since been echoed by commentator after commentator."

While agrarianism quickened a generation of southern writers with its vision of southern tradition beset by change, southern regionalism quickened a generation of social scientists with its vision of the "Problem South." The school of southern regionalism was based in the University of North Carolina at Chapel Hill and was led chiefly by the sociologists Howard W. Odum and Rupert B. Vance. They inspired no single manifesto but their most important works were Vance's *Human Geography of the South* (1932) and Odum's *Southern Regions of the United States* (1936). Odum proposed to overcome the divisiveness of traditional sectionalism by presenting regional diversity as a national strength. He explored the social problems plaguing the South, and argued that rational planning would aid the "Problem South" and develop its rich potential.

With remarkable speed after 1920 Mencken's cultural Sahara turned into a forest populated with nests of singing birds. "One may reasonably argue," wrote the critic Howard Mumford Jones in 1930, "that the South is the literary land of promise today." Just the previous year two vital figures had emerged: Thomas Wolfe, with *Look Homeward, Angel,* and William Faulkner, with *Sartoris* and *The Sound and the Fury.* Fame rushed in first on Wolfe and his native Asheville, North Carolina, which became in the last golden October of the 1920s a classic example of the scandalized community. "Against the Victorian morality and the Bourbon aristocracy of the South," Wolfe had "turned in all his fury," his former classmate, Jonathan Daniels, wrote. The reaction was not an uncommon response to the works of the southern renaissance, created by authors who had outgrown their hometowns and looked back from new perspectives acquired in travel and education.

For all his gargantuan lust for experience and knowledge, his demonic drive to escape the encircling hills for the "fabled" world outside, his agonized search for some "lost lane-end into heaven," Wolfe never completely severed his roots in the South. *Look Homeward, Angel,* his first novel, remained his most successful; it was the lyrical and searching biography of Eugene Gant's (actually Wolfe's) youth in Altamont (Asheville) and his college days in Pulpit Hill (Chapel Hill). It established him as "the giant among American writers of sensitive youth fiction." Three later books, two edited posthumously from a mountain of manuscript after his untimely death at age thirty-seven, traced his further wanderings as Eugene Gant in *Of Time and the River* (1935), and as George Webber in *The Web and the Rock* (1939) and *You Can't Go Home Again* (1940).

William Faulkner himself ranked Wolfe first among contemporary novelists because he "made the best failure. . . . My admiration for Wolfe is that he tried to get it all said; he was willing to throw away style, coherence, all the rules of preciseness, to try to put all the experience of the human heart on the head of a pin, as

William Faulkner. [University of Virginia]

it were." Faulkner's own achievement, more than Wolfe's, was rooted in the world that produced him. Born near Oxford, Lafayette County, Mississippi, he grew up there and transmuted his hometown into Jefferson, Yoknapatawpha County, in his fiction. After a brief stint with the Royal Canadian Air Force he passed the postwar decade in what seemed to fellow townsmen an aimless drifting. He briefly attended classes at the University of Mississippi, worked at odd jobs, and went to New Orleans where he wrote *Soldiers' Pay* (1926), a caricature of the New Orleans bohemians yachting on Lake Pontchartrain. Between books he shipped out briefly for Europe, and after knocking around the Gulf Coast, returned to Oxford.

There, in writing *Sartoris* (1929), he began to discover that his "own little postage stamp of native soil was worth writing about" and that he "would never live long enough to exhaust it." In this book a postwar wasteland stood out the more starkly against a legend of past glory in the Sartoris family. Young Bayard Sartoris, denied the romantic end that befell his twin brother, who had been shot down over France, pursued a kind of gallant death wish by automobile and airplane until he found release in a plane crash. With *Sartoris* and the creation of his mythical land of Yoknapatawpha, Faulkner kindled a blaze of creative energy. Next, as he put it, he wrote his gut into *The Sound and the Fury*, again the story of a demoralized family. It was one of the triumphs of the modernist style, but early readers, taking their cue from the title instead of the critics, found it signified nothing.

Faulkner's creative frenzy continued through the writing of *As I Lay Dying* (1930) and *Light in August* (1932). He began to fill in the early history of Yoknapatawpha with *Absalom! Absalom!* (1936), a story which unfolded slowly as Quentin Compson, in midnight conversations with his Canadian roommate at Harvard, attempted to reconstruct the story of Sutpen Hundred from bits and pieces of information he had picked up. The process, familiar to historians, was disconcerting to readers looking for the completed narrative. Faulkner rounded out further the history of Yoknapatawpha and the conflict between tradition and the modern world. *The Hamlet* (1940), *The Town* (1957), and *The Mansion* (1950) followed the rise of Flem Snopes and his myriad relatives, who lacked an ethical code and aimed to displace the old families who still clung to shopworn tradition.

Most critics at first missed what Faulkner was attempting. Some viewed him as an exemplar of what Ellen Glasgow called "Southern Gothic," the leader in a "cult of cruelty." Others found disturbing his obscurity, the slow unfolding of meaning, convoluted syntax, and runaway rhetoric of his novels. *Absalom! Absalom!*, one critic complained, used the"non-Stop or Life Sentence," a method of "Anti-Narrative, a set of complex devices used to keep the story from getting told." But that, of course, was Faulkner's point—to vary the usual strategies of rhetoric so that new insights overtook the reader by surprise. Not until the mid–twentieth century did critics generally begin to grasp that Faulkner, in composing his mythical history of Yoknapatawpha, had become also—certainly among Americans—the most skillful creator of modernist styles in the novel during the first half of the twentieth century.

DOCUMENTARY EXPRESSION IN THE THIRTIES Somewhere between belles lettres and academic treatise fell a literature of social exploration and descriptive journalism that formed the southern expression of what Alfred Kazin called the "now innocent, now calculating, now purely rhetorical, but always significant experience in national self-discovery that occurred in the 1930s." The New Deal, through the Works Progress Administration's Federal Writers' Project, among other things contributed to the collection of a "vast granary of facts" in fifty-one state and territorial guidebooks, catalogs of archives, collections of folklore and folksongs, and even records of tombstone inscriptions. The Writers' Project pioneered in the oral history of the "inarticulate." In *These Are Our Lives* (1939), the Writers' Project in North Carolina, Tennessee, and Georgia gathered case histories of workers, sharecroppers, and Negroes in a form that Charles A. Beard called "literature more powerful than anything I have read in fiction, not excluding Zola's most vehement passages." *Lay My Burden Down* (1944) presented the life stories of former slaves as recorded by Writers' Project interviewers.

Two women at a convention of former slaves. The period saw Americans reflecting on their culture and history. [Library of Congress]

A new genre of documentary literature teamed social reporters with photographers: Erskine Caldwell and Margaret Bourke-White, *You Have Seen Their Faces* (1937) and *Say, Is This the USA?* (1941); Dorthea Lange and Paul S. Taylor, *An American Exodus* (1939); and James Agee and Walker Evans, *Let Us Now Praise Famous Men* (1941). The last of these, a sensitive and effective evocation of tenant life in Alabama, got little notice at the time but gradually came to be recognized as a unique masterpiece of documentation and art. Under the direction of Roy Stryker the Farm Security Administration built up an enormous photographic documentation of everyday life in America, making familiar in the credits such names as Dorothea Lange and Ben Shahn. Pare Lorenz pioneered the motion picture documentary in *The Plow That Broke the Plains* and *The River*.

In the 1930s America experienced what *Fortune* magazine called "a sort of cultural revolution," largely through the WPA projects in writing, arts, music, theater, and historical research. Americans learned that, like it or not, they had a culture and had had one all along—it had simply been overlooked. Now Americans tried to make up for lost time by tracking the culture down, recording, restoring, and celebrating it. They became intrigued with American art of all kinds, and particularly that least influenced by Europe: primitive, folk, or as it was called most often, "popular" art. American artists, such as Grant Wood and other regionalists, turned their attention to their homeland.

America's "cultural nationalism" in the 1930s would have been "thin and elitist" without the WPA, the historian William Stott wrote, but the "cultural revolution would have happened without the WPA arts projects or indeed any governmental impetus. Its causes—the Depression, America's isolation in a menacing world, the Russian and German examples—were more compelling than any Washington could legislate." And so the two decades of the 1920s and 1930s, times of unusually creative vitality, ended with Americans engaged in the rediscovery of America.

FURTHER READING

The standard surveys of the interwar period cover many of the trends discussed in the chapter. Start with William Leuchtenberg's *The Perils of Prosperity, 1914–1932* (1958).° Still appealing is Frederick Lewis Allen's longtime favorite, *Only Yesterday* (1931).° Allen covers some cultural developments for the 1930s in *Since Yesterday* (1939).° Also helpful are the chapters on the 1920s in Otis L. Graham, Jr.'s *The Great Campaigns: War and Reform in America, 1900–1928* (1971),° and George E. Mowry and Blaine Brownell's *The Urban Nation, 1920–1980* (1980).° The best single introduction to the culture of the 1920s is Loren Baritz, ed. *The Culture of the Twenties* (1969).° A good accompaniment is Richard H. Pells's *Radical Visions and American Dreams: Culture and Social Thought in the Depression Years* (1973).°

Don S. Kirschner's *City and Country: Rural Responses to Urbanization in the 1920s* (1970) highlights many of the cultural tensions which plagued the decade, and John Higham's *Strangers in the Land: Patterns of American Nativism, 1860–1925* (1955),° handles immigration restrictions. For analysis of the more extreme nativist measures, see David Chalmers's *Hooded Americanism: The History of the Ku Klux Klan* (1965)° and Kenneth T. Jackson's *The Ku Klux Klan in the Cities, 1915–1930* (1967). Religious trends are handled in George M. Marsden's *Fundamentalism and American Culture* (1980) and Normal Furniss's *The Fundamentalist Controversy* (1954). Lawrence Levine's *Defender of the Faith: William Jennings Bryan, the Last Decade, 1915–1925* (1965), and Ray Ginger's *Six Days or Forever? Tennessee v. John Scopes* (1958)° cover the antievolution fight in Dayton, while Willard B. Gatewood's *Preachers, Pedagogues, and Politicians* (1966) examines the same controversy in North Carolina. Two contrasting views of prohibition are in Andrew Sinclair's *Prohibition: The Era of Excess* (1962)° and Norman Clark's *Deliver Us from Evil* (1976).° Humbert S. Nelli's *The Business of Crime* (1976) examines those who profited from bootlegging, including Al Capone, while Edward M. Morgan's *The Legacy of Sacco and Venzetti* (1948) chronicles the fate of those accused radicals.

Other social groups also receive scholarly treatment. For blacks, see Charles Kellogg's *NAACP* (1967), for his analysis of the pioneering court

°These books are available in paperback editions.

cases. Gilbert Osofsky's *Harlem: The Making of a Ghetto, 1890–1930* (1966),° Nathan J. Huggins's *Harlem Renaissance* (1972),° and Jervis Anderson's *This Was Harlem: A Cultural Portrait, 1900–1950* (1981),° cover the impact of the Great Migration. For political implications, see Theodore G. Vincent's *Black Power and the Garvey Movement* (1971) and Randall Burkett's *Garveyism as a Religious Movement* (1978). Also valuable are the relevant sections of James Bouchat's *Alley Life in Washington: Family, Community, Religion, and Folk Life in the City, 1850–1980* (1980).

The impact of transportation is gauged in John Roe's *The Road and the Car in American Life* (1971) and Reynold M. Wik's *Henry Ford and Grassroots America* (1973).° Stuart Ewen looks at the effect of mass advertising in *Captains of Consciousness* (1976). Motion pictures are the subject of Robert Sklar's *Movie-Made America* (1975) and Larry May's *Screening out the Past* (1980).

Woman's suffrage is treated extensively in J. Stanley Lemon's *The Woman Citizen: Social Feminism in the 1920s* (1973) and Susan D. Becker's *The Origins of the Equal Rights Amendment: American Feminism between the Wars* (1981). Lois Banner's *American Beauty* (1983) and Elaine Tyler May's *Great Expectations: Marriage and Divorce in Post-Victorian America* (1980) trace changing attitudes about the role of women. Paula S. Fass's *The Damned and the Beautiful: American Youth in the 1920s* (1977)° traces the social attitudes of youth in general.

Much of the theoretical basis for the chapter's discussion of "modernism" comes from Daniel J. Singal's *The War Within: From Victorian to Modernist Thought in the South, 1919–1945* (1982).° Also valuable are Mortin G. White's *Social Thought in America: The Revolt against Formalism* (1957), Arthur A. Ekrich's *Ideologies and Utopias: The Impact of the New Deal on American Thought* (1969), and Edward A. Purcell, Jr.'s *The Crisis of Democratic Theory: Scientific Naturalism and the Problem of Values* (1973). A good introduction to the impact of Darwin is Cynthia E. Russett's *Darwin in America* (1976). For Einstein, see Cornelius Lanczos's *The Einstein Decade, 1905–1915* (1974). Nathan G. Hale, Jr.'s *Freud and America* (1971) examines the impact of psychoanalysis.

Alfred Kazin's *On Native Grounds* (1942)° is a good introduction to the literature of the period. Also valuable is Frederick J. Hoffman's *The Twenties: American Writing in the Postwar Decade* (1962). Studies on individual authors include Eugene Levy's *James Weldon Johnson* (1973),° Hendy D. Piper's *F. Scott Fitzgerald: A Critical Portrait* (1972), Carlos H. Baker's *Hemingway: The Writer as Artist* (1956),° Mark Schorer's *Sinclair Lewis* (1961), Cleanth Brooks's *William Faulkner: The Yoknapatawpha Country* (1963),° C. Hugh Holman's *The Loneliness at the Core: Studies in Thomas Wolfe* (1975), and Townsend Ludington's *John Dos Passos: A Twentieth Century Odyssey* (1980). For the influence of Mencken, see Fred C. Hobson's *Serpent in Eden: H. L. Mencken and the South* (1974).° Louis D. Rubin examines the Fugitives of Vanderbilt in *The Wary Fugitives* (1978).°

27

TO NORMALCY—AND BACK

PROGRESSIVISM DISSOLVED AND TRANSFORMED

The progressive coalition which had reelected Woodrow Wilson in 1916 proved to be a fragile, temporary thing, and by 1920 it had dissolved. It came apart because radicals and other opponents of the war grew disaffected with America's entrance into the conflict and by the war's aftermath, because organized labor was unhappy with the administration's unsympathetic attitude toward the strikes of 1919–1920, and because farmers of the Plains and West thought that wartime price controls had discriminated against them. Intellectuals and elements of the middle class also drifted away from their former support of progressivism. The intellectuals became disillusioned with democracy because of popular support for prohibition and the antievolution movements. The larger middle class became preoccupied with building a new business civilization "based not upon monopoly and restriction," in the words of the historian Arthur Link, "but upon a whole new set of business values— mass production and consumption, short hours and high wages, full employment, welfare capitalism." Progressivism's final triumphs at the national level were already pretty much foregone conclusions before the war's end: the Eighteenth Amendment, ratified in 1919, which imposed national prohibition, and the Nineteenth Amendment, ratified in 1920, which extended women's suffrage to the entire country.

Progressivism, however, did not disappear in the 1920s. Progressives dominated Congress during much of the decade even while the White House was in conservative hands. The progressive impulse for "good government" and public services remained strong, especially at the state and local levels, where movements for good roads, education, public health, and social welfare all gained momentum during the decade. The progressive impulse for reform, however, was transformed into the drive for moral righteousness and conformity animating the Ku Klux Klan and the fundamentalist movement. Prohibition, at first a direct outgrowth of the reform spirit, came to be increasingly associated with the narrow intolerance of the times.

"NORMALCY"

HARDING'S ELECTION   Amid the postwar tumult another presidential season approached. The country was now weary of crusades and no leader was likely to sound the trumpet of reform. Wilson was ill, Theodore Roosevelt had died in 1919, and World War I had produced no military hero of presidential stature. Herbert Hoover, still in his mid-forties, came out of the war with a brilliant record as director of food policies and war relief, but he was not in the race. Even his party affiliation was unknown until, after sweeping the Democratic presidential preference primary in Michigan, he announced that he would refuse a Democratic nomination.

When the Republicans met in Chicago in June 1920 the Old Guard was ready to reclaim its heritage. The regulars found their man in Ohio's Sen. Warren Gamaliel Harding, who had set the tone of his campaign in May, when he told a Boston audience: "America's present need is not heroics, but healing; not nostrums, but normalcy; not revolution, but restoration; not agitation, but adjustment; not surgery, but serenity; not the dramatic, but the dispassionate; not experiment, but equipoise; not submergence in internationality, but sustainment in triumphant nationality." His speeches, said Wilson's treasury secretary, William G. McAdoo, were "an army of pompous phrases moving over the landscape in search of an idea."

Still, Harding caught the mood of the times, a longing for "normalcy" which was unfriendly to ideas. The Republican convention, as Harding's campaign manager, Harry Daugherty, had predicted, reached a deadlock which was broken when a group of tired men sat down in a "smoke filled room" and chose its candidate. Harding fit the bill because, though he might not set the pulses pounding, nobody was mad at him. He had all the classic attributes of availability. The vice-presidential choice fell on Calvin Coolidge, who had caught the public fancy with his pronouncement opposing the Boston Police Strike.

The Democrats met at San Francisco later in June in the first convention west of the Rockies. Their choice lay among three leading candidates: A. Mitchell Palmer, whose Red Scare had peaked too soon; William Gibbs McAdoo, Wilson's son-in-law, who was hobbled by Wilson's stubborn hope that the Democrats would again turn to him; and James Cox, former newsman and former governor of Ohio, who won the nomination on the forty-fourth ballot. For vice-president the convention named Franklin D. Roosevelt, who as assistant secretary of the navy occupied the same position his Republican cousin had held before him. Wilsonians tried to make the vote the "solemn referendum" their leader wanted, but the platform, while broadly endorsing the New Freedom, did not fully endorse the League of Nations. Cox waged an active campaign while the Republicans kept Harding home to conduct a front-porch campaign in the McKinley style —they even redid Harding's porch to look like McKinley's. The Republican platform was a masterpiece of evasion which pledged the party to "agreement among the nations to preserve the peace of the world" but "without the compromise of national independence." The phrasing satisfied both reservationists and irreconcilables. Harding himself scaled the clouded heights of obfuscation on the issue, denouncing Wilson's covenant but talking vaguely about a real "association of nations."

The issue was too foggy for a "solemn referendum." Besides, the Democrats' fate was sealed by the breakup of the Wilsonian coalition. In the words of William Allen White, Americans in 1920 were "tired of issues, sick at heart of ideals, and weary of being noble." Wilson therefore became the Republicans' target rather than Cox, who remained a nonentity, and the country voted overwhelmingly for a "return to normalcy." Harding got 16 million votes, about 61 percent of the total, to 9 million for Cox. Harding's electoral margin was 404 to 127. Cox carried no state outside the Solid South, even there losing Tennessee. In the minority again, the Democrats had returned to normalcy too.

EARLY APPOINTMENTS AND POLICY Harding in office had much in common with Ulysses Grant. His cabinet, like Grant's, mixed some of the "best minds" in the party, whom he had promised to seek out, with some of the worst, cronies who sought him out. Charles Evans Hughes, like Grant's Hamilton Fish, became a distinguished secretary of state. Herbert Hoover in the Commerce Department, Andrew W. Mellon in Treasury, and Henry A. Wallace in Agriculture were men who functioned efficiently and made policy on their own. Of the others, Secretary of the Interior Albert B. Fall landed in prison and Attorney-General Harry

M. Daugherty only narrowly escaped. Many lesser offices went to members of the soon notorious "Ohio Gang," headed by Daugherty, a group with which Harding met in a "Little House on H Street" to get away from the pressures of the White House.

Until he became president, politics had been a joy for Harding. He was the party hack par excellence, "bloviating" (a verb of his own making, which meant speaking with gaseous eloquence) on the stump, jollying it up in the clubhouse and cloakroom, hobnobbing with the great and near-great in Washington. As president, Harding was very simply in over his head, and self-doubt overwhelmed him. "I don't think I'm big enough for the Presidency," he confided to a friend. Woodrow Wilson had said once that it seemed impossible to get an explanation to lodge in Senator Harding's head, and President Harding later confessed as much to his secretary: "I don't know what to do or where to turn in this taxation matter. Somewhere there must be a book that tells all about it. . . . There must be a man in the country somewhere who could weigh both sides and know the truth. . . . But I don't know where to find him. . . . My God, this is a hell of a place for a man like me to be." How much better to get away with the "Ohio Gang," who shared his taste for whiskey, poker, and women. Alice Roosevelt Longworth, Theodore Roosevelt's oldest daughter, witnessed one poker session in the president's study. "Harding wasn't a bad man," she said later. "He was just a slob."

Harding and his friends set a pro-business tone such as had been absent from the White House since McKinley. Big business, whipping-boy of the progressives, had won respectability and acceptance by expanding production during the war and by

Warren Harding "bloviating" on the stump. [Ohio Historical Society]

building a New Era of prosperity after the postwar slump in 1921. Secretary of the Treasury Mellon pushed vigorously and persistently a Republican policy of economy and tax reduction. To get a better handle on expenditures he persuaded a lukewarm Congress to pass the Budget and Accounting Act of 1921, which embodied an idea advanced ten years before by Taft's Commission on Efficiency and Economy. The act created a new Bureau of the Budget, headed by a Chicago banker Charles G. Dawes, to prepare a unified budget, and a General Accounting Office, headed by a comptroller general to audit the accounts. General tax reductions from the wartime level seemed called for, but Mellon insisted that they should go mainly to the rich, on the Hamiltonian principle that wealth in the hands of the few would augment the general welfare through investment in gainful enterprise. Mellon's admirers tagged him "the greatest Secretary of the Treasury since Alexander Hamilton."

A group of western Republicans and southern Democrats fought a dogged battle to preserve the progressive principle built into wartime taxes, but Mellon, in office through the 1920s, eventually carried his points. In 1921 at his behest Congress repealed the wartime excess-profits tax, but balked at the request to lower the maximum rate on personal income from 65 to 32 percent that year and 25 percent thereafter. Instead the lawmakers held the maximum rate at 50 percent, and raised the corporate tax from 10 to $12\frac{1}{2}$ percent while granting some relief to lower income groups with higher exemptions for heads of family and dependents. Subsequent revenue acts lowered the maximum rate to 40 percent in 1924 and 20 percent in 1926. The act of 1926 extended further benefits to high-income groups by lowering estate taxes and repealing the gift tax. In the end, however, the progressive principle was at least in part retained, since the graduated tax was never rolled back to the prewar level of 7 percent. Unfortunately, much of the money released to wealthy people by these acts seems to have augmented the speculative excess of the late 1920s as much as it augmented gainful enterprise. Mellon, however, did balance the federal budget for a time. Governmental expenditures fell from $6.4 billion in 1920 to $3.4 billion in 1922, and to a low of $3 billion in 1927. The national debt went down from $25.5 billion in 1919 to $16.9 billion in 1929.

Mellon favored the time-honored Republican policy of high tariffs, and innovations in the chemical and metal industries revived the argument for protection of infant industries. The Emergency Tariff Act of 1921, which reflected a new protectionism in the depressed farm belts of the West, levied high duties on farm products but had little effect since few major cash crops competed with foreign goods in the home market. The Fordney-McCumber Tariff of 1922 increased rates severely on chemical and metal products as a safeguard against the revival of German industries which had previously commanded the field. In general it restored to industry the protection which had prevailed before the Underwood-Simmons Tariff of 1913. To please the farmers the new act further extended the duties on farm products.

Higher tariffs, however, had ramifications which had never prevailed before and which were not quickly perceived. During the war the United States had been transformed from a debtor to a creditor nation. In former years foreign capital had flowed into the United States, playing an important role in the economic expansion of the nineteenth century. But the private and public credits given the Allies during the war had reversed the pattern. Mellon insisted that the European powers must repay all that they had borrowed, and Coolidge is supposed to have said, "Well, they hired the money, didn't they?" Both, however, were unmindful that the tariff walls erected around the country made it all the harder for other nations to sell in the United States and thus acquire the dollars or credits with which to repay their war debts. For nearly a decade further extensions of American loans and investments sent more dollars abroad, postponing the reckoning.

Neither Harding nor his successor Coolidge could dissolve the regulatory agencies, but by naming commissioners who were less than sympathetic to regulation they rendered these agencies ineffective. Harding named conservative advocates of big business to the Interstate Commerce Commission, the Federal Reserve Board, and the Federal Trade Commission. In 1925 Coolidge made William E. Humprey, former congressman from Washington, chairman of the FTC. The commission, Humphrey asserted, would not be used "as a publicity bureau to spread socialistic propaganda." He and his colleagues, in a departure from Wilson's principle of "pitiless publicity," decided to withhold publicity on all cases until they were settled. While this was defensible, the commission also skirted the edge of legality in giving its support to agreements which allowed trade associations to avoid certain kinds of competition. Sometimes these included secret clauses forbidding price cutting. "Congress," said the chairman, ". . . satisfied its dogmatic tendencies by ordering all sorts of investigations—which come to nothing." Sen. George Norris characterized the new appointments as "the nullification of federal law by a process of boring from within."

Bargain Day in Washington. *The Harding administration, according to this cartoon, put the government up for sale.* [Library of Congress]

A CORRUPT ADMINISTRATION These conservatives were at least operating out of conviction. The "Ohio Gang," however, used White House connections to line their own pockets. In 1923 Harding learned that Charles R. Forbes of the Veterans Bureau was systematically looting medical and hospital supplies. Forbes fled to Europe and resigned. His general counsel, Charles Cramer, committed suicide in Harding's old house in Washington. Not long afterward Jesse Smith, a close crony of Attorney-General Daugherty, also shot himself. Smith, who held no appointment, had set up an office in the Justice Department from which he peddled influence for a fee. Daugherty himself was implicated in the fraudulent handling of German assets seized after the war. When this was discovered, he refused to testify on the ground that he might incriminate himself. Twice brought to court, he was never indicted for want of evidence, possibly because he had destroyed pertinent records. These were but the most visible among many scandals that touched the Justice Department, the Prohibition Bureau, and other agencies under Harding.

But one major scandal rose above all these petty peculations. Teapot Dome, like the Watergate Apartments fifty years later, became the catchword for an epoch of corruption. An oil deposit under the sandstone Teapot Rock in Wyoming, Teapot Dome had been set aside as a naval reserve, along with the Elk Hills deposit in California. Early in Harding's term Navy Secretary Edwin N. Denby transferred them to the control of the Interior Department under Albert B. Fall. The move seemed at the time a sensible attempt to unify control over public reserves, and

Denby regarded it so. But once Fall had control, he signed contracts letting private interests exploit the deposits: Harry Sinclair's Mammoth Oil Company at Teapot Dome and Edward L. Doheny's Pan-American Petroleum and Transport Company at Elk Hills. Fall argued that these contracts were in the government's interest. It was harder for Fall to explain, however, why he acted in secret, without allowing competitive bids.

Suspicion grew when Fall's standard of living suddenly rose. It turned out that he had taken loans of about $100,000 (which came in "a little black bag") from Sinclair and $300,000 from Doheny. As the scandal unraveled, Fall emerged as a figure of tragic weakness. Once wealthy, he had lost extensive mine holdings in the Mexican Revolution, which left him with little more than an expensive dream ranch in New Mexico. Desperate for money, he took loans extended by two old friends—he and Doheny had once worked together in the mines. For the rest of his life Fall insisted that the loans were unrelated to the leases, and that he had contrived a good deal for the government, but at best the circumstances revealed a fatal blindness to his impropriety.

The question of bribery aside, his actions activated the hostility of conservationists. Fall, like Ballinger before him, had regarded conservation as the doctrine of easterners indifferent to jobs and development in the West. After Senator La Follette demanded a senatorial investigation, a committee under Thomas J. Walsh of Montana laid out the whole mess during 1924 to the accompaniment of public outrage.

Harding himself was spared the humiliation of public disgrace. How much he knew is still not clear, but he knew enough to become visibly troubled. "My God, this is a hell of a job!" he confided to the editor William Allen White. "I have no trouble with my enemies, I can take care of my enemies all right. But my damn friends, my God-damn friends, White, they're the ones that keep me walking the floor nights!" In June 1923 Harding left on what would be his last journey, a western speaking tour and a trip to Alaska. Sailing to Alaska, he fell into conversation with Commerce Secretary Herbert Hoover: "If you knew of a great scandal in our administration," he asked, "would you for the good of the country and the party expose it publicly or would you bury it?" Hoover replied quickly: "Publish it, and at least get credit for integrity on your side." But little time was left to Harding. Back in Seattle he fell ill with what was diagnosed first as ptomaine poisoning, but was actually a heart attack. He recovered briefly, then died in a San Francisco hotel of either coronary or cerebral thrombosis.

Not since the death of Lincoln had there been such an outpouring of grief for a "beloved President," for the kindly, ordinary man with the face of a Roman senator, the man who found it in his heart (as Wilson had not) to pardon Eugene Debs and receive him at the White House, and to pressure the steel magnates into giving up their barbarous seven-day week. As the black-streamered funeral train moved toward Washington, then back to Ohio, millions stood by the tracks to honor their lost leader. Eventually, however, grief yielded to scorn and contempt. For nearly a decade the revelations of scandal were paraded before committees and then courts. Harding's long affair with Nan Britton came to light, first the birth of their illegitimate child and later their pathetic couplings among the overshoes in a White House closet. Shortly before the centennial of his birth, Harding's love letters to another man's wife surfaced. For years his friends tried in vain to get his successors to dedicate to him a marble memorial in Marion, Ohio. Finally, in the spring of 1931 Herbert Hoover came to honor "a man whose soul was seared by a great disillusionment."

"SILENT CAL"   Some kind of charmed existence seemed to put Calvin Coolidge in the right place at the right time. The news of Harding's death came when he was visiting his father in the mountain village of Plymouth, Vermont, his birthplace. There at 2:47 on the morning of August 3, 1923, by the light of a kerosene lamp, Col. John Coolidge administered the oath of office to his son in a commonplace room which doubled as living room and office. A day later the new president would have been visiting the baronial estate of Guy Currier at Peterboro. The atmosphere there might better have symbolized the era of business prosperity over which Coolidge would preside, but the rustic simplicity of Plymouth, the very name itself, evoked just the image of roots and solid integrity that the country would long for amid the coming disclosures of corruption. The new first lady, Grace Coolidge, was as unpretentious as her husband, and Alice Roosevelt Longworth found the new atmosphere of the White House "as different as a New England front parlor is from the back room in a speakeasy."

Americans took to their hearts the unflappability of "Silent Cal," his gargantuan midday naps, and the pictures of him fishing, pitching hay, and wearing Indian bonnets while primly clad in business suit and necktie. His taciturn nature became the subject of affectionate humor, often no doubt apocryphal, as in the story of a dinner guest who told Coolidge of a bet that she could make him say three words. "You lose," he replied. "Mr. Coo-

Calvin Coolidge dresses up for the photographers. [Brown Brothers]

lidge's genius for inactivity is developed to a very high point," the journalist Walter Lippmann wrote. "It is a grim, determined, alert inactivity, which keeps Mr. Coolidge occupied constantly." That too suited the mood of the country, which chuckled over the story of the president's awakening from his daily nap and slyly asking: "Is the country still there?" The Coolidge luck held out for the duration of his term. After him, and in at least some measure because of him, the luck of the whole nation ran out.

The change in the White House was more a matter of style than substance. Like Harding, Coolidge embraced the orthodox creed of business. "The business of America is business," he intoned. "The man who works there worships there." It was the business philosophy of the 1880s, absorbed at Amherst where he was taught to associate "the rich, the wise, and the good." At White House functions the rich nearly monopolized the guest lists.

THE 1924 ELECTION   Coolidge was also married to politics, and proved better at it than Harding. He distanced himself from the Harding scandals, and put in charge of the prosecutions two lawyers of undoubted integrity. Yet he kept Daugherty as attorney-general until growing evidence of Daugherty's complicity led to his removal in March 1924. In his place Coolidge named the former dean of the Columbia Law School, Harlan Fiske Stone, once a fellow student at Amherst. Coolidge quietly took control of the Republican party machinery and seized the initiative in the campaign for nomination, which he won with only token opposition. For vice-president the convention chose Charles G.

Dawes, former director of the budget, now fresh from a successful settlement of the German reparations issue.

The Coolidge luck held as the Democrats fell victim to internal dissensions. The source of the party's trouble was its uneasy alliance of incongruous elements which lent much truth to Will Rogers's classic statement: "I am a member of no organized political party. I am a Democrat." A deep alienation was growing up between the metropolis of the Roaring Twenties and the more traditional hinterland, a gap that the Democratic party could not bridge.

The rival candidacies of William Gibbs McAdoo and Alfred E. Smith magnified the divisions in the party. A spate of Republican scandals should have helped a progressive Democrat, but McAdoo, who as a lawyer had represented Edward L. Doheny, was tainted. Oscar Underwood of Alabama, hoping to benefit from party divisions, urged the Democrats to revive a plank from the 1856 platform that had condemned Know-Nothing bigotry. By convention time all the major candidates supported the plank, but the Underwood and Smith forces made the issue one of condemning the Ku Klux Klan by name, a move defeated on a very close vote. The quarrel over this led to the symbolic spectacle of the aging William Jennings Bryan goaded and heckled by Tammany gallants in the galleries of Madison Square Garden. McAdoo and Smith canceled each other out, and it took 103 ballots to bestow the tarnished nomination on John W. Davis, a Wall Street lawyer from West Virginia who could hardly outdo Coolidge in conservatism. For a token balance the convention chose Nebraska Gov. Charles W. Bryan, brother of William Jennings, as its vice-presidential nominee.

Meanwhile a new farmer-labor coalition was mobilizing a third-party effort. In 1922 the railroad unions, smarting from administration opposition, sponsored a Conference for Progressive Political Action which got the support of many farmers who were suffering from price declines at the time. Active on a nonpartisan basis, in 1922 the group had helped defeat a number of Old Guard Republicans. In Minnesota a new Farmer-Labor party during 1922 and 1923 elected two United States senators, a congressman, and some lesser officeholders. Meeting in Cleveland on July 4, 1924, the conference reorganized as the Progressive party and nominated Robert M. La Follette for president and Sen. Burton K. Wheeler (Mont.) for vice-president. La Follette also won the support of Minnesota's Farmer-Labor party, the Socialist party, and the American Federation of Labor.

In the campaign Coolidge chose to focus on La Follette, whom he called a dangerous radical who would turn America into a "communistic and socialistic state." The country preferred to "keep cool with Coolidge," who swept both the popular and electoral votes by decisive majorities. Davis took only the Solid South, and La Follette carried only his native Wisconsin. The popular vote went 15.7 million for Coolidge, 8.4 million for Davis, and 4.8 million for La Follette—the largest popular vote ever polled by a third-party candidate. The electoral result was 382 to 136 to 13.

THE NEW ERA

Businessmen interpreted the Coolidge victory as a vindication of their leadership, and Coolidge saw in the surging prosperity of the time a confirmation of his philosophy. In fact the prosperity and technological achievements of the time had much to do with Coolidge's victory over the Democrats and Progressives. Those in the large middle class who before had formed an important part of the Progressive coalition were now absorbed instead in the new world created by advances in communications, transportation, and business organization.

The gross national product had reached a peak of $88.9 billion in 1920; after a slump to $74 billion in 1921 and 1922, the GNP grew steadily to $104.4 billion in 1929. Per-capita income went from $672 in 1922 to $857 in 1929. A larger public than ever before had the money and leisure to taste of the affluent society, and a growing advertising industry fueled its appetites. By the mid-1920s advertising had grown into both a major industry, with a volume of $3.5 billion, and a major institution of social control. Oldtime values of thrift and saving gave way to a new economic ethic which made spending a virtue. The innovation of installment buying made increased consumption feasible for many.

MOVIES, RADIO, AND THE ECONOMY Consumer-goods industries fueled much of the boom from 1922 to 1929. Moderately priced creature comforts, including such items as hand cameras, wristwatches, cigarette lighters, vacuum cleaners, washing machines, and linoleum, became increasingly available. Inventions in communications and transportation, such as motion pictures, radio, telephones, and automobiles, not only fueled the boom but brought transformations in society.

In the 1890s a quick sequence of inventions had made it possible for a New York audience to see the first picture show in 1896. The first full-length story depicted in a movie was *The Great Train Robbery* in 1903. By 1905 the first movie house opened in Philadelphia, and within three years there were nearly 10,000. By the teens Hollywood had become the center of movie production, grinding out serials, features, westerns, and the timeless two-reel comedies of Mack Sennett's Keystone Studios, where a raft of slapstick comedians, most notably Charlie Chaplin, perfected their art into a form of social criticism. The twelve-reel *Birth of a Nation*, directed in 1915 by D. W. Griffith, became a triumph of cinematic art which marked the arrival of the modern motion picture and at the same time perpetuated a grossly distorted image of Reconstruction. Based on Thomas Dixon's novel *The Clansman*, the movie was replete with stereotypes of villainous Radicals, sinister mulattoes, blameless southerners, and faithful "darkies." The film grossed $18 million and revealed the industry's enormous potential. By the mid-1930s every large American city and most small towns had theaters, and movies replaced oratory as the chief mass entertainment of Americans. A further advancement in technology came with the "talkies." The first movie with sound accompaniment was Warner Brothers' *Don Juan* (1926), but the success of talking pictures was established by Warners' *The Jazz Singer* (1927), starring Al Jolson.

Charlie Chaplin in The Kid, *1921. [Museum of Modern Art / Film Stills Archive]*

A farm family gathered around the radio, Hood River County, Oregon, July 1925. [National Archives]

Radio broadcasting had an even more spectacular growth. Except for experimental broadcasts, radio served only the function of communication until 1920. In August of that year WWJ in Detroit began transmitting news bulletins from the Detroit *Daily News*, and in November KDKA in Pittsburgh, owned by the Westinghouse Company, began regular programs. The first radio commercial was aired by WEAF in New York, in 1922. By the end of that year there were 508 stations and some 3 million receivers in action. In 1926 the National Broadcasting Company, a subsidiary of RCA, began linking stations into a network; the Columbia Broadcasting System entered the field the next year. In 1927 a Federal Radio Commission was established to regulate the industry; in 1934 it became the Federal Communications Commission, with authority over other forms of communication as well.

AIRPLANES, AUTOMOBILES, AND THE ECONOMY Advances in transportation were startling in this period. Wilbur and Orville Wright of Dayton, Ohio, built and flew the first airplane at Kitty Hawk, North Carolina, on December 17, 1903, but the use of planes advanced slowly until the outbreak of war in 1914, after which the Europeans rapidly developed the plane as a military weapon. When the United States entered the war it still had no combat planes—American pilots did battle in craft of British or French make. An American aircraft industry developed during the war but foundered in the postwar demobilization. Under the

Orville Wright pilots the first flight of a power-driven airplane, while Wilbur runs alongside. [National Archives]

Kelly Act of 1925, however, the government began to subsidize the industry through airmail contracts. This encouragement was greatly strengthened by the Air Commerce Act of 1926, which started a program of federal aid to air transport and navigation, including aid in establishing airports.

A psychological boost to aviation came in May 1927 with the solo flight of Charles A. Lindbergh, Jr., from New York to Paris in thirty-three hours and thirty minutes. The drama of the deed, which won him a prize of $25,000, was heightened by the fact that he was flying blind through a fog for part of the way and at times dropped to within ten feet of the water before sighting the Irish coast and regaining his bearings. The parade down Broadway in his honor surpassed even the celebration of the Armistice. The New York City Department of Sanitation estimated that 1,800 tons of ticker tape and shredded paper fell on Lindbergh's parade while only 155 tons showered the Armistice celebration.

By 1930 the industry had forty-three airlines which carried 385,000 passengers over routes of 30,000 miles. Another great impetus came after 1936 when the slow Ford trimotor plane was displaced by the more efficient twin-engine Douglas DC-3 as the chief carrier. In 1940, nineteen airlines carried 2.8 million passengers over routes of 43,000 miles.

By far the most significant development of the time, economic and social, was the automobile. The first motor car had been manufactured for sale in 1895, but in 1900 the census did not even give the industry a separate listing. The founding of the Ford Motor Company in 1903 revolutionized the industry. Ford's reliable Model T (the celebrated "tin lizzie") came out in 1908 at a price of $850 (in 1924 it would sell for $290). In 1916 for the first time the number of cars manufactured passed 1 million; by 1920 more than 8 million were registered, and in 1929 more than 23 million. The production of automobiles consumed large parts of the nation's steel, rubber, glass, and textile output, among other materials. It gave rise to a gigantic market for oil products just as the Spindletop gusher (1901) in Texas heralded the opening of vast southwestern oilfields. It quickened the movement for good roads, financed in large part from a gasoline tax, speeded transportation, encouraged the sprawl of suburbs, and sparked real-estate booms in California and Florida. The car provided liberation for "flaming youth."

The good-roads movement became the automobile-age equivalent of the nineteenth-century railroad movement. Through it the automobile industry received indirect subsidies greater than all government aid to railroads, which had now begun their decline. Road building ranked first or second in state budgets by the end of the 1920s, and the legislative lobbies of road builders and truckers supplanted those of the railroads in influence.

By virtue of its size and importance the automobile industry became the salient example of mass production. When Ford brought out the Model T in 1908, demand ran far ahead of production. Ford and his partner James Couzens then called in a factory expert named Walter E. Flanders as a production manager. By rearranging the plant and putting in new equipment, Flanders met his goal of producing 10,000 cars in twelve months (with two days to spare), earning his bonus of $20,000. The next year Ford's new Highland Park plant was planned with job analysis in mind. In 1910 gravity slides were installed to move parts

Ford Motor Company's Highland Park Plant, 1913. Gravity slides and chain conveyors aided the mass production of automobiles.
[The Henry Ford Museum]

from one workbench to the next, and by the end of 1913 the system was complete, with endless chain conveyors pulling the parts along feeder lines and the chassis down the final-assembly line.

Flanders, the creator of this modern miracle, was in turn a disciple of Frederick W. Taylor (1856–1915), the original "efficiency expert." In the 1880s, working as a foreman for the Midvale Steel Company, Taylor decided that the prevailing practice of having foremen pressure workers for greater output merely resulted in conflict: "Throughout American industry, management's concept of a proper day's work was what the foreman could drive workers to do and the workers' conception was how little they could do and hold their jobs." By the 1890s Taylor's ideas had drawn attention and he had set up shop as a consulting engineer in Philadelphia. In 1895 he outlined his ideas in a paper, "A Piece Rate System," read to the American Society of Mechanical Engineers. The basic principle was to use the carrot instead of the stick, to determine the maximum speed at which work could be done and then offer the incentive of higher piece rates to workers who could attain larger output. His book *The Principles of Scientific Management* (1911) summed up his ideas, which stressed proper organization, improvement of factory arrangement, the use of standardized tools and equipment, proper routing and scheduling of work, and the development of planning departments. "Taylorization" caught on widely in the business world and efficiency experts became a normal part of the business scene. Labor tended to view them with skepticism, and in some cases careless or deliberate planning resulted only in ruthless speedups and more of the conflict that Taylor himself deplored. In the 1920s southern textile workers took to calling such bastard efficiency programs the "stretchout."

STABILIZING THE ECONOMY   The drive for efficiency manifest once in the progressive impulse was now powering the wheels of mass production and consumption, and had become a cardinal belief of Republican leaders. Herbert Hoover, who served as secretary of commerce through the Harding-Coolidge years, was himself an engineer who had made a fortune in far-flung mining operations in Australia, China, Russia, and elsewhere. Out of his experiences in business and his management of Belgian relief, the Food Administration, and other wartime activities, Hoover had developed a philosophy which he set forth in his book *American Individualism* (1922). The idea might best be called "cooperative individualism," or in one of his favorite terms, "associationalism." The principle also owed something to his Quaker upbringing, which taught him the Friends' combination of the work ethic and mutual help. When he applied it to the relations of government and business, Hoover prescribed a kind of middle way between the regulatory and trust-busting traditions, a way of voluntary cooperation.

As secretary of commerce, Hoover was a human dynamo who made the trifling Commerce Department into the most dynamic agency of two listless administrations. During a period of governmental retrenchment he was engaged in expansion. Through an enlarged Bureau of Foreign and Domestic Commerce he sought out new opportunities and markets for business. A Division of Simplified Practice in the Bureau of Standards sponsored more than a thousand conferences on design, production, and distribution, and carried forward the wartime move toward standardization of everything from automobile tires and paving bricks to bedsprings and toilet paper, and reduced in number the different kinds of bolts, nuts, and screws. "When I go to ride in an automobile," Hoover told the author Sherwood Anderson, "it does not matter to me that there are a million automobiles on the road just like mine. I am going somewhere and I want to get there in what comfort I can and at the lowest cost." In 1926 Hoover created a Bureau of Aviation and the next year set out to bring order into the new field of radio with the Federal Radio Commission.

Through conferences and organized public relations, techniques that he had used as food administrator, Hoover promoted his ideas. Most of all he endorsed the burgeoning trade-association movement. The organization of trade associations in business became his favorite instrument for "stabilization" to avoid the waste inherent in competition. Through such associations businessmen in a given field would gather and disseminate information on everything: sales, purchases, shipments, production, and prices. This information allowed them to lay plans with more confidence, the advantages of which included predictable costs, prices, and markets, as well as more stable employment and wages. Sometimes abuses crept in as trade associations skirted the edge of legality by price-fixing and other monopoly practices, but the Supreme Court in 1925 held the practice of sharing information as such to be within the law.

As to the great business combinations themselves, the Supreme Court held to the "rule of reason" it had pronounced in dissolving the Standard Oil Company in 1911. In 1920 the Court found the United States Steel Company an acceptable combination under that rule. After that, wrote two constitutional historians, "almost any monopoly could put up a plausible argument for its social responsibility and thus claim to be a 'reasonable' combination."

THE BUSINESS OF FARMING   Agriculture remained a weak point in the economy, in many ways as weak as its position in the 1890s, when cities flourished and agriculture languished. Briefly after the war the farmers' hopes soared on wings of prosperity. The wartime boom lasted into 1920, and then prices collapsed. Wheat went in eighteen months from $2.50 a bushel to less than $1; cotton from 35¢ per pound to 13¢. Low prices persisted into 1923, especially in the wheat and corn belts, and after that improvement was spotty. A bumper cotton crop in 1926 resulted only in a price collapse and an early taste of depression in much of the South, where foreclosures and bankruptcies spread.

Yet in many ways farmers shared the business outlook of the New Era. Farms, like corporations, were getting larger, more efficient, and more mechanized. By 1930 about 13 percent of all farmers had tractors, and the proportion was even higher on the western Plains. After 1925 the introduction of the smaller Farmall tractor encouraged greater use of the machine on the smaller farms and hilly lands of the Southeast. Better plows, drills, cultivators, planters, and other machines were part of the mechanization process which accompanied improved crops, fertilizers, and animal breeding.

Farm organizations of the 1920s moved away from the alliance with urban labor that marked the Populist era and toward a new view of farmers as businessmen. During the postwar farm depression the idea of marketing cooperatives became the farmer's equivalent of the businessman's trade-association movement. The great promoter of the cooperative movement was a young spellbinder, Aaron Sapiro, a California lawyer who had risen from poverty to success as organizer of marketing associations in raisins, eggs, and other specialties. Much in demand as a speaker in the early 1920s, he infected farm groups with his own zeal for regional commodity-marketing associations; ironclad contracts with producers ("horse-high, bull-strong, and pig-tight") to deliver their crops over a period of years; and "orderly marketing," which required standards and grades, efficient handling and advertising, and a businesslike setup with professional technicians and executives. His program, Sapiro said, "turned the interest of the average farmer from a wild sort of indefinite political hankering to some real intelligent attention to the economic phases of his problem."

While industry boomed, agriculture remained weak in the 1920s. [Library of Congress]

Among the various farm groups, one did carry into the twentieth century the oldtime gospel of Populism. The Farmers' Union, founded in Texas in 1902 by former Allianceman Newt Gresham, had a mercurial growth in the Southeast much like the Alliance's, but emerged in the 1920s mainly as a western wheatbelt group. It was soon overshadowed by the American Farm Bureau Federation, a new group representing the "businesslike" attitude of commercial agriculture in the New Era. Founded in 1920 at a meeting in Chicago, the Farm Bureau was an unexpected outgrowth of the farm demonstration movement. It grew from committees (usually called "bureaus") formed to support county agents and from state federations of those committees. Its philosophy stemmed in part from association with business leaders who supported the bureaus, but in larger part from the predominance of the larger commercial farmers in its membership, a situation that in turn reflected the county agents' practice of working with the more successful farmers in order to make a better showing in their demonstrations. Farm Bureau strength in the Midwest and South represented what by the 1920s was being called a "marriage of cotton and corn."

But if concern with marketing co-ops and other businesslike approaches drew farmers ever farther away from Populism, it was still inevitable that farm problems should invite political solutions. The most effective political response to the crisis of the early 1920s was the formation of the Farm Bloc, a coalition of western Republicans and southern Democrats that put through an impressive, if fairly moderate, program of legislation over a period of three years. The Farm Bloc originated in 1921 in the office of Gray Silver, Washington agent of the Farm Bureau, and eventually mustered some twenty-five senators and about a hundred representatives, led by Arthur Capper of Kansas and L. J. Dickinson of Iowa respectively.

From 1921 to 1923 the Farm Bloc added important legislative achievements to the agrarian program of the Wilson period. It supported a three-year extension of the War Finance Corporation to assist cooperative, storage, and export operations. It pushed passage of the Packers and Stockyards Act (1921) and the Capper-Tincher Grain Futures Act (1922) which sought to prevent collusion designed to keep farm prices down. In addition the Capper-Volstead Cooperative Marketing Act (1922) exempted farm cooperatives from antitrust laws, and the Intermediate Credit Act (1923) set up twelve intermediate credit banks on the model of the Federal Land Banks. The new banks filled the gap of six months to three years between the terms of short-term loans under the Federal Reserve System and long-term loans by the Land Banks, and could lend to cooperative producing and marketing associations.

Meanwhile a new panacea appeared on the horizon. In the spring of 1924 Sen. Charles L. McNary of Oregon and Rep. Gilbert N. Haugen of Iowa introduced the first McNary-Haugen bill. The bill embodied a plan worked out by George N. Peek and Hugh S. Johnson, both of the Moline Plow Company, to secure "equality for agriculture in the benefits of the protective tariff." Complex as it would have been in operation, it was simple in conception: in short, a plan to dump surpluses on the world market in order to raise prices in the home market. The goal was to achieve "parity"—that is, to raise domestic farm prices to a point where they would have the same purchasing power relative to other prices they had had between 1909 and 1914, a time viewed in retrospect as a golden age of American agriculture.

The first bill failed of passage in 1924, but a McNary-Haugen bill passed both houses of Congress in 1927, only to be vetoed by President Coolidge. The process was repeated in 1928. Coolidge pronounced the measure an unsound effort at price-fixing, un-American and unconstitutional to boot. In a broader sense, however, McNary-Haugenism did not fail. The debates made the farm problem into an issue of national policy and defined it as a problem of surpluses. The evolution of the McNary-Haugen plan, moreover, revived the idea of an alliance between the South and West, a coalition which became in the next decade a dominant influence on national farm policy. That policy would follow a different procedure, but its chief focus would be on surpluses, its goal would be "parity," and George N. Peek would preside over its management.

SETBACKS FOR UNIONS   Urban workers shared more than farmers in the affluence of the times. Annual per-capita earnings rose between 1921 and 1928 from an average of $1,171 to $1,408. Without a matching rise in living cost, this meant a gain of about 20 percent in real wages. The benefits of this rise, however, were distributed unevenly. Miners and textile workers suffered a decline in real wages. In these and other trades technological unemployment followed the introduction of new methods and machines, although technology created as well as destroyed jobs. "A workman is far better paid in America than anywhere else in the world," French visitor Andrae Siegfried wrote in 1927, "and his standard of living is enormously higher. The difference, which was noticeable before the War, has been greatly accentuated since, and is now the chief contrast between the old and the new continents. . . . ."

Organized labor, however, did no better than organized agriculture in the 1920s. In fact unions suffered a setback after the growth years of the war. The Red Scare and strikes of 1919 left the uneasy impression that unions and subversion were linked, an idea which the enemies of unions promoted. The brief postwar depression of 1921 further weakened the unions, and they felt the severe impact of open-shop associations which proliferated across the country after the war, led by chambers of commerce and other business groups. In January 1921 the local groups came together at a meeting in Chicago where the open shop was officially designated the "American Plan" of employment. While the open shop in theory implied only the employer's right to hire whom he pleased, in practice it meant discrimination against unionists and refusal to recognize unions even in shops where most of the workers belonged.

Nor were employers always above the use of strong-arm methods, such as requiring "yellow-dog" contracts which forced workers to agree to stay out of unions, using labor spies, exchanging blacklists, and resorting to intimidation and coercion. Some employers tried to kill the unions with kindness. They introduced programs of "industrial democracy" guided by company unions or various schemes of "welfare capitalism" such as profit-sharing, bonuses, pensions, health programs, recreational activities, and the like. The benefits of such programs were often very real.

The mood of the times generally impelled governments as well as business into hostility toward unions. When in 1914 the Clayton Anti-Trust Act pronounced labor not an item of commerce, it was hailed as "Labor's Magna Charta." But this turned out to

make little difference in the courts' willingness to issue labor injunctions. During the 1920s the high court ruled that the act
might limit injunctions against individual workers, but not
against certain union activities. In *Duplex Printing Press Company v. Deering* (1921) the court upheld an injunction against a
secondary boycott (a boycott of one company's product by another company). A more telling blow was struck by an injunction
against the railway shopmen's strike of 1922. The Railway Labor
Board in 1920 had approved a postwar wage cut of 12 percent;
when it approved another such cut two years later, the shopmen
walked out. On September 1, 1922, Attorney-General Daugherty secured a sweeping injunction against picketing, strike
meetings, statements to the public, expenditure of union funds
for strike purposes, or the use of any means of communication by
union leaders. "So long as I can speak for the government of the
United States," said Daugherty, "I will use the power of the government . . . to prevent the labor unions of the country from destroying the open shop." The strike collapsed under the impact
of the injunction, and while the union got contracts from friendly
railroads for about 225,000 workers, some 175,000 were forced
into company unions.

The combined result of prosperity, propaganda, welfare capitalism, and active hostility was a decline in union membership
from about 5 million in 1920 to 3.5 million in 1929. In 1924
Samuel Gompers, founder and longtime president of the AFL,
died; William Green of the mine workers, who took his place,
embodied the conservative, even timid, attitude of unions during
the period. The one outstanding exception to the anti-union policies of the decade was passage of the Railway Labor Act in 1926,
which abolished the Railway Labor Board and substituted a new
Board of Mediation. The act also provided for the formation of
railway unions "without interference, influence, or coercion," a
statement of policy not extended to other workers until the
1930s.

PRESIDENT HOOVER, THE ENGINEER

HOOVER VS. SMITH   On August 2, 1927, while on vacation in the
Black Hills of South Dakota, President Coolidge passed out to reporters slips of paper with the statement: "I do not choose to run
for President in 1928." Exactly what he meant puzzled observers then and has since. Apparently he at least half hoped for a
convention draft, but his statement cleared the way for Herbert
Hoover to mount an active campaign. Well before the June Re-

Herbert Hoover on the campaign trail in 1928. [*Library of Congress*]

publican convention in Kansas City, Hoover was too far in the lead to be stopped by a clutch of favorite sons. For vice-president the party named one of the faithful, Sen. Charles Curtis of Kansas. The platform took credit for prosperity, economy ("raised to a principle of government"), debt and tax reduction, and the protective tariff ("as vital to American agriculture as it is to manufacturing"). It rejected the McNary-Haugen program, but promised a farm board to promote orderly marketing as a way to manage surpluses.

The Democratic nomination was as quickly decided in Houston later in June. Gov. Alfred E. Smith of New York, pronounced the "Happy Warrior" in Franklin D. Roosevelt's nominating speech, faced no effective opposition. The Democrats balanced their ticket by naming Sen. Joseph T. Robinson of Arkansas for vice-president. Their farm plank, while not endorsing McNary-Haugen, did pledge "economic equality of agriculture with other industries." Like the Republicans, the Democrats pledged enforcement of the Volstead Prohibition Act, and aside from calling for stricter regulation of waterpower resources, promised nothing that departed from the conservative position of the Republicans.

The Democratic party had had its fill of factionalism in 1924, and all remained fairly harmonious until the Happy Warrior gave the occasion, if not the cause, for revolt by stating in his acceptance speech a personal desire to liberalize the Volstead Act, and then by selecting for national party chairman John J. Raskob, who was Catholic, wet, a General Motors executive, and at least until recently a Republican. Hoover by contrast had pronounced prohibition "a great social and economic experiment, noble in motive and far-reaching in purpose," and called for a study of enforcement. The two candidates projected sharply different images which obscured the essential likeness of their programs. Hoover was the Quaker son of middle America, the successful businessman, the architect of Republican prosperity, while Smith was the prototype of those things rural–small-town America distrusted: the son of Irish immigrants, Catholic, wet, and a Tammanyite whose East Side twang as he spoke on the "raddio" offended the ears of the hinterland. Outside the large cities all those things were handicaps he could scarcely surmount for all his affability and wit.

In the election Hoover won in the third consecutive Republican landslide, with 21 million popular votes to Smith's 15 million, and an even more top-heavy electoral majority of 444 to 87. Hoover even cracked the Solid South, leaving Smith only a hard core of six Deep South states plus Massachusetts and Rhode Island. The election was above all a vindication of Republican prosperity. As the historian William Leuchtenburg wrote: "If Smith had been Protestant, dry, and born in a log cabin of good yeoman stock, he would still have been defeated." But the shattering defeat of the Democrats concealed a portentous realignment in the making. Smith had nearly doubled the vote for Davis, the Democratic candidate of four years before. Smith's image, though a handicap in the hinterlands, swung big cities back into the Democratic column. In the farm states of the West there were signs that some disgruntled farmers had switched over to the Democrats. A coalition of urban workers and unhappy farmers was in the making.

HOOVER IN CONTROL The year 1929, a fateful milestone in history, dawned with high hopes. Business seemed good, incomes were rising, and the chief author of Republican prosperity was about to enter the White House. "I have no fears for the future of our country," Hoover told the audience at his inauguration. "It is bright with hope." For Hoover the presidency crowned a career of steady ascent, first in mining, then in public service. Hoover's image combined the benevolence fitting for a director of wartime relief and the efficiency of a businessman and administrator. More than most presidents, he had articulated a philosophy of public affairs, to which in his last speech of the 1928 campaign he gave the misleading tag of "rugged individualism." But since he found initiative and enterprise best served by "orderly liberty" and by cooperation, his notion of individualism was less rugged than the slogan suggested.

Hoover approached his new duties much as he might have set about reshaping a mining venture during his days as a consulting engineer. He assigned specific duties to each member of the staff. He promoted voluntary cooperation through "publicity conferences," much as he had done at the Commerce Department. His passion for facts and figures resulted in several major studies of American life at the time: by the Wickersham Commission on Crime and Law Enforcement, and by the Committees on Recent Social Trends, on Recent Economic Change, and on Child Health and Protection—the last a lifetime concern of a man who had himself been orphaned.

Forgotten in the rush of later events would be Hoover's credentials as progressive and humanitarian. Over the objection of Treasury Secretary Mellon, he ordered that publicity be given to large refunds on income, estate, and gift taxes, and announced a plan for tax reductions in the low-income brackets. He took action against corrupt patronage practices, and refused to countenance "red hunts" or interference with peaceful picketing of the White House. He defended his wife's right to entertain the wife of Oscar DePriest, the first black congressman since 1901 and the first ever from the North, sought more money for all-black Howard University, and proposed that the new federal parole board reflect the number of blacks and women in prison. He went along, however, with his party's "lily-white" strategy of ignoring or excluding blacks in most southern states.

His program to stabilize business carried over into his program for agriculture, the most visibly weak sector of the economy. To treat the malady of glutted markets he had two main remedies: federal help for cooperative marketing and higher tariffs on farm products. He pushed through a special session of Congress in June 1929 the Agricultural Marketing Act, which gave support to farm cooperatives by setting up a Federal Farm Board of nine members with a revolving loan fund of $500 million to help cooperatives market the major commodities. The act provided also, at the demand of the farm bloc, a program in which the Farm Board could set up "stabilization corporations" empowered to buy surpluses off the market. Unluckily for any chance of success the plan might have had, it got under way almost simultaneously with the onset of the depression that fall.

Farmers gained even less from tariff revision. What Hoover got after fourteen months of struggle with competing local interest was a general upward revision on manufactures as well as farm goods. The Hawley-Smoot Tariff of June 1930 carried duties to an all-time high. Average *ad valorem* rates went from about 32 to 40 percent, but on actual dutiable imports the average rate was 52.8 percent for the years 1930–1933. Rates went up on some 70 farm products and more than 900 manufactured items. More than 1,000 economists petitioned Hoover to veto the bill because, they said, it would raise prices to consumers, damage the export trade, and thus hurt farmers, promote inefficiency, and provoke foreign reprisals. Events proved them right, but Hoover felt that he had to go along with his party in an election year.

THE ECONOMY OUT OF CONTROL   The tariff did nothing to check a deepening crisis of confidence in the economy. After the slump of 1921 the idea grew that with recovery business had entered a New Era of permanent growth. But real growth propelled an expansive ballyhoo, and a growing contagion of get-rich-quick schemes. Speculative mania fueled the Florida real-estate boom which got under way when the combination of Coolidge prosperity and Ford's "tin lizzies" gave people extra money and made Florida an accessible playground. By 1925 Miami had become a scene of frantic excitement. In the fun-fair of fast turnover the reckless speculator was, if anything, more likely to gain than the prudent investor, and the "binder boys" perfected to a fine art the practice of making money at little or no risk. The principle was to pay a small "binder" fee for an option to buy on promise of a later down payment, then reap a profit by selling binders which might pass through a dozen hands and might or might not convey title. It was the latest in a series of speculative bubbles that had been bursting on the American scene since the British South Sea Bubble of the eighteenth century. By mid-1926, when there were no more "bigger fools" left to whom one could "pass the baby," the Florida bubble burst.

For the losers it was a sobering lesson, but it proved to be but a tryout for the Great Bull Market in stocks. Until 1927 stock values had gone up with profits, but then they began to soar on wings of speculation. Mellon's tax reductions had released money which, with the help of aggressive brokerage houses, found its way to Wall Street. Instead of trading binders on real estate, one could buy stock on margin—that is, make a small down payment and borrow the rest from a broker who held the stock as security against a down market. Brokers' loans rose steadily from about $3.5 million in June 1927 to $8 million in September 1929.

Gamblers in the market ignored warning signs. By 1927 residential construction and automobile sales were catching up to demand, business inventories rose, and the rate of consumer spending slowed. By mid-1929 production, employment, and other signs of economic activity were declining. Still the market rose. Among the blue chips, American Telephone and Telegraph went from 179½ in March 1928 to 304 on September 3, 1929, which was when the market peaked. Glamor stocks moved much faster: Radio Corporation of America, for example, rose from under 100 to over 500 during the same period.

By 1929 the market was functioning in a fantasy world. Conservative financiers and brokers who counseled caution found their feeble admonitions lost in the hubbub of the market. The president worried too, and urged stock exchange and Federal Reserve officers to discourage speculation. In August the Federal Reserve Board raised the rate on loans to member banks (the rediscount rate) to 6 percent, but with no effect. On September 4, stock prices wavered, and the day after that they dropped. Investment advisor Roger Babson recalled the Florida boom and said on September 5: "Sooner or later a crash is coming, and it may be terrific." What was promptly dubbed the Babson Break opened a season of fluctuations. The Great Bull Market staggered on into October, trending downward but with enough good days to keep hope alive. On October 22 Charles E. Mitchell, president of the National City Bank, returning from Europe, told reporters: "I know of nothing fundamentally wrong with the stock market or with the underlying business and credit structure."

THE CRASH AND ITS CAUSES   The next day prices crumbled, and the day after that a wild scramble to unload stocks lasted until word arrived that leading bankers had formed a pool to stabilize prices. Prices steadied for the rest of the week, but after a weekend to think the situation over, stockholders began to unload on Monday. The New York *Times* index of industrials went down 49 points. On Tuesday, October 29, the most devastating single day in the market's history, the index dropped another 43 points. The market reported sales of 16.4 million shares (at the time 3

Wall Street on October 29, 1929. Confusion prevailed on the street and in the markets. [Culver Picture Service]

million shares traded was a busy day) and some issues went begging for buyers. The plunge in prices fed on itself as brokers sold the shares they held for buyers who failed to meet their obligations. During October stocks on the New York Exchange fell in value by 37 percent.

The first impulse of business and government leaders was to express hope. According to President Hoover, "the fundamental business of the country" was sound. John D. Rockefeller issued his first public statement in decades: ". . . my son and I have for some days been purchasing sound common stocks." The comedian Eddie Cantor retorted: "Sure, who else has any money left?" Some speculators who got out of the market went back in for bargains but found themselves caught in a slow, tedious erosion of values. By March 1, 1933, the value of stocks on the New York Exchange was less than a fifth of the value at the market's peak. The New York *Times* stock average, which stood at 452 on September 3, 1929, bottomed at 52 in July 1932.

Caution became the watchword for consumers and businessmen. Buyers held out for lower prices, orders fell off, wages fell or ceased altogether, and the decline in purchasing power brought further cutbacks in business. From 1929 to 1932 Americans' personal incomes declined by more than half, from $82 million to $40 million. Unemployment continued to rise. Farmers, already in trouble, faced catastrophe.

The crash had revealed the fundamental business of the country to be unsound. Most harmful was the ability of business to maintain prices and take profits while holding down wages and the cost of raw materials, with the result that about one-third of the personal income went to only 5 percent of the population. By plowing profits back into expansion, business brought on a growing imbalance between rising productivity and declining purchasing power. As the demand for goods declined, the rate of investment in new plant began to decline. For a time the softness of purchasing power was concealed by greater use of installment buying, and the deflationary effects of high tariffs were concealed by the volume of loans and investments abroad which supported foreign demand for American goods. But the flow of American capital abroad began to dry up when the stock market began to look more attractive. Swollen profits and dividends, together with the Mellon tax policies, enticed the rich into market speculation. When trouble came, the bloated corporate structure collapsed.

Governmental policies also contributed to the debacle. Mellon's tax reductions brought oversaving, which helped diminish demand. The growing money supply fed the fever of speculation.

Hostility toward labor unions discouraged collective bargaining and may have worsened the prevalent imbalances in income. High tariffs discouraged foreign trade. Lax enforcement of anti-trust laws encouraged concentration, monopoly, and high prices.

HOOVER'S EFFORTS AT RECOVERY   Not only did the policies of public officials help bring on economic collapse, but few public leaders acknowledged the crisis: all that was needed, they thought, was a slight correction of the market. Those who held to the dogma of laissez-faire thought the economy would cure itself. The best policy, Secretary Mellon advised, would be to "liquidate labor, liquidate stocks, liquidate the farmers, liquidate real estate." Hoover himself had little patience with speculators, but he was unwilling now to sit by and let events take their course. Hoover in fact did more than any president had ever done before in such dire economic circumstances. Still, his own philosophy, now hardened into dogma, set limits to governmental action, and he was unready to set it aside even to meet an emergency.

As food administrator and promoter of voluntary associations Hoover had insisted on strong public relations departments. He believed also that the nation's fundamental business structure was sound and that the country's main need was confidence. In speech after speech Hoover exhorted the public to keep up hope, and summoned businessmen and labor leaders for talks at the White House. Hoover asked businessmen to keep the mills and shops open, maintain wage rates, and spread the work to avoid layoffs—in short to let the first shock fall on corporate

An incredulous citizen watches as Hoover fills the Christmas stocking with business confidence. It proved cold comfort. [Library of Congress]

profits rather than on purchasing power. In return union leaders, who had little choice, agreed to refrain from wage demands and strikes. As it happened, however, words were not enough, and the prediction that good times were just around the corner (actually made by Vice-President Charles Curtis though attributed to Hoover) eventually became a sardonic joke.

Hoover did more than try to reassure the American public. He hurried the building of public works in order to provide jobs, but state and local cutbacks more than offset federal spending. At Hoover's demand the Federal Reserve returned to an easier credit policy, and Congress passed a modest tax reduction to put more purchasing power in people's pockets. The Federal Farm Board stepped up its loans and its purchases on farm surpluses only to face bumper crops in 1930 despite droughts in the Middle West and Southwest. The high Hawley-Smoot Tariff, proposed at first to help farmers, brought reprisals abroad, devastating foreign trade.

As always, depression hurt the party in power. At the Democratic National Committee, publicity director Charles Michelson exploited Hoover's predicament for all it was worth, and more. But Michelson's role in building the depression image of Hoover has been overblown. In 1930, the Second Year of the Abolition of Poverty (as one newsman put it), the floundering president was easy game. During the war, "to Hooverize" had signified patriotic sacrifice; now the president's name signified distress. Near the city dumps, along the railroad tracks, the dispossessed huddled in shacks of tarpaper and galvanized iron, old packing boxes, abandoned cars. These squalid settlements became "Hoovervilles." A "Hoover blanket" was a newspaper; a "Hoover flag," an empty pocket turned inside out; "Hoover wagons" were cars pulled by mules; "Hoover hogs" were jackrabbits. In November 1930 the Democrats gained their first national victory since 1916, winning a majority in the House and enough gains in the Senate to control it in coalition with western agrarians.

One irony of the time was that the great humanitarian of wartime relief was recast as the stubborn opponent of depression relief. But Hoover was still doing business at the same old stand: his answer remained voluntarism. When Col. Arthur H. Woods, head of the Emergency Committee for Employment, strongly recommended a governmental program of $840 million for road building and other public works, the president turned it down. His annual message to Congress in December 1930 demanded that each community and state undertake the relief of distress "with that sturdiness and independence which built a great Nation." Edmund Wilson, then early in his career as a literary critic, found it "a reassuring thought, in the cold weather, that the emaciated men in the bread lines, the men and women beggars in the streets, and the children dependent on them, are all having their fibre hardened."

In the first half of 1931 economic indicators rose, renewing hope for an upswing. Then, as recovery beckoned, another shock fell. In May 1931 the failure of Austria's largest bank, the Credit Anstalt, triggered panic in central Europe. On June 20, to halt the domino effect of spreading defaults, President Hoover proposed a one-year moratorium on both reparations and war-debt payments. The moratorium, as it happened, became permanent simply by process of default. In July the major European nations accepted the moratorium and later also a temporary "standstill" on settlement of private obligations between banks. The general shortage of exchange drove Europeans to withdraw their gold from American banks and dump their American securities. One after another European country abandoned the gold standard and devalued its currency. In September even the Bank of England went off the gold standard. The United States meanwhile slid into the third bitter winter of depression.

CONGRESSIONAL INITIATIVES   With a new Congress in session, demands for federal action impelled Hoover to stretch his philosophy to its limits. He was ready now to use governmental resources at least to shore up the financial institutions of the country. Eugene Meyer, Jr., former head of the War Finance Corporation, prompted Hoover to bring back the agency for a new purpose. In January 1932 the new Congress set up the Reconstruction Finance Corporation (RFC) with $500 million (and authority to borrow $2 billion more) for emergency loans to banks, life insurance companies, building and loan societies, farm mortgage associations, and railroads. Under former Vice-President Charles G. Dawes, it authorized $1.2 billion in loans within six months. The RFC staved off bankruptcies, but Hoover's critics found in it favoritism to business, the most damaging instance of which was a $90-million loan to Dawes's Chicago bank, made soon after he left the RFC in June 1932. The RFC nevertheless remained a key agency through the New Deal and World War II.

Further help to the financial structure came with the Glass-Steagall Act of February 1932, which broadened the definition of commercial loans which the Federal Reserve would support.

The new arrangement also released about $750 million in gold formerly used to back Federal Reserve Notes, countering the effect of foreign withdrawals and domestic hoarding of gold at the same time that it enlarged the supply of credit. For homeowners the Federal Home Loan Bank Act of July 1932 created with Hoover's blessing a series of discount banks for home mortgages. They provided for savings and loan and other mortgage agencies a service much like that the Federal Reserve System provided to commercial banks.

All these measures reflected a dubious "trickle-down" theory, Hoover's critics said. If government could help banks and railroads, asked New York's Sen. Robert G. Wagner, "is there any reason why we should not likewise extend a helping hand to that forlorn American, in every village and every city of the United States, who has been without wages since 1929?" By 1932 members of Congress were filling the hoppers with bills for federal relief. At that point Hoover might have pleaded "dire necessity" and, backed by his reputation in the field, taken the leadership of the relief movement and salvaged his political fortunes.

Instead he held back and only grudgingly edged toward federal relief. House Speaker John Nance Garner of Texas, with his own eye cocked to the White House, proposed a $1-billion bond issued for federal public works, another $1 billion for RFC loans to state and local public works, and $100 million for distribution to the needy. Senator Wagner proposed even more, but a compromise bill that came out of conference committee met a presidential veto. Then on July 21, 1932, Hoover signed the Emergency Relief and Construction Act, which avoided a direct federal dole but gave the RFC $300 million for relief loans to the states, authorized loans of up to $1.5 billion for state and local public works, and appropriated $322 million for federal public works.

Relief for farmers had long since been abandoned. The Grain and Cotton Stabilization Corporations set up under the Farm Board had lost $345 million in futile efforts to buy up surpluses. In mid-1931 they quit buying altogether and helplessly watched prices slide. In 1919 wheat had fetched $2.16 a bushel; by 1932 it had sunk to 38¢. Cotton reached a high of 41.75¢ a pound in 1919; before the 1932 harvest it went to 4.6¢. Other farm prices declined comparably. Net cash income for farmers slid from $12 billion in 1929 to $5.3 billion in 1932. Between 1930 and 1934 nearly a million farms passed from their owners to the mortgage holders.

FARMERS AND VETERANS IN PROTEST   Faced with the loss of everything, farmers began to defy the law. Angry mobs stopped foreclosures and threatened to lynch the judges sanctioning them. In Nebraska farmers burned corn to keep warm. In Iowa, Milo Reno, once head of the state's Farmers Union, formed the militant Farmers' Holiday Association which called a farmers' strike and forcibly blocked deliveries of produce. Dairymen dumped milk into roadside ditches. On the whole, like voluntary efforts to reduce acreage, the strikes failed, but they vividly dramatized the farmer's mood.

In the midst of the crisis there was desperate if nebulous talk of revolution. "Folks are restless," Mississippi's Gov. Theodore Bilbo told reporters in 1931. "Communism is gaining a foothold. . . . In fact, I'm getting a little pink myself." Bilbo was doing his usual put-on, but across the country the once-obscure Communist party began to draw crowds to its rallies and willing collaborators into its Unemployed Councils and "hunger marches." In Alabama it formed a Share Croppers Union and reaped a propaganda windfall when the party went to the defense of the Scottsboro Boys, nine black itinerants accused on flimsy evidence of raping two white girls atop a gondola car of gravel in northern Alabama. Around Harlan, Kentucky, desperate coal miners embraced the Communist-run National Mine Workers' Union, which fell victim to guns and whips and ultimately to the rock-ribbed faith of miners who heard leaders "denounce our government and our flag and our religion." For all the sound and fury, few were converted to the Communist view. Party membership never rose much above 100,000.

Visions of disorder took shape when unemployed veterans converged on Washington in the spring of 1932. The "Bonus Expeditionary Force" budded first in the brain of Walter W. Waters in Portland, Oregon, but after his first contingent of 330 arrived late in May, the number grew quickly to more than 15,000. Their purpose was to get immediate payment of the bonus which Congress had voted in 1924. It took the form of endowment life insurance payable in 1945—or earlier to the heirs of veterans who died before that date. In 1931, over Hoover's veto, Congress had authorized loans of up to 50 percent of the value of each insurance certificate, but the veterans now wanted everything in cash. The House approved a bonus bill introduced by Wright Patman of Texas, but when the Senate voted it down in June most of the veterans went home. The rest, having no place to go, camped in vacant government buildings and in a shantytown on Anacostia Flats, within sight of the Capitol.

Hunger marchers demonstrating in Washington, D.C., for unemployment insurance, December 1931. [Library of Congress]

The chief of the Washington police, once the youngest brigadier-general of the American Expeditionary Force (the name given to American forces in Europe during the war), gave them a friendly welcome and won their trust. But a fearful White House fretted. Eager to disperse them, Hoover got Congress to vote funds, in the form of loans against the bonus certificates, to buy their tickets home. More left, but others stayed even after Congress adjourned, hoping at least to meet with the president. Late in July the administration ordered the government buildings cleared. In the ensuing melee, one policeman panicked, fired into the crowd, and killed two veterans. This "riot" afforded the excuse that Secretary of War Patrick J. Hurley had been seeking, and the president acceded to his request to move in about 700 soldiers under Gen. Douglas MacArthur, aided by junior officers Dwight D. Eisenhower and George S. Patton, Jr. The soldiers easily drove out the unarmed veterans and their families and burned the shacks. Among the evicted was Joe Angelo of New Jersey, who had received the Distinguished Service Cross for a wartime exploit that saved the life of George Patton. The one fatality—from tear gas—was eleven-week-old Bernard Myers, born at Anacostia.

General MacArthur said the "mob," animated by "the essence of revolution," was about to seize control of the government. The administration insisted that the Bonus Army consisted mainly of Communists and criminals, but neither a grand jury nor the Veterans Administration could find evidence to support the charge. One observer wrote before the incident: "There is about the lot of them an atmosphere of hopelessness, of utter despair, though not of desperation. . . . they have no enthusiasm whatever and no stomach for fighting."

Their mood, and the mood of the country, was much like that of Hoover himself. He worked hard, but took no joy from his labors. "I am so tired," he sometimes said, "that every bone in my body aches." He was, as William Allen White said, "constitutionally gloomy, a congenital pessimist who always saw the doleful side of any situation." A private meeting with Hoover, Secretary of State Stimson said, was "like sitting in a bath of ink." News conferences became more strained and less frequent. When friends urged him to seize the leadership he said, "I can't be a Theodore Roosevelt," or "I have no Wilsonian qualities." The gloom, the sense of futility, communicated itself to the country. In a mood more despairing than rebellious, people waited to see what another presidential campaign would bring forth.

FURTHER READING

The most recent synthesis of events following the First World War is Ellis W. Hawley's *The Great War and the Search for a Modern Order: A History of the American People and Their Institutions, 1917–1933* (1979). A more traditional narrative is John D. Hicks's *Republican Ascendancy, 1921–1933* (1960). Two short introductions to the period are William E. Leuchtenberg's *The Perils of Prosperity, 1914–1932* (1958),° and Paul A. Carter's *The Twenties in America* (1968). The chapter on the 1920s in Blaine Brownell and George E. Mowry's *The Urban Nation, 1920–1960* (1965),° explains the influence of the twenties on later events.

Presidential politics has attracted many scholars. Introductions to Harding include Francis Russell's *The Shadow of Blooming Grove: Warren G. Harding in His Times* (1968), Robert K. Murray's *The Harding Era: Warren G. Harding and His Administration* (1969), and Andrew Sinclair's *The Available Man: The Life behind the Masks of Warren Gamaliel Harding* (1965). For Coolidge, see Donald R. McCoy's *Calvin Coolidge: The Silent President* (1967) and William Allen White's *A Puritan in Babylon* (1940). Studies on Hoover include Joan Hoff Wilson's *Herbert Hoover: Forgotten Progressive* (1975), David Burner's *Herbert Hoover: The Public Life* (1978), and George Nash's *The Life of Herbert Hoover—The Engineer* (vol. 1, 1983).

Studies of other prominent 1920s figures include Oscar Handlin's *Al Smith and His America* (1958), William Harbaugh's *Lawyer's Lawyer: The Life of John W. Davis* (1973), LeRoy Ashby's *The Spearless Leader: Senator Borah and the Progressive Movement in the 1920s* (1972), and David P. Thelen's *Robert M. La Follette and the Insurgent Spirit* (1978).

°These books are available in paperback editions.

Other works on politics include Burl Noggle's *Teapot Dome: Oil and Politics in the 1920s* (1962),° David Burner's *The Politics of Provincialism: The Democratic Party in Transition, 1918–1932* (1967), and James Gilbert's *Designing the Industrial State: The Intellectual Pursuit of Collectivism in America, 1880–1940* (1972). Alan Lichtman's *Prejudice and the Old Politics* (1978) and George B. Tindall's *The Emergence of the New South, 1914–1945* (1967),° cover the election of 1928. John D. Hicks and Theodore Saloutos's *Twentieth Century Populists: Agricultural Discontent in the Midwest, 1900–1939* (1964), and Gilbert Fite's *George Peek and the Fight for Farm Parity* (1954) discuss the Farm Bloc. William Chafe's *The American Woman: Her Changing Social, Economic, and Political Roles* (1970)° is a good introduction to the achievement of suffrage.

An overview of the depression is found in C. P. Kinderberger's *The World in Depression* (1973). A review of the economics of the 1920s is given in George Soule's *Prosperity Decade* (1947) and John Kenneth Galbraith's *Money: Whence It Came, Where It Went* (1975). Galbraith also details the fall of the stock market in *The Great Crash of 1929* (1955).° Another interpretation is given in Peter Temin's *Did Monetary Forces Cause the Great Depression?* (1976).° Albert Romesco's *The Poverty of Abundance: Hoover, the Nation, and the Great Depression* (1965), Jordan A. Schwartz's *Interregnum of Despair: Hoover's Congress and the Depression* (1970), Roger Daniels's *The Bonus March* (1971), and Donald Lisio's *The President and Protest* (1974) all explore what Hoover did and did not do during the crisis. John A. Garraty's *Unemployment in History: Economic Thought and Public Policy* (1979) explores what the nation thought about its plight.

28

FRANKLIN D. ROOSEVELT
AND THE NEW DEAL

FROM HOOVERISM TO THE NEW DEAL

FDR'S ELECTION   On June 14, 1932, while the Bonus Army was
still encamped in Washington, Republicans gathered in Chicago
to renominate Hoover and Curtis. The proceedings were apathetic and dreary, enlivened only by debate over a prohibition
plank, the final version of which straddled the issue. The delegates went through the motions in a mood of defeat. The Democrats, in contrast, converged on Chicago late in June confident
that they would nominate the next president. New York Gov.
Franklin D. Roosevelt was already the front-runner with most of
the delegates lined up, but he still faced an uphill battle for a
two-thirds majority. Al Smith, long a favorite of the party machines, felt entitled to one more chance at the White House. But
Smith's time had passed; he could not even control his own
state's delegation. Among the favorite sons only House Speaker
John Nance Garner of Texas had any serious chance. After a
Garner delegation won the California primary, the Texan was in
a position to deadlock the convention, but the memory of the
1924 deadlock remained strong. When Rep. Sam Rayburn described the line-up on the telephone, Garner replied: "All right,
release my delegates. . . . Hell, I'll do anything to see the Democrats win one more national election." Thus Roosevelt went over
the top on the fourth ballot; Garner's reward was the vice-presi-
dency, an office he later pronounced "not worth a pitcher of
warm spit."

In a bold gesture, Roosevelt flew to Chicago and appeared before the convention in person to accept the nomination instead of awaiting formal notification. "Let it . . . be symbolic that . . . I broke traditions," he told the delegates. "Republican leaders not only have failed in material things, they have failed in national vision, because in disaster they have held out no hope. . . . I pledge you, I pledge myself to a new deal for the American people." What the New Deal would be Roosevelt himself had little idea as yet, but unlike Hoover, he was flexible and willing to experiment. What was more, his ebullient personality communicated joy and hope. His campaign song was "Happy Days Are Here Again."

Roosevelt was strengthened also by his background and experience. Born to a comfortable fortune in 1882, he had the advantage of a proper education at Groton School and Harvard, topped off by the Columbia Law School. Although raised a Democrat, he admired his distant cousin Theodore and up to a point his career retraced the same path. Elected to the New York state legislature in 1910, he caught the public eye by opposing Tammany's candidate for the United States Senate. In 1912 he backed Wilson, and for both of Wilson's terms was his assistant secretary of the navy. Then in 1920, largely on the strength of his name, he became Cox's running mate. In defeat the parallel with Theodore ended, and the following year his career seemed cut short by an attack of poliomyelitis which left him permanently crippled, unable to stand or walk without braces. But the struggle for recovery transformed the once supercilious young aristocrat into one of the most outgoing political figures of the century. Justice Oliver Wendell Holmes, Jr., later summed up his qualities this way: "A second-class intellect—but a first-class temperament."

For seven years he fought his way back to health and in 1928 emerged again on the national scene to nominate Al Smith in Houston. At Smith's urging he ran for governor of New York to strengthen the ticket and won while Smith was losing the state. Reelected by a whopping majority of 700,000 in 1930, he became a shining beacon for 1932.

Partly to dispel doubts about his health, Roosevelt set forth on a grueling campaign tour. His other purposes were to pin responsibility for the depression on Hoover and the Republicans, and to define the New Deal. Always deft at picking other men's brains, he relied mainly on a panel of advisors from Columbia University: Raymond Moley, G. Rexford Tugwell, and A. A. Berle, Jr. In turn this Brain Trust, as newsmen quickly dubbed it, tapped other sources in preparing drafts for major speeches. Roosevelt

*Gov. Franklin D. Roosevelt, the Democratic nominee,
campaigning in Topeka, Kansas. Roosevelt's confidence
inspired voters. [Wide World Photos]*

of course tempered their ideas to political realities, often fuzzing
them over to avoid offending any large bloc of voters, and usually
hedged his bets by offering alternative courses of action.

Like Hoover, Roosevelt made the requisite promise to balance
the budget, but he left open the loophole that he would incur
deficits to prevent starvation and dire want. On the tariff he was
evasive. On farm policy he offered several options pleasing to
farmers and ambiguous enough not to alarm city-dwellers. He
did come out unequivocally for strict regulation of utilities and
for at least some development of public power, and he consistently stood by his party's pledge to repeal the Prohibition
Amendment. At the Commonwealth Club in San Francisco the
candidate gazed into a clouded crystal ball and announced that
economic expansion, like Frederick Jackson Turner's frontier,
had come to an end. Such opinions prevailed widely at the time.
A mature economy would require national planning, Roosevelt
said. "The country needs, and, unless I mistake its temper, the
country demands bold, persistent experimentation. . . . Above
all, try something."

What came across to voters, however, was less the content of
his speeches than the confidence of the man. His most banal utterances seemed somehow significant. Hoover by contrast had
no confidence. He could turn a neat phrase, but many elegant
passages suffered from the pedestrian manner of his delivery.
Democrats, he argued, ignored the international causes of the
depression. They were taking a reckless course. Roosevelt's evasive stand on the tariff, he said, made the Democratic candidate
look like a chameleon on plaid. Roosevelt's policies, he warned,

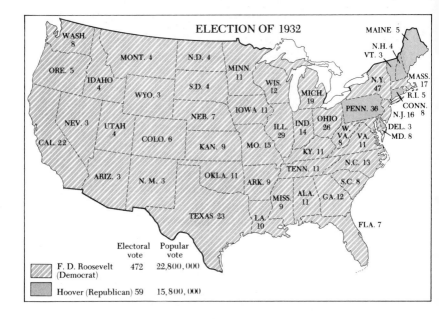

ELECTION OF 1932

	Electoral vote	Popular vote
F. D. Roosevelt (Democrat)	472	22,800,000
Hoover (Republican)	59	15,800,000

"would destroy the very foundations of our American system." Pursue them, and "grass will grow in the streets of a hundred cities, a thousand towns." But few were listening. Amid the persistent depression the country wanted a new course, a new leadership, a new deal.

Many thoughtful observers were disappointed in both candidates. They agreed with Walter Lippmann's earlier judgment that Roosevelt was "a pleasant man, who, without any important qualifications for the office, would very much like to be President." Those who believed only a radical departure would suffice went over to Socialist Norman Thomas, who polled 882,000 votes, and some went on to Communist William Z. Foster, who got 103,000. The wonder is that a desperate people did not turn in greater numbers to radical candidates. Instead they swept Roosevelt into office by 22.8 million votes to Hoover's 15.8 million. Hoover carried only four states in New England plus Pennsylvania and Delaware, losing in the electoral college by 472 to 59.

THE INAUGURATION For the last time the country waited four long months, until March 4, for a new president and Congress to take office. The Twentieth Amendment, ratified on February 6, 1933, provided that the president would take office thereafter on January 20 and the newly elected Congress on January 3. Before the end of November the president-elect went to the White House for an inconclusive conference. Hoover proposed a joint effort, but only on his own terms, so Roosevelt, like Lincoln, warily avoided commitment until power was his own. With policy abandoned to drift, the bleak winter of 1932–1933 became what one historian called "the interregnum of despair." Amid spreading destitution and misery, unemployment continued to rise and panic struck the banking system. Depositors increasingly played it safe by taking their cash out and squirreling it away. In Michigan, where automobile production was severely curtailed, the threat of runs on the banks impelled the governor to extend the Lincoln's Birthday closing indefinitely. As panic spread, governors of other states also found excuses for banking holidays. When the Hoover administration ended, four-fifths of the nation's banks were closed and the country was on the brink of economic paralysis.

A profound crisis of confidence prevailed when Roosevelt took the oath of office on March 4, 1933, but it was tempered by a mood of expectancy. The new president exploited both with a spirit of assurance that conveyed a new sense of vigor and action. First, he asserted a "firm belief that the only thing we have to fear is fear itself—nameless, unreasoning, unjustified terror which paralyzes needed efforts to convert retreat into advance." Roosevelt promised to fill the vacuum of leadership: "The money changers have fled from their high seats in the temple of our civilization. We may now restore that temple to the ancient truths." He would not merely exhort, he promised: "This nation asks for action, and action now!" He warned that emergency measures might call for a temporary departure from the normal balance of executive and legislative authority. If need be, he said, "I shall not evade the clear course of duty. . . . I shall ask the Congress for the remaining instrument to meet the crisis—broad executive power to wage a war against the emergency as great as the power that would be given me if we were in fact invaded by a foreign foe." It was a measure of the country's mood that this call received the loudest applause.

Roosevelt was not the first to resort to what the historian William Leuchtenburg has called "the analogue of war." Time and again the nation's mobilization for World War I was held up as a model for action in the new crisis. The Reconstruction Finance Corporation, started under Hoover but sometimes called the first New Deal agency, was but the War Finance Corporation reborn. Many of Roosevelt's appointees had been involved in the mobilization. George Peek and Hugh S. Johnson, for instance, had once worked for the War Industries Board; soon they would head the New Deal farm and industrial recovery programs.

STRENGTHENING THE MONETARY SYSTEM   The first order of business for the new administration was to unclog the channels of finance. On his second day in office, Roosevelt called Congress to meet in special session on March 9, and then declared a four-day banking holiday, invoking powers under the Trading with the Enemy Act of 1917. It took Congress only seven hours to pass the Emergency Banking Relief Act, which permitted sound banks to reopen under license from the Treasury and provided managers for those that were still in trouble. On March 12, in the first of his radio "fireside chats," the president told his audience it was safer to "keep your money in a reopened bank than under the mattress." The following day, deposits in reopened banks exceeded withdrawals, and by March 15 banks controlling nine-tenths of the nation's banking resources were once again open. The crisis had ended and the new administration was ready to get on with its broader program.

In rapid order Roosevelt undertook to meet two specific pledges in the Democratic platform. At his behest, on March 20 Congress passed an Economy Act granting the executive the power to cut salaries, reduce payments to veterans for non-service-connected disabilities, and reorganize agencies in the interest of economy. On March 22 the Beer-Wine Revenue Act amended the Volstead Act to permit sale of beverages with an alcoholic content of 3.2 percent. The Twenty-first Amendment, already submitted by Congress to the states on February 20, would be declared ratified on December 5, thus ending the "noble experiment" that was prohibition.

The measures of March were but the beginning. During the session from March 9 to June 16, the so-called Hundred Days, Congress received and enacted fifteen major proposals from the president, leaving a record unlike anything seen before in American history:

March 9	The Emergency Banking Act
March 20	The Economy Act
March 31	Establishment of the Civilian Conservation Corps
April 19	Abandonment of the gold standard
May 12	The Federal Emergency Relief Act
May 12	The Agricultural Adjustment Act, including the Thomas amendment which gave the president powers to expand the money supply
May 12	The Emergency Farm Mortgage Act, providing for the refinancing of farm mortgages

May 18   The Tennessee Valley Authority Act, providing for the unified development of the Tennessee Valley
May 27   The Truth-in-Securities Act, requiring full disclosure in the issue of new securities
June 5   The Gold Repeal Joint Resolution, which abrogated the gold clause in public and private contracts
June 13   The Home Owners' Loan Act, setting up the Home Owners' Loan Corporation to refinance home mortgages
June 16   The National Industrial Recovery Act, providing for a system of industrial self-regulation under federal supervision and for a $3.3-billion public works program
June 16   The Glass-Steagall Banking Act, separating commercial and investment banking and establishing the Federal Deposit Insurance Corporation
June 16   The Farm Credit Act, which reorganized the agricultural credit system
June 16   The Railroad Coordination Act, setting up a federal coordinator of transportation

With the banking crisis over, there still remained an acute debt problem for farmers and homeowners, and a lingering distrust of the banks which might yet be aroused again. On March 27, by executive decree, Roosevelt reorganized all farm credit agencies into the Farm Credit Administration (FCA). By the Emergency Farm Mortgage Act (May 12) and the Farm Credit Act (June 16) Congress confirmed that action and authorized extensive refinancing of farm mortgages at lower interest rates. Within seven months the FCA loaned farmers more than $100 million, nearly four times as much as all the land-bank loans made the previous year. The Home Owners' Loan Act (June 13) provided a similar service to city-dwellers through the new Home Owners' Loan Corporation (HOLC)—something which, incidentally, Hoover had vainly urged on Congress in 1931. The Glass-Steagall Banking Act (June 16) further shored up confidence in the banking system. It created the Federal Deposit Insurance Corporation (FDIC) to guarantee bank deposits of up to $5,000. To prevent speculative abuses, it separated investment and commercial banking corporations and extended the Federal Reserve's regulatory power over credit. The Federal Securities Act (May 27) required the full disclosure of information about new stock and bond issues, at first by registration with the Federal Trade Commission, later with the Securities and Exchange Commission (SEC), which was created on June 6, 1934, to regulate the stock and bond markets.

Throughout 1933 Roosevelt tinkered with devaluation of the currency as a way to raise prices and thus ease the debt burden.

Just Another Hole, *a skeptical view of FDR's attempts to boost the economy by devaluing the currency, thereby raising prices. [Lute Pease, Newark* Evening News*]*

Having already placed an embargo on the withdrawal of gold deposits at the outset of his administration, on April 5 he used powers granted by the Emergency Banking Act to order all gold turned in to the Federal Reserve Banks, except small amounts for industrial, professional, or artistic uses. On April 19 the government officially abandoned the gold standard: the consequent decline in the value of the dollar increased the prices of commodities and stocks at home. The Gold Repeal Joint Resolution (June 5) canceled the gold clause in federal and private obligations, made all contracts payable in legal tender, and thus completed the abandonment of the gold standard. The experiment ended when Congress passed the Gold Reserve Act of January 30, 1934, which authorized the president to impound all gold in the Federal Reserve Banks and reduce the theoretical gold value of the dollar. By executive order he set the price of an ounce of gold at $35, which reduced the dollar's gold content as compared to its gold content the previous October. It was done, Roosevelt said, "to make possible the payment of . . . debts at more nearly the price level at which they had been incurred." Prices did rise, and the high price set on gold drew most of the world's supply to the United States, where it was buried in the vaults at Fort Knox, Kentucky.

Another time-honored inflationary device was the coinage of silver, and for a time the ghost of William Jennings Bryan stalked the halls of Congress. A silver bloc, led by Elbert Thomas of Oklahoma, pursued the goal of "reflation" by authorizing free coinage of silver. In May 1933 the silverites got a compromise amendment to the farm bill giving the president discretionary authority to reduce further the gold content of the dollar and to purchase silver for coinage. The president used the first but refused to act on the second. Eventually, however, he yielded to pressure from the farm and Rocky Mountain states and accepted the Silver Purchase Act, passed on June 19, 1934. Under this measure the Treasury was in effect required to buy the entire output of American silver mines. By presidential order of August 9, 1934, the government bought the silver with certificates at the rate of $1.29 an ounce, thereby making twenty-seven ounces of silver equal in value to one ounce of gold (a 27:1 ratio). Since the total stock of silver was by then too small to have much inflationary effect, the result was mainly to memorialize Bryan and to subsidize the silver mines.

RELIEF MEASURES   In 1933 the relief of personal distress was an urgent priority, as it would remain until World War II. A first step toward such relief came with the creation in March of the Civilian Conservation Corps (CCC), which was designed to give work relief to young men aged eighteen to twenty-five, and incidentally to remove them from the job market. Beginning on a cold, rainy day in April 1933 when a caravan of motor trucks set out from Washington to put up the first CCC camp in Virginia's George Washington National Forest, nearly 3 million young men took to the woods to work at a variety of jobs in forests, parks, recreational areas, and soil conservation projects at a nominal pay of $30 a month. Directed by army officers and foresters, they worked under a semi-military discipline and provided perhaps the most direct analogue of war in the whole New Deal.

The Federal Emergency Relief Administration (FERA), created on May 12, 1933, with an authorization of $500 million, addressed the broader problems of human distress. Harry L. Hopkins, an indefatigable social worker who had directed Roosevelt's state relief program in New York, pushed the program

October 17, 1934. The depression was more than the collapse of prices and markets, and New Deal relief efforts recognized this. [Library of Congress]

with a seemingly boundless nervous energy, all the while giving off (in the words of one observer) "a suggestion of quick cigarettes, thinning hair, dandruff, brief sarcasm, fraying suits of clothes, and a wholly understandable preoccupation." The FERA continued and expanded the assistance that had begun under Hoover's RFC, but with a difference. Federal monies flowed to the states in grants rather than "loans." While FERA continued to channel aid through state agencies to relief clients mainly in direct payments, Hopkins enlarged its scope by gradually developing work programs for education, student aid, rural rehabilitation, and transient relief. He pushed an "immediate work instead of dole" approach on local officials, but they preferred the dole as an easier and quicker way to reach the needy.

The first large-scale experiment with work relief came with formation of the Civil Works Administration (CWA) during the winter of 1933–1934, when it had become apparent that even the largesse of the FERA would not prevent widespread privation. Created in November 1933, the CWA provided jobs and wages to those able to work. It was conceived and implemented in haste, and many of its projects were "make-work" jobs such as leaf-raking and ditch-digging; but it spent over $900 million (mostly in wages) for a variety of useful projects, from highway repairs to teaching jobs that helped keep the schools open. The CWA, unlike the FERA, was a federal operation from top to bottom. The CWA was abandoned in the spring of 1934, having served its purpose of helping people weather the winter; but Roosevelt and Hopkins continued to believe that work-relief was preferable to the dole, which they believed to have a debilitating effect psychologically on recipients.

Recovery through Regulation

Beyond rescuing the banks and providing relief lay the long-term goals of recovery for agriculture and business. Members of Roosevelt's Brain Trust and others who influenced policies during the "hundred days" were heirs largely to an earlier Roosevelt's New Nationalism, whether avowedly so or not. They held the trend toward economic concentration to be inevitable. They also believed that the mistakes of the 1920s showed that the only way to operate an integrated economy at capacity and in the public interest was through regulation and organized central planning, not through trust-busting. The success of centralized planning during World War I reinforced such ideas. New farm and recovery programs sprang from their beliefs.

AGRICULTURAL RECOVERY: THE AAA   Early on, the Department of Agriculture produced an omnibus farm bill in consultation with farm leaders, and on March 16 the president urgently submitted it to Congress. The Agricultural Adjustment Act, signed into law on May 12, contained nearly every major device applicable to farm relief including authority to dump surpluses abroad, but only some of its provisions were implemented. The core of the act was a plan to compensate farmers for voluntary cutbacks in production. The goal was to restore farm prices to "parity," or the same level they had reached during the farmers' golden age of 1909–1914 (1919–1929 for tobacco). The act covered seven "basic commodities," a number later enlarged, and the money for benefit payments came from a processing tax levied on each —at the cotton gin, for example, or the flour mill.

By the time Congress acted, the growing season was already advanced. "Wherever we turn," said George N. Peek, first head of the Agricultural Adjustment Administration (AAA), ". . . we have in prospect a race with the sun." The most urgent problem was the prospect of another bumper cotton crop, and the AAA reluctantly resolved to sponsor a plow-under program. Using county demonstration agents the AAA signed up bewildered farmers. Trouble came sometimes from balky mules, trained to avoid trampling the crop, and occasionally from stubborn tenants who, like the oldtime Populists, could not understand how prosperity could come from creating an artificial scarcity. To destroy a growing crop was a "shocking commentary on our civilization," Agriculture Secretary Henry A. Wallace lamented. "I could tolerate it only as a cleaning up of the wreckage from the old days of unbalanced production." Even more troubling was the spectacle of some 6 million little pink pigs slaughtered "before they could reach the full hogness of their hogdom." It could be justified, Wallace said, only as a means of helping farmers to do with pigs what steelmakers did with pig iron—cut production to fit the market.

It worked temporarily. Cotton farmers got about $112 million in benefit payments, and the crop was reduced by about 4 million bales below the estimate. Cotton prices rose above 11¢ per pound in July (parity was 12.7¢), but sagged again as the crop came in. In an effort to take up the slack, in October 1933 the president set up the Commodity Credit Corporation (another CCC!) which extended loans first on cotton and later on other crops kept in storage and off the market. In principle, if not in form, it was a revival of the old Farmers' Alliance–Populist subtreasury plan. With loans averaging 10¢ per pound on the 1933 crop and 12¢ per pound in 1934, it pegged the prices at those levels because no farmer had to sell for less. But the carry-over from the crops of previous years still weighed the prices down. Another drastic step was taken on April 21, 1934, with passage of the Bankhead Cotton Control Act, which set marketing quotas at 10 million bales in 1934 and 10.5 million in 1935; farmers who tried to sell more than their share of the quota would be stopped by a prohibitive tax. The Kerr-Smith Tobacco Control Act of 1934 applied similar quotas to tobacco.

In 1933 widespread drought in the wheat belt reduced production and removed any need to plow up growing wheat, but benefit payments went to farmers who agreed to cut their wheat acreage in 1934 and 1935. Crop reductions were also brought about in corn, rice, and dairy products. Through a variety of causes—acreage reduction, drought, benefit payments, and currency devaluation—farm income increased from $5.5 billion in 1932 to nearly $8.7 billion in 1935.

Then on January 6, 1936, in the Hoosac Mills Case *(United States v. Butler)* the Supreme Court, by a vote of 6 to 3, held the AAA's processing tax unconstitutional because farm production was intrastate and thus beyond the reach of the power to regulate interstate commerce. In a sharp dissent, Justice Harlan Fiske Stone protested that "the present levy is held invalid, not for any want of power in Congress to lay such a tax" and argued that it came "within the specifically granted power to levy taxes to 'provide for the general welfare.' " But the decision stood. The administration hastily devised a new plan in the Soil Conservation and Domestic Allotment Act, which it pushed through Congress in six weeks. The new act, which became law on February 29, 1936, omitted processing taxes and acreage quotas, but provided benefit payments for soil conservation practices which took land out of soil-depleting staple crops—thus indirectly achieving crop reduction. Since the money came out of general funds and not from taxes, this approach was not vulnerable to suit. The act boosted a developing conservation movement directed by the Soil Conservation Service, which had been created in 1935.

The act was an almost unqualified success as an engineering and educational project because it went far to heal the scars of erosion and the plague of dust storms. But soil conservation nevertheless failed as a device for limiting production. With their worst lands taken out of production, farmers cultivated their fertile acres more intensively. In response, Congress passed the second Agricultural Adjustment Act (February 16, 1938), which reestablished the earlier programs but left out the processing taxes. Benefit payments would come from general funds. By the time the second AAA reached a test in the Supreme Court, changes in the Court's personnel had changed its outlook. This time the law was upheld as a legitimate exercise of the inter-state-commerce power. Agriculture, like manufacturing, was now held to be in the stream of commerce.

INDUSTRIAL RECOVERY: THE NRA   For industry, the counterpart to the AAA was the National Recovery Administration (NRA), and the counterpart to AAA chief George Peek was NRA chief Hugh S. Johnson, Peek's former associate at the Moline Plow Company. The recovery act was hastened into being when Senate passage of a bill limiting the workweek to thirty hours, intro-duced by Sen. Hugo Black (D-Ala.), indicated a mood of impa-tience with continued unemployment, which the thirty-hour week was supposed to relieve. The administration quickly planned and submitted a more comprehensive bill that emerged on June 16, 1933, as the National Industrial Recovery Act (NIRA), the two major parts of which dealt with recovery and public works. The latter part, Title II, created the Public Works Administration (PWA) with $3.3 billion for public buildings, highway programs, flood control, and other improvements. The purpose was to "prime the pump" of business with new expen-ditures and provide jobs for the unemployed. Under the direc-tion of Interior Secretary Harold L. Ickes, the PWA indirectly served the purpose of work relief, although Ickes directed it to-ward well-planned permanent improvements rather than the provision of hasty make-work.

The purposes of the NRA, briefly stated, were twofold: first, to stabilize business with codes of "fair" competitive practice, and second, to generate more purchasing power by providing jobs, defining labor standards, and raising wages. Three related streams of thought merged in the creation of the NRA. One was Theodore Roosevelt's New Nationalism. The second was the idea that the New Deal was the analogue of war, that it could re-peat the miracles wrought by the War Industries Board. Another source for the NRA was the trade-association movement, cham-pioned by Hoover in the 1920s and carried beyond his ideas of voluntary association now by force of law. The NRA also enlisted trade union hopes for protection of basic hour and wage stan-dards and liberal hopes for comprehensive planning.

In each major industry, committees representing manage-ment, labor, and government drew up the codes of fair practice. General Johnson turned to existing trade associations for help in drafting them. A plan submitted by the Cotton Textile Institute, for instance, became the basis for Code No. 1, which imposed restraints on plant expansion, limited operations to eighty hours a week, and required reports on operations every four weeks. The labor standards featured in every code set a forty-hour week and minimum weekly wages of $13 ($12 in the South, where living standards were considered lower) which more than doubled earnings in some cases. Announcement of a proviso against child labor under the age of sixteen set off roars of applause in the hearing room. It did "in a few minutes what neither law nor constitutional amendment had been able to do in forty years," Johnson said.

As the drafting of other codes began to drag, Johnson proposed a "blanket code" pledging employers generally to observe the same labor standards as applied to cotton textiles. In mid-July he launched a crusade to whip up popular support for the NRA and its symbol of compliance, the "Blue Eagle," which had been modeled on an Indian thunderbird and embellished with the motto "We do our part." The eagle was displayed in show windows and stamped on products. It was a gamble, but the public responded. The climax to Johnson's effort came early in September when a Blue Eagle parade down New York's Fifth Avenue drew a quarter of a million marchers. Some 2 million employers signed the pledge, and the impact of the campaign broke the logjam in code making.

For a time it worked, perhaps because a new air of confidence

That Ought to Jolt Him. *The NRA eagle jolts the depression with jobs and wages, 1933. [Library of Congress]*

had overcome the depression blues and the downward spiral of wages and prices had ended. But as soon as recovery began, the honeymoon was over. The daily annoyances of code enforcement inspired growing hostility among businessmen. Charges mounted that the larger companies dominated the code authorities, that allocations froze the existing industrial structure and limited production, and that price-fixing robbed small producers of the chance to compete. In 1934 an investigating committee under Clarence Darrow, the noted lawyer, substantiated at least some of the charges. Limiting production, moreover, had discouraged investment. By 1935 the NRA had developed more critics than friends. When it died in May 1935, struck down by the Supreme Court as unconstitutional, few paused to mourn.

The NRA experiment was generally put down as a failure, but it left an enduring mark. With dramatic suddenness, the codes had set new standards, such as the forty-hour week and the end of child labor, from which it was hard to retreat. The NRA's endorsement of collective bargaining spurred the growth of unions. The codes, moreover, advanced trends toward stabilization and rationalization that were becoming the standard practice of business at large and that, despite misgivings about the concentration of power, would be further promoted by trade associations and by outright integration.

REGIONAL PLANNING: THE TVA   But the eclectic philosophy of the New Deal embraced more than the restrictive approaches of the NRA. The creation of the Tennessee Valley Authority (TVA) was a truly bold venture. Among the measures of the Hundred Days, most of which were efforts to salvage the wreckage of depression, TVA became a massive monument of growth, a living rebuttal to the idea that the economy had reached its full measure of mature development. It was the product neither of a single imagination nor of a single concept, but of an unfolding progression of purposes. In 1916, when the government started power and nitrate plants at Muscle Shoals, Alabama, strengthening national defense was the aim. New objectives unfolded in succession: the plants could produce nitrate fertilizers as well as nitrate explosives, general industrial development, and cheap public power to be used as a "yardstick" for private utility rates. Water-power development pointed in turn to navigation, the control of stream flow for both power and flood control, and to conservation of soil and forests to prevent silting. The chain of connections led ultimately to the concept of overall planning for an entire watershed, which included a total drainage area of 41,000 square miles overlapping seven states, four-fifths the size of England.

Through the 1920s Nebraska Sen. George W. Norris had fought conservative administrations in an effort to sell the Alabama project, but never got sufficient support for the objective of providing public power. In 1932, however, he backed Roosevelt, and then won the new president's support for a vast enlargement of the Muscle Shoals project.

Muscle Shoals, Roosevelt said, "gives us the opportunity . . . of setting an example of planning, not just for ourselves but for generations to come, tying in industry and agriculture and forestry and flood prevention . . . over a distance of a thousand miles." On May 18, 1933, Congress created the TVA as a multipurpose public corporation. Mobilizing local support under TVA Director David E. Lilienthal's slogan of "grass-roots democracy," the TVA won almost universal loyalty among the people of the region. By 1936 the TVA board had six dams completed or under way, and a masterplan to build nine high dams on the main river, which would create the "Great Lakes of the South," and other dams on the tributaries. The agency, moreover, opened the

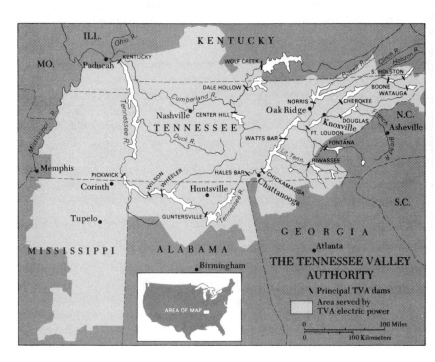

rivers for navigation, fostered soil conservation and forestry, experimented with fertilizers, drew new industry to the region, and sent cheap power pulsating through the valley. Cheap public power, Lilienthal's main passion, became more and more TVA's reason for being—a purpose that would become all the more important during World War II. TVA's success at generating greater power consumption and lower rates awakened private utilities to the mass consumer markets. Cheap power transported farmers of the valley from the age of kerosene to the age of electricity. "The women went around turning the switches on and off," said a Farm Bureau man who witnessed the transition. "The light and wonder in their eyes was brighter than that from the lamps." TVA's first rural cooperative, set up at Corinth, Mississippi, in 1934, pointed the way to the electrification of the nation's farms in the decade that followed. The Rural Electrification Administration (REA), formed as a relief agency by presidential order in 1935, achieved a permanent statutory basis in 1936. By 1940 it had extended loans of more than $321 million to rural cooperatives.

LAUNCHING THE SECOND NEW DEAL

During Roosevelt's first year in office his programs and his personal charms aroused massive support. The president's travels and speeches, his twice-weekly press conferences, and his "fireside chats" over the radio generated vitality from a once-remote White House. In the congressional elections of 1934 the Democrats actually increased their strength in both House and Senate, an almost unprecedented midterm victory for the party in power. When it was over only seven Republican governors remained in office throughout the country.

Criticism of the New Deal was muted or reduced to helpless carping. But as the sense of crisis passed, the spirit of unity relaxed. In August 1934 a group of conservative businessmen and politicians, including Al Smith and John W. Davis, two previous Democratic presidential candidates, formed the American Liberty League to oppose New Deal measures and to "teach the necessity of respect for the rights of person and property."

THUNDER ON THE LEFT   But if there was any real threat to Roosevelt in those years, it came from the hucksters of social nostrums, old and new. The most flamboyant of the group, by far, was Louisiana's "Kingfish," Sen. Huey P. Long, Jr. First as governor, then as political boss of the state, he had delivered to its citizens

The "Kingfish," Huey Long of Louisiana. [Keystone Photos]

tax favors, roads, schools, free textbooks, charity hospitals, and generally better public services, all at the cost of corruption and personal dictatorship. Louisiana, however, became only the base from which he ventured out to conquer other worlds. The vehicle was Long's Share Our Wealth program, first unveiled in 1932 and refined over the next three years. In one version Long proposed to liquidate large personal fortunes, guarantee every family an allowance of $5,000, every worker an annual income of $2,500, grant pensions to the aged, reduce the hours of labor, pay veterans' bonuses, and assure a college education for every qualified student. His book *Every Man a King* (1933) held out the promise of economic security for all. Whether he had a workable plan or not, his scheme dramatized a fundamental issue in a society that had solved the problem of production but not that of distribution, an issue few politicians were so imprudent as to tackle directly. By early 1935 Huey Long was claiming 27,431 Share Our Wealth Clubs and a file of 7.5 million names.

Another scheme came from a California doctor, Francis E. Townsend. Outraged by the sight of three haggard old women raking through garbage cans in Long Beach, Townsend proposed pensions for the aged. In January 1934 he and Robert Clements, a real-estate promoter, founded Old Age Revolving Pensions, Limited, to promote the Townsend Plan of paying $200 a month to every citizen over sixty who retired from employment and promised to spend the money within the month. The plan had the lure of providing both security for the aged and job openings for the young. As the Townsend Clubs grew, critics noted that the cost would be more than half the national income. "I'm not in the least interested in the cost of the plan," Townsend blandly told a House committee.

A third huckster of panaceas, Father Charles E. Coughlin, the "radio priest" of the Shrine of the Little Flower in Royal Oak, Michigan, founded the National Union for Social Justice in 1934. In broadcasts over the CBS network, he specialized in schemes for the coinage of silver and attacks on bankers which carried growing overtones of anti-Semitism.

Coughlin, Townsend, and Long drew support largely from a lower middle class squeezed by the depression. Of the three, Long had the widest following. A canvass by the Democratic National Committee showed that he could draw 5–6 million votes as a third-party candidate for president, perhaps enough to undermine Roosevelt's chances of reelection.

A new militancy and new drives to organize labor added to the "thunder on the left." Beset by pressures from both ends of the political spectrum, Roosevelt drifted through months of hesitation before deciding to "steal the thunder" from the left with new programs of reform and social security. Political pressures impelled Roosevelt, but so did the growing influence of Justice Brandeis, Felix Frankfurter, and the Frankfurter protégés (the "little hot dogs") Thomas G. Corcoran, a presidential assistant, and Benjamin V. Cohen at Interior. These men urged Roosevelt to be less cozy with big business and to push for restored competition and heavy taxes on large corporations.

LIGHTNING FROM THE COURT What finally galvanized the president into action was the behavior of the Supreme Court. Early in 1935 the Court for the first time struck down a piece of New Deal legislation, a provision of the National Industrial Recovery Act forbidding interstate shipment of "hot oil"—oil produced in excess of quotas set by the states. A few weeks later the gold resolution of 1933, which abandoned the gold standard, was barely upheld on a close vote of 5 to 4. Then on May 27, 1935, the Court in three decisions annulled a farm mortgage relief act, found that the president had used his removal power wrongfully, and killed the National Industrial Recovery Act by unanimous vote.

In *Schechter Poultry Corporation v. United States*, quickly tagged the "sick chicken" case, the defendants, who sold to kosher retailers, had been convicted of selling an "unfit chicken" and violating other code provisions as well. The high court ruled that Congress had delegated too much power to the executive when it granted the code-making authority and had exceeded its power under the commerce clause. Chief Justice Hughes's opinion held that the poultry in question had "come to permanent rest within the state," although it had been moved across state lines. In a press conference soon afterward, Roosevelt said: "We have been relegated to the horse-and-buggy definition of interstate commerce." The same line of reasoning, he warned, might endanger much of the New Deal program.

LEGISLATIVE ACHIEVEMENTS   In June Roosevelt ended the stalemate in Congress and launched the so-called Second New Deal with demands for "must" legislation, most of which was already pending. Congress passed these measures with a rush:

July 5	The Wagner National Labor Relations Act, guaranteeing the right of labor to organize and bargain collectively
August 14	The Social Security Act, providing unemployment and old-age insurance and public welfare programs
August 23	The Banking Act of 1935, strengthening the Federal Reserve System
August 28	The Wheeler-Rayburn Public Utility Holding Company Act, preventing the pyramiding of holding companies
August 30	The Revenue Act of 1935, the "Soak the Rich" tax
August 30	The Guffey-Snyder Coal Act, setting up the "little NRA"

The National Labor Relations Act, often called the Wagner Act, gave workers the right to bargain through unions of their own choice and prohibited employers from interfering with union activities. A National Labor Relations Board of five members could supervise plant elections and certify unions as bargaining agents where a majority of the workers approved. The board could also investigate the actions of employers and issue "cease and desist" orders against specified unfair practices. Under the protection of the law, union activities quickly intensified.

The Wagner Act salvaged the labor guarantees of Section 7a of the National Industrial Recovery Act, while other measures revived other parts of the NIRA. The Public Contracts Act applied NRA wage and hour standards to work under government contracts. The Guffey-Snyder Coal Act established for the coal industry alone a "little NRA," but it too fell before the Supreme Court in 1936 and never became operative. The Guffey-Vinson Coal Act of 1937 set up a Bituminous Coal Commission which enforced minimum prices and certain fair-marketing rules, but that act expired in 1943. The oil code gave way in August 1935 to an interstate compact among seventeen oil states by which they agreed to standard practices regulated by the states.

The Social Security Act of 1935, Roosevelt said, was the New Deal's "cornerstone" and "supreme achievement." In common parlance "social security" came to mean the national Old-Age and Survivors' Insurance, under which workers and employers contributed payroll taxes to cover annuities paid to those who retired after age sixty-five. But that was only one of the act's three major provisions. The act also set up a shared federal-state plan of unemployment insurance and committed the national government to a broad range of welfare activities. The principle was that "unemployables"—people who were unable to work— would remain a state responsibility while the national government would provide work relief for the able-bodied. To that end the law inaugurated grants-in-aid for three public assistance programs—old age assistance, aid for dependent children, aid for the blind—and further aid for maternal, child welfare, and public health services. Congress had already passed in April a $4.8-billion bill providing work relief for jobless workers. To manage these programs, the Works Progress Administration (WPA), headed by Harry L. Hopkins, replaced the Federal Emergency Relief Administration. The act did not provide a dole which, Roosevelt told Congress, had been "a narcotic, a subtle destroyer of the human spirit. . . ."

"Yes, You Remembered Me"

The social legislation of the Second New Deal prompted this cartoon of FDR as the friend of "The Forgotten Man." [Library of Congress]

Hopkins favored the lighter public works which would provide jobs quickly, with the consequence that some jobs appeared to be make-work or mere "leaning on shovels." But before its death in World War II the WPA left permanent monuments on the landscape in the form of buildings, bridges, hard-surfaced roads, airports, and schools. The WPA employed a wide range of talents, often saving them from atrophy, in the Federal Theater Project, the Federal Art Project, and the Federal Writers' Project. The National Youth Administration, under WPA, gave part-time employment to students, set up technical training programs, and provided aid to jobless youth. Although WPA took care of only about 3 million out of some 10 million jobless at any one time, in all it tided some 9 million clients over desperate times before it expired in 1943.

The Banking Act of 1935 strengthened the control of the Federal Reserve Board over rediscount rates and reserve requirements, and diminished the power of private bankers in the money market. It accomplished this by concentrating in the board's hands all open-market operations—that is, the buying or selling of government securities to increase (by buying) or decrease (by selling) the money supply. The act greatly strengthened the board's control of the whole monetary system.

The Public Utility Holding Company Act struck at financial corruption in the public utility industry. Like railroads in the 1800s, utilities in their early stages of growth had spawned buccaneers interested more in manipulation than in good business. The act passed despite the high-pressure lobbying tactics of the utilities which, Rep. Sam Rayburn said later, could "produce more noise and fewer votes than any crowd I ever saw."

The final measure endorsed by Roosevelt and the last of the major laws passed during this period was the Revenue Act of 1935, sometimes called the Wealth Tax Act, but popularly known as the "Soak-the-Rich" tax. In asking for the law, Roosevelt told Congress: "Our revenue laws have operated in many ways to the unfair advantage of the few, and they have done little to prevent an unjust concentration of wealth and economic power." The Revenue Act raised surtax rates on incomes above $50,000, and steeply graduated taxes on incomes above $5 million to a maximum of 75 percent on incomes above $5 million. Estate and gift taxes went up, as did the corporate tax on all but small corporations—those with less than $50,000 income. Congress even added to Roosevelt's recommendations an "excess profits" levy on corporate earnings above 10 percent.

The Philadelphia *Inquirer* accused the president of "a bald political stroke . . . to lure hosannas from the something-for-nothing followers of Huey Long, 'Doc' Townsend . . . and the whole tribe of false prophets.'' By "soaking" the rich and enacting Social Security he did indeed steal much of the thunder from the left, although the results fell short of the promise. The new tax law failed to increase revenue significantly, nor did it result in a redistribution of income: the wealthiest 1 percent of the nation in fact slightly increased its share of the wealth after the tax took effect. At the same time the hoopla over "soaking the rich" obscured the more significant impact of both the Social Security payroll tax, which was regressive—that is, it fell more heavily on lower incomes—and the policy of returning indigents to the care of the states. Most states, insofar as they assumed this burden, raised the needed revenue with sales taxes, which were also regressive. Such taxes impeded recovery by reducing total purchasing power.

The viewpoint of the time was that Roosevelt had moved in a radical direction. But the extent of the new departure taken by the Second New Deal is easy to exaggerate. Such measures as work relief, Social Security, utility regulation, and progressive income taxes had long been in the works in Congress. The president himself had little use for theoretical speculation. He was still pursuing the bold experiments he promised before the election. "Roosevelt's program," the historian William E. Leuchtenburg has written, "rested on the assumption that a just society could be secured by imposing a welfare state on a capitalist foundation."

THE ELECTION OF 1936 Whatever economic or philosophical judgment might be passed on the New Deal program, Roosevelt's political instincts were acute. Businessmen fumed over his tax and spending policies. The wealthy resented their loss of status and the growing power of government and labor. They vented an intemperate rage against Roosevelt, whom they called "a traitor to his own class," and against all the works of the New Deal. So many landmarks of a once stable and secure world now seemed threatened, from the gold standard itself to a man's right to run his business as he saw fit. Hoover called the New Deal an attack on "the whole philosophy of individual liberty." Visitors at the home of J. P. Morgan, Jr., were cautioned not to mention Roosevelt's name lest it raise his blood pressure. But the conservative coalition of business and wealth, by its incoherent rage, made a perfect foil for the confident president.

The popularity of the president and his policies impelled the

Come along, we're going to the Trans-Lux to hiss Roosevelt. *Peter Arno's 1936 cartoon satirizes the resentment felt by many of the wealthy for Roosevelt.* [© The New Yorker]

Republican convention in 1936 to avoid candidates too closely identified with the "hate-Roosevelt" contingent. The party chose Gov. Alfred M. Landon of Kansas, a former Bull Moose Progressive, who had fought the Ku Klux Klan, supported civil liberties, and favored regulation of business. While conservative in matters of finance, Landon had endorsed many programs of the New Deal. The most progressive Republican candidate in years, he was probably more liberal than most of his backers, and clearly more so than the party's platform, which accused the New Deal of usurping power. For vice-president the party nominated the more conservative Frank Knox, a newspaper publisher, former Bull Mooser, and one of the original Rough Riders.

Landon started the campaign on a moderate note, arguing that a Republican president could achieve the objectives of the New Deal more efficiently and thriftily. But as the campaign progressed, his statements became more and more conservative. Before the end, Republican party leaders even tried to make an issue of the Social Security program, which they denounced as dangerous "regimentation." The Social Security Act, said Knox, "puts half the working people of America under federal control." Republican Chairman John D. M. Hamilton warned that every worker would have to wear metal dogtags bearing his Social Security number.

Such appeals carried little weight. The chief hope of the Republicans was that the followers of Coughlin, Townsend, and other dissidents would combine to draw enough votes away from Roosevelt to throw the election to them. But that possibility faded when an assassin gunned down Huey Long. Coughlin,

Townsend, and a remnant of the Long movement did support Rep. William Lemke of North Dakota on a Union party ticket, but it was a forlorn and foredoomed effort that polled only 882,000 votes.

In 1936 Roosevelt was able to forge a new electoral coalition which would affect national politics for years to come. While holding the support of most traditional Democrats North and South, FDR made strong gains among beneficiaries of the farm program in the West. In the northern cities he held on to the strong support of ethnic groups helped by New Deal welfare measures and afforded greater recognition in appointments. Middle-class voters, whose property had been saved by New Deal measures, flocked to Roosevelt's support, along with intellectuals stirred by the ferment of new ideas in government. The revived labor movement threw its support to Roosevelt, and Socialist voters deserted Norman Thomas for the New Deal coalition. In the most profound new departure of all, black voters for the first time cast the majority of their ballots for a Democratic president. "My friends, go home and turn Lincoln's picture to the wall," Robert L. Vann of the Pittsburgh *Courier* told black Republicans. "That debt has been paid in full." In perhaps the most seismic and enduring change in the political landscape during the 1930s, a majority of politically active blacks moved away from their traditional adherence to the Republican party.

Roosevelt campaigned with tremendous buoyancy. In his acceptance speech to the Democratic convention in Philadelphia he dropped efforts to reassure businessmen. As the Americans of 1776 had sought freedom from political autocracy, he said, the Americans of 1936 sought freedom from the "economic royalists" who had created "a new despotism." "They complain that we seek to overthrow the institutions of America. What they really complain of is that we seek to take away their power." The campaign closed on an even more strident note, when Roosevelt spoke at Madison Square Garden: "I should like to have it said of my first Administration that in it the forces of selfishness and of lust for power met their match. I should like to have it said of my second administration that in it these forces met their master."

On November 3 the election went as Democratic Chairman James A. Farley had predicted. Roosevelt carried every state except Maine and Vermont with a popular vote of 27.7 million to Landon's 16.7 million, and won what was the closest to a unanimous electoral vote since Monroe's victory in 1820, by 523 to 8. Democrats would dominate Republicans in the new Congress, by 77 to 19 in the Senate and 328 to 107 in the House. The editor William Allen White of Emporia, Kansas, wrote: "The water of liberalism has been dammed up for forty years by the two major parties. The dam is out. Landon went down the creek in a torrent." Roosevelt himself said he felt as if he had experienced "baptism by total immersion."

SECOND-TERM SETBACKS AND INITIATIVES

But as Jefferson and Jackson found (and Lyndon Johnson and Richard Nixon also discovered), some malevolent fate often seems to have it in for presidents who win such victories, and Roosevelt found himself deluged in a sea of troubles over the next year. Roosevelt's Second Inaugural Address, given on January 20, 1937, suggested that he was ready to move toward even further reform. The challenge of American democracy, he said, was that millions of citizens "at this very moment are denied the greater part of what the very lowest standards of today call the necessities of life. . . . I see one-third of a nation ill-housed, ill-clad, ill-nourished." The election of 1936 had been a mandate for extensive reform, he argued; and the overwhelming Democratic majorities in Congress ensured passage. But one major roadblock stood in the way: the Supreme Court.

THE COURT-PACKING PLAN   By the end of the 1936 term the Court had ruled against New Deal laws in seven of the nine major cases it reviewed. Having struck down both major accomplishments of the First New Deal, the AAA and the NRA, the Court moved on in 1936 to rule against the Guffey Coal Act. In the spring of 1936 it denied that states had the power to fix minimum wages. Since it had already ruled, in 1923, that the federal government had no such power, it had left, as Roosevelt protested, a " 'no-man's land,' where no Government—State or Federal" could act. Suits against the Social Security and Wagner Labor Relations Acts now pended. Given the established trend of rulings, often by margins of 5 to 4 or 6 to 3, the Second New Deal seemed in danger of being nullified like the first.

For that reason, Roosevelt and Attorney-General Homer Cummings decided to do something about the Court. Avenues of action included seeking a constitutional amendment, or having Congress limit the cases subject to the Court's review. Roosevelt and Cummings took neither of these courses, deciding finally to change the Court by enlarging it, a move for which there was ample precedent and power. Congress, not the Constitution, determined the size of the Court, which at different times had numbered six, seven, nine, and ten justices, and in 1937 numbered nine. On February 5 Roosevelt sent his plan to Congress, without having consulted congressional leaders or more than a few within his administration. He wanted to create up to fifty new federal judges, including six new Supreme Court justices, and to diminish the power of the judges who had served ten or more years or reached the age of seventy.

The "court-packing" maneuver, as opponents quickly tagged it, handed a viable issue to men who previousy had shunned a fight with Roosevelt. The plan was a shade too contrived. In implying that some judges were impaired by senility, it affronted the elder statesmen of Congress, and especially Louis D. Brandeis, who was both the oldest and the most liberal of the justices. It ran headlong into a deep-rooted veneration of the courts and aroused fears that another president might use the precedent for quite different purposes. Sen. Carter Glass of Virginia feared "the reversal of those decisions of the Court that saved the civilization of the South," by which he meant decisions upholding white supremacy. The newsman Oswald Garrison Villard warned, on the other hand, that "a future Woodrow Wilson could pack the Supreme Court so that no Negro could get within a thousand miles of justice. . . ." In the Senate the Republicans shrewdly stood aside while the Democrats plunged into a family squabble.

As it turned out, no direct vote ever tested senatorial convictions on the matter. Unforeseen events blunted Roosevelt's drive to change the Court. A sequence of Court decisions that spring reversed previous judgments in order to uphold a Washington state minimum-wage law, the Wagner Act, and the Social Security Act. Chief Justice Charles Evans Hughes testified that the Court had kept up with its docket. Conservative Justice Willis Van Devanter resigned, and Roosevelt named to the vacancy one of the most consistent New Dealers, Sen. Hugo Black of Alabama. In mid-July the sudden death of Senate Majority Leader Joseph T. Robinson redirected attention to the divisive struggle for leadership, and the court bill went back to the Judiciary Committee, which had reported it unfavorably in the first place.

Finally, in August, Vice-President Garner arranged a settlement providing reforms in court procedures and more generous retirement provisions, but adding no new judges. Roosevelt later claimed he had lost the battle but won the war. The Court had reversed itself on important New Deal legislation, and Roosevelt was able to appoint justices in harmony with the New Deal. But

Roosevelt's "court-packing" scheme aroused strong opposition from fellow Democrats. The Democratic donkey here kicks up a storm. [Library of Congress]

it was a pyrrhic victory which sowed dissension in his party and blighted Roosevelt's own prestige. For the first time Democrats in large numbers deserted the "champ," and the opposition found an issue on which it could openly take the field. During the first eight months of 1937 the momentum of Roosevelt's great 1936 victory was lost.

A NEW DIRECTION FOR LABOR   Rebellions erupted on other fronts even while the Court bill pended. Under the impetus of the New Deal the moribund labor movement stirred anew. When Section 7a of the National Industrial Recovery Act demanded in every industry code a statement of the workers' right to organize, alert unionists quickly translated it to mean "The President wants you to join the union." John L. Lewis of the United Mine Workers was among the first to exploit the spirit of the Blue Eagle. Leading a union decimated by depression, he rebuilt it from 150,000 members to 500,000 within a year. Spurred by the mine workers' example, Sidney Hillman of the Amalgamated Clothing Workers and David Dubinsky of the International Ladies Garment Workers joined Lewis in promoting a campaign to organize workers in the mass-production industries. As leaders of some of the few industrial unions in the AFL, they found the craft unions to be obstacles to organizing the basic industries.

In 1934 they persuaded the AFL and its president William Green to charter industrial unions in the unorganized industries. But Green and other craft unionists saw these "federal" unions as temporary pools from which to draw members into the crafts. Lewis and the industrial unionists saw them as a chance to organize on a massive scale. In 1935, with passage of the Wagner Act, action began in earnest. The industrial unionists formed a Committee for Industrial Organization (CIO) and craft unionists began to fear submergence by the mass unions. Jurisdictional disputes divided them, and in 1936 the AFL expelled the CIO unions, which then formed a permanent structure called after 1938 the Congress of Industrial Organizations. The rivalry spurred both groups to greater efforts.

The CIO's major organizing drives in automobiles and steel began in 1936, but until the Supreme Court upheld the Wagner Act in 1937 there was little compliance with unions on the part of industry. There was instead widespread use by industry of blacklisting, private detectives, labor spies, vigilante groups, and intimidation. Early in 1937 automobile workers spontaneously adopted a new technique, the "sit-down strike," in which workers refused to leave the shop until the employers granted collective bargaining. Many employers and much of the public saw in such revolutionary tactics a threat to property rights, an alarming gesture of contempt for authority, and further evidence of the New Deal's evil influence. Union leaders, fearing a backlash of public opinion, frowned on the tactic, but it brought the first union victory in a major industry. In February 1937 General Motors recognized the United Automobile Workers as bargaining agent for its employees. The following month, United States Steel capitulated to the Steel Workers Organizing Committee (later the United Steelworkers of America), granting it recognition, a 10 percent wage hike, and a forty-hour week.

Having captured two giants of heavy industry, the CIO went on in the next few years to organize much of industrial America: rubber, oil, electronics, and a good part of the textile industry, in which unionists had to fight protracted struggles to organize scattered plants. The laggard pace in textiles denied the CIO a major victory in the South comparable to its swift conquest of autos and steel, but even there a labor movement appeared that was at last something more than a vehicle for sporadic revolt. Some of the giants of heavy industry held out for yet a few years. The "Little Steel" companies, led by Tom Girdler of Republic Steel, and the Big Four meat-packers remained adamant, but all had capitulated by the end of 1941. Violence punctuated these struggles, most vividly at Girdler's Republic Steel plant in Chicago where police killed ten strikers on Memorial Day in 1937. Company guards brutally beat up Walter Reuther and other organizers at Henry Ford's River Rouge plant in Detroit. In Harlan County, Kentucky, deputized company hoodlums conducted a reign of terror until the NLRB forced operators to bargain with the United Mine Workers late in 1938.

Union organizing drives were helped by the sympathy or at least neutrality of public officials. In Michigan, for instance, Gov. Frank Murphy refused to use troops against sit-down strikers. The Wagner Act put the power of the federal government behind the principle of unionization. In the Congress, a Senate subcommittee under Robert M. La Folette, Jr., exposed practices of violence against unions, while President Roosevelt, though opposed to the tactic, refused to use force against sit-downers. The unions, he said, would soon learn that they could not continue to use a "damned unpopular" tactic. Roosevelt himself had come late to the support of unions and sometimes took exception to their behavior. In the fall of 1937 he became so irritated with the warfare between Lewis and Girdler that he pronounced "a plague on both your houses." The grandiloquent Lewis responded: "It ill behooves one who has supped at labor's table and who has been sheltered in labor's house to curse with equal fervor and fine impartiality both labor and its adversaries when they become locked in a deadly embrace." In 1940 an angry Lewis would back the Republican presidential candidate, but he would be unable to carry labor with him. As workers became more organized, they became more identified with the Democratic party.

A SLUMPING ECONOMY   Beset by the divisive effects of the Court fight and the sit-down strikes, the New Deal in the fall of 1937 also faced a renewed depression. The years 1935 and 1936 had been marked by steady economic improvement. By the spring of 1937 output had moved above the 1929 level. Then in August the economy suddenly cracked, and in the following months it slid into a deep business slump, which the press called a "recession" to distinguish it from the "depression." Actually the collapse was sharper than that in 1929. The Dow-Jones stock averages fell from 190 in August to 115 in October. The New York *Times* business index in the same period went from 110 to 85, back to the level of 1935. By the end of the year 2 million people had been thrown out of work; scenes of the earlier depression reappeared.

The prosperity of early 1937 had been achieved largely through governmental spending. On top of relief and public-works outlays, Congress in 1936 had provided for cash payments of veterans' bonuses upon demand. But in June 1937 Roosevelt, worried about deficits and inflation, ordered sharp cuts in spending. At the same time the Treasury began to diminish disposable income by collecting $2 billion in Social Security taxes.

In 1937, the "American Way" remained out of reach for many. [Photograph by Margaret Bourke-White, Life magazine, © 1965, Time, Inc.]

Private spending could not fill the gap left by reductions in government spending, and business still lacked the faith to risk large investments. The result was the slump of 1937.

The recession brought to a head a fierce debate within the administration. One group, led by Treasury Secretary Henry Morgenthau, Jr., favored less spending and a balanced budget. The slow pace of recovery, Morgenthau thought, resulted from the reluctance of business to invest, and that in turn from fear that federal spending would bring inflation and heavy taxes. The other group, which included Harry Hopkins and Harold Ickes, argued for renewed spending. The recession, they noted, had come just when the budget was brought into balance. "The Government," said another supporter of this view, "must be the compensatory agent in this economy; it must unbalance its budget during the deflation and create surpluses in periods of great business activity."

This view echoed that of the English economist John Maynard Keynes, who had given extended development to the idea in his book *The General Theory of Employment, Interest and Money* (1936). Keynesian economics offered a convenient theoretical justification for what New Dealers had already done in pragmatic response to existing conditions. Many, if not most, of the liberals attracted by Keynesian fiscal policies also subscribed to Brandeisian opposition to monopoly, which held that competition provided the best condition for a thriving economy. "Administered" prices, they argued, held back recovery. When demand slackened, large-scale industries could maintain their prices while cutting production and employment. This camp called for antitrust investigations and action. Their views marked a sharp break with the early New Deal's emphasis on regulation.

ECONOMIC POLICY AND REFORM   Roosevelt waited as the rival theorists sought his approval. "As I see it," Morgenthau remarked, "what you are doing now is treading water . . . to wait to see what happens this spring." Roosevelt responded: "Absolutely." When spring failed to bring recovery, Roosevelt endorsed the ideas of the spenders and antitrusters. On April 14, 1938, he asked Congress to adopt a large-scale spending program, and Congress voted $33 billion mainly for public works by the PWA and the WPA, with lesser amounts for other programs. In a short time the increase in spending reversed the economy's decline, but the recession and Roosevelt's reluctance to adopt the massive spending called for in Keynesian theory forestalled the achievement of full recovery by the end of the decade. Only during World War II would full production and full employment be achieved.

On April 29, two weeks after his spending message, Roosevelt asked Congress to look into the concentration of economic power. Congress responded by setting up the Temporary National Economic Committee, which drew half its members from Congress and half from federal agencies, with Sen. Joseph O'Mahoney of Wyoming as chairman. It was the first major inquiry of the sort since the Pujo committee reported on the money trust in 1912. Over a period of three years the TNEC produced thirty-nine volumes of testimony and forty-three monographs, a treasure trove of information on the economy. Meanwhile Thurman Arnold, named chief of the Justice Department's Antitrust Division in 1938, swung into action. Within five years he filed almost as many antitrust suits as had been brought previously since passage of the Sherman Act in 1890, but neither he nor the TNEC was able to accomplish much of substance before national defense took precedence. Like earlier antitrust efforts, this one turned out to be largely ceremonial.

The Court fight, the sit-down strikes, and the recession in 1937 all undercut Roosevelt's prestige and dissipated the mandate of the 1936 elections. When the 1937 session ended, the only major new reforms enacted for the benefit of the "ill-housed, ill-fed, and ill-clad" were the Wagner-Steagall National

Housing Act and the Bankhead-Jones Farm Tenant Act. In 1938 came three more major reforms, the last of the New Deal era: the second Agricultural Adjustment Act, the Food, Drug and Cosmetic Act, and the Fair Labor Standards Act.

The Housing Act set up the United States Housing Authority (USHA) in the Department of the Interior, which extended long-term loans to local agencies willing to assume part of the cost for slum clearance and public housing. The agency also subsidized low rents. Later, during World War II, it financed housing in connection with defense projects.

The Farm Tenant Act addressed the problem of rural poverty, which in some ways the New Deal's larger farm program had aggravated. Tenants were supposed to be kept on in spite of government-sponsored cutbacks in production, but landlords often made the most of cutbacks by evicting workers and withholding their shares of benefit payments. Social scientists and journalists called attention to the problem, and in northeastern Arkansas tenant farmers themselves found voice when they organized the Southern Tenant Farmers' Union (STFU) in 1934. The union, however, was never able to function effectively in collective bargaining with what one of its founders, H. L. Mitchell, called "an industry that is disorganized, pauperized and kept alive only by government subsidy." But the union did focus public attention on the problem. Some programs offered loans and grants to keep farmers off the relief rolls, and several cooperative farming communities grew up with New Deal support. These scattered efforts were regrouped into the Resettlement Administration (RA), created by executive order in 1935.

Then, on the recommendation of a President's Committee on Farm Tenancy, Congress in 1937 passed the Tenant Act, administered by a new agency, the Farm Security Administration (FSA). The program made available rehabilitation loans to shore up marginal farmers and prevent their sinking into tenancy. It also made loans to tenants for purchase of their own farms. But the idea of small homesteads by the late 1930s was, as the STFU warned, "an economic anachronism, doomed to failure." American mythology still exalted the family farm, but in reality the ever-larger agricultural unit predominated. In the end the FSA proved to be little more than another relief operation which tided a few farmers over difficult times. A more effective answer to the problem, sadly, awaited mobilization for war, which took many tenants off into the military services or defense industries, broadened their horizons, and taught them new skills.

The Agricultural Adjustment Act of 1938 was a response to renewed crop surpluses and price declines during the recession. It reenacted the basic devices of the earlier AAA, with some new twists. Before government could apply marketing quotas to a given crop, for instance, it had to hold a plebiscite among the growers and win a two-thirds majority. The new Food, Drug and Cosmetic Act broadened the coverage of the 1906 Pure Food and Drug Act and forbade the use of false or misleading advertising. Enforcement of the advertising provision became the responsibility of the Federal Trade Commission. The Fair Labor Standards Act applied to enterprises which operated in or affected interstate commerce. It set a minimum wage of 40¢ an hour and a maximum workweek of forty hours, to be put into effect over several years. The act also prohibited child labor under the age of sixteen, and in hazardous occupations under eighteen.

The Legacy of the New Deal

SETBACKS FOR THE PRESIDENT   As the New Deal turned its focus less on recovery and more on reform, an effective opposition emerged within the president's party, especially in the southern wing. Local power elites in the South felt that the New Deal jeopardized their position. They felt threatened too when in 1936 the Democratic convention eliminated the two-thirds rule for nominations, thereby removing the South's veto power, and seated Negro delegates. Southern Democrats were at best uneasy bedfellows with organized labor and blacks. Consequently some of them drifted toward coalition with conservative Republicans. By the end of 1937 a conservative bloc, if unorganized and mutable, had appeared.

In 1938 the conservative opposition stymied an executive reorganization bill amid cries that it would lead to dictatorship. They also secured drastic cuts in the undistributed-profits and capital-gains taxes to help restore business "confidence." The House set up a Committee on Un-American Activities chaired by Martin Dies of Texas who took to the warpath against Communists. Soon he began to brand New Dealers as Red Dupes. "Stalin baited his hook with a 'progressive' worm," Dies wrote in 1940, "and New Deal suckers swallowed bait, hook, line, and sinker."

As the political season of 1938 advanced Roosevelt unfolded a new idea as momentous as the Court plan—a proposal to reshape the Democratic party in the image of the New Deal. On June 24 he announced his purpose to intervene in Democratic primaries as the party leader, "charged with the responsibility of carrying out the definitely liberal declaration of principles set forth in the 1936 Democratic platform." The effort ended in a standoff. The administration ousted only one of its opponents, John O'Connor of New York, chairman of the House Rules Committee; the opposition displaced Sen. James Pope of Idaho. Administration defeats in efforts to unseat Sen. Walter George of Georgia, "Cotton Ed" Smith of South Carolina, and Millard Tydings of Maryland broke the spell of presidential invincibility, or what was left of it. As in the Court fight, Roosevelt had risked his prestige while handing his adversaries persuasive issues. His opponents tagged his intervention in the primaries an attempted "purge"; the word evoked visions of Adolf Hitler and Josef Stalin, tyrants who had purged their Nazi and Communist parties in blood.

The elections of November 1938 handed the administration another setback, a result partly of the friction among Democrats. Their majority in the House fell from 229 to 93, in the Senate from 56 to 42. The margins remained large, but the president headed a restive and divided party. In his State of the Union message in January 1939 Roosevelt for the first time proposed no new reforms, but spoke of the need "to invigorate the process of recovery, in order to *preserve* our reforms." In 1939 the administration won an extension of Social Security and finally put through its reorganization plan. Under the Administrative Reorganization Act the president could "reduce, coordinate, consolidate, and reorganize" the agencies of government. Plans proposed by the president became effective in sixty days unless disapproved by concurrent resolution of Congress.

But the opposition was now able to cut relief expenditures, eliminate the Federal Theater Project, reject Roosevelt appointments, and abolish the undistributed-profits tax. The House set up an investigation of the NLRB under the hostile Howard W. Smith of Virginia, and attempted to narrow the scope of the wage-hour law. The conservative coalition and the administration had reached a standoff.

EMERGENCE OF THE BROKER STATE   The New Deal had lost momentum, but it had wrought some enduring changes. By the end of the 1930s the power of the national government was vastly enlarged over what it had been in 1932. Government had taken on the duty of ensuring the economic and social stability of the country. It had established minimum standards for labor conditions and public welfare. It had helped middle-class Americans hold on to their savings, their homes, and their farms. The protection afforded by deposit insurance, unemployment pay, and Social Security pensions would come to be universally accepted as a safeguard against such disasters as the depression.

Roosevelt had steered a course between the extremes of laissez-faire and socialism. The first New Deal had experimented for a time with a managed economy under the NRA, but had abandoned that experiment for a turn toward enforcing competition and priming the economy with government spendings. The effect of heavy governmental expenditures, which finally produced full employment during World War II, seemed to confirm the arguments of Keynesians.

But the old progressive formulation of regulation versus trust-busting had finally been superseded by the rise of the "broker state," a government which mediated among major interest groups. Government's role was to act as an honest broker protecting a variety of interests, not just business but workers, farmers, consumers, small business, and the unemployed.

Roosevelt himself, impatient with theory, was a pragmatist in developing policy: he kept what worked and discarded what did not. The result was, paradoxically, both profoundly revolutionary and profoundly conservative. The New Deal left America greatly changed in many ways, its economy more socialized than before. At the same time it left the basic capitalistic structure of the economic system in place. "For a permanent correction of grave weaknesses in our economic system," Roosevelt said, "we have relied on new applications of old democratic processes."

FURTHER READING

A sound introduction to the decade of the New Deal is in William E. Leuchtenberg's *Franklin D. Roosevelt and the New Deal, 1932–1940* (1963).° Arthur M. Schlesinger, Jr., provides a more detailed account in *The Age of Roosevelt* (3 vols.; 1957–1960). A more critical interpretation of the same policies can be found in Paul Conkin's *The New Deal* (1968).° Valuable for a balance of interpretation is Otis L. Graham, Jr.'s *The New Deal: The Critical Issues* (1971). Also helpful is Frank Friedel's *Launching the New Deal* (1973), particularly for its coverage of the One Hundred Days.

Susan Estabrook Kennedy's *The Banking Crisis of 1933* (1973) details the effects of the Banking Holiday and subsequent reforms. James T. Patterson's *The New Deal and the States* (1969) examines how initial welfare aid was channeled into local agencies. Van L. Perkins looks at

°These books are available in paperback editions.

farming in *Crisis in Agriculture* (1969), and Sidney Baldwin explores the plight of tenant farmers in *Poverty and Politics: The Rise and Decline of the Farm Security Administration* (1968). Michael Parrish's *Security Regulation and the New Deal* (1970) and Ellis Hawley's *The New Deal and the Problem of Monopoly* (1966) analyze government attempts to forestall another market crash. Robert F. Himmelberg's *The Origins of the National Recovery Act* (1976) and Bernard Bellush's *The Failure of the NRA* (1977) study government relations with business. John Salmond's *The Civilian Conservation Corps* (1967) is insightful. Social Security is covered in Roy Lubove's *The Struggle for Social Security, 1900–1937* (1968). For ideas of leading New Dealers, see Elliot Rosen's *Hoover, Roosevelt, and the Brains Trust* (1977), Otis L. Graham, Jr.'s *Toward a Planned Society: From Roosevelt to Nixon* (1976), and Marion Clawson's *New Deal Planning: The National Resources Planning Board* (1981). The bureaucratic side of reform is handled in Richard Polenberg's *Reorganizing Roosevelt's Government: The Controversy over Executive Reorganization, 1936–1939* (1966).

The New Deal can also be understood by studying its chief proponents. Frank Freidel's *Franklin D. Roosevelt* (4 vols.; 1952–1973) and Arthur Schlesinger's aforementioned *The Age of Roosevelt* are multivolume, detailed works. James MacGregor Burns's *Roosevelt: The Lion and the Fox* (1956)° is an astute political analysis. More personal is Joseph P. Lash's *Eleanor and Franklin: The Story of Their Relationship Based on Eleanor Roosevelt's Private Papers* (1971).° Some of Roosevelt's New Deal lieutenants have compiled memoirs about the decade. Among the better are Raymond Moley's *After Seven Years* (1937), Frances Perkins's *The Roosevelt I Knew* (1946), and Rexford G. Tugwell's *The Democratic Roosevelt* (1957). Studies about leading New Deal lieutenants include Paul A. Kurzman's *Harry Hopkins and the New Deal* (1974), George Martin's *Madam Secretary: Frances Perkins* (1976), and Linda J. Lear's *Harold L. Ickes: The Aggressive Progressive, 1874–1933* (1981). Peter H. Iron's *The New Deal Lawyers* (1982) studies those lieutenants as a social group. An interesting contrast is found in a study of how old Progressives reacted to New Deal reform; see Otis L. Graham, Jr.'s *Encore for Reform* (1967).

For scholarship about the various groups involved in the New Deal, consult Raymond Walters's *Negroes and the Great Depression* (1970), Harvard Sitkoff's *A New Deal for Blacks* (1978),° James T. Patterson's *Congressional Conservatism and the New Deal* (1967), and John M. Allswang's *A House of All People: Ethnic Politics in Chicago, 1890–1936* (1971). Works on the critics of the New Deal include T. Harry Williams's *Huey Long* (1969),° Abraham Holzman's *The Townsend Movement* (1963), Charles J. Tull's *Father Coughlin and the New Deal* (1965), and Alan Brinkley's *Voices of Protest: Huey Long, Father Coughlin, and the Great Depression* (1982).° For radical leftist reactions to reform, see Irving Howe's *The American Communist Party* (1957) and David Shannon's *The Socialist Party of America* (1955).

One particular interest group which was both supportive and critical of New Deal policies was organized labor, treated in books such as Irving Bernstein's *Turbulent Years: A History of the American Worker, 1933–1941* (1970), Sidney Fine's *Sitdown: The General Motors Strike of 1936–1937* (1969), Melvyn Dubofky and Warren Van Tine's *John L. Lewis: A Biography* (1977), and Jerold S. Auerbach's *Labor and Liberty: The La Follette Committee and the New Deal* (1966).

One region of the nation—the South—particularly concerned the New Dealers. The fullest introduction to the New Deal in the South remains the relevant chapters in George B. Tindall's *The Emergence of the New South, 1914–1945* (1967).° How the president dealt with the South is handled in Frank Friedel's *F.D.R. and the South* (1965). A more critical view of the New Deal's limitations is found in Paul Mertz's *The New Deal and Southern Rural Poverty* (1978). How southern farmers fared is examined in David E. Conrad's *The Forgotten Farmers: The Story of the Sharecroppers in the New Deal* (1972), Donald Grubb's *Cry from the Cotton: The Southern Tenant Farmers Union and the New Deal* (1971), and Pete Daniel's *The Shadow of Slavery: Peonage in the South, 1901–1969* (1972).° Thomas McCraw's *TVA and the Power Fight* (1971) and Phillip J. Funigiello's *Toward a National Power Policy: The New Deal and Electric Utility Industry, 1933–1941* (1973), detail federal efforts in public power regulation. Dan T. Carter provides an insightful analysis of the influence of the 1930s reforms on race relations in *Scottsboro: A Tragedy of the American South* (1969).°

For the cultural impact of the New Deal, consult Charles C. Alexander's *Nationalism in American Thought, 1930–1945* (1969), Richard H. Pells's *Radical Visions and American Dreams: Cultural and Social Thought in the Depression Years* (1973), Jane DeHart Mathews's *The Federal Theatre, 1935–1939* (1967), and Richard D. McKinzie's *The New Deal for Artists* (1973).

29

FROM ISOLATION TO
GLOBAL WAR

Postwar Isolationism

THE LEAGUE AND THE U.S.   In the late 1930s, as the winds of war swept Asia and Europe, the focus of American politics moved abruptly from domestic to foreign affairs. Another Democratic president had to shift attention from reform to preparedness and war. But between Wilson and Roosevelt lay two decades of isolation from foreign connections. The postwar mood of 1920 set the pattern. The voters expressed their yearning for normalcy, and President-elect Harding lost little time in indulging it by disposing of the League of Nations. "You just didn't want a surrender of the United States . . ." he told the people in his victory speech. "That's why you didn't care for the League, which is now deceased." The spirit of isolation found other expressions as well: the higher tariff walls, the Red Scare, the rage for "100 percent Americanism," and tight immigration laws by which a nation of immigrants all but shut the door to any more newcomers.

The United States may have felt the urge to leave a wicked world to its own devices, but it could hardly stop the world and get off. American business, despite the tariff walls, now had worldwide connections. American investments and loans abroad put in circulation the dollars that purchased American exports. Overseas possessions, moreover, directly involved the country in world affairs, especially in the Pacific. Even the League of Nations was too great a fact entirely to ignore, although messages from the League at first went unanswered by American diplomats. As late as 1922 Joseph C. Grew, then American ambassador to Switzerland, confessed anxiety that a reporter who saw him waiting for a friend outside League headquarters in Geneva might reveal the indiscretion. Before that year was out, however, the United States had "unofficial observers" at the League, and after 1924 gradually entered into joint efforts on such matters as the international trade in drugs and arms, the traffic in women and children, and a variety of economic, cultural, and technical conferences.

Americans had mixed feelings about adherence to the World Court. The Permanent Court of International Justice, established by the League at The Hague in 1922, was open to any country, whether a member of the League or not. The idea of bringing foreign disputes before a panel of jurists appealed to legal-minded Americans; the United States had in fact urged the idea at the Hague Peace Conferences of 1899 and 1907. Still, it smacked too much of extranational authority for isolationists, even though its jurisdiction was always optional. Repeated efforts to join the World Court therefore met with rebuff from the Senate. Franklin D. Roosevelt pressed the issue in 1935, and the Senate voted 52 to 36 in favor, but fell short of a two-thirds majority. American judges served on the Court panel, but the United States stayed out.

WAR DEBTS AND REPARATIONS Probably nothing did more to heighten American isolationism—or anti-American feeling in Europe—than the war-debt tangle. When in 1917 the Allies had begun to exhaust private credit in the United States, the government then advanced them funds first for the war effort and then for postwar reconstruction. A World War Foreign Debt Commission, created by Congress in 1922, renegotiated the Allied debt to America to a total of about $11.5 billion. Adding the interest payable over sixty-two years to this principal, the Allied debt came to something over $22 billion.

To Americans at large it all seemed a simple matter of obligation, but Europeans commonly had a different perception. In the first place, Americans who thought their loan money had flowed to Europe were wrong: most of it went toward purchases in the United States, which fueled the wartime boom. Then, too, the Allies held off the enemy at great cost of blood and treasure while the United States was raising an army. American states, the British noted, had been known to repudiate debts to British investors; and the French pointed out that they had never been repaid for help in the American Revolution. But most difficult were the practical problems of repayment. To get dollar exchange,

The War Debt Controversy. *The ghost of a French soldier asks America, "In your accounting, have you included my blood and that of my brother soldiers?" [Library of Congress]*

European debtors had to sell their goods to the United States, but tariff walls went higher in 1921 and 1922, and again in 1930, making debt payment problematic. Payment in gold would have undermined the European currencies. When the United States refused to relent, French newspapers rechristened Uncle Sam "l'Oncle Shylock."

The French and British insisted that they could pay America only as they collected reparations from Germany. Twice during the 1920s the resulting strain on Germany brought the structure of international payments to the verge of collapse, and both times the Reparations Commission called in private American bankers to work out rescue plans.

The whole structure finally did collapse during the Great Depression. In 1931 President Hoover negotiated a moratorium on both German reparations and Allied payment of war debts, thereby indirectly accepting the connection between the two. The purpose, among other things, was to shore up American private loans of several billion dollars in Germany, which for the time had kept the international credit structure intact. Once the United States had accepted the connection between reparations and war debt, the Allies virtually cancelled German reparations, reducing them in the Lausanne Agreement of 1932 to only $750 million, which was never paid. At the end of 1932, after Hoover's debt moratorium ended, most of the European countries defaulted on their war debts to the United States; by 1934 all but Finland had defaulted. In retaliation, Congress passed the Johnson Debt Default Act of 1934, which prohibited private loans to any such government.

ATTEMPTS AT DISARMAMENT Yet, for all the isolationist sentiment of the time, Wilsonian idealism had struck a responsive chord in the American people. A lingering doubt, tinged with guilt, haunted Americans about their rejection of the League. Before long the Harding people hit upon a happy substitute—disarmament. The conviction had grown after World War I that large armaments had been the war's cause, and that arms limitation would bring peace. The United States had no intention of maintaining a large army, but under the building program begun in 1916 the United States constructed a navy second only to that of Britain. Neither the British nor the Americans had much stomach for the cost of a naval armaments race with the other, but both shared a common concern with the alarming growth of Japanese power.

During and after the war Japanese-American relations grew increasingly strained. The United States objected to continued Japanese encroachments in Asia. In 1902 Japan had made a defensive alliance with Great Britain, directed then at Russia but invoked in 1914 against Germany in order to pick up German concessions and territories in the Far East. The Japanese quickly took the Shantung Peninsula and the islands of Micronesia, which Germany had purchased not long before from Spain. The Paris Peace Conference reluctantly confirmed Japanese seizure of the Shantung Peninsula, and the League of Nations authorized a Japanese mandate of Micronesia north of the equator. Occupation of Micronesia put the Japanese squarely athwart eastern approaches to the Philippines.

During the war the Japanese had seized the chance for further moves against China. In 1915 the cabinet at Tokyo issued what came to be known as the Twenty-one Demands, which would have brought China virtually under Japanese control. The United States protested, and fortunately the Japanese decided not to force their most rigorous demands. In 1917, after the United States entered the war, Viscount Kikujiro Ishii visited Washington to secure American recognition of Japan's position in Asia, dropping hints that Germany had several times tried to get Japan to quit the war. To forestall such a result, Secretary of State Lansing entered an ambiguous agreement that "territorial propinquity creates special relations between countries" and therefore "Japan has special interests [translated by the Japanese as 'paramount interests'] in China." Americans were unhappy with the Lansing-Ishii Agreement, but it was feared that this was the only way to keep Japan in the war.

To deal with the growing strains, late in 1920 Sen. William E. Borah (R-Ida.), an irreconcilable on the Versailles Treaty, sponsored a resolution for a conference on arms reductions. President Harding then invited nine principal powers to a conference on arms and also on Pacific and East Asian affairs. The Washington Armaments Conference met on November 11, 1921, in time for the delegates to attend the interment of the Unknown Soldier at Arlington National Cemetery.

President Harding delivered a formal address to open the conference. Then American Secretary of State Charles Evans Hughes, in what was expected to be a perfunctory greeting, suddenly announced that "the way to disarm is to disarm." The only way out of an armaments race, he said, "is to end it now." He proceeded to offer concrete suggestions which ultimately became the basis of agreement. It was one of the most dramatic moments in American diplomatic history. In less than fifteen minutes, one electrified reporter said, Hughes had destroyed more tonnage "than all the admirals of the world have sunk in a cycle of centuries."

The upshot was that delegates from the United States, Britain, Japan, France, and Italy reached agreement on a Five-Power Naval Treaty incorporating Hughes's plan for tonnage limits and a naval holiday of ten years during which no capital ships (battleships and aircraft carriers) would be built. These powers also agreed to refrain from further fortification of their Pacific possessions: Japan in all areas except those adjacent to the homeland; Britain and the United States in areas east of Singapore and west of Hawaii, as far north as the Aleutians. The result was to expose Hong Kong and the Philippines in the event of war, but Hong Kong was clearly indefensible and the Philippines only slightly less so given the Japanese presence in Micronesia. The agreement in effect partitioned the world: United States naval power became supreme in the Western Hemisphere, Japanese power in the western Pacific, British power from the North Sea to Singapore.

Two other major agreements came out of the Washington Conference. With the Four-Power Treaty, the United States, Britain, Japan, and France agreed to respect each other's possessions in the Pacific, and to refer any disputes or any outside threat to consultation. In return for this guarantee Britain and Japan abrogated their alliance dating from 1902. The Nine-Power Treaty for the first time formally pledged the signers to support the Open Door and the territorial integrity of China. The powers, in addition to those signing the Five-Power Treaty, were China, Belgium, Portugal, and the Netherlands.

With these agreements in hand within a year of Harding's inauguration, his people could boast of a brilliant diplomatic stroke which relieved American taxpayers of the need to pay for an enlarged navy, and which anticipated potential conflicts in the Pacific. Having learned from one of Wilson's errors, Hoover named to the delegation two senators, one from each party: Henry Cabot Lodge and Oscar W. Underwood. A grateful Senate approved the naval treaty with one dissenting vote. The Four-Power Treaty aroused real opposition, but finally passed with the support of Democrats after the Senate tacked on a reservation that "there is no commitment to armed force, no alliance, no obligation to join in any defense."

There was the rub. Though the agreements tapped a deep urge toward peacemaking, they were uniformly without obligation and without teeth. The signers of the Four-Power Treaty agreed only to consult, not to help each other, a point that was clear even before the Senate tacked on its reservation. The formal endorsement of the Open Door in the Nine-Power Treaty was just as ineffective, and the American people remained unwilling as yet to uphold the principle with anything but pious affirmation. The naval disarmament treaty set limits only on capital ships; the race to build cruisers, destroyers, submarines, and other smaller craft continued. In 1930 a London Naval Conference attempted to set tonnage limits on smaller craft, but failed when Japan withdrew from the agreement four years later. Thus twelve years after the Washington Conference the dream of naval disarmament died.

During and after the "war to end war" the ideal of abolishing war caught the American imagination. Peace societies thrived and spawned innumerable programs, foremost among them the Carnegie Endowment for International Peace, founded in 1910. In 1921 a wealthy Chicagoan named Salmon Levinson founded the American Committee for the Outlawry of War. "We can outlaw this war system just as we outlawed slavery and the saloon," said Colonel Robins, active in many reform causes and one of the more enthusiastic converts.

THE KELLOGG-BRIAND PACT   The glorious vision of abolishing war at the stroke of a pen culminated in the signing of the Kellogg-Briand Pact in 1928. This unique treaty started with an initiative from French Foreign Minister Aristide Briand, who had busied himself winning allies against a possible resurgence of German power. In 1927 Briand proposed to Secretary of State Frank B. Kellogg not an alliance but an agreement that the two countries would never go to war with each other. This innocent-seeming proposal was actually a clever ploy to draw the United States into the French security system by the back door. In any future war, for instance, such a pact would inhibit the United States from re-

Plans for international disarmament, popular in the 1920s, proved impractical. [New York Public Library]

prisals against any French intrusions on neutral rights. Kellogg gave the idea a cool reception, and was outraged to discover that Briand had urged leaders of the American peace movements to put pressure on the government to sign.

Finally Kellogg turned the tables on Briand. He countered with a scheme to have all nations brought into the pact, an idea all the more acceptable to the peace movements. Caught in a trap of his own making, the French foreign minister finally relented. The Pact of Paris (its official name), signed on August 27, 1928, solemnly declared that the signatories "condemn recourse to war . . . and renounce it as an instrument of national policy." Eventually sixty-two powers adhered to the pact, but all explicitly or tacitly reserved "self-defense" as an escape hatch. The United States Senate included a reservation declaring the Monroe Doctrine necessary to self-defense, and then ratified the agreement by a vote of 85 to 1. Carter Glass of Virginia, who voted for "this worthless, but perfectly harmless peace treaty," wrote a friend later that he feared it would "confuse the minds of many good people who think that peace may be secured by polite professions of neighborly and brotherly love."

His judgment aptly described the euphoric assumptions of many Americans at the time. The treaty proved to be the grandest illusion in an age of illusions. Its "only discernible influence," the historian Robert H. Ferrell wrote, "was to inaugurate a fashion whereby wars would be fought under justification of national defense and without formal declaration of hostilities." Such a war broke out just a year later in Manchuria, where Russian forces quickly put down a Chinese effort to regain control of the Chinese Eastern Railway. When Hoover's secretary of state, Henry L. Stimson, called the Soviet Union's attention to the Pact of Paris, Soviet Foreign Minister Litvinov called attention to the fact that the United States had not yet recognized the Soviet government, and scorned the presumption of Stimson's communication.

THE "GOOD NEIGHBOR" POLICY In Latin America the spirit of peace and noninvolvement helped allay resentments against the Colossus of the North, which had freely intervened in the Caribbean during the first two decades of the century. The Harding administration agreed in 1921 to pay the republic of Colombia the $25 million they had once demanded for canal rights. In 1924 American forces left the Dominican Republic, occupied since 1916, although United States officials continued to collect customs duties there until 1941.

The marines left Nicaragua in 1925, but returned a year later with the outbreak of disorders and civil war. There in 1927, Coolidge's personal representative Henry L. Stimson brought both parties into an agreement for American-supervised elections, but one rebel leader, César Augusto Sandino, held out and the marines stayed until 1933. The unhappy legacies of this intervention were enmity toward the United States and a Nicaraguan National Guard, created to keep order after the marines left, but used in 1936 to set up the dictatorship of Anastasio Somoza. These legacies continue to have their effects down to the present day.

The troubles in Nicaragua increased strains in relations with Mexico. Relations were already troubled by repeated Mexican threats to expropriate American oil properties under the Constitution of 1917, which nationalized all mineral and oil resources in the country. In 1927, however, Coolidge sent his Amherst classmate Dwight L. Morrow as ambassador, and Morrow so mollified the Mexicans by his gestures of friendship that a year later he was able to get an agreement protecting American rights acquired before 1917. Expropriation did in fact occur in 1938, but the Mexican government then agreed to reimburse American owners.

In 1928, with problems apparently clearing in Mexico and Nicaragua, President Coolidge traveled to Havana to open the Pan-American Conference, sixth in a series that dated from Blaine's first conference in 1889–1890. It was an unusual gesture of friendship, and so was the choice of Charles Evans Hughes, the former secretary of state, to head the American delegation. Hughes announced United States' withdrawal from Nicaragua and Haiti as soon as possible, although he did block a resolution declaring that "no state has the right to intervene in the affairs of another."

At the end of 1928 President-elect Hoover began a tour of ten Latin American nations. Once in office he reversed Wilson's policy of refusing to recognize "bad" regimes and reverted to the older policy of recognizing governments in power. In 1930 he gained more goodwill points by permitting publication of a 236-page memorandum drawn up in 1928 by Undersecretary of State J. Ruben Clark. The Clark Memorandum denied that the Monroe Doctrine justified American intervention in Latin America. It stopped short of repudiating intervention on any grounds, but that fine point hardly blunted the celebration in Latin America. Although Hoover never endorsed the Clark Memorandum, he never intervened in the area. Before he left office, steps had already been taken to withdraw American forces from Nicaragua and Haiti.

Franklin D. Roosevelt likewise embraced "the policy of the good neighbor" and soon advanced it in practice. In December 1933 at the seventh Pan-American Conference in Montevideo, Uruguay, Secretary of State Cordell Hull supported a resolution saying "No state has the right to intervene in the international or external affairs of another." Under Roosevelt the marines completed their withdrawals from Nicaragua and Haiti, and in 1934 the president negotiated with Cuba a treaty which abrogated the Platt Amendment and thus ended the last formal claim to a right of intervention in Latin America. Roosevelt reinforced hemispheric goodwill in 1936, when he opened the Pan-American Conference in Buenos Aires with a speech declaring that outside aggressors "will find a Hemisphere wholly prepared to consult together for our mutual safety and our mutual good."

War Clouds

JAPANESE INCURSIONS IN CHINA   The lessening of irritants in the Western Hemisphere proved an exception in an otherwise dismal world scene, as war clouds deepened over Europe and Asia. Actual conflict came first in Asia, where unsettled conditions in China had invited foreign encroachments since before the turn of the century. The tottering Manchu dynasty had collapsed in 1911 and the series of governments that followed in Peiping exercised only nominal authority over local warlords. Finally the Kuomintang (or National Party) under Dr. Sun Yat-sen and, later, Chiang Kai-shek, extended its power from a southern base around Canton to take Peiping in 1928 and set up a new capital in Nanking. But when the new government tried to extend its power in Manchuria it ran into the vested interest of the Russians and Japanese there. Its effort to take over the Chinese Eastern Railway in 1929 led to a short undeclared war with Russia and humiliation for the Kuomintang. More important, Chinese nationalist aspirations convinced the Japanese that their own extensive rights in Manchuria, including the South Manchurian Railway, were in danger.

The Japanese army at the time had a nationalist movement of its own, led by a strong cadre of young officers devoted to the vague idea of a "Showa restoration" (Showa being the reign name of Emperor Hirohito) which would overturn corrupt politicians and bring about a moral regeneration for Japan. Economic pressures strengthened this nationalist movement, for Japan was suffering from the Great Depression and Chinese boycotts of Japanese goods. Manchuria offered both a tempting target and a promising market. Japanese occupation of Manchuria began with the Mukden Incident of September 18, 1931, an explosion which destroyed a section of track near that city. The Japanese "Kwantung Army," based in Manchuria to guard the railway, blamed the incident on the Chinese and used it as a pretext to begin its occupation, which it extended during the winter of 1931–1932 to all of Manchuria, including the Russian sphere of influence. In 1932 the Japanese converted Manchuria into the puppet empire of "Manchukuo" and resurrected the former boy emperor of China, deposed in 1911, to head the new state. The Manchuria Incident, as the Japanese called their undeclared war, was a flagrant breach of the Nine-Power Treaty, the Kellogg-Briand Pact, and Japan's pledges as a member of the League of Nations. But when China asked the League and the United States for help, neither was ready to take effective action. President Hoover was unwilling to invoke either military or economic sanctions. Secretary of State Stimson, who would have preferred to do more, issued a statement in January 1932 warning that the United States refused to recognize any treaty, agreement, or situation which violated American treaty rights, the Open Door, or the territorial integrity of China, or any situation brought about by violation of the Kellogg-Briand Pact. This statement, later known as the Stimson Doctrine, had no effect on Japanese action, for later in the same month the Japanese navy attacked and briefly occupied Shanghai.

Indiscriminate bombing of Shanghai's civilian population aroused indignation, but no further Western action. When the League of Nations condemned Japanese aggression in February 1933, Japan's response was to withdraw from the League and keep the islands of Micronesia as a souvenir. During the spring of

Japan's seizure of Manchuria in 1931 prompted this American condemnation. [Granger Collection]

1933 hostilities in Manchuria gradually subsided and ended with a truce on May 31, 1933. Then an uneasy peace settled upon East Asia for four years, during which the leaders of Japan's military further extended their political sway.

ITALY AND GERMANY   The rise of the Japanese militarists paralleled the rise of warlike dictators in Italy and Germany. In 1922 Benito Mussolini had seized power in Italy. A one-time Socialist leader, Mussolini had broken with the party over its antiwar stand, and after returning from World War I as a wounded veteran, had organized the Fascist movement, which was based on a composite faith in nationalism and socialism. The movement's name came from the ancient Roman *fasces,* a symbol of authority consisting of a bundle of sticks bound around an axe. The program, and above all Mussolini's promise to restore order in a country fragmented by dissension, enjoyed a wide appeal. Once in power, Mussolini largely abandoned the socialist part of his platform and gradually suppressed the opposition. By 1925 he wielded dictatorial power as Il Duce (the leader) in a one-party state.

To most Americans there was always something ludicrous about the magniloquent Mussolini posing jut-jawed on the balcony of the Palazzo Venezia. Italy afforded but a limited power base in the total European picture. But Germany was another matter, and Americans were not amused, even at the beginning, by Il Duce's counterpart, Adolf Hitler, despite his Charlie Chaplin moustache. Hitler's National Socialist (Nazi) party duplicated the major features of Italian Fascism, including the ancient Roman salute. Hitler, having failed to duplicate Mussolini's success in a premature *Putsch* in 1923, did manage to win a foothold for his party in the German Reichstag (parliament). The impo-

Mussolini and Hitler. [Wide World Photos]

tence of the Weimar Republic in the face of world depression finally offered his opening. Made chancellor on January 30, 1933, he moved swiftly to intimidate the opposition, won dictatorial powers from a subservient Reichstag on March 24, and after the death of President Hindenburg in 1934 assumed the title of Reichsführer (national leader) with absolute powers. The Nazi police state cranked up the engines of tyranny, persecuting Jews, whom Hitler blamed for all Germany's troubles, and rearming in defiance of the Versailles Treaty. Hitler flouted international agreements, pulled Germany out of the League of Nations in October 1933, and frankly proclaimed that he meant to extend control over all German-speaking peoples. Despite one provocation after another the European democracies seemed to lack the will to resist.

THE MOOD IN AMERICA Americans, absorbed by the problems of the depression, chose to retreat all the more into isolationism during the early 1930s. In the campaign of 1932 Roosevelt had found it prudent to renounce his Wilsonian past and state that he now opposed joining the League of Nations. Once in office he rejected an early chance to deal with economic problems on an international basis. Hoover, convinced that the depression called for world action, had pledged the United States to participate in the London Economic Conference on reparations. The conference of sixty-four nations was to deal with the related issues of currency stabilization, world trade, and war debts. But when a group of gold-bloc nations (led by France) insisted on a return to the gold standard, Roosevelt demurred and the conference ended in futility. The president wanted to be free to experiment with currency manipulation as a device to fight the depression. Roosevelt's action dealt a severe blow to international cooperation. The epilogue was Europe's final default on the war debts, and further American drift toward isolation.

The chief exception to the administration's isolationism was Secretary of State Cordell Hull's grand scheme of reciprocal trade agreements. Hull, a former Tennessee judge and congressman, held to the firm conviction that to release the fetters on world trade would advance understanding and peace. His economic thinking, said one historian, was "a blend of Adam Smith and the cotton South." In 1934 the administration threw its support behind Hull's pet project, and over the objections of business interests and Republicans Congress adopted the Trade Agreements Act, which authorized the president to lower tariff rates as much as 50 percent for countries which made similar concessions on American products. Agreements were made with fourteen countries by the end of 1935, and twenty-nine by 1945. The economic results are hard to measure, since the following years were so troubled.

Another scheme for building foreign markets, diplomatic recognition of Soviet Russia, won more support in business quarters than had the reciprocity plan. The vast expanse of Russia stirred fantasies of a trade boom, much as China had at the turn of the century. By 1933 the reasons for American refusal to recognize the Bolshevik regime had grown stale. Japanese expansionism in Asia, moreover, gave Russia and the United States a common concern. Given an opening by the shift of opinion, Roosevelt invited Maxim Litvinov, Soviet commissar for foreign affairs, to visit Washington. After nine days of talks, a formal exchange of notes on November 16, 1933, signaled the renewal of diplomatic relations. Litvinov promised that his country would abstain from propaganda in the United States, extend religious freedom to Americans in the USSR, and reopen the question of czarist debts.

THE EXPANDING AXIS   But a catastrophic chain of events in Asia and Europe sent the world hurtling toward disaster. In 1934 Japan renounced the Five-Power Naval Treaty. In 1935 Mussolini commenced an Italian conquest of Ethiopia. The same year a referendum in the Saar Basin, held in accordance with the Versailles Treaty, delivered that coal-rich region into the hands of Hitler. In 1936 Hitler reoccupied the Rhineland with armed forces, in violation of the Versailles Treaty but without any forceful response from the French. (It is now known that such a response would have forced him to break down.) The year 1936 also brought the Spanish Civil War, which began with an uprising of the Spanish armed forces in Morocco, led by Gen. Francisco Franco. In three years Franco had established a fascist dictatorship with help from Hitler and Mussolini while the democracies stood by and left the Spanish Republic to its fate. On July 7, 1937, Japanese and Chinese troops came into conflict at the Marco Polo Bridge near Peiping. The incident quickly developed into a full-scale war which the Japanese persisted in calling the "China Incident." It was the beginning of World War II in Asia, two years before war came to Europe. That same year Japan joined Germany and Italy in the "Anti-Comintern Pact," allegedly directed at the Communist threat, thus establishing the Rome-Berlin-Tokyo "Axis."

By 1938 the peace of Europe trembled in the balance. Having rebuilt German military force, Hitler forced the *Anschluss* (union) of Austria with Germany in March 1938, and six months

AGGRESSION IN EUROPE
— Aggressive moves
Axis Powers

The swastika, symbol of Nazi Germany, about to crush Poland. [D. R. Fitzpatrick, St. Louis Post Dispatch]

later took the Sudeten territory from Czechoslovakia after signing an agreement at Munich under which Britain and France abandoned a country that had probably the second-best army in central Europe. The mountainous Sudetenland, largely German in population, was vital to the defense of Czechoslovakia. Having said this was his last territorial demand, Hitler in March 1939 occupied the remainder of Czechoslovakia. In quick succession the Spanish Republic finally collapsed on March 28 and Mussolini seized the kingdom of Albania on April 7. Finally, during the summer Hitler heated up a "war of nerves" over control of the free city of Danzig and the Polish Corridor, and on September 1 launched his conquest of Poland. A few days before, he had reached a nonaggression pact with Russia. Having deserted Czechoslovakia, Britain and France now honored their commitment to go to war if Poland were invaded.

DEGREES OF NEUTRALITY   During these years of deepening crisis, the Western democracies remained infirm of purpose, hoping in vain that each concession would appease the appetites of fascist dictators. The response of the United States was to retreat more deeply into isolation. The prevailing mood was reinforced by a Senate inquiry into the role of bankers and munitions makers in World War I. Under Sen. Gerald P. Nye of North Dakota, a progressive Republican, the committee sat from 1934 to 1937, and after hauling to the witness stand J. P. Morgan, Jr., and the du Pont brothers, among others, reached the foregone conclusion that bankers and munitions makers had made scandalous profits from the war. Although Nye never showed that greed for profit had actually impelled Wilson into war, millions of Americans became convinced that Uncle Sam had been duped by the "merchants of death."

Historians then rehashing the European origins of World War I challenged the idea of German war guilt; some condemned America's entry into the war. In one of the bestsellers of the time, *The Road to War: America, 1914–1917* (1935), Walter Millis, a freelance journalist and historian, argued that a combination of British propaganda, economic involvement with the Allies, and Wilson's uneven response to British and German violations of neutrality had sucked the United States into a war it should have kept out of. In 1934 Charles Warren, assistant attorney-general under Wilson, wrote in the journal *Foreign Affairs* that modern warfare had rendered obsolete old notions of freedom of the seas. If the United States wanted to remain neutral in the current crisis, therefore, it would have to keep Americans out of war zones, keep belligerent vessels out of American ports, embargo arms shipments, and set quotes on the export of contraband. Such ideas became official policy as war enveloped Asia and Europe.

Like generals who are said to be always preparing for the last war, Congress occupied itself with keeping out of the last war. Neutrality laws of the 1930s moved the United States back toward Jefferson's embargo policies and complete isolation from the quarrels of Europe. Americans wanted to keep out of war, but their sympathies were more strongly than ever with the Western democracies, and the triumph of fascist aggression aroused growing fears for national security.

On August 31, 1935, President Roosevelt signed the first in a series of neutrality acts, one which anticipated Italy's invasion of Ethiopia. The Neutrality Act of 1935 forbade the sale of arms and munitions to all belligerents whenever the president proclaimed that a state of war existed. Americans who traveled on belligerent ships thereafter did so at their own risk. Roosevelt would have preferred discretionary authority to levy an embargo only against aggressors, but reluctantly accepted the act because it would be effective only six months, and for the time being "meets the need of the existing situation." That is, it would actually be enforced against Italy in its war with Ethiopia. When he signed the act on August 31, Roosevelt nevertheless urged reconsideration of the arms embargo on all belligerents: "History is filled with situations that call for some flexibility of action. It is conceivable that situations may arise in which the wholly inflexible provisions . . . of this act . . . might drag us into war instead of keeping us out."

On October 3, 1935, Italy invaded Ethiopia and the president invoked the act. One shortcoming in its provisions became apparent right away: the key problem was neither arms traffic nor passenger travel, but trade in contraband not covered by the Neutrality Act. Secretary of State Hull warned, however, that anybody trading with the belligerents, meaning in effect Italy since there was little trade with Ethiopia, did so at his own risk. He asked, moreover, for a "moral embargo" on oil and other products. Sanctions imposed under the Neutrality Act had no deterrent effect on Mussolini or his suppliers. In the summer of 1936 Il Duce completed his conquest of Ethiopia.

When Congress reconvened in January 1936, it fell into a three-cornered debate among the advocates of mandatory embargoes, flexible embargoes aimed at aggressors, and traditional neutrality. After six weeks Congress simply extended the arms embargo and added a provision forbidding loans to belligerents. Then in July 1936, while Italian troops mopped up the last resistance in Ethiopia, the Spanish Army revolted in Morocco. Ironically, Roosevelt now became more isolationist than some of the isolationists. Although the Spanish Civil War involved a fascist uprising against a recognized, democratic government, Roosevelt accepted the French and British position that only nonintervention would localize the fight. There existed, moreover, a strong bloc of pro-Franco Catholics in America who feared that the Spanish Republic was a threat to the church. They feared Communist influence in the Spanish government; intrigues by Spanish Communists did prove divisive and the Soviet Union in fact did supply aid to the Republic, but nothing like the quantity of German and Italian aid to Franco.

Roosevelt asked for another "moral embargo" on the arms trade, and asked Congress to extend the neutrality laws to cover civil wars. Congress did so in January 1937 with only one dissenting vote—although many, including Senator Nye, had second thoughts later about leaving the Spanish Republic thus to its fate. The Western democracies then stood witness while German and Italian soldiers, planes, and armaments supported Franco's overthrow of Spanish democracy, which was completed in 1939.

In the spring of 1937 isolationism reached a peak. The Gallup poll found that 94 percent of its respondents preferred efforts to keep out of war over efforts to prevent war. That same spring Congress passed yet another neutrality law, which continued restraints on arms sales and loans, forbade Americans to travel on belligerent ships, and forbade the arming of American merchant ships trading with belligerents. The president also got discre-

"Come on in. I'll treat you right. I used to know your daddy." *This Pulitzer Prize–winning cartoon by Clarence Bachelor reflects American isolationism of the 1930s. [New York* News*]*

tionary authority to require that goods other than arms or munitions exported to belligerents be placed on a cash-and-carry basis. This was an ingenious scheme to preserve a profitable trade without running the risk of war.

The new law had its first test on July 7, 1937, when Japanese and Chinese forces clashed at the Marco Polo Bridge west of Peiping. Since neither side declared war, Roosevelt was able to use his discretion about invoking the neutrality law. He decided to wait, and in fact never invoked it. This was because its net effect would have favored the Japanese, since China had greater need of arms but few means to get supplies past the Japanese Navy. A flourishing trade in munitions to China flowed around the world as ships carried arms across the Atlantic to England, where they were reloaded on British ships bound for Hong Kong. Roosevelt, by inaction, had challenged strict isolationism.

He soon ventured a step further. On October 5, 1937, Roosevelt delivered a forthright denunciation of the "reign of terror and international lawlessness" in which 10 percent of the world's population threatened the peace of the other 90 percent. "When an epidemic of physical disease starts to spread, the community approves and joins in a quarantine of the patients in order to protect the health of the community. . . ." There should also be a quarantine against nations "creating a state of international anarchy and instability from which there is no escape through mere isolation or neutrality." On the whole, public reaction to the speech was mixed. The president quickly backed off from its implications and refused to spell out any specific program. The day after his address, the League of Nations condemned Japanese aggression and called for a conference of the

Nine-Power Treaty signatories. The meeting, held at Brussels in November 1937, did nothing but reaffirm the principle of the Open Door Policy and then adjourn.

Three weeks after the Brussels Conference, on December 12, 1937, Japanese planes bombed and sank the American gunboat *Panay*, which had been lying at anchor in the Yangtze River and prominently flying the American flag, and then attacked three Standard Oil tankers. Two members of the *Panay* crew and an Italian journalist died; thirty more were injured. Though the Japanese government was quick to apologize and pay the reparations demanded—nearly $2¼ million—the incident reinforced American animosity toward Japan. The private boycott of Japanese goods spread, but isolationist sentiment continued strong, as was vividly demonstrated by support for the Ludlow Amendment in Congress. The proposed constitutional amendment would have required a referendum for a declaration of war except in case of attack on American territory. Only by the most severe pressure from the White House, and a vote of 209 to 188, was consideration of the measure stopped in January 1938.

Still, the continuing Japanese war against China brought public outrage and protests from Secretary Hull. On July 1, 1938, after nearly a year of war in China, the government notified domestic aircraft manufacturers and exporters that it opposed sales to those guilty of attacks on civilian populations. To have imposed an outright embargo would have violated a commercial treaty of 1911 with Japan, but after another year, on July 26, 1939, the United States gave six-months' notice of the termination of the treaty—thus clearing the way for an embargo on war materials.

By then Hitler had brought Europe into war. After the German occupation of Czechoslovakia, Roosevelt no longer pretended impartiality in the impending struggle. He urged Congress to repeal the embargo and permit the United States to sell arms on a cash-and-carry basis to Britain and France, but to no avail. "You haven't got the votes," Vice-President Garner told him, "and that's all there is to it." When the German attack on Poland came on September 1, 1939, Roosevelt proclaimed neutrality, but in a radio talk said that he did not, like Wilson, ask Americans to remain neutral in thought because "even a neutral has a right to take account of the facts."

Congress, summoned into special session on September 21, was asked once again to amend the Neutrality Act. "I regret the Congress passed the Act," the president said. "I regret equally that I signed the Act." This time he got what he wanted by winning the support of conservative Democrats who had opposed his domestic policies. Under the Neutrality Act of 1939 the Allies could come, buy for cash, and take away arms or anything else they wanted. American ships, on the other hand, were excluded from belligerent ports and from specified war zones. Roosevelt then designated as a war zone the Baltic Sea and the waters around Great Britain and Ireland from Norway south to the coast of Spain. One ironic effect of this move was to relieve Hitler of any inhibitions against using unrestricted submarine warfare to blockade Britain.

American attitudes continued to vacillate. As the war crisis developed, an isolationist policy of hands-off prevailed. Once the great democracies of western Europe faced war, American public opinion, appalled at Hitler's tyranny, came to support measures short of war to help their cause. "What the majority of the American people want," the editor Freda Kirchwey wrote in the *Nation*, "is to be as unneutral as possible without getting into war." On October 3, while Congress debated repeal of the arms embargo, the foreign ministers of the American republics adopted the Declaration of Panama, which created a "chastity belt" around the Americas, south of Canada, a zone 300 to 1,000 miles wide in which belligerents were warned not to pursue naval action. For a time it seemed possible that the Western Hemisphere could remain insulated from the war. After Hitler overran Poland in less than a month, the war settled into an unreal stalemate that began to be called the "Phony War." What lay ahead, it seemed, was a long war of attrition in which Britain and France would have the resources to outlast Hitler. The illusion lasted through the winter.

THE STORM IN EUROPE

BLITZKRIEG   In the spring of 1940 the winter's long *Sitzkrieg* suddenly erupted into *Blitzkrieg*—lightning war. At dawn on April 9, without warning, Nazi troops entered Denmark and disembarked along the Norwegian coast. Denmark fell in a day, Norway within a few weeks. On May 10 Hitler released his dive bombers and panzer tank divisions on neutral Belgium and the Netherlands. On May 21 German forces moving down the valley of the Somme reached the English Channel, cutting off a British force sent to help the Belgians and French. A desperate evacuation from the beaches at Dunkirk enlisted every available boat from warship to tug. Some 338,000 men, including a few French, escaped to England. Having outflanked the forts on

France's defense perimeter, the Maginot Line, the German forces rushed ahead, cutting the French armies to pieces and spreading panic by strafing refugees in a deliberate policy of terror. On June 10 Mussolini entered the war. "I need only a few thousand dead to enable me to take my seat . . . at the peace table," Il Duce said. Speaking at the University of Virginia the same day, Roosevelt grimly ad libbed: "The hand that held the dagger has plunged it into the back of France." On June 14 the swastika flew over Paris. On June 22 French delegates, in the presence of Hitler, submitted to his terms in the same railroad car at Compiègne in which German delegates had signed the Armistice of 1918.

AMERICA'S GROWING INVOLVEMENT   Britain stood alone, but in Parliament Prime Minister Winston Churchill, who had replaced Chamberlain amid the *Blitzkrieg*, breathed defiance. "We shall go on to the end," he said; "we shall never surrender." Even if the home islands should fall, the Empire "would carry on the struggle, until, in God's good time, the New World with all its power and might, steps forth to the rescue and liberation of the Old." Despite the grim resolution of the British, America seemed suddenly vulnerable as Hitler turned his air force against Britain. President Roosevelt, who in his annual budget had requested $1.9 billion for defense, now asked for more, and called for the production of 50,000 combat planes a year. By October 1940 Congress had voted more than $17 billion for defense. In response to Churchill's appeal for military supplies, the War and Navy Departments began releasing stocks of arms, planes, and munitions to the British. They resorted to a World War I law which permitted the government to trade in equipment for newer models—the manufacturers could then send the trade-ins to Britain on a cash-and-carry basis.

America continued to prepare its defense. On June 15, 1940, the president set up the National Defense Research Committee under Dr. Vannevar Bush of the Carnegie Institution to coordinate military research, including a secret look into the possibility of developing an atomic bomb, suggested the previous fall by Albert Einstein and other scientists. To bolster national unity, on June 19 Roosevelt named two Republicans to the defense posts in his cabinet: Henry L. Stimson as secretary of war and Frank Knox as secretay of the navy. On July 20 Roosevelt signed a bill authorizing a two-ocean navy at a cost of $4 billion, and on July 30 delegates to the Pan-American Conference approved the Declaration of Havana, under which the republics might take over and administer European possessions that were in danger of falling into unfriendly hands. In August the United States and Canada set up a Permanent Joint Board on Defense. At the end of the month units of the National Guard began to be inducted into federal service.

The summer of 1940 brought the desperate Battle of Britain, in which the Royal Air Force, with the benefit of the new technology of radar finding, outfought the numerically superior German Luftwaffe and finally forced the Germans to give up plans to invade. Submarine warfare meanwhile strained the resources of the battered Royal Navy. To relieve the pressure, Churchill urgently requested the transfer of American destroyers. Secret negotiations led to an executive agreement on September 2, under which fifty "overaged" destroyers went to the British in return for ninety-nine-year leases on naval and air bases in Newfoundland, Bermuda, the Bahamas, Jamaica, St. Lucia, Trinidad, Antigua, and British Guiana. It was, Roosevelt declared expansively, "the most important action in the reinforcement of our national defense that has been taken since the Louisiana Purchase." Two weeks later, on September 16, 1940, Congress adopted the first peacetime conscription in American history. The Burke-Wadsworth Act called for the registration of all men aged twenty-one to thirty-five for a year's military service within the United States.

The new state of affairs prompted vigorous debate between "internationalists" who believed national security demanded aid to Britain and isolationists who charged that Roosevelt was drawing the United States into a needless war. In May 1940 the nonpartisan Committee to Defend America by Aiding the Allies was organized with the Kansas journalist William Allen White as chairman. It drew its strongest support from the East and West Coasts and the South, and included among its members General Pershing, Harold Ickes, Harry Hopkins, and Henry Stimson. In June, moreover, thirty men known as the Century Group, after the New York club where they met, urged immediate declaration of war on Germany. One of them was Walter Millis, whose book on World War I had done so much five years earlier to bolster isolationism.

In July 1940, on the other hand, isolationists formed the America First Committee. The organizer was a Yale law student, R. Douglas Stuart, Jr., whose father was president of the Quaker Oats Company. The group included midwestern businessmen like Gen. Robert Wood of Sears, Roebuck, and Jay Hormel, the meat-packer, as well as the historian Charles A. Beard, Herbert Hoover, and Charles A. Lindbergh. Before the end of 1941 the committee had about 450 chapters around the country, but probably two-thirds of its members lived within a 300-mile radius of Chicago. The isolationists argued that the war involved, in Senator Borah's words, "nothing more than another chapter in the bloody volume of European power politics," and that a Nazi victory, while distasteful, would pose no threat to national security.

A THIRD TERM FOR FDR   In the midst of these developments the quadrennial presidential campaign came due. Isolationist sentiment was strongest in the Republican party and both the leading Republican candidates were noninterventionists, but neither loomed as a man of sufficient stature to challenge the "champ," assuming Roosevelt decided to run again. Sen. Robert A. Taft of Ohio, son of the former president, lacked popular appeal, and New York District Attorney Thomas E. Dewey, who had won fame as a "racket buster," at thirty-eight seemed young and unseasoned. This left an opening for an inspired group of political amateurs to promote the dark-horse candidacy of Wendell L. Willkie. Willkie seemed at first an unlikely choice: a former Democrat who had voted for Roosevelt in 1932, a utility president who had fought TVA, but in origins a Hoosier farm boy whose disheveled charm inspired strong loyalty. He was "a simple, barefoot Wall Street lawyer," in the devastating phrase of Interior Secretary Harold L. Ickes. Unlike the front-runners, he openly supported aid to the Allies, and the Nazi *Blitzkrieg* had brought many other Republicans to the same viewpoint. As late

GOP presidential nominee Wendell L. Willkie parading through Elwood, Indiana, 1940. [Wide World Photos]

as April Willkie did not have a single delegate, but when the Republicans met at Philadelphia on June 28, six days after the French surrender, the convention was stampeded by the cry of "We Want Willkie" from the galleries. Sen. Charles L. McNary of Oregon was the choice for vice-president.

The Nazi victory also ensured another nomination for Roosevelt. The president cultivated party unity behind his foreign policy and kept a sphinx-like silence about his intentions. Amid the uncertainty no other hopefuls rose high enough to challenge him. The world crisis reconciled southern conservatives to the man whose foreign policy at least they supported. At the July convention in Chicago Roosevelt won nomination for a third term with only token opposition from Farley and Garner. The vice-presidential nod went to Agriculture Secretary Henry A. Wallace. A former Republican with a reputation more for mysticism than for politics, Wallace was anathema to the professionals, but they swallowed hard and took him.

Through the summer Roosevelt assumed the role of a man above the political fray, busy rather with urgent matters of defense and diplomacy: Pan-American agreements for mutual defense, the destroyer-bases deal, and visits to defense facilities which took the place of campaign trips. Willkie inspired a more intense personal devotion than any Republican candidate since Theodore Roosevelt, but he had trouble positioning himself since there was little on which he disagreed with Roosevelt. The New Deal programs were too popular, in any case, to oppose head-on.

Like Landon, Willkie was reduced to attacks on New Deal red tape, and promises to run the programs better. A widespread reluctance to violate the tradition against a presidential third term strengthened his argument that new blood was needed in the White House. In the end, however, he switched to an attack on Roosevelt's conduct of foreign policy. In October he warned: "If you re-elect him you may expect war in April, 1941." To this Roosevelt responded, "I have said this before, but I shall say it again and again and again: Your boys are not going to be sent into any foreign wars." Three days before the election he declared in Buffalo: "Your President says this country is not going to war." Neither man distinguished himself with such hollow statements, since both knew the risks of all-out aid to Britain, which both supported.

Roosevelt won the election by a comfortable margin of 27 million votes to Willkie's 22 million, and a wider margin of 449 to 82 in the electoral college. The popular vote was closer than any presidential vote since 1916. Given the dangerous world situation a majority of the voters agreed with the Democrats' slogan: "Don't switch horses in the middle of the stream."

THE ARSENAL OF DEMOCRACY   Bolstered by the mandate for an unprecedented third term, Roosevelt moved quickly for greater measures of aid to Britain. Since the outbreak of war Roosevelt had corresponded with Winston Churchill, who as first lord of the Admiralty used the signature "Navy Person"; as prime minister he became "Former Naval Person." Soon after the election Churchill informed Roosevelt that British credit was fast running out. Since direct American loans would arouse memories of earlier war-debt defaults—the Johnson Act of 1934 forbade such loans anyway—the president created an ingenious device to bypass that issue and yet supply British needs, the "lend-lease" program.

In a fireside chat on December 29, 1940, he told the nation that it must become "the great arsenal of democracy" because of the threat of Britain's fall. In his annual message to Congress on January 6, 1941, he warned that only the British navy stood between America and the peril of attack. Greater efforts to bolster British defenses were therefore in order: "They do not need manpower. They do need billions of dollars worth of the weapons of defense." At the end of the speech he enunciated the Four Freedoms for which the democracies fought: freedom of speech, freedom of worship, freedom from want, and freedom from fear. The Lend-Lease Bill, introduced in Congress on January 10, authorized the president to sell, transfer, exchange, lend, lease, or otherwise dispose of arms and other equipment and supplies to "any country whose defense the President deems vital to the defense of the United States."

For two months a bitter debate over the bill raged in Congress and the country. Isolationists saw it as the point of no return. "The lend-lease-give program," said Sen. Burton K. Wheeler, "is the New Deal's triple A foreign policy; it will plow under every fourth American boy." Roosevelt pronounced this "the rottenest thing that has been said in public life in my generation." Administration supporters denied that lend-lease would lead to war, but it did manifestly increase the risk. On March 11, 1941, as "An Act to Promote the Defense of the United States," lend-lease became law. The next day the president asked that the program be funded with an appropriation of $7 billion, the largest single appropriation in American history to that time, more than ninety times the national debt refunded by Alexander Ham-

Women Pray for Defeat of Lend-Lease Bill. *These women shared Senator Wheeler's fear that lend-lease would "plow under every fourth American boy." [Wide World Photos]*

ilton in 1790. Congress complied, and Britain and China became the first beneficiaries.

While the nation debated, the war was spreading. In October 1940 when the presidential campaign approached its climax, Mussolini launched attacks on Greece and, from Italian Libya, on the British in Egypt. But he had bitten off more than he could chew, and his forces had to fall back in both cases. In the spring of 1941 Hitler came to his aid. German forces under Gen. Erwin Rommel joined the Italians in Libya, forcing the British, whose resources had been drained to help Greece, to withdraw into Egypt.

In April lightning attacks by Nazi panzer divisions overwhelmed Yugoslavia and Greece, and by the end of May airborne forces subdued the Greek island of Crete, putting Hitler in a position to menace the entire Middle East. With Hungary, Rumania, and Bulgaria forced into the Axis fold, Hitler controlled nearly all of Europe. Then, on June 22, 1941, he suddenly fell upon Russia. Frustrated in the purpose of subduing Britain, he thought to eliminate the potential threat on his rear with another lightning stroke. The Russian plains offered an ideal theater for *Blitzkrieg,* or so it seemed, and Russian resources were a seductive lure. With Rumanian and Finnish allies, the Nazis moved on a 2,000-mile front from the Arctic to the Black Sea with seeming invincibility until, after four months, the Russian soldiers rallied in front of Leningrad, Moscow, and Sevastopol. During the winter of 1941–1942 Hitler began to learn the bitter lesson the Russians taught Napoleon in 1812.

Winston Churchill had already decided to offer British support to Russia in case of such an attack. "If Hitler invaded Hell," he said, "I would make at least a favorable reference to the Devil in the House of Commons." Roosevelt adopted the same policy, offering American aid two days after the attack. Stalinist Russia, so long as it held out, ensured the survival of Britain. American aid was now indispensable to Europe's defense, and the logic of lend-lease led on to deeper American involvement. In order to deliver aid to Britain, goods had to be maneuvered through the U-boat "wolf packs" in the North Atlantic. So on April 11, 1941, Roosevelt informed Churchill that the United States Navy would extend its patrol areas in the North Atlantic out to 26° West Longitude, nearly all the way to Iceland.

In August 1941 Roosevelt and Churchill held a secret rendezvous in Placentia Bay, Newfoundland, alternately aboard the American cruiser *Augusta* and the British battleship *Prince of Wales*. There they drew up a statement of principles that came to be known as the Atlantic Charter, issued as a press release on August 14. In effect the "common principles" upon which the parties based "their hopes for a better future for the world" amounted to a joint statement of war aims, its eight points a mixture of the idealistic goals of the New Deal and Wilson's Fourteen Points. It called for the self-determination of all peoples, equal access to raw materials, economic cooperation, freedom of the seas, and a new system of general security. In September it was announced that fifteen anti-Axis nations, including the Soviet Union, had endorsed the statement.

Thus Roosevelt had led the United States into a joint statement of war aims with the anti-Axis powers. It was not long before shooting incidents involved Americans in the North Atlantic. As early as May 21, 1941, in fact, a German U-boat had sunk the American merchantman *Robin Moor* off the coast of Brazil, in retaliation for which Roosevelt froze all German and Italian assets in the United States, as well as those of Axis-controlled countries, and closed down German and Italian consulates. On September 4 came the first attack on an American warship, when a German submarine fired two torpedoes at the destroyer *Greer*. The president announced a week later orders to "shoot on sight" any German or Italian raiders ("rattlesnakes of the Atlantic") which ventured into American defensive waters. Five days later the United States Navy announced convoying all the way to Iceland. Then on October 17, while the destroyer *Kearny* was attacking German submarines, it sustained severe damage and loss of eleven lives from a German torpedo.

In his Navy Day speech of October 27 Roosevelt asserted that

"America has been attacked" and that "the shooting has started." Three days later, on the night of October 30, a submarine torpedoed and sank the destroyer *Reuben James*, with a loss of ninety-six officers and men, while it was on convoy duty west of Iceland. This act hastened Congress into making changes in the neutrality act already requested by the president. On November 17 the legislation was in effect repealed when the bans on arming merchant vessels and allowing them to enter combat zones and belligerent ports were removed. Step by step the United States had given up neutrality and embarked on naval warfare against Germany. Still, the American people hoped to avoid taking the final step into all-out war. The decision for war, when it came, came in an unexpected quarter—the Pacific.

THE STORM IN THE PACIFIC

JAPANESE AGGRESSION   After the Nazi victories in the spring of 1940, relations with Japan also took a turn for the worse. Japanese militarists, bogged down in the vastness of China, now eyed new temptations: French Indochina, the Dutch East Indies, British Malaya, and Burma. Here they could cut off one of China's last links to the west, the Burma Road. What was more, they could incorporate into their "Greater East Asia Co-Prosperity Sphere" the oil, rubber, and other strategic materials which the crowded homeland lacked. As it was, they depended on the United States for important supplies, including 80 percent of their oil. During the summer of 1940 Japan forced the helpless French government at Vichy to permit the construction of Japanese airfields in northern Indochina and to cut off the railroad into South China. The United States responded with a loan to China and the Export Control Act of July 2, 1940, which authorized the president to restrict the export of arms and other strategic materials to Japan. Gradually Roosevelt extended embargoes on aviation gas, scrap iron, and other supplies.

On September 27, 1940, the Tokyo government signed a Tripartite Pact with Germany and Italy, by which each pledged to declare war on any nation which attacked any of them. The pact could have been directed against either the United States or Russia. The Germans hoped to persuade Japan to enter Siberia when their forces entered Russia from the west. The Soviet presence in Siberia did inhibit the Japanese impulse to move southward, but on April 13, 1941, while the Nazis were sweeping through the Balkans, Japan signed a nonaggression pact with

JAPANESE EXPANSION
BEFORE PEARL HARBOR

Territory under Japanese control, Dec. 7, 1941

Dates indicate year of acquisition or occupation

U.S.S.R.

KAMCHATKA PEN. (U.S.S.R.)

MONGOLIA

Lupin

Khabarousk

SAKHALIN, 1905

KURILE ISLANDS, 1875

Amur R.

Harbin

MANCHURIA 1932

Vladivostok

Mukden

KWEISUI, 1937

PEKING 1937

KOREA PROTECTORATE, 1905 ANNEXED, 1910

C H I N A

PORT ARTHUR 1905

SHANTUNG PEN. 1905

Yenan

KAIFENG 1938

Tokyo

Yellow R.

HANKOW 1938

Nanking

J A P A N

ICHANG, 1940

Chungking

SHANGHAI, 1937

Yangtze R.

NACHANG, 1939

HANGCHOW, 1937

RYUKYU ISLANDS, 1879

BONIN IS. 1876

AMOY, 1938

PESCADORES, 1895

VOLCANO IS. 1891

MARCUS, 1899

SWATOW, 1939

CANTON, 1938

FORMOSA (TAIWAN), 1895

BURMA

Hanoi

Hong Kong

KWANGCHOW (Fr.), 1940

HAINAN, 1939

P A C I F I C

O C E A N

THAILAND

FRENCH INDOCHINA, 1940

Saigon

MARIANA ISLANDS

GUAM (U.S.)

PHILIPPINE ISLANDS (U.S.)

M I C R O N E S I A

OCCUPIED, 1914, MANDATED, 1922

MARSHALL ISLANDS

BRITISH MALAYA

Singapore

Mekong R.

C A R O L I N E   I S L A N D S

0   1000 Miles
0   1000 Kilometers

D U T C H   E A S T   I N D I E S

Russia and, once the Nazis invaded Russia in June, the Japanese were freed of any threat from the north.

Their first move southward came on July 25, 1941, when Japan announced that it was assuming a protectorate over all of French Indochina. Roosevelt took three steps in response on the next day: he froze all Japanese assets in the United States; he restricted exports of oil to Japan; and he took the armed forces of the Philippines into the Army of the United States and put their commander, Gen. Douglas MacArthur, in charge of all United States forces in the Far East. By September the oil restrictions had tightened into an embargo. The commander of the Japanese navy estimated that their oil reserves would last two years at most, eighteen months in case of an expanded war. Forced by the embargo to secure other oil supplies, the Japanese army and navy began to lay plans for attacks on the Dutch and British colonies to the south.

Actions by both sides put the United States and Japan on the way to a war which neither wanted. In his regular talks with the

Japanese ambassador, Secretary of State Cordell Hull took the position that Japanese withdrawal from Indochina and China was the price of renewed trade. Though the United States was under no obligation to fuel the Japanese war machine, a more flexible position might have strengthened the moderates in Japan. The Japanese were not then pursuing a concerted plan of aggression comparable to Hitler's. The Japanese military had stumbled crazily from one aggression to another without approval from the government in Tokyo. Premier Konoye, however, while known as a man of liberal principles who preferred peace, caved in to pressures from the warlords.

The Japanese warlords, for their part, seriously misjudged the United States. The desperate wish of Americans to stay out of war might still have enabled the Japanese to conquer the British and Dutch colonies before an American decision to act. But the warlords decided that they dared not leave the American navy intact and the Philippines untouched on the flank of their new lifeline to the south.

TRAGEDY AT PEARL HARBOR   Thus a tragedy began to unfold with a fatal certainty mostly out of sight of the American people, whose attention was focused on the war in the Atlantic. Late in August Prince Konoye proposed a personal meeting with President Roosevelt. Hull smelled a rat. On his advice, Roosevelt refused to go unless agreement on fundamentals could be reached in advance. Soon afterward, on September 6, an imperial conference approved preparations for an attack and gave Premier Konoye six more weeks to reach a settlement. The Japanese emperor's clear displeasure with the risks of an attack afforded the premier one last chance to pursue a compromise, but the stumbling block was still the presence of Japanese troops in China. In October he urged War Minister Hideki Tojo (nicknamed "The Razor") to consider withdrawal while saving face by keeping some troops in North China. Tojo retorted that at times one must have the courage to take the plunge—or as he put it, to jump off Kiyomizu (a mountainside Buddhist temple in Kyoto). Faced with this rebuff, and Tojo's threat to resign and bring down the cabinet, Konoye himself resigned on October 15; Tojo became premier the next day. The war party was now in complete control.

On the very day that Tojo became premier a special envoy, Saburo Kurusu, conferred with Hull and Roosevelt in Washington. His arrival was largely a cover for Japan's war plans, although neither he nor Ambassador Nomura knew that. On November 20 they presented Tojo's final proposal. Japan would occupy no more territory if the United States would cut off aid to China, restore trade, and help Japan get supplies from the Dutch Indies. In that case Japan would pull out of southern Indochina immediately and abandon the remainder once peace had been established with China—presumably on Japanese terms. Tojo expected the United States to refuse such demands. On November 26 Hull repeated the demand that Japan withdraw altogether from China. That same day a Japanese naval force left its rendezvous at Hitokappu Bay on one of the remote Kurile Islands. Six carriers, two battleships, and an escort of cruisers, destroyers, and submarines headed silently across the North Pacific, through rough waters deserted by shipping in the late fall, toward Pearl Harbor.

Washington already knew that war was imminent. Reports of troop transports moving south from Formosa prompted Washington to send war warnings to Pearl Harbor and Manila, and to the British government. The massive movements southward clearly signaled attacks on the British and the Dutch. American leaders had every reason to expect war in the southwest Pacific, but none expected that Japan would commit most of its carriers to another attack 5,000 miles away at Pearl Harbor.

On the morning of December 7, 1941, American cryptanalysts decoded the last part of a fourteen-part Japanese message breaking off the negotiations. Nomura was instructed to deliver the message at 1:00 P.M. (7:00 A.M. in Honolulu), about a half hour before the blow fell, but delays in decoding the message held up delivery until more than an hour later than scheduled. Gen. George Marshall and Adm. Harold R. Stark sent out an alert at noon that something was about to happen, but the message, which went by commercial wire because radio contacts were broken, arrived in Hawaii eight and a half hours later.

It was still a somnolent Sunday morning when the first Japanese planes roared down the west coast and the central valley of Oahu to begin their assault. At 7:53 A.M. the flight commander, Mitsuo Fuchida, rounded Barber's Point and sounded the cry "Tora! Tora! Tora!" ("Tiger! Tiger! Tiger!"), the signal that the attackers had taken the American Pacific fleet by surprise. For nearly two hours the Japanese planes kept up their attack on an unready Pacific fleet. Of the eight battleships in Pearl Harbor, three were sunk, one grounded, one capsized, and the others badly battered. Altogether nineteen ships were sunk or disabled. At the adjoining Hickam Field and other airfields on the island the Japanese found planes parked wing to wing, and destroyed in all about 150 of them. Few were able to get airborne, and Japa-

Pearl Harbor. The view from this attacking Japanese airplane shows American ships in vulnerable positions. [National Archives]

nese losses numbered fewer than thirty planes. Before it was over the raid had killed more than 2,400 American servicemen and civilians, and wounded 1,178 more. The surprise attack fulfilled the wildest dreams of its planners, but it fell short of total success in two ways. The Japanese ignored shore installations and oil tanks, without which the surviving ships might have been forced back to the West Coast, and they missed the American aircraft carriers which were out on mission at the time. In the naval war to come, these carriers would be decisive.

Later the same day (December 8 in the western Pacific) Japanese forces began assaults on the Philippines, Guam, and Midway, and on the British forces in Hong Kong and the Malay Peninsula. With one stroke the Japanese had silenced America's debate on neutrality, and a suddenly unified nation prepared for the struggle. The next day President Roosevelt delivered his war message to Congress:

> Yesterday, December 7, 1941—a date which will live in infamy—the United States of America was suddenly and deliberately attacked by naval and air forces of the Empire of Japan. . . .
>
> The facts of yesterday speak for themselves. The people of the United States have already formed their opinions and well understand the implications to the very life and safety of our Nation. . . .

Congress voted for the war resolution unanimously, with the sole exception of Rep. Jeanette Rankin, who was unable in conscience to vote for war in 1917 or 1941. For several days it was uncertain whether war with the other Axis powers would follow. The defensive Tripartite Pact carried no obligation for them to enter, but Hitler, impatient with American aid to Britain, willingly joined his Oriental allies. On December 11 Germany and Italy declared war on the United States. The separate wars in Asia and Europe had become one global war.

FURTHER READING

Selig Adler's *The Uncertain Giant: American Foreign Policy between the Wars* (1966) provides a detailed narrative of the events covered in this chapter. For a focus on the 1920s, see L. Ethan Ellis's *Republican Foreign Policy, 1921–1933* (1968). John E. Wiltz's *From Isolation to War, 1931–1941* (1968), and Robert Dallek's *Franklin D. Roosevelt and American Foreign Policy, 1932–1945* (1979),° cover the 1930s. A number of revisionists stress the economic bases of foreign policy: see William Appleman Williams's *The Tragedy of American Diplomacy* (1962), Joan Hoff Wilson's *American Business and Foreign Policy, 1920–1931* (1971), and Michael J. Hogan's *Informal Entente: The Private Structure of Cooperation in Anglo-American Economic Diplomacy, 1918–1929* (1977).

Other scholars have concentrated on specific policies of the 1920s. Thomas H. Buckley's *The United States and the Washington Conference, 1921–1922* (1970), and Raymond G. O'Connor's *Perilous Equilibrium: The United States and the London Naval Conference* (1962) examine disarmament. Keith Nelson's *Victors Divided: America and the Allies in Germany, 1918–1923* (1975), deals with the reparations issue. For a study of the Kellog-Briand pact, see Robert H. Ferrell's *Peace in Their Time: The Origins of the Kellog-Briand Pact* (1962).°

For American relations in the Pacific during the period, see Warren I. Cohen's *America's Response to China: An Interpretative History of Sino-American Relations* (1971) and Akira Iriye's *After Imperialism: The Search for a New Order in the Far East, 1921–1933* (1965).

For relations with countries south of the border, see David Green's *The Containment of Latin America* (1971), Bryce Wood's *The Making of the Good Neighbor Policy* (1961), and Alexander DeConde's *Herbert Hoover's Latin American Policy* (1951). Diplomacy in Europe is examined in Arnold A. Offner's *American Appeasement: United States Foreign Policy and Germany, 1933–1938* (1969), Brice Harris, Jr.'s *The United States and the Italo-Ethiopian Crisis* (1964), and Allen Guttman's *The Wound in the Heart: America and the Spanish Civil War* (1962).

For the eventual entry of the United States into World War II, see the two volumes of *The World Crisis and American Foreign Policy* by William L. Langer: *The Challenge to Isolationism, 1937–1940* (1952), and *The Undeclared War, 1940–1941* (1953). Other interpretations of Roosevelt

°These books are available in paperback editions.

and diplomacy include Robert A. Divine's *Roosevelt and World War II* (1969),° James MacGregor Burns's *Roosevelt: The Soldier of Freedom* (1970), and Lloyd C. Gardner's *Economic Aspects of New Deal Diplomacy* (1964). Other scholars concentrate on American relations with Great Britain: see David Reynolds's *The Creation of the Anglo-American Alliance, 1937–1941: A Study in Competitive Cooperation* (1981), C. A. McDonald's *The United States, Britain, and Appeasement, 1936–1939* (1981), and Joseph P. Lash's *Roosevelt and Churchill* (1976).°

How some dissenting Americans reacted to the Roosevelt policies is traced by Wayne S. Cole in *Gerald P. Nye and American Foreign Relations* (1962) and *America First: The Battle against Intervention, 1940–1941* (1967). Also helpful is Ellsworth Barnard's *Wendell Willkie: Fighter for Freedom* (1966). An unusual approach to the impact of foreign policy is found in David H. Culbert's *News for Everyman: Radio and Foreign Affairs in Thirties America* (1976). For Lend-Lease and the domestic reaction, see Warren F. Kimball's *The Most Unsordid Act: Lend-Lease, 1939–1941* (1969).

Two introductions to Pearl Harbor are Roberta Wohlstetter's *Pearl Harbor, Warning and Decision* (1962) and Gordon W. Prange's *At Dawn We Slept: The Untold Story of Pearl Harbor* (1981).° The Japanese perspective is given in Robert J. Burtow's *Tojo and the Coming of the War* (1961). Bruce M. Russell's *No Clear and Present Danger: A Skeptical View of United States Entry into World War II* (1972) provides a critical account.

30

THE WORLD AT WAR

AMERICA'S EARLY BATTLES

SETBACKS IN THE PACIFIC   For months after Pearl Harbor the news from the Pacific was "all bad," as President Roosevelt frankly confessed. On the first day of the war American planes in the Philippines were caught lined up at Clark Field near Manila despite ten hours' notice of the attack on Pearl Harbor—an event that defies plausible explanation. That same day enemy planes sank the British battle cruiser *Repulse* and the battleship *Prince of Wales* near Singapore while Japanese land forces entered Malaya and Thailand. Thailand prudently surrendered, becoming a passive ally of the Japanese. In quick sequence these Allied outposts fell to the enemy before the end of December: Guam, Wake Island, the Gilbert Islands, and Hong Kong. Rabaul in New Britain fell in January 1942, Singapore and Java in February. Adm. Thomas C. Hart's tiny Asiatic Fleet, with British and Dutch help, fought holding actions in the Dutch East Indies through January and February, all of them defeats climaxed by the disastrous Battle of the Java Sea (February 27 to March 1). The fall of Rangoon on March 9 cut off the Burma Road, the main link to Nationalist China.

In the Philippines, where General MacArthur abandoned Manila on December 27, the main American forces, outmanned and outgunned, held out on Bataan Peninsula until April 9, and then on "The Rock," the fortified island of Corregidor. MacArthur slipped away in March, when he was ordered out to Australia to take command of Allied forces in the Southwest Pacific. By May 6, when American forces surrendered Corregidor, Japan controlled a new empire that stretched from Burma eastward through the Dutch Indies and on out to Wake Island and the Gilberts.

If the Japanese had been willing to quit while they were ahead, they might have consolidated an almost impregnable empire with the resources they had seized. But the Japanese navy succumbed to what one of its admirals later called "victory disease." Though the Supreme Command decided to stop at the gates of India, behind the mountain barriers of Burma, it resolved to push on into the South Pacific, isolate Australia, and strike again at Hawaii. The aim was to draw out and destroy the American navy before the productive power of the United States could be brought to bear on the war effort.

A Japanese mistake and a stroke of American luck, however, enabled the United States Navy to frustrate the plan. Japan's failure to destroy the shore facilities at Pearl Harbor left the base relatively intact, and most of the ships damaged on December 7 lived to fight another day. The aircraft carriers at sea during the attack spent several months harassing Japanese outposts in the Gilberts and Marshalls. Their most spectacular exploit, an air raid on Tokyo itself launched on April 18, 1942, was delivered by Col. James H. Doolittle's B-25 bombers which took off from the carrier *Hornet* and, unable to land on its deck, proceeded to China. The raid caused only token damage, but did much to lift American morale amid a series of defeats elsewhere.

Japanese advances were finally halted in two decisive naval battles, the first of which started the day after Corregidor fell. The Battle of the Coral Sea (May 7–8, 1942) stopped a fleet convoying Japanese troop transports toward Port Moresby, on the southern coast of New Guinea. Planes from the *Lexington* and *Yorktown* sank one Japanese carrier, damaged another, and destroyed smaller ships. American losses were greater, and included the carrier *Lexington*, but the Japanese transports had to turn back. Port Moresby was secured, thwarting the Japanese advance on Australia.

MIDWAY: A TURNING POINT   Less than a month after the Coral Sea engagement Adm. Isoruku Yamamoto, the Japanese naval commander, decided to force a showdown in the central Pacific. With nearly every capital ship under his personal command, he headed for Midway Island, from which he hoped to render Pearl Harbor helpless. This time it was the Japanese who were the victims of surprise. American cryptanalysts had by then broken their naval code, and Adm. Chester Nimitz, commander of the central Pacific, knew what was up. He reinforced Midway with planes and the carriers *Enterprise, Hornet,* and *Yorktown.*

The first Japanese foray against Midway, on June 4, severely damaged the island, but at the cost of about a third of the Japanese planes. Before another attack could be mounted, American torpedo planes and dive bombers had caught three of the four Japanese carriers in the process of servicing their planes. The first wave of slow American torpedo bombers was almost all shot down, but dive bombers disabled the carriers *Akagi, Kaga,* and *Soryu,* and left them to sink. The fourth, the *Hiryu,* managed to send up planes which disabled the *Yorktown,* but American planes found and sank the *Hiryu* that afternoon. A Japanese submarine later sank the *Yorktown.* The only other major American loss was a destroyer. Yamamoto had to retreat, and the Japanese navy, having lost its four best aircraft carriers, all veterans of Pearl Harbor, was forced into retreat less than six months after the attack on Hawaii. The Japanese scored one dubious success, a diversionary action which captured the Aleutian Islands of Attu and Kiska in a vain effort to draw the navy off from Midway. The Japanese defeat was the turning point of the Pacific war, a loss they were never able to make up.

SETBACKS IN THE ATLANTIC   Early setbacks in the Pacific were matched by setbacks in the Atlantic. Since the *Blitzkrieg* of 1940 German submarine "wolf-packs" had issued out of bombproof pens on the French coast, wreaking havoc in the North Atlantic. In January 1942, after an ominous lull, German submarines suddenly appeared off American shores and began to sink coastal shipping, much of it tankers. Fourteen ships went down off the United States coast that month, and twelve in Canadian waters. By February nineteen had been sunk in the Caribbean and Gulf of Mexico. Until April and May, when coastal cities were blacked out, passing freighters and tankers were like sitting ducks, silhouetted against the horizon. From January through June 1942 nearly 400 ships were lost in American waters before effective countermeasures brought the problem under control. Adm. Ernest J. King, who became the commander of the United States Navy on December 20, 1941, hastened the building of small escort vessels, meanwhile pressing into patrol service all kinds of surface craft and planes, some of them civilian. During the second half of 1942 he brought the losses down to a negligible number.

MOBILIZATION AT HOME

The Pearl Harbor attack ended not only the long debate between isolation and intervention but also the long depression decade of the 1930s, and with the same finality with which the market crash of 1929 ended the prosperity decade of the 1920s. There was no doubt that the war effort would require all of America's huge productive capacity and full employment of the workforce. Soon after Pearl Harbor, Winston Churchill recalled that, thirty years before, Edward Grey had compared the United States to a gigantic boiler: "Once the fire is lighted under it, there is no limit to the power it can generate."

Mobilization was in fact already farther along than preparedness had been in 1916–1917. Selective services had been in effect for more than a year, and the army had grown to more than 1.4 million men by June 30, 1941. Congress quickly repealed the ban on sending draftees outside the Western Hemisphere and extended their service to six months after the end of the war. Men between eighteen and forty-five became subject to service. Altogether more than 15 million men and women served in the armed forces.

ECONOMIC CONVERSION The economy too was already partially mobilized by lend-lease and defense efforts. As early as May 1939 the president had named a War Resources Board to study supply needs. In May 1940, while *Blitzkrieg* enveloped France, Roosevelt revived the National Defense Advisory Commission, from which evolved multiple bureaus of war production and controls. The War Powers Act of December 18, 1941, gave the president a mandate to reshuffle government agencies, and a Second War Powers Act, of March 1942, empowered the government to allot materials and facilities as needed for defense, with penalties for those who failed to comply.

The War Production Board (WPB), created in January 1942 under Donald Nelson of Sears, Roebuck, became the new counterpart to Bernard Baruch's War Industries Board in directing industrial conversion to war production. Auto makers switched to producing tanks, makers of shirts switched to mosquito netting, model train plants to hardware, and the makers of refrigerators, stoves, and cash registers to munitions. The Reconstruction Finance Corporation, a depression agency, now financed war plants. For a year the War Production Board oversaw a wild scramble of manufacturers for available supplies. As War Secretary Stimson put it, it was "like . . . hungry dogs quarreling over a very inadequate bone" until the WPB instituted its Controlled Materials Plan, which allocated scarce items to claimants according to its best judgment of need.

Some shortages called for more heroic efforts. The government named special administrators, or "czars," to promote production of rubber and oil. Rubber Director William Jeffers, president of Union Pacific Railroad, pushed construction of synthetic rubber plants, which by 1944 produced 800,000 tons, or 87 percent of the country's requirements. Tire rationing began in December 1941, and gasoline rationing at the end of 1942. Since German sinkings of coastal tankers placed an unusual burden on railways in getting oil to the East Coast, Petroleum Administrator Harold Ickes hastened construction of the "Big Inch" pipeline, which was twenty-four inches in diameter and ran 1,250 miles from the Texas oilfields to the New York–Philadelphia region. Begun in the summer of 1942, it was finished a year later. Through the Office of Scientific Research and Development Dr. Vannevar Bush mobilized thousands of "scientists against time" to create and modify radar, sonar, the proximity fuse, the bazooka, means to isolate blood plasma, and myriads of other innovations.

The pressure of wartime needs and the stimulus of government spending sent the gross national product soaring from $100.6 billion in 1940 to $213.6 billion in 1945. Government expenditures during the war years rose from $20 billion in calendar year 1941 to $97.2 billion in 1944. From July 1, 1940, to June 30, 1946, expenditures totaled $337 billion, of which $304 billion went to the war effort. The figure for total expenditures was twice as great as the total of all previous federal spending in the history of the republic, and about 10 times what America spent in World War I, and 100 times the expenditures during the Civil War.

FINANCING THE WAR   To cover the war's huge cost the president preferred taxes to borrowing. "I would rather pay one hundred percent of taxes now than push the burden of this war onto the shoulders of my grandchildren," he said in December 1942. Taxes also had the merit of relieving upward pressures on prices. The wartime Congress, however, dominated by conservatives, feared taxes more than deficits and refused to go more than half-way with Roosevelt's fiscal prudence. The Revenue Act of 1942 provided for only about $7 billion in increased revenue, less than half that recommended by the Treasury. It also greatly broadened the tax structure by lowering exemptions from $750 to $500 for single persons, and from $1,500 to $1,200 for married persons. Whereas in 1939 only about 4 million people filed returns, the new act, in the words of a tax historian, "made the Federal income tax a genuine mass tax." By 1943 the idea was gaining ground of putting all tax collections on a current basis through regular payroll deductions, which would further fight inflation. Before the year was out the plan had been adopted.

In February 1944 a rebellion against an administration request for a tax increase to combat inflation and finance the war led Roosevelt to veto a tax bill. It was "a tax relief bill . . . not for the needy, but for the greedy," the president said. Sen. Alben Barkley angrily resigned as Senate majority leader, only to be reelected unanimously, and both houses promptly overrode the veto by large votes. Still, a few months later an act for the next fiscal year reduced the basic tax rate from 6 to 3 percent while raising surtaxes to 91 percent in the highest bracket.

The result was that the government covered about 45 percent of its 1939–1946 costs with tax revenues. Roosevelt would have preferred to cover more, but the figure compared favorably with 30 percent for World War I and 23 percent for the Civil War. To cover the rest of its costs the government borrowed from the public. War-bond drives, including a Victory Drive in 1945, induced citizens to put aside more than $150 billion in bonds rather than use it to bid up prices. Financial institutions picked up most of the rest of the government's debt. In all, by the end of the war the national debt had grown to about $260 billion, about

Mobilization for war deflected many New Deal efforts. [Library of Congress]

six times its size at the time of Pearl Harbor. One of its effects was to make converts to the Keynesian argument that government spending would end the depression.

The basic economic problem was no longer finding jobs but finding workers for the booming shipyards, aircraft factories, and powder mills. Millions of people were brought fully into the economic system who before had lived on its margin, which leveled out somewhat the economic pyramid. Between 1939 and 1944 the share of the income going to the wealthiest 5 percent declined from 23.7 to 16.8 percent. Stubborn poverty did not disappear, but for most of those who stayed home the war spelled neither hardship nor suffering but better life than ever before, despite shortages and rationing.

ECONOMIC CONTROLS Increased incomes and spending during the war conjured up the spectre of inflation. Some of the available money went into taxes and war bonds, but even so, more was sent chasing after civilian goods just as production was converting to war needs. Such consumer durables as cars, washing machines, and nondefense housing in fact ceased to be made at all. It was apparent that only strict restraints would keep prices from soaring out of sight. The administration, having set out in 1933 to raise prices, now reversed its ground and set out to hold them down. In April 1941 Roosevelt had created the Office of Price Administration (OPA) under Leon Henderson, a New Deal economist. By July 1941 Roosevelt was seeking statutory price controls and finally, in January 1942, Congress authorized the OPA for the first time to set price ceilings. While some increases were deemed necessary as incentives to production, the General Maximum Price Regulation of April 1942 froze prices at the highest level they had reached in March 1942. With prices frozen, goods had to be allocated through rationing, which began with auto tires in December 1941 and was gradually extended to other goods in short supply, with coupons doled out for sugar, coffee, gasoline, and meats.

Wages and farm prices were not controlled, however, and this complicated things. War prosperity offered farmers a chance to redress the balance from two decades of distress, and farm-state congressmen fought to raise both floors and ceilings on farm prices. Price supports continued for basic crops, and the Emergency Price Control Act limited farm-price ceilings to no less than 110 percent of parity. Some farm prices rose to 150 percent of parity. Higher food prices reinforced worker demands for higher wages, and the War Labor Board tried to hold the line with the Little Steel formula of July 1942, which permitted wage increases in line with the 15 percent increase in the cost of living since January 1941. The WLB, however, had jurisdiction only over wage increases resulting from labor disputes.

Under the Stabilization Act of October 1942 the president got new authority to control wages and farm prices, which he took back to simple parity. At the same time he set up the Office of Economic Stabilization under James F. Byrnes, who left his seat on the Supreme Court to coordinate the effort. Stabilization proved to be one of the most complex jobs of the war effort, subject to constant sniping by special interests. By December 1942 Leon Henderson had offended so many congressmen by his zeal to keep prices down that he was forced to resign. Chester Bowles, who replaced him at the OPA, proved equal to the challenge.

Both business and workers chafed at the wage and price controls. On occasion the government was forced to seize industries threatened by strike. The coal mines and railroads both came under government operation for a short time in 1943, and in 1944 the government briefly took over Montgomery-Ward Company. Soldiers had to carry its chairman bodily out of his office when he stubbornly defied orders of the War Labor Board. Despite these problems, stabilization was on the whole a success story. Roosevelt's "hold-the-line" order of April 8, 1943, freezing prices, wages, and salaries, finally brought the price level to a plateau for the rest of the war. By the end of the war consumer prices had risen about 31 percent, a far better record than the wartime rise of 62 percent before the Armistice of 1918.

SOCIAL EFFECTS: WOMEN   The war became an important watershed in the changing status of women. The proportion of women

A Women's Army Corps poster. [State Historical Society of Wisconsin]

*Women at work on the noses of fighter planes at Douglas Aircraft, 1943.
"Stars over Berlin and Tokyo will soon replace these factory lights
reflected" on the plane noses. [National Archives]*

working had barely altered from 1910 to 1940, but at a time
when millions of men were going into military service the demand for labor shook up old prejudices about sex roles in the
workplace—and in the military. Nearly 200,000 women went
into the Women's Army Corps (WAC) and the navy's equivalent,
Women Accepted for Volunteer Emergency Service (WAVES).
Lesser numbers joined the Marine Corps, the Coast Guard, and
the Women's Auxiliary Ferrying Squadron (WAFS) of the Army
Air Force. By the end of the war over 6 million women had entered the workforce, an increase in general of over 50 percent
and in manufacturing alone of some 110 percent. Old barriers
fell overnight as women entered employment of all sorts, becoming toolmakers, machinists, crane operators, lumberjacks,
stevedores, blacksmiths, and railroad track workers. Such arduous occupations were no longer reserved for men.

By 1944 women made up 14 percent of all workers in shipbuilding and 40 percent in aircraft plants. Rosie the Riveter
symbolized women in war work, and her real counterparts
performed so well in jobs once thought unsuited for women that
attitudes about the abilities of women were permanently altered.
One striking feature of the new scene was the larger proportion
of older, married women in the workforce. In 1940 about 15.2
percent of married women went into gainful employment; by
1945 it was 24 percent. In the workforce as a whole, married
women for the first time outnumbered single women. Attitudes
sharply changed from those of the depression days, when over

80 percent of Americans opposed work by married women; by 1942 a poll showed 60 percent in favor of hiring married women in war industries. Defense jobs, however, were the ones most vulnerable to postwar cuts.

SOCIAL EFFECTS: BLACKS   Potentially the most inflammable issue ignited by the war was that of black participation in the defense effort. From the start black leaders demanded full recognition in the armed forces and defense industries. Eventually about a million Negroes served in the armed forces, in every branch and every theater. But they served usually in segregated units which mirrored the society from which they came. Every army camp had its little Harlem, its separate facilities, its periodic racial "incidents." The most important departure was a 1940 decision to give up segregation in officer candidate schools, except those for air force cadets. A separate flight school at Tuskegee, Alabama, trained about 600 Negro pilots, many of who saw action over Europe.

War industries were even less accessible to black influence and pressure, although government policy theoretically opposed discrimination. In February 1941 A. Philip Randolph, head of the Brotherhood of Sleeping Car Porters, organized a March on Washington Movement to demand an end to discrimination in defense industries. As the movement grew, its leaders promised to mobilize 100,000 marchers. The administration, alarmed at the prospect of a mass descent on Washington, struck a bargain. The Randolph group called off its march in return for Executive Order 8802, which forbade discrimination in defense work and training programs by requiring a nondiscrimination clause in defense contracts, and set up the Committee on Fair Employment Practices (FEPC). The FEPC's authority was chiefly moral, since

A unit of black soldiers about to conduct religious services, [Photoworld/FPG]

it had no power to enforce directives. It nevertheless offered willing employers the chance to say they were following government policy in giving jobs to black citizens, and no doubt persuaded others to go along. About 2 million blacks were working in war plants by the end of 1944. The demand for black labor revived migration out of the South, which had lagged during the depression, and large numbers of blacks now headed for the Far West as well as the North. States with the largest proportionate gains of black population in the 1940s were, in order, California, Michigan, Oregon, Washington, Utah, Colorado, Wisconsin, Illinois, and New York.

Blacks quickly broadened their drive for wartime participation into a more inclusive social and political front. Early in 1942 the Pittsburgh *Courier* endorsed the "Double V," which stood for victory at home and abroad. The slogan became immensely popular in black communities, and reflected a growing urge to rid the world not just of Hitler but of Hitlerism, as one editor put it. Blacks began to challenge more openly all kinds of discrimination, including racial segregation itself. "It was as if some universal message had come through to the great mass of Negroes," the sociologist Howard Odum wrote in 1943, "urging them to dream new dreams and to protest against the old order." Confirmation of his observation came in *What the Negro Wants* (1944), a symposium to which the University of North Carolina Press invited fourteen blacks of various viewpoints to contribute. The editor and black historian Rayford W. Logan noted "surprising unanimity" among the contributors, all of whom "want Negroes eventually to enjoy the same rights, opportunities and privileges that are vouchsafed to all other Americans." A foundation was being laid for a great expansion of civil-rights efforts after the war. Membership in the NAACP grew during the war from 50,000 to 450,000. Blacks could look forward to greater political participation after the Supreme Court, in *Smith v. Allwright* (1944), struck down Texas's white primary on the grounds that Democratic primaries were part of the election process and thus subject to the Fifteenth Amendment.

The growing militancy of blacks of course aroused antagonism from some whites. Racial violence this time did not approach the level of that in World War I, but growing tensions on a hot summer afternoon in Detroit sparked incidents on crowded Belle Isle, an offshore park in the Detroit River. Fighting raged through June 20–21, 1943, until federal troops arrived on the second evening to stop it. Twenty-five blacks and nine whites had been killed.

The first day of evacuation from the Japanese quarters in San Francisco, April 1942. Photo by Dorothea Lange. [National Archives]

SOCIAL EFFECTS: JAPANESE-AMERICANS   The record on civil liberties during World War II was on the whole better than that during World War I, if only because there was virtually no opposition to the war effort after the attack on Pearl Harbor. Neither German-Americans nor Italian-Americans faced the harassments meted out to their counterparts in the previous war; few had much sympathy for Hitler or Mussolini. The shameful exception to an otherwise improved record was the treatment given to more than 100,000 Americans of Japanese descent who were forcibly removed from homes and businesses on the West Coast to "War Relocation Camps" in the interior. They were not disloyal, but victims of fear and racial prejudice. In 1983, more than forty years later, the federal government agreed with this view, and proposed granting those Nisei still living $20,000 each in compensation.

In Hawaii, a far more sensitive area, the Japanese formed the largest single ethnic group in a mixed population. These Japanese were plagued by rumors of sabotage at Pearl Harbor and on the mainland, all unfounded. In fact Japanese Hawaiians and mainlanders made up two of the most celebrated infantry units in the war, fighting with distinction on the Italian front. Other thousands of Nisei served as interpreters and translators, the "eyes and ears" of the American armed forces in the Pacific.

DOMESTIC CONSERVATISM   In domestic politics the wartime period was marked by a growing conservatism. Discontent with price controls, labor shortages, rationing, and a hundred other petty vexations spread. In 1942 the congressional elections registered a national swing against the New Deal. Republicans gained forty-six seats in the House and nine in the Senate, chiefly in the Middle States farm areas. Democratic losses outside the South strengthened the southern delegation's position within the party, and the delegation itself reflected conservative victories in southern primaries. A coalition of conservatives proceeded to eviscerate "nonessential" New Deal agencies. In 1943 Congress abolished the Work Projects Administration, the National Youth Administration, and the Civilian Conservation Corps, began to dismantle the Farm Security Administration, and liquidated the National Resources Planning Board by refusing it funds.

Organized labor, despite substantial gains during the war, was vulnerable to the conservative trend. In the spring of 1943, when John L. Lewis led the coal miners out on strike, widespread resentment led Congress to pass the Smith-Connally War Labor Disputes Act, which authorized the government to seize plants useful to the war, required prestrike plebiscites, and forbade unions to make political contributions. The intended effect of the act was somewhat blunted by the tendency of unionists to vote routinely for strikes as a bargaining ploy. In 1943 a dozen states adopted laws variously restricting picketing and other union activities, and in 1944 Arkansas and Florida by constitutional amendment set in motion a wave of "right-to-work" legislation which outlawed the closed shop and other union security devices.

Congress generally cooperated with the administration's war effort. The Senate War Investigating Committee under Harry S Truman of Missouri devoted itself to rooting out waste and inefficiency in the war effort. Unity on foreign relations persisted through the war, and in 1943 both houses of Congress passed resolutions in favor of an international peacekeeping organization after the war.

The Allied Drive toward Berlin

By mid-1942 the "home front" began to get news from the war fronts that some of the lines were holding at last. Japanese naval losses at the Coral Sea and Midway had secured Australia and Hawaii. By midyear Admiral King's motley fleet of air and sea subchasers was ending six months of happy hunting for U-boats off the Atlantic coast. This was all the more important because war plans called for the defeat of Germany first.

WAR AIMS AND STRATEGY There were many reasons for the priority of defeating Hitler. Nazi forces in western Europe and the Atlantic posed a more direct threat to the Western Hemisphere;

German war potential was greater and German science was more likely to come up with some devastating new weapon. Lose in the Atlantic, Gen. George Marshall said, and you lose everywhere. Hitler's attack on Russia in June 1941 strengthened the argument. Once defeat Germany, strongest of the Axis powers, and Japan would face overwhelming force. Despite the understanding, Japanese attacks involved Americans directly in the Pacific war from the start, and as a consequence, during the first year of fighting more Americans went to the Pacific than across the Atlantic.

The Pearl Harbor attack brought Prime Minister Churchill quickly to Washington for lengthy talks about a common war plan. Out of these exchanges came several major and a number of minor decisions, including the one, urged by General Marshall, to name a supreme commander in each major theater of war. Each commander would be subject to orders from the British-American Combined Chiefs of Staff with headquarters in Washington. Marshall, Adm. Ernest J. King, and Army Air Force Gen. H. H. "Hap" Arnold thereafter met periodically with their British counterparts to review strategy. Other joint boards allotted munitions, raw materials, and shipping. American and British war plans thereafter proceeded in close concert, and often launched joint operations, especially against Germany. No such concert was ever effected with Russia, which fought its own war on the eastern front, separate except for the coordinated timing of some major offensives. In Washington on January 1, 1942, representatives of twenty-six governments then at war with the Axis signed the Declaration of the United Nations, affirming the Principles of the Atlantic Charter, pledging their full resources to the war, and promising not to make separate peace with the common enemies. Finally, in the course of their talks the British and American leaders reaffirmed the priority of war against Germany.

Agreement on war aims, however, was not agreement on strategy. Roosevelt and Winston Churchill, meeting at the White House again in June 1942, could not agree on where to hit first. American military planners wanted to strike directly across the English Channel before the end of 1942, secure a beachhead, and move against Germany in 1943. The British preferred to keep the Germans off balance with hit-and-run raids and air attacks, while continuing to build up their forces. With vivid memories of the last war, the British feared a mass bloodletting in trench warfare if they struck prematurely. When General Marshall argued in London for an early assault on the score of German strength, Lord Cherwell told him: "It's no use—you are arguing against the casualties on the Somme." The Russians, bearing the brunt of the German attack in the East, insisted that the Western Allies must do something to relieve the pressure. Finally, the Americans accepted Churchill's proposal to invade French North Africa.

THE NORTH AFRICA CAMPAIGN   It was not only the Russians who needed a diversion, but British forces defending Egypt against invaders from Libya. If German Gen. Erwin Rommel's Afrika Korps took Alexandria and Suez, little more than distance would stand between them and India, where they could link up with the Japanese. Late in October 1942 Gen. Sir Bernard Montgomery began a counterattack on Rommel at El-Alamein. On November 8, 1942, Anglo-American forces under the command of Gen. Dwight D. Eisenhower landed at Casablanca in Morocco and at Oran and Algiers in Algeria. Completely surprised, French forces under the Vichy government (which collaborated with the Germans) had little will to resist. Hitler therefore occupied the whole of France and sent German forces into French Tunisia. By chance Adm. Jean-François Darlan, second to Marshal Petain in the collaborationist Vichy government, was visiting in Algiers and was persuaded to order a cease-fire on November 11.

Since Darlan seemed the man the French forces would most likely obey, a deal was struck to make him the leader of the French in the North African colonies. A military expedient which probably saved thousands of Allied lives, this deal with a former Nazi collaborator was widely criticized in America and Britain until the assassination of Darlan on Christmas Eve relieved the Allies of the embarrassment. Gen. Henri Giraud, who had escaped a Nazi prison, took his place. Still, Gen. Charles De Gaulle, leader of the "Free French" who had escaped to England, had little influence in North Africa. Not until October 1944 did the United States formally recognize him as leader of the French nation.

Farther east the tide had turned and General Montgomery was pushing Rommel back across Libya, but green American forces were held in stalemate by seasoned Nazis pouring into Tunisia. Before spring, however, Montgomery had taken Libya and the Germans were caught in a gigantic pincers. By April Montgomery had linked up with American forces and one month later, on May 7, 1943, Bizerte fell to the Americans and Tunis to the British. The remaining Germans made a last stand on Cape Bon. Hammered from all sides, unable to retreat across the Mediterra-

WAR IN EUROPE AND AFRICA,
1942-1945

Axis Powers at outbreak of war

Maximum extent of Axis military power

Allies

Neutral countries

Allied offensives

Heaviest Allied aerial bombing

Inside limit of German U-boat operations

nean, an army of 275,000 surrendered on May 13, 1943, leaving all of North Africa in Allied hands.

While the battle of Tunisia was still shaping up, in January 1943 Roosevelt and Churchill and the Combined Chiefs of Staff met at Casablanca to plan the future. Stalin declined to leave Russia for the meeting but continued to press for a second front in Europe. For the time, however, the decision was reached to postpone the cross-Channel invasion further, and to carry out Churchill's scheme to attack what he called the "soft underbelly of the Axis" by invading Sicily. Admiral Nimitz and General MacArthur were authorized meanwhile to start an offensive in the Pacific islands. Top priority, however, went to an antisubmarine campaign in the Atlantic. Before leaving Casablanca, Roosevelt announced, with Churchill's endorsement, that the war would end only with the "unconditional surrender" of all enemies. An echo of Ulysses Grant's ultimatum at Fort Donelson, the formula was designed to reassure Stalin and to quiet suspicions aroused by the Darlan deal that the Western Allies might negotiate separately with the enemy. The announcement owed a good bit also to the determination that, as Roosevelt put it, "every person in Germany should realize that this time Germany is a defeated nation." This dictum was later criticized for having stiffened enemy resistance, but probably had little effect; in fact neither the Italian nor Japanese surrender would be totally unconditional.

THE BATTLE OF THE ATLANTIC While the battles raged in North Africa the more crucial Battle of the Atlantic reached its climax on the high seas. Several factors brought success to the Allied effort. Patrols by land-based planes covered much of the Atlantic from airfields in Britain and the Western Hemisphere, and in 1943 Portugal permitted American planes to operate from the Azores, thereby closing the last gap in coverage in the North Atlantic. Scientists perfected a variety of new detection devices: radar, which the British had already used to advantage in the air Battle of Britain, bounced radio waves off objects above the surface and registered their positions on a screen; sonar gear detected sound waves from submerged U-boats, and sonobuoys, dropped from planes, radioed back their findings; advanced magnetic equipment enabled aircraft to detect objects under water. New escort carriers ("baby flat-tops") and improvements in depth charges added to the effectiveness of convoys.

By April 1943 there were in the western half of the North Atlantic at any time an average of 31 convoys with 145 escorts and 673 merchant ships, as well as 120 other ships traveling alone and a number of heavily escorted troopships. None of the troopships going to Britain or the Mediterranean was lost, although submarines sank three en route to Greenland and Iceland. The U-boats kept up the Battle of the Atlantic until the war's end; when Germany finally collapsed at least forty-nine were still at sea. But Adm. Karl Doenitz, their commander, later admitted that the Battle of the Atlantic was lost by the end of May 1943. In his memoirs he credited the difference largely to radar. What he did not know then was that the Allies had a secret weapon. By early 1943 their cryptanalysts were routinely reading messages from Doenitz and telling their sub-hunters where to look for the German prey.

SICILY AND ITALY   The North African campaign won, the Allies got ready to attack Sicily, and decided at Casablanca. On July 10 about 250,000 British and American troops landed on Sicily, the largest single amphibious action in the war to that time, scoring a complete surprise. Gen. George Patton's American Seventh Army landed on the southwest coast, and after a fierce battle at the beachhead, moved swiftly across the island to take Palermo twelve days later. Montgomery's British Eighth Army encountered more stubborn resistance near Syracuse, but the entire island was in Allied hands by August 17, although some 40,000 Germans escaped to the mainland.

The collapse in Sicily ended Mussolini's twenty years of Fascist rule. Italians never had much heart for the war into which he had dragged them. On July 25, 1943, King Victor Emmanuel III notified the dictator of his dismissal as premier. A new regime under the elderly Marshal Pietro Badoglio, former chief of the general staff, startled the Allies when it offered not only to surrender but to switch sides in the war. Unfortunately, mutual suspicions prolonged talks until September 3, while the Germans poured reinforcements into Italy and seized key points. In the confusion the Italian army disintegrated, although most of the navy escaped to Allied ports. A few army units later joined the Allied effort, and a good many of the soldiers joined bands of partisans who fought behind the German lines. Mussolini, plucked from imprisonment by a German airborne raid, became head of a shadowy puppet government in northern Italy.

Landings on the mainland therefore did not turn into a walkover. British forces invading the foot of the peninsula in early September landed unopposed, but the main landing at Salerno on September 9 encountered heavy resistance. In hope of scoring a surprise, the invaders omitted preliminary bombardment, leaving intact the German defenses. The American Fifth Army under Gen. Mark Clark, with British troops in the assault force, nevertheless secured beachheads within a week and by October 1 were in Naples. The Germans had reduced much of the city to rubble, but the bay and port facilities were soon cleared and back in operation. Before the end of September British forces had crossed the peninsula to Foggia, on the Adriatic. From there Allied fighters could cover the front and bombers could raid Nazi facilities in the Balkans as far as the Ploesti oilfields in Rumania.

Rome was the next objective, but mountainous country stood in the way. Fighting stalled in the Appenines where the German Gustav Line held the Allies through the winter of 1943–1944 in some of the most miserable, mud-soaked, and frostbitten fighting of the war. Cartoonist Bill Mauldin's Willie and Joe, in the GI newspaper *Yank,* slogged their way to fame in the Italian campaign as typical dogface infantrymen who distilled a saving humor out of their plight. On January 22, 1944, the Allies attempted an end-run by landing at Anzio, behind the German lines near Rome. This time they surprised the enemy, but failed to move quickly enough to the commanding Alban Heights. At Anzio they held on only by dogged determination until a series of savage attacks broke the Gustav Line in mid-May 1944 and lifted the siege. On June 4, 1944, Mark Clark's Fifth Army was in Rome, which fortunately had escaped the destruction visited on Naples, or on the Benedictine abbey at Monte Cassino. The capture of Rome provided only a brief moment of glory, for the long-awaited cross-Channel landing in France came two days later. Italy, always a secondary front, faded from the limelight of world attention as the GIs labored 150 miles northward to the Gothic Line, where the Germans staged a last-ditch defense for yet another bleak winter.

STRATEGIC BOMBING OF EUROPE   Behind the long-postponed landings on the Normandy beaches lay months of preparation. While waiting, the United States Army Air Force and the Royal Air Force (RAF) carried the battle into Hitler's "Fortress Europe." In April 1942 advance units of the Eighth Air Force embarked for Britain by sea, and soon afterward planes began to be ferried across the North Atlantic by air. On July 4, 1942, six American crews took part in a raid on airfields in Holland; on August 17, 1942, heavy bombers staged the first all-American raid on freight yards in Rouen, France, and in October began hitting submarine pens in the Bay of Biscay. Late in January 1943 came the first American raid on Germany itself, on the port of Wilhelmshaven.

By 1943 American strategic bombers were full-fledged partners of the RAF in the effort to pound Germany into submission. The RAF, to cut losses during the hard days after the fall of

"Joe, yestiddy ya saved my life an' I swore I'd pay ya back. Here's my last pair of dry socks." *Mauldin's Willie and Joe. [Bill Mauldin and Wil-Jo Associates, Inc.]*

France, had confined itself mostly to night raids, and continued now to specialize in nocturnal attacks. The Americans believed that they could be more effective with high-level daylight precision bombing. Between them the AAF and RAF kept German defenders on the watch day and night.

Yet despite the widespread damage it caused, the strategic air offensive ultimately failed to cut severely into German production or, as later studies found, to break civilian morale. German production in fact increased until the last few weeks of the war. Heavy Allied losses persisted through 1943. In six days of October, raids deep inside the continent, climaxed by an attack on ball-bearing works at Schweinfurt, resulted in the loss of 148 bombers, mainly from German fighters. By the end of 1943, however, jettisonable gas tanks permitted escort fighters to go as far as Berlin and back. In the "Big Week" of February 20–25, 1944, 3,300 heavy bombers of the Eighth Air Force, and 500 from the Fifteenth Air Force in Italy, focused their attack on aircraft plants. Badly damaged, the German aircraft industry continued to turn out planes to the end, but heavy losses of both planes and pilots forced the German Luftwaffe to conserve its strength and cease challenging every Allied mission.

Berlin, the air strategists assumed, was one target the German fighters would have to protect. But in March the capital became the object of repeated Allied raids, and the resultant losses left German fighters ever more reluctant to rise to the bait. The horror at enemy attacks on civilians earlier in the war proved no barrier to a response in kind. Germany, Churchill said, was reaping the whirlwind. With air supremacy assured, the Allies were free to concentrate on their primary urban and industrial targets, and when the time came, to provide cover for the Normandy landings. On April 14, 1944, General Eisenhower assumed control of the Strategic Air Forces for use in the Normandy landings, less than two months away. On D-Day he told the troops: "If you see fighting aircraft over you, they will be ours."

THE TEHERAN MEETING   By the summer of 1943 the growing American presence in Britain, combined with successes in the Battle of the Atlantic and the strategic bombing, finally brought Churchill around on the cross-Channel invasion. Late in the fall he and Roosevelt finally had their first joint meeting with Josef Stalin in Teheran, Iran. A preliminary meeting of foreign ministers was held in Moscow during late October 1943, with Secretary of State Hull and Foreign Ministers Anthony Eden and V. M. Molotov. On one point they could not reach agreement: the Russians refused to recognize the Polish government-in-exile at London. But when Hull and Eden gave assurance that a cross-Channel invasion was coming, the Russians in return promised to enter the war against Japan after Germany's defeat. The ministers also agreed to begin plans for an international organization, and at Eden's suggestion they set up a European Advisory Commission in London to lay plans for postwar Germany. It was this body that later fixed the zones of occupation.

On the way to the Teheran meeting with Stalin, Churchill and Roosevelt met in Cairo with Generalissimo Chiang Kai-shek from November 22 to 26. The resultant Declaration of Cairo

Premier Stalin (left), President Roosevelt, and Prime Minister Churchill at the Teheran conference, November 1943. [Library of Congress]

(December 1, 1943) affirmed that war against Japan would continue until Japan's unconditional surrender, that all Chinese territories taken by Japan would be restored to China—including Formosa and the Pescadores—that Japan would lose the Pacific islands acquired after 1941, and that "in due course Korea shall become free and independent."

During November 28 to December 1 the Big Three leaders conferred in Teheran. Their chief subject was the planned invasion of France and a Russian offensive timed to coincide with it. Stalin repeated his promise to enter the war against Japan, and the three leaders reaffirmed the foreign ministers' decision in favor of planning an international organization. At further discussions in Cairo (December 4–6) Roosevelt and Churchill decided to put General Eisenhower in command of the cross-Channel invasion.

D-DAY AND AFTER   In January 1944 General Eisenhower arrived in London to take command at Supreme Headquarters, Allied Expeditionary Forces (SHAEF). Already battle-tested in North Africa and the Mediterranean, he now faced the supreme test of Operation "Overlord," the cross-Channel assault on Hitler's "Atlantic Wall." In April and May while the vast invasion forces made final preparations, the Allied air forces disrupted the transportation network of northern France, smashing railroads, bridges, and rolling stock. By early June all was ready, and after postponement for one day because of weather, D-Day fell on June 6, 1944.

The invasion hit not across the narrow stretch from Dover to Calais, where the elaborate activity of Gen. George Patton's Third Army had led the Germans to expect it, but along sixty

Gen. Dwight D. Eisenhower instructing paratroopers just before they board their airplanes to begin the D-Day assault. [Library of Congress]

The Allied beachhead in Normandy. [Maritime Administration]

miles of beach in Normandy. Airborne forces dropped behind the beaches during the night while planes and battleships pounded the coastal defenses. At dawn the invasion fleet of some 4,000 ships began to pour out their cargoes of troops and supplies on the shore. On Utah Beach, at the base of the Cotentin Peninsula, the American invaders made it in against relatively light opposition, but farther east, on a four-mile segment designated Omaha Beach, bombardment had failed to take out German defenders and the Americans were caught by heavily mined water. They then had to make it across a fifty-yard beach exposed to crossfire from concrete pillboxes before they could huddle under a sea wall and begin to root out the defenders. Still farther east, British forces had less difficulty on Gold, Juno, and Sword beaches, but found themselves subjected to bitter counterattack by German forces determined to hold Caen Beach.

Within two weeks the Allies had landed a million men and seized a beachhead sixty miles wide and five to fifteen miles deep. Before the end of June they had swept up the peninsula to the port of Cherbourg, only to find the harbor so completely blocked that it took two months to clear. But they continued to pour men and matériel onto the beaches, and contrived man-made harbors by scuttling old ships to create breakwaters. On into July the Allies edged inland through the Norman marshes and hedgerows. On July 19, 1944, Gen. Omar Bradley's troops took St. Lo, a transportation hub for roads and railroads into the heart of France. Marshals Gerd von Rundstedt, the German commander, and Erwin Rommel, now in charge of Army Group B, advised withdrawal to defenses behind the Seine, but an enraged Hitler removed both men and issued disastrous orders to contest every inch of land. Rommel, convinced that all was lost, began to intrigue for a separate peace until he was arrested and granted the option of suicide. Other like-minded officers, convinced that the war was hopeless, tried to kill Hitler at his headquarters on July 20, but the Führer survived the bomb blast and hundreds of conspirators and suspects were tortured to death.

Meanwhile, the Führer's tactics brought calamity to the German forces in western France. On July 25 Gen. Omar Bradley's First Army broke through west of St. Lo and, soon augmented by George Patton's Third Army, the American forces broke out westward into Brittany and eastward toward Paris. Patton moved east and north to link up with British forces coming south from Caen, and the two caught the German Seventh and Fifth Panzer Armies in a trap. Only remnants managed to escape through the Falaise Gap before the pincers closed on August 19. Meanwhile on August 15 a joint American-French invasion force landed on the French Mediterranean coast, took Marseille and Toulon in a walkover, and raced up the Rhône Valley. German resistance in France collapsed. A Free French division under Gen. Jacques Le Clerc, aided by American forces, had the honor of liberating Paris on August 25. German forces retired pell-mell toward the prewar Siegfried Line or Westwall at the German border, and in a rush by mid-September most of France and Belgium were cleared of enemy forces. By this time the Americans were in Aachen, the old seat of Charlemagne's empire, the first German town to fall.

SLOWING MOMENTUM   Things had moved so much faster than expected, in fact, that the Allies were running out of gas. Neither their plans nor their supply system could keep up with the movement. General Montgomery, whose British and Canadian forces had been the pivot of the Allied sweep, had moved forward into Belgium, where they took Antwerp. From there, he argued, a quick fatal thrust toward Berlin could end things. On the right flank, General Patton was just as sure he could take the American Third Army all the way. Eisenhower reasoned, however, that prudence demanded getting his supply lines in order first, which required clearing stubborn Germans out of the Scheldt estuary and opening a supply channel to Antwerp—a long, hard battle which lasted until the end of November. Before giving up his original plan, however, Montgomery tried one sharp thrust at Arnhem to make a bridgehead across the Rhine. His force proved inadequate, with the consequence that airborne forces dropped behind the German lines were cut off and decimated. Another winter of fighting would remain before the German collapse.

LEAPFROGGING TO TOKYO

Even in the Pacific, relegated to lower priority, Allied forces had brought the war within reach of the enemy homeland by the end of 1944. The war's first American offensive in fact had been in the southwest Pacific. There the Japanese, stopped at Coral Sea and Midway, had thrust into the southern Solomons, and were building an airstrip on Guadalcanal from which they could attack transportation routes to Australia. On August 7, 1942, two months before the North Africa landings, the First Marine Division under Gen. Alexander A. Vandegrift landed on Guadalcanal and seized the airstrip while other marines secured nearby Tulagi and its port.

These quick victories, however, provoked a savage Japanese response. Reinforcements poured in via the "Tokyo Express" down the central channel, the Solomons "Slot," and the opposing navies challenged each other in a confusing series of battles that battered both so badly the sailors named the Savo Island Sound "Iron Bottom Bay." But while the Americans had lost heavily, they delivered such punishment to Japanese carrier groups, already battered at Midway, that the Japanese navy remained on the defensive for the rest of the war. The marines, helped by reinforcements, finally cleared the steaming jungles of Japanese. By February 1943 only stragglers were left.

MACARTHUR IN NEW GUINEA   Meanwhile American and Australian forces under General MacArthur had begun to push the Japanese out of their advanced positions on the north coast of New Guinea. These battles, fought through some of the hottest, most humid and mosquito-infested swamps in the world, bought advances at a heavy cost, but by the end of January 1943 the eastern tip of New Guinea up to Huon Gulf was secured.

At this stage came a critical decision on strategy. MacArthur proposed to advance westward along the northern coast of New Guinea toward the Philippines and ultimately Tokyo. Admiral Nimitz, with headquarters at Pearl Harbor, argued for a sweep through the islands of the central Pacific ultimately toward Formosa and China. In March 1943 the Combined Chiefs of Staff, meeting in Washington, agreed to MacArthur's plan and allotted resources for the purpose. Soon afterward they agreed that Nimitz should undertake his sweep too, for the central Pacific island complex would expose MacArthur's northern flank to a constant threat if it were left in Japanese hands.

A new tactic expedited the movement. During the air Battle of the Bismarck Sea (March 2–3, 1943) Gen. George Kennedy's bombers sank eight Japanese troopships and ten warships bringing reinforcements. Thereafter the Japanese dared not risk sending transports to points under siege, making it possible to use the tactic of bypassing Japanese strongholds, neutralizing them with air and sea power, and moving on, leaving them to die on the vine. Adm. Theodore S. Wilkinson called it "leapfrogging," or in a new twist on baseball language, "hitting 'em where they ain't." Premier Tojo later acknowledged the strategy as a major cause of Allied victory. Meanwhile, in mid-April, before the offensive got under way, fighters from Henderson Field on Guadalcanal shot down a plane which American codebreakers knew was carrying Admiral Yamamoto into Bougainville. The death of Japan's naval commander, the planner of the Pearl Harbor attack, was a shattering blow to Japanese morale.

The first strong point left stranded by the leapfrog strategy was Rabaul, New Britain, bastion of the "Bismarck Barrier" which threatened the flank of MacArthur's advance across New Guinea. The offensive got under way first with sharp amphibious and naval thrusts to secure the northern Solomons. After successful naval actions in the Solomons Slot (in one of which *PT 109*, Lt. John Fitzgerald Kennedy's torpedo boat, went down) American forces controlled the waters in the area. On November 1 an amphibious force landed on an undefended coast of Bougainville in the northern Solomons and carved out a beachhead from which fighters and bombers brought Rabaul under daily attack. A Japanese fleet that moved to challenge the operation was decisively beaten in the Battle of Empress Augusta Bay on November 2, 1943. In New Guinea, MacArthur's forces moved into command of the coast opposite Cape Gloucester, New Britain. Occupation of Arawe and Cape Gloucester in December secured the passageway to the north coast of New Guinea and the western Pacific. When the Admiralty Islands were taken in March 1944, the isolation of Rabaul was complete and nearly 100,000 Japanese were stranded. Thus by early 1944 the Bismarcks Barrier was broken.

NIMITZ IN THE CENTRAL PACIFIC   Admiral Nimitz's parallel advance through the central Pacific had as its first target two tiny atolls in the Gilberts: Makin and Tarawa. After advance bombing raids by the Seventh Air Force, mounted from Canton and Funa Futi in the Phoenix and Ellice Islands, a fleet of 200 ships delivered infantry and marines ashore at dawn on November 20, 1943.

KAMCHATKA PEN. (U.S.S.R.)

ALASKA (U.S.A.)

ALEUTIAN ISLANDS

ATTU

KISKA

1943

ISLANDS

LIMIT OF JAPANESE CONTROL

THE WAR IN THE PACIFIC, 1942-1945

Areas controlled by Japan, 1942

Major Allied offensives

Major Allied air offensives

Major battle

P A C I F I C

MIDWAY

H A W A I I A N

I S L A N D S

Pearl Harbor

OAHU

WAKE

1944

ENIWETOK

MARSHALL

KWAJALEIN

ISLANDS

S L A N D S

MAKIN

TARAWA

GILBERT

ISLANDS

1943

EQUATOR

O

C

E

A

N

Rabaul

BOUGAINVILLE

NEW

RITAIN

SOLOMON

ISLANDS

GUADALCANAL

1942

NEW

HEBRIDES

FIJI

ISLANDS

CORAL SEA

NEW

CALEDONIA

True at equator

0   1000 Miles

0   1000 Kilometers

Makin, where the Japanese had only a small force, was soon cleared; after three days Gen. Ralph Smith radioed the terse message, "Makin taken." Tarawa, with its concrete bunkers behind a long coral reef and beach obstructions of wire and logs, was one of the most heavily protected islands in the Pacific. There nearly 1,000 American soldiers, sailors, and marines lost their lives rooting out a determined resistance by 4,000 Japanese who refused to surrender. The Gilberts provided costly lessons in amphibious operations, one of which was to confirm the value of bypassing strong points. The islands also provided airfields from which the Seventh Air Force began softening up strong points in the Marshall Islands. Japanese planes completely abandoned the region.

Invasion of the Marshalls, the next step "up the ladder" to Tokyo, began on January 31, 1944, at Kwajalein and Eniwetok, both of which were soon taken. During these operations a carrier raid wrought heavy destruction on enemy ships and aircraft at Truk, the Japanese "Pearl Harbor" in the Carolines. Then Truk, like Rabaul, was bypassed. The Americans took Saipan in the Marianas on June 15, which brought the new American B-29 bombers within striking distance of Japan itself. The Japanese navy therefore had to resist with all it had, which was not enough despite its crash program to build new carriers.

In the Battle of the Philippine Sea, the grand "Marianas Turkey Shoot" fought mostly in the air on June 19 and 20, 1944, the Japanese lost three more carriers, two submarines, and over 300 planes, at the cost of only 17 American planes. The battle secured the Marianas, and soon B-29s were winging their way to the first systematic bombings of the Japanese homeland. Defeat in the Marianas finally brought home to General Tojo the realization that the war was lost. On July 18, 1944, he and his entire cabinet resigned, and Gen. Kunikai Koiso became the new premier.

THE BATTLE OF LEYTE GULF   With New Guinea and the Marianas all but conquered, President Roosevelt met with General MacArthur and Admiral Nimitz in Honolulu on July 27–28, 1944, to decide the next major step. Previous plans had marked China as the essential springboard for invading Japan, but a Japanese offensive in April 1944 had taken most of the south China airfields from which American air power had operated. This strengthened MacArthur's standing opinion that the Philippines would provide a safer staging area than Formosa. Sentimental and political considerations, as well as military, tipped the decision his way. After securing his flanks with the capture of Morotai in the Moluccas and Peleliu in the Palaus—the latter was the scene of some of the bloodiest fighting of the war, ground out in heat up to 115°—MacArthur made his move into the Philippines on October 20, landing first on the island of Leyte. Wading ashore behind the first landings, he issued an announcement: "People of the Philippines: I have returned. . . . Rally to me. . . . Let no heart be faint."

The Japanese, knowing that loss of the Philippines would cut them off from the oil and other essential resources of the East Indies, brought in fleets from three directions. The three encounters that resulted on October 25, 1944, came to be known collectively as the Battle of Leyte Gulf. Just after midnight the southern force made premature contact with American PT-boats, and then with destroyers, cruisers, and battleships. After an old-fashioned naval battle, only two Japanese ships were left to retire, with carrier planes in hot pursuit. The northern force from Formosa, designed to decoy the American fleet from the scene, worked all too well. Admiral Halsey, commanding the Third Fleet, headed north to sink the approaching carriers.

After dawn the major Japanese force, although hit by American submarines and planes, threaded through San Bernadino Straight and, off Samar Island, ran into American forces. Inadequately protected by three destroyers and four destroyer escorts, Rear Adm. Clifton Sprague put up a desperate fight against superior firepower. Two destroyers and one escort went down, but Sprague's forces disabled a Japanese cruiser and so upset the enemy battle line that a confused Admiral Kurita broke off back to San Bernadino Straight. He later claimed that an intercepted message persuaded him that massive American reinforcements were on the way.

The third major engagement took place off Cape Engano, Luzon, where Admiral Halsey closed on the northern force with overwhelming superiority. American planes sank four Japanese carriers and a destroyer before the fleet broke off to chase Admiral Kurita, but too late. In one day the Battle of Leyte Gulf had grown into the largest naval engagement in history. The Japanese had lost most of their remaining sea power and the ability to protect the Philippines. The battle brought the first of the suicide attacks by Japanese pilots who crash-dived into Sprague's baby carriers, sinking one and seriously damaging others. The "Kamikaze" units, named for the "Divine Wind" that saved Japan from Mongol invasion in 1281, were able to inflict severe damage on the American navy until the end of the war.

A New Age Is Born

ROOSEVELT'S FOURTH TERM   In 1944, war or no war, the calendar dictated another presidential election. This time the Republicans turned to the former crime-fighter and New York governor, Thomas E. Dewey, as their candidate. They balanced the moderately progressive Dewey with conservative John W. Bricker of Ohio as their vice-presidential nominee. Once again no Democratic challenger rose high enough to contest Roosevelt, but a fight did develop over the second spot on the ticket. Vice-President Wallace had earned the enmity of both southern conservatives and northern city bosses who feared his ties with labor, but Roosevelt finally rejected James F. Byrnes, the favorite of these groups. The outcome was the compromise choice of Missouri Sen. Harry S Truman.

Dewey ran under the same handicap as Landon and Willkie before him. He did not propose to dismantle Roosevelt's programs, but argued that it was time for younger men to replace the tired old leaders of the New Deal. Roosevelt betrayed decided signs of illness and exhaustion, but nevertheless carried the battle to the enemy. His most memorable thrust was at a Teamsters Union dinner in Washington, where FDR responded in mock outrage to stories that he had sent a destroyer to the Aleutians to pick up his Scottie, Fala. The president did not resent the attacks, he said, but as for Fala, "his Scotch soul was furious. He has not been the same dog since." On November 7, 1945, Roosevelt was once again elected, this time by a popular margin of 25.6 million to 22 million and an electoral vote of 432 to 99.

CONVERGING FRONTS   After their quick sweep across France, the Allies lost momentum in the fall of 1944 and settled down to slugging at the frontiers of Germany. Along this line the armies fought it out all winter. Bradley's Ninth Army joined the First to capture the Roer River dams by early December. Patton's Third Army, farther south, captured the Lorraine fortress city of Metz and pushed into the Saar while General Devers's Sixth Army Group took Strasbourg in Alsace and moved up the Rhine.

Then the Germans sprang a surprise in the rugged Ardennes Forest, where the Allied line was thinnest. Hitting on December 16, 1944, under clouds which prevented air reconnaissance, they advanced along a fifty-mile front in Belgium and Luxembourg. In ten days they penetrated nearly to the Meuse River on their way to Antwerp, which had been recently captured by the

Canadians, but they stalled at Bastogne. Reinforced by the Allies just before it was surrounded, Bastogne held for six days against all the Germans could bring against it. On December 22 Gen. "Tony" McAuliffe of the 101st Airborne gave his memorable answer to the demand for surrender: "Nuts." His situation remained desperate until the next day when the clouds lifted, allowing Allied airpower to hit the Germans and drop in supplies. On December 26 the Fourth Armored Division broke through to the relief of Bastogne, but it would be mid-January 1945 before the previous lines were restored.

Germany's sudden thrust upset Eisenhower's timetable, but the outcome shook German power and morale. Their effort had weakened the eastern front, and in January the Russians began their final offensive. The western offensives started in February. Advancing all along the front, the Allies by early March had reached the banks of the Rhine nearly all the way from Holland to Switzerland. On March 6 they took Cologne, and the next day, by remarkable luck, the Allies seized the bridge at Remagen before the Germans could blow it up. Troops poured across the Rhine there and soon afterward at other points.

The Allies then encircled the Ruhr Valley, center of Germany's heavy industry. Hodges's First Army on the south and Simpson's Ninth on the north in quick sweeps closed the pincers on some 400,000 German soldiers in the region and pounded them into submission. By mid-April resistance there was over. Meanwhile the Russian offensive had also reached Germany itself, after taking Warsaw on January 17 and Vienna on April 13.

YALTA AND THE POSTWAR WORLD   As the final offensives got under way, the Yalta Conference (February 4–11, 1945) brought the Big Three leaders together again in a czar's palace at the Crimean resort. While the focus at Teheran in 1943 had been on wartime strategy, it was now on the shape of the postwar world. Two aims loomed large in Roosevelt's thinking. One was the need to ensure that the Soviet Union join the war against Japan. The other was based on the lessons he drew from the previous World War. Just as the Neutrality Acts of the 1930s were designed with lessons from the previous war in mind, thoughts about the future were now influenced by memories of the interwar years. Americans, the historian Ernest May has written, visualized World War II as parallel to World War I. "They expected its aftermath to be in most respects the same. And they defined statesmanship as doing those things which might have been done to prevent World War II from occurring." Chief among the mis-

The first session of the Yalta Conference, convened in February 1945 to shape the postwar world. Stalin (left), FDR (upper right), and Churchill (lower right) confer. [National Archives]

takes to be remedied this time were the failure of the United States to join the League of Nations and the failure of the Allies to maintain a united front against the German aggressors.

The Yalta meeting began by calling for a conference on world organization to be held in the United States, beginning on April 25, 1945. The Yalta conferees decided also that Russia would have three votes in the organization's General Assembly and that substantive decisions in the Security Council would require the acquiescence of its five permanent members: the United States, Britain, Russia, France, and China.

GERMANY AND EASTERN EUROPE   With Hitler's "Thousand-Year Reich" stumbling to its doom, arrangements for the postwar governance of Germany had to be made. The war map dictated the basic pattern of occupation zones: Russia would control the east and the Western Allies would control the rich industrial areas of the west. Berlin, isolated within the Russian zone, would be subject to joint occupation. At the behest of Churchill and Roosevelt, liberated France got a zone along its border and also in Berlin. Similar arrangements were made for Austria, with Vienna like Berlin under joint occupation within the Russian zone. Russian demands for reparations of $20 billion, half of which would go to Russia, were referred to a Reparations Commission in Moscow. The commission never reached agreement, although the Russians made off with untold amounts of machinery and equipment from their occupation zone.

With respect to eastern Europe, where Russian forces were

advancing on a broad front, there was little the Western Allies could do to influence events. Roosevelt was inhibited by his wish to win Russian cooperation in the fight against Japan and in the effort to build the proposed United Nations organization. Poland became the main focus of Western concern. Britain and France had gone to war in 1939 to defend Poland and now, six years later, the course of the war had left Poland's fate in the hands of the Russians. Events had long foreshadowed the outcome. Controversy over the Katyn Forest massacre of 1940, in which the Russians had gunned down over 14,000 Polish officers, led the Russians in 1943 to break relations with the Polish government-in-exile in London. When Russian forces reentered Poland in 1944, the Soviets placed civil administration under a Committee of National Liberation in Lublin, a puppet regime representing few Poles. When Soviet troops reached the gates of Warsaw, the underground resistance in the city rose against the Nazi occupiers. The underground, however, held allegiance to the London government-in-exile. The Russians then stopped their offensive for two months while the Nazis wiped out thousands of Poles, potential rivals to the Lublin puppet government.

That optimism about postwar cooperation could survive such events was a triumph of hope over experience. The attitude was remotely reminiscent of 1919, when Wilson made concessions to win approval of the League of Nations in the hope that the League could later remedy any injustices which had crept into the peace settlement. But in any case the Western Allies could do no more than acquiesce or stall. On the Soviet proposal to expand the Lublin Committee into a provisional government together with representatives of the London Poles, they acquiesced. On the issue of Poland's boundaries, they stalled. The Russians proposed to keep eastern Poland, offering land taken from Germany as compensation. Roosevelt and Churchill accepted the proposal, but considered the western boundary at the Oder–Western Neisse Rivers only provisional. The peace conference at which the western boundary of Poland was to be settled never took place because of later disagreements. The presence of the London Poles in the provisional government only lent a tone of legitimacy to a regime dominated by the Communists, who soon ousted their rivals.

The Big Three promised to sponsor free elections, democratic governments, and constitutional safeguards of freedom throughout the rest of Europe. The Yalta Declaration of Liberated Europe reaffirmed faith in the principles of the Atlantic Charter and the United Nations, but in the end it made little difference. It may have postponed Communist takeovers in eastern Europe for a few years, but before long Communist members of coalition governments had their hands on the levers of power and ousted the opposition. Aside from Czechoslovakia, though, the countries of eastern Europe lacked strong democratic traditions in any case. And Russia, twice invaded by Germany in the twentieth century, had good reason for wanting buffer states between it and the Germans.

YALTA's LEGACY The Yalta agreements were later attacked for giving eastern Europe over to Soviet domination. But the course of the war shaped the actions at Yalta. By suppressing opposition, moreover, the Soviets were not acting under the Yalta accords, but in violation of them.

Perhaps the most bitterly criticized of the Yalta understandings was a secret agreement on the Far East, not made public until after the war. As the Big Three met, fighting still raged in the Philippines and Burma. The Joint Chiefs of Staff still estimated that Japan could hold out for eighteen months after the defeat of Germany. Costly campaigns lay ahead and the atomic bomb was still an expensive gamble on the unknown. Roosevelt accepted Stalin's demands on postwar arrangements in the Far East, subject technically to later agreement by Chiang Kai-shek. Stalin wanted continued Russian control of Outer Mongolia through its puppet People's Republic there, acquisition of the Kurile Islands from Japan, and recovery of rights and territory lost after the Russo-Japanese War in 1905, which included the southern half of Sakhalin Island, control of Port Arthur (Dairen), and joint Soviet-Chinese operation of the major railroads in Manchuria. Stalin in return promised to enter the war against Japan two or three months after the German defeat, to recognize Chinese sovereignty over Manchuria, and to conclude a treaty of friendship and alliance with the Chinese Nationalists. Later Roosevelt's concessions would appear in a different light, but given their geographical advantages in Asia as in eastern Europe, the Soviets were in a position to get what they wanted in any case.

THE THIRD REICH COLLAPSES The collapse of Nazi resistance was imminent, but President Roosevelt did not live to join the celebrations. All through 1944 his health had been declining, and photographs from early 1945 revealed a very sick man. Roosevelt had always before been able to recharge his batteries with brief rests, and in the spring of 1945 he went to his second home in Warm Springs, Georgia, to rest up for the Charter Conference of the United Nations at San Francisco. On April 12, 1945, while he was drafting a Jefferson Day speech, a cerebral hemorrhage brought sudden death. The last words he wrote into the speech were: "The only limit to our realization of tomorrow will be our doubts of today. Let us move forward with strong and active faith."

The collapse of Hitler's Germany came less than a month later. The Allied armies rolled up almost unopposed to the Elbe River, where they met advanced detachments of Russians at Torgau on April 25. Three days later Italian partisans caught and killed Mussolini and his mistress as they tried to flee. In Berlin, which was under siege by the Russians, Hitler married his mistress, Eva Braun, in an underground bunker on the last day of April just before killing her and himself in a suicide pact. On May 2 Berlin fell to the Russians. That same day German forces in Italy surrendered. Adm. Karl Doenitz, Hitler's designated successor, desperately tried to surrender to the Western Allies, but Eisenhower declined to act except in concert with the Russians. Finally, on May 7 Marshal Alfred Jodl signed an unconditional surrender in Allied headquarters at Rheims. So ended the Thousand-Year Reich, little more than twelve years after its Führer came to power.

Massive celebrations of victory in Europe on V-E Day, May 8, 1945, were tempered by the tragedies that had engulfed the world: mourning for the lost president and the death and mutilation of untold millions. Most shocking was the discovery of the Nazi Holocaust, scarcely believable until the Allied armies came upon the death camps in which the Nazis had sought to apply their "final solution" to the Jewish "problem": the wholesale extermination of some 6 million Jews along with more than 1 million others who had incurred the Nazi contempt and displeasure for one reason or another. The sobering thought that the defeat of Japan remained to be accomplished cast a further pall over the celebrations.

A GRINDING WAR   American forces continued to penetrate and disrupt the Japanese Empire in the early months of 1945, but at heavy cost. Stubborn opposition by the Japanese slowed the reconquest of the Philippines. Japanese forces in Manila held out until March 4. By July 1 the Sixth Army had those parts of Luzon it most needed, but about 50,000 Japanese continued to fight until the end of the war. While fighting went on in the Philippines, on February 19, 1945, marine assault forces invaded Iwo Jima, a speck of volcanic rock in the Bonin group, 750 miles from Tokyo. It was needed to provide fighter escort for bombers over

Japan and a landing strip for disabled B-29s. Nearly six weeks were required to secure an island five miles square from defenders hiding in an underground labyrinth. The cost was more than 20,000 American casualties and nearly 7,000 dead.

The fight for Okinawa, beginning on Easter Sunday, April 1, was even bloodier. The largest island in the Ryukyu chain, Okinawa was large enough to afford a staging area for invasion. It was the largest amphibious operation of the Pacific war, involving some 300,000 line and service troops. From a beachhead on the northern coast the invaders fought their way south through rugged terrain. Desperate Japanese counterattacks inflicted heavy losses on land, by air, and by sea. Kamikaze planes came in by the hundreds. Finally, the battleship *Yamato*, a survivor of Leyte Gulf, left Kyushu with nine other ships—the remnant of a once-great navy—with fuel only for a one-way trip, all that was available. American seaplanes intercepted the pathetic armada, sank the *Yamato* and two other warships, and badly damaged the rest. It was the end of the Japanese navy, but the fight for Okinawa raged until late June, when the bloody attrition destroyed any further Japanese ability to resist. The fighting brought nearly 50,000 American casualties; the dead included their commander, Gen. Simon B. Buckner, Jr., and one of the GIs' favorite correspondents, Ernie Pyle. The Japanese lost an estimated 140,000 dead, but more than 10,000 surrendered. Casualties included about 42,000 Okinawans.

The campaign was significant mainly for wearing down the remaining defenses of the Japanese. Now American ships could roam the coastline of Japan, shelling targets ashore. American planes bombed at will and mined the waters of the Inland Sea. Tokyo, Nagoya, and other major cities were devastated by firestorms from incendiary bombs, made all the worse by the prevalence of wooden structures in earthquake-prone Japan. Still, it seemed that ahead lay further beachheads and more bitter fighting against the same suicidal fury that had made Okinawa so costly a conquest. But as the irony of timing would have it, Okinawa was never needed as a staging area. When the Americans invaded Okinawa the emperor named a new premier, and when resistance on the island collapsed he instructed the new premier to seek peace terms. Washington had picked this up by decoding Japanese messages, which suggested either an effort to avoid unconditional surrender or perhaps just a stall.

THE ATOMIC BOMB By this time, however, a new force had changed all strategic calculations: President Truman had just got word of the first atomic explosion, the result of several years of intensive work. The strands of scientific development that led to the bomb ironically ran back to Germany. Except for the Nazi bigotry that drove scientists into exile, Germany might well have developed the atomic bomb first. Early in 1939 a German scientific journal revealed that the uranium atom had been split at the Kaiser Wilhelm Institute in Berlin; experiments in Denmark and the United States soon confirmed the finding. On October 11, 1939, President Roosevelt learned of the matter when an emissary, Dr. Alexander Sachs, delivered a letter from Albert Einstein and a memorandum from Dr. Leo Szilard, explaining the potential of nuclear fission and warning that the Germans might steal the march. Roosevelt quickly set up a committee to coordinate information in the field, and in 1940 some army and navy funds were diverted into research which grew ultimately into the $2 billion top-secret Manhattan Project.

On August 13, 1942, the Army Engineers set up the Manhattan Engineering District under Brig.-Gen. Leslie R. Groves to direct development and production of the bomb. On December 2, 1942, Dr. Enrico Fermi and other scientists achieved the first atomic chain reaction in a squash court at the University of Chicago's Stagg Field, removing any remaining doubts of the bomb's feasibility. Gigantic plants sprang up at Oak Ridge, Tennessee, and Hanford, Washington, to make plutonium, while a group of physicists under Dr. J. Robert Oppenheimer worked out the scientific and technical problems of bomb construction in a laboratory at Los Alamos, New Mexico. On July 16, 1945, the first atomic fireball rose from the New Mexico desert. The awestruck Oppenheimer said later that in the observation bunker "A few

"I am become death, the shatterer of worlds." [Library of Congress]

people laughed, a few people cried, most people were silent. There floated through my mind a line from the Bhagavad-Gita in which Krishna is trying to persuade the prince that he should do his duty: 'I am become death, the shatterer of worlds.' " Colleagues crowded forward with their congratulations: "Oppie," said one, "now we're all sons of bitches."

The question of how to use this awful weapon had already come before a committee of officials and scientists. Some of the scientists, awed at the ghastly prospect, favored a demonstration in a remote area, but the decision went for military use because only two bombs were available, and even those might misfire. More consideration was given to the choice of targets. Four cities had been reserved from conventional bombing as potential targets. After Secretary Stimson eliminated Kyoto, the ancient capital and center of many national and religious treasures, priority went to Hiroshima, center of war industries, headquarters of the Second General Army, and command center for the homeland's defenses.

On July 25, 1945, President Truman, then at the Big Three Conference in Potsdam, Germany, ordered the bomb dropped if Japan did not surrender before August 3. The next day the heads of the American, British, and Chinese governments issued the Potsdam Declaration demanding that Japan surrender or face "prompt and utter destruction." The deadline passed, and at 9:15 A.M. on August 6, 1945, a B-29 out of Tinian, the *Enola Gay*, with a crew commanded by Col. Paul W. Tibbetts, dropped the bomb over Hiroshima. A sudden flash wiped out four square miles of the city, wrecked the defense headquarters, wiped out most of the Second General Army, and killed in all more than 60,000 people. Dazed survivors wandered the streets, so painfully burned that their skin began to peel in large strips. In one of history's most pungent ironies, Capt. Mitsuo Fuchida, flight commander of the Pearl Harbor attack, flew into Hiroshima Airport that morning and found himself facing "a procession of people who seemed to have come out of Hell." Even those who appeared unhurt began mysteriously to sicken and die, the first victims of a deadly radiation which blighted lives for years to come. In the United States, Americans greeted the first news with elation: it promised a quick end to the long nightmare of war. Only later would the awareness dawn that it marked the start of a more enduring nightmare, the atomic age.

Three days later Russia hastened to enter the war, and a few hours after that, about noon on August 9, the second bomb exploded over the port city of Nagasaki, legendary home of Ma-

Nagasaki, blasted by the atomic bomb. [George Silk, Life magazine, © *1971 Time Inc.]*

dame Butterfly and once the isolated kingdom's only window to the world, killing 36,000 more. That night the emperor urged his cabinet to accept the inevitable and surrender on the sole condition that he remain as sovereign. The next day the United States government, to facilitate surrender and an orderly transition, announced its willingness to let him keep the throne, but under the authority of an Allied supreme commander. Frantic exchanges ended with Japanese acceptance on August 14, 1945, when the emperor himself broke precedent to record a radio message announcing the surrender to his people. Even then a last-ditch palace revolt had to be squashed. After preliminary arrangements by Japanese emissaries in Manila, an American advance party arrived at Atsugi airfield on August 28 and General MacArthur came in two days later to take up residence at the New Grand Hotel. On September 2, 1945, he and other allied representatives accepted Japan's formal surrender on board the battleship *Missouri.* MacArthur then settled in at his headquarters in the Dai Ichi, "Building One," facing the Imperial Palace across the street, behind its moat. Just seventy-seven years after the Meiji Restoration had overthrown the last Tokugawa shogun, Japan had a new American shogun.

THE FINAL LEDGER Thus ended the most deadly conflict in human history. No effort to tabulate a ledger of death and destruction can ever take the full measure of the war's suffering, nor hope to be more than an informed guess as to the numbers involved. One estimate has it that 70 million in all fought in the war, at a cost in human lives of 17 million military dead and more than 18 million civilian dead. Material costs were also enormous, perhaps $1 trillion in military expenditures and twice that in property losses. The Soviet Union suffered the greatest losses of all, over 6 million military deaths, over 10 million civilians dead, and at least 25 million left homeless. World War II was more costly for the United States than any other of the country's foreign wars: 294,000 battle deaths and 114,000 other deaths. But in proportion to population, the United States suffered a far smaller loss than any of the major allies or enemies, and American territory escaped the devastation visited on so many other parts of the world.

The war's end opened a new era for the United States. It accelerated the growth of American power while devastating all other world powers, leaving the United States economically and militarily the strongest nation on earth. But Russia, despite its human and material losses, emerged from the war with much new territory and enhanced influence, making it the greatest power on the whole Eurasian land mass. Just a little over a century after Alexis de Tocqueville predicted that western Europe would come to be overshadowed by the power of the United States and Russia, his prophecy had come to pass.

FURTHER READING

Two surveys which detail American involvement in the global conflict are John Morton Blum's *V Was for Victory: Politics and American Culture during World War II* (1976)° and Martha Hoyle's *A World in Flames: A History of World War II* (1970). Albert R. Buchanan's *The United States and World War II* (2 vols.; 1962) is more thorough, particularly on the military aspects of the struggle.

Russell F. Weigley's *The American Way of War: A History of United States Military Strategy and Policy* (1973) provides a scholarly assessment of why the war was fought as it was. Gordon Wright's *The Ordeal of Total War, 1939–1945* (1968), surveys the conflict in Europe, while Charles B. McDonald's *The Mighty Endeavor: American Armed Forces in the European Theatre in World War II* (1969) concentrates on American involvement there. Another perspective on the European conflict can be found in the memoirs of Dwight D. Eisenhower, *Crusade in Europe*

°These books are available in paperback editions.

(1948). Stephen Ambrose's *The Supreme Commander: The War Years of General Dwight D. Eisenhower* (1970) takes a look at Eisenhower's contribution. Books on specific campaigns in Europe include Trumball Higgins's *Soft Underbelly: The Anglo-American Controversy and the Italian Campaign, 1939–1945* (1968), Cornelius Ryan's *The Longest Day* (1959),° on the D-Day operation, and his *The Last Battle* (1966) and John Toland's *The Last Hundred Days* (1966), both on the last days of the Nazi resistance. Two other views of the European conflict can be found in the memoirs of Omar Bradley, *A General's Life: An Autobiography* (1983), and Forrest C. Pogue's *George C. Marshall* (3 vols.; 1963–1973). The Pacific theater is reviewed in Samuel E. Morison's *Strategy and Compromise: The Two-Ocean War* (1963), which covers naval operations, and D. Clayton James's *The Years of MacArthur* (1970, 1975), which concentrates on land strategy. Other perspectives on the war in the Far East are considered by Barbara Tuchman in *Stilwell and the American Experience in China, 1911–1945* (1971), John Toland's *The Rising Sun: The Decline and Fall of the Japanese Empire* (1970),° and Edwin P. Hoyt's *How They Won in the Pacific: Nimitz and His Admirals* (1970).

Overviews of the war on the home front include Gerald D. Nash's *The Great Depression and World War II: Organizing America* (1979), Richard Polenberg's *The War and Society* (1972), Richard Lingeman's *Don't You Know There's a War On* (1970), and the aforementioned Blum volume. The economic measures taken to undergird the war effort are viewed in Eliot Janeway's *Struggle for Survival* (1951), Chester Bowles's *Promise to Keep* (1971), Lester V. Chandler's *Inflation in the United States, 1940–1948* (1951), and John Kenneth Galbraith's *A Life in Our Times* (1982). Carl Degler treats the new working environment for women in *At Odds: Women and the Family in America from the Revolution to the Present* (1980).° Neil Wynn looks at the participation of blacks in *The Afro-American and the Second World War* (1976). The story of the oppression of Japanese-Americans is told by Roger Daniels in *Concentration Camps USA: Japanese Americans and World War II* (1971) and by Audie Girdner and Anne Loftis in *The Great Betrayal: The Evacuation of the Japanese-Americans during World War II* (1969).

Sound introductions to American diplomacy during the conflict can be found in Gaddis Smith's *American Diplomacy during the Second World War, 1941–1945* (1965), and Robert Beitzell's *The Uneasy Alliance: America, Britain, and Russia, 1941–1943* (1972). Gabriel Kolko's *The Politics of War: The World and United States Foreign Policy, 1943–1945* (1968) is a revisionist view. To understand the role Roosevelt played in policy-making, consult Raymond G. O'Connor's *Diplomacy for Victory: Franklin D. Roosevelt and Unconditional Surrender* (1971), Joseph P. Lash's *Roosevelt and Churchill* (1976), James MacGregor Burns's *Roosevelt: The Soldier of Freedom* (1970), and Robert A. Divine's *Roosevelt and World War II* (1969).° Diane Shaver Clemens is critical of Roosevelt in *Yalta* (1970).

An introduction to the issues and events which led to the deployment of atomic weapons is traced by Herbert Feis in *The Atomic Bomb and the End of World War II* (1966). Also helpful are Greg Herken's *The Winning Weapon* (1980),° Martin Sherwin's *A World Destroyed: The Atomic Bomb and the Grand Alliance* (1975), and Neill Davis's *Lawrence and Oppenheimer* (1968). Gar Alperovitz's *Atomic Diplomacy: Hiroshima and Potsdam* (1965), Michael Sherry's *Preparing for the Next War: American Plans for Postwar Defense, 1941–1945* (1977), and Richard G. Hewlett and Oscar E. Anderson's *A History of the United States Atomic Energy Commission: The New World, 1939–1946* (1962) and *Atomic Shield, 1947–1952* (1969), detail how the bomb helped shape American postwar policy.

Ruth B. Russell's *A History of the United Nations Charter* (1958) and Robert A. Divine's *Second Chance: The Triumph of Internationalism during World War II* (1967) chronicle America's emergence as a postwar world leader. Martin Gilbert's *Auschwitz and the Allies* (1981)° explains how the Holocaust shaped postwar attitudes.

31

THE FAIR DEAL
AND CONTAINMENT

DEMOBILIZATION UNDER TRUMAN

TRUMAN'S UNEASY START "Who the hell is Harry Truman?" Admiral Leahy, the president's chief-of-staff asked Roosevelt in the summer of 1944. The question unwittingly echoed a campaign slogan of exactly a century before: "Who is James K. Polk?" The question was on more lips when, after less than twelve weeks as vice-president, Harry Truman took the presidential oath on April 12, 1945. It may have recurred two days later, when he impulsively began his first speech to Congress and House Speaker Sam Rayburn interrupted sotto voce: "Just a minute. Let me present you, will you, Harry?" Clearly he was not Franklin Roosevelt, and that was one of the burdens he would bear. "With Roosevelt you'd have known he was President even if you hadn't been told," the journalist Merle Miller wrote years later. "He looked imperial, and he acted that way, and he talked that way. Harry Truman, for God's sake, looked and acted and talked like—well, like a failed haberdasher"—which he was.

In their origins Roosevelt and Truman came from different worlds. For Truman there had been no inherited wealth, no early contact with the great and near-great, no European travel, no Groton, no Harvard—indeed, no college at all. Born in 1884 in the western Missouri town of Lamar, Truman had pioneer grandparents from Kentucky and a Southern Baptist background. He grew up in Independence, once the staging area for the Oregon and Santa Fe Trails, but by the time of his youth an unglamorous satellite to Kansas City. Too nearsighted to join in the activities of other boys, Truman became bookish, introverted, and withdrawn. But after high school he moved to his grandfather's farm near Grandview, worked at a variety of jobs, became active in the National Guard, Masons, Democratic party, and other groups, grew into an outgoing young man, and learned the salty language that seasoned his speech in later years.

During World War I he served in France as captain of an artillery company. Afterward he and a partner went into the haberdashery business, but the business failed in the recession of 1922 and Truman after that became a professional politician under the tutelage of Kansas City boss Tom Pendergast. Elected county judge in 1922, he was defeated in 1924 and elected once again in 1926. In 1934 Missouri sent him to the United States Senate, where he remained fairly obscure until he became chairman of the committee to investigate war mobilization.

Something about Harry Truman evoked the spirit of Andrew Jackson: his decisiveness, his feisty character, his pungent language, his truculent prickliness, his family loyalty. But that was a side of the man that the American people came to know only as he settled into the job. On his first full day as president, he was still awestruck. "Boys, if you ever pray, pray for me now," he told a group of reporters. "I don't know whether you fellows ever had a load of hay fall on you, but when they told me yesterday what had happened, I felt like the moon, the stars and all the planets had fallen on me."

Truman's accession heartened the conservatives who had helped engineer his nomination. Six weeks after Roosevelt's death the Speaker of Mississippi's House of Representatives said Truman had "begun well and is making rapid progress towards returning this country to Fundamental Americanism." But as the newsman and then presidential assistant Jonathan Daniels put it, the men who put Truman in "knew what they wanted but did not know what they were getting." What they were getting was a man who favored much of the New Deal and was even prepared to extend it, but at the same time was uneasy with many New Dealers. "He was not of their clan and kidney," newsman Cabell Phillips put it. Within ninety days he had replaced much of the Roosevelt cabinet with his own choices. These included fewer Missourians and "cronies" than his detractors claimed, but on the whole they were more conservative in outlook and included enough mediocrities to lend credence to the criticism. Truman suffered the further handicap of seeming to be a caretaker for the remainder of Roosevelt's time. Few, including Truman himself at first, expected him to serve another term.

Truman's domestic policies remained unformulated while he wrestled with problems of war and peace. He gave one significant clue, however, on September 6, 1945, four days after the Japanese surrender, when he sent Congress a comprehensive peacetime program which in effect proposed to continue and enlarge the New Deal. Its twenty-one points included expansion of unemployment insurance, extension of the Employment Service, a higher minimum wage, a permanent Fair Employment Practices Commission, slum clearance and low-rent housing, regional development of the nation's river valleys, and a public works program. "Not even President Roosevelt asked for so much at one sitting," said House Republican leader Joseph Martin. "It's just a plain case of out-dealing the New Deal." Beset by other problems, Truman was unable to set priorities on his demands. The result was a domestic cold war between the president and a Congress which was dominated, as it had been since 1938, by a conservative coalition. Indeed, like Cleveland in the 1890s, Truman managed for a time to offend businessmen, farmers, and workers alike.

CONVERTING TO PEACE   The raucous celebrations that greeted Japan's surrender signaled the habitual American response to victory: a rapid demobilization and a return to more congenial pursuits. Given the character and experience of the American

The Eldridge General Store, Fayette County, Illinois. Postwar America quickly demobilized, turning its attention to the pursuit of abundance. [University of Louisville Photographic Archives]

people, any other outcome would have been unlikely. The president and Congress were besieged by demands for bringing the boys home. By midsummer 1946 the wartime army and navy had been reduced to 1.5 million and 700,000 respectively. By 1947 the total armed forces were down to 1.5 million and Congress had decreed further cuts, reducing their number to little more than 1 million. In his memoirs Truman termed this "the most remarkable demobilization in the history of the world, or 'disintegration' if you want to call it that." It was in fact the same pattern that had prevailed since the days of the colonial wars, and it went on for several years despite mounting tensions. By early 1950 the army had fallen to 600,000 men in ten active divisions.

The veterans returned to schools, new jobs, wives, and babies. Population growth, which had dropped off sharply in the depression decade, now soared: the population increase of 8.9 million during the 1930s exploded to a growth of 19 million in the 1940s. The birth rate per 1,000 of total population grew from 19.4 in 1940 to above 24 per annum by 1946, and did not begin to show a decline until the 1960s. Americans born during this postwar period composed what came to be known as the baby-boom generation.

The end of the war, with its sudden demobilization and recon-

The electronic numerical integrator and computer, or ENIAC, 1946. Developed for the Army Ordnance Department by Dr. J. Presper Eckert, Jr., the ENIAC and its progeny would have profound consequences for the later twentieth-century world. [Library of Congress]

version to a peacetime economy, brought sharp dislocations but not the postwar depression that many feared. The economic impact of demobilization was cushioned by numerous shock-absorbers: unemployment pay and other Social Security benefits; the Servicemen's Readjustment Act of 1944, known as the "GI Bill of Rights," under which more than $13 billion was spent for veterans on education, vocational training, medical treatment, unemployment insurance, and loans for building homes or going into business; and most important, the pent-up demand for consumer goods that was fueled by wartime incomes. Instead of sinking into depression, businesses seized upon options to buy up properties from the Defense Plant Corporation and began a spurt of private investment in new plant and equipment. Gross national product first exceeded the 1929 level in 1940, when it reached $100.6 billion, but by annual increases (except in 1946) it had grown to $347 billion by 1952, Truman's last full year in office.

CONTROLLING INFLATION   The problem Truman faced was not depression but inflation, one problem which President Roosevelt had not encountered. The historian Barton Bernstein summed up the political burden imposed by this difference: "Whereas the politics of depression generally allowed the Roosevelt administration, by bestowing benefits, to court interest groups and contribute to an economic upturn, the politics of inflation required a responsible government like Truman's to curb wages, prices, and profits and to deny the growing expectations of rival groups." The political problems inherent in fighting inflation were worsened by Truman's early inexperience and uncertainty.

Released from wartime restraints, the demands of businessmen and workers alike conspired to frustrate efforts at controlling rising prices. Truman endorsed demands for wage increases and argued that they were needed to cushion the shock of conversion and to sustain purchasing power. He felt that there was "room in the existing price structure" for business to grant such increases, a point management refused to concede. Within six weeks of war's end, corporations confronted a wave of union demands. In November 1945 Truman, like Wilson in 1919, called a labor-management conference to formulate a labor policy; it had as little result as the one in 1919.

A series of strikes followed. The United Automobile Workers walked out on General Motors, with Walter Reuther, head of the union's General Motors division, arguing that the company could afford a 30 percent pay raise without raising car prices. (The company denied this claim.) A strike in the steel industry finally gave rise to a formula for settling most of the disputes. President Truman suggested a pay raise of 18½¢ per hour, which the Steel Workers accepted but United States Steel refused. To break the logjam the administration in February agreed to let the company increase its prices. That pattern then became the basis for settlements in other industries, and also set a dangerous precedent of price-wage spirals that would plague consumers in the postwar world.

Major disputes soon developed in the coal and railroad industries. John L. Lewis of the United Mine Workers wanted more than the 18½¢-per-hour wage increase. He demanded also improved safety regulations and a union health and welfare fund financed by a royalty on coal. Mine owners refused the demands, and a strike followed. The government responded by using wartime powers to seize the mines. Interior Secretary Julius A. Krug then accepted nearly all the union's demands. In the rail dispute the unions and management reached an agreement, but two brotherhoods, the trainmen and locomotive engineers, held out for rule changes as well as higher wages. Truman seized the roads in May and won a five-day postponement of a strike. But when the brotherhoods' leaders refused to budge further, the president went before Congress in a burst of fury against their "obstinate arrogance" and demanded authority to draft strikers into the armed forces. In the midst of the speech he was informed that the strike had been settled, but after telling a jubilant Congress, he went on with his message. The House passed a bill including the president's demands, but with the strike settled, it died in the Senate.

Into 1946 the wartime Office of Price Administration managed to maintain some restraint on price increases while gradually ending the rationing of most goods, and Truman asked for a one-year renewal of its powers. But during the late winter and spring of 1946 the business community mounted a massive campaign against price controls and other restraints. Just a week before controls were to expire at the end of June, Congress passed a bill to continue the OPA but with such cumbersome new procedures as to cripple the agency. Truman vetoed the bill, allowing the controls to end. Congress finally extended the controls on July 25, but by then the cost of living had already gone up by 6 percent. When in August the OPA restored controls on meat prices, farmers responded by withholding beef from the market until they succeeded in forcing a reversal on October 15. After the congressional elections of 1946 Truman gave up the battle altogether, ending all controls except those on rents, sugar, and rice.

PARTISAN COOPERATION AND CONFLICT   But the legislative history of 1946 was not all deadlock and frustration. Out of the turmoil Congress and the administration extracted two signal new departures, the Employment Act of 1946 and the creation of the Atomic Energy Commission. A program of "full employment" had been a Democratic promise in the campaign of 1944, a pledge reaffirmed by Truman in 1945. The administration then backed an employment bill which proposed that the government make an annual estimate of the investment and production necessary to ensure full employment, and key its spending to that estimate in order to raise production to the full-employment level. Conservatives objected to what they regarded as carte blanche for defecit spending, and proposed a nonpartisan commission to advise the president on the status of the economy. Compromise resulted in the Employment Act of February 1946, dropping the commitment to full employment and instead setting up a three-member Council of Economic Advisers to make continuing appraisals of the economy and advise the president in an annual economic report. A new congressional Joint Committee on the Economic Report would make proposals for implementing the program.

With regard to the new force that atomic scientists had released upon the world, there was little question that the public welfare required the control of atomic energy through a governmental monopoly. Disagreements over the degree of military versus civilian control were resolved when Congress, in August 1946, created the civilian Atomic Energy Commission. The president alone was given power to order the use of atomic weapons in warfare. Subject to "the paramount objective of assuring the common defense and security," the act declared a policy of peaceful development "so far as practicable . . . toward improving the public welfare, increasing the standard of living, strengthening free competition in private enterprise, and promoting world peace." Technical problems and high costs, however, would delay for two decades the construction of nuclear powerplants, and even yet questions of feasibility, security, and public safety from radioactive pollution are unresolved.

As congressional elections approached in the fall of 1946, discontent ran high, most of it directed against the administration. Truman caught the blame for labor problems from both sides. A speaker at the CIO national convention tagged Truman "the No.

1 strikebreaker," while much of the public, angry at striking unions, laid the blame for strikes at the White House door. In September 1946 Truman fired Henry Wallace as secretary of commerce in a disagreement over foreign policy, thus offending the Democratic left. At the same time the administration was plagued by Republican charges that Communists had infiltrated the government. Coastal states were unhappy over his claim that federal authority governed use of the continental shelf, as were oil companies which preferred to deal with the states on offshore drilling rights. Republicans had a field day coining slogans. "To err is Truman" was credited to Martha Taft, wife of Sen. Robert Taft. But most effective was the simple "Had enough?" attributed to a Boston ad agency: their message was that the Democrats had simply been in too long. Then in August came the cattlemen's embargo on meat. "This is going to be a damn *beefsteak* election," said House Speaker Sam Rayburn. Truman's removal of price controls on meat only worsened his image of vacillation. In the end, Republicans won majorities in both houses of Congress for the first time since 1928.

Given the head of steam built up against organized labor, the new Congress was sure to take up restrictive legislation, and seventeen such bills were indeed introduced on the first day of the new session. The feeling of many that labor "bosses" had grown too strong encouraged moves to restrict their actions, just as business abuses against labor were restricted under the Wagner Act of 1935. The result was the Taft-Hartley Act of 1947, which banned any closed shop (in which nonunion workers could not be hired) but permitted a union shop (in which workers newly hired were required to join the union), unless banned by state law. It included provisions against "unfair" union pactices such as secondary boycotts, jurisdictional strikes (by one union to exclude another from a given company or field), "featherbedding" (pay for work not done), refusal to bargain in good faith, and contributing to campaigns. Unions' political action committees were allowed to function, but on a voluntary basis only, and union leaders had to take oaths that they were not members of the Communist party. Employers were permitted to sue unions for breaking contracts, to petition the NLRB for votes for or against the use of specific unions as collective-bargaining agents, and to speak freely during union campaigns. The act forbade strikes by federal employees, and imposed a "cooling-off" period of eighty days on any strike which the president found to be dangerous to the national health or safety.

Truman's veto of the bill, which unions called the "slave-labor act," restored his credit with labor, and many unionists who had gone over to the Republicans in 1946 returned to the Democratic fold. But the bill was passed over Truman's veto, and as it turned out, had a less than ruinous effect on unions. Its most severe impact probably was on the CIO's "Operation Dixie," a drive to win for unions a more secure foothold in the South. By 1954 fifteen states, mainly in the South, had used the Taft-Hartley Act's authority to enact "right-to-work" laws forbidding the union shop and other union security devices.

Truman clashed with the Republicans on other domestic issues as well, including tax reduction passed by Congress but successfully vetoed twice by Truman on the principle that in times of high production and employment the federal debt should be reduced. In 1948, however, Congress finally managed to override his veto of a $5-billion tax cut at a time when government debt still ran high. The controversy over the tax cut highlighted a soft point in Keynesian economics. In times of depression there was strong political support for increasing governmental expenditures, but in prosperous times support was weak for the taxes needed to reduce the deficits created by government spending. Truman paid the political price for this weakness in economic theory.

The conflicts between Truman and Congress which were so visible in the 1948 campaign obscured the high degree of bipartisan cooperation marking matters of governmental reorganization and foreign policy. After a postwar congressional investigation into the Pearl Harbor disaster made plain a fatal lack of coordination among the armed forces and intelligence services, a bipartisan majority in Congress set out to correct this problem by passing the National Security Act in July 1947. The act created a National Military Establishment, headed by a secretary of defense with subcabinet departments of army, navy, and air force, and a new National Security Council (NSC) which included the president, heads of the defense departments, the secretary of state, and the head of the National Security Resources Board (later the Office of Defense Mobilization). The act made permanent the Joint Chiefs of Staff, which had been a wartime innovation, and established the Central Intelligence Agency (CIA), descended from the wartime Office of Strategic Services (OSS), to coordinate intelligence. There was at the time no intention to have the CIA engage in covert actions as the OSS had done in the war, nor any purpose that it engage in domestic activities. But the act included two gigantic loopholes which would in time allow the CIA to engage in both: authority to perform "such other functions and duties related to intelligence" as the NSC might direct, and responsibility for "protecting intelligence sources and methods."

Congress also adopted President Truman's proposal for a change in the presidential succession. The existing law of 1886 put the secretary of state next in line after the vice-president, to be followed by other cabinet members according to rank, determined by the order in which their offices had been created. The Presidential Succession Act of 1947 inserted the Speaker of the House and the president pro tempore of the Senate ahead of the secretary of state, on the principle that the presidency should first go to elected rather than appointed officers. Congress itself took the initiative in adopting the Twenty-second Amendment, ratified in 1951, which limited presidents after Truman to two terms. Under the Legislative Reorganization Act of 1946 Congress also recast its own organization, reducing the number of standing committees in each house and requiring lobbyists to register and report their expenses.

Finally, President Truman promoted friendly partisan relations by bringing former President Hoover out of retirement to investigate programs of overseas relief, and then in 1947 to head a Commission on Organization of the Executive Branch. The Hoover Commission's 1949 reports led to extensive changes in governmental structure, most of them adopted under the Reorganization Act of 1949, which permitted the president to make organizational changes subject to a veto by either house. Of thirty-six plans submitted by Truman, Congress rejected only the creation of a new Department of Welfare.

The Cold War

BUILDING THE U.N. During World War II no one spouted slogans about making the world safe for democracy or that this was a war to end all wars. At the same time many came to reject isolationism and the disillusionment of an earlier time. As it turned out, however, the hope that the wartime concert of the United Nations would carry over into the postwar world proved but another great illusion. The pragmatic Roosevelt shared no such illusion. To the contrary, the historian Robert Dallek has argued: "His desire for a new world league . . . rested less on a faith in Wilsonian collective security than on the belief that it was a necessary vehicle for permanently involving the United States in world affairs." He expected that the Great Powers in the postwar world would have spheres of influence, but felt he had to obscure such *Realpolitik* with an organization "which would satisfy widespread demand in the United States for new idealistic or universalist arrangements for assuring the peace."

In the 1941 Atlantic Charter, Roosevelt and Churchill had looked forward to a "permanent system of general security." Its name derived later from the declaration of the "United Nations," signed at Washington on January 1, 1942, by twenty-six countries at war with the Axis powers. In the autumn of 1943 both houses of Congress passed a resolution introduced by William Fulbright of Arkansas favoring "international machinery with power adequate to establish and to maintain a just and lasting peace." That same autumn the foreign ministers of the "Big Four" (the United States, Russia, Britain, and China) issued the Declaration of Moscow calling for an international organization, and in the 1944 elections the platforms of both major parties endorsed the principle.

On April 25, 1945, two weeks after Roosevelt's death and two weeks before the German surrender, delegates from fifty nations at war with the Axis met in San Francisco's Opera House to draw up the charter of the United Nations. These fifty were joined by Poland as charter members, with the provision that additional members could be admitted by a two-thirds vote of the General Assembly. This body, one of the two major agencies set up by the charter, included delegates from all member nations and was to meet annually in regular session to approve the budget, receive annual reports from U.N. agencies, and choose members of the Security Council and other bodies. The Security Council, the other major charter agency, would remain in permanent session and had "primary responsibility for the maintenance of international peace and security." Its eleven members included six elected for two-year terms and five permanent members: the United States, Russia, Britain, France, and China. Each permanent member had a veto on any question of substance, though not of procedure. The Security Council might investigate any dispute, recommend settlement or reference to the International Court, and take measures including a resort to military force.

Four other agencies rounded out the structure: an International Court of Justice at The Hague; a Secretariat to administer the U.N.; a Trusteeship Council to oversee administration of former Italian and Japanese colonies and the former mandates of the League of Nations; and an Economic and Social Council which might conduct studies, make recommendations, and draw agreements to bring into relationship with the U.N. existing international bodies such as the Food and Agricultural Organization, the United Nations Relief and Rehabilitation Administration (established in 1943), the International Monetary Fund, the International Bank for Reconstruction and Development (the World Bank), and the International Labor Office. All but the last of these had been created by negotiations during the war to provide relief and to ensure the stability of international finances after the war.

The United States Senate, in sharp contrast to the reception it gave the League of Nations, ratified the U.N. charter by a vote of 89 to 2 after only six days of discussion. The organization held its first meeting at London in 1946, and the next year moved to temporary quarters at Lake Success, New York, pending completion of its permanent home in New York City.

TRYING WAR CRIMINALS   There was also a consensus that those responsible for the atrocities of World War II should face trial and punishment. The Potsdam Conference, among other things, gave final approval to the principle of war-crimes trials, for which a commission in London had been preparing since 1943. Both German and Japanese officials went on trial for crimes against peace, against humanity, and against the established rules of war. At Nuremberg, Germany, site of the annual Nazi party rallies, twenty-two major German offenders faced an International Military Tribunal. After a ten-month trial filled with massive documentation of Nazi atrocities, the court sentenced twelve to death, three to life imprisonment, and four to shorter terms. In Tokyo, a similar tribunal put twenty-five Japanese leaders on trial from May to November 1946, and pronounced sentences of

The Nuremberg Trials. *At far left sit the high-ranking Nazis on trial, including Albert Speer (second row, third from right) and, in dark glasses, Hans Frank. [Signal Corps Photo]*

death on seven (including General Tojo), life imprisonment on sixteen, and committed two for a term of years. Other international tribunals tried thousands of others, while many accused war criminals were remanded to the courts of the countries in which they had committed their crimes. Altogether well over 2,000 war-crimes trials are estimated to have taken place, not counting those in Russia and the East Bloc countries.

Critics argued that the trials set an unfortunate precedent of victors' taking revenge on the defeated. They argued as well that the convictions were condemnations *ex post facto*, for crimes against which no law existed at the time they were committed. Supporters responded by pointing to the Pact of Paris outlawing war, to the Geneva Convention for care of the sick and wounded prisoners, the Hague declarations on the rules of war, and the fact that crimes against humanity such as murder, rape, and pillage were already crimes under the laws of the countries where they occurred.

DIFFERENCES WITH THE SOVIETS   There were signs of trouble in the grand alliance as early as the spring of 1945 as Russia moved to set up compliant governments in eastern Europe, violating the Yalta promises of democratic elections. On February 1 the Polish Committee of National Liberation, a puppet group already claiming the status of provisional government, moved from Lublin to Warsaw. In March the Soviets installed a puppet premier in Rumania. Protests at such actions led to Russian counterprotests that the British and Americans were negotiating German surrender in Italy "behind the back of the Soviet Union" and that German forces were being concentrated against Russia. A few days before his death, Roosevelt responded to Stalin: "I cannot avoid a feeling of resentment toward your informers . . . for such vile misrepresentations."

Such was the atmosphere when Truman entered the White House. A few days before the San Francisco conference, Truman gave Soviet Foreign Minister Molotov a dressing down in Washington on the Polish situation. "I have never been talked to like that in my life," Molotov said. "Carry out your agreements," Truman snapped, "and you won't get talked to like that." On May 12, 1945, four days after victory in Europe, Winston Churchill sent a telegram to Truman: "What is to happen about Europe? An iron curtain is drawn down upon [the Russian] front. We do not know what is going on behind. . . . Surely it is vital now to come to an understanding with Russia, or see where we are with her, before we weaken our armies mortally. . . ." Nevertheless, as a gesture of goodwill, and over Churchill's protest, the

American forces withdrew from the occupation zone assigned to Russia at Yalta. Americans were still hopeful that the Yalta agreements would be carried out, at least after a fashion, and even more hopeful for Russian help against Japan.

Although the Russians admitted British and American observers to their sectors of eastern Europe, there was little the Western powers could do to prevent Russian hegemony even if they had not let their military powers dwindle. The presence of Soviet armed forces frustrated the efforts of non-Communists to gain political influence. Coalition governments appeared temporarily as an immediate postwar expedient, but the Communists followed a long-range strategy of ensconcing themselves in the interior ministries in order to control the police. Opposition political leaders found themselves under accusation, "confessions" were extorted, and the leaders of the opposition were either exiled, silenced, executed, or consigned to prison.

Secretary of State James F. Byrnes, who had replaced Edward Stettinius on June 30, 1945, struggled on through 1946 with the problems of postwar settlements. As early as September 1945 the first meeting of the Council of Foreign Ministers broke up because of Byrnes's fruitless demand that the governments of Rumania and Bulgaria be broadened. A series of almost interminable meetings of the Council of Foreign Ministers wrangled over border lines and reparation from Hitler's satellites, finally producing treaties for Italy, Hungary, Rumania, Bulgaria, and Finland. The treaties, signed on February 10, 1947, in effect confirmed Russian control over eastern Europe, which in Russian eyes seemed but a parallel to American control in Japan and Western control over most of Germany and all of Italy. The Yalta guarantees of democracy in eastern Europe had turned out much like the Open Door Policy in China, little more than pious cant subordinate to the pressures of *Realpolitik*. Byrnes's impulse to brandish the atomic bomb only added to the irritations, intimidating no one.

The United States, together with Britain and Canada (partners in developing the atomic bomb), had exclusive possession of atomic weapons at the time, but in 1946 proposed to internationalize the control of atomic energy through a plan presented to the U.N. Atomic Energy Commission. Under the plan, drawn up chiefly by Dean Acheson and David E. Lilienthal, an International Atomic Development Authority would have a monopoly of atomic explosives and atomic energy. The Russians, fearing Western domination of the agency, proposed instead simply to outlaw the manufacture and use of atomic bombs, with enforcement vested in the Security Council and thus subject to a veto. Later they conceded the right of international inspection, but still refused to give up the veto, and the American government rejected the arrangement, which it considered a compromise of international control. The plan was a failure, another manifestation of the inability to find any common ground for agreement on far-reaching issues.

CONTAINMENT By the beginning of 1947 relations with the Soviet Union had become very troubled. A year before, Stalin had already pronounced international peace impossible "under the present capitalist development of the world economy." His statement impelled George F. Kennan, counselor of the American Embassy in Moscow, to send an 8,000-word dispatch in which he sketched the roots of Russian policy and warned that the Soviet Union was "committed fanatically to the belief that with the U.S. there can be no permanent *modus vivendi*, that it is desirable and necessary that the internal harmony of our society be disrupted, our traditional way of life be destroyed, the international authority of our state be broken, if Soviet power is to be secure."

More than a year later, by then back at the State Department in Washington, Kennan spelled out his ideas for a proper response to the Soviets in a July 1947 article published anonymously in *Foreign Affairs*. "It is clear," he wrote, "that the main element of any United States policy toward the Soviet Union must be that of a long-term, patient but firm and vigilant containment of Russian expansive tendencies. . . . such a policy has nothing to do with outward histrionics: with threats or blustering or superfluous gestures of outward 'toughness.' " Americans, he argued, could hope for a long-term moderation of Soviet ideology and policy, so that in time tensions with the West would lessen. There was a strong possibility "that Soviet power, like the capitalist world of its conception, bears within it the seeds of its own decay, and that the sprouting of those seeds is well advanced."

Kennan's statement on containment supplied the rationale for the radical new departure in American foreign policy which America's political leaders had already decided to take. Behind this shift in policy lay a growing fear that Russian aims reached beyond eastern Europe, posing dangers in the eastern Mediterranean, the Middle East, and western Europe itself. The first major postwar crisis occurred in Iran, which borders the Soviet Union on the south and provided important trade routes to the

USSR. Soviet troops had been stationed in northern Iran while British-American troops were in the south, and all were supposed to pull out six months after the war. But the Soviets remained beyond the deadline of March 2, 1946, all the while stirring revolts in the northern provinces. The crisis finally blew over when a Soviet-Iranian agreement brought Russian withdrawal in early May.

Meanwhile the USSR was looking for a breakthrough into the Mediterranean, long important to Russia for purposes of trade and defense. After the war the USSR began to press Turkey for territorial concessions and the right to build naval bases on the Bosporus, an important gateway between the Black Sea and the Mediterranean. In August 1946 civil war broke out in Greece between a government backed by the British and a Communist-led faction, the EAM, which held the northern part of Greece and drew supplies from Yugoslavia, Bulgaria, and Albania. In February 1947 the British ambassador informed the American government that the British could no longer bear the economic and military burden of aiding Greece. When Truman conferred with congressional leaders on the situation, Arthur H. Vandenberg, chairman of the Senate Foreign Relations Committee, advised: "Scare the hell out of the American people." On March 12, 1947, President Truman appeared before Congress to ask $400 million for economic aid to both Greece and Turkey, and power to send American personnel to train their soldiers.

THE TRUMAN DOCTRINE AND THE MARSHALL PLAN   In his speech Truman stated what quickly came to be known as the Truman Doctrine, which was so far-reaching because it justified aid to Greece and Turkey in terms more active than Kennan's idea of containment and more general than this specific case warranted. "I believe," Truman declared, "that it must be the policy of the United States to support free peoples who are resisting attempted subjugation by armed minorities or by outside pressures." In May 1947, with the support of Senator Vandenberg, Congress passed the Greek-Turkish aid bill, and by 1950 had spent $659 million on the program. Turkey achieved economic stability, and Greece defeated the Communist insurrection in October 1949, partly because President Tito of Yugoslavia had broken with the Russians in the summer of 1948 and ceased to aid the EAM in mid-1949.

The Truman Doctrine was the beginning, or at least the open acknowledgment, of a contest which Bernard Baruch named in April 1947 in a speech to the legislature of his native South Car-

The Taskmaster. *Postwar Europe was a land of devastation. [Jacob Burck in the Chicago Sun-Times]*

olina: "Let us not be deceived—today we are in the midst of a cold war." Signs were growing that Greece and Turkey were but the front lines of a struggle that would involve western Europe as well. There wartime damage and dislocation had devastated factory production, and severe drought in 1947, followed by a severe winter, destroyed crops. Europe had become, in Winston Churchill's words, "a rubble heap, a charnel house, a breeding ground of pestilence and hate." Amid the chaos the Communist parties of France and Italy were flourishing, having gained credibility by working in the wartime resistance. Aid from the United Nations had staved off starvation, but had provided little basis for economic recovery.

In the spring of 1947 William L. Clayton, the State Department's chief advisor on economic affairs, reported to George C. Marshall, who had replaced Byrnes as secretary of state in January, that the United States had underestimated the extent of wartime damage in Europe. Only a program of massive aid could rescue western Europe from disaster. Late in May the Policy Planning Staff, under George Kennan, brought forth a plan which Secretary Marshall presented at the Harvard Commencement on June 5. Taking Kennan's lead, Marshall avoided the ideological overtones of the Truman Doctrine. "Our policy," Marshall said, "is directed not against country or doctrine, but against hunger, poverty, desperation, and chaos." Marshall offered aid to all European countries, including Russia, and called upon them to take the lead in judging their own needs. On June 27 the foreign ministers of France, Britain, and Russia met in London to discuss Marshall's overture. Molotov arrived with eighty advisors, but during the talks got word from Moscow to withdraw from this "imperialist" scheme. Two weeks later a meeting of delegates from western Europe formed a Committee of European Economic Cooperation (CEEC), which had a plan ready by September.

In December Truman submitted his proposal for the European Recovery Program to Congress. Two months later, a Communist coup d'état in Czechoslovakia ended the last remaining coalition government in eastern Europe. Coming just ten years after Munich, the seizure of power in Prague assured congressional passage of the Marshall Plan. From 1948 until 1951 the Economic Cooperation Administration (ECA), which managed the Marshall Plan, poured about $12 billion into European recovery through the CEEC.

DIVIDING GERMANY   The breakdown of the wartime alliance left the problem of postwar Germany unsettled. The German economy had stagnated, requiring the American army to carry a staggering burden of relief. In September 1946 Secretary Byrnes had said in a speech at Stuttgart that the zonal boundaries should not be regarded "as self-contained economic and political units," and in December of that year the Americans and British united their zones economically. Slowly, zones of occupation evolved into functioning governments. In February 1948 the British and Americans united their zones into what came to be called "Bizonia," which the French joined to create "Trizonia" in June. The West Germans were then invited to organize state governments and elect delegates to a federal constitutional convention.

Soviet reactions to the Marshall Plan and the unification of West Germany were sharp, and they were quickly focused on Berlin. In April 1948 the Russians began to restrict the flow of traffic into West Berlin; on June 23 they stopped all traffic. The blockade was designed to leave the allies no choice but to give up either Berlin or the plan to unify West Germany. But Gen. Lucius D. Clay, American commander in Germany, proposed to stand firm. "When Berlin falls, Western Germany will be next," he told the Pentagon. "If we mean . . . to hold Europe against communism, we must not budge."

Truman agreed, and after considering the use of armed convoys to supply West Berlin, opted for a massive airlift. At the time this seemed an enormous and perhaps impossible task, requiring, according to General Clay's estimate, 4,500 tons of supplies a day. But by quick work the allied air forces brought in planes from around the world and by October 1948 were flying in nearly 5,000 tons of food and equipment a day. Altogether, from June 1948 to mid-May 1949, the Berlin Airlift carried in

OCCUPATION OF GERMANY AND AUSTRIA

French zone   British zone   U.S. zone   Soviet zone

more than 1.5 million tons of supplies, or above a half ton for each of the 2.5 million West Berliners. Gen. Frank L. Howley, American commandant in Berlin, meanwhile got in a few licks at his Russian counterpart by cutting off a gas main that ran through the American sector to Marshal Vasily Sokolovsky's house, forcing him to move. When Sokolovsky's aides tried to truck his furniture through the American zone, Howley seized the furniture.

Finally, on May 12, 1949, after extended talks, the Russians lifted the blockade in return for a meeting of the Council of Foreign Ministers in Paris. This was purely a face-saving gesture, and the meeting resulted in no important decision on Germany. That same May, West Germany adopted a constitution, and before the end of the year the German Federal Republic had a government functioning under Christian Democratic Chancellor Konrad Adenauer. At the end of May 1949 a German "Democratic" Republic arose in the eastern zone, making the division of Germany a permanent fact. West Germany gradually acquired more authority, until the Western powers recognized its full sovereignty in 1955.

BUILDING NATO   As relations between the Soviets and western Europe chilled, transatlantic unity ripened into an outright military alliance. By March 1948, Britain, France, and the "Benelux" countries (Belgium, the Netherlands, and Luxembourg) had signed a fifty-year treaty of alliance and economic cooperation, the Brussels Pact. That June the Senate passed a resolution introduced by Senator Vandenberg authorizing the administration to develop a collective defense pact under Article 51 of the U.N. Charter. Negotiations for an Atlantic alliance got under way in July. On April 4, 1949, the North Atlantic Treaty was signed at Washington by representatives of twelve nations: the five Brussels Pact countries plus the United States, Canada, Denmark, Iceland, Italy, Norway, and Portugal. Greece and Turkey joined the alliance in 1952. The treaty pledged that an attack against any one of the signers would be considered an attack against all, and provided for a council of the North Atlantic Treaty Organization (NATO) which could establish other necessary agencies. In September 1950 the council decided to create an integrated defense force for western Europe and later named General Eisenhower to head the Supreme Headquarters of the Allied Powers in Europe (SHAPE). In 1955 the Warsaw Treaty Organization appeared as the eastern European counterpart to NATO. Senate ratification of the North Atlantic Treaty by a vote of 82 to 13 suggested that the isolationism of the prewar period no longer exerted a hold on the American people.

One other foreign-policy decision with long-term consequences came during the eventful year 1948. Palestine, as the

NATO, a hopeful sign for the West. [*The Hartford* Courant]

biblical Holy Land had come to be known, had been long occupied by Arabs, and was under Turkish suzerainty until the
League of Nations made it a British mandate after World War I.
Over the early years of the twentieth century many Zionists, who
advocated a Jewish state in the region, had migrated there. Still
more came after the British entered, and a greatly increased
number came (illegally, under British rule) after World War II.
Offered tenuous promises by the British of a national homeland,
the Jewish inhabitants demanded their own state. Late in 1947
the U.N. General Assembly voted to partition Palestine into Jewish and Arab states, but this met with fierce Arab opposition. Finally, the British mandate expired without firm action by the
U.N. to enforce its decision, and on May 14, 1948, Jewish
leaders proclaimed the independence of the state of Israel. President Truman, who had been in close touch with Jewish leaders,
ordered recognition of the new state within minutes—the
United States became the first nation so to act. The neighboring
Arab states reacted by going to war against Israel, which, however, held its own. U.N. mediators gradually worked out truce
agreements with Israel's Arab neighbors and an uneasy peace
was restored by May 11, 1949, when Israel was admitted as a
member of the United Nations. But the hard feelings and intermittent warfare between Israel and the Arab states have festered
ever since, complicating American foreign policy, which has
tried to maintain friendship with both sides.

HARRY GIVES 'EM HELL

SHAPING THE FAIR DEAL   The determination Truman projected in
foreign affairs had not yet altered his image on the domestic
front. By early 1948, after three years in the White House, Truman had yet to shake the impression that he was not up to the
job. The columnists Joseph and Stuart Alsop wrote before the
Democratic convention that Truman would be running "the lone-
liest campaign in recent history." Rather than go with a loser,
New Deal stalwarts and party regulars tried to draft General Eisenhower or Justice William O. Douglas, but in vain. The Democratic party seemed about to fragment: southern conservatives
took umbrage at Truman's outspoken support of civil rights,
while the left flared up in 1946 over his firing Secretary of Commerce Henry A. Wallace after a speech critical of the administration's policy. "Getting tough," Wallace had argued, "never
brought anything real and lasting—whether for school yard bul-

lies or world powers. The tougher we get, the tougher the Russians will get." The left itself was splitting between the Progressive Citizens of America (PCA), formed in December 1946, which gave ear to Wallace, and the Americans for Democratic Action (ADA), formed in January 1947, which also criticized Truman but took a firm anti-Communist stance.

Unknown to all these groups, Truman had a game plan for 1948; it had been outlined in a forty-three-page memorandum written by his aide, Clark Clifford, a young lawyer from St. Louis. Much of what later seemed desperate impulse actually followed Clifford's design, which urged an aggressive effort to shore up the New Deal coalition. Truman needed the midwestern and western farm belts, and happily had fairly strong support among farmers. In metropolitan areas the trick was to carry the labor and the black vote, which Truman wooed by working closely with unions and liberals, and pressing the cause of civil rights. The Solid South, Clifford predicted, could be counted on to stay in the Democratic column. The Republicans would choose Thomas E. Dewey again, and Wallace, running on a third-party Progressive ticket, would be badly compromised by Communist support. With the South and West, Truman could afford to lose some New Deal strongholds in the East and still win. On nearly every point, Clifford called the turn. He erred chiefly in underrating the rebellion that took four Deep South states out of Truman's camp.

The grand new departure in Clifford's design was its forthright emphasis on civil rights—a politically advantageous issue now that so many blacks had migrated to northern cities in states with large electoral votes. Truman's motivations in embracing the issue were complex. When in 1946 he appointed the President's Committee on Civil Rights, a panel of distinguished citizens, black and white, North and South, he acted not only in response to the pressures of black organizations, but apparently also out of outrage at several recent attacks on blacks. The committee's report, *To Secure These Rights* (1947), touched on virtually every category of racial discrimination and called for the "elimination of segregation based on race, color, creed, or national origin, from American life."

Like other presidents, Truman used his State of the Union message in January 1948 to set the agenda for an election year. The speech offered something to nearly every group the Democrats hoped to win over. The first goal, Truman said, was "to secure fully the essential human rights of our citizens" and promised a special message later on civil rights. "To protect human resources," Truman asked for federal aid to education, increased and extended unemployment and retirement benefits, a comprehensive system of health insurance, more federal support for housing, and extension of rent controls. He continued to pile on the demands: for reclamation projects, more rural electrification, a higher minimum wage, laws to admit thousands of displaced persons to the United States, money for the Marshall Plan, a "cost of living" tax credit, and much more. As Senator Taft put it, the speech "raised all the ghosts of the old New Deal with new trappings that Tugwell and Harry Hopkins never thought of." On February 2 Congress received Truman's message on civil rights, which called for a broad range of actions, none of which he seriously hoped to get out of Congress. On July 26, however, he did ban racial discrimination in hiring federal employees, and four days later ordered an end to segregation in the armed forces.

THE 1948 ELECTION   The Republican Congress for the most part spurned the Truman program, which it would later regret. Republican presidential hopefuls, scenting victory in November, entered a scramble for the nomination: Senator Taft, former Minnesota Gov. Harold E. Stassen, California Gov. Earl Warren, Governor Dewey, and an array of favorite sons. At the Philadelphia convention in June Dewey won the nomination on the third ballot and designated Governor Warren as his running mate. The platform endorsed most of the New Deal reforms as an accomplished fact and approved the administration's bipartisan foreign policy, but as Landon had in 1936, promised to run things more efficiently.

In July a glum Democratic convention gathered in Philadelphia, expecting to do little more than go through the motions, only to find itself doubly surprised: first by the battle over the civil rights plank, and then by Truman's acceptance speech. To keep from stirring southern hostility any further, the administration sought a platform plank that opposed discrimination only in general terms. ADA leaders, however, sponsored a plank which called on Congress for specific action and commended Truman "for his courageous stand on the issue of civil rights." Speaking last in favor of the change, Minneapolis Mayor Hubert H. Humphrey electrified the delegates and set off a ten-minute demonstration: "The time has arrived for the Democratic party to get out of the shadow of states' rights and walk forthrightly into the bright sunshine of human rights." Segregationist delegates from Alabama and Mississippi walked, instead, out of the convention.

After the convention had nominated Truman, and as his running mate, Sen. Alben Barkley, the president appeared on the rostrum during the wee hours of the morning to give his acceptance speech. It was a new Truman, showing a new fighting style in his speeches. To overcome Truman's tendency to read speeches in a flat drone, his staff encouraged him to talk off-the-cuff from a brief outline. "Senator Barkley and I will win this election and make the Republicans like it," he said, "don't you forget it!" Near the end he sprang a bombshell. On July 26, known in Missouri as "Turnip Day," he would call Congress back into session "to get the laws the people need," many of which the Republican platform had endorsed.

On July 17 a group of rebellious southerners met in Birmingham and nominated South Carolina Gov. J. Strom Thurmond on a States' Rights Democratic ticket, quickly dubbed the "Dixiecrat" ticket by a headline writer on the Charlotte *News*. The Dixiecrats' dream was to draw enough electoral votes to preclude a majority for either major party, throwing the election into the House where they might strike a sectional bargain like that of 1877. A few days later, on July 23, the left wing of the Democratic party gathered in Philadelphia to name Henry A. Wallace on a Progressive party ticket. These splits in the Democratic ranks seemed to spell the final blow to Truman. The special session of Congress petered out in futility.

But Truman, undaunted, set out on a 31,000-mile "whistle stop" train tour during which he castigated the "do-nothing" Eightieth Congress to the accompaniment of cries from his audiences: "Pour it on, Harry!" and "Give 'em hell, Harry." And Harry would respond: "I don't give 'em hell. I just tell the truth and they think it's hell." Dewey, in contrast, ran a restrained campaign, designed to avoid rocking the boat. By so doing he

Students parade for Strom Thurmond at the States' Rights Convention in Birmingham, Alabama, July 1948. [United Press International]

The Man Who "Done
His Damndest."
*Truman's victory was a
huge upset. [United Press
International]*

may have snatched defeat from the jaws of victory. In trying to look "presidential," the dapper Dewey came across, in Alice Roosevelt Longworth's deadly simile, looking like the groom on the wedding cake. He deliberately studded his speeches with high-toned platitudes hailing the "creative genius" of a free people, damning the "prophets of gloom," and staying for the most part on what a reporter called "a high road of rich baritone homilies." In Phoenix he disclosed that "America's future—like yours in Arizona—is still ahead of us."

To the end the polls and the pundits predicted a sure win for Dewey, and most speculation centered on his cabinet choices. But on election day Truman chalked up the biggest upset in American history, taking 24.2 million votes (49.5 percent) to Dewey's 22 million (45.1 percent) and winning a thumping 303 to 189 margin in the electoral college. Thurmond and Wallace each got more than a million votes, but the revolt of right and left worked to Truman's advantage. The Dixiecrat rebellion reassured black voters who had questioned the Democrats' commitment to civil rights, while the Progressive movement made it hard to tag Truman as "soft on Communism." Thurmond carried the four Deep South states in which his name was accompanied on the ballot by the Democratic party symbol (in Alabama one could not vote for Truman) and walked off with 39 electoral votes, including one from a Tennessee elector who repudiated his state's decision for Truman. Thurmond's success started a momentous disruption of the Democratic Solid South, which in a series of elections now divided its vote. But Truman's victory also carried Democratic majorities into Congress, where the new group of senators included Hubert Humphrey, Tennessee's Estes Kefauver, and by eighty-seven votes, "Landslide Lyndon" B. Johnson of Texas.

The outcome seemed a vindication for the New Deal and a

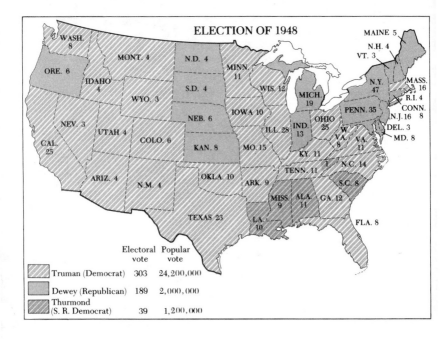

ELECTION OF 1948

	Electoral vote	Popular vote
Truman (Democrat)	303	24,200,000
Dewey (Republican)	189	2,000,000
Thurmond (S. R. Democrat)	39	1,200,000

mandate for liberalism and Truman so regarded it. "We have rejected the discredited theory that the fortunes of the nation should be in the hands of a privileged few," he said in January 1949. His State of the Union message repeated substantially the agenda he had set forth a year previously. "Every segment of our population and every individual," he said, "has a right to expect from his government a fair deal." Whether consciously or not he had invented a tag, the "Fair Deal," to set off his program from the New Deal.

The president won some of his Fair Deal proposals, but they were mainly extensions or enlargements of New Deal programs already in place: a higher minimum wage, bringing more people under Social Security, extension of rent controls, farm price supports at 90 percent of parity, a sizable slum-clearance and public housing program, and more money for the Reclamation Bureau, the TVA, rural electrification, and farm housing. Despite Democratic majorities, however, the conservative coalition was able to resist any drastic new departures in domestic policy. Congress gave the cold shoulder to civil rights bills, national health insurance, federal aid to education, and Agriculture Secretary Charles F. Brannan's plan to provide subsidies that would hold up farm incomes rather than farm prices. Congress also turned down Truman's demand for repeal of the Taft-Hartley Act.

THE COLD WAR HEATS UP

Global concerns, never far from center stage in the postwar world, plagued Truman's second term as they had his first. In his inaugural address Truman called for foreign policy to rest on four pillars: the United Nations, the Marshall Plan, NATO, and a "bold new plan" for technical assistance to underdeveloped parts of the world, a sort of global Marshall Plan which came to be known simply as "Point Four." Under the Technical Cooperation Administration, this program to aid the postwar world began in 1950 with a modest outlay of $35 million.

"LOSING" CHINA AND THE BOMB   One of the most intractable problems, the China tangle, was fast coming unraveled in 1949. The Chinese Nationalists (Kuomintang) of Chiang Kai-shek had at first accepted the help of Communists, but expelled them from their ranks in 1927. When a new leader, Mao Tse-tung, began to rebuild the Communist party by organizing the peasants instead of urban workers, the Nationalists drove him out of Kiangsi province in the south. After an arduous trek, which the Communists later romanticized as the "Long March" of 1934–1935, they entrenched themselves in northern China at Yenan in Shensi province. The outbreak of war with Japan in 1937 relieved them of pressure from the Nationalists, and at the same time enabled them to assume a patriotic stance by fighting the Japanese. During the war Roosevelt, and apparently Stalin as well, believed that the Nationalists would organize China after the war.

The commanders of American forces in China long found Chiang hard to get on with and were driven to the same conclusion as many foreign service officers: that Chiang's government was hopelessly corrupt, tyrannical, and inefficient. After the war, American forces nevertheless ferried Nationalist armies back into the eastern and northern provinces as the Japanese withdrew, and themselves temporarily occupied some of the major coastal cities in China. United States' policy during and immediately after the war was to promote peace and coalition between the factions in China, but sporadic civil war broke out late in 1945.

It soon became a losing fight for the Nationalists, as the Communists radicalized the land-hungry peasantry. In October 1948 the Communists took Mukden; three months later they were in Peking and Tientsin, beginning another long march southward. By December 1949 they had taken Canton and the Nationalist

Gen. Mao Tse-tung reviews troops of the Chinese Communist Army, 1949. [Photoworld]

government had fled to the island of Formosa, which it renamed Taiwan.

From 1945 through 1949 the United States had funneled some $2 billion in aid to the Nationalists, to no avail. Administration critics asked bitterly: "Who lost China?" and a State Department white paper put the blame on Chiang for his failure to hold the support of the Chinese people. In fact it is hard to imagine how the United States government could have prevented the outcome short of military intervention, which would have been very risky and unpopular. The United States continued to recognize the Nationalist government on Taiwan as the rightful government of China, delaying formal relations with Red China for thirty years until 1979. Seeking to shore up friendly regimes in Asia, in February 1950 the United States recognized the French-supported regime of Emperor Bao Dai in Vietnam and shortly afterward extended aid to the French in their battle against Ho Chi Minh's guerrillas there.

As China fell to the Communists, American intelligence in September 1949 found an unusual radioactivity in the air, evidence that the Soviets had set off an atomic bomb. The American nuclear monopoly had lasted just four years, but under the umbrella of security that it seemed to offer, the wartime military establishment had been allowed to dwindle. In a crisis, this left American leaders the choice of doing nothing or cremating millions of people. The discovery of the Russian bomb set off an intense reappraisal of the strategic balance in the world, causing Truman in 1950 to end a dispute among his scientific advisors by ordering the construction of a hydrogen bomb, a weapon far more frightful than the Hiroshima bomb, lest the Russians make one first. The discovery also led the National Security Council to give the president a top-secret document, NSC-68, which called for rebuilding conventional military forces to provide options other than nuclear war. This represented a major departure from America's time-honored aversion to keeping large standing armies in peacetime, and was a very expensive proposition. But the American public was growing more accustomed to the nation's world role, and the invasion of South Korea by Communist forces from the north then clinched the issue.

WAR IN KOREA   The division of Korea at the end of World War II, like the division of Germany, began as a temporary expedient and ended as a permanent fact. In the hectic days of August 1945 a State-War-Navy Coordinating Committee adopted a hasty proposal to divide Korea at the Thirty-eighth Parallel. The Soviets accepted to the surprise of Dean Rusk and others involved. Since they bordered on Korea, the Russians could quickly have occupied the whole country. With the onset of the Cold War, it became clear that agreement on unification was no more likely in Korea than in Germany, and by the end of 1948 separate regimes had appeared in the two sectors and occupation forces had withdrawn. American leaders then inadvertently may have given false impressions to the Communists. General MacArthur during 1949 and Secretary of State Dean Acheson in January 1950 omitted both Korea and Formosa (Taiwan) from an America defense perimeter which included the Philippines, the Ryukyu Islands, and Japan. The weakened state of the American military may have contributed to the impression that South Korea was vulnerable.

For whatever reasons, North Korean forces crossed the boundary on June 24, 1950, and swept quickly down the peninsula. President Truman responded decisively. Korea might have been outside America's defense perimeter, but its southern tip was dangerously close to Japan. Besides, American foreign policy was still much subject to what might be called the "Munich syndrome," or what General MacArthur called "history's clear lesson . . . that appeasement but begets new and bloodier war." Failure to act, Truman reasoned, would embolden Communist leaders "to override nations closer to our own shores."

An emergency meeting of the U.N. Security Council quickly censured the North Korean "breach of peace." The Soviet delegate, who held a veto power, was at the time boycotting the council because it would not seat Red China in place of Nationalist China. On June 27, its first resolution having been ignored, the Security Council called on U.N. members to "furnish such assistance to the Republic of Korea as may be necessary to repel the armed attack and to restore international peace and security in the area." Truman then ordered American air, naval, and ground forces into action. In all, some fourteen other U.N. members sent in military units, the largest from Britain and Turkey, and five sent medical units. Later, when the U.N. voted a unified command, General MacArthur was designated to take charge. The war remained chiefly an American affair, and one that set a precedent of profound consequence: war by order of the president rather than by vote of Congress. It had the sanction of the U.N. Security Council, to be sure, and could be considered a "police action," not a war. And other presidents had ordered American troops into action without a declaration of war, but never on such a scale.

For three months things went badly indeed for the Republic of Korea (ROK) and U.N. forces. By September they were barely hanging on to the Pusan perimeter in the southeast corner of Korea. Then, in a brilliant ploy, on September 15 MacArthur landed a new force to the North Korean rear at Inchon, port city of Seoul. Synchronized with a breakout from Pusan, the sudden blow stampeded the enemy back across the border. At this point George Kennan argued that the U.N. forces should stop at the

Thirty-eighth Parallel and negotiate, but a decision was taken on MacArthur's assurance to push on and seek to reunify Korea. The Russian delegate was back in the Security Council, wielding his veto, so on October 7 the United States got approval for this course from the U.N. General Assembly, where the veto did not apply. United States forces had already crossed the boundary by October 1, and now continued northward against minimal resistance. President Truman, concerned over broad hints of intervention by Red China, flew out to Wake Island for a conference with General MacArthur on October 15. There the general discounted chances that the Red Army would act, but if it did, he predicted "there would be the greatest slaughter."

That same day Peking announced that China "cannot stand idly by." But by October 20 U.N. forces had entered Pyongyang, the North Korean capital, and on October 26 the most advanced units had reached Chosan on the Yalu River border with China. MacArthur now predicted total victory by Christmas, but on the night of November 25 Chinese "volunteers" counterattacked, and massive "human wave" attacks, with the support of tanks and planes, turned the tables on the U.N. forces, sending them into a desperate retreat just at the onset of winter. It had become "an entirely new war," MacArthur said. Soon he was putting out word that the fault for the war's continuance lay with the administration for requiring that he conduct a limited war. He proposed raids on China's "privileged sanctuary" in Manchuria, a blockade of China, and an invasion of the mainland by the Taiwan Nationalists, but Truman resisted. MacArthur seemed to have forgotten altogether his one-time reluctance to bog the country down in a major war on the Asian mainland.

The landing at Inchon, September 1950. [Hank Walker, Life *magazine, © 1978 Time Inc.]*

Truman stood firmly against leading the United States into the "gigantic booby trap" of war with China, and the U.N. forces soon rallied. By January 1951 U.N. troops under Gen. Matthew Ridgway finally secured their lines below Seoul, and then launched a counterattack that carried them back across the Thirty-eighth Parallel in March. When Truman seized the chance and offered negotiations to restore the boundary, MacArthur undermined the move by issuing an ultimatum for China to make peace or be attacked. Truman decided then that MacArthur would have to go. On April 5, on the floor of the House, Republican Minority Leader Joseph Martin read a letter in which MacArthur criticized the president and said that "there is no substitute for victory." Such an act of open insubordination left the commander-in-chief no choice but to accept MacArthur's policy or fire him. Civilian control of the military was at stake, Truman later said, and he did not let it remain at stake very long. The Joint Chiefs of Staff all backed the decision, and on April 11, 1951, the president removed MacArthur from all his commands and replaced him with Matthew B. Ridgway.

Truman's action set off an immediate uproar in the country, and a tumultuous reception greeted MacArthur upon his return home for the first time since 1937. MacArthur's speech to a joint session of Congress provided the climactic event. "Once war is forced upon us," he said, "there is no alternative than to apply every available means to bring it to a swift end. War's very object is victory. . . . Why, my soldiers asked of me, surrender military advantages to an enemy in the field? I could not answer them." MacArthur ended the speech in memorable fashion. He recalled a barracks ballad of his youth "which proclaimed most proudly that old soldiers never die, they just fade away." And like the old soldiers of that ballad, he said, "I now close my military career and just fade away, an old soldier who tried to do his duty as God gave him the light to see that duty." A Senate investigation, with Richard Russell of Georgia in the chair, brought out the administration's arguments, best summarized by Gen. Omar Bradley, chairman of the Joint Chiefs of Staff. "Taking on Red China," he said, would lead only "to a larger deadlock at greater expense." The MacArthur strategy "would involve us in the wrong war at the wrong place at the wrong time and with the wrong enemy." Americans, nurtured on classic western showdowns in which good always triumphed over evil, found the logic of limited war hard to take, but also found Bradley's logic persuasive.

On June 24, 1951, the Soviet representative at the United Nations proposed a cease-fire and armistice along the Thirty-eighth

Parallel; Secretary of State Acheson accepted in principle a few days later with the consent of the U.N. China and North Korea responded favorably—at the time General Ridgway's "meat-grinder offensive" was inflicting severe losses—and truce talks started on July 10, 1951, only to drag out for another two years while the fighting continued. The chief snags were prisoner exchanges and the insistence of South Korea's President Syngman Rhee on unification. By the time a truce was finally reached on July 26, 1953, Truman had relinquished the White House to Dwight D. Eisenhower. The truce line followed the front at that time, mostly a little north of the Thirty-eighth Parallel, with a demilitarized zone of four kilometers separating the forces; repatriation of prisoners would be voluntary, supervised by a neutral commission. No final peace conference ever took place, and Korea, like Germany, remained divided. The war had cost the United States more than 33,000 battle deaths and 103,000 wounded and missing. South Korean casualties, all told, were about 1 million, and North Korean and Chinese casualties an estimated 1.5 million.

ANOTHER RED SCARE   In calculating the costs of the Korean War one must add in the far-reaching consequences of the Second Red Scare, which had grown since 1945 as the domestic counterpart to the Cold War abroad and reached a crescendo during the Korean conflict. Since 1938, a House Committee on Un-American Activities had kept up a drumfire of accusations about subversives in government. In 1945 government agents found that secret American documents had turned up in the offices of a Communist-sponsored magazine, and in 1946 more dramatic revelations came from a Canadian royal commission which uncovered several spy rings in the Canadian bureaucracy. On March 21, 1947, just nine days after he announced the Truman Doctrine, the president signed an executive order setting up procedures for an employee loyalty program in the federal government. Every person entering the civil employ of the government would be subject to an investigation. By early 1951 the Civil Service Commission had cleared over 3 million people, while over 2,000 had resigned and 212 had been dismissed for doubtful loyalty, but no espionage ring was uncovered. The program covered all government employees, not just those in sensitive positions.

The Truman program was designed partly if not mainly to protect the president's political flank, but it failed of that purpose, mainly because of disclosures of earlier Communist penetrations into government that were few in number but sensational in character. The loyalty review program may in fact have heightened the politically explosive hysteria over Communist infiltration.

Perhaps the single case most damaging to the administration involved Alger Hiss, president of the Carnegie Endowment for International Peace, who had served in several government departments, and while in the State Department had been secretary-general of the United Nations charter conference. Whittaker Chambers, a former Soviet agent and later an editor of *Time* magazine, told the House Un-American Activities Committee in 1948 that Hiss had given him a number of secret documents ten years earlier, when Chambers worked for the Soviets. Hiss sued for libel, and Chambers produced microfilms of the State Department documents Hiss had passed on to him. Before a federal grand jury Hiss denied the accusation, whereupon he was indicted for perjury and, after one mistrial, convicted in January 1950. The charge was perjury, but he was convicted of lying about espionage—for which he could not be tried because the statute of limitations on the crime had expired. Most damaging to the administration was the fact that President Truman, taking at face value the many testimonials to Hiss's integrity, called the charges against him a "red herring." Secretary of State Dean Acheson compounded the damage when, meaning to express compassion, he said: "I do not intend to turn my back on Alger Hiss." The Hiss affair had another political consequence: it raised to national prominence a young California congressman, Richard M. Nixon, who doggedly insisted on pursuing the case and then exploited the anti-Communist cause to win election to the Senate in 1950.

More cases surfaced. In 1949, the government brought about the conviction of eleven top Communist party leaders under the Smith Act of 1940, which outlawed any conspiracy to advocate the overthrow of the government. The Supreme Court upheld the law under the doctrine of a "clear and present danger," which overrode the right to free speech. In 1950, the government disclosed the existence of a British-American spy network which had fed information about the development of the atomic bomb to Russia. These disclosures led to the arrest of, among others, Klaus Fuchs in Britain and Julius and Ethel Rosenberg in the United States. The Rosenbergs, convicted of espionage in wartime, were executed in 1953. The importance of the secrets they transmitted is doubtful. In a time of less excitement their sentence might well have been commuted.

MCCARTHY'S WITCH-HUNT Such revelations encouraged politicians to exploit public fears. If a man of such respectability as Hiss were guilty, many wondered, who then could be trusted? The United States, which bestrode the world like a colossus in 1945, had since "lost" eastern Europe and Asia, and "lost" its atomic secrets to Russia. (Physicists, however, insisted that there was nothing secret about the basic principles underlying the bomb.) Early in 1950 the hitherto obscure Sen. Joseph R. McCarthy suddenly surfaced as the shrewdest and most ruthless exploiter of such anxieties. Seeking a way to augment his chances of reelection in 1952, he took up the cause, or at least the pose, of anticommunism. He began with a speech at Wheeling, West Virginia, on February 9, 1950, in which he said that the State Department was infested with Communists and that he held in his hand a list of their names. Later there was confusion as to whether he had said 205, 81, 57, or "a lot" of names, and even whether the sheet of paper carried a list. But such confusion always pursued McCarthy's charges.

Challenged to provide names, he finally pointed to Owen Lattimore of the Johns Hopkins University, an Asian expert, as head of "the espionage ring in the State Department." A special committee under Sen. Millard Tydings looked into the matter and pronounced McCarthy's charges "a fraud and a hoax." McCarthy then turned, in what became his common tactic, to other charges, other names. Whenever his charges were refuted, he loosed a scattershot of new charges. In his hit-and-run tactics, McCarthy displayed the instincts of Shakespeare's Iago, planting suspicions without proof and growing ever more impudent. "He lied with wild abandon," the commentator Richard Rovere wrote; "he lied without evident fear; . . . he lied vividly and with bold imagination; he lied, often, with very little pretense of telling the truth."

McCarthy never uncovered a single Communist agent in gov-

Sen. Joseph McCarthy.
[United Press International]

ernment. But with the United States at war with Korean Communists in mid-1950, he continued to mobilize true believers. In the elections of 1950 he intervened in Maryland and helped defeat the conservative Senator Tydings with trumped-up charges that Tydings was pro-Communist. Republicans, even for a time a man of such probity as Robert Taft, encouraged him to keep up the game. By 1951 he was riding so high as to list Gens. George C. Marshall and Dwight D. Eisenhower among the disloyal. He kept up his campaign without successful challenge until the end of the Korean War. But all his discoveries, according to Richard Rovere, added up to "nothing more exciting than a Major Peress [a "pink" army dentist], a citation of Corliss Lamont [a Soviet apologist] in a bibliography, a girl who had heard talk of unwedded bliss in a propaganda agency, a novel by a Communist on a library shelf, and an ex-Communist here and there in some minor agency. He did no better than that."

Under the influence of anti-Communist hysteria the Congress in 1950 passed the McCarran Internal Security Act over President Truman's veto.The act made it unlawful "to combine, conspire, or agree with any other person to perform any act which would substantially contribute to . . . the establishment of a totalitarian dictatorship." Communist and Communist-front organizations had to register with the attorney-general. Aliens who had belonged to totalitarian parties were barred from admission to the United States, a provision that discouraged any temptation for Communists to defect to the United States. Enforcement was placed under a Subversive Activities Control Board.

The McCarran Act, Truman said in his veto message, would "put the Government into the business of thought control." He might in fact have said as much about the Smith Act of 1940, or even his own program of loyalty investigations. In the mid-1950s, looking back over the recent era of hysteria, John Lord O'Brian, once an advisor to Hoover's attorney-general, said, "in reality we have been establishing something like a new system of preventive law applicable to the field of ideas and essentially different from traditional American procedures."

During the late summer of 1951, while the off-and-on peace negotiations continued in Korea, the United States buttressed its defense perimeter through treaties with offshore allies which, just six years after the end of the war, now included Japan. On September 8, 1951, in the San Francisco Opera House, the United States and forty-eight other nations—the USSR declined to participate—signed a peace treaty with Japan, which recognized restoration of Japan's sovereignty but stripped the empire of all claims to Korea, Formosa, the Pescadores, the Kuriles, Sakhalin, and the Pacific islands formerly held under League of Nations mandate. These, along with the Ryukyu and Bonin Islands, now passed to a U.N. trusteeship under the United States. By another treaty signed with Japan that same day, the United States was permitted to maintain armed forces in the defeated country. Just a week earlier, on September 1, as the delegates gathered for the peace conference, the United States, Australia, and New Zealand entered a Tripartite Security Treaty which provided for mutual defense. Two days before that, on August 30, the presidents of the United States and the Philippines signed a similar agreement in Washington.

ASSESSING THE COLD WAR In retrospect the onset of the Cold War takes on an appearance of terrible inevitability. American and Soviet misunderstanding of each other's motives was virtually unavoidable. America's preference for international principles, such as self-determination and democracy, conflicted with Stalin's preference for international spheres of influence. Russia, after all, had been invaded by Germany twice in the first half of the twentieth century, and Soviet leaders wanted tame buffer states on their borders for protection. The people of eastern Europe, as usual, were caught in the middle. But the Communists themselves held to a universal principle: world revolution. And since the time of President Monroe, Americans had bristled at the thought of foreign intervention in their own sphere of influence, the Western Hemisphere. After the war the United States moved to make the Monroe Doctrine multilateral. Under the Act of Chapultepec (1945) all American states except Argentina agreed that an attack on one would be taken as an attack on all. The Treaty of Rio de Janeiro (1947), with Argentina now included, repeated the principle and imposed an obligation on all to aid any fellow American state attacked, whether from outside the hemisphere or by another American state.

If international conditions set the stage for the Cold War, the actions of political leaders and thinkers set events in motion. President Truman, in following the advice Senator Vandenberg gave during the crisis in Greece and Turkey, may have scared hell out of the American people all too well. The loyalty program, following hot on the heels of the Truman Doctrine, may have spurred on the anti-Communist hysteria of the times. George Kennan's policy of containment itself proved hard to contain, its author later confessed, in part because he failed at the outset to spell out its limits explicitly. "Repeatedly," Kennan wrote in his *Memoirs*, ". . . I expressed in talks and lectures the view that there were only five regions of the world—the United States, the United Kingdom, the Rhine valley with adjacent industrial areas, the Soviet Union, and Japan—where the sinews of military strength could be produced in quantity; I pointed out that only one of these was under Communist control; and I defined the main task of containment, accordingly, as one of seeing to it that none of the remaining ones fell under its control."

The years after World War II were unlike any other postwar years in American history. Having taken on global burdens, the nation had become, if not exactly a "garrison state," at least a country committed for the first time to a major and permanent National Military Establishment, along with the attendant National Security Council, Central Intelligence Agency, and by presidential directive in 1952, the enormous National Security Agency, entrusted with extensive monitoring of media and communications for foreign intelligence. The new policy initiatives of the Truman years had led the country to abandon its long-standing aversion to peacetime alliances not only in the NATO pact but in the agreements with Japan, the Philippines, and the other American states. It was a far cry from the world of 1796, when George Washington in his Farewell Address warned his countrymen against "those overgrown military establishments which . . . are inauspicious to liberty" and advised his country "to steer clear of permanent alliances with any portion of the foreign world."

FURTHER READING

The Cold War, like Reconstruction, is an area of American history still hotly debated by scholars. Traditional interpretations by Herbert Feis in *From Trust to Terror: The Onset of the Cold War, 1945–1950* (1970), and John L. Gaddis in *The United States and the Origins of the Cold War, 1941–1947* (1972),° can be balanced with the revisionists Walter LaFeber in *America, Russia, and the Cold War, 1945–1980* (1981),° and Gabriel Kolko in *The Limits of Power: The World and United States Foreign Policy, 1945–1954* (1972). Two more encompassing works, which also balance the two sides of argument, are the traditional John L. Gaddis's *Strategies of Containment: A Critical Appraisal of Postwar American National Security Policy* (1982) and the more revisionist Norman A. Graebner's *The Age of Global Power: The United States since 1938* (1979).

°These books are available in paperback editions.

Other scholars concentrate on more specific events in the buildup of international tensions. Lynn Etheridge Davis's *The Cold War Begins: Soviet-American Conflict over Eastern Europe* (1974), George C. Herring, Jr.'s *Aid to Russia, 1941–1946* (1973), Thomas G. Paterson's *Soviet-American Confrontation* (1973), and Bruce Kuklick's *American Policy and the Division of Germany* (1972) deal with initial tensions at the close of the war. Herbert Feis's *Between War and Peace: The Potsdam Conference* (1960) examines Truman's attitude. How tensions widened to other areas of the world is shown in Bruce R. Kuniholm's *The Origins of the Cold War in the Near East: Great Power Conflict and Diplomacy in Iran, Turkey, and Greece* (1980). For the foundations of the Truman Doctrine, consult Lawrence S. Wittner's *American Intervention in Greece, 1943–49* (1982), and William Roger Louis's *Imperialism at Bay: The United States and the Decolonization of the British Empire* (1978). For the Marshall Plan, two helpful books are Hadley Arkes's *Bureaucracy, the Marshall Plan, and the National Interest* (1974) and Robert H. Ferrell's *George C. Marshall* (1966). For subsequent tensions and policy, see W. Phillips Davison's *The Berlin Blockade* (1958) and Robert E. Osgood's *NATO* (1962). Also helpful on defensive arrangements in Europe is John Bayliss's *Anglo-American Defence Relations, 1939–1980: The Special Relationship* (1981). For the Truman administration's reliance on the atomic bomb monopoly, see Joseph I. Lieberman's *The Scorpion and the Tarantula: The Struggle to Control Atomic Weapons, 1945–1949* (1970), Alexander L. George and Richard Smoke's *Deterrence and American Foreign Policy: Theory and Practice* (1975), Michael Mandelbaum's *The Nuclear Question: The United States and Nuclear Weapons, 1946–1976* (1979), and Daniel Yergin's *Shattered Peace: The Origins of the Cold War and the National Security State* (1977).°

A solid study of the career bureaucrats who helped shape policy is Lloyd C. Gardner's *Architects of Illusion: Men and Ideas in American Foreign Policy, 1941–1949* (1970). Those who opposed such policies are the subject of Thomas G. Paterson's *Cold War Critics: Alternatives to American Foreign Policy in the Truman Years* (1972) and Robert J. Maddox's *The New Left and the Origins of the Cold War* (1973).

Two favorable biographies of Truman are Margaret Truman's *Harry S. Truman* (1973) and Merle Miller's *Plain Speaking: An Oral Biography of Harry S. Truman* (1974).° Other scholars view Truman through his activities as president; they include Robert J. Donovan's *Conflict and Crisis: The Presidency of Truman, 1945–1948* (1977),° Bert Cochran's *Truman and the Crisis Presidency* (1973), and Alonzo L. Hamby's *Beyond the New Deal: Harry S. Truman and American Liberalism* (1973).

The domestic policies of the Fair Deal receive analysis in William C. Berman's *The Politics of Civil Rights in the Truman Administration* (1970), Richard O. Davis's *Housing Reform during the Truman Administration* (1966), Richard M. Dafiumes's *Desegregation of the United States Armed Forces* (1969), Maeva Marcus's *Truman and the Steel Seizure* (1977), and R. Alton Lee's *Truman and Taft-Hartley* (1967). Other scholars concentrate on the difficulties Truman had with the conservatives in Congress, including Charles D. Hadley's *Transformations of the American Party System: Political Coalitions from the New Deal to the 1970s* (1978), Ronald Radosh's *Prophets on the Right: Profiles of Conservative Critics of American Globalism* (1975), and Susan Hartmann's *Truman and the Eightieth Congress* (1971). For the fabled election of 1948, see Richard N. Smith's *Thomas E. Dewey and His Times* (1982), Norman D. Markowitz's *The Rise and Fall of the People's Century: Henry A. Wallace and American Liberalism, 1941–1948* (1974), Allen Yarnell's *Democrats and Progressives: The 1948 Election as a Test of Postwar Liberalism* (1974), and Samuel Lubell's *The Future of American Politics* (1952).

For an introduction to the tensions in Asia, see Akira Iriye's *The Cold War in Asia* (1974). More specific to China are Ely J. Kahn, Jr.'s *The China Hands: America's Foreign Service Officers and What Befell Them* (1975), Kenneth E. Shewmaker's *Americans and the Chinese Communists, 1927–1945* (1971), and Tang Tsou's *America's Failure in China, 1941–1950* (1971). For the Korean conflict, see Bruce Cumming's *The Origins of the Korean War: Liberation and the Emergence of Separate Regimes, 1945–1947* (1980), Joseph C. Goulden's *Korea: The Untold Story of the War* (1982), and David Rees's *Korea: The Limited War* (1964). The high command perspective is shown in Robert Smith's *MacArthur in Korea: The Naked Emperor* (1982), William Manchester's *American Caesar: Douglas MacArthur, 1880–1960* (1978),° John W. Spanier's *The Truman-MacArthur Controversy* (1965), and Trumball Higgins's *Korea and the Fall of MacArthur* (1960).

The anti-Communist syndrome which helped produce McCarthy is surveyed in David Carter's *The Great Fear: The Anti-Communist Purge under Truman and Eisenhower* (1978).° Other works on the topic include Athan Theoharis's *Seeds of Repression: Harry S. Truman and the Origins of McCarthyism* (1971), Richard Freeland's *The Truman Doctrine and the Origins of McCarthyism* (1972), Alan Harper's *The Politics of Loyalty: The White House and the Communist Issue, 1946–1952* (1968), and Mary S. McAuliffe's *Crisis on the Left: Cold War Politics and American Liberals, 1947–1954* (1978). Richard Freeland's *Men against McCarthy* (1976), Edwin R. Bagley's *Joe McCarthy and the Press* (1981),° and Thomas C. Reeves's *The Life and Times of Joe McCarthy* (1982)° cover McCarthy himself. For the Rosenberg trial, consult Walter and Miriam Schneir's *Invitation to an Inquest* (1972). Allen Weinstein's *Perjury! The Hiss-Chambers Conflict* (1978)° covers that subject well.

For the rise of the intelligence network, see Thomas F. Troy's *Donovan and the CIA: A History of the Establishment of the Central Intelligence Agency* (1981) and Anthony C. Brown's *The Last Hero: Wild Bill Donovan* (1982).

32

CONFLICT AND DEADLOCK:
THE 1950s

"Time for a Change"

By 1952 the Truman administration had piled up a heavy burden of political liabilities. Its bold stand in Korea had brought a bloody stalemate abroad, renewed wage and price controls at home, reckless charges of subversion and disloyalty, and the exposure of corrupt lobbyists and influence peddlers who rigged favors in Washington. The disclosure of "the Mink Dynasty" and the "five percenters" led Truman to fire nearly 250 employees of the Bureau of Internal Revenue and, among others, an assistant attorney-general in charge of the Justice Department's Tax Division. But doubts lingered that Truman, protégé of the Kansas City Pendergast machine, would ever finish the housecleaning. There were two Trumans, the newscaster Elmer Davis had said: "The White House Truman does all the big things right, and the courthouse Truman does all the little things wrong." But by 1952 few things, big or little, seemed to be going right. The country had bogged down in "Plunder at home, blunder abroad."

EISENHOWER'S POLITICAL RISE   It was, in another maxim of the day, "time for a change," and South Dakota's Sen. Karl Mundt had a simple formula for Republican victory: $K_1 C_2$—Korea, communism, and corruption. The GOP (Grand Old Party, or Republican party) field quickly narrowed to two men, Sen. Robert A. Taft and Gen. Dwight D. Eisenhower, with General MacArthur alert for a deadlock. The party wheelhorses turned instinctively to Taft, "Mr. Republican," long a faithful party worker. Taft had become the foremost spokesman for domestic conservatism and for a foreign policy which his enemies branded isolationist. A man of stubborn integrity, he did not usually trim his sails to the prevailing winds. He had openly opposed the war-crimes trials, for instance, arguing that they were *ex post facto* and a dangerous precedent. His conservatism left room for federal aid to education and public housing, and his foreign policy, a "unilateralist" one, favored an active American role in opposing communism but opposed "entangling alliances" such as NATO. He joined the "Asia Firsters" in stressing the strategic importance of the Pacific area, but warned against the dangers of a land war on the Asian mainland. In Korea, he felt, the time had come to go all out for victory or to withdraw completely.

But Taft inspired little enthusiasm beyond the party regulars. He projected an image of little glamor, and as a leader used to taking controversial stands, he had made enemies. The eastern, internationalist wing of the party turned instinctively to Eisenhower, then the NATO commander. As a war hero he had the glamor that Taft lacked, and his captivating and unpretentious manner inspired support. His leadership had been tested in the fires of war, but as a professional soldier he had escaped the scars of political combat. He stood, therefore, outside and above the vulgar arena of public life, although his political instincts and skills were sharpened during his successful army career.

Eisenhower nevertheless seemed genuinely immune to the presidential bug until Sen. Henry Cabot Lodge, Jr., and others appealed to his sense of duty: only he could stop Taft and the isolationists. In January 1952 the general affirmed that he was a Re-

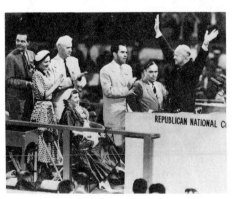

Dwight D. Eisenhower (right) and Richard M. Nixon (third from right), the Republican standard-bearers for 1952. [United Press International]

publican and in the following months permitted his name to be entered in party primaries. In June he left his NATO post and joined the battle in person. An outpouring of public enthusiasm began to overwhelm Republican party regulars. Bumper stickers across the land announced simply, "I like Ike." The closely divided convention resolved itself into a series of contests between rival delegations which the younger Taft could not control. Eisenhower won the nomination on the first ballot. He balanced the ticket by choosing as his running mate a youthful Californian, the thirty-nine-year-old Sen. Richard M. Nixon, who had built a career on opposition to "subversives" and gained his greatest notoriety as the member of the House Un-American Activities Committee most eager in the pursuit of Alger Hiss.

THE 1952 ELECTION   The Twenty-second Amendment, ratified in 1951, in a belated thrust at Roosevelt forbade any president to seek a third term. The amendment exempted the incumbent, but weary of the war, harassed by charges of subversion and corruption in government, his popularity declining, Truman chose to withdraw and his exit threw the Democratic race wide open. An early lead was mustered by Tennessee's Estes Kefauver, who had chaired a nationally televised investigation of organized crime. Sporting a coonskin cap, the symbol of his campaign, Kefauver worked the streets and shook every hand in reach. But his primary victories failed to move Democratic party regulars. Truman preferred Gov. Adlai E. Stevenson of Illinois but, rebuffed by the governor's insistent refusal, threw his support to Vice-President Alben W. Barkley. Just before the convention, however, a group of "certain self-appointed political labor leaders" told Barkley he was too old (at seventy-five) and asked him to withdraw. When he did, Truman threw his support again to Governor Stevenson, who aroused the delegates with an eloquent speech welcoming them to Chicago. On the third ballot the convention drafted Stevenson, who then chose Sen. John J. Sparkman of Alabama as his running mate.

The campaign matched two of the most magnetic personalities ever pitted in a presidential contest. Both men attracted new followings among people previously apathetic to politics, but the race was uneven from the start. Eisenhower, though a political novice, was a world figure who had been in the public eye for a decade. Stevenson, the politician, was hardly known outside of Illinois and never able to escape the burden of Truman's liabilities. The genial general, who had led the crusade against Hitler, now opened a domestic crusade to clean up "the mess in Washington." To this he added a promise, late in the campaign, that as president-elect he would go to Korea to secure "an early and honorable" peace. The Democrats' charge that he was grandstanding had little impact in the face of his long military experience. Stevenson's forte was a lofty eloquence spiced with a quick wit, but his resolve to "talk sense" and "tell the truth to the American people" came across as just a bit too aloof, a shade too intellectual. The Republicans hastened to cast him in the role of an "egghead," a latter-day Hamlet, in contrast to Eisenhower, the man of the people, the man of decision and action.

The war hero triumphed in a landslide of 33.9 million votes to Stevenson's 27.3 million, and 442 electoral votes to Stevenson's 89. The election marked a turning point in Republican fortunes in the South: for the first time since the heyday of the Whigs the South was moving toward a two-party system. Stevenson carried only eight southern states plus West Virginia; Eisenhower picked up five states in the outer South: Florida, Oklahoma, Tennessee, Texas, and Virginia. In the former Confederacy the Republican ticket garnered 48.9 percent of the votes. The "nonpolitical" Eisenhower had made it respectable, even fashionable, to vote Republican in the South. Elsewhere, too, the general made inroads in the New Deal coalition, attracting supporters among the ethnic and religious minorities in the major cities.

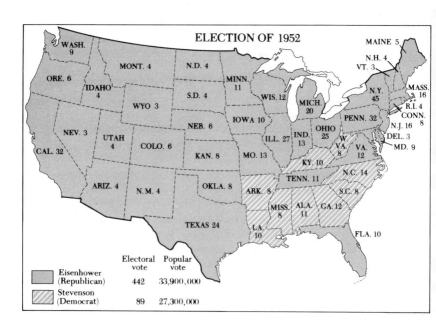

The voters, it turned out, liked Ike better than they liked his party. Democrats retained most of the governorships, lost control of the House by only eight votes, and broke even in the Senate, where only the vote of the vice-president ensured Republican control. The congressional elections two years later would weaken the Republican grip on Congress, and Eisenhower would have to work with a Democratic Congress until he left office.

IKE   Born in Dennison, Texas, on October 14, 1890, Dwight David Eisenhower grew up in Abilene, Kansas, near the geographical center of the country and Harry Truman's hometown of Independence, Missouri. Young Eisenhower's first memory of presidential politics was a torchlight parade in 1896, but after graduating from West Point he went on to spend nearly his entire adult life in the military service. He spent World War I stateside as a tank instructor, and then worked his way through the ranks. He served as staff officer to General MacArthur in Washington and the Philippines. After Pearl Harbor, Gen. George C. Marshall made Brigadier-General Eisenhower his chief of operations. Later, as a major-general, he took command of American forces in the European theater and directed the invasion of North Africa in November 1942. In 1944 he assumed the post of supreme commander of allied forces in preparation for the invasion of the continent. After the war, by then a five-star general of the armies, he became chief of staff and supreme commander of NATO forces, with a brief interlude in between as president of Columbia University.

Eisenhower's inauguration brought a change in style to the White House. The contrast in character between the feisty Truman and the avuncular Ike was reinforced by a contrast in philosophy and approach to the presidency. Eisenhower's military experience developed in him an instinct for methodical staff work. He met with the cabinet and the National Security Council nearly every week, and relied heavily on them as consultative bodies. Under the direction of his chief assistant, former New Hampshire Gov. Sherman Adams, the flow of routine paperwork reached the Oval Office digested into single-page summaries. "I count the day lost," Adams said, "when I have not found some new way of lightening the President's load."

Such procedures, it seemed, tended to isolate the president from conflicting viewpoints and to reduce the policy choices available to him. The public image of Ike confirmed that view, but it endeared him all the more to the people as a man who rose above politics. He was unpretentious, an ardent golfer, a common man who read little but western novels, uninformed on the currents of intellectual and artistic life, and given to copybook maxims: "Everybody ought to be happy every day. Play hard, have fun doing it, and despise wickedness." George Kennan said: "He was the nation's number one Boy Scout."

But those who were closer to him have presented another side to the man. When provoked he could release a massive temper and scalding profanity. While Ike talked with genuine feeling about such traditional virtues as duty, honesty, and thrift, he was not above a calculated dissimulation. The scrambled syntax in which he answered reporters' questions was sometimes deliberate evasion. Eisenhower deliberately toned down eloquent passages which speech writers tried to smuggle into his public utterances, although he had written florid speeches for General MacArthur. One recent student of Eisenhower's techniques has spoken of a "hidden-hand presidency" in which Ike deliberately cultivated an image of passivity to hide his active involvement in policy decisions.

"DYNAMIC CONSERVATISM" AT HOME   Like Ulysses Grant, however, Eisenhower betrayed a weakness for men with money. His cabinet, a column in the *New Republic* quipped, consisted of "eight millionaires and a plumber." The plumber, Secretary of Labor Martin Durkin, was gone in eight months, charging that the administration had reneged on a promise to change the Taft-Hartley Act. Charles E. Wilson, president of General Motors, became secretary of defense and two auto distributors, Douglas McKay and Arthur Summerfield, became secretary of the interior and postmaster-general respectively. The New Dealers, Adlai Stevenson wryly remarked, "have all left Washington to make way for the car dealers."

Unaccustomed to the glare of Washington publicity, several cabinet members succumbed to foot-in-mouth disease. It was perhaps innocent enough for Charles E. Wilson to say at his confirmation hearings, "I thought what was good for our country was good for General Motors, and vice versa," except that it was readily translated into: "What is good for General Motors is good for the country." Douglas McKay put it more baldly: "We're here in the saddle as an Administration representing business and industry." Treasury Secretary George Humphrey, head of Mark Hanna's old coal and oil firm in Cleveland, put Andrew Mellon's picture on the wall, and replied when asked if he had read Hemingway's *The Old Man and the Sea:* "Why would anybody be interested in some old man who was a failure and never amounted to anything anyway?"

Eisenhower called his program "dynamic conservatism," which meant being "conservative when it comes to money and liberal when it comes to human beings." Stevenson conjectured: "I assume what it means is that you will strongly recommend the building of a great many schools to accommodate the needs of our children, but not provide the money." Budget cutting was a high priority for the new administration, which set out after both domestic programs and national defense. Eisenhower warned repeatedly against the dangers of "creeping socialism," "huge bureaucracies," and budget deficits. But though Eisenhower chipped away at New Deal programs, his presidency in the end served rather to legitimate the New Deal.

In 1953 Eisenhower won quick congressional approval for turning over to the coastal states the oil-rich "tidelands" which the Supreme Court had awarded to the federal government. Eisenhower also abolished the Reconstruction Finance Corporation, ended wage and price controls, and reduced farm price subsidies. Eisenhower also moved the government away from the Roosevelt-Truman commitment to public power. In fact, had Ike had his way the government would have sold the TVA. The Republican Congress rejected a proposal in 1953 to build a new TVA steam plant to supply the power needs of Memphis, Tennessee, and thereby release power to serve the AEC's atomic weapons plant at Paducah, Kentucky. Opposed to any further expansion of TVA, the administration instead got behind a plan of the Dixon-Yates utility syndicate to build a private plant. Controversy over the proposal dragged out for two years until investigations revealed that the government consultant who recommended the plant was vice-president of an investment firm handling Dixon-Yates securities.

The embarrassed administration then seized upon an alternative, a municipal powerplant with which the city of Memphis promised to supply the need. Another protracted struggle over public power ended differently when the Idaho Power Company won a license to build three small dams on the Snake River in place of a gigantic federal dam proposed for Hell's Canyon. Still another step away from public power came with the Atomic Energy Act of 1954, which opened the door for construction of private nuclear powerplants under AEC license and safeguards.

In fiscal policy the administration found its passion for budget cutting encumbered by unyielding facts. Its first budget had already been prepared by Truman's men, providing for expenditures of $80 billion and a deficit of $9.9 billion, which Eisenhower's heroic efforts reduced by only $4.4 billion. In 1954 Treasury Secretary George Humphrey formulated tax reductions which resembled Andrew Mellon's programs of the 1920s in providing benefits mainly to corporations and individuals in the upper brackets. The new budget slashed expenditures by $6.5 billion, nearly 10 percent, and Humphrey joined with the Federal Reserve Board in tightening credit and raising interest rates to avert inflation. But the business slump which followed reduced government revenues, making it harder to balance the budget. After that experience Eisenhower's fiscal and monetary policies became less doctrinaire and more flexible. The government accepted easier credit and deficits as necessary "countercyclical" methods. The Keynesian Age, if not yet acknowledged, endured.

In some ways, moreover, the administration not only maintained the New Deal but extended its reach, especially after 1954 when it had the help of Democratic Congresses. Amendments to the Social Security Act in 1954 and 1956 brought coverage to millions in categories formerly excluded: professional people, domestic and clerical workers, farm workers, and members of the armed forces. In 1959 the program's benefits went up 7 percent. The federal minimum wage rose in 1955 from 75¢ to $1 an hour. Federal expenditures for public health rose steadily in the Eisenhower years and the president went so far as to endorse federal participation in health insurance, but Congress twice refused to act. Low-income housing continued to be built, although on the much-reduced scale of some 35,000 units annually.

Some farm-related programs were expanded during the Eisenhower years. The Rural Electrification Administration announced on its twenty-fifth birthday in 1960 that 97 percent of American farms had electricity. The Farmers Home Administration and a Rural Development Program continued the program of loans to support farm ownership and improvements, although on a much smaller scale than the New Deal's Farm Security Administration. Cordell Hull's program of reciprocal trade agreements was regularly renewed. Under the Agricultural Trade Development and Assistance Act of 1954 the government undertook on a large scale to finance the export of surplus farm products in exchange for foreign currencies, an idea much like the McNary-Haugen scheme of the 1920s. Surpluses were exported also as gifts to needy nations and to provide milk for schoolchildren. By an amendment to the act in 1959, surpluses became available to the needy by issuing food stamps redeemable at grocery stores.

Despite Eisenhower's general disapproval of public power

programs, he continued to support public works for which he saw a legitimate need. Indeed two such programs left major monuments to his presidency: the St. Lawrence Seaway and the Interstate Highways. The St. Lawrence Seaway, designed to open the Great Lakes to ocean-going ships by means of locks and dredging, had languished in Congress since the time of President Hoover because of opposition by eastern business and railroad interests afraid of the competition. In 1954 Eisenhower finally broke the opposition by pointing to Canadian determination to go ahead anyway and to the growing need of American steel producers for Laurentian ore as the Mesabi deposits gave out. Congress then approved joint participation with the Canadians, and five years later the seaway was open. The Federal Aid Highway Act of 1956 authorized the federal government to put up 90 percent of the cost of building 42,500 miles of limited-access interstate highways to serve the needs of commerce and defense, as well as private convenience. The states put up the remaining 10 percent. It was only afterward that people realized that the huge national commitment to the automobile might have come at the expense of America's railroad system, already in a state of advanced decay.

CONCLUDING AN ARMISTICE   America's new position in the postwar world, however, continued to absorb Eisenhower's attention. The most pressing problem when he entered office was the continuing, painful deadlock in the Korean peace talks. The main stumbling block at Panmunjom was the insistence of North Korea and Red China that all prisoners be returned regardless of their wishes. To break the deadlock, Eisenhower resolved upon a bold stand. In mid-May 1953 he stepped up aerial bombardment of North Korea, then had Secretary of State Dulles convey to Peking through the Indian government a secret threat to remove all limits on weapons and targets. It was a thinly veiled warning of atomic warfare against Red forces, perhaps even against China itself. Whether for that reason or others, negotiations then moved quickly toward an armistice along the established battle line just above the Thirty-eighth Parallel, and toward a complicated arrangement for prisoner exchange which allowed captives to accept or refuse repatriation.

On July 26, 1953, President Eisenhower announced the conclusion of the armistice. But most of the Korean peninsula was devastated. Whether or not Eisenhower had pulled a masterful bluff in getting the armistice has never become clear; no one knows whether or not he actually would have forced the issue with atomic weapons. Perhaps the more decisive factors in bringing about a settlement were the size of Chinese Communist losses, which even they found unacceptable, and the new spirit of uncertainty and caution felt by Russian Communists after the death of Josef Stalin on March 5, 1953—six weeks after Ike's inauguration.

CONCLUDING A WITCH-HUNT   The Korean armistice helped to end another dismal episode: the meteoric career of Sen. Joseph R. McCarthy, which had flourished amid the anxieties of wartime. Eventually the logic of McCarthy's tactics led to his self-destruction, but not before he had left still more personal careers and reputations in ruins. The Republicans thought their victory in 1952 would curb his recklessness, and Senator Taft sought to deflect him into the chairmanship of the Permanent Investigation Subcommittee of the Senate Committee on Government Operations, but merely provided him a platform and staff resources. McCarthy's new sensations overshadowed those of the regular subversive-hunting committees of the House and Senate.

When Eisenhower nominated Charles E. Bohlen, a career diplomat, as ambassador to Russia, McCarthy and other Senate militants attacked Bohlen for association with the Yalta "betrayal." Not only had Bohlen been Roosevelt's interpreter there, he had even defended the Yalta agreements before a Senate committee. The intervention of Senator Taft brought Senate approval of the nomination, but thirteen members persisted in voting against Bohlen. McCarthy then began to fill the headlines with gossip and innuendoes about the State Department's Voice of America. During the summer of 1953 he sent two youthful assistants, Roy M. Cohn and G. David Schine, on a junket to Europe to purge the libraries of the International Information Agency. "Subversive works," such as the writings of Emerson and Thoreau, were removed from shelves and in some cases burned. Dulles ordered American information centers abroad to exclude the works of "any Communists, fellow travellers, et cetera."

McCarthy finally overreached himself when he tried to peddle the absurdity that the United States Army itself was "soft" on communism. The cases in point, it seemed, were a "pink" dentist at Fort Monmouth, New Jersey, since given an honorable discharge, and the army's refusal to give special treatment to a draftee, G. David Schine, McCarthy's former assistant, who was being held "hostage." A confusing tangle of charges and countercharges led to televised hearings by McCarthy's subcommittee, with Sen. Karl Mundt temporarily in the chair. From April

"Here Goes"

The Army-McCarthy hearings of 1954 marked the end of the senator's influence. [Copyright 1954 by Herblock in the Washington Post*]*

22 to June 17, 1954, the Army-McCarthy hearings displayed McCarthy at his capricious worst, bullying witnesses, dragging out lengthy irrelevancies, repeatedly calling "point of order." He became the perfect foil for the army's gentle but unflappable counsel, Joseph Welch of Boston, whose rapier wit repeatedly drew blood. When a witness used the word "pixie," McCarthy demanded a definition and Welch sweetly explained that a pixie was "a kind of fairy." But when McCarthy tried to smear one of Welch's young associates, the counsel went into a cold rage: "Until this moment, Senator, I think I never really gauged your cruelty or your recklessness. . . . Have you no sense of decency, sir, at long last?" When the audience burst into applause, the confused senator was reduced to whispering, "What did I do?"

Apparently he never found out, but at that point the house he had thrown together began to crash around his ears. He descended into new depths of scurrility, now directed at his own colleagues, calling Ralph Flanders of Vermont "senile" and Robert C. Hendrickson of New Jersey "a living miracle . . . the only man who has lived so long with neither brains nor guts." On December 2, 1954, the Senate voted 67 to 22 to "condemn" McCarthy for contempt of the Senate. Samuel J. Ervin, Jr., of North Carolina, a newly appointed senator, accused him of "disorderly conduct by flyblowing . . . a strong Anglo-Saxon word, but a very expressive one." McCarthy was finished, and increasingly took to alcohol. Three years later, at the age of forty-eight, he was dead.

The witch-hunt was over. McCarthyism, Ike joked, had become McCarthywasm, though not for those whose reputations and careers had been wrecked. To the end Eisenhower kept his resolve not to "get down in the gutter with that guy" and sully the dignity of the presidency, but he did work resolutely against McCarthy behind the scenes. Eisenhower shared, nevertheless, the deeply held conviction of many citizens that espionage posed a real danger to national security. He denied clemency to Julius and Ethel Rosenberg, convicted of transmitting atomic secrets to the Russians, on the grounds that they "may have condemned to death tens of millions of innocent people." They went to the electric chair at Sing-Sing Prison on June 19, 1953.

INTERNAL SECURITY   Even earlier, Eisenhower stiffened the government security program which Truman had set up six years before. Executive Order 10450, dated April 27, 1953, broadened the basis for firing government workers by replacing Truman's criterion of "disloyalty" with the new category of "security risk." Under the new edict federal workers lost their jobs because of dubious associations or personal habits that might make them careless or vulnerable to blackmail. In December 1953 the AEC removed the security clearance of the physicist J. Robert Oppenheimer, the "father of the atomic bomb," on the grounds that he had expressed qualms about the hydrogen bomb in 1949–1950 and had associated with Communists or former Communists in the past. Lacking evidence of any disloyalty or betrayal, the AEC nevertheless branded him a "security risk" because of "fundamental defects in his character."

The Supreme Court, however, modified some of the more extreme expressions of the Red Scare. In September 1953 Chief Justice Frederick M. Vinson died and Eisenhower chose former Gov. Earl Warren of California to take his place, a decision the president later pronounced the "biggest damnfool mistake I ever made." Warren, who had seemed safely conservative while active in politics, proved to have a social conscience and a streak of libertarianism which Eisenhower's next appointee, William I. Brennan, Jr., shared. The "Warren Court" (1953–1969), under the chief justice's influence, became an important agency of social and political change on through the 1960s. In connection with security programs and loyalty requirements, the Court veered back in the direction of traditional individual rights. In *Yates v. United States* (1957) an opinion by Justice John Marshall Harlan narrowly construed the Smith Act of 1940 to apply to those advocating revolutionary action, not those merely teaching revolutionary doctrine in the abstract. This, plus other decisions setting rigid standards for evidence, rendered the Smith

Act a dead letter. In *Pennsylvania v. Nelson* (1956) the Court banned state prosecution for subversion against the United States since Congress had preempted that field. Much later, in *Albertson v. Subversive Activities Control Board* (1965), the Warren Court held that the McCarran Act's requirement that Communist party leaders register with the board violated the Fifth Amendment guarantee against self-incrimination. This left the board little to do until it was abolished in 1973.

DULLES AND FOREIGN POLICY   The Eisenhower administration promised new departures in foreign policy under the direction of Secretary of State John Foster Dulles. Grandson of one former secretary of state and nephew of another, Dulles had pursued a lifetime career as an international lawyer and sometime diplomat. At the age of nineteen he had been secretary to the Chinese delegation at the 1907 peace conference at The Hague; in 1919 he had assisted the American delegates at the Versailles Conference. As counselor to the Truman State Department he had, among other things, negotiated the Japanese peace treaty of 1951. Son of a minister and himself an active Presbyterian layman, Dulles, in the words of British Ambassador Sir Oliver Franks, resembled those old zealots of the wars of religion who "saw the world as an arena in which the forces of good and evil were continuously at war."

The foreign policy planks of the 1952 Republican platform, which Dulles wrote, showed both the moralist and the tactician at work. The policy of containment was needlessly defensive, Dulles thought. This conviction meshed nicely with the conventional wisdom of the right wing that Yalta was perhaps a betrayal, at best a blunder. The 1952 platform, therefore, promised to "repudiate all commitments . . . such as those of Yalta which aid Communist enslavement" and to end "the negative, futile and immoral policy of 'containment' which abandons countless human beings to a despotism and godless terrorism. . . ." A new policy of liberation, the platform promised, "will inevitably set up strains and stresses within the captive world which will make the rulers impotent to continue in their monstrous ways and mark the beginning of the end."

The policy came perilously close to proclaiming a holy war, but Dulles took care to explain that he did not intend forcible liberation. Soon it became apparent that it was less a policy than a web of rhetoric to catch ethnic voters whose homelands had fallen captive. The Republican party's new Ethnic Origins Division made the most of it. Eisenhower in his inaugural address promised to "unleash" Chiang Kai-shek—that is, cancel the Seventh Fleet's orders to prevent his invading the Chinese mainland. The fleet's more realistic mission of protecting Taiwan continued, however.

When it came to repudiating Yalta, the administration drew back. Ike was conscious of his own vulnerability as the commander who had implemented the agreement and who had stopped American forces short of Berlin and Prague. The administration's Captive Peoples Resolution merely rejected any misuse of the Yalta agreements, "which have been perverted to bring about the subjugation of free peoples." The real betrayal, in short, had been Russian violation of the Yalta accords. Even that resolution died in congressional committee. That the liberation rhetoric rang false became more evident in June 1953 when workers in East Germany rebelled against working conditions and food shortages. When Russian tanks rolled over the demonstrators, the administration did nothing except to deplore the situation. For three years more Dulles was able to maintain the belief that his rhetoric was undermining the Communist hold on eastern Europe—until suppression of the 1956 uprising in Hungary underscored the danger of stirring futile hopes among captive peoples.

COVERT ACTIONS   Insofar as interventions occurred, they were covert operations by the Central Intelligence Agency in countries outside the Soviet sphere. Under Eisenhower, Allen Dulles, brother of the secretary of state, rose from second in command to chief of the CIA. A veteran of the wartime Office of Strategic Services, he had already had a hand in beefing up the CIA's capacity for cloak-and-dagger operations. In two cases early in the Eisenhower years this capability was actually used to overthrow governments believed hostile to American interests: in Iran (1953) and in Guatemala (1954).

In Iran, Premier Mohammed Mossadegh, a seventy-year-old nationalist, whipped up popular feeling against British control of Iranian oil production and then expropriated the foreign properties. In thus challenging Western interests he had the support of the Tudeh, Iran's Communist party, and left the impression that he either had gone over to their side or would become their dupe. In these circumstances, Allen Dulles sent a crack agent, Kermit Roosevelt (Theodore Roosevelt's grandson), along with Col. H. Norman Schwartzkopf, who had helped the shah of Iran, Mohammed Reza Pahlavi, to organize his secret police. Armed chiefly with about a million dollars, they stirred up street demonstrations against Mossadegh which, reinforced by soldiers loyal to the shah, toppled the premier, sent him to jail, and brought the young shah back from exile in Rome. A new premier made an arrangement under which the British and Americans each got 40 percent of Iran's oil production, the Dutch 14 percent, and the French 6 percent.

In Guatemala, Jacobo Arbenz Guzman had become president in an election in which he had Communist backing. While the administration lacked evidence that Arbenz was a Communist, Ambassador John Peurifoy said "he talked like a Communist, he thought like a Communist, and he acted like a Communist, and if he is not one, he will do until one comes along." Critics of the intervention contended that Arbenz's chief sin was that he had expropriated 225,000 acres of United Fruit Company land. He had also secured weapons from East Germany with which to arm a peasant militia. With Eisenhower's consent the CIA chose one Col. Carlos Castillo Armas to stage a coup from a base in Honduras. The operation, however, was mainly a war of nerves, with rumors spread by clandestine radio stations and token raids on Guatemala City run by surplus planes from World War II. Arbenz panicked, resigned, and fled the country. Defenders of the action were those who agreed with the conclusion of a committee commissioned to investigate the CIA in 1955: "It is now clear that we are facing an implacable enemy whose avowed objective is world domination by whatever means and at whatever cost. There are no rules in such a game. Hitherto acceptable norms of conduct do not apply."

BRINKSMANSHIP Actually, Dulles made no significant departure from the strategy of containment created under Acheson and Truman. Instead he institutionalized containment in the rigid mold of his Cold War rhetoric and extended it into the military strategy of deterrence. He betrayed a fatal affinity for colorful phrases which left him, according to Arthur Larsen, "perpetually poised between a cliché and an indiscretion." To his lexicon of "liberation" and "roll back," Dulles added two major new contributions while in office: "massive retaliation" and "going to the brink."

"Massive retaliation" is actually a shorthand version of Dulles's phrase "massive retaliatory power," a description of the "New Look" in military strategy, an effort to get, in the slogan soon current, "more bang for the buck" or "more rubble for the ruble." Budgetary considerations lay at the root of military plans, for Eisenhower and his cabinet shared the fear that in the effort to build a superior war power the country could spend itself into bankruptcy. During 1953 new members of the Joint Chiefs of Staff, headed by Adm. Arthur W. Radford, set to work on planning a new military posture. The heart of their New Look was the assumption that nuclear weapons could be used in limited-war situations, allowing reductions in conventional forces and thus budgetary savings. Dulles, who announced the policy on January 12, 1954, explained that savings would come "by placing more reliance on deterrent power, and less dependence on local defensive power." No longer could an enemy "pick his time and place and method of warfare." American responses would be "by means and at places of our choosing." No longer would "the Communists nibble us to death all over the world in little wars," Vice-President Nixon explained in March 1954.

By this time both the United States and Russia had exploded hydrogen bombs. With the new policy of deterrence, what Winston Churchill called a "balance of terror" had replaced the old "balance of power." The threat of nuclear holocaust was terrifying, but the notion that the United States would risk such a disaster in response to local wars had little credibility.

Dulles's policy of "brinksmanship" depended for its strategic effect on those very fears of nuclear disaster. Dulles argued in 1956 that in following a tough policy of confrontation with communism, one sometimes had to "go to the brink" of war: "The ability to get to the verge without getting into war is the necessary art. If you cannot master it, you inevitably get into war. . . . We walked to the brink and we looked it in the face. We took strong action." The first occasion on which a firm stand had

"Don't Be Afraid—I Can Always Pull You Back"

Secretary of State Dulles pushes a reluctant America to the brink of war. [Herblock's Special for Today (New York: Simon & Schuster, 1958)]

halted further aggression had been America's threat in 1953 to break the Korean stalemate by removing restraints from the armed forces. The second had come in 1954, when aircraft carriers moved into the South China Sea "both to deter any Red Chinese attack against Indochina and to provide weapons for instant retaliation. . . ."

INDOCHINA: THE BACKGROUND TO WAR   Dulles's reference to Indochina was an oversimplification: it neglected the complexity of the situation there, which presented a special if not unique case of the nationalism which swept the old colonial world of Asia and Africa after World War II, damaging both the power and prestige of the colonial powers. By the early 1950s most of British Asia was independent or on the way: India, Pakistan, Ceylon (later Sri Lanka), Burma, and the Malay States (later the Federation of Malaysia). The Dutch and French, however, were less ready than the British to give up their colonies and thus created a dilemma for American policy-makers. Americans sympathized with colonial nationalists who sometimes invoked the example of 1776, but Americans also wanted Dutch and French help against communism. The Truman administration felt obliged to answer their pleas for aid. Both the Dutch and the French were obliged to reconquer areas which had passed from Japanese occupation into the hands of local patriots. In the Dutch East Indies the Japanese had created a puppet Indonesian Republic which emerged from World War II virtually independent. The Dutch effort to regain control met resistance which exploded into open warfare.

Eventually, American pressure persuaded the Dutch to accept self-government under a Dutch-Indonesian Union in 1949, but that lasted only until 1954 when the Republic of Indonesia became independent. In April 1955 the Bandung Conference in Indonesia, attended by delegates from twenty-nine independent countries of Asia and Africa, signaled the emergence of a "Third World" of underdeveloped countries, unaligned with either the United States or the Soviet bloc. Among other actions the conference condemned "colonialism in all its manifestations," a statement which implicitly condemned both the USSR and the West.

French Indochina, created in the nineteenth century out of the old kingdoms of Cambodia, Laos, and Vietnam, offered a variation on Third World nationalism. During World War II Japanese control of the area had required their support of pro-Vichy French civil servants and opposition to the local nationalists. Chief among the latter were the Vietminh (Vietnamese League for Independence), who fell under the influence of Communists

Ho Chi Minh. [Warder Collection]

led by Ho Chi Minh. At the end of the war this group controlled part of northern Vietnam, and on September 2, 1945, Ho Chi Minh proclaimed a Democratic Republic of Vietnam, with its capital in Hanoi.

Ho's declaration borrowed clearly from Thomas Jefferson, opening with the words "We hold these truths to be self-evident. That all men are created equal." American officers were on the reviewing stand in Hanoi and American planes flew over the celebration. Ho had received secret American help against the Japanese during the war, but bids for further aid after the war went unanswered. Vietnam took low priority in American diplomatic concerns at the time.

In March 1946 the French government, preoccupied with domestic politics, recognized Ho's new government as a "free state" within the French union. Before the year was out, however, Ho's forces came into conflict with French efforts to establish another regime in the southern provinces, and this clash soon expanded into the First Indochina War. In June 1949, having set up former native kings as puppets in Laos and Cambodia, the French installed Bao Dai of an old Vietnamese ruling family as emperor of Vietnam. The victory of the Chinese Communists later in 1949 was followed by Red China's diplomatic recognition of the Vietminh government in Hanoi, and then the recognition of Bao Dai by the United States and Britain.

The Vietminh movement thereafter became more completely dominated by Ho Chi Minh and his Communist associates, and more dependent on Russia and Red China for help. In 1950, with the outbreak of fighting in Korea, the struggle in Vietnam took on more and more the appearance of a battleground in the Cold War. When the Korean War ended, American aid to the French in Vietnam, begun by the Truman administration, continued. By the end of 1953 the Eisenhower administration was paying about two-thirds of the cost of the French effort, or about $1 billion annually. By 1954 the United States found itself at the edge of the "brink" to which Dulles later referred. A major French force had been sent to Dien Bien Phu, near the Laos border, in the hope of luring Vietminh guerrillas into a set battle and grinding them up with superior firepower. The French instead found themselves trapped by a superior force which threatened to overrun their stronghold.

In March 1954 the French government requested an American air strike to relieve the pressure. The request had been encouraged by Adm. Arthur W. Radford, chief of staff, who argued for raids by B-29s from the Philippines covered by carrier-based fighters. The forceful chief of staff won the support of Dulles and Vice-President Nixon. Army Gen. Matthew B. Ridgway, however, disagreed. Effective action, he feared, would require American ground forces, which were not up to the assignment. Eisenhower himself seemed to endorse forceful action when he advanced his "domino theory" to a news conference on April 7, 1954: "You have a row of dominoes set up, you knock over the first one, and what will happen to the last one is the certainty that it will go over very quickly." He was nevertheless playing a cautious game. When congressional leaders expressed reservations, he took a stand against American action unless the British lent support. When they refused, he backed away from unilateral action.

THE GENEVA ACCORDS AND U.S. POLICY   On May 7, 1954, the massive attacks loosed by Vietminh Gen. Vo Nguyen Giap finally overwhelmed the last French resistance at Dien Bien Phu. It was the very eve of the day an international conference at Geneva took up the question of Indochina. Six weeks later, as French forces continued to meet defeats in the Red River Delta, a new French government under Premier Pierre Mendès-France promised to get an early settlement. On July 20 representatives of France, Britain, Russia, the People's Republic of China, and the Vietminh reached agreement on the Geneva Accords, and the next day produced their Final Declaration which proposed to neutralize Laos and Cambodia and divided Vietnam at the Seventeenth Parallel. The Vietminh would take power in the north and the French would remain south of the line until elections in

1956 should reunify Vietnam. American and South Vietnamese representatives refused either to join in the accord or to sign the Final Declaration, with the result that Russia and China backed away from their earlier hints that they would guarantee the settlement. In the end, nobody at all signed the Declaration and participants confined themselves to unilateral statements in which they endorsed or dissociated themselves from particular parts of the Geneva Accords.

The American response was an effort to set up mutual defense arrangements for Southeast Asia. On September 8, 1954, at a meeting in Manila, the United States joined seven other countries in an agreement that Dulles wanted known as the Manila Defense Accord (MANDAC), but which the press quickly labeled as the Southeast Asia Treaty Organization (SEATO). The impression that it paralleled NATO was false, for the Manila Accord was neither a common defense organization like NATO nor was it primarily Asian. The signers agreed that in case of attack on one, the others would act according to their "constitutional practices," and in case of threats or subversion they would "consult immediately." The members included only three Asian countries—the Philippines, Thailand, and Pakistan—together with Britain, France, Australia, New Zealand, and the United States. India and Indonesia, the two most populous countries in the region, refused to join. A special protocol added to the treaty extended coverage to Indochina. The treaty reflected what Dulles's critics called "pactomania," which by the end of the Eisenhower administration contracted the United States to defend forty-three other countries.

Eisenhower announced that though the United States "had not itself been party to or bound by the decision taken at the [Geneva] Conference," any renewal of Communist aggression "would be reviewed by us as a matter of grave concern." In Vietnam, when Ho Chi Minh took over the north, those who wished to leave for South Vietnam did so with American aid. Power in the south gravitated to a new premier imposed on Emperor Bao Dai by the French at American urging: Ngo Dinh Diem, who had opposed both the French and the Vietminh, took office during the Geneva talks. Before that he had been in exile at a Catholic seminary in New Jersey. In October 1954 Eisenhower offered to assist Diem "in developing and maintaining a strong, viable state, capable of resisting attempted subversion or aggression through military means." In return the United States expected "needed reforms." American aid was forthcoming in the form of CIA and military cadres charged with training Diem's armed forces and police.

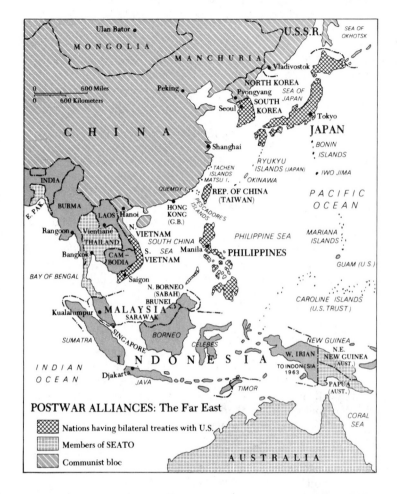

POSTWAR ALLIANCES: The Far East

Nations having bilateral treaties with U.S.

Members of SEATO

Communist bloc

Instead of instituting reforms, however, Diem tightened his grip on the country, suppressing opposition on both right and left, offering little or no land distribution, and permitting widespread corruption. In 1956 he refused to join in the elections to reunify Vietnam, and after French withdrawal from the country, ousted Bao Dai and installed himself as president. His efforts to eliminate all opposition played into the hands of the Communists, who found recruits and fellow travelers among the discontented. By 1957 guerrilla forces known as the Vietcong had begun attacks on the government, and in 1960 the resistance emerged as the National Liberation Front. As guerrilla warfare gradually disrupted the country, the Eisenhower administration was helpless to do anything but "sink or swim with Ngo Dinh Diem."

QUEMOY AND MATSU   Having backed away from the "brink" in Vietnam, Eisenhower and Dulles soon found themselves approaching another. Just before the Manila conference in September 1954, Red Chinese artillery began shelling the Quemoy islands at the entrance to Amoy harbor, and soon afterward brought under fire the nearby Matsu and Tachen groups, all of which were held by Chiang Kai-shek's Nationalists. On his way back from Manila Dulles stopped in Taipei and worked out a mutual defense treaty which bound the United States to defend Taiwan and the nearby Pescadores Islands, and which bound Taiwan to undertake offensive action only with American consent. The treaty omitted mention of the offshore islands, and the mainland Chinese continued their pressure, occupying one of the Tachens. In January 1955 the president secured in Congress a resolution giving him full power to go to the defense of Taiwan and the Pescadores, and also authorizing him to secure and protect "such related positions of that area now in friendly hands" in order to defend Taiwan. Congress's endorsement was overwhelming—the resolution drew only three negative votes in each house—for so sweeping a grant of power.

The Red Chinese kept up their activity nonetheless, and under pressure from the American government the Nationalists evacuated the Tachens as indefensible. But Quemoy and Matsu became symbols of the will to protect Taiwan, and were perhaps strategically useful too. In any case Adm. Robert B. Carney, chief of naval operations, "leaked" word to newsmen that the administration was considering a plan "to destroy Red China's military potential and thus end its expansionist tendencies." Soon afterward the Chinese backed away from the brink. At the Bandung Conference in April, with diplomatic encouragement from other Asian nations, Premier Chou En-lai said Red China was ready to discuss the Formosa Strait issue directly with the United States. In May 1955 representatives of the two governments began meetings in Geneva, and the guns fell silent.

A THAW IN THE COLD WAR   The quiet in the Formosa Strait was but one signal of a "thaw" in the Cold War. Europe remained the chief focus of American foreign policy, and there friendly gestures came from the Soviet government and the Communist party secretary Nikita Khrushchev, who had come out on top in the post-Stalin power struggles. While American and Chinese officials were discussing Quemoy and Matsu, the Soviets agreed to the Austrian State Treaty, ending the four-power occupation of that little country and restoring its independence as a neutral but

Western-oriented state. At Geneva, during July 18–23, 1955, President Eisenhower, British Prime Minister Anthony Eden, and Premiers Edgar Fauré of France and Nikolai Bulganin of the Soviet Union held the first summit conference since the one at Potsdam ten years before, but unlike the Potsdam meeting this one was strictly a cosmetic affair. The leaders displayed cheerful grins and conveyed a mood of affability that had newsmen writing about the amicable "spirit of Geneva." But they decided nothing of substance on any of the major issues they discussed.

The high point of the conference came on July 21, when Eisenhower set forth what came to be called his "Open Skies" proposal, a prelude to disarmament by which Russia and the United States would give each other "a complete blueprint of four military establishments from beginning to end," and would each open its skies to the other for aerial surveillance. Khrushchev, who was present at the meeting, told the president privately that it was "a very transparent espionage device." It would give Americans information they did not already have while providing the Russians little they did not already know. In consequence the conference did nothing except to lay the groundwork for cultural and diplomatic exchanges. The conference left behind a vague aura of peace, but it also made clear the arrival of a thermonuclear stalemate.

An H-Bomb hideaway. The Geneva Conference marked a thaw in the Cold War, but the continuing threat of nuclear war caused many Americans to invest in underground fallout shelters such as the Kidde Kokoon, designed to protect "a family for three to five days after an H bomb blast." [United Press International]

"THE AFFLUENT SOCIETY"

THE CONSUMER ECONOMY The warm afterglow of Geneva made the prospect of nuclear conflict seem remote. With the guns silent in Vietnam and the Formosa Strait, the world enjoyed its first season of peace in nearly two decades, while a flourishing economy ushered the United States into what the economist John Kenneth Galbraith soon called the "affluent society." The consumer culture which had emerged in the 1920s now resumed the growth stunted by depression and war. Pent-up demand and wartime savings triggered the postwar prosperity, which was maintained by Cold War outlays and increased consumer buying. Advertising and credit spurred the process, and credit cards, used at least since the 1930s, proliferated with advances in plastics and computers.

The electronic computer, the first of which was built in 1945, went on the market in the 1950s. But at this time consumers were more interested in new products such as television, transistorized FM radios, electric floor polishers, electric can openers, electric pencil sharpeners, antibiotics, and automatic car transmissions. Consumers enjoyed easy access to these goods in the new drive-in shopping malls spreading in the suburbs. Government expenditures for the St. Lawrence Seaway, the interstate highways, new rocketry, and the space program created new boom towns. The increased demand for housing called forth arrays of homogenized houses, typified by the sprawling Levit-towns in Pennsylvania and Long Island, or by Daly City, California, where the snuggeries perched along the hillsides inspired a

Dr. Jonas Salk. Salk's polio vaccine, developed in the mid-1950s, proved effective in preventing infection by the crippling viral disease. [March of Dimes, Birth Defects Foundation]

popular song, "Little Boxes": "And they're all made out of ticky-tacky and they all look just the same."

At the same time relaxed trade restrictions encouraged Americans to enjoy a variety of exotic foreign products and fashions. The reciprocal trade agreements started by Cordell Hull in 1934 were expanded into a multilateral policy under the General Agreement on Tariffs and Trade signed at Geneva in 1947. By 1960 the average level of American duties was down to about 12 percent from above 50 percent in 1930. The flow of American funds abroad made the dollar the chief medium of international exchange.

The United States now had by far the most productive economy in the world. In 1955, with about 6 percent of the world's population, the nation produced nearly half the world's goods. The median family income rose from $3,083 in 1949 to $5,657 in 1959, a rise, when corrected for inflation, still of some 48 percent. Inflation, measured at a low 1.6 percent annually from 1948 to 1963, was kept in check by efforts to hold the line on governmental expenditures. These efforts contributed to recessions in 1949, 1953–1954, 1957–1958, and 1960–1961. Despite the visible rise in wealth, the American economy grew more slowly from 1948 to 1960 than most other major world economies: its growth rate was 2.9 percent compared to 8.7 percent for Japan, 7.2 percent for Germany, 5.8 percent for Italy, 4.2 percent for France, and 2.7 percent for Great Britain. But America had started from a much higher plateau after the war, and the 1960s would bring a renewed spurt of economic growth.

STIRRINGS IN CIVIL RIGHTS   If the Eisenhower presidency seems an interlude of relative tranquility between two decades of domestic and foreign strife it should be remembered that those years saw the onset of a revolution in race relations which historians have come to call the Second Reconstruction. Eisenhower entered office committed to civil rights in principle, and did push the issue in areas of federal authority. During his first three years public services in Washington, D.C., were desegregated, as were navy yards and veterans hospitals. Beyond that, however, two aspects of the president's philosophy inhibited vigorous action: his preference for state or local action, and his doubt that law could be effective in such matters. "I don't believe you can change the hearts of men with laws or decisions," he said. For the time, then, leadership in the civil rights field came from the judiciary more than from the executive or legislative branch of the government.

Segregation began to be tested in the courts by the NAACP in the late 1930s. [Library of Congress]

In the 1930s the NAACP had resolved to test the "separate but equal" doctrine which had upheld racial segregation since the *Plessy* decision in 1896. Charles H. Houston, dean of the Howard University Law School, laid the plans and his former student, Thurgood Marshall, served as chief NAACP lawyer. They decided to begin with the expensive field of postgraduate study. At the time no southern or border state provided such study for blacks, although some offered grants for them to go out of state. In the case of Lloyd L. Gaines (1938) the Supreme Court ruled that such a grant failed to provide the equal protection of the laws required under the Fourteenth Amendment. Missouri hastily improvised a separate law school, but before Gaines's lawyers could resolve the issue, he mysteriously vanished. In *Ada Lois Sipuel v. Board of Regents* (1948) the court found a black woman entitled to attend the University of Oklahoma Law School in the absence of a separate facility, and in *Sweatt v. Painter* (1950) ruled that a separate law school in Texas failed to measure up because of intangible factors, such as its isolation from most of the future lawyers with whom its graduates would interact.

THE BROWN DECISION   By that time challenges to segregation in the public schools were rising through the appellate courts. Five such cases, from Kansas, Delaware, South Carolina, Virginia, and the District of Columbia—usually cited by reference to the first, *Brown v. Board of Education of Topeka, Kansas*—came to the Supreme Court for joint argument in 1952. Chief Justice Earl Warren wrote the opinion, handed down on May 17, 1954, in which a unanimous Court declared that "in the field of public education the doctrine of 'separate but equal' has no place." In support of its opinion the Court cited current sociological and psychological findings presented by the eminent Kenneth Clark, a black psychologist. It might well have cited historical evidence that Jim Crow facilities had been seldom equal and often not available to blacks at all. A year later, after further argument, the Court directed "a prompt and reasonable start toward full compliance"; the process should move "with all deliberate speed."

The white South's first response was relatively calm, deceptively so as it happened. Eisenhower refused to take any part in leading white southerners toward compliance. Privately he remarked: "I am convinced that the Supreme Court decision *set back* progress in the South *at least fifteen years.* The fellow who tries to tell me you can do these things by *force* is just plain *nuts.*" While token integration began as early as 1954 in the border states, hostility mounted in the Deep South and Virginia, led by the newly formed Citizens' Councils and similar groups. Before the end of 1955, moderate sentiment in the South gave way to reaction. Virginia's Sen. Harry F. Byrd supplied a rallying cry: "Massive Resistance." State legislatures passed pupil assignment laws and adopted other dodges, all futile, to interpose their power between the courts and the schools. In March 1956, 101 southern members of Congress lent their names to a "Southern Manifesto" which denounced the Court's decision as "a clear abuse of judicial power." At the end of 1956, in six southern states, not a single black child attended school with whites. In several of the others the degree of desegregation was minuscule.

THE MONTGOMERY BUS BOYCOTT At the end of 1955 the drive for civil rights took a new turn in Montgomery, Alabama, "the cradle of the Confederacy." There, on December 1, 1955, Mrs. Rosa Parks was arrested for refusing to give up her seat on a city bus to a white man. The next night black community leaders met in the Dexter Avenue Baptist Church to organize a massive bus boycott under the Montgomery Improvement Association.

In Dexter Avenue's twenty-six-year-old pastor, Martin Luther King, Jr., the movement found a charismatic leader who spoke eloquently in cadences familiar to the Bible Belt. He brought the movement a message of nonviolent, passive resistance compounded from the Gospels, the writings of Thoreau, and the example of Mahatma Gandhi in India. "We must use the weapon of love," he told his people. "We must realize so many people are taught to hate us that they are not totally responsible for their hate." To his antagonists he said: "We will soon wear you down by our capacity to suffer, and in winning our freedom we will so appeal to your heart and conscience that we will win you in the process."

The bus boycott achieved a remarkable solidarity. Blacks in Montgomery formed car pools, hitchhiked, or simply walked. But the white town fathers, who were not so quickly worn down, held out against the boycott and against the pleas of a bus company tired of losing money. The boycotters finally won through the federal courts a case they had initiated against bus segregation, and on December 20, 1956, the Supreme Court let stand without review an opinion of a lower court that "the separate but equal doctrine can no longer be safely followed as a correct statement of the law." The next day King and other blacks boarded the buses, but they still had a long way to travel before Jim Crow could be laid finally to rest. Trying to keep alive the spirit of the bus boycott, King and a group of associates in 1957 organized the Southern Christian Leadership Conference (SCLC).

Despite Eisenhower's reluctance to take the lead in desegregating schools, he had no problem with supporting the right to vote. In 1956, hoping to exploit divisions between northern and southern Democrats and to reclaim some of the black vote for Republicans, Eisenhower proposed legislation which became the Civil Rights Act of 1957. The first civil rights law passed since Reconstruction, it finally got through the Senate, after a year's delay, with the help of Majority Leader Lyndon B. Johnson, who won southern acceptance by watering the act. Still, it established for a period of two years the Civil Rights Commission, which was later extended indefinitely, and a new Civil Rights Division in the Justice Department, which could seek injunctions to prevent interference with the right to vote. The SCLC promptly announced a campaign to register 2 million black voters. The Civil Rights Act of 1960 provided for federal court referees to register blacks where a court found a "pattern and practice" of discrimination, and also made it a federal crime to interfere with any court order or to cross state lines to destroy any building.

LITTLE ROCK   There had been sporadic violence in resistance to civil rights efforts, but a few weeks after the 1957 act passed, the governor of a state for the first time stood in outright defiance of the law. Arkansas Gov. Orval Faubus called out the National Guard to prevent nine black students from entering Little Rock's Central High School under federal court order. A conference between the president and the governor proved fruitless, but on court order Faubus withdrew the Guard. When the students tried to enter the school, a hysterical mob outside forced their removal for their own safety. At that point Eisenhower, who had said two months before that he could not "imagine any set of circumstances that would ever induce me to send federal troops,"

Federal troops at Little Rock High School. [Burt Glinn, Magnum Photos]

ordered a thousand paratroopers to Little Rock to protect the students, and placed the National Guard on federal service. The soldiers stayed through the school year.

The following year Faubus peremptorily closed the high schools of Little Rock, and court proceedings dragged on into 1959 before the schools could be reopened. The year 1959 proved an important turning point, for in that year massive resistance in Virginia collapsed when both state and federal courts struck down state laws which had cut off funds from integrated schools. Thereafter, massive resistance for the most part was confined to the Deep South where five states, from South Carolina west through Louisiana, still held out against even token integration.

A LANDSLIDE FOR IKE   When President Eisenhower suffered a "moderately severe" coronary seizure during a Colorado vacation in September 1955, some journalists felt that he could not have chosen a more opportune time: there was no immediate crisis on the horizon. He recovered quickly and was getting back in harness within a month. In February 1956, after his doctor pronounced him recovered, the president announced his decision to run again. A serious operation for ileitis, an inflammation of the intestine, in June 1956 did not change his plans. In August the Republican convention renominated him by acclamation and, despite a quixotic effort by Harold Stassen to dump Nixon, again named him as the vice-presidential candidate. The party platform endorsed Eisenhower's "modern Republicanism."

The Democrats turned again to Stevenson, who had campaigned vigorously in the primaries against Sen. Estes Kefauver. After Stevenson freed the convention to name its own candidate for vice-president, the delegates chose Kefauver by a narrow margin over young Sen. John F. Kennedy. The platform evaded the civil rights issue and otherwise stuck to Democratic staples: less "favoritism" to big business, repeal of the Taft-Hartley Act, parity for farmers, tax relief for those in low-income brackets.

Neither candidate generated much excitement during the campaign. The Democrats did what they could with the issue of the president's health, but centered their fire on the heir apparent, Richard Nixon, a "man of many masks." Stevenson aroused little enthusiasm for two controversial proposals: to drop conscription and rely on an all-volunteer army, and to ban H-bomb tests by international agreement. Both involved military questions which put Stevenson at a disadvantage by pitting his judgment against that of a successful general.

During the last week of the campaign the season of world peace was broken by shooting wars along the Suez Canal and in the streets of Budapest. The two crises made it possible for Stevenson to declare the administration's foreign policy "bankrupt." Most voters, however, seemed to reason that the crises spelled a poor time to switch horses, and they handed Eisenhower a landslide victory. He lost one border state, Missouri, but in carrying Louisiana became the first Republican to win a Deep South state since Reconstruction; nationally, he carried all but seven states. The decision was unmistakably clear: he won more than 35.6 million popular votes to a little over 26 million for Stevenson, 457 electoral votes to the Democrat's 73.

A SEASON OF TROUBLES

CRISIS IN THE MIDDLE EAST   The twin crises in the Suez and Hungary were unrelated but occurred almost as if placed in malicious juxtaposition by some evil force. The attack on Egypt by Britain, France, and Israel disrupted the Western alliance and damaged any claim to moral outrage at Russian actions in Hungary. For the Soviets, the Suez War afforded both a smokescreen for the subjugation of Hungary and a chance to enlarge their influence in the Middle East, an increasingly important source of oil.

After 1953 the Eisenhower-Dulles policy in the region departed from the Truman-Acheson focus on Israel and distanced itself from British-French economic interests in order to cultivate Arab friendship. To forestall Russian penetration, Dulles in 1955 completed his line of alliances across the "northern tier" of the Middle East. Under American sponsorship Britain joined the Moslem states of Turkey, Iraq, Iran, and Pakistan in the Middle East Treaty Organization (METO), or Baghdad Pact, as the treaty

POSTWAR ALLIANCES:
Europe, North Africa, The Middle East

Members of NATO

Members of CENTO

Arab League

Communist bloc
(Warsaw Pact)

was commonly called. By linking the easternmost NATO state (Turkey) to the westernmost SEATO state (Pakistan), METO had a certain superficial logic, but after Iraq, the only Arab member, withdrew in 1959 it became clear that the whole thing had been moribund from the start. Below the northern tier, moreover, the Arab states remained aloof from the organization. These were the states of the Arab League (Egypt, Jordan, Syria, Lebanon, and Saudi Arabia), which had warred on Israel in 1948–1949 and remained committed to its destruction.

The most fateful developments in the region turned on the rise of Egyptian Gen. Gamal Abdel Nasser, leader of the army officers who overthrew King Farouk in 1952. The bone of contention was the Suez Canal, which had opened in 1869 as a joint French-Egyptian venture. But in 1882 the British government had acquired the largest block of stock and from the next year on British forces were posted there to protect the British Empire's "lifeline" to India and other colonies. When Nasser's new regime pressed for the withdrawal of British forces from the canal zone, Eisenhower and Dulles supported its demand, and in 1954 an Anglo-Egyptian treaty provided for British withdrawal within twenty months. Nasser, like other leaders of the Third World, remained unaligned in the Cold War and sought to play both sides off against each other. In 1955 Nasser made a deal for Czech armaments in return for Egyptian cotton. The United States, meanwhile, courted Egyptian support by offering the prospect of American assistance in building a great hydroelectric plant at Aswan on the Nile River.

From the outset the administration's proposal was opposed by Jewish constituencies concerned with Egyptian threats to Israel, and by southern congressmen who feared the competition from Egyptian cotton produced by irrigation at Aswan. When Nasser then increased trade with the Soviet bloc and recognized Red China, Dulles abruptly canceled the loan offer in July 1956. The outcome was far from a triumph of American diplomacy. The chief victims, it turned out, were Anglo-French interests in the Suez. Unable to retaliate against the United States, Nasser nationalized the Suez Canal Company and earmarked its revenues for the Aswan project, thereby enhancing his prestige in the Arab world. The British and French, directly challenged and faced with loss of control of the crucial Suez Canal, reacted strongly. Fruitless negotiations dragged out through the summer, and finally, on October 29, Israeli forces invaded the Gaza Strip and the Sinai peninsula. The Israelis invaded ostensibly to root out Arab guerrillas, but actually to synchronize with the British and French, who began bombing Egyptian air bases and on November 3 occupied Port Said. Their actions, the British and French claimed, were meant to protect the canal against the opposing belligerents.

The Suez War put the United States in a quandary. Either the administration could support its Western allies and see the troublesome Nasser crushed, or it could stand on the United Nations

The Twentieth Century Dilemma. *The Suez crisis forced America into a difficult choice.[Long in the Minneapolis* Tribune]

Charter and champion Arab nationalism against imperialistic aggression. The latter course was adopted, with the unusual result that Russia sided with the United States' position. Once the threat of American embargoes had forced Anglo-French-Israeli capitulation, the Russians capitalized on the situation by threatening to use missiles against the Western aggressors. This belated bravado won for Russia some of the credit in the Arab world for what the United States had done.

REPRESSION IN HUNGARY   All the while, Khrushchev was engaged in the subjugation of Hungary, a sharp reversal to the campaign of "de-Stalinization" he had launched in his "secret" speech on the crimes of the Stalin era, delivered at the Communist Party Congress in February 1956. Khrushchev joined this confession of Communist tyranny with hints of relaxed policies and suggestions that different countries might take "separate roads to socialism." In the satellite countries this put Stalinist leaders on the defensive and emboldened the more independent national leaders. In June riots in the Polish city of Poznan led to the rise of Wladyslaw Gomulka, a Polish nationalist, to leadership of the Polish Communist party. Gomulka managed to win a greater degree of independence by avoiding an open break with the Russians.

In Hungary, however, a similar movement got out of hand. On October 23 fighting broke out in Budapest, followed by the installation of Imre Nagy, a moderate Communist, as head of the government. Again the Russians seemed content to let "de-Stalinization" follow its course, and on October 28 they withdrew their forces from Budapest. But Nagy's announcement three days later that Hungary would withdraw from the Warsaw Pact brought Russian tanks back into Budapest. They installed a more compliant leader, Janos Kadar, and hauled Nagy off to Moscow, where a firing squad executed him in 1958. It was a tragic dénouement to a movement that, at the outset, promised the sort of moderation which might have vindicated Kennan's policy of "containment," if not Dulles's notion of "liberation."

LEGISLATIVE STUMBLING   In the euphoria of his landslide victory on November 6, Eisenhower said on election night: "I think that modern Republicanism has now proved itself. And America has approved of modern Republicanism." He later defined this as "the political philosophy that recognizes clearly the responsibility of the Federal Government to take the lead in making certain that the productivity of our great economic machine is distributed so that no one will suffer disaster, privation, through no fault of his own." Eisenhower Republicans, it seemed clear, had assimilated the New Deal as an accomplished fact. But decisive as was the vote for Eisenhower, the winner's coattails failed to swing a congressional majority for his own party in either house, the first time this had happened since the election of Zachary Taylor.

A season of troubles followed Eisenhower's smashing victory. It began with the "great budget battle" of 1957. In January the president sent up to Capitol Hill a $71.8-billion budget for fiscal 1958, up $3 billion from the previous year, the biggest peacetime budget ever. The size of the budget, which increased foreign aid, military spending, and allocations for atomic energy, housing, public works, and education, startled and alarmed even the president, who had little time to cut it back. Eisenhower sent the bill to Congress, still hopeful that continued prosperity and high revenues would supply a surplus.

On the day the budget went to Congress, January 16, 1957, Secretary of the Treasury George Humphrey told reporters "there are a lot of places in this budget that can be cut," and suggested that if government could not reduce the "terrific" tax burden "you will have a depression that will curl your hair." Eisenhower claimed to share Humphrey's desire to reduce the budget, but the spectacle of a treasury secretary challenging the budget on the day it went to Congress conveyed an impression of divided purpose and conflict in the administration. Both Democrats and Old Guard Republicans declared an open season on the administration's budget requests, and in the end they hacked out about $4 billion, including heavy cuts in foreign aid, the United States Information Agency, and the Defense Department. By the time the battle was over in August, an economic slump had set in and tax revenues dropped. In spite of the cuts, the administration projected a $500-million deficit.

SPUTNIK On October 4, 1957, came the Soviet launching of the first man-made satellite, called *sputnik,* an acronym for the Russian phrase "fellow traveler of earth." Sputnik I weighed 194 pounds, but less than a month later the Soviets launched a capsule of 1,120 pounds, and it carried a dog wired up for monitoring. Americans, until then complacent about their technical primacy, suddenly discovered an apparent "missile gap." If the Russians were so advanced in rocketry, then perhaps they could hit American cities just as Nazi rockets had hit London in 1945. All along Eisenhower knew that the "gap" was more illusory than real, but could not reveal that high-altitude American U-2 spy planes were gathering this information. Even so, American missile development was in a state of disarray, with a tangle of

By the Rocket's Red Glare. *The Soviet success in space shocked Americans. [Poinier in the Detroit News]*

agencies and committees engaged in waste and duplication. To the embarrassment of the administration, Sen. Lyndon B. Johnson's Preparedness Subcommittee of the Armed Services Committee laid out the facts about all this. The launching of Explorer I, the first American satellite, on January 31, 1958, did not quiet the outcry.

Russia's success with Sputnik launched efforts in America to enlarge defense spending, to offer NATO allies intermediate-range ballistic missiles (IRBMs) pending development of long-range intercontinental ballistic missiles (ICBMs), to set up a new agency to coordinate space efforts, and to establish a crash program in science education. The "sputnik syndrome," compounded by a sharp recession through the winter of 1957–1958, loosened the purse strings of economy-minded congressmen, who added to the new budget more than Eisenhower wanted for both defense and domestic programs. During 1958 Britain, Italy, and Turkey accepted American Thor and Jupiter missiles on their territory. In July 1958 Congress created the National Aeronautics and Space Agency (NASA) to coordinate research and development in the field. Before the end of the year NASA had a program to put a manned craft in orbit, but the first manned flight, by Commander Alan B. Shepard, Jr., did not take place until May 5, 1961. Finally, in September 1958 Congress enacted the National Defense Education Act, which authorized federal grants especially for training in mathematics, science, and modern languages, as well as for student loans and fellowships.

CORRUPT PRACTICES   During the first two years of Eisenhower's second term, public confidence in his performance, as registered by opinion polls, dropped sharply from 79 percent to 49 percent. Emotional issues such as civil rights and defense policy had compounded his troubles. The president's image was further tarnished when congressional investigations revealed that the administration, which had promised to clean up "the mess in Washington," was itself touched by scandals, one of which involved Sherman Adams, the White House "chief of staff." Adams, it seemed, had done little more than open some doors at the Securities and Exchange Commission and the Federal Trade Commission with introductions for Boston industrialist Bernard Goldfine, but he had taken gifts of a fur coat and an Oriental rug from Goldfine. In September 1958 the president reluctantly accepted Adams's resignation. Republicans also faced the growing opposition of farmers, angry with cuts in price supports, and labor, angry because many Republicans had made "right-to-work" (or open-shop) laws a campaign issue in 1958. The Democrats came out of the midterm elections with nearly two-to-one majorities in Congress: 282 to 154 in the House, 64 to 34 in the Senate.

Eisenhower would be the first president to face three successive Congresses controlled by the opposition party. One consequence was that the president could manage few new departures in domestic policy. The most important legislation of the last two years in the Eisenhower presidency were the Landrum-Griffin Labor-Management Act of 1959, the Civil Rights Act of 1960, and the admission of the first states not contiguous to the continental forty-eight. Alaska became the forty-ninth state on January 3, 1959, and Hawaii the fiftieth on August 21, 1959.

The Landrum-Griffin Act of September 14, 1959, aimed at controlling union corruption, was actually a compromise between the views of its House sponsors and the somewhat less stringent views of Sen. John F. Kennedy and some of his colleagues. It reflected, nevertheless, popular feeling against racketeering and monopolistic practices in unions, especially the Teamsters, which had been revealed by an extensive Senate probe directed by John L. McClellan of Arkansas. The act safeguarded democratic procedures, penalized the misuse of union funds and coercion of members, and excluded from office persons convicted of certain crimes. The act also strengthened restrictions on secondary boycotts and blackmail picketing. Most of its provisions were directed against unfair union practices, but the act also monitored employer payments to union officers or labor-management consultants.

FESTERING PROBLEMS ABROAD   Once the Suez and Hungary crises faded from the front pages, Eisenhower enjoyed eighteen months of smooth sailing in foreign affairs. A brief flurry occurred in May 1958 over hostile demonstrations in Peru and Venezuela against Vice-President Nixon, who was on a goodwill tour of eight Latin American countries. Then in July 1958 the Middle East flared up again. By this time the president had secured from Congress authority for what came to be called the Eisenhower Doctrine, which promised to extend economic and military aid to Middle East nations, and to use armed forces if necessary to assist any such nation against armed aggression from any Communist country.

President Nasser of Egypt meanwhile had emerged from the Suez crisis with heightened prestige, and in February 1958 created the United Arab Republic (UAR) by merger (a short-lived one) with Syria. Then on July 14 a leftist coup in Iraq, supposedly inspired by Nasser and the Russians, threw out the pro-Western government and killed King Faisal, the crown prince, and the premier. In Lebanon, already unsettled by internal conflict, President Camille Chamoun appealed to the United States for support against a similar fate. Eisenhower immediately ordered 5,000 marines into Lebanon on July 15, where they limited themselves to the capital, Beirut, and its airfield. He proposed to go no farther because, he said later, if the government could not hold out with such protection, "I felt we were backing up a government with so little popular support that we probably should not be there." British forces meanwhile went into Jordan at the request of King Hussein. Once the situation stabilized, and the Lebanese factions reached a compromise, American forces (up to 15,000 at one point) withdrew in October.

East Asia heated up again when, on August 23, 1958, Red China renewed its bombardment of the Nationalists on Quemoy and Matsu. In September the American Seventh Fleet began to escort Nationalist convoys, but stopped short of entering Chinese territorial waters. To abandon the islands, President Eisenhower said, would amount to a "Western Pacific 'Munich.' " But on October 1 he suggested that a cease-fire would provide "an opportunity to negotiate in good faith." Red China ordered such a cease-fire on October 6, and on October 25, which happened to be the day the last American forces left Lebanon, said that it would reserve the right to bombard the islands on alternate days. With that strange stipulation the worst of the crisis passed, but the problem continued to fester.

The problem of Berlin festered too; Premier Khrushchev called it a bone in his throat. West Berlin provided a "showplace" of Western democracy and prosperity, a listening post for Western intelligence, and a funnel through which news and propaganda from the West penetrated what Winston Churchill called "the iron curtain." Although East Germany had sealed its western frontiers, refugees could still pass from East to West

Berlin. On November 10, 1958, at a Soviet-Polish friendship rally in Moscow, Khrushchev threatened to transfer Soviet obligations in the occupation to East Germany. After the deadline he set, May 27, 1959, Western occupation authorities would have to deal with the East German government, in effect recognizing it, or face the possibility of another blockade.

But Eisenhower refused to budge from his position on Berlin. At the same time he refused to engage in saber-rattling or even to cancel existing plans to reduce the size of the army. As Stephen Ambrose, an Eisenhower biographer, wrote: "He thought the greatest danger in the Berlin crisis was that the Russians would frighten the United States into an arms race that would bankrupt the country." Khrushchev, it turned out, was no more eager for confrontation than Eisenhower. In talks with British Prime Minister Harold Macmillan, he suggested that the main thing was to begin discussions of the Berlin issue, and not the May 27 deadline. Macmillan in turn won Eisenhower's consent to a meeting of the Big Four foreign ministers.

There was little hope of resolving different views on Berlin and German reunification, but the talks distracted attention from Khrushchev's deadline of May 27: it passed almost unnoticed. In September, after the Big Four talks had adjourned, Premier Khrushchev paid a visit to the United States, going to New York, Washington, Los Angeles, San Francisco, and Iowa, and dropping in on Eisenhower at Camp David. In talks there Khrushchev endorsed "peaceful coexistence," and Eisenhower admitted that the Berlin situation was "abnormal." They agreed that the time was ripe for a summit meeting in the spring.

THE U-2 SUMMIT The summit meeting, however, blew up in Eisenhower's face. On May 1, 1960, near Sverdlovsk, east of the Urals, a Soviet rocket brought down an American U-2 spy plane. Such planes had been flying missions over Russia for three and a half years. Khrushchev played up the news for domestic consumption to keep in good standing with Soviet "hard-liners." He set out to entrap Eisenhower and succeeded, by announcing first only that the plane had been shot down. When the State Department insisted that there had been no attempt to violate Soviet airspace, Khrushchev then announced that the Soviets had pilot Francis Gary Powers, "alive and kicking," and his pictures of military installations. On May 11 Eisenhower finally took personal responsibility—an unprecedented action for a head of state—and justified the action on grounds of national security. "No one wants another Pearl Harbor," he said. In Paris, five days later, Khrushchev withdrew an invitation for Eisenhower to visit the USSR and called on the president to repudiate the U-2 flights and "pass severe judgment on those responsible." When Eisenhower refused, Khrushchev left the meeting.

Eisenhower's frustration in Paris was magnified by several foreign-policy setbacks he encountered as his term drew to a close. Another came a month afterward when he set out in June on a tour to Formosa, the Philippines, and Japan. Japan had just agreed to a new military treaty which extended the American right to station armed forces in Japan indefinitely, subject to renunciation on one-year's notice. Although the treaty removed all remnants of Japan's status as an occupied country, neutralists and pacifists—together with a small number of Communists—argued that the treaty would draw Japan into the Cold War. Others complained that the treaty did not return the Ryukyu and Bonin Islands to Japanese administration. Massive anti-American riots and demonstrations reached such a level that on June 16 Premier Nobusuke Kishi notified Eisenhower in Manila that the Japanese government could not guarantee his safety. He had no choice but to fly back home. Premier Kishi then resigned.

CASTRO'S CUBA   But the greatest thorn in Eisenhower's side was the Cuban regime of Fidel Castro, which came to power on January 1, 1959, after three years of guerrilla warfare against the dictator Fulgencio Batista. In their struggle against Batista, Castro's forces had the support of many Americans who hoped for a new day of democratic government in Cuba. When American television picked up trials and executions conducted by the victorious Castro, such hopes were dashed. Staged like a Roman holiday before crowds of howling spectators, the trials vented anger against Batista's officials and police, but offered little in the

Cuban Premier Fidel Castro. [Magnum Photos]

way of legal procedure or proof. Castro, moreover, planned a social revolution and opposed the widespread foreign control of the Cuban economy. When he began programs of land reform and nationalization of foreign-owned property, relations worsened. Some observers believed, however, that by rejecting Castro's requests for loans and other help the American government lost a chance to influence the direction of the revolution, and by acting on the assumption that Communists already had the upper hand in his movement the administration may have ensured that fact.

Castro, on the other hand, showed little reluctance to accept the Communist embrace. In February 1960 he entered a trade agreement to swap Cuban sugar for Soviet oil and machinery. In July, after Cuba had seized three British-American oil refineries which refused to process Soviet oil, Eisenhower cut sharply the quota for Cuban sugar imports. Premier Khrushchev in response warned that any military intervention in Cuba would encounter Russian rockets. In October 1960 the United States suspended imports of Cuban sugar and embargoed most shipments to Cuba. One of Eisenhower's last acts as president was to suspend diplomatic relations with Cuba on January 3, 1961. In the hope of creating "some kind of non-dictatorial 'third force,' neither Castroite nor Batistiano," as Eisenhower put it, the president authorized the CIA to begin training a force of Cuban refugees (some of them former Castro stalwarts) for a new revolution. But the final decision on its use would rest with the next president, John F. Kennedy.

ASSESSING THE EISENHOWER YEARS

The Eisenhower years have not drawn much acclaim from journalists and historians. One journalist called Ike's administration "the time of the great postponement," during which the president "lived off the accumulated wisdom, the accumulated prestige, and the accumulated military strength of his predecessors" and left domestic and foreign policies "about where he found them in 1953." Yet even these critics granted that Eisenhower had succeeded in ending the war in Korea and settling the dust raised by McCarthy. But if he had failed to end the Cold War and in fact had institutionalized it as a global confrontation, he sensed the limits of American power and kept its application to low-risk situations. If he took few initiatives in addressing the social problems that would erupt in the 1960s, he left the major innovations of the New Deal in place and thereby legitimized them. If he tolerated unemployment of as much as 7 percent at times, he kept inflation to an average rate of 1.6 percent during his terms. His farewell address to the American people, delivered on radio and television three days before he left office, showed his remarkable foresight in his own area of special expertise, the military.

Like Washington, Eisenhower couched his wisdom largely in the form of warnings: that America's "leadership and prestige depend, not merely upon our unmatched material strength, but on how we use our power in the interests of world peace and human betterment"; that the temptation to find easy answers should take into account "the need to maintain balance in and among national problems"; and above all that Americans "must avoid the impulse to live only for today, plundering, for our own ease and convenience, the precious resources of tomorrow."

As a soldier, Eisenhower highlighted perhaps better than anyone else could have the dangers of a military establishment in a time of peace. "This conjunction of an immense military establishment and a large arms industry is new in the American experience," he said. "In the councils of government we must guard against the acquisition of unwarranted influence, whether sought or unsought, by the military-industrial complex. The potential for the disastrous rise of misplaced power exists and will persist." With the new importance of technology, "a government contract becomes virtually a substitute for intellectual curiosity" in directing university research. This new circumstance created the dual danger "of domination of the nation's scholars by Federal employment," and the shaping of policy by "a scientific-technological elite."

His great disappointment as he lay down his responsibilities, Eisenhower said, was his inability to affirm "that a lasting peace is in sight," only that "war has been avoided." But he prayed "that, in the goodness of time, all peoples will come to live together in a peace guaranteed by the binding force of mutual respect and love."

FURTHER READING

Two scholars admirably document the political and cultural trends of the 1950s—William E. Leuchtenberg in *A Troubled Feast: American Society since 1945* (1979)° and Godfrey Hodgson in *America in Our Time: From World War II to Nixon, What Happened and Why* (1976).°

Scholarship on Eisenhower is extensive. The best overview of the

°These books are available in paperback editions.

period is Charles A. Alexander's *Holding the Line: The Eisenhower Era, 1951–1961* (1975). Other studies include Herbert S. Parmet's *Eisenhower and the American Crusade* (1972), Peter Lyon's *Eisenhower: Portrait of a Hero* (1974), James L. Sundquist's *Politics and Policy: The Eisenhower, Kennedy, and Johnson Years* (1968), Arthur Larsen's *Eisenhower: The Person Nobody Knew* (1968), and Blanche Wiesen's *The Declassified Eisenhower: A Divided Legacy* (1981). For the manner in which Eisenhower conducted foreign policy, see in particular Robert A. Divine's *Eisenhower and the Cold War* (1981) and Richard A. Aliano's *American Defense Policy from Eisenhower to Kennedy* (1975).

The conservatism of the 1950s is documented best in studies of Congress and its members. A good start is James T. Patterson's *Mr. Republican: A Biography of Robert A. Taft* (1975). Also helpful are Gary W. Reichard's *The Reaffirmation of Republicanism: Eisenhower and the Eighty-third Congress* (1975) and George B. Nash's *The Conservative Intellectual Movement in America: Since 1945* (1976).° How the liberals fared in the 1950s is included in John Bartlow Martin's *The Life of Adlai E. Stevenson* (2 vols.; 1976–1977), which is also the best work on Eisenhower's two-time opponent. Also see Joseph B. Gorman's *Kefauver: A Political Biography* (1971).

Among the numerous titles on the Cold War listed in Chapter 31, several cover the Eisenhower years, including John L. Gaddis's *Strategies of Containment: A Critical Appraisal of Postwar American National Security Policy* (1982) and Norman A. Graebner's *The Age of Global Power: The United States since 1938* (1979). The role played by the secretary of state is analyzed in Townsend Hoopes's *The Devil and John Foster Dulles* (1973) and Louis Gerson's *John Foster Dulles* (1973).

Specific Eisenhower decisions also have received scrutiny. Chester Cooper's *The Lion's Last Roar: Suez, 1956* (1978), and Hugh Thomas's *Suez* (1967) cover Eisenhower's handling of the crisis. For the buildup of American involvement in Indochina, consult James P. Harrison's *The Endless War: Fifty Years of Struggle in Vietnam* (1982), Melvin Gurov's *The First Vietnamese Crisis* (1967), and George C. Herring's *America's Longest War: The United States and Vietnam, 1950–1975* (1979).° For negotiations on use of the atomic bomb, see Robert A. Divine's *Blowing in the Wind: The Nuclear Test Ban Debate, 1954–1960* (1978). How the Eisenhower Doctrine came to be implemented is traced in Stephen Ambrose's *Rise to Globalism: American Foreign Policy, 1938–1980* (1981).° For intelligence activities during the Eisenhower administration, consult Harry Rositzke's *The CIA's Secret Operations: Espionage, Counterespionage, and Covert Action* (1977) and Richard H. Immerman's *The Central Intelligence Agency in Guatemala* (1982).

Two introductions to the impact wrought by the Warren Supreme Court during the 1950s are Alexander Bickel's *The Supreme Court and the Idea of Progress* (1970)° and Paul Murphy's *The Constitution in Crisis Times* (1972).° Also helpful are Archibald Cox's *The Warren Court: Constitutional Decision as an Instrument of Reform* (1968)° and Phillip B. Kurland's *Politics, the Constitution, and the Warren Court* (1970). Biographical studies of the chief justice include John D. Weaver's *Warren* (1967), Leo Katcher's *Earl Warren* (1967), and G. Edward White's *Earl Warren: A Public Life* (1982). A masterful study of the important Warren Court decision on school desegregation is Richard Kluger's *Simple Justice: The History of Brown v. Board of Education and Black America's Struggle for Equality* (1975).°

A good follow-up to the Kluger work is Benjamin Muse's *Ten Years of Prelude: The Story of Integration since the Supreme Court's 1954 Decision* (1964). Other surveys of the era include John Hope Franklin's *From Slavery to Freedom: A History of Negro Americans* (1974),° Charles F. Kellogg's *NAACP* (1967), and Harvard Sitkoff's *A New Deal for Blacks: The Emergence of Civil Rights as a National Issue* (1978). For the story from Montgomery, see David L. Lewis's *King: A Critical Biography* (1970)° and Stephen B. Oates's *Let the Trumpet Sound: The Life of Martin Luther King, Jr.* (1982).° William H. Chafe's *Civilities and Civil Rights: Greensboro, North Carolina, and the Black Struggle for Freedom* (1980)° examines how one community dragged its feet on the Brown implementation order. J. B. Martin's *The Deep South Says Never* (1957) and Anthony Lewis's *Portrait of a Decade: The Second American Revolution* (1964) look at massive resistance on a regional level.

In addition to the surveys by Leuchtenberg and Hodgson cited above, other scholars have examined 1950s culture and society. John Kenneth Galbraith's *The Affluent Society* (1958)° and *The New Industrial State* (1971)° are studies of the influence exerted by corporate managers in shaping American policies and values. How the corporate ethic was itself shaped by overseas conditions is treated in Mira Wilkin's *The Maturing of Multinational Enterprise: American Business Abroad from 1914 to 1970* (1974). For religion, consult W. L. Miller's *Piety along the Potomac: Notes on Politics and Morals in the Fifties* (1964). For the suburban society, the best case study is Zane L. Miller's *Suburb: Neighborhood and Community in Forest Park, Ohio, 1935–1976* (1981). Bruce Cook's *The Beat Generation* (1971) examines the roots of the youth rebellion which surfaced after 1960. Views of women in the 1950s can be found in Carl N. Degler's *At Odds: Women and the Family in America from the Revolution to the Present* (1980)° and Sheila M. Rothman's *Woman's Proper Place: A History of Changing Ideas and Practices, 1870 to the Present* (1978).

33

INTO THE MAELSTROM:
THE SIXTIES

Eisenhower's misgiving about the military-industrial complex sounded a warning that countered the complacency and buoyant optimism of the 1950s. By the end of that decade a chorus of voices was deploring the triumph of materialistic values that arrived with what John Kenneth Galbraith had labeled "the affluent society." If we are so rich, social critics wondered, why do we feel so poor? "With the supermarket as our temple and the singing commercial as our litany," asked Adlai Stevenson, "are we likely to fire the world with an irresistible vision of America's exalted purposes and inspiring way of life?"

Eisenhower greeted these lamentations in the traditional way: he named a presidential commission to study the matter. *Goals for Americans: A Report of the President's Commission on National Goals* (1960) appeared just as Eisenhower was leaving office. The commission saw no need to worry. The gross national product had more than doubled since the end of the war and there was no reason to doubt its continued growth. If government investment in education kept pace with the economy, one could expect a new cadre of professionals—doctors, economists, social workers—to solve the problems that came with prosperity. The only real danger came from abroad, in the form of Communist aggression and subversion. The report contrasted the Communist ideal of the state with the American ideal of the individual. How a nation of 180 million individuals could achieve a sense of collective purpose while still pursuing their unbridled self-interest was, appropriately, a matter best left to the individuals themselves.

But the members of the commission were better historians than prophets. As the complacent 1950s yielded to another decade, few if any people foresaw the collapse of consensus, the hopes dashed, the ironic turns of fortune ahead. An alert prophet might have found a sign in an unlikely quarter—the Woolworth lunch counter in Greensboro, North Carolina, where just one month into the 1960s, on February 1, four black freshmen from a nearby college sat down and asked for coffee. It took them nearly six months to get service, but by then they had set in motion the completion of a Second Reconstruction and had introduced two salient styles of the 1960s: civil disobedience and the youth rebellion, two protean phenomena that would assume many different shapes before the decade ended.

DEMOGRAPHIC AND ECONOMIC TRENDS

"A NEW GENERATION" John Fitzgerald Kennedy's election to the presidency in 1960 was symbolic in several ways. Most obviously, Kennedy was young and visibly vigorous, at forty-three the youngest person ever elected president. Eisenhower at seventy was then the oldest man ever to occupy the White House. When Kennedy told the inaugural crowd that "the torch has been passed to a new generation of Americans," he was on the mark in both a political and a demographic sense.

The much-mentioned "generation gap" that came to popular attention in the 1960s had a solid foundation in population statistics. Between 1945 and 1960 America's total population increased by almost 40 million. In the 1950s alone the population went up by 28 million, an 18.5 percent increase that was the largest since the peak years of immigration in the first decade of the twentieth century. Much of America's social history since the 1940s has been the story of the "baby boom" generation and its progress through life. The population explosion created a massive demand for family housing in the 1950s and thereby spurred the remarkable growth of suburbs, and the highways and cars required for transport to them. By the 1960s the population explosion had generated a demand for new high schools and colleges, a rise in auto accidents and "juvenile delinquency," and toward the end of the decade, a glutted job market and a high rate of unemployment among people in their teens and twenties. The youth culture that attracted so much attention in the 1960s was not the figment of some Madison Avenue imagination, although advertisers responded quickly to the rapidly growing youth "market." America's population was dominated by a generation that was accustomed to affluence, nurtured on the homogenizing effects of television, unexposed to depression or major wartime dislocations, aware of the Cold War primarily as a battle of words and gestures without immediate consequences for them, and secure in the belief that nuclear annihilation was a remote and unreal possibility.

Meanwhile the older generation fell roughly into two groups. Americans aged fifty or over, who had been born well before the depression, constituted a disproportionately large group, reflecting the relatively high birth rates of the 1910s. This group created a demand for retirement condominiums in Florida and Arizona, more geriatric wards and medical facilities, and legislation to benefit "senior citizens." Another large age cohort born in the 1920s was reaching age forty. The generation born during the depression, however, was somewhat smaller, reflecting the decline in births during that time of economic distress. Mostly in their thirties during the 1960s, this group, because of their small numbers, experienced less competition for executive and professional jobs. Born and raised with memories of the Great Depression and World War II, and finding in the 1960s easy access to prosperity and enhanced status, this group had few reasons to complain about the justice of "the system." As the products of the postwar "baby boom" passed through high school and college, it was this older generation, so different in size and experience, that held the lucrative jobs which younger Americans coveted. Here was one powerful reason for the rallying cry of the young: "Never trust anyone over thirty."

The "baby boom" of the postwar decades made a mockery of most earlier predictions about the ultimate size of the United States' population. Earlier forecasters had tended to expect a leveling-off at about 150 million in 1970. Instead the population reached 205 million that year and was still growing. A dramatic slowing of the upward trend occurred during the 1960s when, despite an increase of 24 million people, the percentage increase was only 13.3, the lowest in American history except for the depression. In fact the birth rate in 1968 reached the lowest level ever recorded in America, 17.5 births per 1000 population. The rate rose slightly above that the next two years, then fell even lower on through the 1970s.

As the average size of families declined, so did the demand for new housing, appliances, and durable goods. Reliable and handy contraceptives, especially "the pill," allowed prospective parents to opt for a second car or a better home rather than another child, and permitted working wives to choose a career over extended childrearing. The dip in the birth rate also made the notion of "zero population growth," a goal of liberal reformers from the mid-1960s on, seem within reach by the middle of the next century.

CITIES AND SUBURBS   Almost the entire population increase of the 1950s and 1960s (97 percent) was an urban phenomenon. The flight from the farm accelerated in the postwar years: 20 million Americans left the land for the city between 1940 and 1970. The old America of small towns and family farms, Norman Rockwell's vision of picket fences and cracker-barrel conversations in the general store, became more quaintly nostalgic with each passing year. In 1870 about three-fourths of the American people were classified as rural residents; exactly one century later the residential patterns had reversed themselves and three-fourths of the population lived in towns and cities. Much of the urban population growth occurred in the South, the Southwest, and the West, in an arc that stretched from the Carolinas down through Texas and into California, diverse states that by the 1970s were being lumped together into the "Sunbelt." The surging cities of the old Spanish borderlands included Atlanta, Miami, Dallas, Houston, San Antonio, Phoenix, and Los Angeles. But the Northeast remained the most densely populated area; by the early 1960s, 20 percent of the total population lived in the land corridor that stretched from Boston to Norfolk, Virginia.

While more concentrated in cities, Americans were simultaneously spreading out within metropolitan areas. In 1950 the Census Bureau redefined the term "urban" to include suburbs as well as central cities. In fact the real postwar population growth was suburban rather than urban. In the 1960s eight of the ten largest cities in the United States actually lost population, yet all of the metropolitan areas surrounding these cities (except for one, Pittsburgh) grew in size. By 1970 more Americans lived in suburbs (76 million) than central cities (64 million). The most striking example of urban sprawl occurred in southern California, where Los Angeles became a centerless collection of freeways and fast-food restaurants that spread from Santa Barbara to the Mexican border, over 200 miles to the south. At the other end of the continent, Manhattan actually lost population in the 1960s and sections of the Bronx became rat-infested wastelands that resembled the bombed-out cities of Europe after World War II.

Sheer statistics cannot convey the magnitude of the social problems that the new urban demography had created by the 1960s. The suburbs had become rings of affluence around cores of poverty. In such suburbs as Darien, Connecticut, Shaker

Herblock's cartoon Vicious Circle *captures the plight of the cities in the 1960s and 1970s. [Herblock in the* Washington Post, *March 23, 1969]*

Heights, Ohio, and Kenilworth, Illinois, mothers drove children to new schools and shopping malls in wood-paneled station wagons. Meanwhile in the center cities of New York, Cleveland, and Chicago, trash piled up on the sidewalks and "white flight" left black and Puerto Rican youth mired in what the anthropologist Oscar Lewis called "the culture of poverty." In 1965, when a massive power failure in the Northeast plunged New York City into darkness for one evening, some observers took it as evidence that Gotham was dead and beyond any hope of recovery. But nine months later, hospitals reported a flood of new births, thereby demonstrating that the darkness had inspired fresh feats of human communication and adaptation. Such signs of hope, however, were but minor incidents in the larger pattern of urban segregation. America's urban geography had become a series of concentric circles, with the central cities bull's-eyes of festering racial and economic problems.

THE POSTWAR ECONOMY   The dominant theme in the story of the American economy during the postwar years was growth, unprecedented rates of sustained growth that produced a cornucopia of goods and services and the highest standard of living ever experienced by so many people in the history of the planet. The gross national product went from a low of $58 billion in 1932 to

$211.9 billion in 1945. This growth was primarily a result of wartime mobilization, but in the next twenty-five years the growth continued without the stimulus of all-out war, nearly doubling by 1960 to $503.7 billion and reaching the verge of $1 trillion by 1970. Between 1932 to 1970 America's per capita income rose almost tenfold, from $401 to $3,945. By 1970 the gap between living standards in the United States and the rest of the world had become a chasm: with 6 percent of the world's population, Americans produced and consumed two-thirds of the world's goods.

Some older Americans who remembered the Great Depression warned that the upward cycle that began in 1897 had come to disaster in 1929. Perhaps, they warned, the economic growth from 1945 to 1970 would end the same way. But the federal government now assumed the responsibility for managing or "fine-tuning" the economy during times of potential recession or depression. The timely manipulation of fiscal and monetary policies to stimulate economic growth in sluggish phases had proven successful on several occasions in the late 1940s and throughout the 1950s. And when President John Kennedy increased government spending and cut taxes in 1963, the "Eisenhower recession" ended and the economy took off on a growth spurt that lasted through the 1960s. Secretary of Labor W. Willard Wirtz later called it "the ultimate triumph of the spirit of John Maynard Keynes over the stubborn shade of Adam Smith."

But the incredible wealth generated by the postwar expansion was not filtering evenly throughout the society. True, the unrelenting growth of the economy improved the material well-being of all sectors of the society. This was what Kennedy meant when he observed that "a rising tide raises all boats." Nevertheless, in 1960 the top 5 percent of the population received about 20 percent of the wealth while the bottom 20 percent received only 5 percent. The American social structure was less like a pyramid than a diamond. The great mass of citizens, about half the population, were members of that amorphous American entity called "the middle class," which was the chief beneficiary of the postwar boom. In 1947 only 8.9 percent of American families had an annual income of $10,000 or more. By 1968, even after allowing for inflation, 36.9 percent were in that category. By 1970 there were five times as many Americans in college as in 1940; about four times as many Americans owned cars.

A major cause of the Great Depression had been a distribution of income so unbalanced in favor of the wealthy that levels of consumption were inadequate to keep the economy moving. The apparently insatiable appetite of middle-class Americans who came of age in the 1950s and 1960s virtually guaranteed that underconsumption would not afflict the economy. Moreover, income had become more evenly spread during and immediately after World War II. But between 1950 and 1970 the distribution of income changed hardly at all. During that time the people at the bottom of American society had their standard of living raised relative to the rest of the world, but their position relative to the middle class did not improve at all: the bottom 20 percent of the population continued to claim only 5 percent of the wealth throughout the administrations of Eisenhower, Kennedy, and Johnson. In 1968 an estimated 25 million Americans still lived below the "poverty line," even though another 14 million had moved above the line since Kennedy's election. Pockets of poverty, often in the central cities and in such rural areas as Appalachia, persisted despite national prosperity. And the increasingly gaudy affluence of middle-class life—"two cars in the garage, a television in each room, a kitchen full of modern appliances and a mind empty of inspiration" was how one cynic put it—presented poor Americans with a vision of the good life that kept receding into the middle distance.

The New Frontier

KENNEDY VS. NIXON   The presidential election of 1960 pitted two candidates who seemed to symbolize the unadventurous politics of the 1950s. Neither Richard M. Nixon nor John F. Kennedy seemed an embodiment of national purpose. Though better known than Kennedy because of his eight years as vice-president, famous for his debate with Soviet Premier Nikita Khrushchev in the exhibit of an American kitchen in Moscow, Nixon had also developed the reputation of a cunning chameleon, the "Tricky Dick" who concealed his duplicity behind a series of masks. "Nixon doesn't know who he is," Kennedy told an aide, "and so each time he makes a speech he has to decide which Nixon he is, and that will be very exhausting."

Kennedy himself seemed equally calculating. Despite an abundance of assets, including a record of heroism in the Pacific, an attractive young wife, a Harvard education, a large and rich family, and an engaging wit, Kennedy's record in the Senate was undistinguished. Author of a Pulitzer Prize–winning study of political leaders who "made the tough decisions" entitled *Profiles in Courage* (1956), Kennedy, said the Washington pundits, had shown more profile than courage during the McCarthy years and had a weak record on civil rights. Eric Sevareid, a television commentator who covered the campaign, likened both candidates to the kind of banal young men he remembered prancing about fraternity rows in college "thinking the proper thoughts, cultivating the proper people. I always sensed that they would end up running the big companies in town," said Sevareid, "but I'm damned if I ever thought one of them would end up running the country."

During his campaign for the Democratic nomination Kennedy had shown that he had the energy to match his ambition. As the first Catholic to run for the presidency since Al Smith, Kennedy realized that he had to dispel the impression that his religion was a major political liability. "If the nomination ever goes into a back room," he told a friend, "my name will never emerge." By the time of the Los Angeles convention in August he had traveled over 65,000 miles, visited 25 states, and made over 350 speeches. Hubert Humphrey, the liberal senator from Minnesota, was knocked out of the race in the West Virginia primary. Stuart Symington, the early favorite, conceded that Kennedy had shown "just a little more courage, stamina, wisdom and character than the rest of us." In his acceptance speech Kennedy found the rhetoric that would stamp the rest of his campaign and his presidency: "We stand today on the edge of a New Frontier—the frontier of unknown opportunities and perils—a frontier of unfulfilled hopes and threats."

Two events shaped the campaign that fall. First, in a speech before the Houston Ministerial Association on September 12, Kennedy confronted the question of his Catholicism directly. In America, he told the Protestant clergy, "the separation of church and state is absolute" and "no Catholic prelate would tell the President—should he be a Catholic—how to act and no Protestant minister should tell his parishioners for whom to vote." The religious question thereafter drew little public attention; Kennedy had neutralized it. Second, Nixon violated one of the cardinal rules of politics when he agreed to debate his less known opponent on television. In the first of four debates a national audience of 70 million saw Nixon, still weak from a recent illness, looking haggard and uneasy before the camera. Kennedy, on the other hand, displayed a poise that made him seem equal, if not superior, in his fitness for the office. Kennedy immediately shot up in the polls and was never headed. Reporters discovered that he had "charisma" and noted the bobby-soxers who greeted his arrival at campaign stops with what Theodore White called "the ups and downs of a thoroughly sexy oscillation." In the words of a bemused southern senator, Kennedy combined "the best qualities of Elvis Presley and Franklin D. Roosevelt."

The fourth debate, October 21, 1960. Kennedy's forthrightness impressed viewers and voters. [United Press International]

When the votes were counted Kennedy and his running-mate, Lyndon B. Johnson of Texas, had won the closest presidential election since 1888. Kennedy's winning margin was only 118,574 votes out of the 68 million cast. His wide margin in the electoral vote, 303 to 219, belied the paper-thin margin in several key states, especially Illinois, where Mayor Richard Daley's Democratic machine appeared to have lived up to its legendary campaign motto: "In Chicago we tell our people to vote early and to vote often." Nixon had in fact carried more states than Kennedy, sweeping most of the West, and holding four of the six southern states Eisenhower had carried in 1956. Kennedy's majority was built out of victories in southern New England, the populous Middle Atlantic states, and key states in the South where black voters had provided the crucial margin of victory.

THE NEW ADMINISTRATION Kennedy's cabinet appointments put an accent on youth and "Eastern Establishment" figures. Adlai Stevenson was favored by liberal democrats for secretary of state, but Kennedy chose Dean Rusk, a career diplomat who then headed the Rockefeller Foundation. Stevenson got the relatively minor post of ambassador to the United Nations. Robert S. McNamara, one of the "whiz kids" who had reorganized the Ford Motor Company with his "systems analysis" techniques, was asked to bring his managerial magic to bear on the Department of Defense. C. Douglas Dillon, a banker and a Republican, was made secretary of the treasury in an effort to assure conservative businessmen. When critics attacked the appointment of Kennedy's thirty-five-year-old brother Robert as attorney-general, the president quipped, "I don't see what's wrong with giving Bobby a little experience before he goes into law practice."

McGeorge Bundy, whom Kennedy called "the second smartest man I know," was made special assistant for national security affairs, lending additional credence to the impression that foreign policy would remain under tight White House control. John Kenneth Galbraith recommended Walter Heller, an outspoken advocate of Keynesian policies, as chairman of the Council of Economic Advisors. Theodore Sorenson, the former campaign head, became special counsel and chief speechwriter. House Speaker Rayburn expressed to Lyndon Johnson a wry "wish just one of them had run for sheriff once."

The inaugural ceremonies set the tone of elegance and youthful vigor that would come to be called the "Kennedy style." The bracing and glittering atmosphere of snow-clad Washington seemed to symbolize fresh promise. After Robert Frost paid tribute to the administration in verse, Kennedy dazzled listeners with epigrammatic eloquence that recalled the speeches of Lincoln and Jefferson. "Let the word go forth from this time and place," he proclaimed, "Let every nation know, whether it wishes us well or ill, that we shall pay any price, bear any burden, meet any hardship, support any friend, oppose any foe, to assure the survival and success of liberty. And so, my fellow Americans:

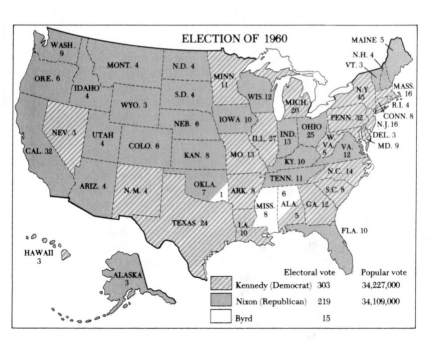

ELECTION OF 1960

	Electoral vote	Popular vote
Kennedy (Democrat)	303	34,227,000
Nixon (Republican)	219	34,109,000
Byrd	15	

Kennedy and wife Jacqueline at the inauguration, January 20, 1961. [Paul Schutzer, Life magazine, © 1961 Time Inc.]

ask not what your country can do for you—ask what you can do for your country." Spines tingled at the time; Kennedy, the journalist I. F. Stone wrote, was the first of all the presidents to be a Prince Charming. But years later, especially after the disastrous involvement in Vietnam, the speech would appear less a vibrant new message than a call to arms reminiscent of the anti-Communist tirades of John Foster Dulles.

THE KENNEDY RECORD   Historical evaluation of Kennedy's brief presidency, like reaction to his inaugural address, has oscillated widely in the past two decades between mindless celebration and bitter denunciation; it is only now beginning to settle into a more balanced assessment. It is clear, for example, that Kennedy's domestic record was mixed. Despite a few dramatic gestures of support toward civil rights leaders, he never grasped the significance of the most widespread reform movement of the decade. The Congress, although overwhelmingly Democratic, remained in the grip of a conservative coalition that blocked Kennedy's effort to increase federal aid to education, provide health insurance for the aged, and create a new Department of Urban Affairs to address the problems of the central cities. The Senate killed his initiatives in behalf of unemployed youth, migrant workers, and mass transit. When in January 1963 Kennedy finally came around to the advice of his Keynesian advisors and submitted a drastic tax cut of $13.6 billion, Congress blocked that as well. Four days before his death the *Congressional Quarterly* calculated that Kennedy had won acceptance for only one-third of his legislative program.

Administration proposals, nevertheless, did win some notable victories in Congress. Those involving defense and foreign policy generally won favor; indeed defense appropriations exceeded administration requests. On foreign aid there were some cuts, but Congress readily approved the proposals for a Development Loan Fund to help underdeveloped countries, broad "Alliance for Progress" programs to help Latin America, membership in the Organization for Economic Cooperation and Development (OECD) in which Canada and eighteen western European countries collaborated on improving world trade and helping underdeveloped nations, and the celebrated Peace Corps, created in March 1961 to supply volunteers for educational and technical services abroad. Kennedy's biggest legislative accomplishment in any field probably was the Trade Expansion Act of 1962, which after the "Kennedy Round" of negotiations in 1964–1967 eventually led to tariff cuts averaging 35 percent between the United States and the European Common Market.

In the field of domestic social legislation the administration did score a few legislative victories, most of them during this first year, 1961. They included a new Housing Act which afforded nearly $5 billion for urban renewal over four years, a raise in the minimum wage from $1 to $1.25 and its extension to more than 3 million additional workers, the Area Redevelopment Act of May 1961 which provided nearly $400 million in loans and grants to "distressed areas," an increase in Social Security benefits, and additional funds for sewage treatment plants. Kennedy also won support for an accelerated program to reach the moon before the end of the decade. Upon hearing that Kennedy wanted to beat the Russians there, Eisenhower shook his head: "Anybody who would spend $40 billion on a race to the moon for national prestige is nuts."

FOREIGN FRONTIERS

EARLY SETBACKS Kennedy's record in foreign affairs was also mixed, though more spectacularly so. He had made the existence of a "missile gap" a major part of his campaign. Upon taking office he discovered that there was no "missile gap"—the United States was far ahead of the Soviets in nuclear weaponry—but that there was an ongoing training exercise under the supervision of the CIA designed to prepare 1500 anti-Castro Cubans for an invasion of their homeland. The Joint Chiefs of Staff assured Kennedy that the plan was feasible; diplomatic advisors assured him that the invasion would inspire indigenous uprisings against Castro. In retrospect, it is clear that the scheme, poorly planned and poorly executed, had about as much chance of succeeding as John Brown's raid on Harper's Ferry a little over a century earlier. When the invasion force landed at the Bay of Pigs in Cuba on April 19, 1961, it was subdued in three days and 1,200 men were captured. Cyrus Sulzberger, the New York *Times* columnist, lamented that the United States "looked like fools to our friends, rascals to our enemies, and incompetents to the rest." It was hardly an auspicious way for the new president to demonstrate his mastery of foreign policy. "Victory has a thousand fathers," Kennedy said sadly, "but defeat is an orphan."

Two months after the Bay of Pigs debacle Kennedy met Russian Premier Khrushchev in Vienna, Austria. It was a tense confrontation during which Khrushchev threatend to limit Western access to Berlin, the divided city located deep within East Germany. Kennedy was shaken by the aggressive Soviet stand, but returned home determined to demonstrate American resolve. He called up reserve and national guard units and asked Congress for another $3.2 billion in defense funds. The Soviets responded by throwing up the Berlin Wall, begun with barbed wire on August 13, eventually solidified into a cinder-block barrier which cut off movement between East and West Berlin. Although no shooting incident triggered an accidental war, the Berlin Wall plugged the most accessible escape hatch for East Germans, showed Soviet willingness to challenge American resolve in Europe, and became another intractable barrier to the opening of new frontiers.

THE MISSILE CRISIS   A year later Khrushchev posed another challenge, this time not on the exposed periphery of American power but near its heart, ninety miles off the coast of Florida. Kennedy's unwillingness to commit the forces necessary to overthrow Castro and his acquiescence in the Berlin Wall seemed to signify a failure of will, and the Russians apparently reasoned that they could install missiles in Cuba with relative impunity. While such missiles would hardly alter the military balance, they would come from a direction not covered by radar systems and arrive too quickly for warning. More important to Kennedy's eyes was the psychological effect of American acquiescence to a Soviet presence on its doorstep. This might weaken the credibility of the American deterrent for Europeans and demoralize anti-Castro elements in Latin America. At the same time the installation of missiles served Khrushchev's purpose of demonstrating his toughness to both Chinese and Russian critics of his earlier advocacy of peaceful coexistence. But he misjudged the American response.

On October 14, 1962, American intelligence discovered from

photographs made on high-altitude U-2 flights that Russian missile sites were under construction in Cuba. From the beginning the administration was determined that they had to go; the only question was how. In a series of secret meetings the Executive Committee of the National Security Council narrowed the options down to a choice between a "surgical" air strike and a blockade of Cuba. The decision went for a blockade, which was carefully disguised by the euphemism "quarantine," since a blockade was technically an act of war. It offered the advantage of forcing the Soviets to shoot first, if it came to that, and leaving open the further options of stronger action. Monday, October 22, began one of the most anxious weeks in world history. On that day the president announced to members of Congress and then to the public the discovery of the missile sites in Cuba; he also announced the quarantine.

Tensions grew as Khrushchev blustered that Kennedy had pushed mankind "to the abyss of a world missile-nuclear war." Soviet ships, he declared, would ignore the quarantine. But on Wednesday, October 24, five Soviet ships, presumably with missiles aboard, stopped short of the quarantine line. Two days later an agent of the Russian embassy privately approached John Scali, a television newscaster, with a proposal for an agreement: Russia would withdraw the missiles in return for a public pledge by the United States not to invade Cuba. Secretary of State Rusk sent back word that the administration was interested, but told Scali: "Remember, when you report this, that eyeball to eyeball, they blinked first." The same evening Kennedy received two mes-

Russian missiles under construction at San Cristobal, Cuba, October 23, 1962. [U.S. Air Force]

sages from Khrushchev, the first repeating the offer reported by Scali, the second demanding removal of American missiles from Turkey. The two messages probably reflected divided counsels in the Kremlin. Ironically, Kennedy had already ordered removal of the outmoded missiles in Turkey, but he refused now to act under the gun. Instead he followed Robert Kennedy's suggestion that he respond favorably to the first letter and ignore the second. On Sunday, October 28, Khrushchev agreed to remove the missiles and added a conciliatory invitation: "We should like to continue the exchange of views on the prohibition of atomic and thermonuclear weapons, general disarmament, and other problems relating to the relaxation of international tension."

In the aftermath, the level of tension between the United States and Russia was quickly lowered. Kennedy, aware that Khrushchev had problems with his own hawks in the Kremlin, cautioned his associates against any gloating over the favorable settlement and began to explore in correspondence the opening provided by the premier's invitation. Several symbolic steps were taken to relax tensions: an agreement to sell Russia surplus wheat, the installation of a "hot line" between Washington and Moscow to provide instant contact between the heads of government, and the removal of obsolete missiles from Turkey, Italy, and Britain. On June 10, 1963, the president announced in a speech at American University that discussions with the Soviets would soon begin, and called upon the nation to reexamine its attitude toward peace, the Soviet Union, and the Cold War. In Moscow, Averell Harriman negotiated a treaty with Russian and British representatives to stop nuclear testing in the atmosphere. The treaty, ratified in September 1963, did not provide for on-site inspection nor did it ban underground testing, which continued, but it promised to end the dangerous pollution of the atmosphere with radioactivity. The treaty was an important symbolic and substantive move toward détente. As Kennedy put it: "A journey of a thousand miles begins with one step." Unfortunately it was a small step, and one that not everybody chose to take. Neither France nor China, which now had atomic capabilities, agreed to go along.

KENNEDY AND VIETNAM   In Southeast Asia events were moving toward what would become within a decade the greatest American foreign policy debacle of the century. During John Kennedy's "thousand days" in office the turmoil of Indochina never preoccupied the public mind for any extended period, but it dominated international diplomatic debates from the time the administration entered office. The landlocked kingdom of Laos, along with Cambodia, had been declared neutral in the Geneva Accords of 1954, but had fallen into a complex struggle for power between the Communist Pathet Lao and the Royal Laotian Army. There matters stood when Eisenhower left office and told Kennedy: "You might have to go in there and fight it out." Adm. Arleigh Burke, chairman of the Joint Chiefs of Staff, argued in favor of a stand against the Pathet Lao, even at the cost of direct intervention. After a lengthy consideration of alternatives, Washington decided to favor a neutralist coalition which would preclude American military involvement in Laos, yet prevent a Pathet Lao victory. The Soviets, who were extending aid to the Pathet Lao, indicated a readiness to negotiate, and in May talks began in Geneva with the veteran diplomat Averell Harriman leading the American delegation. After more than a year of tangled negotiations the three factions in Laos agreed to a neutral coalition. American and Russian aid to the opposing parties was supposed to end, but both countries kept up covert operations, while North Vietnam kept open the Ho Chi Minh trail through eastern Laos, over which it supplied its Vietcong allies in South Vietnam.

There things kept getting worse under the leadership of Premier Ngo Dinh Diem, despite encouraging reports from Gen. Paul Harkins, the military commander of American "advisors" in South Vietnam. At the time the problem was less the scattered guerrilla attacks than Diem's failure to deliver social and economic reforms and his inability to rally popular support. His repressive tactics, directed not only against Communists but also against Buddhists and other critics, played into the hands of his enemies. In 1961 White House assistant Walt Rostow and Gen. Maxwell Taylor became the first in a long train of presidential emissaries to South Vietnam's capital, Saigon. Focusing on the military situation, they proposed a major increase in the American military presence. Kennedy refused, but continud to dispatch more "advisors" in the hope of stabilizing the situation: when he took office there had been 2,000; by the end of 1963 there were 16,000, none of whom had been committed to battle.

By 1963 sharply divergent reports were coming in from the country. Military advisors, their eyes on the inflated "kill ratios" reported by the Army of the Republic of Vietnam (ARVN), drew optimistic conclusions of progress. Political reporters like David Halberstam of the New York *Times*, watching the reactions of the Vietnamese people, foresaw continued deterioration without the promised political and economic reforms. By mid-year growing Buddhist demonstrations made the discontent more plainly visible. The spectacle of Buddhist monks immolating themselves in protest brought from Diem's sister-in-law only sarcasm about "barbecued monks." By the fall of 1963 the administration had decided that Diem was a lost cause. When dissident generals proposed a coup d'état, American ambassador Henry Cabot Lodge assured them that Washington would not stand in the way. On November 1 they seized the government and murdered Diem, though without American approval. But the generals provided no more stability than earlier regimes, as successive coups set the country spinning from one military leader to the other.

KENNEDY'S ASSASSINATION Kennedy seemed to be facing up to the intractability of the situation in Vietnam by the fall of 1963. In September he declared of the South Vietnamese: "In the final analysis it's their war. They're the ones who have to win it or lose it. We can help them as advisors but they have to win it." And the following month he had McNamara and Taylor announce the administration's intention to withdraw United States' forces from South Vietnam by the end of 1965. What Kennedy would have done has remained a matter of endless controversy among historians, endless because it is unanswerable and unanswerable because on November 22, 1963, while visiting Dallas, he was shot in the neck and head by Lee Harvey Oswald, whose motives remain unknown, and died almost immediately. Kennedy's death, then the murder of Oswald by Jack Ruby, a Dallas nightclub owner, were shown over and over again on televison, the medium that had so helped Kennedy's rise to the presidency and that now captured his death and the moving funeral at Arlington Cemetery, thereby assuring his enshrinement in the public imagination as a martyred leader. Shortly afterward Jacquelyn Kennedy reminisced for a reporter. At night they would play records, and the song he loved most came from a current Broadway hit *Camelot*, based on the legends of King Arthur: "'Don't let it be forgot, that once there was a spot, for one brief shining moment, that was known as Camelot'—and it will never be that way again." A Gallup poll in 1976 showed that a majority of Americans regarded Kennedy as the greatest of all American presidents.

Lyndon Johnson and the Great Society

Lyndon Johnson took the oath as president of the United States on board the plane that took John Kennedy's body back to Washington. At age fifty-five he had spent twenty-six years on the Washington scene and had served nearly a decade as Demo-

Kennedy's vice-president, Lyndon B. Johnson, takes the presidential oath as Air Force One *returns from Dallas with Jacqueline Kennedy (right), the presidential party, and the body of the assassinated president. [Wide World Photos]*

cratic leader in the Senate, where he had displayed the greatest gift for compromise since Henry Clay. Johnson brought to the White House a change of style as sharp as that which had come with Kennedy. The first southern president since Woodrow Wilson, he harbored always, like another southern president, Andrew Johnson, a sense of being the perpetual "outsider" despite his long experience with power. And indeed he was so regarded by "insiders" who, charmed by Kennedy's Boston Irish accent, could never warm to the man who, a probably fictional lady in Texas was supposed to have said, spoke without an accent.

Those who viewed Johnson as a stereotypical southern conservative reckoned without his long-standing admiration for Franklin Roosevelt, the depth of his concern for humble people, and his commitment to the cause of civil rights. "By political background, by temperament, by personal preference," wrote the journalist Philip Geyelin, Johnson was "the riverboat man. He was brawny and rough and skilled beyond measure in the full use of tricky tides and currents, in his knowledge of the hidden shoals. He was a swashbuckling master of the political midstreams—but only in the crowded, well-traveled and familiar inland waterways of domestic politics." In foreign affairs he was, like Wilson, a novice.

POLITICS AND POLICY   Quite naturally, domestic politics became his first priority. Johnson exploited the national grief after the assassination by declaring that Kennedy's cabinet and advisors would stay on and that his legislative program, stymied in several congressional committees, would be passed. Given to ceaseless work, fourteen hours or more a day, Johnson loved the kind of political infighting and legislative detail that Kennedy loathed. "Not a sparrow falls," reported one aide, "that he doesn't know about." Recalcitrant congressmen and senators were brought to the White House for what became famous as "the Johnson Treatment." The columnists Rowland Evans, Jr., and Robert D. Novak described the experience: "He moved in close, his face a scant millimeter from his target, his eyes widening and narrowing, his eyebrows rising and falling. From his pockets poured clippings, memos, statistics. Mimicry, humor, and the genius of analogy made the Treatment an almost hypnotic experience and rendered the target stunned and helpless." The logjam in the Congress that had blocked Kennedy's program broke under Johnson's forceful leadership and a torrent of legislation poured through. Virtually the entire agenda of twentieth-century liberalism would be enacted.

Before the year 1963 was out Congress finished action on the pending foreign aid bill and a plan to sell wheat to the Soviet Union. But America's commitment to foreign aid pointed up its own people's needs. In January 1964 the Council of Economic Advisors reported that 9.3 million American families, about 20 percent of the population, was below the "poverty line" of $3,000 per year for a family of four. "Unfortunately, many Americans live on the outskirts of hope," Johnson told the Congress in his first State of the Union message on January 8, 1964, "some because of their poverty and some because of their color, and all too many because of both." At the top of his agenda he put the stalled measures for tax reduction and civil rights, then added to his "must" list a bold new idea which bore the LBJ brand: "This Administration today, here and now, declares unconditional war on poverty in America." The particulars were to come later, the product of an administration task force already at work before Johnson took office.

To get the tax cut, Johnson emphasized fiscal responsibility. Advisors told him that a budget of $108 billion could be defended, but the budget had never before exceeded $100 billion, and Johnson pressed to keep it below that level, dramatizing his determination by the gesture of turning off unneeded lights in the White House. The budget submitted in January was a surprisingly low $97.9 billion, a figure which reduced the projected deficit by one-half. With congressional conservatives like Sen. Harry F. Byrd mollified, the tax reduction of more than $10 billion passed in February, and the increasing purchasing power thus generated started one of the longest sustained booms in American history.

The administration's task force on poverty had its Economic Opportunity Bill ready to submit in March. The bill was an omnibus measure that incorporated a wide range of programs: a Job Corps for youths aged sixteen to twenty-one, job-training programs, work-study projects for students, grants to farmers and rural business, loans to those willing to hire the hard-core unemployed, the Volunteers in Service to America (VISTA, a "domestic Peace Corps"), and the Community Action Program, which would provide "maximum feasible participation" of the poor in directing programs designed for their benefit. Speaking at Ann Arbor, Michigan, in May 1964, Johnson called for a "Great Society" resting on "abundance and liberty for all. The Great Society demands an end to poverty and racial injustice, to which we are fully committed in our time." It was liberalism triumphant.

THE 1964 ELECTION   In the Republican party, on the other hand, a new frenzy of activity was developing on the right. For years the conviction had grown within the party that it had fallen into the hands of an eastern establishment that had given in to the same internationalism and big-government policies as liberal Democrats. Ever since 1940, so the theory went, the party had nominated "me-too" candidates who merely promised to run more efficiently the programs that Democrats promoted. Offer the voters "a choice, not an echo," they reasoned, and a conservative majority would assert itself. Left leaderless by the death of Robert Taft in 1953, the Republican Right began to drift toward varieties of dogmatic conservatism, ranging from a kind of "aristocratic" intellectual "new conservatism" which found voice in the *National Review,* edited by William F. Buckley, Jr., to the John Birch Society, founded by Robert Welch, a New England candy manufacturer given to accusing such distinguished citizens as Eisenhower, Dulles, Chief Justice Warren, and Gen. George Marshall of supporting a Communist conspiracy.

By 1960 Arizona's Sen. Barry Goldwater had begun to emerge as the leader of the Republican Right. In his book *The Conscience of a Conservative* (1960), Goldwater proposed abolition of the income tax, sale of the TVA, and a drastic overhaul of Social Security. Almost from the time of Kennedy's victory in 1960 a movement to draft Goldwater got under way, mobilizing right-wing activists to capture party caucuses and contest primaries. In 1964 they took an early lead before party regulars knew what was happening. Goldwater's chief opponent, Nelson Rockefeller, then governor of New York, stigmatized by a recent divorce and remarriage, never caught up. Goldwater swept the all-important California primary and his forces controlled the Republican convention when it gathered in Los Angeles. Johnson, the incumbent, was conceded the Democratic nomination from the start, and after rebuffing a move to make Robert F. Kennedy his running mate, chose Hubert H. Humphrey of Minnesota, a prominent liberal senator who had led the civil rights forces of the 1948 convention, and a man whose reputation far outshone that of his Republican counterpart, William E. Miller, an obscure congressman from upstate New York.

By the end of the campaign Goldwater had achieved a position of splendid isolation on the far right of the political spectrum. He had an unusual gift for frightening voters. Accusing the administration of waging a "no-win" war in Vietnam, he urged wholesale bombing of North Vietnam and left the impression of being trigger-happy. In Tennessee he urged the sale of TVA; in St. Petersburg, Florida, a major retirement community, he questioned Social Security. He had voted against both the nuclear test ban and the Civil Rights Act, the latter on constitutional principle. Although that principle was not segregation, he was not without reason identified with the segregationist forces. During the campaign Sen. J. Strom Thurmond, the greatest Dixiecrat (conservative southern Democrat) of them all, announced his conversion to the "Goldwater Republican Party."

Johnson appealed to the great consensus that spanned most of the political spectrum. He responded to Goldwater's bellicose rhetoric on Vietnam with a pledge that won great applause at the time and much comment later: "We are not about to send American boys nine or ten thousand miles from home to do what Asian boys ought to be doing for themselves"—a statement reminiscent of the assurance which Johnson's idol, Franklin Roosevelt, voiced regarding the European war in 1940. Much of the campaign could be summed up in the Goldwater slogan "In your heart you know he's right," and the Democratic riposte "In your heart you know he might."

The result was a landslide. Johnson polled 61 percent of the total votes; Goldwater carried only Arizona and five states in the Deep South, where race remained the salient issue. Vermont went Democratic for the first time ever in a presidential election. Johnson won the electoral vote by a whopping 482 to 52. In the Senate the Democrats increased their majority by two (68 to 32) and in the House by thirty-seven (295 to 140). The columnist

Walter Lippman noted: "The returns prove the falsity of the claim . . . that there is a great, silent majority of 'conservative' Republicans who will emerge as the Republican party turns its back on 'me-tooism' and offers them a 'choice.' The Johnson majority is indisputable proof that the votes are in the center." Even so, LBJ was aware that a mandate such as he had received could quickly erode. He told aides, "every day I'm in office, I'm going to lose votes. I'm going to alienate somebody. . . . We've got to get this legislation fast. You've got to get it during my honeymoon."

LANDMARK LEGISLATION A flood of Great Society legislation poured through the Eighty-ninth Congress at a pace unseen since Franklin Roosevelt's Hundred Days. Priority went to health insurance and aid to education, proposals that had languished since President Truman advanced them in 1945. For twenty years the proposal for a comprehensive plan of medical insurance had been stalled by the American Medical Association. But now that Johnson had the votes, the AMA joined Republicans in boarding the bandwagon for a bill serving those over age sixty-five. The AMA proposed, in addition to hospital insurance, a program for payment of doctor bills and drug costs with the government footing half the premium. The act that finally emerged went well beyond the original program. Rep. Wilbur Mills's Ways and Means Committee not only incorporated the new proposal into the Medicare program for the aged, but added another program, dubbed Medicaid, for federal grants to states that would help cover medical payments for the indigent. President Johnson signed the bill on July 30 in Independence, Missouri, with eighty-one-year-old Harry Truman looking on.

Five days after he submitted his Medicare program, Johnson sent to Congress his proposal for $1.5 billion in federal aid to elementary and secondary education. Such proposals had been ignored since the 1940s, blocked alternately by issues of segregation or separation of church and state. The first had been laid to rest, legally at least, by the Civil Rights Act of 1964. Now Oregon's Sen. Wayne Morse and Secretary of Health, Education and Welfare Wilbur Cohen devised a means of extending aid to "poverty-impacted" school districts regardless of their public or parochial character. This measure Johnson signed in the dilapidated one-room schoolhouse he had first attended, with his first-grade teacher looking on.

The momentum generated by the progress of these measures had already begun to carry others along, and the momentum continued through the following year. Before the Eighty-ninth Congress adjourned, it had established a record in the passage of landmark legislation unequaled since the time of the New Deal. Altogether the tide of Great Society legislation had carried 435 bills through the Congress. Among them was the Appalachian Regional Development Act of 1966, which provided $1.1 billion for programs in remote mountain coves. The Housing and Urban Development Act of 1965 provided aid for construction of 240,000 units of housing and $2.9 billion for urban renewal. Funds for rent supplements for low-income families followed in 1966, and in that year a new Department of Housing and Urban Development appeared, headed by Robert C. Weaver, the first black cabinet member. Johnson had, in the words of one Washington reporter, "brought to harvest a generation's backlog of ideas and social legislation."

FROM CIVIL RIGHTS TO BLACK POWER

THE CIVIL RIGHTS MOVEMENT   Part of the harvest was the legislation which provided the legal capstone to the Second Reconstruction. But an explanation of the civil rights movement that focused on the corridors of Congress would be something like an explanation of a hurricane that focused on the Weather Bureau. Federal legislation, and the presidential leadership provided by both Kennedy and Johnson, lagged behind the grass-roots reform movement that had begun in the South when Rosa Parks refused to move to the rear of the bus in 1955, triggering the Montgomery, Alabama, bus boycott which catapulted Martin Luther King into prominence. King's philosophy of "militant nonviolence" inspired thousands to challenge Jim Crow practices with direct action. At the same time lawsuits to desegregate the schools had activated thousands of parents and young people. The momentum built up to the first genuine mass movement in the history of black Americans when the four black students sat down and demanded service at Woolworth's lunch counter in Greensboro, North Carolina, on February 1, 1960. Within a week the "sit-in" movement had spread to six more towns in the state, and within a month to towns in six more states. In April 1960 the student participants, black and white, formed the Student Nonviolent Coordinating Committee (SNCC), which worked with King's Southern Christian Leadership Conference (SCLC) to spread the movement. The "sit-ins" at restaurants became "kneel-ins" at churches and "wade-ins" at pools, and everywhere the protestors refused to retaliate, even when struck with clubs or burned with lighted cigarettes. The editor of the conservative Richmond *News Leader* conceded admiration for their courage:

> Here were the colored students, in coats, white shirts, ties, and one of them was reading Goethe, and one was taking notes from a biology text. And here, on the sidewalk, outside, was a gang of white boys come to heckle, a ragtail rabble, slack-jawed, black-jacketed, grinning fit to kill, and some of them, God save the mark, were waving the proud and honored flag of the Southern States in the last war fought by gentlemen.

In May of 1961 the Congress of Racial Equality (CORE) sent a group of black and white "freedom riders" on buses to test both a Supreme Court decision, *Morgan v. Virginia* (1946), which had prohibited discrimination against interstate travelers, and an order of the Interstate Commerce Commission which had banned segregation on buses and trains and in terminals since 1955. First in Anniston, Alabama, and then in Birmingham and Montgomery mobs assaulted the travelers and burned one of the buses.

Then in 1962 Gov. Ross Barnett of Mississippi defied a court order and refused to allow James H. Meredith to enroll at the University of Mississippi. Federal marshalls entered the campus to enforce the law. They lined up around Lyceum Hall, the administration building, only to be assaulted by a mob which grew more violent as night fell. Ironically, the protesters were urged on by Edwin Walker, a retired general who had commanded the federal troops at Little Rock's Central High in 1957. Once again federal troops had to break up a mob, but only after two deaths and many injuries. Meredith was registered at "Ole Miss" the next morning.

In April of 1963 King launched a series of nonviolent demonstrations in Birmingham, where Police Commissioner Eugene "Bull" Connor proved the perfect foil for King's tactics. Connor used attack dogs, tear gas, electric cattle prods, and fire hoses on the protesters while millions of outraged Americans watched the confrontation on television. Martin Luther King, who was arrested and jailed during the demonstrations, wrote his "Letter from the Birmingham Jail," a defense of his nonviolent strategy that became a classic of the civil rights movement. That fall Gov. George Wallace stood in the doorway of a building at the University of Alabama to block the enrollment of several black students but stepped aside in the face of the National Guard. That night President Kennedy spoke eloquently of the moral issue facing the nation: "If an American, because his skin is black, cannot enjoy the full and free life which all of us want, then who among us would be content to have the color of his skin changed and stand in his place? Who among us would be content with the counsels of patience and delay?" Later the same night NAACP official Medgar Evers was shot to death as he returned home in Jackson, Mississippi.

The high point of the phase of the civil rights movement that had begun with the Montgomery bus boycott, a movement with integration as its goal and nonviolent confrontation as its strategy, was reached on August 28, 1963, when over 200,000 blacks and whites marched down the Mall in Washington, D.C., toward the Lincoln Memorial singing "We Shall Overcome." The March on Washington was the largest civil rights demonstration in American history. Standing in front of Lincoln's statue, King delivered one of the memorable public speeches of the century: "Even though we face the difficulties of today and tomorrow, I still have a dream. It is a dream chiefly rooted in the American dream . . . one day . . . the sons of former slaves and the sons of former slave-owners will be able to sit together at the table of brotherhood." That the time had not yet arrived, however, became clear a little over two weeks later when a bomb exploded in a Birmingham church killing four black girls who had arrived early for Sunday school.

The widespread demonstrations across the South became a series of local defeats that eventually inspired a national triumph. The intransigence and violence that civil rights workers encountered won converts to their cause all across the country. President Kennedy endorsed a pending omnibus civil rights bill

Martin Luther King, Jr. (second from right), and other prominent civil rights leaders at the head of the March on Washington for Jobs and Freedom, August 28, 1963. [National Archives]

during the Birmingham demonstrations. After Kennedy's death President Johnson, who had maneuvered through the Senate the Civil Rights Acts of 1957 and 1960, called for passage of the pending bill as a memorial to the fallen leader. With bipartisan support he weakened the grip of the House Rules Committee and finally broke the Senate filibuster which was mounted by a diminishing band of bitter-enders. "Nothing," said Republican Senate leader Everett Dirksen, quoting the French writer Victor Hugo, "is so powerful as an idea whose time has come." On July 2 Johnson signed the Civil Rights Act of 1964, the most far-reaching civil rights measure ever enacted by the Congress. The act outlawed discrimination in hotels, restaurants, and other public accommodations. It required that literacy tests for voting be administered in writing, and defined as literate anybody who had finished the sixth grade. The attorney-general could now bring suits for school desegregation, relieving parents of a painful necessity. Federally assisted programs and private employers alike were required to eliminate discrimination. An Equal Employment Opportunity Commission (the old Fair Employment Practices Committee reborn) administered a ban on job discrimination by race, religion, national origin, or sex.

Early in 1965 King announced a drive to register the 3 million blacks in the South who had not registered to vote. In Selma, Alabama, the focus at the outset, he found in Sheriff Jim Clark a foil as perfect as Birmingham's police chief. On March 7 civil rights protesters began a march to Montgomery, only to be met and violently dispersed by state troopers and a mounted posse at the Edmund Pettus Bridge across the Alabama River. A federal judge, Frank M. Johnson, Jr., agreed to allow the march, and President Johnson provided protection with National Guardsmen and army military police. By March 25, when the demonstrators reached Montgomery, some 35,000 people were with them, and King addressed them from the steps of the state capitol. That night snipers shot and killed a white woman from Detroit who was driving a marcher home. Several days before the march President Johnson went before Congress with a moving plea which reached its climax when he slowly intoned the words of the movement hymn: "And we shall overcome." The resulting Voting Rights Act of 1965, passed to ensure all the right to vote, rejected the old case-by-case procedures and authorized the attorney-general to dispatch federal examiners to register voters. In states or counties where fewer than half the adults had voted in 1964, the act suspended literacy tests and other devices commonly used to defraud citizens of the vote. By the end of the year some 250,000 blacks were newly registered.

"BLACK POWER"   A new phase in the civil rights movement began on August 11, 1965, less than a week after the passage of the Voting Rights Act. The Watts area of Los Angeles exploded in a frenzy of black riots and looting. When the uprising ended, there were thirty-four dead, almost 4,000 rioters in jail, and property damage exceeding $35 million. Liberal commentators were both stunned and surprised, since the riots occurred in the wake of the greatest legislative victories for black Americans since the first Reconstruction. Moreover, Watts was not an outrageous slum. The national Urban League in fact had rated Los Angeles as the most prosperous and desirable city for black urban residents in the United States. But events did not stand still to await white liberal comprehension. Chicago and Cleveland, along with forty other American cities, had racial riots in the summer of 1966. The following summer Newark and Detroit burst into flames. Detroit provided the most graphic example of urban violence, as tanks rolled through the streets and soldiers from the 101st Airborne used machine guns to deal with snipers in the tenements. *Pravda,* the official Soviet newspaper, ran the story with accompanying pictures of the carnage on its front page. Firemen who tried to put out the flames in several of the urban riots were showered by bricks and bottles thrown by the very people whose houses were burning.

In retrospect, it was predictable that the civil rights movement would focus on the plight of urban blacks. By the middle 1960s about 70 percent of the black population lived in metropolitan areas, most of them in central-city ghettos that had been bypassed by the postwar prosperity. And again it seems clear, in retrospect, that the nonviolent tactics which had worked in the rural South would not work in the northern cities, where the

Detroit's black ghetto exploded in rioting on Sunday, July 23, 1967. [Wide World Photos]

problems were de facto segregation resulting from residential patterns, not de jure segregation amenable to changes in law, and where white ethnic groups did not have the cultural heritage which southern whites shared with blacks. "It may be," wrote a contributor to *Esquire,* "that looting, rioting and burning . . . are really nothing more than radical forms of urban renewal, a response not only to the frustrations of the ghetto but to the collapse of all ordinary modes of change, as if a body despairing of the indifference of doctors sought to rip a cancer out of itself." A special Commission on Civil Disorders headed by Gov. Otto Kerner of Illinois noted that, unlike earlier race riots, the urban upheavals of the middle 1960s were initiated by blacks themselves; earlier riots had been started by whites, which had then provoked black counterattacks. Now blacks visited violence and destruction on themselves in an effort to destroy what they could not stomach and what civil rights legislation seemed unable to change.

By 1966 "Black Power" had become the new rallying cry. Radical members of SNCC had become estranged from Martin Luther King's theories of militant nonviolence. As King became the center of attention from the white media, SNCC members began to refer to him cynically as "de Lawd." When Stokely Carmichael, a twenty-five-year-old graduate of Howard University, became head of SNCC in May 1966, the separatist philosophy of black power became official and whites were ousted from the organization. "We reject an American dream defined by white people and must work to construct an American reality defined by Afro-Americans," said a SNCC position paper. H. Rap Brown, who succeeded Carmichael as head of SNCC in 1967, even urged blacks to "get you some guns" and "kill the honkies." Meanwhile Carmichael had moved on to the Black Panther party, a self-professed group of urban revolutionaries founded in Oakland, California, in 1966 and headed by Huey P. Newton and Eldridge Cleaver. Under their leadership the Black Panthers echoed the separatist demands of Marcus Garvey, terrified the public by wearing bandeleros and carrying rifles, but eventually fragmented in spasms of violence.

Perhaps the most articulate spokesman for black power was one of the earliest, Malcolm X (formerly Malcolm Little, with the "X" denoting his lost African surname). Malcolm had risen from a ghetto childhood of narcotics and crime to become the chief disciple of Elijah Muhammad, the Black Muslim prophet who rejected Christianity as "the religion of white devils." "Yes, I'm an extremist," Malcolm acknowledged in 1964. "The black race in the United States is in extremely bad shape. You show me a black man who isn't an extremist and I'll show you one who needs psychiatric attention." By 1964 Malcolm had broken with Elijah Muhammad and founded his own organization, which was committed to the establishment of alliances between the blacks of the United States and the nonwhite peoples of the world. But just after the publication of his *Autobiography* in 1965, Malcolm was gunned down in the Audubon Ballroom in Harlem by Black Muslim assassins. With him went the most effective voice for urban black militancy since Marcus Garvey.

Black power was a slogan more than a philosophy. The conclusion of the Kerner Commission on Civil Disorders was harsh but accurate: "Black Power rhetoric and ideology actually expresses a lack of power. . . . Powerless to make any fundamental changes in the life of the masses . . . many advocates of Black Power have retreated into an unreal world, where they see an outnumbered and poverty-stricken minority organizing itself independently of whites and creating sufficient power to force white Americans to grant its demands." But if Lyndon Johnson's Great Society encountered harsh realities in American cities, it was running into even harsher realities in the Vietnamese countryside.

THE TRAGEDY OF VIETNAM

DIMENSIONS OF A WAR At the time of President Kennedy's death there were 16,000 American troops in Vietnam. Johnson inherited a commitment to prevent a Communist takeover in South Vietnam along with a reluctance to assume the military burden for fighting the war. One president after another did just enough to stall off the prospect of being charged with having "lost" Vietnam. Such an outcry, Johnson feared, would undermine his influence and endanger his Great Society programs in Congress. Therefore he found himself drawn inexorably deeper into intervention in Asia. During the presidential campaign of 1964 Johnson had opposed the use of American combat troops and had privately described Vietnam as "a raggedy-ass fourth-rate country" not worthy of American blood and treasure. Nevertheless, by the end of 1965 there were 184,000 American troops in Vietnam; in 1966 the troop level reached 385,000; and by 1969, the height of the American presence, 542,000. By the time the last American troops left in March 1973, 51,000 Americans had died in combat and another 270,000 had been wounded. The war had cost the American taxpayers $150 billion, generated economic dislocations that destroyed many

Great Society programs, produced 570,000 draft offenders and 563,000 less-than-honorable discharges from the service, toppled Johnson's administration, and divided the country as no event in American history had since the Civil War.

ESCALATION   The official sanction for "escalation"—a Defense Department term coined in the Vietnam era—was the Tonkin Gulf Resolution, voted by Congress on August 7, 1964. Johnson told a national television audience that two American destroyers, the U.S.S. *Maddox* and *C. Turner Joy*, had been attacked by North Vietnamese vessels on August 2 and 4 in the Gulf of Tonkin off the coast of North Vietnam. Although Johnson described the attack as unprovoked, in truth the destroyers had been monitoring South Vietnamese attacks against two North Vietnamese islands—attacks planned by American advisors. The Tonkin Gulf Resolution authorized the president to "take all necessary measures to repel any armed attack against the forces of the United States and to prevent further aggression." Only Sen. Wayne Morse of Oregon and Sen. Ernest Gruening of Alaska voted against the resolution, which Johnson thereafter interpreted as equivalent to a congressional declaration of war.

Soon after Johnson's landslide victory over Goldwater in 1964, the crucial decisions that shaped American policy in Vietnam for the next four years were made. On February 5 Vietcong guerrillas killed 8 and wounded 126 Americans at Pleiku. Further attacks on Americans later that week led Johnson to order operation "Rolling Thunder," the first sustained bombings of North Vietnam, which were intended to stop the flow of soldiers and supplies into the south. Six months later a task force headed by Adam Yarmolinsky, a former Pentagon planner in the Kennedy years, conducted an extensive study of the bombing's effects on the supplies pouring down the "Ho Chi Minh Trail" from North Vietnam through Laos. Yarmolinsky concluded that there was "no way" to stop the traffic.

In March 1965 the new American army commander in Vietnam, Gen. William C. Westmoreland, requested and got the first installment of combat troops, who waded ashore at Da Nang. By the summer American troops were engaged in "search and destroy" operations, thus ending the fiction that American soldiers were only "advisors." And as combat operations increased, so did the mounting list of American casualties, announced each week on the nightly news along with the "body count" of alleged Viet Cong dead. "Westy's War," although fought with helicopter gunships, chemical defoliants, and napalm, became like the trench warfare of World War I—a war of attrition.

THE CONTEXT FOR POLICY Johnson's decision to "Americanize" the war, so ill-starred in retrospect, was consistent with the foreign policy principles pursued by all American presidents after World War II. The version of the containment theory articulated in the Truman Doctrine, endorsed by Eisenhower and Dulles throughout the 1950s, and reaffirmed by Kennedy, pledged United States opposition to the advance of communism anywhere in the world. "Why are we in Vietnam?" Johnson asked rhetorically at Johns Hopkins University in 1965. "We are there because we have a promise to keep. . . . To leave Vietnam to its fate would shake the confidence of all these people in the value of American commitment." Secretary of State Dean Rusk repeated this rationale before countless congressional committees, warning that Thailand, Burma, and the rest of Southeast Asia would fall to communism if American forces withdrew. American military intervention in Vietnam was not an aberration, but a logical culmination of the assumptions widely shared by the foreign policy establishment and leaders of both political parties since the early days of the Cold War.

If Vietnam was not an aberration, *The Pentagon Papers* subsequently made clear that the United States did not "stumble into a quagmire." Undersecretary of State George Ball consistently warned of disaster: "Once on the tiger's back we cannot be sure of picking the place to dismount." Or as Maxwell Taylor, ambassador to South Vietnam during the crucial 1964–1965 period, put it: "Once we brought troops in, it was the nose of the camel." It was also clear to Johnson and his advisors from the start that American military involvement could not reach levels that would provoke the Chinese or Soviets into direct intervention. And this meant, in effect, that military victory in any traditional sense of the term was never possible. "It was startling to me to find out," said the new secretary of defense Clark Clifford in 1968, "that we had no military plan to end the war." The goal of the United States was not to win the war, but to prevent the North Vietnamese and Viet Cong from winning. This meant that America would have to maintain a military presence as long as the enemy retained the will to fight.

As it turned out, American support for the war eroded faster than the will of the North Vietnamese leaders to tolerate casualties. Opposition to the war on college campuses began in 1965 with "teach-ins" at the University of Michigan. And in January 1966 Sen. J. William Fulbright of Arkansas, chairman of the Senate Foreign Relations Committee, began congressional investigations into American policy. George Kennan, the founding father of the containment doctrine, told Fulbright's committee that the doctrine was appropriate for Europe, but not Southeast Asia. Gen. James Gavin testified that Westmoreland's military strategy had no chance of achieving victory. By 1967 opposition to the war had become so pronounced that antiwar demonstrations in New York and at the Pentagon attracted massive support. Nightly television accounts of the fighting—Vietnam was the first war to receive extended television coverage—stripped the war of any nobility and made official optimism appear fatuous. By May 1967 even Secretary of Defense McNamara was wavering: "The picture of the world's greatest superpower killing or injuring 1000 noncombatants a week, while trying to pound a tiny backward nation into submission on an issue whose merits are hotly disputed, is not a pretty one."

VIETNAM, 1966

□ Major U.S. bases

0 ——— 200 Miles

0 ——— 200 Kilometers

THE TURNING POINT   On January 31, 1968, the first day of the Vietnamese New Year (Tet), the Viet Cong defied a holiday truce to launch assaults on American and South Vietnamese forces throughout South Vietnam. The city of Hue fell to the Communists and Viet Cong units temporarily occupied the grounds of the American embassy in Saigon. General Westmoreland proclaimed the Tet offensive a major defeat for the Viet Cong, and most students of military strategy later agreed with him. But while Viet Cong casualties were enormous, the impact of the events on the American public were more telling. *Time* and *Newsweek* soon ran antiwar editorials urging American withdrawal. Walter Cronkite, the dean of American television journalists, confided to his viewers that he no longer believed the war was winnable. "If I've lost Walter," Johnson was reported to say, "then it's over. I've lost Mr. Average Citizen." Polls showed that Johnson's popularity declined to 35 percent, lower than any president since Truman's darkest days.

Johnson was increasingly isolated. Clark Clifford, the new secretary of defense, reported to Johnson that a task force of prominent soldiers and civilians saw no prospect for a military victory. Even Dean Acheson, the preeminent cold warrior, believed that the cause was hopeless. Robert Kennedy was reportedly considering a run for the presidency in order to challenge Johnson's Vietnam policy. And Sen. Eugene McCarthy of Minnesota had already made the decision to oppose Johnson in the primaries. With antiwar students rallying to his candidacy, McCarthy polled 42 percent of the vote to Johnson's 48 percent in New Hampshire's March primary. It was a remarkable showing for a little-known senator, even though Johnson was a write-in candidate. Each presidential primary now promised to become a referendum on Johnson's Vietnam policy. In Wisconsin, scene of the next primary, Johnson's political advisors forecast a humiliating defeat: "We sent a man [to campaign for Johnson] and all we've heard from him since is a few faint beeps, like the last radio signals from the Bay of Pigs."

Despite Johnson's troubles in the conduct of foreign policy, he remained a master at reading the political omens. On March 31 he went on national television to announce a limited halt to the bombing of North Vietnam and fresh initiatives for a negotiated cease-fire. Then he added a dramatic postscript: "I have concluded that I should not permit the Presidency to become involved in the partisan divisions that are developing in this political year. Accordingly, I shall not seek, and I will not accept, the nomination of my party for another term as your President."

Although American troops would remain in Vietnam for five more years and the casualties would continue, the quest for military victory had ended. Now the question was how the most powerful nation in the world could extricate itself from Vietnam with a minimum of damage to its prestige.

SIXTIES CRESCENDO

A TRAUMATIC YEAR   History seemed to move at a fearful pace throughout the 1960s, but 1968 was a year of extreme turbulence even for that decade. On April 4, only four days after Johnson's announced withdrawal, Martin Luther King was gunned down while standing on the balcony of his motel in Memphis, Tennessee. The assassin, James Earl Ray, had expressed hostility toward blacks, but debate still continues over whether he was a pawn in an organized conspiracy. King's death set off an outpouring of grief among whites and blacks. It also set off riots in over sixty American cities, with the most serious occurring in Chicago and Washington, D.C. Two months later, on June 6, Robert Kennedy was shot in the head by a young Palestinian, Sirhan Sirhan, who resented Kennedy's strong support of Israel. Kennedy's death occurred at the end of the day on which he had convincingly defeated Eugene McCarthy in the California primary, thereby assuming leadership of the antiwar forces in the race for the Democratic nomination for president. David Halberstam thought back to the assassinations of John Kennedy and Malcolm X, then the violent end of King, the most influential black leader of the twentieth century, and then Robert Kennedy,

America's violent underside became all too apparent in the 1960s. [Cartoon by Franklin— Daily Mirror, London]

"ALWAYS THERE IS A BLACK SPOT IN OUR SUNSHINE— IT IS THE SHADOW OF OURSELVES."—CARLYLE the heir to leadership of the Kennedy clan. "We could make a calendar of the decade," Halberstam wrote, "by marking where we were at the hours of those violent deaths."

Although the Democratic nomination was now a foregone conclusion—Hubert Humphrey was virtually assured of winning as the candidate most acceptable to regular Democrats—the forces converging on Chicago in August possessed energies that had been seething and simering throughout the decade. Bizarre activists like Jerry Rubin, the "Yippie" leader who threatened to put LSD into Chicago's water supply, were but the extreme fringe of a movement of alienated Americans, most of them young, that resembled a religious crusade more than a political movement. In the last two years of the decade, first at the Democratic convention in Chicago and then at the Woodstock Festival in upstate New York in August 1969, what soon became known as "the counterculture" expressed itself in varieties of protest, public singing, drug use, and sexual experimentation.

THE COUNTERCULTURE   The explicitly political strain of the counterculture had its origins on college campuses and in the civil rights movement. In 1962 the Students for a Democratic Society (SDS) was organized in Michigan and issued the Port Huron Statement: "We are the people of this generation, bred in at least moderate comfort, housed in universities, looking uncomfortably to the world we inherit." In 1964 students at the University of California at Berkeley initiated the Free Speech Movement, a protest in behalf of student rights that quickly escalated into a more general criticism of the modern university, the impersonal character of bureaucracy, and as it spread to colleges throughout the country, a hostility to all established institutions. Disaffected and radical students flowed into the antiwar movement but focused their anger most frequently on the institutions closest to them, the colleges and universities. The eventful spring of 1968 witnessed the disruption of Columbia University until police forcibly ejected student protesters who had seized the offices of campus officials. Harvard and Cornell were afflicted with similar disruptions within the next two years. The New Left, as it came to be called, was a predominantly white, middle-class movement, populated by idealistic young Americans who had developed a sense of themselves as a discrete generation in rebellion against authorities of all kinds. Campus parietals, government policies in Vietnam, the draft, and parental restrictions on dress and hair length all provoked their censure.

Drugs and rock music were more important than political ideology to the "hippies," the direct descendants of the "beatniks" of the 1950s and the flaming youth of the 1920s who drank gin, bobbed their hair, and danced the Charleston. "Tune in, turn on, drop out" became a slogan popularized by Timothy Leary, a Harvard professor turned high priest of the drug culture. Hallucinogenic drugs were necessary to strip away what Theodore Roszak, the friendly chronicler of the counterculture, called "the myth of objective consciousness" and "the scientific world view with its entrenched commitment to an egocentric and cerebral mode of consciousness." Rock concerts that featured Janis Joplin or Jimi Hendrix became "happenings" in which the youth culture flaunted its freedom. By the end of the 1960s *Rolling Stone* magazine warned that pretensions of artistic purity ignored the commercial corruption of heroes like Hendrix and Bob Dylan, and groups like the Beatles: "The difference between a rock star and a robber baron is six inches of hair." As the Democratic convention convened in Chicago, disc jockeys debated whether the Beatles' song "Revolution I" was counterrevolutionary ("But if you go carrying a picture of Chairman Mao, you ain't gonna make it with anyone anyhow"). Many disc jockeys preferred the new tune by the Rolling Stones that began "The time is right for fighting in the streets."

CHICAGO AND MIAMI   While Democratic delegates gathered inside the convention hall at Chicago, 24,000 police and National Guardsmen and a small army of television reporters stood watch over an eclectic gathering of protesters herded together miles away in a public park. The counterculture was represented by antiwar groups carrying signs supporting the Viet Cong and by

The violence at the 1968 Democratic National Convention in Chicago seared the nation. [R. Malloch, Magnum Photos]

the Yippies, who staged a "Festival of Life" intended to contrast with "Lyndon and Hubert's celebration of death." Mayor Richard Daley, who had given "shoot-to-kill" orders to police during the April riots protesting King's assassination, warned that he would not tolerate disruptions. But riots broke out in front of the Conrad Hilton Hotel and were televised nationwide. As police tear gas and billy clubs struck demonstrators, others took up the chant "The whole world is watching."

The liberal tradition represented by the Democratic party was clearly in disarray, a fact that gave heart to the Republicans who gathered in Miami to nominate Richard Nixon. Only six years earlier, after he had lost the California gubernatorial race, Nixon had told reporters, "You won't have Nixon to kick around anymore, because, gentlemen, this is my last press conference." But by 1968 he had become a preeminent spokesman for all the values the counterculture was against. Russell Baker of the New York *Times* said the Miami convention had been "planned in advance by six bores and a sadist." And Norman Mailer, who covered both conventions to gather material for a book on American politics, likened the convention in Miami to a Rotarian gathering in a cemetery. But Nixon and the Republicans were offering a vision of stability and order that a majority of Americans—soon to be called "the silent majority"—wanted desperately.

George Wallace, the governor of Alabama who had made his reputation as a defender of segregation, became a third candidate in the campaign on the American Independent party ticket. Wallace moderated his position on the race issue, but appealed even more candidly than Nixon to the fears generated by protesters, the welfare system, and the growth of the federal government. Although never a possible winner, Wallace's candidacy did pose the possibility of denying Humphrey or Nixon an electoral majority and thereby throwing the choice into the House of Representatives, which would have provided an appropriate climax to a chaotic year.

NIXON AGAIN   It did not happen that way. Nixon enjoyed an enormous lead in the polls, which narrowed as the election approached. Wallace's campaign was hurt by his running mate, retired Air Force Gen. Curtis LeMay, who favored expanding the war in Vietnam and spoke approvingly of using nuclear weapons. (It was reported that LeMay was the model for the deranged general in the film *Doctor Strangelove*.) In October, Humphrey announced that he would stop bombing North Vietnam "as an acceptable risk for peace." Eugene McCarthy, who

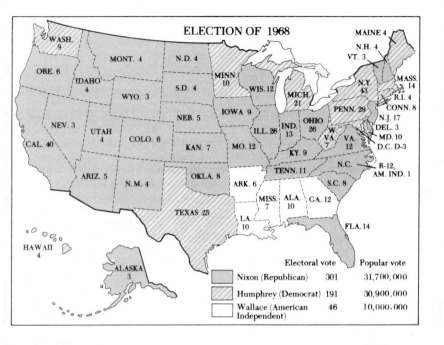

ELECTION OF 1968

	Electoral vote	Popular vote
Nixon (Republican)	301	31,700,000
Humphrey (Democrat)	191	30,900,000
Wallace (American Independent)	46	10,000,000

had been strangely silent and had even spent some time cloistered in a Benedictine monastery, eventually came out in support of Humphrey. "I believe the Vice-President is a man who can be relied on to tell the difference between the pale horse of death and the white horse of victory," said McCarthy. "I am not sure Nixon can make that distinction."

Nixon and Gov. Spiro Agnew of Maryland, his running mate, eked out a narrow victory by about 800,000 votes, a margin of about one percentage point. The electoral vote was more decisive, 301 to 191. Wallace won 10 million votes, 13.5 percent of the total, for the best showing by a third-party candidate since Robert La Follette in 1924. All but one of Wallace's 46 electoral votes were from the Deep South. Nixon swept all but four of the states west of the Mississippi. Humphrey's support came almost exclusively from the Northeast.

And so at the end of a turbulent year near the end of a traumatic decade, power passed peacefully to a president who was associated with the complacency of the 1950s. A nation that had seemed on the verge of consuming itself in spasms of violence looked to Richard Nixon to provide what he had promised in the campaign: "peace with honor" in Vietnam and a middle ground on which a majority of Americans, silent or otherwise, could come together.

FURTHER READING

A number of scholars have chronicled the events of the 1960s, often with analysis based on their personal experiences from the decade. Among the most popular of these works is William L. O'Neill's *Coming Apart: An Informal History of America in the 1960s* (1971).° More concise is William Leuchtenberg's *A Troubled Feast: American Society since 1945* (1979),° which depicts well how the events of the 1950s led into the conflicts of the 1960s. Godfrey Hodgson's *America in Our Time: From World War II to Nixon, What Happened and Why* (1976),° is detailed and probes the underlying forces which led to discontent. Other overviews include Morris Dickstein's *Gates of Eden: American Culture in the Sixties* (1977),° Ronald Berman's *America in the Sixties* (1968),° and Jim F. Heath's *Decade of Disillusion: The Kennedy-Johnson Years* (1975).

For the context of the Camelot years, consult first James L. Sundquist's *Politics and Policy: The Eisenhower, Kennedy, and Johnson Years* (1968).° Herbert Parmet traces the influence of Kennedy in two volumes, *Jack: The Struggle of John Fitzgerald Kennedy* (1980) and *JFK: The Presidency of John Fitzgerald Kennedy* (1983). Favorable memoirs from White House staffers include Arthur M. Schlesinger, Jr.'s *A Thousand Days: John F. Kennedy in the White House* (1965)° and Theodore C. Sorenson's *Kennedy* (1965). A former New Frontiersman, Roger Hilsman offers an argument about Kennedy's effectiveness in *To Move a Nation: The Politics of Policy in the Administration of John F. Kennedy* (1967).° Less favorable assessments come from Henry Fairlie's *The Kennedy Promise* (1973) and Bruce Miroff's *Pragmatic Illusions: The Presidential Politics of John F. Kennedy* (1976). For details of the assassination, see William Manchester's *The Death of the President* (1967).° Anthony Summer's *Conspiracy* (1980)° reviews best the many theories about the death of Kennedy, including the evidence provided in the official Warren Report.

There are fewer works about Kennedy's successor, but many are solidly detailed. Lyndon Johnson's own *The Vantage Point: Perspectives on the Presidency, 1963–1969* (1971),° can be balanced with Doris Kearns's *Lyndon Johnson and the American Dream* (1976).° Also helpful is Merle Miller's *Lyndon: An Oral Biography* (1980).° Tom Wicker's *JFK and LBJ: The Influence of Personality upon Politics* (1968)° examines Johnson's effective control of Congress. Eric Goldman's *The Tragedy of Lyndon Johnson* (1969)° is critical of Johnson's Vietnamese escalation. Ronnie Dugger's *The Politician: The Life and Times of Lyndon Johnson* (1982) depicts in detail Johnson's early career, as does the first volume of Robert Caro's biography, *The Years of Lyndon Johnson* (1982).°

Among the works which interpret the policy of the liberals are W. W. Rostow's *The Diffusion of Power, 1957–1972* (1972), and Robert Lekachman's *The Age of Keynes* (1966).° Also helpful is the memoir of a

°These books are available in paperback editions.

leading Keynesian, John Kenneth Galbraith, *A Life in Our Times* (1981). For liberal social programs, consult the assessment of the Great Society by Sar Levitan and Robert Taggart, *The Promise of Greatness* (1976).° Very helpful for background on the formation of this policy is James T. Patterson's *America's Struggle against Poverty, 1900–1980* (1981). The polemical literature of the period is also helpful; see Daniel Moynihan's *Maximum Feasible Misunderstanding: Community Action in the War on Poverty* (1970)° and Kenneth Davies's *The Paradox of Poverty in America* (1969). For the way social policy affected cities, see Mark I. Gelfand's *A Nation of Cities* (1975) and Sam Bass Warner's *The Urban Wilderness* (1972).°

For the foreign policy of the liberals, see Louise Fitzsimmon's *The Kennedy Doctrine* (1972) and Richard Walton's *Cold War and Counter-revolution: The Foreign Policy of John F. Kennedy* (1972).° To learn more about Kennedy's problems in Cuba, see Haynes Johnson's *The Bay of Pigs* (1964). Herbert S. Dinerstein analyzes the Soviet perspective in *The Making of a Missile Crisis* (1976). For the Alliance of Progress, see Jerome Levinson and Juan de Onis's *The Alliance That Lost Its Way* (1970). Jerome Slater's *Intervention and Negotiation* (1970) depicts Johnson's use of military force in Santo Domingo. Also helpful on foreign policy are Warren Cohen's *Dean Rusk* (1980) and Leonard Silk and Mark Silk's *The American Establishment* (1980).

The establishment's policy in Vietnam has received voluminous treatment from all political perspectives. Three of the most popular negative accounts of the struggle are Chester L. Cooper's *The Lost Crusade* (1970), Frances Fitzgerald's *Fire in the Lake: The Vietnamese and the Americans in Vietnam* (1972),° and David Halberstam's *The Best and the Brightest* (1972).° Subsequent surveys of American involvement include Paul Kattenberg's *The Vietnam Trauma in American Foreign Policy, 1945–1980* (1980), and James Pinckeney Harrison's *The Endless War: Fifty Years of Struggle in Vietnam* (1982). Works which see American policy in a favorable light include Norman Podhoretz's *Why We Were in Vietnam* (1982), Guenter Lewy's *America in Vietnam* (1978),° and Leslie Gelb and Richard Bett's *The Irony of Vietnam: The System Worked* (1979).° The life of the common soldier is depicted in Peter Goldman and Tony Fuller's *Charlie Company: What Vietnam Did to Us* (1983) and Robert Pison's *The End of the Line: The Siege of Khe Sanh* (1982).

For an overview of the antiwar movement spawned by the Vietnam War, see Todd Gitlin's *The Whole World Is Watching* (1981). Other works on anti-war protest include Kirkpatrick Sales's *SDS* (1973),° Theodore Roszak's *The Making of the Counterculture* (1969),° Irwin Unger's *The Movement* (1974),° Lawrence Lader's *Power on the Left* (1979), and Thomas Powers's *The War at Home* (1974). Richard Flack's *Youth and Social Change* (1971) and William Strauss's *Change and Circumstance* (1978) are particularly detailed about opposition to compulsory military service.

Many scholars have dealt with various aspects of the civil rights movement and race relations of the 1960s. A recent introduction to the period is Sar A. Levitan, William B. Johnson, and Robert Taggart's *Still a Dream: The Changing Status of Blacks since 1960* (1975).° Studies of the national politics of civil rights include Carl Brauer's *John F. Kennedy and the Second Reconstruction* (1977)° and Lee Rainwater and William L. Yancey's *The Moynihan Report and the Politics of Controversy* (1967). Two biographies of Martin Luther King, Jr., are helpful: Stephen B. Oates's *Let the Trumpet Sound* (1982)° and David Lewis's *King: A Critical Biography* (1970).° David J. Garrow has two specialized studies of King, *Protest at Selma* (1978)° and *The FBI and Martin Luther King, Jr.: From "Solo" to Memphis* (1981).° King is also enlightening in his own book *Why We Can't Wait* (1964).° Other personalities in the civil rights movement are studied in Charles F. Kellogg's *NAACP* (1967), August Meier and Elliott Rudwick's *CORE* (1973),° and Howard Zinn's *SNCC: The New Abolitionists* (1964). For legal turns the civil rights movement took during the 1960s, see J. Harvie Wilkinson's *From Brown to Bakke: The Supreme Court and School Integration, 1954–1978* (1978). William Chafe's *From Civilities to Civil Rights: Greensboro, North Carolina, and the Black Struggle for Freedom* (1980)° details the original sit-ins.

For race relations subsequent to the Civil Rights Act, consult Theodore Draper's *The Discovery of Black Nationalism* (1970). Important books by blacks during the period include Alex Haley (ed.), *The Autobiography of Malcolm X* (1965),° Eldridge Cleaver's *Soul on Ice* (1967),° George Jackson's *Soledad Brother* (1970),° and Stokely Carmichael and Charles Hamilton's *Black Power* (1967).° Also valuable is Archie Epp's *Malcolm X and the American Negro Revolution* (1969). For background on the urban riots, see Robert Fogelson's *Violence as Protest* (1971) and Joe R. Feagin and Harlin Hahn's *Ghetto Revolts* (1973). Claude Brown's *Manchild in the Promised Land* (1975)° explores the world of ghetto life.

For the tumultuous events of the 1968 campaign, start with Theodore H. White's *The Making of the President, 1968* (1969).° Less favorable to Nixon is Joe McGinnis's *The Selling of the President* (1969).° For the McCarthy movement, see Norman Ben Stavis's *We Were the Campaign* (1969). Arthur M. Schlesinger, Jr.'s *Robert Kennedy and His Times* (1978)° and Marshall Frady's *Wallace* (1976)° report the campaign from the viewpoint of other candidates.

34

THE 1970s AND BEYOND: THE SEARCH FOR STABILITY

The sixties was a state of mind as well as a discrete decade. For some Americans the 1960s ended with the assassinations of Martin Luther King and Robert Kennedy in 1968. For others the end came in 1973, when they inched their cars into gas stations and discovered that scarcity had replaced abundance at the fuel pump. For many Americans, however, the Vietnam War was the dominant event of the decade. Until the war was ended and all American troops had returned home, the nation found it difficult to achieve the equilibrium and moderation that the new president had promised. In his State of the Union message of 1970, President Nixon called on Americans to pursue "the lift of a driving dream," a memorable phrase that reporters asked him to define. "Well, before we can get the lift of a driving dream," Nixon explained, "we have to get rid of the nightmares we inherited. One of the nightmares is a war without end."

Nixon and Vietnam

GRADUAL WITHDRAWAL   During the campaign of 1968 Nixon had claimed to have a secret plan that would bring "peace with honor" in Vietnam. After the election Clark Clifford, the former secretary of defense, went to Henry Kissinger, the professor of international relations at Harvard who had been tapped to serve as Nixon's special assistant for national security affairs, and suggested that "within ninety days of taking office, Mr. Nixon could announce that he was starting the withdrawal of American troops and would continue to withdraw them until they were all gone." Clifford's advice was similar to the suggestion put forward by Sen. George Aiken of Vermont that "we declare victory and leave." But neither Nixon nor Kissinger found such advice acceptable. Kissinger insisted that the war in Indochina was a mere "sideshow" of considerably less significance than American interests in Europe and the Middle East, but American withdrawal from Vietnam was agonizingly slow nonetheless. Like several preceding administrations, the Nixon administration, even while withdrawing American forces, held to a policy that it was contrary to the national interest to let the North Vietnamese dominate Indochina. When a settlement was finally reached in 1973, another 20,000 Americans had died, the morale of the American army was shattered, millions of additional Asians were killed or wounded, and fighting in fact continued in Southeast Asia. In the end, Nixon's policy gained nothing he could not have accomplished in 1969.

The new Vietnam policy of the Nixon administration moved along three separate fronts. First, American negotiators in Paris insisted on the withdrawal of Communist forces from South Vietnam and the preservation of the American-supported regime of President Nguyen Van Thieu. The North Vietnamese and Viet Cong negotiators insisted on the retention of a military presence in the south and the reunification of the Vietnamese people under a government dominated by the Communists. There was no common ground on which to come together. It required months before the parties could even agree on the shape of the table around which they would meet.

Second, Nixon sought to undercut domestic unrest over the war. He reduced the number of American troops in Vietnam, justifying the reduction as the natural result of "Vietnamization"— the equipping and training of the South Vietnamese to assume the burden of ground combat in place of Americans. From a peak of 540,000 in 1969, American combat troops were withdrawn at a gradual and steady pace that matched almost precisely the pace of the American buildup from 1965 to 1969. By 1973 only 50,000 American troops remained in Vietnam. Nixon also established a lottery system that clarified the likelihood of being drafted—only those with low lottery numbers would have to go —and in 1973 he did away with the draft altogether by creating an all-volunteer army. Nixon was more successful in achieving the goal of reducing antiwar activity than at forcing concessions from the North Vietnamese in Paris.

Third, while reducing the number of American combat troops, Nixon and Kissinger actually expanded the air war in an effort to persuade the enemy to come to terms. On March 18, 1969, American planes began "Operation Menu," a fourteen-month-long bombing of Communist sanctuaries in Cambodia. Congress did not learn of these secret raids until 1970, although the total tonnage of bombs dropped was four times that dropped on Japan during World War II. Then on April 30, 1970, Nixon went on television to announce what he called an "incursion" into Cambodia by United States troops to "clean out" Communist staging areas. The head of Cambodia's government for two decades, Prince Norodom Sihanouk, had previously objected to such raids into his country, but Sihanouk had been replaced in a coup by Gen. Lon Nol earlier in the spring, clearing the way for the American invasion. Finally, on December 18, 1972, the president ordered the saturation bombing of Hanoi and Haiphong, the two largest cities in North Vietnam. These so-called Christmas bombings by B-52s, and the simultaneous mining of North Vietnamese harbors, aroused worldwide protest. "Civilized man will be horrified," read a New York *Times* editorial. Captured American pilots—fifteen of the giant B-52s were shot down—were paraded before television cameras to express regret at the civilian deaths and carnage, which the Pentagon described as the unfortunate consequence of North Vietnamese decisions to place military targets, such as airfields and munitions depots, in the middle of highly populated areas.

DIVISIONS AT HOME   The effect of America's gradual withdrawal on the morale and reputation of the American military was devastating. Beginning in 1969, when it became clear that military victory was no longer the goal, whole combat units refused to obey orders to fight. "No one wants to be the last grunt to die in this lousy war," said one soldier. In May 1969 the newspaper *GI Says* offered a bounty of $10,000 for the murder of the officer who ordered the assault on "Hamburger Hill," where 476 American soldiers had died to capture a position which was abandoned the following day. Between 1969 and 1971 there were 730 reported "fragging" incidents, efforts to kill or injure officers, usually with fragmentation grenades. Even the old marching chants became cynical, as troops shouted, "If I die in a combat zone, box me up and ship me home," while keeping cadence. Drugs became a major problem. In 1971 four times as many American troops were hospitalized for drug abuse as for combat-related wounds. "In Vietnam," wrote Col. Robert

The face of a "nightmare war," south of the demilitarized zone, Vietnam. [Larry Burrows, Life magazine, © Time Inc.]

Heinl, Jr., the army "is numbly extricating itself from a nightmare war . . . foisted on them by bright civilians who are now back on campus writing books about the folly of it all."

And back on the homefront the public learned of previously suppressed events in Vietnam that caused even the staunchest supporters of the war to wince. Late in 1969 the story of the My Lai massacre broke in the press and plunged the country into two years of exposure to the gruesome tale of Lt. William Calley, who ordered the murder of over 200 civilians in My Lai village in March 1968. Twenty-five army officers were charged with complicity in the massacre and subsequent cover-up, but only Calley was convicted; Nixon eventually granted him parole.

Perhaps the loudest public outcry against Nixon's Indochina policy occurred in the wake of the Cambodian "incursion." Nixon's television speech of April 30, 1970, sounded the tocsin: "we will not be defeated. . . . If, when the chips are down, the world's most powerful nation . . . acts like a pitiful, helpless giant, the forces of totalitarianism and anarchy will threaten free nations and free institutions throughout the world." Campuses across the country exploded in what William J. McGill, the president of Columbia University, called "the most disastrous month of May in the history of American higher education." Hundreds of colleges and universities closed down. At Kent State University the Ohio National Guard was called in to quell rioting in which the campus Reserve Officer Training Corps (ROTC) building was burned. The young guardsmen panicked and opened fire on the demonstrators, killing four bystanders. Eleven days later, on May 15, Mississippi highway patrolmen riddled a dormitory at Jackson State College with bullets, killing two black students.

Although an official investigation of the Kent State episode condemned the "casual and indiscriminate shooting," polls indicated that the American public supported the actions by the National Guard; students had "got what they were asking for." In New York City, antiwar demonstrators who gathered to protest the deaths at Kent State and the invasion of Cambodia were attacked by "hard-hat" construction workers, who forced the student protesters to disperse and then marched on City Hall to raise the flag that had been lowered to half-staff in mourning for the Kent State victims.

The following year, in June 1971, the New York *Times* began publishing excerpts from a secret Defense Department study commissioned by Robert McNamara before his departure from government. The so-called *Pentagon Papers*, leaked to the press by a former Defense Department official, Daniel Ellsberg, confirmed what many critics of the war had long suspected: as in the case of American naval aid to Britain in 1941, Congress and the people had not received the full story on the Gulf of Tonkin incident of 1964; and as in 1940–1941, contingency plans for American entry into the war were being drawn up while Johnson was promising the American people that combat troops would never be sent to Vietnam. Moreover there was no plan for bringing the war to an end so long as the North Vietnamese persisted. The Nixon administration attempted to block publication of the *Pentagon Papers*, arguing that they endangered national security and that their publication would prolong the war. By a vote of 6 to 3 the Supreme Court ruled against the government. Newspapers throughout the country began publication the next day.

"Son. . . !" "Dad. . . !"
The Vietnam War caused
vehement divisions between
"hawks" and "doves," old and
young, even parents and
children. [Conrad in the Los
Angeles Times*]*

WAR WITHOUT END   The mounting social divisions at home and
the approach of the 1972 presidential elections combined to
produce a shift in the American negotiating position in Paris. In
the summer of 1972 Henry Kissinger began meeting privately
with Le Duc Tho, the North Vietnamese negotiator, and
dropped his insistence on the removal of all North Vietnamese
troops from the south before the withdrawal of American troops.
On October 26, only a week before the American presidential
election, Kissinger announced: "Peace is at hand." But the Thieu
regime in South Vietnam objected to the plan for a cease-fire,
fearful that the presence of North Vietnamese troops in the south
virtually guaranteed an eventual Communist victory. The talks
broke off on December 16 and the next day the B-52 raids on
Hanoi and Haiphong began. The "Christmas bombings" stopped
on December 30, and the resumption of talks in Paris soon followed. On January 27, 1973, the United States signed an
"agreement on ending the war and restoring peace in Vietnam."
While Nixon and Kissinger both claimed that the bombing had
brought North Vietnam to its senses, in truth the North Vietnamese never altered their basic stance; they kept troops in the south
and remained committed to the reunification of Vietnam under
one government. What had changed since the previous fall was
the willingness of the South Vietnamese to accept these terms,
albeit reluctantly, on the basis of Nixon's promise that the United
States would respond "with full force" to any violation of the
agreement.

On March 29, 1973, the last American combat troops left
Vietnam. And on that same day the last of several hundred American prisoners-of-war, most of them downed pilots, were released from Hanoi. Within a period of months the cease-fire in
Vietnam ended, however, the war between north and south resumed, and the military superiority of the Communist forces
soon became evident. In Cambodia and Laos, where fighting had
been more sporadic, Communist victory also seemed inevitable.
In March 1975 the North Vietnamese launched a full-scale offensive against the south, which appealed to Washington for assistance. Congress refused. The much-mentioned "peace with
honor" had proven to be, in the words of one CIA official, only a
"decent interval"—enough time for the United States to extricate itself from Vietnam before the collapse of the South Vietnamese government. On April 30 Americans watched on
television as North Vietnamese tanks rolled into Saigon, soon to
be named Ho Chi Minh City, and helicopters lifted the officials in
the American embassy to ships waiting offshore. In those last des-

As Saigon falls to the North Vietnamese, mobs scale the 14-foot wall of the U.S. Embassy to reach helicopters for evacuation, May 1, 1975. [World Photos]

perate moments, crying South Vietnamese hung on the landing gear of the helicopters as they took off; a sign in the embassy courtyard read "Turn off the light at the end of the tunnel when you leave."

The longest and most controversial war in American history was over, leaving in its wake a bitter legacy that was a mirror-image of the goals that the United States had cited as justifications for involvement ten years earlier. The war fought to prevent the "domino effect" in Asia had left Communists in control of Vietnam, Laos, and Cambodia, and threatening in Thailand. The war described as a noble crusade in behalf of democratic ideals instead suggested that democracy was not easily transferrable to Third World regions that lacked any historical experience with liberal values and representative government. The war designed to serve as a showcase for American military power instead eroded respect for the military so thoroughly that many young Americans came to regard military service as corrupting and ignoble. The war fought to show the world that the United States was united in its convictions, divided Americans more drastically than any event since the Civil War, and prompted European nations to doubt American reliability and revolutionary leaders in the Third World to mock American pretensions.

Little wonder that the dominant reaction to the war's end was the urge to "put Vietnam behind us," in President Gerald Ford's phrase, and forget. Although subsequent debates over American foreign policy in the Middle East, Africa, and Latin America frequently involved recourse to "the lessons of Vietnam," the phrase was used by different factions for diametrically opposed purposes, ranging from refusal to commit American troops and resources in El Salvador to an insistence on massive military commitments unfettered by any diplomatic restrictions that might preclude outright victory. "In the end, then," wrote Leslie H. Gelb, a longtime student of American policy on the Vietnam era, "there was no end at all."

NIXON AND MIDDLE AMERICA

Richard Nixon had been elected in 1968 as the representative of "Middle America," the champion of those middle-class citizens fed up with the politics and promises of the 1960s. The Nixon cabinet and White House staff reflected their values. The chief figures were John Mitchell, the gruff attorney-general who had made his fortune as a municipal bond lawyer in Nixon's old firm; H. R. Haldeman and John Ehrlichman, advisers on domestic policy whose major experience before their association with the Nixon campaign had been in advertising; William Rogers, the secretary of state, an oldtime Nixon friend whose control over foreign policy was quickly preempted by Henry Kissinger; and Melvin Laird, the secretary of defense, who also found his influence undercut by Kissinger's access to the White House. Robert Finch, the secretary of health, education and welfare, and Walter Hickle, the secretary of the interior, demonstrated instincts for independence that soon led to their resignations. The cabinet was all white, all male, all Republican. "There are no blooded patricians in the lot," said *Time* magazine, "just strivers who have acted out the middle-class dream."

DOMESTIC AFFAIRS   If a balanced assessment of the Kennedy foreign policy is only now becoming possible, a detached evaluation of the domestic record of the Nixon administration remains out of reach, in part because the Watergate scandal affixed a stigma on Nixon's administration that colors all judgments, in part because the major legislative achievements happened largely in spite of rather than because of Nixon's efforts. Nixon was the first new president since 1849 to confront a Congress in which both houses were under the control of the opposition party. It therefore followed that he focused his energies on foreign policy, where presidential initiatives were less encumbered and where he, in tandem with Kissinger, achieved several stunning breakthroughs. The domestic front became a holding action in which Nixon, like Eisenhower before him, found it difficult to stop the march of liberal programs.

Despite the efforts of the Nixon administration, the civil rights legislation enacted during the Johnson years continued to take

In July 1969, a program begun by Kennedy reached its goal: putting a man on the moon. [NASA]

effect. "There are those who want instant integration and those who want segregation forever," said Nixon in September of 1969. "I believe we need to have a middle course between these extremes." In practice this "middle course" took the shape of a concerted effort in 1970 to block congressional renewal of the Voting Rights Act and to delay implementation of court orders requiring the desegregation of school districts in Mississippi. "For the first time since Woodrow Wilson," said the head of the NAACP, "we have a national administration that can be rightly characterized as anti-Negro." Sixty-five lawyers in the Justice Department signed a letter of protest against the administration's stance and Robert Finch eventually resigned from the cabinet in protest. Congress then extended the Voting Rights Act over Nixon's veto. The Supreme Court, in the first decision made under the new Chief Justice Warren Burger—a Nixon appointee—ordered the integration of the Mississippi schools. In *Alexander v. Holmes County Board of Education* (1969) a unanimous Court ordered a quick end to segregation. Fifteen years after the original school desegregation cases, the standard of "all deliberate speed" no longer applied. During Nixon's first term more schools were desegregated than in all the Kennedy-Johnson years combined.

Nixon's attempts to block desegregation efforts in urban areas also failed. The Burger Court ruled unanimously in *Swann v. Charlotte-Mecklenburg Board of Education* (1971) that cities must bus students out of their neighborhoods if this was necessary to achieve integration. As it happened, one little-noticed result was that the change caused shorter bus trips, on average, for

Charlotte-Mecklenburg students. Protest over desegregation now began to manifest itself more in the North than in the South as white families in Boston, Denver, and other cities denounced the destruction of "the neighborhood school"; and angry parents in Pontiac, Michigan, fire-bombed school buses. Sensing the anxieties that white parents felt about the busing issue, Nixon asked Congress to impose a moratorium on all busing orders by the federal courts. The House of Representatives, equally attuned to voter outrage at busing, went along. But in the Senate, Walter Mondale of Minnesota and Jacob Javits of New York led a filibuster that blocked the president's antibusing bill. Busing opponents won a limited victory when the Supreme Court ruled, in *Milliken v. Bradley* (1974), that desegregation plans in Detroit requiring the transfer of students from the inner city to the suburbs were unconstitutional. This landmark decision, along with the *Bakke v. Board of Regents of California* (1978) decision which restricted the use of quotas to achieve racial balance, marked the transition of desegregation from an issue of simple justice to a more tangled thicket of conflicting group and individual rights.

The shift of the Supreme Court toward a more moderate posture was a clear Nixon legacy, although even here the president got only part of what he wanted. The Warren Court had become a bastion of liberal values and a visible symbol of all that the "silent majority" loved to hate. Not only had its civil rights decisions disrupted traditional social patterns in the North as well as the South, but its stand on civil liberties had offended the sensibilities of almost all the groups that voted for Nixon. In *Engel v. Vitale* (1962) the Court had ruled that a school prayer adopted by the New York State Board of Regents violated the constitutional prohibition against an established religion. In *Baker v. Carr* (1962) the Court had ordered the Tennessee state legislature to apportion representation in accord with the "one man, one vote" principle. In *Gideon v. Wainwright* (1963) the Court required that every felony defendant be provided a lawyer regardless of the defendant's ability to pay. And in *Miranda v. Arizona* (1966) the Court had confirmed the obligation of police to inform arrested suspects of their rights. This litany of liberal decisions had made the Warren Court a prime target for mostly middle-class Americans who resented what they regarded as the federal government's excessive protection of the "undeserving."

Fate and the aging of the justices on the Warren Court gave Nixon the chance to make four new appointments. His first,

Warren Burger, caused no uproar. But Nixon's next two nominations generated opposition in the Senate. Clement F. Haynsworth, a federal appeals court judge from South Carolina, had the support of the American Bar Association but drew fire from civil rights groups and labor unions for his conservative record. There was no question of Haynsworth's integrity, but the Senate rejected him when it learned that he had heard a case involving a subsidiary of a corporation in which he owned a small amount of stock. The nomination of G. Harold Carswell, a judge of the Florida appeals court, created even more opposition. Carswell had not only been an out-and-out defender of white supremacy, but he was acknowledged by all parties to be singularly lacking in distinction. By a vote of 51 to 45 the Senate rejected Carswell. Nixon, who was accused by several senators of tarnishing the image of the Court in order to pursue his "Southern Strategy" for reelection, condemned the Senate rejection as "an act of regional discrimination." But he took care thereafter to nominate jurists of stature for the Supreme Court: Harry Blackmun, a compatriot of Burger's from Minnesota; Lewis F. Powell, Jr., a respected conservative judge from Virginia; and William Rehnquist, an articulate, conservative lawyer in the Justice Department. None encountered serious opposition in the Senate. And none, save perhaps Rehnquist, would consistently support Nixon's interpretation of the Constitution.

Nixon had also promised to "get tough on crime," a promise difficult to fulfill because criminal statutes were local and state concerns. In July 1969, however, he proposed a crime bill for the District of Columbia designed to clarify his administration's tough stance and thereby assume symbolic leadership as "the nation's number one cop." The bill empowered judges to jail suspects for sixty days before trial ("preventive detention") and allowed policemen to break into houses without a warrant ("no knock"). Sen. Samuel J. Ervin, Jr., of North Carolina called it "A bill to repeal the fourth, fifth, sixth and eighth amendments to the Constitution." Afraid of appearing "soft" on crime, Congress passed the bill, but its influence on state and local laws proved negligible.

The single most innovative piece of domestic legislation proposed by the administration was the Family Assistance Plan, a proposal to overhaul the welfare system and cut out several layers of the bureaucracy created by Great Society programs. Daniel Patrick Moynihan, head of the Council on Urban Affairs, drafted the plan, which called for direct grants of $1,600 to poor families: in short, a guaranteed income floor. The idea had support among a wide range of experts, including some conservatives, but the plan's constituency had little political clout. The Family Assistance Plan went down to defeat in the Congress, in part because Nixon had insisted that it was "workfare and not welfare." In truth the plan was unadulterated welfare—a guaranteed income—but liberals in Congress, befuddled by Nixon's characterization of the plan, or miffed that it did not go far enough, joined with conservatives in an unusual alliance to kill the bill.

Nixon invented several names for his domestic program. At one point it was called the "New Federalism," which would "start resources and power flowing back from Washington to the people." To that end he proposed, and got from Congress in 1972, a five-year revenue-sharing plan which would distribute $30 billion of federal revenues to the states for use as they saw fit. At another point Nixon called for a "New American Revolution" to revive traditional values. These catch-phrases never caught on, as had the "New Frontier" or the "Great Society," because Nixon's domestic program was essentially defensive and negative.

In the fall of 1969 Nixon sent Vice-President Spiro Agnew on a national speaking tour to stigmatize the opposition. Agnew and a clutch of White House speechwriters described war protesters as "anarchists and ideological eunuchs," the liberal news media as "an effete corps of impudent snobs" and "nattering nabobs of negativism." It was time, said Agnew, "to rip away the rhetoric and divide on authentic lines. . . . When the president said 'bring us together,' he meant the functioning, contributing portions of the American citizenry." But while Agnew turned phrases, the Democratic Congress moved forward with new legislation: the right of eighteen-year-olds to vote in national elections (1970), extended to all elections by the Twenty-sixth Amendment (1971); an increase in Social Security benefits and food-stamp funding; passage of the Occupational Safety and Health Act (1970), the Clean Air Act (1970), new acts to control water pollution (1970 and 1972), and the Federal Election Campaign Act (1972).

ECONOMIC MALAISE   The economy proved even less responsive to conservative rhetoric than the Democratic Congress. The inflation rate began to rise in 1967, when it was at 3 percent. By 1973 it was at 9 percent; a year later it was at 12 percent, and it remained in double digits for most of the 1970s. The Dow-Jones average of major industrial stocks, at 985 a month after Nixon's election, fell to 631 on May 26, 1970, its steepest decline in over thirty years. In 1970 real gross national product (adjusted for inflation) declined for the first time since 1958, and the following year American imports exceeded exports for the first time since 1893. Meanwhile unemployment, at a low of 3.3 percent when Nixon took office, climbed to 6 percent by the end of 1970 and threatened to keep rising. Somehow the American economy was undergoing a recession and inflation at the same time. Economists coined the term "stagflation" to describe the syndrome which defied the orthodox laws of economics.

The economic malaise had at least three deep-rooted causes. First, the Johnson administration had attempted to pay for both the Great Society and the war in Vietnam without a major tax increase, generating huge federal deficits, a major expansion of the money supply, and the inevitable price inflation. Second, and more important, by the late 1960s American goods faced stiff competition in international markets from West Germany, Japan, and other emerging industrial powers. No longer was American technological superiority unquestioned. Third, the American economy had depended heavily on cheap sources of energy; no nation was more dependent on the automobile and the automobile industry, and no nation was more careless in its use of fossil fuels in factories and homes. Just as domestic petroleum reserves began to dwindle and dependence on foreign sources increased, the Organization of Petroleum Exporting Countries (OPEC) combined to use their oil as a political and economic weapon. In 1973 when the United States sent massive aid to Israel after a devastating Syrian-Egyptian attack on Yom Kippur, the holiest day in the Jewish calendar, OPEC announced in October that it would not sell oil to nations supporting Israel and that it was raising its prices by 400 percent. Motorists faced long lines at gas stations, schools and offices closed down, factories cut production, and the inflation rate took off as if fueled by all the oil not being delivered to the United States.

Stagflation posed a new set of economic problems, but Nixon responded erratically and ineffectively with the old remedies. First, he tried to reduce the federal deficit by raising taxes and cutting the budget. When the Democratic Congress refused to cooperate with this approach, he followed the advice of Milton Friedman, the conservative economist at the University of Chicago, and encouraged the Federal Reserve Board to reduce the money supply by raising interest rates. The stock market immediately collapsed and the economy plunged into the "Nixon recession."

In 1969, when asked about wage and price controls, Nixon had been unequivocal: "Controls. Oh, my God, no! I was a lawyer for the OPA [Office of Price Administration] during the war and I know all about controls. . . . We'll never go to controls." But on August 15, 1971, he reversed himself, probably under the influence of John Connally, the aggressive new secretary of the treasury. He froze all wages and prices for ninety days and announced that the United States would no longer convert dollars into gold for foreign banks. This ended an era that had begun with the international agreement reached at Bretton Woods, New Hampshire, in 1944. The United States had made the dollar convertible to gold at $35 an ounce, thereby setting a firm standard by which other currencies were measured. Now the dollar, its link to gold cut, drifted lower on world currency exchanges. After ninety days Nixon established mandatory guidelines for subsequent wage and price increases under the supervision of a federal agency. Still the economy floundered. When administration economists kept predicting an imminent upturn, journalists recalled General Westmoreland's predictions of victory in Vietnam. By 1973 the wage and price guidelines were made voluntary, and therefore almost entirely ineffective.

Nixon Triumphant

CHINA If the ailments of the economy proved more than Nixon could remedy, in foreign policy his administration managed to diagnose and treat American relations with the major powers of the Communist world—China and the Soviet Union—and to shift fundamentally the pattern of the Cold War. In July 1971 Henry Kissinger made a secret trip to Peking° to explore the possibility of American recognition of China. Since 1949, when Mao Tse-tung's revolutionary movement overturned the government of Chiang Kai-shek, the United States had refused to recognize Communist China, preferring to regard the exiled regime on Taiwan as the legitimate government of China. In one simple but stunning stroke, Nixon and Kissinger ended two decades of diplomatic isolation for the People's Republic of China and drove a wedge between the two chief bastions of communism in the world.

° The traditional spellings are used here. After Mao's death the Chinese government adopted the "Pinyin" transliterations that are used today: Peking = Beijing; Mao Tse-tung = Mao Zedong; and Chou En-lai = Zhou Enlai.

President Nixon and the chairman of the Chinese Communist party, Mao Tse-tung, February 22, 1972. [United Press International]

In February 1972 Americans watched on television as their president visited famous Chinese landmarks, which had been invisible to the West for over two decades, and drank toasts with Premier Chou En-lai and Mao Tse-tung. The United States and China agreed to scientific and cultural exchanges, steps toward the resumption of trade, and the eventual reunification of Taiwan with the mainland. A year after the Nixon visit, "liaison offices" were established in Washington and Peking that served as unofficial embassies, and in 1979 diplomatic recognition was formalized. Richard Nixon, the former anti-Communist crusader who had condemned the State Department for "losing" China in 1949, accomplished a diplomatic feat his more liberal predecessors could not.

DÉTENTE In truth, China welcomed the breakthrough in relations with the United States because its rivalry with the Soviet Union, with which it shared a long border, had become more bitter than its rivalry with the West. The Soviet leaders, troubled by the Sino-American agreements, were also anxious for an easing of tensions now that they had, as the result of a huge arms buildup following the Cuban missile crisis, achieved virtual parity with the United States in nuclear weapons. Once again the president surprised the world, by announcing that he would visit Moscow in May 1972 for discussions with Leonid Brezhnev, the Soviet premier. The high theater of the China visit was repeated in Moscow, with toasts and elegant dinners between world leaders who had previously regarded one another as incarnations of evil.

What became known as "détente" with the Soviets offered the

promise of a more orderly and restrained competition between the two superpowers. Nixon and Brezhnev signed agreements reached at the Strategic Arms Limitation Talks (SALT) which negotiators had been working on since 1969 in Helsinki and Vienna. The SALT agreement did not end the arms race, but it did set limits to the number of intercontinental ballistic missiles (ICBMs) and sharp limits to the construction of antiballistic missile systems (ABMs). In effect the Soviets were allowed to retain a greater number of missiles with greater destructive power while the United States retained a lead in the total number of warheads. No limitations were placed on new weapons systems, though each side agreed to work toward a permanent freeze on all nuclear weapons. The Moscow summit also produced new trade agreements, including an arrangement whereby the United States sold almost one-quarter of its wheat crop to the Soviets at a favorable price. American farmers rejoiced, since the wheat deal assured them a high price for their crop, but domestic critics grumbled that the deal would raise food prices in the United States and rescue the Russians from troublesome economic problems.

SHUTTLE DIPLOMACY   The Nixon-Kissinger initiatives in the Middle East were less dramatic and conclusive than the China or Russia agreements, but did show that America recognized Arab power in the region and its own dependence on the oil from Islamic states fundamentally opposed to Israel. After the Six-Day War of 1967, in which Israeli forces routed the armies of Egypt, Syria, and Jordan, Israel seized territory from all three Arab nations. Moreover the Palestinian refugees, many of them homeless since the creation of Israel in 1948, were made much more numerous by the Israeli victory in 1967. When Israel recovered from the initial shock of the surprise Yom Kippur War of 1973, Kissinger negotiated a cease-fire and exerted pressure to prevent Israel from seizing additional Arab territory. American reliance on Arab oil led to closer ties with Egypt and its president, Anwar el-Sadat, and more restrained support for Israel. Kissinger, whose "shuttle diplomacy" among the capitals of the Middle East won acclaim from all sides, failed to find a comprehensive formula for peace in the troubled region and ignored altogether the Palestinian problem, but did lay groundwork for the subsequent accord between Israel and Egypt in 1977.

THE 1972 ELECTION   Nixon's foreign policy achievements allowed him to stage the campaign of 1972 as a triumphal procession. At the Republican convention Nixon's nomination was a foregone conclusion. Film stars who symbolized the certitudes of an earlier era—John Wayne, Jimmy Stewart, Glenn Ford— delivered patriotic endorsements. The main threat to Nixon's re-election came from George Wallace, who had the potential as a third-party candidate to deprive the Republicans of conservative votes and thereby throw the election to the Democrats or the Democratic-controlled Congress. But on May 15, 1972, Wallace was shot and left permanently paralyzed below the waist by Arthur Bremer, a white midwesterner anxious to achieve a grisly brand of notoriety. Wallace was forced to withdraw from the campaign.

Meanwhile the Democrats were further ensuring Nixon's victory by nominating Sen. George S. McGovern of South Dakota, a crusading liberal who embodied antiwar and social welfare values associated with the turbulence of the 1960s. At the Democratic convention in Chicago McGovern's nomination was made easier by party reforms which increased the representation of women, blacks, and minorities, but which alienated the party regulars. Mayor Richard Daley of Chicago was actually ousted from the convention, and the AFL-CIO refused to endorse the Democratic candidate. McGovern also suffered from his handling of the crisis that developed when it was revealed that his running mate, Sen. Thomas Eagleton of Missouri, had undergone shock treatments for emotional disturbances. McGovern first announced complete support for Eagleton, then bowed to critics and dropped him in favor of Sargent Shriver, leaving an impression of vacillation and indecisiveness.

The campaign was an exercise in futility for McGovern, while Nixon made only a few formal political trips and cast himself in the role of "global peacekeeper." Nixon won the greatest victory of any Republican presidential candidate in history, winning 521 electoral votes to only 21 for McGovern. The popular vote was equally decisive: 45.9 million to 28.4 million, a margin of 60.8 percent that was second only to Johnson's victory over Goldwater in 1964. During the course of the campaign McGovern complained about the "dirty tricks" of the Nixon administration, most especially the curious incident in which a group of burglars was caught red-handed breaking into the Democratic National Committee headquarters in the Watergate apartment complex in Washington. McGovern's accusations seemed shrill and biased at the time, the lamentations of an obvious loser. Nixon and his staff made plans for "four more years" as the investigation of the fateful Watergate break-in proceeded apace.

WATERGATE

Under the relentless prodding of Judge John J. Sirica, one of the burglars began to tell the full story of the Nixon administration's complicity in the Watergate episode. James W. McCord, a former CIA agent and security chief for the Committee to Re-elect the President (CREEP), was the first in a long line of informers and penitents in a melodrama which unfolded over the next two years and which mixed the special qualities of soap opera and Machiavellian intrigue. It ended in the first resignation of a president in American history, the conviction and imprisonment of twenty-five officials of the Nixon administration, including four cabinet members, and the most serious constitutional crisis since the impeachment trial of Andrew Johnson.

UNCOVERING THE COVER-UP   The trail of evidence pursued first by Judge Sirica, then a grand jury, then a Senate investigation committee headed by Sen. Samuel J. Ervin, Jr., of North Carolina, led directly to the White House. Sen. Howard Baker of Tennessee, a member of the Ervin Committee, put the crucial questions succinctly: "What did the President know and when did he know it?" There was never any evidence that Nixon ordered the break-in or that he was aware of plans to burglarize the Democratic National Committee. What the evidence did show conclusively was that from the start Nixon was personally involved in the cover-up of the incident, that he used his presidential powers to discredit and block the investigation, and most alarming, that the Watergate burglary was merely one small part of a larger pattern of corruption and criminality sanctioned by the Nixon White House.

The White House had become committed to illegal tactics in May 1970 when the New York *Times* broke the story of the secret bombings in Cambodia. Nixon had ordered illegal telephone taps on several newsmen and government employees suspected of leaking the story. The covert activity against the press and critics of Nixon's Vietnam policies increased in 1971 during the crisis generated by the publication of the *Pentagon Papers*, when a team of burglars under the direction of White House adviser John Ehrlichman had broken into a psychiatrist's office in an effort to obtain damaging information on Daniel Ellsberg. By the spring of 1972 Ehrlichman commanded a team of "dirty tricksters" who performed various acts of sabotage against prospective Democratic candidates for the presidency, including falsely accusing Hubert Humphrey and Sen. Henry Jackson of sexual improprieties, forging press releases, setting off stink-bombs, and associating the opposition candidates with racist remarks. By the time of the Watergate break-in, the money to finance such "pranks" was being illegally collected through the Committee to Re-elect the President and placed under the control of the White House staff.

The cover-up unraveled further in April 1973 when L. Patrick Gray, acting director of the FBI, resigned after confessing that he had confiscated and destroyed several incriminating documents. On April 30 Ehrlichman and Haldeman resigned, together with Attorney-General Richard Kleindienst. Then the Ervin Committee heard John Dean, whom Nixon had dismissed as counsel to the president, testify that there had been a cover-up and that Nixon had approved it. In another "bombshell" disclosure Alexander Butterfield, a White House aide, told the committee that Nixon had installed a taping system in the White House—many of the conversations about Watergate had been recorded.

A year-long battle for the "Nixon tapes" began. The Harvard law professor Archibald Cox, who had been appointed by Nixon as special prosecutor to handle the Watergate case, took the president to court in October 1973 in order to obtain the tapes. Nixon, pleading "executive privilege," refused to release the tapes and ordered Cox fired. In what became known as the "Saturday Night Massacre," Attorney-General Elliot Richardson and Deputy Attorney-General William Ruckelshaus resigned rather than execute the order. Cox's replacement as special prosecutor, Leon Jaworski, proved no more pliable than Cox, and also took the president to court. On July 24, 1974, the Supreme Court voted unanimously that the president must surrender the tapes. A few days later the House Judiciary Committee voted to recommend three articles of impeachment: obstruction of justice through the payment of "hush money" to witnesses and the witholding of evidence; using federal agencies to deprive citi-

Sen. Sam Ervin, chairman of the Senate Watergate Committee, swears in the ex-White House Counsel John Dean, whose testimony linked President Nixon to the cover-up. [United Press International]

Having resigned his office, Richard Nixon waves farewell outside the White House, August 9, 1974. [Wide World Photos]

zens of their constitutional rights; and defiance of Congress by withholding the tapes. But before the House of Representatives could meet to vote on impeachment, Nixon handed over the complete set of White House tapes. On August 9, 1974, fully aware that the evidence on the tapes implicated him in the cover-up, he resigned from office, the only president ever to do so.

EFFECTS OF WATERGATE Nixon was not succeeded by Spiro Agnew because Agnew himself had been forced to resign in October 1973 when it became known that he had accepted bribes from contractors before and during his term as vice-president. The vice-president at the time of Nixon's resignation was Gerald Ford, the former minority leader in the House whom Nixon had appointed, with the approval of Congress, under provisions of the Twenty-fifth Amendment, which had been ratified in 1964 in the wake of President Kennedy's assassination. Ford insisted that he had no intention of pardoning Nixon, who was still liable for criminal prosecution. "I do not think the public would stand for it," said Ford. But a month after Nixon's resignation the new president explained that a pardon was necessary to end the national obsession with the Watergate scandals.

Many concluded that Nixon and Ford had made a deal, though there was no evidence to confirm the speculation. President Ford testified personally to a congressional committee: "There was no deal, period." But Watergate spawned a wave of cynicism. In the spring of 1974 polls showed that a majority of Americans believed that Nixon was lying about his complicity, but that four out of five judged him as no more guilty of wrongdoing than his presidential predecessors. The Watergate scandals and Nixon's resignation seemed to justify the most distrustful appraisals of American leaders and political institutions; little wonder that less than half the eligible electorate would vote in the next presidential election. Apart from Nixon's illegal action, the language used in the White House and made public in the tapes stripped away the veils of mystery surrounding national leaders and left even the die-hard defenders of presidential authority shocked at the crudity and duplicity of Nixon and his subordinates. If there was a silver lining in this dark cloud, it was the vigor and resiliency of the institutions that had brought a president down—the press, Congress, the courts, and an aroused public opinion.

Although many observers attributed Watergate to the idiosyncracies of one man, Richard Nixon, claiming that his entire political career revealed a quest for hidden enemies, Congress responded to the revelations of Watergate with several pieces of legislation designed to curb executive power in the future. The War Powers Act (1973) required the president to consult with Congress before sending American troops into combat abroad and to withdraw troops after sixty days unless Congress specifically approved their stay. In an effort to correct abuses of campaign funds, Congress enacted legislation in 1974 that set new ceilings on contributions and expenditures. And in reaction to the Nixon claim of "executive privilege," Congress strengthened the Freedom of Information Act to preclude the government from denying access to official documents "arbitrarily or capriciously."

REFORM SEVENTIES STYLE

While a president was being toppled, while Henry Kissinger was shuttling from the Paris peace talks to the Mideast, and while the nation was doing its best to forget the war in Vietnam, several social movements were gliding through the America of the 1970s with a life and momentum of their own. Women, Hispanics, and American Indians rode the waves created in the 1960s toward fresh goals. And the protection of the environment emerged as the prototypical reform movement in post-1960s America, demanding limitations rather than liberation and calling for a fatalistic acceptance of difficult economic and environmental "trade-offs."

THE WOMEN'S MOVEMENT   The movement for women's rights had roots in the rebellious sixties, and even deeper roots in the suffrage movements of the nineteenth century. But in the 1970s women achieved significant political and economic gains, overshadowing those of other minority groups which had occupied center stage in the 1960s but then suffered "benign neglect" in the Nixon years. This was in keeping with a century-old pattern in which women's rights blossomed during the latter stages of liberal reform movements: the Seneca Falls movement during the abolitionist crusade against slavery; the suffrage movement during the progressive era; and now the modern feminist movement in the wake of the civil rights and antiwar protests of the 1960s.

Betty Friedan's *The Feminine Mystique* (1963) launched the new phase of female protest. Friedan called attention to the fact that women had actually lost ground during the years after World War II, when "Rosie the Riveter" allegedly went home from the wartime assembly line and settled down before the television set in suburbia to watch "Queen for a Day" and care for the kids. In Friedan's view, the American middle-class home had become "a comfortable concentration camp" where women suffocated in an atmosphere of mindless consumption and affluent banality. The major rallying cry for the National Organization for Women (NOW), founded in 1966 by Friedan and soon regarded as the NAACP of the women's movement, became Title VII of the Civil Rights Act of 1964, which forbade discrimination in the workplace on the basis of sex. This title had been added to the original legislation by Rep. Howard Smith of Virginia, who had presumed that such a provision would make the bill so absurd as to kill it in Congress. NOW spearheaded efforts to end job discrimination, to legalize abortion, and to obtain federal and state support for child-care centers.

Statistical evidence confirmed that such bread-and-butter reforms spoke to a national need: in 1963 the average woman wage-earner made only 63¢ for every $1 a man earned; in the 1950s women comprised a smaller portion of the college population than they had in the 1920s. By the early 1970s Congress and the Supreme Court began to respond to pressure from women's groups committed to the cause of sexual equality. Under Title IX of the Educational Amendments Act of 1972, colleges were required to institute programs of "affirmative action" to ensure equal opportunity for women. In the same year Congress overwhelmingly approved the Equal Rights Amendment, which had been bottled up in a House committee for almost half a century, and the Supreme Court, in *Roe v. Wade*, struck down state laws forbidding abortions during the first three months of pregnancy. Meanwhile the educational bastions of male segregation, including Yale and Princeton, led a new movement for coeducation that swept the country. "If the 1960s belonged to blacks," said one feminist, "the next ten years are ours."

By the end of the decade divisions within the women's movement between moderate and radical feminists, as well as the movement's failure to broaden its appeal much beyond the confines of the middle class, caused reform efforts to stagnate. The Equal Rights Amendment, which had once seemed a straightforward assertion of equal opportunity ("Equality of rights under the law shall not be denied or abridged by the United States or by any State on account of sex") and assured of ratification, was stymied in several state legislatures. Despite a congressional extension of the normal time allowed for ratification, by 1982 it died several states short of passage. And the very success of NOW's efforts to change abortion laws generated a powerful reaction, especially among Catholics and fundamentalist Protestants, who mounted a "right to life" crusade of enormous power.

But the successes of the women's movement seemed likely to endure despite setbacks and long after the militant rhetoric had evaporated. For in fact women were not just another minority group pursuing the traditional path of liberal reform. They were a majority: they constituted 51 percent of the population. Their political power, only partially mobilized in the 1970s, had enormous potential for achieving social change. Moreover, their growing presence in the labor force assured women of a greater share of economic and political influence. In the year of the bicentennial, over half the married women in America and nine of ten women college graduates were employed outside the home, a development that one economist called "the single most outstanding phenomenon of this century." Many career women did not regard themselves as feminists; they took jobs because they and their families needed the money to survive or to achieve higher levels of material comfort. But regardless of their motives, traditional sex roles and childrearing practices were being changed to accommodate the two-career family. Indeed the two-career family had replaced the established pattern of male breadwinner and female housekeeper as the new American norm. "The classic differences between masculinity and femininity are disappearing," observed one sociologist, "as both sexes in the adult generation take on the same roles in the labor market." This quiet revolution continued apace into the 1980s.

HISPANICS In the 1970s Hispanics also emerged as a new and powerful force that politicians could no longer ignore. In the 1960s the chief focus of attention was Cesar Chavez, who almost single-handedly founded the United Farm Workers (UFW) in California, then launched a series of strikes for an increase in the wages and benefits of migrant workers. By 1970 the UFW had won recognition from California's grape growers and national visibility for the plight of Hispanic farm laborers through well-publicized boycotts of table grapes and lettuce. By the middle 1970s the UFW was challenged less by the growers than by competition from the Teamsters Union, which attempted to muscle the UFW aside.

But the chief strength of the Hispanic movement lay less in the duplication of civil rights strategies than in the sheer growth of the Hispanic population. In 1960 Hispanics had numbered slightly more than 3 million; by 1970 they had increased to 9 million, and by 1980 they numbered 20 million, making them the largest minority in America after blacks. The most numerous among them were Mexican-Americans, or Chicanos, who were concentrated in California and the Southwest. Next came the Puerto Rican population, most of whom lived in New York City and the Connecticut Valley. Finally there were the Cubans, many refugees from Castro's regime, who were concentrated in southern Florida.

Although affluent Hispanics became influential in Miami and Los Angeles, the vast bulk of the Hispanic population were poor, deprived, and often isolated from the mainstream of American life by the language barrier. Bilingualism—the belief that Hispanics were entitled to schooling in Spanish as well as English—divided the Hispanic community between those who wished to cultivate their heritage and those who feared that failure to adopt English as their primary language would block their social advance. By 1980, however, aspiring presidential candidates were openly courting the Hispanic vote, promising support for urban renewal projects in New York and amnesty programs for illegal immigrants in Texas, and delivering rousing anti-Castro speeches in Miami. The voting power of Hispanics and their concentration in states with key electoral votes had helped give the Hispanic point of view political clout.

NATIVE AMERICANS   In addition to women and Hispanics, American Indians—some of whom preferred to call themselves Native Americans—emerged as a new political force in the 1970s. The Indian population grew in the 1960s, but remained tiny by national standards, totaling about 800,000 in 1970. Two conditions conspired to make Indian rights a priority: first, white Americans felt a deep and centuries-old sense of guilt for the destructive policies of their ancestors toward a people who had, after all, been here first; second, the plight of the Indian minority was more desperate than that of any other minority group in the country. Indian unemployment was ten times the national rate, their life expectancy was twenty years lower than the national average, and the suicide rate was a whopping one hundred times higher than the rate for whites. If blacks had extracted a deserved promise of compensation for past injustices from whites in the 1960s, Indians felt that they had an even more compelling claim on white consciences in the 1970s.

At first the Indian militants copied the tactics of civil rights and black power activists. In 1968 the American Indian Movement (AIM) was founded. The leaders of AIM occupied Alcatraz Island in San Francisco Bay in 1969, claiming the site "by right of discovery." And in 1972 an Indian "sit-in" at the Bureau of Indian Affairs in Washington attracted national attention to their cause. But the most celebrated protest occurred at Wounded Knee, South Dakota, in January 1973. It dramatized the impoverished conditions of Indians living on the reservations near Wounded Knee, which also happened to be the site of the infamous massacre of Sioux Indians by federal troops in 1890.

Soon Indian protesters discovered a more effective tactic than direct action and "sit-ins." They went into the federal courts armed with copies of the treaties signed by nineteenth-century American government officials and demanded that the violations of these treaties become the basis for restitution. In Alaska, Maine, and Massachusetts they won significant settlements that provided legal recognition of their tribal rights and financial compensation at levels that upgraded the standard of living on several reservations.

THE ENVIRONMENTAL MOVEMENT   The sudden emergence of widespread support for environmental protection in the early 1970s was a product of many Americans' recognition that there were limits to growth. The realization that cities and industrial development were damaging the physical environment and altering the earth's ecology was not new: Rachel Carson's *Silent Spring* (1962) had sounded the warning years earlier. But in Nixon's first term Congress took concerted action, passing several acts to protect and clean up the environment, and blocking support for development of the supersonic transport (SST) plane on grounds that its sonic boom would disrupt the atmosphere. The administration at the same time created by executive order the Environmental Protection Agency, a consolidation of existing agencies,

An Earth Day demonstration dramatizing the dangers of air pollution, April 1972. [Wide World Photos]

to oversee federal guidelines for air pollution, toxic wastes, and water quality.

The energy crisis that struck home after the Arab oil boycott and the OPEC price increase heightened the public awareness that natural resources were not infinitely expendable. "Although it's positively un-American to think so," said one sociologist, "the environmental movement and energy shortage have forced us all to accept a sense of our limits, to lower our expectations, to seek prosperity through conservation rather than growth." Historians, always interested in precedents, recalled Frederick Jackson Turner's observation that the disappearance of the frontier in the 1890s marked a new epoch in American history by ending the geographic expansion over the continent. Richard Nixon had "promised to bring us together," noted one critic of the new mood, "but he didn't tell us that we would be gathering around diminished energy supplies, a no-growth economy and a reduced sense of national power."

Although the environmental movement cut across class, racial, and ethnic lines by appealing to the collective interests of all Americans in clean air and water, it simultaneously aggravated the competition between regional vested interests. In Texas, where the oil lobby resented controls on gas prices and speed limits, bumper stickers read: "Drive fast, freeze a Yankee." In Tennessee, where a federal dam project was halted because it threatened the snail darter—a species of fish—with extinction, local developers took out ads asking residents to "tell the government that the size of your wallet is more important than some two-inch-long minnow."

As stagflation persisted into the middle and late 1970s, corporate criticism that environmental regulations were cutting into jobs and profit margins began to sound more persuasive, especially when the staggering cost of cleaning up accumulated toxic wastes became known. "Why worry about the long run," said one unemployed steelworker in 1976, "when you're out of work right now." Faith in the ability of the federal government to monitor environmental safeguards dissipated in the wake of the crisis at the nuclear power plant at Three Mile Island, Pennsylvania, in March 1979, when a combination of faulty equipment and inadequate safety provisions caused the radioactive core of the plant to overheat, threatening a large portion of the northeastern United States with radiation poisoning. Exposure of corrupt practices within the EPA during the Reagan administration also hurt the environmental cause. Polls showed that protection of the environment remained a high priority among a majority of Americans, but that few were willing to suffer a cutback in their standard of living to achieve that goal. "It was," bemoaned one journalist, "as if passengers knew they were boarding the *Titanic*, but preferred to jostle with one another for first class accommodations so they might enjoy as much of the voyage as possible."

DRIFTING: FORD AND CARTER

During Nixon's last year in office the Watergate crisis so dominated the Washington scene that the major domestic and foreign problems received little executive attention. Henry Kissinger assumed virtually complete control over the management of foreign policy, watching helplessly as the South Vietnamese forces began to crumble before North Vietnamese attacks, attempting with limited success to establish a framework for peace in the Middle East, and supporting the CIA role in overthrowing Salvador Allende, the popularly elected Marxist president of Chile who was subsequently murdered and replaced by Gen. Augusto Pinochet, a military dictator supposedly friendly to the United States. The persistent combination of inflation and recession and the mounting energy crisis received little attention.

THE FORD YEARS Gerald Ford inherited these simmering problems. An amiable and eminently honest man, Ford enjoyed widespread popular support for only a short time. His pardon of Nixon on September 8, 1974, generated a storm of criticism. And as president he soon took on the posture he had developed as a conservative minority leader in the House: nay-saying leader of the opposition who simply did not believe that the federal government should exercise much power over domestic affairs. In

President Gerald Ford, a week after taking office. [United Press International]

his fifteen months as president Ford vetoed thirty-nine bills, thereby outstripping Herbert Hoover's veto record in less than half the time. By resisting congressional pressure to reduce taxes and increase federal spending, he succeeded in plummeting the economy into the deepest recession since the Great Depression. Unemployment jumped to 9 percent in 1975 and the federal deficit hit a record $60 billion the next year. When New York City announced that it was near bankruptcy, unable to meet its payrolls and bond payments, Ford vowed "to veto any bill that has as its purpose a federal bailout of New York City." But he relented after the Senate and House banking committees guaranteed the loan; New York was, at least temporarily, saved from insolvency. Ford rejected wage and price controls to curb inflation, preferring voluntary restraints which he tried to bolster by passing out "WIN" buttons, symbolizing his campaign to "Whip Inflation Now." The WIN buttons instead became a national joke and a popular symbol of Ford's ineffectiveness in the fight against stagflation.

In foreign policy, Ford retained Henry Kissinger as secretary of state and attempted to pursue Nixon's goals of stability in the Middle East, rapprochement with China, and détente with the Soviet Union. Late in 1974 Ford met with Leonid Brezhnev at Vladivostok in Siberia and accepted the framework for another arms-control agreement that was to serve as the basis for SALT II. Meanwhile Kissinger's tireless shuttling between Cairo and Tel Aviv produced an agreement: Israel promised to return to Egypt most of the Sinai territory captured in the 1967 war, and the two nations agreed to rely on negotiations rather than force to settle future disagreements. These limited but significant achievements should have enhanced Ford's image, but they were drowned in the sea of criticism and carping that followed the collapse of South Vietnam in May 1975.

Not only had a decade of American effort in Vietnam proven futile, but the Khmer Rouge, the Cambodian Communist movement, had also won a resounding victory, plunging that country into a fanatical bloodbath. And the Arab oil cartel was threatening another boycott while other Third World nations denounced the United States as a depraved and declining imperialistic power. Daniel Patrick Moynihan, the new American ambassador to the United Nations, attempted to answer these shrill accusations with his own unique blend of Irish passion and patriotic stridency, but succeeded in further antagonizing American relations with the developing countries. Ford also lost his patience, sending in the Marines to rescue the crew of the American merchant ship *Mayaguez*, which had been captured by the Cambodian Communists in May 1975. This vigorous move won popular acclaim until it was disclosed that the Cambodians had already agreed to release the captured Americans; the marines killed in the operation had died needlessly.

THE 1976 ELECTION   The Democrats could hardly wait for the 1976 election. Ford managed to beat off a powerful challenge for the nomination from the right wing of the Republican party, who rallied behind the former California governor and Hollywood actor, Ronald Reagan. Since even the Republicans were divided over Ford's leadership, and since Ford's failure to solve the economic and energy problems was beyond dispute, the Democratic nominee seemed a shoo-in for the presidency. "We could run an aardvark this year," said one Democratic leader, "and win."

His party chose an obscure former naval officer turned peanut farmer who had served one term as governor of Georgia. Jimmy Carter campaigned harder than any of the other Democratic hopefuls; he capitalized on the post-Watergate cynicism by promising "I will never tell a lie to the American people" and citing his inexperience in the byways of Washington politics as an asset. With the help of a skilled Atlanta advertising executive, Gerald Rafshoon, and by dint of full-time campaigning for over a year, the Georgian outdistanced his better known rivals and sewed up the nomination before the convention. Facing the prospect of the first president from the Deep South since 1849, and the first ever born and bred in that particular briar patch, the media suffered a surfeit of "southern fried chic." Reporters marveled at a Baptist candidate who claimed to be "born-again," and began to speculate that Carter's native region harbored some

Georgia's Jimmy Carter campaigned full-time for a year before winning the Democratic nomination. [Library of Congress]

forgotten virtues down home, after all. Sen. Sam Ervin's performance at the Watergate hearings had prepared the way.

To the surprise of many pundits Carter drew together the New Deal coalition of southern whites, blacks, urban labor, and ethnic groups to win 41 million votes to Ford's 39 million, and a narrow electoral majority of 297 to 241. Polls showed that the Carter victory was attributable to a heavy turnout of blacks in the South, where Carter swept every state but Virginia. Carter also benefited from the appeal of Walter F. Mondale, his liberal running mate and a favorite among blue-collar workers and the urban poor. He lost most of the trans-Mississippi West, but no other Democratic candidate had made much headway there since Harry Truman in 1948. The big story of the election was the low voter turnout. "Neither Ford nor Carter won as many votes as Mr. Nobody," said one reporter, commenting on the fact that almost half the eligible voters, alienated by Watergate and the lackluster candidates, chose to sit out the election.

CARTER'S TERM During the televised debates between the presidential candidates in 1976, Jimmy Carter had chided Ford by saying, "Anything you don't like about Washington, I suggest you blame on him." Once in office, Carter suffered the fate of all American presidents since Kennedy: after an initial honeymoon, during which Carter displayed folksy charms by walking down Pennsylvania Avenue after his inauguration rather than riding, and wearing cardigan sweaters during televised "fireside chats," his popularity and political effectiveness waned. Soon *Newsweek* was referring to the "corn bread-and-cardigan atmospherics" and television journalists were noting that, during one "fireside chat," the fire actually went out. The truth was that, like Ford before him, Carter faced an almost insurmountable set of domestic and international problems. He was expected to cure the economic recession and inflation at a time when all industrial economies were shaken by a shortage of energy and confidence. He was expected to reassert America's global power at a time of waning respect for America's international authority. And he was expected to do this, as well as buoy the national spirit, through a set of political institutions in which many Americans had lost faith. In short, Carter was predestined to fail at an impossible task.

During the first two years of his term Carter enjoyed several successes, most reflecting the values of moderate liberalism. His administration included more blacks and women than ever before in history; his appointment of Andrew Young, a former follower and protégé of Martin Luther King, as ambassador to the United Nations attracted the most attention. He created a federal task force to study the problem of Vietnam-era draft evaders and eventually offered amnesty to the thousands of young Americans who had fled the country rather than serve in Vietnam. He reformed the civil service and created new cabinet-level Departments of Energy and Education. And he pushed several significant environmental bills through Congress, including a bill to establish controls over strip mining, a "superfund" of $1.6 billion to clean up chemical waste sites, and a proposal to protect over 100 million acres of Alaskan land from development.

Carter's political predicament began to become clear in the debate over energy policy. Borrowing a phrase from William James, the president declared that solving the energy problem was "the moral equivalent of war" and presented the Congress with what he called "a comprehensive energy program" that would assure victory. Carter, like Hoover, served at a time of diminishing resources, and like that other engineer-businessman, had a distaste for "stroking" congressmen or wheeling and dealing to get legislation through. The energy bill passed in August 1978 was a gutted version of the original, reflecting the power of both conservative and liberal special-interest lobbies. One Carter aide said that the energy bill looked like it had been "nibbled to death by ducks."

Carter also urged the coupling of deregulation of the oil industry, which would increase prices and encourage domestic oil discovery, with a "windfall profits tax" on the oil companies, whose profits would skyrocket as a result of deregulation. Liberal congressmen resented deregulation because it meant higher prices for consumers. Conservatives opposed the windfall profits tax. The result was a bill that made no one happy. With party discipline in the Congress in a shambles and each special-interest group clamoring for its own program, the White House was forced to create what one Carter aide described as a "roll-your-own majority" for each presidential proposal. And Carter, unlike Wilson, FDR, and LBJ, was ill-equipped at maneuvering his proposals around congressional obstacles.

In the summer of 1979, when renewed violence in the Middle East produced a second fuel shortage, motorists were forced to wait in long lines again for limited supplies of gas that they regarded as excessively expensive. Opinion polls showed Carter with an approval rating of 26 percent, lower than Nixon during the worst moments of the Watergate crisis. Carter called his advisors to an extraordinary retreat at Camp David, Maryland, and emerged ten days later proclaiming a "crisis of confidence" and a need for "a rebirth of the American spirit." He also called for a "new and positive energy program." But motorists in the gas lines traded jokes about Carter's "born-again energy theology" and Congress only partially funded the major feature of his new plan—a federal agency to encourage development of synthetic fuels.

Several of Carter's early foreign policy initiatives also got caught in political crossfires. Soon after his inauguration Carter vowed that "the soul of our foreign policy" should be the defense of human rights abroad. But the human rights campaign came under attack from several sides: those who feared it sacrificed a detached appraisal of national interest for high-level moralizing, and those who pointed to the administration's inconsistency in applying the standard. But foreign policy always turns on multiple considerations, and the Carter policy was a reaffirmation of American ideals which heartened prisoners of conscience around the world.

Similarly, Carter's successful negotiation of treaties to turn over control of the Panama Canal to the government of Panama came under intense attack. Republican Ronald Reagan claimed that the Canal Zone was sovereign American soil purchased "fair and square" in Theodore Roosevelt's administration. (In the congressional debate one senator quipped, "We stole it fair and square, so why can't we keep it?") Carter argued that recognition of the limitations on American influence in Latin America, and the deep resentment toward American colonialism in Panama, left the United States with no other choice. The Senate ratified the treaties by a paper-thin margin (68 to 32, two votes more than the required two-thirds), but conservatives lambasted

Carter for surrendering American authority in a strategically critical part of the world. Finally, Carter completed the restoration of diplomatic relations with China, a process that had begun under Nixon. But because the Sino-American agreement of December 1978 required the United States to sever diplomatic relations with Taiwan, conservative critics condemned the agreement as a "sell-out" of the Taiwanese and another instance of American international withdrawal from past commitments.

ACHIEVEMENT AND FAILURE The crowning achievement of the Carter foreign policy, which even his most devoted critics applauded, was the arrangement of a peace agreement between Israel and Egypt. In November 1977 President Anwar el-Sadat flew to Tel Aviv at the invitation of Israeli Prime Minister Menachem Begin. Sadat's bold act, and his accompanying announcement that Egypt was now willing to recognize the legitimacy of the Israeli state, opened up diplomatic opportunities that Carter and Secretary of State Cyrus Vance quickly pursued. In September 1978 Carter invited Sadat and Begin to the presidential retreat at Camp David for two weeks of difficult negotiations. The first part of the eventual agreement called for Israel to return all land in the Sinai in exchange for Egyptian recognition of Israel's sovereignty. This agreement was successfully implemented in April 1982 when the last Israeli settler vacated the Sinai. But the second part of the agreement, calling for Israeli willingness to negotiate with Sadat to resolve the Palestinian refugee dilemma, began to unravel soon after the Camp David summit. By the time Begin and Sadat returned to Washington on March 26, 1979, to sign the formal treaty, Begin had already made clear his refusal to block new Israeli settlements on the West Bank of the Jordan River, which Sadat had regarded as a prospective homeland for the Palestinians, and most of the Arab nations had condemned Sadat as a traitor to their Islamic cause. Still, Carter and Vance were responsible for a dramatic display of high-level diplomacy that, whatever its limitations, made an all-out war between Israel and the Arab world less likely in the foreseeable future.

Carter's crowning failure, which even his most avid supporters acknowledged, was his management of the economy. In effect he inherited a bad situation and left it worse. Carter employed the same economic policies as Nixon and Ford to fight stagflation, but he reversed the order of the federal "cure," preferring to fight unemployment first with a tax cut and increased public spending. Unemployment declined slightly, from 8 to 7 percent in 1977, but inflation soared; at 5 percent when he took office, it reached 10 percent in 1978 and kept going. During one month in 1980 it measured an annual rate of no less than 18 percent. Like previous presidents, Carter then reversed himself to fight the other side of the economic malaise. By midterm he was delaying tax reductions and vetoing government spending programs that he had proposed in his first year. The result, however, was the worst of both possible worlds—a deepened recession with unemployment at 7.5 percent in 1980, mortgage rates at 15 percent, and interest rates at an all-time high of 20 percent; and a runaway inflation averaging between 12 and 13 percent. It was as if a seriously ill patient had been wheeled from one physician to another, receiving from each medication that worsened the original ailment, and then was told there was nothing else that medical science could do.

The conclusion of the SALT II treaty with the Soviets put Carter's leadership to the test just as the mounting economic problems made him the subject of biting editorial cartoons nationwide. Like SALT I, the new agreement did not do much to slow down the nuclear arms race. It placed a ceiling of 2,250 bombers and missiles on each side and set limits on the number of warheads and new weapons systems. In order to quell his conservative critics, who charged that SALT II would give the Soviets a decided advantage in the number and destructive power of land-based missiles, Carter announced that the United States would build a new missile system, called the MX, that would be housed in a vast maze of underground tunnels connected by railroad, creating a sort of "nuclear shell game" that would prevent Soviet planners from knowing where to strike. Liberal critics called the MX plan "a combination of Disneyworld and Armageddon" and criticized the SALT II agreement as "a step sideways rather than backwards in the arms race." Conservatives questioned the whole idea of détente, arguing that the Soviets would never have signed the agreement if it did not guarantee them nuclear superiority. Whether or not the SALT II treaty would pass the Senate became an open question.

The question became moot in December 1979 when the Soviet army invaded Afghanistan in order to rescue the faltering Communist government there, which was being challenged by Muslim rebels. Carter immediately shelved SALT II, suspended shipments of grain to the Soviet Union, and began a campaign for an international boycott of the 1980 Olympics, which were to be held that summer in Moscow. Zbigniew Brzezinski, Carter's hard-line national security advisor, won out over Cyrus Vance in the behind-the-scenes shuffling for influence and persuaded the president that the Soviet invasion of Afghanistan was only the first step in a Soviet scheme to dominate the oil-rich Persian Gulf. Calling the Soviet invasion "the gravest threat to world peace since World War II," Carter proclaimed that the United States would oppose by force any further Soviet advances in the Middle East. Military experts claimed that the United States lacked the forces and capability to block a Soviet move into the region, but Carter was determined to assert American power, even if, as one congressman put it, "the act of fighting for the oil would undoubtedly destroy all the oil fields, if not lead to thermonuclear war."

IRAN Then came the Iranian crisis, a year-long cascade of unwelcome events that epitomized the reduced stature of the United States in the world. The crisis began with the fall of the shah of Iran in January 1979. The revolutionaries who toppled the shah rallied around Ayatollah Ruhollah Khomeini, a Muslim religious leader who symbolized the Islamic values the shah had tried to replace with Western ways and whose hatred of the United States dated back to the CIA-sponsored overthrow of Iran's Mossadegh government in 1953. Nor did it help the American image that SAVAK, the shah's ruthless secret police force, was also trained by the CIA. Late in October the exiled shah was allowed to enter the United States in order to undergo treatment for lymphatic cancer. A few days later, on November 4, 1979, a

The year-long Iranian hostage crisis damaged America's prestige and President Carter's chances for reelection. [United Press International]

frenzied mob stormed the American embassy in Teheran and seized the diplomats and staff inside. Khomeini endorsed the mob action and demanded the return of the shah along with all his wealth in exchange for the release of the fifty-three American hostages. In the meantime the Iranian militants staged daily demonstrations for the benefit of worldwide news and television coverage in which the American flag and effigies of the American president were burned and otherwise desecrated.

Carter's range of options was limited. He appealed to the United Nations, protesting what was a clear violation of diplomatic immunity and international law. But Khomeini scoffed at U.N. requests for the release of hostages. Carter then froze all Iranian assets in the United States and appealed to American allies for a trade embargo of Iran. The trade restrictions were only partially effective—even America's most loyal European allies did not want to lose their access to Iranian oil—so Carter authorized a rescue attempt by American commandos in April 1980. Secretary of State Vance resigned in protest against the rescue attempt, and against Carter's sharp turn toward a more hawkish foreign policy. The commando raid was aborted because of helicopter failures, and ended with eight fatalities when another helicopter collided with a transport plane in the desert. Nightly television coverage of the taunting Iranian rebels generated widespread popular craving for action, cries of "Let's nuke the whole damn Iranian country" from frustrated Americans, and a near obsession with the falling fortunes of the United States and the fate of the hostages. The end came after 444 days of captivity when Carter, in his last act as president, released several billion dollars of Iranian assets to ransom the kidnapped hostages. A plane carrying them left Teheran for Algiers moments after Ronald Reagan finished his inaugural address. Carter then flew to Wiesbaden, West Germany, as the new president's envoy to greet the released hostages at an American base.

THE REAGAN RESTORATION

Ronald Reagan had initially appeared as an even more improbable presidential possibility than Jimmy Carter had four years earlier. A small-town midwestern boy who had gone west in the 1930s in search of fame and fortune, Reagan had found both in Hollywood. Though never a major film star, he became president of the Screen Actors Guild and a disciple of New Deal politics. The rhetoric of FDR stayed with him, but in the 1950s, as he toured the small towns and byways of middle America as a representative of General Electric, whose weekly television program he hosted, Reagan's political values changed. In 1964 he delivered a rousing speech on behalf of Barry Goldwater at the Republican convention. But Goldwater's crushing defeat seemed to show that such uncompromising conservatism as Reagan had come to embrace had no prospect of achieving a national following. During two terms as governor of California Reagan combined his fervid commitment to conservative principles with pragmatic skills as a performer and a political realist capable of compromise. Nevertheless, by the middle 1970s Reagan's brand of conservatism still appeared too extreme for a national audience and his "back-to-basics" speeches regularly provoked barbed jokes from journalists: "Ronald Reagan wants to take us back to the fifties," wrote an Associated Press reporter, "back to the 1950's in foreign policy and back to the 1850's in economic and domestic policy."

THE MOVE TO REAGAN   By the late 1970s, on the eve of the presidential election, Reagan had become the beneficiary of two developments that made his conservative vision of America much more than a harmless flirtation with nostalgia. First, the Census of 1980 revealed that the American population (226,505,000) was getting older and was moving in large numbers from the Northeast to the "Sunbelt" states of the South and West. This dual development—a 24 percent increase in the population classified as "elderly" and the steady transfer of political and economic power to regions of the country where hostility to "big government" was a powerful force—meant that demographic forces were carrying the United States toward Reagan's position.

Second, in the 1970s the country experienced a major revival of evangelical religion not unlike the Great Awakenings of the eighteenth and early nineteenth centuries. No longer a local or provincial phenomenon that could be dismissed as "a bunch of Bible thumping lunatics down in the hill country of Tennessee who talk directly with God and play with snakes," Christian evangelicals now owned their own television and radio stations and operated their own schools and universities. A survey in 1977 revealed that more than 70 million Americans described themselves as "born-again" Christians who had "a direct personal relationship with Jesus." The Rev. Jerry Falwell's "Moral Majority" expressed the political sentiments of countless other evangelical groups: free enterprise should remain free, big government should be made little, abortion should be outlawed as murder, the scientific version of evolution should be replaced in schoolbooks by the biblical story of creation, and Soviet expan-

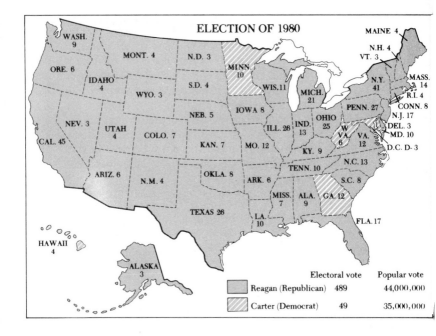

ELECTION OF 1980

	Electoral vote	Popular vote
Reagan (Republican)	489	44,000,000
Carter (Democrat)	49	35,000,000

sion should be opposed as a form of pagan totalitarianism. "You show me one of them liberal 'secular humanists,' " said one evangelical minister, "and I'll show you a fellow on his way to hell." The religious zeal and financial resources of the religious right made them at once formidable and effective opponents of liberal political candidates and programs. As defenders of traditional and local values—prayer in schools, families in which women stayed home to care for children, tough criminal laws—the religious right rallied to Reagan, opposing even the "born-again" Jimmy Carter.

And by 1980 Reagan also benefited from the deep popular disenchantment with the president, whose campaign was burdened by the frustrations of the Iranian hostage crisis, a desperately sick economy, and the party divisions created by Sen. Edward M. Kennedy's luckless quest for the Democratic nomination. On election day Reagan swept to a decisive victory, with 489 electoral votes to 49 for Carter, who carried only six states. The popular vote was equally lopsided: 44 million (51 percent) to 35 million (41 percent), with 7 percent going to John Anderson, an independent Republican who had bolted the party after Reagan's nomination. Reagan had won almost everywhere, in an election with the lowest voter turnout in the twentieth century. He had pulled enough Republican candidates along on his coattails to provide his administration with a Republican majority in the Senate and a House of Representatives that, though still Democratic, was sufficiently conservative to support White House initiatives during his first two years.

EARLY ASSESSMENTS The jury is still out on the achievements of Reagan's presidency. Not enough time has passed since he took office to permit judgments that qualify as history in any meaningful sense of the term. It is possible to conclude with confidence that Ronald Reagan brought to Washington the most conservative philosophy since Calvin Coolidge, whom he admired, that he brought skills as a public speaker and experienced television performer which served him well in presenting his views to the American people, and that, unlike the three previous presidents, he refused to compromise his basic outlook on what ailed the economy or what America's role in the world should be. Drift and equivocation were replaced with confident leadership that even some liberal critics admired. "Reagan is probably taking us down the wrong road," said a New York *Times* columnist, "but he's doing it with the style and grace and 'don't-look-back' bravado that the job requires."

Reagan's economic proposals were pure full-strength conservative medicine for the decade-long stagflation. His "supply-side" economics, soon dubbed "Reaganomics," presumed that the economic problems were a result of government intrusions into the marketplace and excessive taxes on workers and business. So Reagan proposed a three-year rate reduction in personal and corporate income taxes. Since reduced revenues required

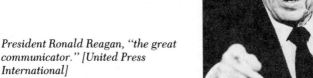

President Ronald Reagan, "the great communicator." [United Press International]

reduced federal expenditures, Reagan and David Stockman, his tough-minded budget director, proposed reductions in welfare, education, and other social services to the amount of $40 billion. Despite loud protests from liberal groups and congressmen, the entire Reagan economic package was passed by the summer of 1981. "Reaganomics" was based on the assumption that the tax cuts to consumers and corporations would stimulate a general economic revival and that prospective deficits would be made up with tax revenue collected in the wake of the recovery. "Reaganomics" in fact resembled the "Mellonomics" of Coolidge's secretary of the treasury in that it emphasized tax cuts to the rich on the assumption that their investments would stimulate the economy.

By the summer of 1983 a major economic recovery was under way, but its duration and the long-term implications of "Reaganomics" were clouded in controversy. The chief culprit was the huge budget deficit of approximately $200 billion, which in part was inherited from Reagan predecessors, in part resulted from Reagan's massive spending on arms and defense, and in part reflected the tardiness of the recovery. A liberal economist likened the American economy under Reagan's management to "a dying man who has stumbled out of the desert and receives a canteen of water, but meanwhile the arrow buried into his back [the deficit] is ignored."

In foreign policy, Reagan believed that Americans had overlearned the lessons of Vietnam and had forgotten the lessons of Munich. He embarked on a major buildup of nuclear and conventional weapons to close the gap that he claimed had developed between Soviet and American military forces, recovering the rhetoric of John Foster Dulles and the Kennedy inaugural address to describe American resolve in the face of "Communist aggression anywhere in the world." Ironically, Reagan's rhetoric was so apocalyptic that it contributed to a sudden and massive upsurge in the protest against nuclear weapons, which focused on a "freeze" on all nuclear weapons development and a declaration of "no first use" in Europe, where the NATO forces relied on tactical nuclear weapons to deter a Soviet invasion.

Détente deteriorated even further under Reagan's tough talk about "Communist imperialism" and in the face of the imposition of martial law in Soviet-controlled Poland in the winter of 1981. The crack-down came after Polish workers, united under the banner of an independent union called Solidarity, challenged the Communist monopoly of power. As in Hungary in 1956 and Czechoslovakia in 1968, there was little the United States could do except register protest and impose economic sanctions against the Communist government of Poland. Even Reagan accepted, albeit reluctantly, the limitations on American policy in central and eastern Europe.

Central America became the region in which Reagan detected the most serious Communist threat and into which he projected the most bellicose version of American resolve. Indeed Central America became to the Reagan administration in the early 1980s what Cuba had become to Kennedy in the early 1960s or Vietnam had become to Johnson in the mid-1960s. The tiny nation of El Salvador, caught up in a brutal struggle between Communist-supported revolutionaries and a repressive government, received American commitments of economic and military assistance. Reagan stopped short of sending American troops, but did increase the number of military advisors to the Salvadoran government. When Jimmy Carter had been confronted with a similar development in Nicaragua in 1979, he had concluded that the leftist takeover was inevitable and had not attempted to save the corrupt Somoza regime, even though Cuban-sponsored Communists were part of the revolutionary group. Critics of Reagan's policy in El Salvador argued that American involvement assured that the revolutionary forces would emerge as the victorious representatives of Salvadoran nationalism. Supporters countered by warning that American failure to act would allow for a repeat of Communist victories in Nicaragua and that Honduras, Guatemala, and then all of Central America would eventually enter the Communist camp.

Under Ronald Reagan the United States moved toward the year in which George Orwell's novel *1984* had foreseen worldwide dictatorship. America's mood most resembled the complacent hedonism of the 1950s. Russell Baker, writing in the New York *Times*, described "the hunt for the ideal restaurant, the perfect head of lettuce, the totally satisfying human relationship" as the current "equivalents of the Eisenhower age's passion for bigger tail fins, dryer martinis, darker steak houses and cozier evenings with the family." The world had changed a great deal since the 1950s, of course, and America was also a more complex and troubled society in which the bitter memories of Vietnam, assassinations, Watergate, and stagflation lingered like bad dreams. For the moment, however, the nation seemed eager to dispel these recent memories and recover the faith of the 1950s. Almost five centuries after Europeans had discovered the North American continent, over two centuries after American colonists had broken free from England, over a century after the sectional crisis had been resolved in civil war, the American people were pausing, wary of the future, looking back.

FURTHER READING

A good start for the events of the Nixon years is the former president's memoirs, *RN: The Memoirs of Richard Nixon* (1978).° Studies of Nixon at the time of his resurgence to power include Garry Wills's *Nixon Agonistes* (1970)° and Paul Hoffman's *The New Nixon* (1970). Fawn Brodie's *Richard Nixon* (1980)° is a critical work based on post-Watergate analysis. James David Barber's *The Presidential Character* (1972)° insightfully compares Nixon to his predecessors in the White House.

No one survey captures all the details of the Watergate scandal. The works of the two *Washington Post* reporters involved, Robert Woodward and Carl Bernstein, recount their role in the events; follow *All the President's Men* (1974)° with *The Final Days* (1976).° Arthur M. Schlesinger, Jr.'s *The Imperial Presidency* (1973)° looks for the scandal's cause in the growing power given the president to conduct foreign affairs. Other views of Watergate can be found in Theodore H. White's *Breach of Faith* (1975),° Jonathan Schell's *The Time of Illusion* (1976),° and Anthony Lukas's *Nightmare* (1976). For the impact of Watergate on the office of the presidency, see T. E. Cronin's *The State of the Presidency* (1975).

For the way the Republicans handled affairs abroad, consult Tad Szulc's *The Illusion of Power: Foreign Policy in the Nixon Years* (1978). Secretary of State Henry Kissinger recounts his role in policy formation in *The White House Years* (1978). Less favorable reports of the Kissinger role appear in David Landau's *Kissinger: The Uses of Power* (1972) and Seymour M. Hersh's *The Price of Power: Kissinger in the Nixon White House* (1983). Also helpful is Lloyd C. Gardner's *The Great Nixon Turnaround* (1975), for background on Nixon's relations with Russia and China.

The loss of Vietnam and the end of American involvement are traced in A. E. Goodman's *The Lost Peace: America's Search for a Negotiated Settlement of the Vietnam War* (1978) and Gareth Porter's *A Peace Denied: The United States, Vietnam and the Paris Agreement* (1975). William Showcross's *Sideshow: Kissinger, Nixon, and the Destruction of Cambodia* (1978)° deals with the broadening of the war, while Larry Berman's *Planning a Tragedy: The Americanization of the War in Vietnam* (1982)° and Leslie Gelb and Richard Betts's *The Irony of Vietnam: The System Worked* (1979)° assess the final impact of American involvement.

For the domestic side of the Nixon years, see R. P. Nathan (ed.), *Monitoring Revenue Sharing* (1975) and Daniel P. Moynihan's *The Politics of a Guaranteed Income: The Nixon Administration and the Family Assistance Plan* (1973).° Also helpful is Otis L. Graham, Jr.'s *Toward a Planned Society: From Roosevelt to Nixon* (1976).

For other views of politics during the 1970s, consult Henry S. Parmet's *The Democrats: The Years after FDR* (1976),° particularly for the McGovern campaign of 1972. Gerald Ford's memoir, *A Time to Heal:*

°These books are available in paperback editions.

The Autobiography of Gerald R. Ford (1979), is illuminating on the post-Watergate years.

The dimension of ethnic politics which figured in the early 1970s is explored in Edgar Litt's *Beyond Pluralism: Ethnic Politics in America* (1970) and Peter Schrag's *The Decline of the WASP* (1971). Ronald Taylor's *Chavez and the Farm Workers* (1975) discusses the ethnic politics of the Southwest. The plight of Indians is traced in Vine De Loria, Jr.'s *Behind the Trail of Broken Treaties* (1974). The feminist movement is depicted in William Chafe's *The American Woman: Her Changing Social, Economic, and Political Roles, 1920–1970* (1972),° and Jo Freeman's *The Politics of Women's Liberation* (1975).

To examine the rise of Jimmy Carter, consult Betty Glad's *Jimmy Carter: In Search of the Great White House* (1980) and Victor Lasky's *Jimmy Carter: The Man and the Myth* (1979). A work critical of the Carter administration is Haynes Johnson's *In the Absence of Power: Governing America* (1980). Zbigniew Brzezinski's *Power and Principle: Memories of the National Security Advisor, 1977–1981* (1983), gives insight to the Carter approach to foreign policy. Background on how the Middle East came to dominate much of American policy is found in Richard Stookey's *America and the Arab States* (1975) and William B. Quandt's *Decade of Decision: American Policy toward the Arab-Israeli Conflict, 1967–1976* (1977).° What followed in the Camp David Accords is handled best by Jimmy Carter in *Keeping Faith: The Memoirs of a President* (1982). Background on the SALT controversy is provided in Harold B. Moulton's *From Superiority to Parity: The United States and the Strategic Arms Race, 1961–1972* (1973).

Many recent books deal with various aspects of contemporary American culture. Zane L. Miller's *Suburb* (1981) and William Kornblum's *Blue-Collar Country* (1974) examine different elements of modern American society. Landon Y. Jones's *Great Expectations: America and the Baby Boom Generation* (1980)° explores how childraising affects current attitudes. Christopher Lasch's *The Culture of Narcissism: American Life in an Age of Diminishing Expectations* (1979)° criticizes the materialist element of modern culture. David Halberstam's *The Powers That Be* (1979)° investigates the influence and operation of mass media. The environmental crisis is treated in William Ophuls's *Ecology and the Politics of Scarcity* (1979) and Thomas R. Dunlop's *DDT: Scientists, Citizens, and Public Policy* (1981). The rise of the computer is traced in Kent C. Redmond's *Project Whirlwind: The History of a Pioneer Computer* (1980) and Geoffrey D. Austrian's *Hermann Hollerith: Forgotten Giant of Information Processing* (1982).

Peter Steinfel's *The Neoconservatives* (1979) heralded the election of conservatives in 1980. Lou Cannon's *Reagan* (1983) is one of the better studies of the president. Robert B. Reich's *The Next American Frontier* (1981)° examines the nation's recent industrial crisis.

APPENDIX

THE DECLARATION OF INDEPENDENCE

WHEN IN THE COURSE OF HUMAN EVENTS, it becomes necessary for one people to dissolve the political bands which have connected them with another, and to assume the Powers of the earth, the separate and equal station to which the Laws of Nature and of Nature's God entitle them, a decent respect to the opinions of mankind requires that they should declare the causes which impel them to the separation.

We hold these truths to be self-evident, that all men are created equal, that they are endowed by their Creator with certain unalienable rights, that among these are Life, Liberty, and the pursuit of Happiness. That to secure these rights, Governments are instituted among Men, deriving their just powers from the consent of the governed. That whenever any Form of Government becomes destructive of these ends, it is the Right of the People to alter or to abolish it, and to institute new Government, laying its foundation on such principles and organizing its powers in such form, as to them shall seem most likely to effect their Safety and Happiness. Prudence, indeed, will dictate that Governments long established should not be changed for light and transient causes; and accordingly all experience hath shown, that mankind are more disposed to suffer, while evils are sufferable, than to right themselves by abolishing the forms to which they are accustomed. But when a long train of abuses and usurpations, pursuing invariably the same Object evinces a design to reduce them under absolute Despotism, it is their right, it is their duty, to throw off such Government, and to provide new Guards for their future security.—Such has been the patient sufferance of these Colonies; and such is now the necessity which constrains them to alter their former Systems of Government. The history of the present King of Great Britain is a history of repeated injuries and usurpations, all having in direct object the establishment of an absolute Tyranny over these States. To prove this, let Facts be submitted to a candid world.

He has refused his Assent to Laws, the most wholesome and necessary for the public good.

He has forbidden his Governors to pass Laws of immediate and pressing importance, unless suspended in their operation till his Assent should be obtained; and when so suspended, he has utterly neglected to attend to them.

He has refused to pass other Laws for the accommodation of large districts of people, unless those people would relinquish the right of Representation in the Legislature, a right inestimable to them and formidable to tyrants only.

He has called together legislative bodies at places unusual, uncomfortable, and distant from the depository of their public Records, for the sole purpose of fatiguing them into compliance with his measures.

He has dissolved Representative Houses repeatedly, for opposing with manly firmness his invasions on the rights of the people.

He has refused for a long time, after such dissolutions, to cause others to be elected; whereby the Legislative powers, incapable of Annihilation, have returned to the People at large for their exercise; the State remaining in the mean time exposed to all dangers of invasion from without, and convulsions within.

He has endeavoured to prevent the population of these States; for that purpose obstructing the Laws of Naturalization of Foreigners; refusing to pass others to encourage their migrations hither, and raising the conditions of new Appropriations of Lands.

He has obstructed the Administration of Justice, by refusing his Assent to Laws for establishing Judiciary powers.

He has made Judges dependent on his Will alone, for the tenure of their offices, and the amount and payment of their salaries.

He has erected a multitude of New Offices, and sent hither swarms of Officers to harass our People, and eat out their substance.

He has kept among us, in times of peace, Standing Armies without the Consent of our legislature.

He has affected to render the Military independent of and superior to the Civil Power.

He has combined with others to subject us to a jurisdiction foreign to our constitution, and unacknowledged by our laws; giving his Assent to their Acts of pretended Legislation:

For quartering large bodies of armed troops among us:

For protecting them, by a mock Trial, from Punishment for any Murders which they should commit on the Inhabitants of these States:

For cutting off our Trade with all parts of the world:

For imposing taxes on us without our Consent:

For depriving us of many cases, of the benefits of Trial by jury:

For transporting us beyond Seas to be tried for pretended offences:

For abolishing the free System of English Laws in a neighbouring Province, establishing therein an Arbitrary government, and enlarging its Boundaries so as to render it at once an example and fit instrument for introducing the same absolute rule into these Colonies:

For taking away our Charters, abolishing our most valuable Laws, and altering fundamentally the Forms of our Governments:

For suspending our own Legislatures, and declaring themselves invested with Power to legislate for us in all cases whatsoever.

He has abdicated Government here, by declaring us out of his Protection and waging War against us.

He has plundered our seas, ravaged our Coasts, burnt our towns, and destroyed the lives of our people.

He is at this time transporting large armies of foreign mercenaries to compleat the works of death, desolation, and tyranny, already begun with circumstances of Cruelty & perfidy scarcely paralleled in the most barbarous ages, and totally unworthy the Head of a civilized nation.

He has constrained our fellow Citizens taken Captive on the high Seas to bear Arms against their Country, to become the executioners of their friends and Brethren, or to fall themselves by their Hands.

He has excited domestic insurrections amongst us, and has endeavoured to bring on the inhabitants of our frontiers, the merciless Indian Savages, whose known rule of warfare, is an undistinguished destruction of all ages, sexes, and conditions.

In every stage of these Oppressions We have Petitioned for Redress in the most humble terms: Our repeated Petitions have been answered only by repeated injury. A Prince, whose character is thus marked by every act which may define a Tyrant, is unfit to be the ruler of a free people.

Nor have We been wanting in attention to our British brethren. We have warned them from time to time of attempts by their legislature to extend an unwarrantable jurisdiction over us. We have reminded them of the circumstances of our emigration and settlement here. We have appealed to their native justice and magnanimity, and we have conjured them by the ties of our common kindred to disavow these usurpations, which, would inevitably interrupt our connections and correspondence. They too must have been deaf to the voice of justice and of consanguinity. We must, therefore, acquiesce in the necessity, which denounces our Separation, and hold them, as we hold the rest of mankind, Enemies in War, in Peace Friends.

WE, THEREFORE, the Representatives of the UNITED STATES OF AMERICA, in General Congress, Assembled, appealing to the Supreme Judge of the world for the rectitude of our intentions, do, in the Name, and by Authority of the good People of these Colonies, solemnly publish and declare, That these United Colonies are, and of Right ought to be FREE AND INDEPENDENT STATES; that they are Absolved from all Allegiance to the British Crown, and that all political connection between them and the State of Great Britain, is and ought to be totally dissolved; and that as Free and Independent States, they have full Power to levy War, conclude Peace, contract Alliances, establish Commerce, and to do all other Acts and Things which Independent States may of right do. And for the support of this Declaration, with a firm reliance on the Protection of Divine Providence, we mutually pledge to each other our Lives, our Fortunes, and our sacred Honor.

The foregoing Declaration was, by order of Congress, engrossed, and signed by the following members:

John Hancock

NEW HAMPSHIRE
Josiah Bartlett
William Whipple
Matthew Thornton

MASSACHUSETTS BAY
Samuel Adams
John Adams
Robert Treat Paine
Elbridge Gerry

RHODE ISLAND
Stephen Hopkins
William Ellery

CONNECTICUT
Roger Sherman
Samuel Huntington
William Williams
Oliver Wolcott

NEW YORK
William Floyd
Philip Livingston
Francis Lewis
Lewis Morris

NEW JERSEY
Richard Stockton
John Witherspoon
Francis Hopkinson
John Hart
Abraham Clark

PENNSYLVANIA
Robert Morris
Benjamin Rush
Benjamin Franklin
John Morton
George Clymer
James Smith
George Taylor
James Wilson
George Ross

DELAWARE
Caesar Rodney
George Read
Thomas M'Kean

MARYLAND
Samuel Chase
William Paca
Thomas Stone
Charles Carroll,
  of Carrollton

VIRGINIA
George Wythe
Richard Henry Lee
Thomas Jefferson
Benjamin Harrison
Thomas Nelson, Jr.
Francis Lightfoot Lee
Carter Braxton

NORTH CAROLINA
William Hooper
Joseph Hewes
John Penn

SOUTH CAROLINA
Edward Rutledge
Thomas Heyward, Jr.
Thomas Lynch, Jr.
Arthur Middleton

GEORGIA
Button Gwinnett
Lyman Hall
George Walton

Resolved, That copies of the Declaration be sent to the several assemblies, conventions, and committees, or councils of safety, and to the several commanding officers of the continental troops; that it be proclaimed in each of the United States, at the head of the army.

ARTICLES OF CONFEDERATION

To ALL TO WHOM these Presents shall come, we the undersigned Delegates of the States affixed to our Names send greeting.

Whereas the Delegates of the United States of America in Congress assembled did on the fifteenth day of November in the Year of our Lord One Thousand Seven Hundred and Seventy-seven, and in the Second Year of the Independence of America agree to certain articles of Confederation and perpetual Union between the States of Newhampshire, Massachusetts-bay, Rhodeisland and Providence Plantations, Connecticut, New York, New Jersey, Pennsylvania, Delaware, Maryland, Virginia, North-Carolina, South-Carolina and Georgia in the Words following, viz.

"Articles of Confederation and perpetual Union between the States of Newhampshire, Massachusetts-bay, Rhodeisland and Providence Plantations, Connecticut, New-York, New-Jersey, Pennsylvania, Delaware, Maryland, Virginia, North-Carolina, South-Carolina and Georgia.

ARTICLE I. The stile of this confederacy shall be "The United States of America."

ARTICLE II. Each State retains its sovereignty, freedom and independence, and every power, jurisdiction and right, which is not by this confederation expressly delegated to the United States, in Congress assembled.

ARTICLE III. The said States hereby severally enter into a firm league of friendship with each other, for their common defense, the security of their liberties, and their mutual and general welfare, binding themselves to assist each other, against all force offered to, or attacks made upon them, or any of them, on account of religion, sovereignty, trade or any other pretence whatever.

ARTICLE IV. The better to secure and perpetuate mutual friendship and intercourse among the people of the different States in this Union, the free inhabitants of each of these States, paupers, vagabonds and fugitives from justice excepted, shall be entitled to all privileges and immunities of free citizens in the several States; and the people of each State shall have free ingress and regress to and from any other State, and shall enjoy therein all the privileges of trade and commerce, subject to the same duties, impositions and restrictions as the inhabitants thereof respectively, provided that such restrictions shall not extend so far as to prevent the removal of property imported into any State, to any other State of which the owner is an inhabitant; provided also that no imposition, duties or restriction shall be laid by any State, on the property of the United States, or either of them.

If any person guilty of, or charged with treason, felony, or other high misdemeanor in any State, shall flee from justice, and be found in any of the United States, he shall upon demand of the Governor or Executive power, of the State from which he fled, be delivered up and removed to the State having jurisdiction of his offence.

Full faith and credit shall be given in each of these States to the records, acts and judicial proceedings of the courts and magistrates of every other State.

ARTICLE V. For the more convenient management of the general interests of the United States, delegates shall be annually appointed in such manner as the legislature of each State shall direct, to meet in Congress on the first Monday in November, in every year, with a power reserved to each State, to recall its delegates, or any of them, at any time within the year, and to send others in their stead, for the remainder of the year.

No State shall be represented in Congress by less than two, nor by more than seven members; and no person shall be capable of being a delegate for more than three years in any term of six years; nor shall any person, being a delegate, be capable of holding any office under the United States, for which he, or another for his benefit receives any salary, fees or emolument of any kind.

Each State shall maintain its own delegates in a meeting of the States, and while they act as members of the committee of the States.

In determining questions in the United States, in Congress assembled, each State shall have one vote.

Freedom of speech and debate in Congress shall not be impeached or questioned in any court, or place out of Congress, and the members of Congress shall be protected in their persons from arrests and imprisonments, during the time of their going to and from, and attendance on Congress, except for treason, felony, or breach of the peace.

ARTICLE VI. No State without the consent of the United States in Congress assembled, shall send any embassy to, or receive any embassy from, or enter into any conference, agreement, alliance or treaty with any king, prince or state; nor shall any person holding any office of profit or trust under the United States, or any of them, accept of any present, emolument, office or title of any kind whatever from any king, prince or foreign state; nor shall the United States in Congress assembled, or any of them, grant any title of nobility.

No two or more States shall enter into any treaty, confederation or alliance whatever between them, without the consent of the United States in Congress assembled, specifying accurately the purposes for which the same is to be entered into, and how long it shall continue.

No State shall lay any imposts or duties, which may interfere with any stipulations in treaties, entered into by the United States in Congress assembled, with any king, prince or state, in pursuance of any treaties already proposed by Congress, to the courts of France and Spain.

No vessels of war shall be kept up in time of peace by any State, except such number only, as shall be deemed necessary by the United States in Congress assembled, for the defence of such State, or its trade; nor shall any body of forces be kept up by any State, in time of peace, except such number only, as in the judgment of the United States, in Congress assembled, shall be deemed requisite to garrison the forts necessary for the defense of such State; but every State shall always keep up a well regulated and disciplined militia, sufficiently armed and accoutred, and shall provide and constantly have ready for use, in public stores, a due number of field pieces and tents, and a proper quantity of arms, ammunition and camp equipage.

No State shall engage in any war without the consent of the United States in Congress assembled, unless such State be actually invaded by enemies, or shall have received certain advice of a resolution being formed by some nation of Indians to invade such State, and the danger is so imminent as not to admit of a delay, till the United States in Congress assembled can be consulted: nor shall any State grant commissions to any ships or vessels of war, nor letters of marque or reprisal, except it be after a declaration of war by the United States in Congress assembled, and then only against the kingdom or state and the subjects thereof, against which war has been so declared, and under such regulations as shall be established by the United States in Congress assembled, unless such State be infested by pirates, in which case vessels of war may be fitted out for that occasion, and kept so long as the danger shall continue, or until the United States in Congress assembled shall determine otherwise.

ARTICLE VII. When land-forces are raised by any State of the common defence, all officers of or under the rank of colonel, shall be appointed by the Legislature of each State respectively by whom such forces shall be raised, or in such manner as such State shall direct, and all vacancies shall be filled up by the State which first made the appointment.

ARTICLE VIII. All charges of war, and all other expenses that shall be incurred for the common defense or general welfare, and allowed by the United States in Congress assembled, shall be defrayed out of a common treasury, which shall be supplied by the several States, in proportion to the value of all land within each State, granted to or surveyed for any person, as such land and the buildings and improvements thereon shall be estimated according to such mode as the United States in Congress assembled, shall from time to time direct and appoint.

The taxes for paying that proportion shall be laid and levied by the authority and direction of the Legislatures of the several States within the time agreed upon by the United States in Congress assembled.

Article IX. The United States in Congress assembled, shall have the sole and exclusive right and power of determining on peace and war, except in the cases mentioned in the sixth article—of sending and receiving ambassadors—entering into treaties and alliances, provided that no treaty of commerce shall be made whereby the legislative power of the respective States shall be restrained from imposing such imposts and duties on foreigners, as their own people are subjected to, or from prohibiting the exportation or importation of and species of goods or commodities whatsoever—of establishing rules for deciding in all cases, what captures on land or water shall be legal, and in what manner prizes taken by land or naval forces in the service of the United States shall be divided or appropriated—of granting letters of marque and reprisal in times of peace—appointing courts for the trial of piracies and felonies committed on the high seas and establishing courts for receiving and determining finally appeals in all cases of captures, provided that no member of Congress shall be appointed a judge of any of the said courts.

The United States in Congress assembled shall also be the last resort on appeal in all disputes and differences now subsisting or that hereafter may arise between two or more States concerning boundary, jurisdiction or any other cause whatever; which authority shall always be exercised in the manner following. Whenever the legislative or executive authority or lawful agent of any State in controversy with another shall present a petition to Congress, stating the matter in question and praying for a hearing, notice thereof shall be given by order of Congress to the legislative or executive authority of the other State in controversy, and a day assigned for the appearance of the parties by their lawful agents, who shall then be directed to appoint by joint consent, commissioners or judges to constitute a court for hearing and determining the matter in question: but if they cannot agree, Congress shall name three persons out of each of the United States, and from the list of such persons each party shall alternately strike out one, the petitioners beginning, until the number shall be reduced to thirteen; and from that number not less than seven, nor more than nine names as Congress shall direct, shall in the presence of Congress be drawn out by lot, and the persons whose names shall be so drawn or any five of them, shall be commissioners or judges, to hear and finally determine the controversy, so always as a major part of the judges who shall hear the cause shall agree in the determination: and if either party shall neglect to attend at the day appointed, without reasons, which Congress shall judge sufficient, or being present shall refuse to strike, the Congress shall proceed to nominate three persons out of each State, and the Secretary of Congress shall strike in behalf of such party absent or refusing; and the judgment and sentence of the court to be appointed, in the manner before prescribed, shall be final and conclusive; and if any of the parties shall refuse to submit to the authority of such court, or to appear or defend their claim or cause, the court shall nevertheless proceed to pronounce sentence, or judgment, which shall in like manner be final and decisive, the judgment or sentence and other procedings being in either case transmitted to Congress, and lodged among the acts of Congress for the security of the parties concerned: provided that every commissioner, before he sits in judgment, shall take an oath to be administered by one of the judges of the supreme or superior court of the State where the cause shall be tried, "well and truly to hear and determine the matter in question, according to the best of his judgment, without favour, affection or hope of reward:" provided also that no State shall be deprived of territory for the benefit of the United States.

All controversies concerning the private right of soil claimed under different grants of two or more States, whose jurisdiction as they may respect such lands, and the states which passed such grants are adjusted, the said grants or either of them being at the same time claimed to have originated antecedent to such settlement of jurisdiction, shall on the petition of either party to the Congress of the United States, be finally determined as near as may be in the same manner as is before prescribed for deciding disputes respecting territorial jurisdiction between different States.

The United States in Congress assembled shall also have the sole and exclusive right and power of regulating the alloy and value of coin struck by their own authority, or by that of the respective States—fixing the standard of weights and measures throughout the United States—regulating the trade and managing all affairs with the Indians, not members of any of the States, provided that the legislative right of any State within its own limits be not infringed or violated—establishing and regulating post-offices from one State to another, throughout all of the United States, and exacting such postage on the papers passing thro' the same as may be requisite to defray the expenses of the said office—appointing all officers of the land forces, in the service of the United States, excepting regimental officers—appointing all the officers of the naval forces, and commissioning all officers whatever in the service of the United States —making rules for the government and regulation of the said land and naval forces, and directing their operations.

The United States in Congress assembled shall have authority to appoint a committee, to sit in the recess of Congress, to be denominated "a Committee of the States," and to consist of one delegate from each State; and to appoint such other committees and civil officers as may be necessary for managing the general affairs of the United States under their direction—to appoint one of their number to preside, provided that no person be allowed to serve in the office of president more than one year in any term of three years; to ascertain the necessary sums of money to be raised for the service of the United States, and to appropriate and apply the same for defraying the public expenses—to borrow money, or emit bills on the credit of the United States, transmitting every half year to the respective States an account of the sums of money so borrowed or emitted,—to build and equip a navy—to agree upon the number of land forces, and to make requisitions from each State for its quota, in proportion to the number of white inhabitants in such State; which requisition shall be binding, and thereupon the Legislature of each State shall appoint the regimental officers, raise the men and cloath, arm and equip them in a soldier like manner, at the expense of the United States; and the officers and men so cloathed, armed and equipped shall march to the place appointed, and within the time agreed on by the United States in Congress assembled: but if the United States in Congress assembled shall, on consideration of circumstances judge proper that any State should not raise men, or should raise a smaller number of men than the quota thereof, such extra number shall be raised, officered, cloathed, armed and equipped in the same manner as the quota of such State, unless the legislature of such State shall judge that such extra number cannot be safely spared out of the same, in which case they shall raise officer, cloath, arm and equip as many of such extra number as they judge can be safely spared. And the officers and men so cloathed, armed and equipped, shall march to the place appointed, and within the time agreed on by the United States in Congress assembled.

The United States in Congress assembled shall never engage in a war, nor grant letters of marque and reprisal in time of peace, nor enter into any treaties or alliances, nor coin money, nor regulate the value thereof, nor ascertain the sums and expenses necessary for the defence and welfare of the United States, or any of them, nor emit bills, nor borrow money on the credit of the United States, nor appropriate money, nor agree upon the number of vessels to be built or purchased, or the number of land or sea forces to be raised, nor appoint a commander in chief of the army or navy, unless nine States assent to the same: nor shall a question on any other point, except for adjourning from day to day be determined, unless by the votes of a majority of the United States in Congress assembled.

The Congress of the United States shall have power to adjourn to any time within the year, and to any place within the United States, so that no period of adjournment be for a longer duration than the space of six months, and shall publish the journal of their proceedings monthly, except such parts thereof relating to treaties, alliances or military operations, as in their judgment require secrecy; and the yeas and nays of the delegates of each State on any question shall be entered on the Journal, when it is desired by any delegate; and the delegates of a State, or any of them, at his or their request shall be furnished with a transcript of the said journal, except such parts as are above excepted, to lay before the Legislatures of the several States.

ARTICLE X. The committee of the States, or any nine of them, shall be authorized to execute, in the recess of Congress, such of the powers of Congress as the United States in Congress assembled, by the consent of nine States, shall from time to time think expedient to vest them with; provided that no power be delegated to the said committee, for the exercise of which, by the articles of confederation, the voice of nine States in the Congress of the United States assembled is requisite.

ARTICLE XI. Canada acceding to this confederation, and joining in the measures of the United States, shall be admitted into, and entitled to all the advantages of this Union: but no other colony shall be admitted into the same, unless such admission be agreed to by nine States.

ARTICLE XII. All bills of credit emitted, monies borrowed and debts contracted by, or under the authority of Congress, before the assembling of the United States, in pursuance of the present confederation, shall be deemed and considered as a charge against the United States, for payment and satisfaction whereof the said United States, and the public faith are hereby solemnly pledged.

ARTICLE XIII. Every State shall abide by the determinations of the United States in Congress assembled, on all questions which by this confederation are submitted to them. And the articles of this confederation shall be inviolably observed by every State, and the Union shall be perpetual; nor shall any alteration at any time hereafter be made in any of them; unless such alteration be agreed to in a Congress of the United States, and be afterwards confirmed by the Legislatures of every State.

And whereas it has pleased the Great Governor of the world to incline the hearts of the Legislatures we respectively represent in Congress, to approve of, and to authorize us to ratify the said articles of confederation and perpetual union. Know ye that we the undersigned delegates, by virtue of the power and authority to us given for that purpose, do by these presents, in the name and in behalf of our respective constituents, fully and entirely ratify and confirm each and every of the said articles of confederation and perpetual union, and all and singular the matters and things therein contained: and we do further solemnly plight and engage the faith of our respective constituents, that they shall abide by the determinations of the United States in Congress assembled, on all questions, which by the said confederation are submitted to them. And that the articles thereof shall be inviolably observed by the States we respectively represent, and that the Union shall be perpetual.

In witness thereof we have hereunto set our hands in Congress. Done at Philadelphia in the State of Pennsylvania the ninth day of July in the year of our Lord one thousand seven hundred and seventy-eight, and in the third year of the independence of America.

THE CONSTITUTION OF
THE UNITED STATES

WE THE PEOPLE OF THE UNITED STATES, in order to form a more perfect Union, establish Justice, insure domestic Tranquility, provide for the common defence, promote the general Welfare, and secure the Blessings of Liberty to ourselves and our Posterity, do ordain and establish this Constitution for the United States of America.

ARTICLE. I.

Section. 1. All legislative Powers herein granted shall be vested in a Congress of the United States, which shall consist of a Senate and House of Representatives.

Section. 2. The House of Representatives shall be composed of Members chosen every second Year by the People of the several States, and the Electors in each State shall have the Qualifications requisite for Electors of the most numerous Branch of the State Legislature.

No Person shall be a Representative who shall not have attained to the Age of twenty five Years, and been seven Years a Citizen of the United States, and who shall not, when elected, be an Inhabitant of that State in which he shall be chosen.

Representatives and direct Taxes shall be apportioned among the several States which may be included within this Union, according to their respective Numbers, which shall be determined by adding to the whole Number of free Persons, including those bound to Service for a Term of Years, and excluding Indians not taxed, three fifths of all other Persons. The actual Enumeration shall be made within three Years after the first Meeting of the Congress of the United States, and within every subsequent Term of ten Years, in such Manner as they shall by Law direct. The Number of Representatives shall not exceed one for every thirty Thousand, but each State shall have at Least one Representative; and until such enumeration shall be made, the State of New Hampshire shall be entitled to chuse three, Massachusetts eight, Rhode-Island and Providence Plantations one, Connecticut five, New-York six, New Jersey four, Pennsylvania eight, Delaware one, Maryland six, Virginia ten, North Carolina five, South Carolina five, and Georgia three.

When vacancies happen in the Representation from any state, the Executive Authority thereof shall issue Writs of Election to fill such Vacancies.

The House of Representatives shall chuse their Speaker and other Officers; and shall have the sole Power of Impeachment.

Section. 3. The Senate of the United States shall be composed of two Senators from each State, chosen by the legislature thereof, for six Years; and each Senator shall have one Vote.

Immediately after they shall be assembled in Consequence of the first Election, they shall be divided as equally as may be into three Classes. The Seats of the Senators of the first Class shall be vacated at the Expiration of the second Year, of the second Class at the Expiration of the fourth Year, and of the third Class at the Expiration of the sixth Year, so that one third maybe chosen every second Year; and if Vacancies happen by Resignation, or otherwise, during the Recess of the Legislature of any State, the Executive thereof may make temporary Appointments until the next Meeting of the Legislature, which shall then fill such Vacancies.

No Person shall be a Senator who shall not have attained to the Age of thirty Years, and been nine Years a Citizen of the United States, and who shall not, when elected, be an Inhabitant of that State for which he shall be chosen.

The Vice President of the United States shall be President of the Senate, but shall have no Vote, unless they be equally divided.

The Senate shall chuse their other Officers, and also a President pro tempore, in the Absence of the Vice President, or when he shall exercise the Office of President of the United States.

The Senate shall have the sole Power to try all Impeachments. When sitting for that Purpose, they shall be on Oath or Affirmation. When the President of the United States is tried, the Chief Justice shall preside: And no Person shall be convicted without the Concurrence of two thirds of the Members present.

Judgment in Cases of Impeachment shall not extend further than to removal from Office, and disqualification to hold and enjoy any Office of honor, Trust or Profit under the United States: but the Party convicted shall nevertheless be liable and subject to Indictment, Trial, Judgment and Punishment, according to Law.

Section. 4. The Times, Places and Manner of holding Elections for Senators and Representatives, shall be prescribed in each State by the Legislature thereof, but the Congress may at any time by Law make or alter such Regulations, except as to the Places of chusing Senators.

The Congress shall assemble at least once in every Year, and such Meeting shall be on the first Monday in December, unless they shall by Law appoint a different Day.

Section. 5. Each House shall be the Judge of the Elections, Returns and Qualifications of its own Members, and a Majority of each shall constitute a Quorum to do Business; but a smaller Number may adjourn from day to day, and may be authorized to compel the Attendance of absent Members, in such Manner, and under such Penalties as each House may provide.

Each House may determine the Rules of its Proceedings, punish its Members for disorderly Behaviour, and, with the Concurrence of two thirds, expel a Member.

Each House shall keep a Journal of its Proceedings, and from time to time publish the same, excepting such Parts as may in their Judgment require Secrecy; and the Yeas and Nays of the Members of either House on any question shall, at the Desire of one fifth of those Present, be entered on the Journal.

Neither House, during the Session of Congress, shall, without the Consent of the other, adjourn for more than three days, nor to any other Place than that in which the two Houses shall be sitting.

Section. 6. The Senators and Representatives shall receive a Compensation for their Services, to be ascertained by Law, and paid out of the Treasury of the United States. They shall in all Cases, except Treason, Felony and Breach of the Peace, be privileged from Arrest during their Attendance at the Session of their respective Houses, and in going to and returning from the same; and for any Speech or Debate in either House, they shall not be questioned in any other Place.

No Senator or Representative shall, during the Time for which he was elected, be appointed to any civil Office under the Authority of the United States, which shall have been created, or the Emoluments whereof shall have been encreased during such time; and no Person holding any Office under the United States, shall be a Member of either House during his Continuance in Office.

Section. 7. All Bills for raising Revenue shall originate in the House of Representatives; but the Senate may propose or concur with Amendments as on other Bills.

Every Bill which shall have passed the House of Representatives and the Senate shall, before it become a Law, be presented to the President of the United States; If he approve he shall sign it, but if not he shall return it, with his Objections to that House in which it shall have originated, who shall enter the Objections at large on their Journal, and proceed to reconsider it. If after such Reconsideration two thirds of that House shall agree to pass the Bill, it shall be sent, together with the Objections, to the other House, by which it shall likewise be reconsidered, and if approved by two thirds of that House, it shall become a Law. But in all such Cases the Votes of both Houses shall be determined by yeas and Nays, and the Names of the Persons voting for and against the Bill shall be entered on the Journal of each House respectively. If any Bill shall not be returned by the President within ten Days (Sundays excepted) after it shall have been presented to him, the Same shall be a Law, in like Manner as if he had signed it, unless the Congress by their Adjournment prevent its Return, in which Case it shall not be a Law.

Every Order, Resolution, or Vote to which the Concurrence of the

Senate and House of Representatives may be necessary (except on a question of Adjournment) shall be presented to the President of the United States; and before the Same shall take Effect, shall be approved by him, or being disapproved by him, shall be repassed by two thirds of the Senate and House of Representatives, according to the Rules and Limitations prescribed in the Case of a Bill.

Section. 8. The congress shall have Power To lay and collect Taxes, Duties, Imposts and Excises, to pay the Debts and provide for the common Defence and general Welfare of the United States; but all Duties, Imposts and Excises shall be uniform throughout the United States.

To borrow Money on the credit of the United States;

To regulate Commerce with foreign Nations, and among the several States, and with the Indian Tribes;

To establish an uniform Rule of Naturalization, and uniform Laws on the subject of Bankruptcies throughout the United States;

To coin Money, regulate the Value thereof, and of foreign Coin, and fix the Standard of Weights and Measures;

To provide for the Punishment of counterfeiting the Securities and current Coin of the United States;

To establish Post Offices and Post Roads;

To promote the Progress of Science and useful Arts, by securing for limited Times to Authors and Inventors the exclusive Right to their respective Writings and Discoveries;

To constitute Tribunals inferior to the supreme Court;

To define and punish Piracies and Felonies committed on the high Seas, and Offences against the Law of Nations;

To declare War, grant Letters of Marque and Reprisal, and make Rules concerning Captures on land and Water;

To raise and support Armies, but no Appropriation of Money to that Use shall be for a longer Term than two Years;

To provide and maintain a Navy;

To make Rules for the Government and Regulation of the land and naval Forces;

To provide for calling forth the Militia to execute the Laws of the Union, suppress Insurrections and repel Invasions;

To provide for organizing, arming, and disciplining, the Militia, and for governing such Part of them as may be employed in the Service of the United States, reserving to the States respectively, the Appointment of the Officers, and the Authority of training the Militia according to the discipline prescribed by Congress;

To exercise exclusive Legislation in all Cases whatsoever, over such District (not exceeding ten Miles square) as may, by Cession of particular States, and the Acceptance of Congress, become the Seat of the Government of the United States, and to exercise like Authority over all Places purchased by the Consent of the Legislature of the State in which the Same shall be, for the Erection of Forts, Magazines, Arsenals, dock-Yards, and other needful Buildings;—And

To make all Laws which shall be necessary and proper for carrying into Execution the foregoing Powers, and all other Powers vested by this Constitution in the Government of the United States, or in any Department or Officer thereof.

Section. 9. The Migration or Importation of such Persons as any of the States now existing shall think proper to admit, shall not be prohibited by the Congress prior to the Year one thousand eight hundred and eight, but a Tax or duty may be imposed on such Importation, not exceeding ten dollars for each Person.

The Privilege of the Writ of Habeas Corpus shall not be suspended, unless when in Cases of Rebellion or Invasion the public Safety may require it.

No Bill of Attainder or ex post facto Law shall be passed.

No Capitation, or other direct, Tax shall be laid, unless in Proportion to the Census or Enumeration herein before directed to be taken.

No Tax or Duty shall be laid on Articles exported from any State.

No Preference shall be given by any Regulation of Commerce or Revenue to the Ports of one State over those of another: nor shall Vessels bound to, or from, one State, be obliged to enter, clear, or pay Duties in another.

No Money shall be drawn from the Treasury, but in Consequence of Appropriations made by Law, and a regular Statement and Account of the Receipts and Expenditures of all public Money shall be published from time to time.

No Title of Nobility shall be granted by the United States: And no Person holding any Office of Profit or trust under them, shall, without the Consent of the Congress, accept of any present, Emolument, Office, or Title, of any kind whatever, from any King, prince, or foreign State.

Section. 10. No State shall enter into any Treaty, Alliance, or Confederation; grant Letters of Marque and Reprisal; coin Money; emit Bills of Credit; make any Thing but gold and silver Coin a Tender in Payment of Debts; pass any Bill of Attainder, ex post facto Law, or Law impairing the Obligation of Contracts, or grant any Title of Nobility.

No State shall, without the Consent of the Congress, lay any Imposts or Duties on Imports or Exports, except what may be absolutely necessary for executing it's inspection Laws: and the net Produce of all Duties and Imposts, laid by any State on Imports or Exports, shall be for the Use of the Treasury of the United States; and all such Laws shall be subject to the Revision and Controul of the Congress.

No State shall, without the Consent of Congress, lay any Duty of Tonnage, keep Troops, or Ships of War in time of Peace, enter into any Agreement or Compact with another State, or with a foreign Power, or engage in War, unless actually invaded, or in such imminent Danger as will not admit of delay.

ARTICLE. II.

Section. 1. The executive Power shall be vested in a President of the United States of America. He shall hold his Office during the term of four

Years, and, together with the Vice President, chosen for the same Term, be elected, as follows.

Each State shall appoint, in such Manner as the Legislature thereof may direct, a Number of Electors, equal to the whole Number of Senators and Representatives to which the State may be entitled in the Congress: but no Senator or Representative, or Person holding an Office of Trust or Profit under the United States, shall be appointed an Elector.

The Electors shall meet in their respective States, and vote by Ballot for two Persons, of whom one at least shall not be an Inhabitant of the same State with themselves. And they shall make a List of all the Persons voted for, and of the Number of Votes for each; which List they shall sign and certify, and transmit sealed to the Seat of the Government of the United States, directed to the President of the Senate. The President of the Senate shall, in the Presence of the Senate and House of Representatives, open all the Certificates, and the Votes shall then be counted. The Person having the greatest Number of Votes shall be the President, if such Number be a Majority of the whole Number of Electors appointed; and if there be more than one who have such Majority, and have an equal Number of Votes, then the House of Representatives shall immediately chuse by Ballot one of them for President; and if no Person have a Majority, then from the five highest on the List the said House shall in like Manner chuse the President. But in chusing the President, the Votes shall be taken by States, the Representation from each State having one Vote; A quorum for this Purpose shall consist of a Member or Members from two thirds of the States, and a Majority of all the States shall be necessary to a Choice. In every Case, after the Choice of the President, the Person having the greatest Number of Votes of the Electors shall be the Vice President. But if there should remain two or more who have equal Votes, the Senate shall chuse from them by Ballot the Vice President.

The Congress may determine the Time of chusing the Electors, and the Day on which they shall give their Votes; which Day shall be the same throughout the United States.

No Person except a natural born Citizen, or a Citizen of the United States, at the time of the Adoption of this Constitution, shall be eligible to the Office of President, neither shall any Person be eligible to that Office who shall not have attained to the Age of thirty five Years, and been fourteen Years a Resident within the United States.

In Case of the Removal of the President from office, or of his Death, Resignation, or Inability to discharge the Powers and Duties of the said Office, the Same shall devolve on the Vice President, and the Congress may by Law provide for the Case of Removal, Death, Resignation or Inability, both of the President and Vice President, declaring what Officer shall then act as President, and such Officer shall act accordingly, until the Disability be removed, or a President shall be elected.

The President shall, at stated Times, receive for his Services, a Compensation, which shall neither be encreased or diminished during the Period for which he shall have been elected, and he shall not receive within that Period any other Emolument from the United States, or any of them.

Before he enters on the Execution of his Office, he shall take the following Oath or Affirmation:—"I do solemnly swear (or affirm) that I will faithfully execute the Office of President of the United States, and will to the best of my Ability, preserve, protect and defend the Constitution of the United States."

Section. 2. The President shall be Commander in Chief of the Army and Navy of the United States, and of the Militia of the several States, when called into the actual Service of the United States; he may require the Opinion, in writing, of the principal Officer in each of the executive Departments, upon any Subject relating to the Duties of their respective Offices, and he shall have Power to grant Reprieves and Pardons for Offences against the United States, except in Cases of Impeachment.

He shall have Power, by and with the Advice and Consent of the Senate, to make Treaties, provided two thirds of the Senators present concur; and he shall nominate, and by and with the Advice and Consent of the Senate, shall appoint Ambassadors, other public Ministers and Consuls, Judges of the supreme Court, and all other Officers of the United States, whose Appointments are not herein otherwise provided for, and which shall be established by Law; but the Congress may by Law vest the Appointment of such inferior Officers, as they think proper, in the President alone, in the Courts of Law, or in the Heads of Departments.

The President shall have Power to fill up all Vacancies that may happen during the Recess of the Senate, by granting Commissions which shall expire at the End of their next Session.

Section. 3. He shall from time to time give to the Congress Information of the State of the Union, and recommend to their Consideration such Measures as he shall judge necessary and expedient; he may, on extraordinary Occasions, convene both Houses, or either of them, and in Case of Disagreement between them, with Respect to the Time of Adjournment, he may adjourn them to such Time as he shall think proper; he shall receive Ambassadors and other public Ministers; he shall take Care that the Laws be faithfully executed, and shall Commission all the Officers of the United States.

Section. 4. The President, Vice President and all civil Officers of the United States, shall be removed from Office on Impeachment for, and Conviction of, Treason, Bribery, or other high Crimes and Misdemeanors.

Article. III.

Section. 1. The judicial Power of the United States, shall be vested in one supreme Court, and in such inferior Courts as the Congress may from time to time ordain and establish. The Judges, both of the supreme and inferior Courts, shall hold their Offices during good Behavior, and shall, at stated Times, receive for their Services, a Compensation, which shall not be diminished during their Continuance in Office.

Section. 2. The judicial Power shall extend to all Cases, in Law and Equity, arising under this Constitution, the Laws of the United States, and Treaties made, or which shall be made, under their Authority;—to all Cases affecting Ambassadors, other public Ministers and Consuls;—to all Cases of admiralty and maritime Jurisdiction;—to Controversies to which the United States shall be a Party;—to Controversies between two or more States;—between a State and Citizens of another State;—between Citizens of different States;—between Citizens of the same State claiming Lands under Grants of different States, and between a State, or the Citizens thereof, and foreign States, Citizens or Subjects.

In all cases affecting Ambassadors, other public Ministers and Consuls, and those in which a State shall be Party, the supreme Court shall have original Jurisdiction. In all the other Cases before mentioned, the supreme Court shall have appellate Jurisdiction, both as to Law and Fact, with such Exceptions, and under such Regulations as the Congress shall make.

The Trial of all Crimes, except in Cases of Impeachment, shall be by Jury; and such Trial shall be held in the State where the said Crimes shall have been committed; but when not committed within any State, the Trial shall be at such Place or Places as the Congress may by Law have directed.

Section. 3. Treason against the United States, shall consist only in levying War against them, or in adhering to their Enemies, giving them Aid and Comfort. No Person shall be convicted of Treason unless on the Testimony of two Witnesses to the same overt Act, or on Confession in open Court.

The Congress shall have Power to declare the Punishment of Treason, but no Attainder of Treason shall work Corruption of Blood, or Forfeiture except during the Life of the Person attainted.

ARTICLE. IV.

Section. 1. Full Faith and Credit shall be given in each State to the public Acts, Records, and judicial Proceedings of every other State. And the Congress may by general Laws prescribe the Manner in which such Acts, Records and Proceedings shall be proved, and the Effect thereof.

Section. 2. The Citizens of each State shall be entitled to all Privileges and Immunities of Citizens in the several States.

A Person charged in any State with Treason, Felony, or other Crime, who shall flee from Justice, and be found in another State, shall on Demand of the executive Authority of the State from which he fled, be delivered up, to be removed to the State having Jurisdiction of the Crime.

No Person held to Service or Labour in one State, under the Laws thereof, escaping into another, shall, in Consequence of any Law or Regulation therein, be discharged from such Service or Labour, but shall be delivered up on Claim of the Party to whom such Service or Labour may be due.

Section. 3. New States may be admitted by the Congress into this Union; but no new State shall be formed or erected within the Jurisdiction of any other State; nor any State be formed by the Junction of two or more States, or Parts of States, without the consent of the Legislatures of the States concerned as well as of the Congress.

The Congress shall have Power to dispose of and make all needful Rules and Regulations respecting the Territory or other Property belonging to the United States; and nothing in this Constitution shall be so construed as to Prejudice any Claims of the United States, or of any particular States.

Section. 4. The United States shall guarantee to every State in this Union a Republican Form of Government, and shall protect each of them against Invasion; and on Application of the Legislature, or of the Executive (when the Legislature cannot be convened) against domestic Violence.

ARTICLE. V.

The Congress, whenever two thirds of both Houses shall deem it necessary, shall propose Amendments to this Constitution, or, on the Application of the Legislatures of two thirds of the several States shall call a Convention for proposing Amendments, which, in either Case, shall be valid to all Intents and Purposes, as Part of this Constitution, when ratified by the Legislatures of three fourths of the several States, or by Conventions in three fourths thereof, as the one or the other Mode of Ratification may be proposed by the Congress; Provided that no Amendment which may be made prior to the Year One thousand eight hundred and eight shall in any Manner affect the first and fourth Clauses in the Ninth Section of the first Article; and that no State, without its Consent, shall be deprived of it's equal Suffrage in the Senate.

ARTICLE. VI.

All Debts contracted and Engagements entered into, before the Adoption of this Constitution, shall be as valid against the United States under this Constitution, as under the Confederation.

This Constitution, and the Laws of the United States which shall be made in Pursuance thereof; and all Treaties made, or which shall be made, under the Authority of the United States, shall be the supreme Law of the Land; and the Judges in every State shall be bound thereby, any Thing in the Constitution or Laws of any State to the Contrary notwithstanding.

The Senators and Representatives before mentioned, and the Members of the several State Legislatures, and all executive and judicial Officers, both of the United States and of the several States, shall be bound by Oath or Affirmation, to support this Constitution; but no religious Test shall ever be required as a Qualification to any Office or public Trust under the United States.

ARTICLE. VII.

The Ratification of the Conventions of nine States, shall be sufficient for the Establishment of this Constitution between the States so ratifying the Same.

Done in Convention by the Unanimous Consent of the States present the Seventeenth Day of September in the Year of our Lord one thousand seven hundred and Eighty seven and of the Independence of the United States of America the Twelfth. In witness thereof We have hereunto subscribed our Names,

G°: WASHINGTON—Presid^t
and deputy from Virginia

New Hampshire	John Langdon Nicholas Gilman	Delaware	Geo: Read Gunning Bed- ford jun John Dickinson Richard Bassett Jaco: Broom
Massachusetts	Nathaniel Gorham Rufus King		
Connecticut	Wm Saml Johnson Roger Sherman	Maryland	James McHenry Dan of St Thos Jenifer Danl Carroll
New York	Alexander Hamilton		
New Jersey	Wil: Livingston David A. Brearley. Wm Paterson. Jona: Dayton	Virginia	John Blair— James Madison Jr.
Pennsylvania	B. Franklin Thomas Mifflin Robt Morris Geo. Clymer Thos. FitzSimons Jared Ingersoll James Wilson Gouv Morris	North Carolina	W^m. Blount Richd Dobbs Spaight. Hu Williamson
		South Carolina	J. Rutledge Charles Cotesworth Pinckney Charles Pinckney Pierce Butler.
		Georgia	William Few Abr Baldwin

AMENDMENTS TO THE CONSTITUTION

ARTICLES IN ADDITION TO, and Amendment of the Constitution of the United States of America, proposed by Congress, and ratified by the Legislatures of the several States, pursuant to the fifth Article of the original Constitution.

AMENDMENT I.

Congress shall make no law respecting an establishment of religion, or prohibiting the free exercise thereof; or abridging the freedom of speech, or of the press; or the right of the people peaceably to assemble, and to petitition the Government for a redress of grievances.

AMENDMENT II.

A well regulated Militia, being necessary to the security of a free State, the right of the people to keep and bear Arms, shall not be infringed.

AMENDMENT III.

No Soldier shall, in time of peace be quartered in any house, without the consent of the Owner, nor in time of war, but in a manner to be prescribed by law.

AMENDMENT IV.

The right of the people to be secure in their persons, houses, papers, and effects, against unreasonable searches and seizures, shall not be violated, and no Warrants shall issue, but upon probable cause, supported by Oath or affirmation, and particularly describing the place to be searched, and the persons or things to be seized.

AMENDMENT V.

No person shall be held to answer for a capital, or otherwise infamous crime, unless on a presentment or indictment of a Grand Jury, except in cases arising in the land or naval forces, or in the Militia, when in actual service in time of War or public danger; nor shall any person be subject for the same offence to be twice put in jeopardy of life or limb; nor shall be compelled in any criminal case to be a witness against himself, nor be deprived of life, liberty, or property, without due process of law; nor shall private property be taken for public use, without just compensation.

AMENDMENT VI.

In all criminal prosecutions, the accused shall enjoy the right to a speedy and public trial, by an impartial jury of the State and district wherein the crime shall have been committed, which district shall have been previously ascertained by law, and to be informed of the nature and cause of the accusation; to be confronted with the witnesses against him; to have compulsory process for obtaining witnesses in his favor, and to have the Assistance of Counsel for his defence.

Amendment VII.

In Suits at common law, where the value in controversy shall exceed twenty dollars, the right of trial by jury shall be preserved, and no fact tried by a jury, shall be otherwise re-examined in any Court of the United States, than according to the rules of the common law.

Amendment VIII.

Excessive bail shall not be required, nor excessive fines imposed, nor cruel and unusual punishments inflicted.

Amendment IX.

The enumeration in the Constitution, of certain rights, shall not be construed to deny or disparage others retained by the people.

Amendment X.

The powers not delegated to the United States by the Constitution, nor prohibited by it to the States, are reserved to the States respectively, or to the people. [The first ten amendments went into effect December 15, 1791.]

Amendment XI.

The Judicial power of the United States shall not be construed to extend to any suit in law or equity, commenced or prosecuted against one of the United States by Citizens of another State, or by Citizens or Subjects of any Foreign State. [January 8, 1798.]

Amendment XII.

The Electors shall meet in their respective states, and vote by ballot for President and Vice-President, one of whom, at least, shall not be an inhabitant of the same state with themselves; they shall name in their ballots the person voted for as President, and in distinct ballots the person voted for as Vice-President, and they shall make distinct lists of all persons voted for as President, and of all persons voted for as Vice-President, and of the number of votes for each, which lists they shall sign and certify, and transmit sealed to the seat of the government of the United States, directed to the President of the Senate;—The President of the Senate shall, in the presence of the Senate and House of Representatives, open all the certificates and the votes shall then be counted;—The person having the greatest number of votes for President, shall be the President, if such number be a majority of the whole number of Electors appointed; and if no person have such majority, then from the persons having the highest numbers not exceeding three on the list of those voted for as President, the House of Representatives shall choose immediately, by ballot, the President. But in choosing the President, the votes shall be taken by states, the representation from each state having one vote; a quorum for this purpose shall consist of a member or members from two-thirds of the states, and a majority of all the states shall be necessary to a choice. And if the House of Representatives shall not choose a President whenever the right of choice shall devolve upon them, before the fourth day of March next following, then the Vice-President shall act as President, as in the case of the death or other constitutional disability of the President.—The person having the greatest number of votes as Vice-President, shall be the Vice-President, if such number be a majority of the whole number of Electors appointed, and if no person have a majority, then from the two highest numbers on the list, the Senate shall choose the Vice-President; a quorum for the purpose shall consist of two-thirds of the whole number of Senators, and a majority of the whole number shall be necessary to a choice. But no person constitutionally ineligible to the office of President shall be eligible to that of Vice-President of the United States. [September 25, 1804.]

Amendment XIII.

Section 1. Neither slavery nor involuntary servitude, except as a punishment for crime whereof the party shall have been duly convicted, shall exist within the United States, or any place subject to their jurisdiction.

Section 2. Congress shall have power to enforce this article by appropriate legislation. [December 18, 1865.]

Amendment XIV.

Section 1. All persons born or naturalized in the United States, and subject to the jurisdiction thereof, are citizens of the United States and of the State wherein they reside. No State shall make or enforce any law which shall abridge the privileges or immunities of citizens of the United States; nor shall any State deprive any person of life, liberty, or property, without due process of law; nor deny to any person within its jurisdiction the equal protection of the laws.

Section 2. Representatives shall be apportioned among the several States according to their respective numbers, counting the whole number of persons in each State, excluding Indians not taxed. But when the right to vote at any election for the choice of electors for President and Vice President of the United States, Representatives in Congress, the Executive and Judicial officers of a State, or the members of the Legislature thereof, is denied to any of the male inhabitants of such State, being twenty-one years of age, and citizens of the United States, or in any way abridged, except for participation in rebellion, or other crime, the basis of representation therein shall be reduced in the proportion which the number of such male citizens shall bear to the whole number of male citizens twenty-one years of age in such State.

Section 3. No person shall be a Senator or Representative in Congress, or elector of President and Vice President, or hold any office, civil or military, under the United States, or under any State, who, having previously taken an oath, as a member of Congress, or as an officer of the United States, or as a member of any State legislature, or as an executive or judicial officer of any State, to support the Constitution of the United States, shall have engaged in insurrection or rebellion against the same, or given aid or comfort to the enemies thereof. But Congress may by a vote of two-thirds of each House, remove such disability.

Section 4. The validity of the public debt of the United States, authorized by law, including debts incurred for payment of pensions and bounties for services in suppressing insurrection or rebellion, shall not be questioned. But neither the United States nor any State shall assume or pay any debt or obligation incurred in aid of insurrection or rebellion against the United States, or any claim for the loss or emancipation of any slave; but all such debts, obligations and claims shall be held illegal and void.

Section 5. The Congress shall have power to enforce, by appropriate legislation, the provisions of this article. [July 28, 1868.]

Amendment XV.

Section 1. The right of citizens of the United States to vote shall not be denied or abridged by the United States or by any State on account of race, color, or previous condition of servitude—

Section 2. The Congress shall have power to enforce this article by appropriate legislation.—[March 30, 1870.]

Amendment XVI.

The Congress shall have power to lay and collect taxes on incomes, from whatever source derived, without apportionment among the several States, and without regard to any census or enumeration. [February 25, 1913.]

AMENDMENT XVII.

The Senate of the United States shall be composed of two senators from each State, elected by the people thereof, for six years; and each Senator shall have one vote. The electors in each State shall have the qualifications requisite for electors of the most numerous branch of the State legislature.

When vacancies happen in the representation of any State in the Senate, the executive authority of such State shall issue writs of election to fill such vacancies: *Provided*, That the legislature of any State may empower the executive thereof to make temporary appointments until the people fill the vacancies by election as the legislature may direct.

This amendment shall not be so construed as to affect the election or term of any senator chosen before it becomes valid as part of the Constitution. [May 31, 1913.]

AMENDMENT XVIII.

After one year from the ratification of this article, the manufacture, sale, or transportation of intoxicating liquors within, the importation thereof into, or the exportation thereof from the United States and all territory subject to the jurisdiction thereof for beverage purposes is hereby prohibited.

The Congress and the several States shall have concurrent power to enforce this article by appropriate legislation.

This article shall be inoperative unless it shall have been ratified as an amendment to the Constitution by the legislatures of the several States, as provided in the Constitution, within seven years from the date of the submission thereof to the States by Congress. [January 29, 1919.]

AMENDMENT XIX.

The right of citizens of the United States to vote shall not be denied or abridged by the United States or by any State on account of sex.

The Congress shall have power by appropriate legislation to enforce the provisions of this article. [August 26, 1920.]

AMENDMENT XX.

Section 1. The terms of the President and Vice-President shall end at noon on the twentieth day of January, and the terms of Senators and Representatives at noon on the third day of January, of the years in which such terms would have ended if this article had not been ratified; and the terms of their successors shall then begin.

Section 2. The Congress shall assemble at least once in every year, and such meeting shall begin at noon on the third day of January, unless they shall by law appoint a different day.

Section 3. If, at the time fixed for the beginning of the term of the President, the President-elect shall have died, the Vice-President-elect shall become President. If a President shall not have been chosen before the time fixed for the beginning of his term, or if the President-elect shall have failed to qualify, then the Vice-President-elect shall act as President until a President shall have qualified; and the Congress may by law provide for the case wherein neither a President-elect nor a Vice-President-elect shall have qualified, declaring who shall then act as President, or the manner in which one who is to act shall be selected, and such person shall act accordingly until a President or Vice-President shall have qualified.

Section 4. The Congress may by law provide for the case of the death of any of the persons from whom the House of Representatives may choose a President whenever the right of choice shall have devolved upon them, and for the case of the death of any of the persons from whom the Senate may choose a Vice-President whenever the right of choice shall have devolved upon them.

Section 5. Sections 1 and 2 shall take effect on the 15th day of October following the ratification of this article.

Section 6. This article shall be inoperative unless it shall have been ratified as an amendment to the Constitution by the legislatures of three-fourths of the several States within seven years from the date of its submission. [February 6, 1933.]

Amendment XXI.

Section 1. The eighteenth article of amendment to the Constitution of the United States is hereby repealed.

Section 2. The transportation or importation into any State, Territory or possession of the United States for delivery or use therein of intoxicating liquors, in violation of the laws thereof, is hereby prohibited.

Section 3. This article shall be inoperative unless it shall have been ratified as an amendment to the Constitution by convention in the several States, as provided in the Constitution, within seven years from the date of the submission thereof to the States by the Congress. [December 5, 1933.]

Amendment XXII.

Section 1. No person shall be elected to the office of the President more than twice, and no person who has held the office of President, or acted as President, for more than two years of a term to which some other person was elected President shall be elected to the office of the President more than once. But this Article shall not apply to any person holding the office of President when this Article was proposed by the Congress, and shall not prevent any person who may be holding the office of President, or acting as President, during the term within which this Article becomes operative from holding the office of President or acting as President during the remainder of such term.

Section 2. This article shall be inoperative unless it shall have been ratified as an amendment to the Constitution by the legislatures of three-fourths of the several states within seven years from the date of its submission to the States by the Congress. [February 27, 1951.]

Amendment XXIII.

Section 1. The District constituting the seat of government of the United States shall appoint in such manner as the Congress may direct:

A number of electors of President and Vice-President equal to the whole number of Senators and Representatives in Congress to which the District would be entitled if it were a State, but in no event more than the least populous State; they shall be in addition to those appointed by the States, but they shall be considered, for the purposes of the election of President and Vice-President, to be electors appointed by a State; and they shall meet in the District and perform such duties as provided by the twelfth article of amendment.

Section 2. The Congress shall have the power to enforce this article by appropriate legislation. [March 29, 1961.]

Amendment XXIV.

Section 1. The right of citizens of the United States to vote in any primary or other election for President or Vice President, for electors for President or Vice President, or for Senator or Representative in Congress, shall not be denied or abridged by the United States or any State by reason of failure to pay any poll tax or other tax.

Section 2. The Congress shall have power to enforce this article by appropriate legislation. [January 23, 1964.]

Amendment XXV.

Section 1. In case of the removal of the President from office or of his death or resignation, the Vice President shall become President.

Section 2. Whenever there is a vacancy in the office of Vice President, the President shall nominate a Vice President who shall take office upon confirmation by a majority vote of both Houses of Congress.

Section 3. Whenever the President transmits to the President pro tempore of the Senate and the Speaker of the House of Representatives his written declaration that he is unable to discharge the powers and duties of his office, and until he transmits to them a written declaration to the contrary, such powers and duties shall be discharged by the Vice President as Acting President.

Section 4. Whenever the Vice President and a majority of either the principal officers of the executive departments or of such other body as Congress may by law provide, transmit to the President pro tempore of the Senate and the Speaker of the House of Representatives their written declaration that the President is unable to discharge the powers and duties of his office, the Vice President shall immediately assume the powers and duties of the office as Acting President.

Thereafter, when the President transmits to the President pro tempore of the Senate and the Speaker of the House of Representatives his written declaration that no inability exists, he shall resume the powers and duties of his office unless the Vice President and a majority of either the principal officers of the executive departments or of such other body as Congress may by law provide, transmit within four days to the President pro tempore of the Senate and the Speaker of the House of Representatives their written declaration that the President is unable to discharge the powers and duties of his office. Thereupon Congress shall decide the issue, assembling within forty-eight hours for that purpose if not in session. If the Congress, within twenty-one days after receipt of the latter written declaration, or, if Congress is not in session, within twenty-one days after Congress is required to assemble, determines by two-thirds vote of both Houses that the President is unable to discharge the powers and duties of his office, the Vice President shall continue to discharge the same as Acting President; otherwise, the President shall resume the powers and duties of his office. [February 10, 1967.]

AMENDMENT XXVI.

Section 1. The right of citizens of the United States, who are eighteen years of age or older, to vote shall not be denied or abridged by the United States or by any State on account of age.

Section 2. The Congress shall have power to enforce this article by appropriate legislation [June 30, 1971.]

PRESIDENTIAL ELECTIONS

Year	Number of States	Candidates	Parties	Popular Vote	% of Popular Vote	Electoral Vote	% Voter Participation
1789	11	**GEORGE WASHINGTON**	No party designations			69	
		John Adams				34	
		Other candidates				35	
1792	15	**GEORGE WASHINGTON**	No party designations			132	
		John Adams				77	
		George Clinton				50	
		Other candidates				5	
1796	16	**JOHN ADAMS**	Federalist			71	
		Thomas Jefferson	Democratic-Republican			68	
		Thomas Pinckney	Federalist			59	
		Aaron Burr	Democratic-Republican			30	
		Other candidates				48	
1800	16	**THOMAS JEFFERSON**	Democratic-Republican			73	
		Aaron Burr	Democratic-Republican			73	
		John Adams	Federalist			65	
		Charles C. Pinckney	Federalist			64	
		John Jay	Federalist			1	

Year	Number of States	Candidates	Parties	Popular Vote	% of Popular Vote	Electoral Vote	% Voter Participation
1804	17	**THOMAS JEFFERSON**	Democratic-Republican			162	
		Charles C. Pinckney	Federalist			14	
1808	17	**JAMES MADISON**	Democratic-Republican			122	
		Charles C. Pinckney	Federalist			47	
		George Clinton	Democratic-Republican			6	
1812	18	**JAMES MADISON**	Democratic-Republican			128	
		DeWitt Clinton	Federalist			89	
1816	19	**JAMES MONROE**	Democratic-Republican			183	
		Rufus King	Federalist			34	
1820	24	**JAMES MONROE**	Democratic-Republican			231	
		John Quincy Adams	Independent Republican			1	
1824	24	**JOHN QUINCY ADAMS**	Democratic-Republican	108,740	30.5	84	26.9
		Andrew Jackson	Democratic-Republican	153,544	43.1	99	
		Henry Clay	Democratic-Republican	47,136	13.2	37	
		William H. Crawford	Democratic-Republican	46,618	13.1	41	

Year	Number of States	Candidates	Parties	Popular Vote	% of Popular Vote	Electoral Vote	% Voter Participation
1828	24	**ANDREW JACKSON**	Democratic	647,286	56.0	178	57.6
		John Quincy Adams	National Republican	508,064	44.0	83	
1832	24	**ANDREW JACKSON**	Democratic	688,242	54.5	219	55.4
		Henry Clay	National Republican	473,462	37.5	49	
		William Wirt	Anti-Masonic	101,051	8.0	7	
		John Floyd	Democratic			11	
1836	26	**MARTIN VAN BUREN**	Democratic	765,483	50.9	170	57.8
		William H. Harrison	Whig			73	
		Hugh L. White	Whig	739,795	49.1	26	
		Daniel Webster	Whig			14	
		W. P. Mangum	Whig			11	
1840	26	**WILLIAM H. HARRISON**	Whig	1,274,624	53.1	234	80.2
		Martin Van Buren	Democratic	1,127,781	46.9	60	
1844	26	**JAMES K. POLK**	Democratic	1,338,464	49.6	170	78.9
		Henry Clay	Whig	1,300,097	48.1	105	
		James G. Birney	Liberty	62,300	2.3		
1848	30	**ZACHARY TAYLOR**	Whig	1,360,967	47.4	163	72.7
		Lewis Cass	Democratic	1,222,342	42.5	127	
		Martin Van Buren	Free Soil	291,263	10.1		

Year	Number of States	Candidates	Parties	Popular Vote	% of Popular Vote	Electoral Vote	% Voter Participation
1852	31	**FRANKLIN PIERCE**	Democratic	1,601,117	50.9	254	69.6
		Winfield Scott	Whig	1,385,453	44.1	42	
		John P. Hale	Free Soil	155,825	5.0		
1856	31	**JAMES BUCHANAN**	Democratic	1,832,955	45.3	174	78.9
		John C. Frémont	Republican	1,339,932	33.1	114	
		Millard Fillmore	American	871,731	21.6	8	
1860	33	**ABRAHAM LINCOLN**	Republican	1,865,593	39.8	180	81.2
		Stephen A. Douglas	Democratic	1,382,713	29.5	12	
		John C. Breckinridge	Democratic	848,356	18.1	72	
		John Bell	Constitutional Union	592,906	12.6	39	
1864	36	**ABRAHAM LINCOLN**	Republican	2,206,938	55.0	212	73.8
		George B. McClellan	Democratic	1,803,787	45.0	21	
1868	37	**ULYSSES S. GRANT**	Republican	3,013,421	52.7	214	78.1
		Horatio Seymour	Democratic	2,706,829	47.3	80	
1872	37	**ULYSSES S. GRANT**	Republican	3,596,745	55.6	286	71.3
		Horace Greeley	Democratic	2,843,446	43.9		
1876	38	**RUTHERFORD B. HAYES**	Republican	4,036,572	48.0	185	81.8
		Samuel J. Tilden	Democratic	4,284,020	51.0	184	
1880	38	**JAMES A. GARFIELD**	Republican	4,453,295	48.5	214	79.4
		Winfield S. Hancock	Democratic	4,414,082	48.1	155	
		James B. Weaver	Greenback-Labor	308,578	3.4		

Year	Number of States	Candidates	Parties	Popular Vote	% of Popular Vote	Electoral Vote	% Voter Participation
1884	38	**GROVER CLEVELAND**	Democratic	4,879,507	48.5	219	77.5
		James G. Blaine	Republican	4,850,293	48.2	182	
		Benjamin F. Butler	Greenback-Labor	175,370	1.8		
		John P. St. John	Prohibition	150,369	1.5		
1888	38	**BENJAMIN HARRISON**	Republican	5,477,129	47.9	233	79.3
		Grover Cleveland	Democratic	5,537,857	48.6	168	
		Clinton B. Fisk	Prohibition	249,506	2.2		
		Anson J. Streeter	Union Labor	146,935	1.3		
1892	44	**GROVER CLEVELAND**	Democratic	5,555,426	46.1	277	74.7
		Benjamin Harrison	Republican	5,182,690	43.0	145	
		James B. Weaver	People's	1,029,846	8.5	22	
		John Bidwell	Prohibition	264,133	2.2		
1896	45	**WILLIAM McKINLEY**	Republican	7,102,246	51.1	271	79.3
		William J. Bryan	Democratic	6,492,559	47.7	176	
1900	45	**WILLIAM McKINLEY**	Republican	7,218,491	51.7	292	73.2
		William J. Bryan	Democratic; Populist	6,356,734	45.5	155	
		John C. Wooley	Prohibition	208,914	1.5		

Year	Number of States	Candidates	Parties	Popular Vote	% of Popular Vote	Electoral Vote	% Voter Participation
1904	45	**THEODORE ROOSEVELT**	Republican	7,628,461	57.4	336	65.2
		Alton B. Parker	Democratic	5,084,223	37.6	140	
		Eugene V. Debs	Socialist	402,283	3.0		
		Silas C. Swallow	Prohibition	258,536	1.9		
1908	46	**WILLIAM H. TAFT**	Republican	7,675,320	51.6	321	65.4
		William J. Bryan	Democratic	6,412,294	43.1	162	
		Eugene V. Debs	Socialist	420,793	2.8		
		Eugene W. Chafin	Prohibition	253,840	1.7		
1912	48	**WOODROW WILSON**	Democratic	6,296,547	41.9	435	58.8
		Theodore Roosevelt	Progressive	4,118,571	27.4	88	
		William H. Taft	Republican	3,486,720	23.2	8	
		Eugene V. Debs	Socialist	900,672	6.0		
		Eugene W. Chafin	Prohibition	206,275	1.4		
1916	48	**WOODROW WILSON**	Democratic	9,127,695	49.4	277	61.6
		Charles E. Hughes	Republican	8,533,507	46.2	254	
		A. L. Benson	Socialist	585,113	3.2		
		J. Frank Hanly	Prohibition	220,506	1.2		
1920	48	**WARREN G. HARDING**	Republican	16,143,407	60.4	404	49.2
		James M. Cox	Democratic	9,130,328	34.2	127	
		Eugene V. Debs	Socialist	919,799	3.4		
		P. P. Christensen	Farmer-Labor	265,411	1.0		
1924	48	**CALVIN COOLIDGE**	Republican	15,718,211	54.0	382	48.9
		John W. Davis	Democratic	8,385,283	28.8	136	
		Robert M. La Follette	Progressive	4,831,289	16.6	13	

Year	Number of States	Candidates	Parties	Popular Vote	% of Popular Vote	Electoral Vote	% Voter Participation
1928	48	**HERBERT C. HOOVER**	Republican	21,391,993	58.2	444	56.9
		Alfred E. Smith	Democratic	15,016,169	40.9	87	
1932	48	**FRANKLIN D. ROOSEVELT**	Democratic	22,809,638	57.4	472	56.9
		Herbert C. Hoover	Republican	15,758,901	39.7	59	
		Norman Thomas	Socialist	881,951	2.2		
1936	48	**FRANKLIN D. ROOSEVELT**	Democratic	27,752,869	60.8	523	61.0
		Alfred M. Landon	Republican	16,674,665	36.5	8	
		William Lemke	Union	882,479	1.9		
1940	48	**FRANKLIN D. ROOSEVELT**	Democratic	27,307,819	54.8	449	62.5
		Wendell L. Willkie	Republican	22,321,018	44.8	82	
1944	48	**FRANKLIN D. ROOSEVELT**	Democratic	25,606,585	53.5	432	55.9
		Thomas E. Dewey	Republican	22,014,745	46.0	99	
1948	48	**HARRY S TRUMAN**	Democratic	24,179,345	49.6	303	53.0
		Thomas E. Dewey	Republican	21,991,291	45.1	189	
		J. Strom Thurmond	States' Rights	1,176,125	2.4	39	
		Henry A. Wallace	Progressive	1,157,326	2.4		
1952	48	**DWIGHT EISENHOWER**	Republican	33,936,234	55.1	442	63.3
		Adlai E. Stevenson	Democratic	27,314,992	44.4	89	

Year	States	Candidates	Party	Popular Vote	% Popular Vote	Electoral Vote	% Voter Participation
1956	48	**DWIGHT D. EISENHOWER**	Republican	35,590,472	57.6	457	60.6
		Adlai E. Stevenson	Democratic	26,022,752	42.1	73	
1960	50	**JOHN F. KENNEDY**	Democratic	34,226,731	49.7	303	64.0
		Richard M. Nixon	Republican	34,108,157	49.5	219	
1964	50	**LYNDON B. JOHNSON**	Democratic	43,129,566	61.1	486	61.7
		Barry M. Goldwater	Republican	27,178,188	38.5	52	
1968	50	**RICHARD M. NIXON**	Republican	31,785,480	43.4	301	60.6
		Hubert H. Humphrey	Democratic	31,275,166	42.7	191	
		George C. Wallace	American Independent	9,906,473	13.5	46	
1972	50	**RICHARD M. NIXON**	Republican	47,169,911	60.7	520	55.5
		George S. McGovern	Democratic	29,170,383	37.5	17	
		John G. Schmitz	American	1,099,482	1.4		
1976	50	**JIMMY CARTER**	Democratic	40,830,763	50.1	297	54.3
		Gerald R. Ford	Republican	39,147,793	48.0	240	
1980	50	**RONALD REAGAN**	Republican	43,901,812	50.7	489	53.0
		Jimmy Carter	Democratic	35,483,820	41.0	49	
		John B. Anderson	Independent	5,719,722	6.6	0	
		Ed Clark	Libertarian	921,188	1.1	0	

Candidates receiving less than 1 percent of the popular vote have been omitted. Thus the percentage of popular vote given for any election year may not total 100 percent.

Before the passage of the Twelfth Amendment in 1804, the Electoral College voted for two presidential candidates; the runner-up became vice president.

ADMISSION OF STATES

Order of Admission	State	Date of Admission	Order of Admission	State	Date of Admission
1	Delaware	December 7, 1787	26	Michigan	January 26, 1837
2	Pennsylvania	December 12, 1787	27	Florida	March 3, 1845
3	New Jersey	December 18, 1787	28	Texas	December 29, 1845
4	Georgia	January 2, 1788	29	Iowa	December 28, 1846
5	Connecticut	January 9, 1788	30	Wisconsin	May 29, 1848
6	Massachusetts	February 7, 1788	31	California	September 9, 1850
7	Maryland	April 28, 1788	32	Minnesota	May 11, 1858
8	South Carolina	May 23, 1788	33	Oregon	February 14, 1859
9	New Hampshire	June 21, 1788	34	Kansas	January 29, 1861
10	Virginia	June 25, 1788	35	West Virginia	June 30, 1863
11	New York	July 26, 1788	36	Nevada	October 31, 1864
12	North Carolina	November 21, 1789	37	Nebraska	March 1, 1867
13	Rhode Island	May 29, 1790	38	Colorado	August 1, 1876
14	Vermont	March 4, 1791	39	North Dakota	November 2, 1889
15	Kentucky	June 1, 1792	40	South Dakota	November 2, 1889
16	Tennessee	June 1, 1796	41	Montana	November 8, 1889
17	Ohio	March 1, 1803	42	Washington	November 11, 1889
18	Louisiana	April 30, 1812	43	Idaho	July 3, 1890
19	Indiana	December 11, 1816	44	Wyoming	July 10, 1890
20	Mississippi	December 10, 1817	45	Utah	January 4, 1896
21	Illinois	December 3, 1818	46	Oklahoma	November 16, 1907
22	Alabama	December 14, 1819	47	New Mexico	January 6, 1912
23	Maine	March 15, 1820	48	Arizona	February 14, 1912
24	Missouri	August 10, 1821	49	Alaska	January 3, 1959
25	Arkansas	June 15, 1836	50	Hawaii	August 21, 1959

POPULATION OF THE UNITED STATES

Year	Number of States	Population	Percent Increase	Population per Square Mile
1790	13	3,929,214		4.5
1800	16	5,308,483	35.1	6.1
1810	17	7,239,881	36.4	4.3
1820	23	9,638,453	33.1	5.5
1830	24	12,866,020	33.5	7.4
1840	26	17,069,453	32.7	9.8
1850	31	23,191,876	35.9	7.9
1860	33	31,443,321	35.6	10.6
1870	37	39,818,449	26.6	13.4
1880	38	50,155,783	26.0	16.9
1890	44	62,947,714	25.5	21.2
1900	45	75,994,575	20.7	25.6
1910	46	91,972,266	21.0	31.0
1920	48	105,710,620	14.9	35.6
1930	48	122,775,046	16.1	41.2
1940	48	131,669,275	7.2	44.2
1950	48	150,697,361	14.5	50.7
1960	50	179,323,175	19.0	50.6
1970	50	203,235,298	13.3	57.5
1980	50	226,504,825	11.4	64.0

PRESIDENTS, VICE-PRESIDENTS, AND SECRETARIES OF STATE

President	Vice-President	Secretary of State
1. George Washington, Federalist 1789	John Adams, Federalist 1789	T. Jefferson 1789 E. Randolph 1794 T. Pickering 1795
2. John Adams, Federalist 1797	Thomas Jefferson, Dem.-Rep. 1797	T. Pickering 1797 John Marshall 1800
3. Thomas Jefferson, Dem.-Rep. 1801	Aaron Burr, Dem.-Rep. 1801 George Clinton, Dem.-Rep. 1805	James Madison 1801
4. James Madison, Dem.-Rep. 1809	George Clinton, Dem.-Rep. 1809 Elbridge Gerry, Dem.-Rep. 1813	Robert Smith 1809 James Monroe 1811
5. James Monroe, Dem.-Rep.-1817	D. D. Tompkins, Dem.-Rep. 1817	J. Q. Adams 1817
6. John Quincy Adams, Dem.-Rep. 1825	John C. Calhoun, Dem.-Rep. 1825	Henry Clay 1825
7. Andrew Jackson, Democratic 1829	John C. Calhoun, Democratic 1829 Martin Van Buren, Democratic 1833	M. Van Buren 1829 E. Livingston 1831 Louis McLane 1833 John Forsyth 1834
8. Martin Van Buren, Democratic 1837	Richard M. Johnson, Democratic 1837	John Forsyth 1837
9. William H. Harrison, Whig 1841	John Tyler, Whig 1841	Daniel Webster 1841

President	Vice-President	Secretary of State
10. John Tyler, Whig and Democratic 1841		Daniel Webster 1841 Hugh S. Legare 1843 Abel P. Upshur 1843 John C. Calhoun 1844
11. James K. Polk, Democratic 1845	George M. Dallas, Democratic 1845	James Buchanan 1845
12. Zachary Taylor, Whig 1849	Millard Fillmore, Whig 1848	John M. Clayton 1849
13. Millard Fillmore, Whig 1850		Daniel Webster 1850 Edward Everett 1852
14. Franklin Pierce, Democratic 1853	William R. D. King, Democratic 1853	W. L. Marcy 1853
15. James Buchanan, Democratic 1857	John C. Breckinridge, Democratic 1857	Lewis Cass 1857 J. S. Black 1860
16. Abraham Lincoln, Republican 1861	Hannibal Hamlin, Republican 1861 Andrew Johnson, Unionist 1865	W. H. Seward 1861
17. Andrew Johnson, Unionist 1865		W. H. Seward 1865
18. Ulysses S. Grant, Republican 1869	Schuyler Colfax, Republican 1869 Henry Wilson, Republican 1873	E. B. Washburne 1869 H. Fish 1869
19. Rutherford B. Hayes, Republican 1877	William A. Wheeler, Republican 1877	W. M. Evarts 1877

President	Vice-President	Secretary of State
20. James A Garfield, Republican 1881	Chester A. Arthur, Republican 1881	J. G. Blaine 1881
21. Chester A. Arthur, Republican 1881		F. T. Frelinghuysen 1881
22. Grover Cleveland, Democratic 1885	T. A. Hendricks, Democratic 1885	T. F. Bayard 1885
23. Benjamin Harrison, Republican 1889	Levi P. Morton, Republican 1889	J. G. Blaine 1889 J. W. Foster 1892
24. Grover Cleveland, Democratic 1893	Adlai E. Stevenson, Democratic 1893	W. Q. Gresham 1893 R. Olney 1895
25. William McKinley, Republican 1897	Garret A. Hobart, Republican 1897 Theodore Roosevelt, Republican 1901	J. Sherman 1897 W. R. Day 1897 J. Hay 1898
26. Theodore Roosevelt, Republican 1901	Chas. W. Fairbanks, Republican 1905	J. Hay 1901 E. Root 1905 R. Bacon 1909
27. William H. Taft, Republican 1909	James S. Sherman, Republican 1909	P. C. Knox 1909
28. Woodrow Wilson, Democratic 1913	Thomas R. Marshall, Democratic 1913	W. J. Bryan 1913 R. Lansing 1915 B. Colby 1920
29. Warren G. Harding, Republican 1921	Calvin Coolidge, Republican 1921	C. E. Hughes 1921
30. Calvin Coolidge, Republican 1923	Charles G. Dawes, Republican 1925	C. E. Hughes 1923 F. B. Kellogg 1925

President	Vice-President	Secretary of State
31. Herbert Hoover, Republican 1929	Charles Curtis, Republican 1929	H. L. Stimson 1929
32. Franklin D. Roosevelt, Democratic 1933	John Nance Garner, Democratic 1933 Henry A. Wallace, Democratic 1941 Harry S Truman, Democratic 1945	C. Hull 1933 E. R. Stettinius, Jr. 1944
33. Harry S Truman, Democratic 1945	Alben W. Barkley, Democratic 1949	J. F. Byrnes 1945 G. C. Marshall 1947 D. G. Acheson 1949
34. Dwight D. Eisenhower, Republican 1953	Richard M. Nixon, Republican 1953	J. F. Dulles 1953 C. A. Herter 1959
35. John F. Kennedy, Democratic 1961	Lyndon B. Johnson, Democratic 1961	D. Rusk 1961
36. Lyndon B. Johnson, Democratic 1963	Hubert H. Humphrey, Democratic 1965	D. Rusk 1963
37. Richard M. Nixon, Republican 1969	Spiro T. Agnew, Republican 1969 Gerald R. Ford, Republican 1973	W. P. Rogers 1969 H. A. Kissinger 1973
38. Gerald R. Ford, Republican 1974	Nelson Rockefeller, Republican 1974	H. A. Kissinger 1974
39. Jimmy Carter, Democratic 1977	Walter Mondale, Democratic 1977	C. Vance 1977 E. Muskie 1980
40. Ronald Reagan, Republican 1981	George Bush, Republican 1981	A. Haig 1981 G. Schultz 1982

INDEX